Australian
Management
essentials

About the Authors

Neil Flanagan and Jarvis Finger are the successful writing team behind several Australian bestsellers including *Management in a Minute*, *Just About Everything a Manager Needs to Know*, *The Manager's 100* and *The Management Bible*.

Australian Management Essentials replaces *The Management Bible*, which was reprinted 13 times, selling more than 30,000 copies.

Neil Flanagan, BA, B Ed St, M Ed Admin, PhD, is a highly regarded management strategist, motivational speaker and bestselling author. His drive-time radio program was syndicated nationally, and he continues to contribute articles to media in Australia.

Jarvis Finger, BA, B Ed, M Ed Admin, FACEL, FQIEA, AFAIM, is a well-known author and editor. A former executive manager in one of Australia's largest public organisations, he is author of a range of management books and regular magazine contributor.

Australian
Management
essentials

Neil Flanagan & Jarvis Finger

WOODSLANE
PRESS

Woodslane Press Pty Ltd
10 Apollo St, Warriewood, NSW 2102
Email: info@woodslane.com.au
www.woodslane.com.au

First published as The Management Bible in 2003
Reprinted 2003, 2004, 2005, 2007 (updated), 2008 (updated) and 2010
Second edition published by Woodslane Press in Australia in 2013
This updated paperback edition published by Woodslane Press in Australia in 2020

©2013 and 2020 Woodslane Press
Text and diagrams © 2003-2010, 2013 and 2020 Neil Flanagan and Jarvis Finger

A catalogue record for this book is available from the National Library of Australia

Printed in Australia by SOS

Foreword

One of the few 'sure things' in life is the need for knowledge. There's no downside to learning—the more you learn, the more competent you become in your personal and professional life. In this regard, management knowledge and expertise can be acquired over many years and in various ways:

- Formal management courses are valuable sources of information— but because the useful lifespan of information is only a few years, it is important to continue to learn once the course is over.
- Conferences, seminars, and workshops are accepted forms of training and information gathering also—and again, to get full value from these events, it is vital that the learning process go on after the formal training has ended.
- In-house support, often focusing on administrative procedures, new technology, and —unfortunately—the latest management fads, can provide information as well, although all too often in a fragmented way.
- Much too can be learnt from others—friends, colleagues, mentors—but your needs will be a competing priority, forcing them to limit any time they spend with you.
- Online resources and websites provide a mass of information—if only you could locate, retrieve, and use the material quickly, when you really need it.
- And, of course, on-the-job experience is a great teacher—but it takes such a long time and can often be mistake-riddled.

But, whatever you do, sooner or later, you're going to be on your own managing as best you can. And that's where *Australian Management Essentials* can be your salvation.

In my career as a management educator, I get to see a wide variety of books and other resources designed to give busy people access to essential management information. *Australian Management Essentials* is one of the most comprehensive collections of hands-on management advice I have seen. For the workplace, it is potentially one of the most useful, because here the authors have gathered together, into one succinct, handy volume, an amazing wealth of management strategies, expertise, advice, and solutions.

It was Albert Einstein who advocated that, rather than take up valuable brain space, information is best stored in a way that makes it, when required, readily accessible, retrievable, and immediately usable. Einstein could see that the exponential growth of knowledge would require more efficient ways of accessing essential information. Not only have the authors of this book taken Einstein's words of wisdom to heart, but they have also presented, in a simple, straightforward, and easy-to-use format, the core information as step-by-step, cross-referenced solutions; and then complemented these strategies with hundreds of valuable side-panel fragments to satisfy both the browser and the serious reader. *Australian Management Essentials* is written and published with the needs of the busy reader in mind.

Australian Management Essentials is clearly an authoritative survival manual for managers of all levels and ages, and I recommend it highly.

Michael R Vitale

Professor Michael Vitale
Asia Pacific Centre, Monash University.
Previously Joint Professor at Melbourne Business School and ANZ School of Government.
Formerly Dean and Director at Australian Graduate School of Management,
University of New South Wales and University of Sydney.

v

Contents

MANAGING RELATIONSHIPS

COMMUNICATING

BUILDING ESSENTIAL SKILLS

PLANNING

STAFF-RELATED ISSUES

MANAGING CONFLICT

MANAGING CRISES

MARKETING

ORGANISATION-WIDE ISSUES

Preface

Four management tales

The tale of the weary axeman

Will Sherwood was a woodsman. One day Will was working in a forest, cutting down a large tree. A stranger happened to be passing by and on meeting the woodsman asked, 'What are you doing?'

'I'm cutting down this tree,' came Will's gruff reply as he continued to chop.

'You look very tired indeed,' the stranger continued. 'And just how long have you been at work here?'

Will downed his axe.

'A long time,' replied the woodsman as he wiped his brow. 'In fact, I've been at it for many hours now, and I'm exhausted. It really is hard work.'

'At the risk of interfering,' suggested the stranger, 'why don't you take a break for a few minutes and sharpen your axe. That'll make your job easier and you'll take less time on the job.'

Will replied, as he again swung his axe into the tree, 'I don't have time to sharpen the axe. I'm too busy chopping!'

Are you like Will Sherwood, the woodsman—too busy to stop doing what you are doing? Or do you make sure you take a breather every now and then to sharpen your axe—or, as Stephen Covey would have it, take time out to 'sharpen the saw'? If your axe isn't sharp, you'll soon become exhausted, run short of ideas, and be unaware of the range of alternative management solutions available to you.

We all need to set aside time to sharpen our axes, and *Australian Management Essentials* provides a wealth of information to help you to do so.

Start sharpening now!

The tale of the smart logger

One of the secrets of good management is to find the essence of each management situation—just like a professional logger clearing a log-jam.

The experienced logger climbs a tall tree and locates the key log, blows it up, and lets the stream clear the rest. An amateur would start at the edge of the log-jam and move each log in turn, eventually getting to and moving the key log. Both approaches work—but the professional's approach is smarter, and saves time and effort.

Nearly all management situations and problems have a key log if only we know where to find it—and that's where *Australian Management Essentials* comes in. It's your short cut to management expertise. Simply consult *Australian Management Essential's* index: it will provide ready access to your 'key' log. As well, the cross references at the top of each page may also prove effective in helping you to clear your management stream.

The tale of the missed opportunity

One of the most remarkable motion pictures ever made by Walt Disney was *The African Lion*. One sequence shows a cheetah accelerating from a walk to a 60 m.p.h. sprint while chasing a nimble member of the deer family. The cat is so intent on the one animal he has selected as his prey that he actually passes other deer frenziedly running in all directions. One of them even runs alongside the cheetah for a while, not realising in his abject terror that the pursuer is his running companion. One swipe from the predator's paw would bring down the nearby prey; but the hunter runs on, eyes fixed on the animal directly ahead. And he catches him.

There is a lesson to be learnt from this. Author and lecturer Edwin Feldman once encapsulated the message precisely: 'We must be so intent on attaining our goals as to be able to ignore distractions—but not to the extent of missing better opportunities.'

Far be it from us to distract you from your daily management grind, but may we suggest that *Australian Management Essentials*, with its wealth of invaluable basic management information and solutions, is one of Feldman's 'opportunities'. As a busy manager, make sure you don't fix your gaze so rigidly on the daily task that you ignore the opportunity this book offers for you to become an even better manager.

The tale of the stubborn calf

Ralph Waldo Emerson had a reputation for being an unruffled, patient, good-tempered man. He was an eminent historian, a noted poet, and a respected American philosopher.

On this particular afternoon, however, he was far from unruffled, patient, and good-tempered.

For nearly half an hour, Emerson and his son, Edward, had been trying to persuade a calf to enter the barn.

No amount of pushing and shoving would entice the animal through the door.

In a final desperate effort, Edward circled the neck of the calf with one arm and Ralph pushed from behind. They struggled to get the obstinate heifer to move, but with each pull and push, the stubborn creature locked its knees and firmly planted all four feet on the ground. Emerson's clothing by now was soaked with bovine sweat; his own streamed down his face. The great Ralph Waldo Emerson, dripping and frustrated, had lost his persistent and sedate spirit.

A young Irish peasant woman happened by. She immediately sensed the Emersons' predicament and asked whether she could be of assistance.

'If you think you can do anything, then you just go right ahead,' came the exasperated reply.

The woman walked around to the front of the calf and stuck her finger into the calf's mouth. The calf followed her into the barn.

The son was amused, and Emerson himself was intrigued by the simple lesson the young peasant girl had taught him.

Some managers are just like the calf. You can prod them, push them, pull them, even kick them—and still they won't give up the way they have traditionally done things—understandably, perhaps. But if you give them, first, a reason they understand and, second, a motive to change their ways, they will peaceably follow.

So let us give you a reason, just in case *you*'re like Emerson's calf... The reason you should treasure *Australian Management Essentials* is that it will provide you with a collection of just about all the essential management advice, expertise, and solutions you'll ever require, and all in one volume! Over 300 major issues covering the whole spectrum of management, and considerable complementary material as well! We are confident you will be hard pressed to find another book as comprehensive.

And a motive for using this treasury of management information? If you dip into *Australian Management Essentials* frequently, or whenever you have a nagging management issue to grapple with, and you put into practice the ideas and strategies offered, you'll soon accumulate the essential know-how on how to manage yourself, your career, your staff, and your organisation far more effectively than you do at present.

Will Rogers, the cowboy philosopher famous for his homespun humour, once observed that a person 'learns only by two things: one is reading and the other is association with smarter people'. We hope that managers everywhere will learn valuable management strategies by reading *Australian Management Essentials*. (We'll leave *you* to find and learn something from someone smarter than yourself, through networking or mentoring.)

Our earlier books—*Management in a Minute, Just about Everything a Manager Needs to Know,* and *The Management Bible* (retitled as *Australian Management Essentials*)—were international bestsellers, and indeed were adopted by a number of corporations as their management manuals.

Those books, too, were evidence of our

guiding principle—the need to separate for busy managers the practical ideas of management from the entangling theory and jargon that so often demotivate hands-on practitioners; and to present the material as step-by-step solutions to everyday management problems and issues.

In the process, we were often reminded of those who went before us in other fields of endeavour—the van Goghs, Renoirs, Chopins, Lincolns—and, although we hesitate to equate our creative talents with theirs, indulge us for a moment…

There are only three pure colours—red, blue, and yellow. But look at what van Gogh and Renoir did with those three colours. There are only seven musical notes, but look at what Chopin, Schubert, and McCartney did with theirs. Lincoln's famous Gettysburg Address contained only 262 words — and 202 of them had only one syllable. Think of the effect those simple, direct words had on civilisation.

We have attempted to distil the essence of management succinctly into one comprehensive volume. Our hope is that managers at all levels and in all fields will treasure our efforts as much as Chopin treasured those seven notes or van Gogh those three basic colours.

You decide.

– Neil Flanagan and Jarvis Finger

The authors

Neil Flanagan

Neil Flanagan, B.A., B.Ed.St., M.Ed.Admin., Ph.D., is a highly regarded management strategist, a sought-after keynote, conference, and motivational speaker, and a best-selling author. His drive-time radio program was syndicated nationally, and he continues to contribute articles to media in Australia.

Neil's approach to strategy draws on the wisdom of the ancient sages, recognised strategists, and his own management experience to help individuals and organisations achieve their highest potential.

His previous books—*Management in a Minute*, *Just about Everything a Manager Needs to Know*, *Creative Debt Collecting*, and *Responsiveness: Double Your Profits in Half the Time*—have all achieved international bestseller status.

Neil's management experience includes education and educational administration, corporate training, human resource management, management strategy, and company directorships. From that experience, and by working closely with managers in those fields, he has developed a clear understanding not only of managers' needs but also of the way busy managers want information presented.

Jarvis Finger

Jarvis Finger, B.A., B.Ed., M.Ed. Admin., FACEA, FQIEA, AFAIM, is a well-known author and editor of a range of management books and magazines.

A former executive manager in one of Australia's largest public organisations, he is the award-winning founder and editor of Australia's best-known management magazine for school administrators, *The Practising Administrator*, and author of several best-selling books on school management—the *Managing Your School* series. Jarvis was awarded the Gold Medal of the Australian Council for Educational Administration for 'his services to the professional literature of educational administration in Australia'. He has also authored a series of books on Queensland's early colonial prison on St Helena Island, on the crimes and criminals of colonial Queensland, and several entertaining paperbacks on education.

Co-author with Neil Flanagan of *Management in a Minute* and *Just about Everything a Manager Needs to Know*, he brings the same writing, presentation, and editing skills to this book that he brought to his earlier bestsellers.

This book's special features

To supplement the core text within a topic, each of the following double-page spreads features 'See also' cross-referencing links and a series of side panels on a range of relevant issues to help you understand and implement the core material presented...

 here's an idea

A practical suggestion to help implement some aspect of the topic

 research says

Brief research findings that elaborate on or reinforce a point made in the topic

 quotable quote

Something worth noting from the literature on the topic

 read further

A recommended book or website that will take you further into the topic

don't forget

Emphasising important points raised in the topic

 viewpoint

An authoritative comment to emphasise an important point made in the topic

 smile & ponder

An anecdote or cartoon that reinforces, with a touch of humour, a point in the topic

 ask yourself

A question that promotes self-examination and reflection, possibly followed by action

it's a fact

A useful piece of corroborative data that clarifies or supports the topic

 mini seminar

A provocative issue that warrants ten minutes'discussion and exploration with colleagues

See also:

This topic cross-referencing feature appears at the top of each right-hand page. The page numbers relevant to the core topic being presented are listed in numerical order—not necessarily in order of priority or importance to the core topic.

How to cultivate a better professional image for yourself

Like it or not, you do have an image: if you do not develop it by intent, then it will develop by default. So the answer is to make sure that the image you project is an asset rather than a liability. But knowing what image you present and how to go about improving it is more difficult than it would seem at first glance. The suggestions that follow are listed to help you enhance your personal image and to influence more positively the way others see you…

1 Know what image you want to project.

What kind of personal image do you want to project? Do you want to impress as a creative, energetic, innovative, and enthusiastic leader? Or as a laid-back, let-it-all-happen, efficient manager? Or as a sensitive, caring people person? Other people read the signals you project so analyse the image you would like to create and set about communicating the right signals to project that image.

2 Attend to your personal appearance.

Dress appropriately and well, as if you have already arrived at the top of your success pyramid. Wear what you consider will meet other people's expectations of you as a successful manager.

Compile and analyse your own personal dress and grooming check list—ties, shoes, hair, accessories, pen, briefcase, glasses, cosmetics, fingernails, jewellery… How do you and others rate your appearance?

3 Be a positive communicator.

What you say and how you say it are important factors in image-building. Have you ever recorded yourself in natural conversation or in reading aloud to consider the loudness, pitch, and tone of your voice; and your articulation and speed? Recordings can reveal much: boring monotone, nasality, stridency, gotta's, dropped g's, overuse of um's and ah's, and y'knows… All can contribute to a negative personal image.

Be a good listener while at the same time keeping your employees and colleagues informed about what is going on in your department or organisation. Spend as much time listening as talking, and make oral and written communication as positive as you can.

4 Check your nonverbal messages.

Your body signals could be impeding your chances of success as a manager. If you feel strong and confident you should stand tall and walk with assurance. If you sit with stooped shoulders or walk with a slow, hesitating gait, you will project an image of one overwhelmed by life and low on self-esteem. Posture and bearing disclose a great deal—as any body language book will tell you.

5 Develop those essential interactive qualities.

Here are important aspects to remember in your dealings with others:

- Always be first to say hello. Offer a firm but not crushing handshake.
- Never be casual with your greeting. Be sincere and meaningful.
- A friendly smile projects an image of trust.
- Use the other person's name in your conversation.
- Do your homework when meeting with someone. Work your knowledge of him or her into the conversation.
- Show that you are interested in what the other person is saying.
- Observe the basic rules of politeness and etiquette.

6 Think about your work environment.

The appearance of your office or workplace says much about you. A cluttered desk, for example, can give others the idea that you are untidy and disorganised. Visitors are most impressed with an 'organised stacks' setting.

7 Always project a professional attitude.

Make certain your name is always associated with honest, ethical behaviour. Strive to develop good personal relationships. Demonstrate integrity, understanding, sensitivity, trust, respect, and competence. Let colleagues know that you are tastefully ambitious and keen to get ahead; but avoid giving the impression that you are prepared to walk over others to get there. Tactfully make your skills and accomplishments known. Admit mistakes and never publicly criticise a superior or colleague. Seize every opportunity to prove that you are a good team player.

8 Be constantly aware of your image.

The key to image-building is to start early. You see, it's easier to build up a positive image before one has been formed in the eyes of others than to change one that is already established. Unfortunately, few of us can begin with a clean slate.

But if you suspect that your present image is not helping you to advance your career, you will need to change it—and this could take some time; well-established behaviours are hard to alter. Be aware always that the way you present yourself to others is one of the most important facets of any leader's makeup. Work at it daily.

In a nutshell, act like a professional and always look the part.

don't forget

Practise what you preach...

If you're an advocate of teamwork, do *you* work well with others?

If you ask your staff to take risks, does *your* behaviour match your words?

If you recommend lifelong learning, do *you* attend seminars to keep up to date in your field?

If you require your staff to keep current by reading the professional literature, do they see evidence that *you* are a reader?

Managers who don't put into practice what they preach lack credibility, and others will be reluctant to follow their advice.

Put this reminder on your office wall: 'Walk the Talk!'

It's all about image!

How to develop a positive mental attitude

We've all met people who seem to have everything going for them—ideal upbringing, seemingly unlimited talents, useful contacts, and so on. But why is it they never seem to get to first base, careerwise? The answer: attitude. It is often their attitude that limits their achievements. Although changing attitudes is not easy, it can be done. Here's a nine-step process that can lead to the development of a positive mental attitude, a will to win, and career success…

Take charge of your attitude.

Religious writer Charles Swindoll, encapsulates it precisely:

> The longer I live, the more I realise the impact of attitude on life. Attitude, to me, is more important than facts. It is more important than the past, than education, than money, than circumstances, than failures, than successes, than what other people think or say or do. It is more important than appearance, giftedness, or skill. It will make or break a company…
>
> The remarkable thing is that we have a choice every day regarding the attitude we will embrace for that day. We cannot change our past…we cannot change the fact that people will act in a certain way. We cannot chance the inevitable. The only thing we can do is play on the one string we have, and that is our attitude …I am convinced that life is 10 per cent what happens to me and 90 per cent how I react to it. And so it is with you… we are in charge of our attitudes.

Practise visualisation.

Visualisation is one of the most powerful techniques of self-image modification because your visual image can become your reality. Management expert Brian Tracy tells us that there are four elements of visualisation and an increase in any one of them will accelerate the rate at which we create the physical equivalent of that mental picture of our life. These four elements are:

- *Frequency.* People who accomplish extraordinary things continually visualise their desired results.
- *Vividness.* This is literally seeing things clearly.
- *Intensity.* When you intensely desire something, it occurs much faster.
- *Duration.* The longer you imagine a desired future event, the more likely it is to appear.

Make affirmations.

Affirmations are strong statements or commands from our conscious to our subconscious mind. They override old information and reinforce new, positive habits of behaviour and thought. Affirmations need to be based on the 3Ps: they must be positive, present tense, and personal. For example, if you're trying to improve your health and general well-being, positive self-talk such as this will help: 'I'm feeling better now', 'I feel young and vital', 'I'm reaching my best weight', and 'I can really feel the difference my exercise program and change in eating habits are having.'

 Affirm aloud.

Begin and end each day verbalising your affirmations. You'll be amazed how much more confidently you will feel and behave when you're feeding yourself the right messages. So, in the days leading up to a job interview, for example, tell yourself, aloud, whenever you get the chance: 'During my interview I will be calm, confident, and in control!' Don't forget: what you 'see' is what you get; what you 'feel' is what you are.

 Act the part.

Walk, talk, and act exactly as if you are the person you want to be. St Thomas Aquinas referred to this philosophy as 'as if'; others call it 'fake it till you make it'. The first step in becoming more confident is to act 'as if' you already are.

 Expose yourself to high-quality information only.

The more you read, listen, watch, and learn about your subject area, the more confident and capable you'll feel. But we need to be discerning about the quality of information we expose ourselves to. Look on information as food: we should be careful to feed ourselves only the best food.

The famous T-Cell study of the 1980s is worth remembering ('T-Cell' being a measure of the blood's healthfulness). The T-Cell of a group actually changed after exposure to varying amounts of positive and negative information. One outcome of the study was that regular exposure to negative information was a health hazard!

 Associate with positive people.

Fly with the eagles instead of scratching with the chooks. Our parents taught us that 'we are judged by the company we keep'. They were right. To meet new, positive people, you have to stop associating with the loser-brigade, those dull excuse-makers who end up dragging you down to their level of complacency and incompetence.

 Imitate positive people.

The qualities we admire and envy in others usually reflect our own under-developed capacities. Imitation is vital to learning. Identify those around you with a positive mental attitude and watch what they do. How do they work, what do they say, how do they carry themselves? Select one small behaviour at a time and emulate it.

 Teach others.

When you attempt to articulate and explain a concept to others, you will understand it and internalise it better yourself. Seize every opportunity to share the notion of 'positiveness' as a way of helping yourself to become even more familiar with it.

---

smile & ponder

A small boy strode through his backyard, baseball cap in place, and carrying a bat and ball.

'I'm the greatest baseball player in the world,' he said proudly.

Then he tossed the ball in the air, swung and missed. Undaunted, he picked up the ball, said to himself, 'I'm the greatest player ever!', threw the ball into the air, swung – and missed again.

He paused for a moment to examine the ball and the bat thoughtfully. Then once again he threw the ball into the air and said, 'I'm the greatest baseball player who ever lived.' He swung the bat hard – and again he missed the ball.

'Wow!' he exclaimed. 'What a pitcher!'

■ Life's all a matter of attitude. There's *always* something to feel positive about.

research says

The Mayo Clinic in Minnesota found that people with an optimistic view live longer and feel healthier and mentally sharper in their later years. Nearly 450 patients were given a personality test in the 1960s, with a follow-up health check 30 years later. Pessimists reported worse mental and physical health.[4]

How to stay healthy

Studies that analyse the attributes of an effective manager invariably list good health as a most important contributing quality. Being healthy promotes a more satisfying and productive work experience for all of us. So, if you want to improve your fitness level and to enjoy a happier, more productive worklife, consider seriously the following suggestions…

1 Be aware of the benefits of good health.

By focusing on your personal health, you can take advantage of the following reported benefits:

- less sickness
- decreased blood pressure
- reduction in cardiac risk factors
- improved oxygen uptake
- reduction in body weight
- improved diet
- improved disposition
- better self-image
- expansion of friendship circles.

Is not this a strong and convincing case for personal health and fitness?

2 Get a regular check-up and fitness assessment.

Pay attention to the warning messages your body sends you—such as migraines, palpitations, stomach upsets—and see your doctor immediately. In fact, a regular medical check-up should be seen as part of your managerial responsibility. Knowledge of health and fitness is expanding daily, and a regular assessment means that you are ensuring you are at least physically prepared for your managerial role.

3 Keep a check on your diet.

Most of your exercise time and effort can be negated by what you eat and drink. In fact, it is a good idea to work on your diet before you get serious about exercising. Eat well-balanced meals as regularly and unhurriedly as you can. Encourage your family to be health conscious by maintaining a nutritionally sound diet. Literature abounds on this topic.

4 Exercise regularly.

Exercise several times a week. Undertake a program that is enjoyable, convenient, and appropriate for your age and state of fitness—perhaps walking, jogging, golf, gym, swimming, or cycling. Self-discipline can sometimes be a problem—which is why some people prefer a specifically designed program with a fitness instructor; others pair up with a colleague and they keep fit together.

The important thing is that exercise should be fun. The moment regular exercising becomes drudgery, it's time to vary your routine. Exercising is not only about staying alive: it's also about *being* alive. And it's an important component in your physical health and work performance.

 ### Get plenty of sleep.

Sleep recharges our batteries. Many people worry about the amount of sleep they get—some think they sleep too much; others worry they are not sleeping enough. How much do you need? Research has shown that the average sleep period is 7 to 8 hours daily. In the washup, it seems to depend on the individual: make sure you get as much sleep as *you* need. What seems to be important is that you sleep soundly.

 ### Try to cut back on the health no-no's.

The health and social consequences of excessive use of tobacco, alcohol, drugs, and medication in the form of tranquillisers, headache pills, and sleeping medication have been well documented elsewhere. Overuse of these substances can affect personal health and, consequently, productivity in the workplace.

 ### Take full advantage of your leisure time.

All work and no play make Jack and Jill dull people. Take the adage to heart. Become involved in a hobby or other interests outside work time— something that distracts you and extends you psychologically, socially and intellectually. But don't get so competitive in your pastime, whether it be Scrabble or golf, that it becomes stressful too. The essential qualities of a leisure-time activity are that it should be relaxing and enjoyable. And don't put off taking your holidays. Getting away from work for a few weeks can make you happier, healthier, and more productive on your return.

 ### Maintain a balanced lifestyle.

The ancient Chinese sages stressed the importance of balance by keeping all things in perspective—friends, finances, fun, faith, family, formal and informal education, and fitness—often referred to as the '7Fs'. Overemphasising any one to the detriment of others can result in disharmony and imbalance.

 ### Resolve to feel how you behave.

Most people have been brought up to *behave how they feel*; that's one reason so many of us feel and act depressed on Monday mornings. Active, energetic, and enthusiastic people can't afford to let feelings dictate their behaviour. A much better alternative is to decide to behave in a certain way and experience the corresponding feelings—that is, *feel how you behave*. Make the change and experience the difference.

---

 smile & ponder

Ulysses S. Grant, the 18th President of the United States, learnt about the game of golf for the first time on a visit to Scotland.

Grant was taken out on the links for a demo. His host placed a ball on the tee and took a mighty swing. The club hit the turf with a heavy thud, sending chunks of earth flying. The ball remained on the tee.

Again the host took a nasty slash at the ball. Again he missed.

A third almighty swish and once more the ball did not budge.

Grant watched the exhibition quietly, until after the sixth futile swoosh at the ball. At that time, so the story goes, he turned to his perspiring host and said: 'There seems to be a good amount of *exercise* in this game. But tell me, what's the purpose of the little white ball?'

■ The key to a productive worklife is to exercise several times a week – even if it simply involves spending half an hour swinging at – and missing – a little white golf ball.

---

smile & ponder

Your body is the baggage you must carry through life. The more excess baggage, the shorter the trip.

How to boost your self-confidence

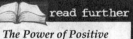

read further

The Power of Positive Thinking by Norman Vincent Peale, 1953.

Success through a Positive Mental Attitude by Napoleon Hill & W. Clement Stone, 1960.

Personal confidence is something most of us would like more of. And where do we turn to get it? To ourselves, of course, by bolstering and developing those areas that need attention. Increasing self-confidence is primarily a matter of finding out what makes us feel good about ourselves and then practising the relevant behaviour patterns. To grow in confidence yourself, here are strategies you might consider...

1 Set realistic targets for yourself.

Self-confidence will not turn you into Superman or Wonderwoman—only allow you to make the best of what you are personally capable of doing. So set reasonable and realistic expectations for yourself, rather than compare yourself with others. Keep upgrading your own standards in lifestyle, behaviour, relationships, and professional achievements.

2 Know what you do best.

If you stop and think about even the small things you do each day, you may be surprised to find some abilities and positive features that you haven't given yourself ample credit for in the past. Try to emphasise the positive at all times—and you'll gain confidence to work on those less positive aspects.

3 Monitor negative thoughts and feelings.

How negative are you about yourself? Do you spend long periods of time worrying about your inadequacies? Do you hold back because you think your report or response is not good enough? Do you compare yourself with another person and always come out second best? Such thinking will get you nowhere. When you find yourself thinking negatively, clench your fist, say 'Stop!' to yourself, and replace negative thoughts with positive ones. Consider your blessings—what and whom you are thankful for, your accomplish-ments, what you have done that you are proud of so far, and your goals, ambitions, and dreams.

4 Heed the advice of Norman Vincent Peale.

Find a copy of Norman Vincent Peale's classic *The Power of Positive Thinking*. Embrace his timeless advice, which includes these five ideas:

• Formulate and stamp indelibly on your mind a mental picture of yourself as succeeding. Hold this picture tenaciously. Never permit it to fade. Always picture 'success' no matter how badly things seem to be going at the moment.

- Whenever a negative thought concerning your personal powers comes to mind, deliberately voice a positive thought to cancel it out.
- Difficulties must be studied and efficiently dealt with to be eliminated, but they must be seen for only what they are. They must not be inflated by fear thoughts.
- Do not be awe-struck by other people or try to copy them. Nobody can be you as efficiently as *you* can. Remember that most people are often as scared as you and as doubtful of themselves.
- Make a true estimate of your own ability—then raise it 10 per cent. Believe in your own powers.

 Look for small victories.

All is not lost if that big achievement eludes you. If everything seems to be falling apart in one area of your life or work, consider your accomplishments in another area. Give yourself a pat on the back for what you have already achieved.

 Learn from your mistakes.

Don't let your mistakes drag you down. Look on each stumble as a learning experience. Ask what went wrong and what you should do next time.

 Look and sound confident.

Learn to walk more erectly and authoritatively in public. No matter how you feel, always act, walk, and dress as if you're feeling on top of the world and master of the task. Others will respond to your positive vibes, and that, in turn, will boost *your*

confidence. Try to delete negative or uncertain words from your conversation—'maybe', 'I'm not sure', and '…but'. Use positive terms such as 'I will' and 'I can'.

 Adopt a confident approach to your day.

Consider the following confidence-boosters:

- Plan a positive experience for the day and look forward to it.
- As you travel to work, at every stop light, get yourself into a positive frame of mind: 'I *can* finish the Gordon report today!'
- At work, get your tasks into priority order and work confidently to your plan.
- Participate actively in meetings.
- Show a colleague how well your day is going.
- At day's end, review your plan and celebrate the crossing-off of tasks completed.
- Reward yourself for a good day's work.

 Please yourself.

Extending yourself just to impress other people runs counter to what self-confidence is all about. You need to spend more time doing things simply because you want to do them, because these are the things you can succeed in. Use them to bolster your confidence when they go well.

 Reward yourself.

Enjoy your successes, however small, and celebrate them by yourself or with others. In this way you will be taking the focus off your inadequacies.

How to gain a reputation for honesty and integrity

Integrity has been defined as 'honesty, soundness, uprightness, true to self or stated values, beliefs, or ethics'. Success will come when employees and customers respect an organisation for its integrity—and that integrity will be reflected in its leadership and management. Image is what people think we are; integrity is what we really are. Indecision over matters of ethics can be fatal for individuals and organisations. The following considerations will help clarify your thinking…

 Develop moral courage.

With moral courage, you will be capable of standing up for what you know to be right, doing the right thing regardless of the consequences, and accepting the blame when you are in the wrong. You will be respected by all if you have strong moral courage. Indeed, it is the very foundation on which integrity rests.

 Practise truthfulness and honesty at all times.

Unless you are honest, you cannot be relied on at all. If you get caught out by your staff or colleagues misrepresenting the facts or covering up a problem, you will lose credibility instantly. Credibility is never easy to repair or regain.

Guard against white lies, too: they often are the crack in the dam wall. Of course, this doesn't mean you should insult or hurt a person by telling the truth—if you can say nothing good about a person, it's best to say nothing at all.

 Take a stand for what you believe is morally right.

Never compromise your high moral standards; never prostitute your principles. Have the courage of your convictions, for your stance in a situation where a tough decision is required can point the way for an entire group. General Norman Schwarzkopf talks about leadership and his Rule 14: 'Do what's right.'

 Practise what you preach.

Make sure your behaviour mirrors your professional attitudes and the high standards laid down by others. You must also follow the rules of your organisation. If you tell your staff to do as you tell them to do, they won't listen if your own actions are different from your words. They'll do as you do or they'll do as they want. Practise what you preach.

 Don't abuse the privileges of your position.

If you divert any of the managerial

resources at your disposal for personal gain, you're risking your reputation and your position. The simple act of having your office secretary type a letter to your brother to organise your family vacation reveals how easily company resources can be abused—people (you and your secretary, both paid by the company), materials (company stationery and a stamp), facilities (use of office facilities), time (yours and your secretary's), and money (the company pays for salaries, facilities, and materials). Petty abuses can so easily lead to much more serious transgressions, such as nepotism, falsifying accounts, padding expense claims, cheating, back-stabbing, disloyalty, or theft of office supplies and equipment. Remember, our personal values become the navigating system that guides us through the seas of temptation.

Make no promise you cannot keep.

If you know you can't live up to your promises, don't make them. You must be as good as your word, and your word must be as good as your bond.

Accept the blame when you are wrong.

It's very hard to criticise a person when that person admits being in the wrong and, when at fault, accepts the blame without question. When you foul up, admit it. Don't try to look for scape-goats, rationalise away your mistakes, or sulk. And never lie. Remember, one lie always seems to lead to another, to another, to another…

Know why it's important.

It's essential to understand why integrity is so important for someone in a position of leadership:

It builds trust. When people know you are not using your position for personal gain or at their expense, you'll gain their trust, confidence, loyalty, and whole-hearted support.

It influences others. As Emerson said: 'Every great institution is the lengthened shadow of a single man. His character determines the character of the organisation.'

It builds for you a reputation, not just an image. Regrettably, some of us work harder on our outside than our inside—forgetting that 'image promises much but produces little; integrity never disappoints', as Thomas Macauley wrote.

It creates high standards. Your own integrity in the workplace will set a positive example for all to follow. By your actions alone, you can inspire your staff to reach your high standards. People do what people see.

It helps you live with yourself. You'll be able to sleep at night.

It doesn't have to be advertised. Integrity is visible in everything you do and soon becomes common knowledge to everyone.

Finally, if you're ever tempted to compromise—as no doubt you will be, always place honour, a sense of duty and moral values above all else. If you do that, you cannot possibly fail yourself, your family, your colleagues, or your organisation.

smile & ponder

Back in the 1930s, so the story goes, a baker in Scotland suspected that a farmer who was supplying his butter was giving him short weight.

Over a period of several weeks he carefully checked the weight and his suspicions were confirmed. This so angered him that he had the farmer arrested.

'I assume you have weights,' said the judge at the farmer's trial.

'No, sir, I don't,' replied the farmer.

'Then how do you weigh the butter you sell?'

'Well,' said the farmer, 'when the baker began buying butter from me, I decided to get my bread from him. I just use the one-pound loaf he sells me as a weight for the butter I sell. If the weight of the butter is wrong, he has only himself to blame.'

■ The moral of the story is that dishonesty will ultimately return to haunt us – which is why managers need to gain a reputation for honesty and integrity.

How to take the initiative and make things happen

What is it that separates the achievers and the go-getters from those managers who sit there, spinning their wheels or worse still, just waiting for something to happen? The real achievers are those who take the initiative and make things happen. Do you want to stand around and wait for something to happen, or do you want to make it happen? The following guidelines are provided for the latter…

Adopt a positive approach at all times.

If you want to be a successful initiator, you must begin by having the right attitude. You must speak and act with confidence, even be a little pushy in your approach. If you assume that your ideas will be listened to and respected, you immediately increase the chances of that happening. If you see the initiative as a possible disaster, a disaster will probably occur.

Your attitude will be contagious. If you exude confidence about the outcome of your initiative, your enthusiasm will be passed on to your staff.

Challenge the routine way of doing things.

It is very comfortable to stop thinking critically about our routine tasks, to go through the motions, to retreat to the familiar. It can be habit-forming.

When did you last look critically at everything you do with the eye of an initiator? Try it for a week. You'll find that some of the best initiatives are small improvements to old routines—the way you run meetings, how you organise your day, when you meet with clients, and so on.

Remember, too, that success is usually a result of being one per cent better at 1000 things than 100 per cent better at one thing. Besides, small initiatives are not as risky; so it is easier to get support from your staff for the changes.

Look for opportunities.

Look for ways of improving things in your workplace. Force yourself to stop for a minute every hour, to step outside yourself, to look at what you're doing and what's going on around you.

Ask yourself: 'What's not working?', 'What could be done better?' By opening your eyes, you'll see opportunities for initiative everywhere. The trick is to discipline yourself to set aside that minute every hour.

Be action-oriented.

Don't wait to be asked, trained, or told. Whenever you see an opportunity to improve the operation of your organisation, pursue it. As Peters and Waterman write in *In Search of Excellence*: 'do it; fix it; try it'. Initiators are thinkers and doers, planners and workers. They get involved using a hands-on approach.

 Look beyond your own world.

Winners learn from winners, so be on the lookout for other organisations' successful ideas. Who's trying what? What's working and what isn't? Proactively seek out 'initiatable ideas'.

Develop your own formal and informal networks through professional organisations, clubs, and so on. The professional journals are goldmines for action-oriented leaders—and they usually come with the whys, wheres, hows, and valuable contacts. Don't limit your horizons. Look beyond the confines of your own organisation.

 Accept the challenges and the risks.

Many of the best opportunities for initiative reside in those activities that others are reluctant to handle. Make a name for yourself: take on the challenge that nobody else wants. That's how successful leaders are made. Remember that every new

initiative involves a risk: theory doesn't always work in practice. But a mistake doesn't mean failure. Mistakes are inevitable; they're also invaluable, apparently, for superachievers in life usually have a long string of failures behind them.

 Foster initiative in others.

As a manager, you must not only take the initiative but must also inspire others of your staff to do so.

One simple way of doing this is to require your employees to come to you, not only with problems, but also with some options and recommended solutions. An added bonus is that you may end up with a better solution than if you were the sole problem-solver. As well, this process creates a wonderful opportunity for staff development.

 And don't forget...

- Some people fight change. Initiators embrace it. They know that change is the one constant in today's world.
- Develop the ability to visualise the steps from idea to fulfilment.
- Be assertive rather than aggressive. Do not alienate your staff members by flaunting your innovative nature.
- A successful initiator relies on imagination, strength of purpose, intelligence—and a little luck.

smile & ponder

When Mother Teresa, whose Missionaries of Charity treated hundreds of thousands of lepers and AIDS victims, visited New York several years ago, she took the initiative and showed how well-focused and confident leadership can turn a vision into reality.

After addressing the United Nations in New York, Mother Teresa visited Sing Sing prison. There she found four inmates there had AIDS. Later, she went to New York's city hall and met Mayor Ed Koch.

She asked Koch to get Governor Mario Cuomo on the phone. 'Governor,' she said, 'I'm just back from Sing Sing, and four prisoners there have AIDS. I'd like to open up an AIDS centre. Would you mind releasing those four prisoners to me?'

No doubt happy to have the four inmates removed from State custody, Cuomo quickly agreed to her suggestion.

'Now let me tell you about the building I have in mind,' she continued. 'I'm sure you wouldn't mind paying for it.'

Ah... Well, of course not. Turning to Koch, she said, 'Today is Monday. I'd like to open the centre on Wednesday. We're going to need some permits cleared. I'm sure you could arrange them for me.'

'As long as you don't have me agreeing to wash the floors,' replied the mayor.

■ A true achiever is an ordinary person with an extraordinary determination, someone prepared to take the initiative and make things happen. Mother Teresa was such a person.

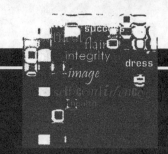

How to stand up for yourself

If you express your beliefs, feelings, and opinions honestly and directly in a socially acceptable manner, you are being assertive. Assertiveness means standing up for yourself but, in the process, respecting the rights of others. To be an effective manager, you will need to act assertively at times—when negotiating, giving or receiving feedback, dealing with staff or customers, or defending your position. Here's how you can become a more effective manager by becoming more assertive…

1 Understand what assertiveness means.

Assertiveness falls midway between aggression and submission.

- Aggressive people are brutally direct, inconsiderate, and domineering when dealing with others.
- Submissive people are the opposite— indirect, subtle, vague, even shy.
- Assertive people are honest, communicate feelings, are direct but tactful, and leave people feeling comfortable and positive.

2 Adopt a clear stance and restate your position regularly.

When resolution is called for, make your stance known from the start and make it obvious that you intend to stand firm. Calmly repeat your position whenever the need arises. By being clear and resolute and refusing to be side-tracked, you avoid unnecessary argument.

3 Know when you need to be assertive.

Some situations will require that you take a stance and stick to it. For example:

- *Saying no.*
  Can you turn down other people's requests assertively? Learn to say no directly and calmly without hesitation and without lengthy excuses or apologies. Don't fall into the trap of being made to feel guilty, manipulated, or coaxed into giving in.

- *Making requests.*
  When you want something, ask for it specifically and directly, rather than hint, manipulate, or demand. To make a request assertively, state your need, ask for action, and give a reason for your request.

- *Giving criticism.*
  The ability to be fair and firm when criticising another person is the hallmark of an assertive manager. Be firm, direct, clear, tactful, and compassionate.

- *Receiving criticism.*
  An assertive person can listen to criticism without becoming aggressive or defensive, can examine that feedback objectively,

and can use the information constructively.

In each of these situations, keep your outcome in mind. Do not engage in a verbal slanging match. Instead, respond positively—either as a gracious loser or as a generous winner.

Learn to communicate assertively.

To be assertive, you need to look assertive, sound assertive, and use assertive language.

Maintain direct and steady eye contact; check that your posture is businesslike; make sure your expression is serious but relaxed; and get rid of those nervous giggles and angry frowns.

Don't shout or mumble; speak steadily and calmly; be sincere; and keep anger, excitement, nervousness, and sarcasm in check. Keep your statements concise, clear, and direct; avoid name-calling and emotive labels such as 'lazy' and 'stupid'; and don't use such indecisive phrases as 'kind of' and 'that's just my view, anyway'.

Become an 'I-person'.

Get into the habit of using 'I' statements. As Elaina Zuker explains:

> When you speak for yourself, you are announcing that you are the expert on you… When you make 'I' statements, you are being responsible for yourself. Take ownership of or responsibility for your statements.
>
> When you speak for yourself as a responsible, assertive communicator, you demonstrate that you are aware

and clear that you are the source of the messages you send, that you are the owner of your perceptions, thoughts, feelings, wants, and actions.[8]

Leave the other person feeling positive.

Where the situation demands, offer and reach agreement on a workable compromise so that neither you nor the other party is confused about any follow-up action to be adopted, and so that the other party can save face.

Or in the words of Lisa Davis:

> Assertive people recognise that the process of negotiation involves working towards an agreement that is favorable for them and reasonably acceptable to the other side. They know that if they negotiate a deal that leaves the other side experiencing the trauma of total defeat, then they are leaving the door open for revenge and retaliation in the future.[9]

And finally…

Gael Lindenfield, author of *Assert Yourself*, advises that, if you want to be assertive, then you must:

- decide what you want
- decide whether it's fair
- ask clearly for it
- not be afraid of taking risks
- be calm and relaxed
- express your feelings openly
- give and take compliments easily
- give and take criticism.

You must not:

- beat about the bush
- go behind people's backs
- bully
- call people names
- bottle up your feelings.

don't forget

Avoid being assertive in the extreme

- Don't let 'assertiveness' go over the top and turn into 'aggression'.
- Workplace bullying can lead to legal actions for discrimination or 'constructive dismissal'.
- Don't use personal threats or intimidation – these can land you in court, too.
- Watch what you say. Name-calling can easily go too far and degenerate into defamation.
- When criticising, use natural justice principles and allow the other person the opportunity to respond.

 quotable quote

Usually we act non-assertively out of fear – the fear of saying what we want will be considered pushy or aggressive. It's not polite. Often we feel like the victim or underdog and are pessimistic. We don't think we'll win anyway, so why try? And non-assertive comments – like 'This is only my opinion' and 'I don't know if anyone will agree with this but…' – convey a lack of self-confidence….

How can we expect people to believe us, or to value what we are saying, if we don't believe in ourselves?[12]

How to model yourself on successful people

Successful people have three things in common: they know where they are now; they know where they want to be; and they move further along the connecting path each day. Their actions become the key determinants of their success. The accumulated messages of their biographies and autobiographies provide added insights into their personal qualities, offering models for you to emulate as you set and chart your own path. Here are those qualities and the actions required...

 quotable quote

Lives of great men all remind us
We can make our lives sublime,
And, departing, leave behind us
Footprints in the sands of time.

– Longfellow

 it's a fact

In his book *Lincoln on Leadership*, Don Phillips saw Abraham Lincoln as a role model for today's leaders...

He managed without overmanaging. Lincoln always gave his generals many suggestions, but never ordered the generals to follow them. He 'empowered' people before that word was even invented.

He got out there with the troops. In an earlier version of 'management by walking around', Lincoln often left the White House to spend time with the troops – more than any other US president has done – and was the first to come under enemy fire.

He knew what he wanted. His 'vision' was set in stone: an undivided union, with no slavery. He gave his followers something to strive for, a reason to keep moving forward.

He never sugarcoated the bad news. 'Honest Abe' gained respect and trust by always telling the truth to his subordinates, even when the truth was bad news.

 ### Know where you're going.

Knowing where you're going is part of the success story. Although your vision will encounter setbacks (we're told envisaged futures usually have less than a 70 per cent chance of being achieved), visions help to transform possibilities into realities. As the saying goes, 'If you don't know where you're going, you'll finish up somewhere else.'

 ### Believe in yourself.

Successful people believe in themselves, confident in the knowledge that they can achieve. Their actions illustrate that belief and provide freedom and power. They let nothing limit their potential. Positive affirmations can be effective means of reinforcing that belief.

Be open to opportunities.

Your openness to opportunities will ensure a continuing flow of them. Do not let negative thoughts and inaction limit your potential to achieve. Some success stories reveal such an abundance of opportunities that choosing which ones to pursue is most difficult. Spreading yourself and your resources too thinly must be avoided.

 ### Set goals that challenge.

Successful people know that what they focus on grows, and goals help to provide the necessary focus and direction. Challenging goals bring out the best in people.

 ### Accept responsibility.

Successful people don't blame others when things don't go as planned. The responsibility for the fulfilment of your dreams is yours. The power to succeed—or to fail—is yours. And no one can take that away.

 ### Build desire.

You have to want something badly enough to let nothing stand in your way. But that does not suggest you should turn to aggression; many success stories are those of quiet achievers. Desire helps to overcome seemingly insurmountable obstacles. Successful people, we're told, help to make things happen.

Strive for excellence.

Achieving excellence is the pinnacle, and it's attained by few. Make sure you go beyond the call of duty, doing more than others expect. Excellence comes from striving, maintaining the highest standards, looking after the smallest detail, and going that extra mile. Successful people never compromise their standards.

Demonstrate courage.

Courage is a special personal quality that helps you to distinguish between what ought to be feared and what need not be feared. Although history's successful people have never backed away from any encounter that threatened their progress, they made certain they were around to 'fight another day'.

Be persistent—and flexible.

The power to hold on in the face of adversity and the power to endure—these are the qualities of a winner. Persistence is the ability to face setbacks without losing sight of your destination. Persistence is the skill of doing everything necessary to reach your goals, including making adjustments based on the feedback received.

Learn from failure.

The law of failure is one of the most powerful of all the success laws: you only really fail when you stop trying. That's why successful people never fail. Setbacks simply provide them with essential feedback to help them chart their course.

Make honesty the best policy.

Cheats may prosper—but not for long. You will be called on daily to choose between honesty and dishonesty, and those choices will contribute to your reputation. With honesty, there is no middle ground; you can't be 'a little honest' or 'slightly dishonest'. You're either honest or dishonest.

Take action.

Action combines all of your insights, experiences, and talents into physical performance. If you've set your vision, selected opportunities, and rallied your courage, determination and desire, then it's time to act. Outlaw procrastination. Successful people know that, without action, nothing happens.

Love what you do.

Love is the most important ingredient of success. Successful people rarely distinguish between work and many of their other activities: they do what they do because they love it. Sharing that passion with a select few makes all the effort worthwhile.

quotable quote

A traveller in ancient Greece met an old man on the road and asked him how to get to Mt Olympus. The old man, who happened to be Socrates, replied, 'If you really want to get to Mt Olympus, just make sure that every step you take is in that direction.[13]

ask yourself

Take some time to think of people who have demonstrated leadership qualities to you. Who are the leaders you know? Make a list of them today. The list could include your boss, co-workers, spouse or relatives, and friends, as well as historical figures, people you've met via books, television, or other media. It makes no difference how long you make your list.

Now, why do you consider the people on your list leaders? What did they do to deserve that honour? List their qualities. Explain your reasoning. To become a leader, you'll need to develop the same or similar qualities.

Would you say you're already on track? How can you speed up that process? And if *you're* not on track, how can you get there? Use your answers to set some targets for your life; then proceed to achieve those targets.

How to dress the part

Former leading image consultant, Mary Spillane, said that 'a poor image is self-defeating; it gets in the way of you projecting your true qualities and abilities. Many of us wish this wasn't the case, that we should be assessed only on our achievements, not on any additional, superficial factor, such as appearance'.[14] But, she insisted, how we are packaged speaks volumes about how we value ourselves and respect others, about our sense of quality, creativity, and professionalism. Appearance matters for aspiring executives—and the following provides some useful introductory advice...

Know why we are reluctant to look the part.

US image consultant Susan Bixler claimed that most aspiring executives fail to maintain a polished professional appearance for four main reasons:

- *Self-consciousness:* many feel they would give the impression of being dressy merely to cover technical deficiencies.
- *Cost:* most believe looking good would be expensive. It doesn't. In fact, you can't afford to dress badly.
- *Time:* most erroneously believe they're too busy to spend time on their appearance.
- *Lack of fashion knowledge.* The literature and the store advisors can help here.

Successful people, Bixler says, counter such views to upgrade their appearance —their most visible credential.

Dress appropriately.

There is near unanimous agreement among experts that dress codes do exist and that, as a rule, they filter down from the top of the organisation. Even then, 'appropriateness' focuses on a variety of factors, including:

- *Your industry.* 'Creative' businesses such as film and advertising want to show flair and creativity, so their people wear bright colours and trendy, bold styles; bankers prefer subdued, high-quality, conservative clothes; real estate agents want to look approachable and favour casual styles.
- *The occasion.* A real estate broker may dress very differently when showing an apartment to an investment banker than when accompanying a rock star.
- *The geographic location:* The dress code of a legal firm's lawyer in Darwin may be far more relaxed than that of a Melbourne colleague in the same organisation.
- *The message you want to send.* Artistic, elegant, conservative, reliable, wealthy, approachable, solid, trendy, male dork, or female bimbo? To create an impression of trustworthiness and reliability, for example, consider conservative business wear, nothing trendy or extreme; simple quality accessories; well-cared-for polished shoes; impeccable grooming, showing attention to detail; regularity of pattern in tie or prints; discreet jewellery and minimal makeup for women; men, clean shaven.

In *Executive Essentials*, Mitchell Posner concludes that, for success in business, 'stay with a conventional look that will not offend others, but will make them notice your good taste, your understated elegance, and your appreciation of fine quality'.

Buy smart and within your budget.

Fortunately, a moderate budget does not preclude looking good—any more than a generous budget guarantees it. The secret is to use your resources, however limited or abundant, wisely. Instead of selecting classic, high quality, coordinated pieces, most people waste much of their clothing budget on such mistakes as:

- a style so trendy that, next season, it can clearly be labelled 'last year's'
- discount store purchases that fade, shrink, hang poorly, or don't last
- mark-downs that don't quite fit—but 'I'll lose a few kilos!'
- fabric that is stiff, itchy, shiny, or cheap
- an unusual colour that coordinates with nothing or makes the wearer look drab, tired, or lit up like a Christmas tree.

In *Executive Style*, Jean Woo advises you to shop wisely—by selecting the right store, keeping your objectives in mind, knowing your budget, setting aside enough time, avoiding sales, being realistic about weight loss or gain, putting function before fashion, and favouring conventional garments rather than trendy ones.

Don't forget those accessories.

Carefully selected, high-quality accessories make a statement. For a woman it may be her jewellery, scarf, and hosiery; for a man his tie, socks, braces, and handkerchief. For both sexes, it might be the watch, the card case, glasses, briefcase, wallet or purse, shoes, belt, or pen. And the literature provides a wealth of advice, e.g.

- Your tie must reach your belt buckle.
- Avoid watches if made of plastic, rubber or diamonds, or more colourful than your tie, or if they make noises or bleep.
- Avoid wearing matching earrings and brooches.
- Confine disposable pens to your desk. Use fountain pens for signatures or high-quality ball-point pens.
- Avoid clunky bangles or noisy charm bracelets.

Seek expert advice through the literature.

Today, many publications offer expert advice on personal appearance and image. Serious image-makers can consult books and magazines for detailed and intricate analyses of such wide-ranging topics as:

- body types, the images they project, and the clothing they require
- the colours and patterns of shirts, suits, ties, and dresses that flatter you, and those that make you look drained or ill
- collars that flatter the shape of your face—and those that don't
- single-breasted v double-breasted suits.

You'll be told why

- a beard in business puts people off
- blue is a good shirt colour for 'warm' men with blue eyes, but should be avoided if you have brown or hazel eyes
- you might consider wearing glasses with clear lenses to look more intelligent, authoritative, even older
- you shouldn't attempt to disguise a balding scalp by combing the remaining strands across it
- the larger the face, the larger the earrings; the shorter the neck, the shorter the earrings
- women in business who don't wear make-up look unpolished and unprofessional.

You will even be introduced to 'sensitive topics like hairy noses, stained teeth, bad breath, receding hair, body odour, fluctuating waistlines, and make-up'.

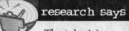

How to show entrepreneurial flair

An entrepreneur is someone who sees an opportunity and creates the organisational structures to pursue it. The entrepreneurial process involves all of the functions, activities, and actions associated with pursuing that opportunity. If you decide to establish your own business or remain where you are, entrepreneurial behaviour can be learnt and used to strengthen your existing management skills—even open new doors for you. Here's how to sharpen your entrepreneurial skills…

1 Develop appropriate personal attributes.

Though entrepreneurs come from a wide variety of backgrounds, the literature can provide an accurate picture of these innovative types.

Wayne Bygraves in *Portable MBA in Entrepreneurship* refers to the *10 Ds* that characterise entrepreneurs: they *d*ream or vision what the future could be like; they're *d*ecisive, and *d*oers, showing *d*edication, *d*etermination, *d*evotion, and attention to *d*etail they're in charge of their *d*estiny, expect *d*ollars as a sign of their success, and *d*istribute ownership of their businesses among key employees.

John Miner in *The Four Roots to Entrepreneurial Success* sees entrepreneurs as having high personal achievement, characterised by a need to succeed, with a strong belief in themselves (that they *can* make a difference), an energetic personal commitment to their organisation (existing or new), a desire for feedback, a desire to plan and set goals, and a preparedness to take the initiative.

How do you measure up?

2 Learn to work with people.

Entrepreneurs are in some respects loners, preferring their own company; but they realise the influence others can have if they are to achieve their goals. They can expect to spend a great deal of their time selling their ideas to others, so it's important to adopt an encouraging style, a sharp human-interest focus, a desire to help others, empathy, and strong positive relationships. They must be willing to persuade others to their way of thinking. Entrepreneurs, being the type of people they are, often rapidly advance in the system; but then, when frustrated by the constraints of the organisation, they reject the system to form their own.

3 Seek innovation and change.

Connecting ideas with opportunities is a form of constant engagement for entrepreneurs (some call it innovating). Because of this desire to innovate, entrepreneurs search out new ideas and encourage new product development. Although entrepreneurs may like to give the impression of being risk-takers, their desire to maintain control ensures that detailed preparation eliminates (or significantly reduces) any risk. They always like to check things out before engaging.

As an entrepreneur, explore ways to obtain the competitive advantage; and be ready to bend, if not break, a few rules. If necessary, be prepared to 'sail close to the wind' and use unconventional persuasive techniques.

Fundamentally, however, the idea of the entrepreneur as a person who always takes high risks is a myth. The leverage that you, as an entrepreneur, can bring to the use of capital is the key to your sustaining success while being both thorough and cautious in your assessment of viable projects.

So the message for you is to aspire to innovate, but make sure you always do your homework first.

Look for role models.

Environmental factors (external influences, if you like) have a significant effect on the development of entrepreneurs. Knowing successful entrepreneurs makes the act of becoming one yourself seem much more credible. Some workplaces—Silicon Valley, for example—tend to attract people with entrepreneurial flair. Though your role model may be working in the industry, don't discount the influence your family and friends can have as well.

Gain industry experience and management know-how.

Industry experience and management know-how—preferably with accountability for profit and loss—are indispensable qualities of successful entrepreneurs. More than 80 per cent of all new businesses are founded in industries the same as, or closely related to, the ones that the entrepreneurs have previously experienced. Additional skills are always a bonus, but make sure you focus your energies in familiar areas where they will get the best results.

Exploit timing.

Timing is more than recognising and responding to windows of opportunity. In fact, successful entrepreneurs resist the temptation to rush into new enterprises before they have had a chance to gather all of the resources they will need. For the entrepreneur, timing is not about speed but selecting the moment of engagement. Be prepared for when your moment arrives.

Make entrepreneurship a lifetime focus.

Leopards don't change their spots, nor entrepreneurs their dreams, desires, ambitions, and decisiveness. If you believe entrepreneurship is your destiny, then go for it!

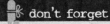 **don't forget**

Consider these characteristics

These are among the characteristics exhibited by individuals with a propensity to act entrepreneurially:

■ *Desire to achieve* – They conquer problems and give birth to a successful venture.

■ *Hard work* – They are workaholics (in many instances they have to be in order to achieve their goals).

■ *Nurture quality* – They take charge of and watch over a venture until it can stand alone.

■ *Accept responsibility* – They are morally, legally and mentally accountable for their ventures.

■ *Reward orientation* – They want to be rewarded handsomely for their efforts… and rewards can come in forms other than money, such as recognition and respect.

■ *Optimism* – They live by the philosophy that this is the best of times and anything is possible.

■ *Orientation to excellence* – They desire to achieve something outstanding that they can be proud of – something first class.

■ *Organisation* – They are good at bringing together the components of a venture by 'taking charge'.

■ *Profit orientation* – They want to make a profit, primarily as a meter to gauge their degree of achievement and performance.[18]

How to beat the Monday-morning blues

A productive, happy, and effective day is usually achieved by starting out fast and peppy in the morning. Unfortunately, the day is often lost to many of us even before we get out of bed: we self-destruct as soon as we wake up, dreading the thought of having to go to work. For most people, Monday mornings in particular can be the most difficult time of all. If you have trouble getting started each week, here is some timely advice on beating those Monday morning blues…

1 Finish as many jobs as possible on Friday.

If you finish as many tasks as you can before the weekend, you will feel much better knowing that these matters are not hanging over for Monday morning.

2 Tidy up your office before leaving on Friday evening.

Never arrive on Monday morning to find the cluttered remnants of the previous week's work.

3 Get Monday off to a flying start on Friday.

Try not to start a project from scratch on Monday. Begin a task on Friday so that you can pick it up when you arrive on Monday morning, thus giving yourself momentum and an immediate sense of accomplishment.

4 Set a new goal for Monday.

On Friday afternoon, write down a simple goal to be tackled first thing Monday morning. It won't hurt to think about Monday's goal while pruning the roses on Sunday.

5 Leave weekend matters to the weekend.

Never carry non-business issues and tasks from your weekend over to Monday morning. Get them out of the way before Monday morning or postpone them until later in the week.

6 Take it easy on Sunday night.

Schedule your weekend activities for Saturday and for Sunday morning and afternoon. Reserve Sunday night for relaxation, winding down weekend activities in preparation for a new working week.

7 Exercise on Monday morning.

Before heading off to work on Monday morning, jog around the block, or try some exercises. Bring some zest back into your life. Keep your body fit so that your emotions and your body don't become drags on your mind.

Get up early on Mondays.

If you sleep in on Monday mornings, you will only be adding to your misery. Rise early, exercise, have breakfast, read the paper, and snap yourself into the routine of the coming week.

 Schedule interesting meetings for Monday mornings.

Good company and stimulating conversation can lift your spirits. If you want to start the week well, schedule a meeting with interesting colleagues.

 Avoid big jobs on Monday morning.

Spread major jobs throughout the week. This strategy will make the thought of going back to work after the weekend less oppressive.

 Plan to vary your activities.

Schedule something enjoyable for Wednesday. On Monday morning, the mid-week reprieve won't seem as far away as Saturday. It could work wonders to improve your outlook.

 Set an example for staff.

The chances are that you're not the only one with Monday morning blues. As Arnold Brown acknowledges:

> For inalienable biological reasons, Monday tends to be the least productive for most people. It's simply natural to feel stress when making the transition from

pleasurable engagement back into work.[59]

But remember that, if the boss suffers from the Monday morning blues, those on staff who *are* enthusiastic may well decide to follow the boss's example. You see, the blues are contagious!

Managers need to set an example. See work as an enjoyable experience, and convey this impression to staff— particularly on Monday mornings.

And don't forget, as well, that there's nothing worse for a worker's motivation than to find a stuffy office first thing on Monday morning. So make sure the air conditioning is switched on well before they arrive.

 And finally...

For a fast and enthusiastic start to any new day, heed the advice of internationally known motivational speaker Tom Hopkins. He suggests:

- Listen to lively, exciting, zingy, upbeat music. It will do wonders for your morning mood.
- Listen to motivational audiobooks that you can alternate with music. Create a playlist of your favourites.
- Psyche yourself up with your own words: 'OK. Today is the most beautiful day I've ever had. Today I must really perform for my staff...'
- Push positive thinking all the way. If enthusiasm doesn't take over, negativism may.
- Start your day the night before.

 it's a fact

I don't like Mondays! – In 1979, these words rang in the ears of Bob Geldof and the Boomtown Rats who turned them into a world-wide number one rock song. The words had been used earlier that year by an American schoolgirl...

It was a Monday morning in January 1979 when sixteen-year-old high school student Brenda Spencer began firing a .22 semi-automatic rifle at her school in Cleveland, Ohio. Miraculously only two people were killed during the shooting spree – the principal and the school janitor. Nine students suffered bullet wounds.

Running back home, Brenda locked herself in and waited. In no time at all, the outside of the house was swarming with heavily armed police and, of course, the media. At last Brenda Spencer was the centre of attention. For two hours she spoke to news reporters by telephone, but in the end there was just one question everybody wanted answered – why did she do such a thing?

Now there are many motives for murder, almost as many motives as there are murderers, but there can be few more fatuous excuses for taking two lives than that offered by Brenda Spencer.

'I just started shooting,' she told the newsmen, 'that's it. I just did it for the fun of it. I just don't like Mondays... I did it because it's a way to cheer the day up. Nobody likes Mondays...'

How to fight fatigue

smile & ponder

It's important to get enough sleep to be productive in the workplace. But if you get caught sleeping at your desk, what are you to say? Try one of these…

■ "They told me at the Blood Bank that this might happen."

■ "This is one of the 7 habits of highly effective people!"

■ "Darn, why did you interrupt me? I almost had our biggest problem figured out."

■ "Someone's put decaf in the wrong pot again…"

■ "Wasn't sleeping! I was trying to pick up my contact lens without using my hands."

■ "I wasn't sleeping. I was meditating on our mission statement."

■ "Amen."

Despite your best efforts to plan your day, there are often additional demands on your time. To cope, you will frequently have to call on your energy reserves to boost your staying power. You can't afford to wilt when the pressure is on—so here are some tips to have you feeling more zip instead of feeling zapped…

1 Understand your rhythms.

It's OK to experience fatigue, because it's natural to get tired at the same time every day—it's part of a rhythm. That's why understanding that rhythm is so important. The best way to cope with your daily rhythm is to work it into your schedule—doing the things that demand the most energy when you're fresh and, conversely, keeping the less demanding tasks for when you're in a trough. And the highs and lows can be different for each individual.

2 Watch what you eat.

You are what you eat, so select foods that keep you competitive. Consider these tips to fuel your brain and body:

- Carbohydrates are good fuel, but a lunch of pasta can slow you down in the afternoon. Stay away from foods high in fat. Food that combines protein with carbohydrates—a chicken sandwich, for example—helps offset fatigue.

- Fresh fruit and vegetables are essential for providing vitamins and minerals, preventing fatigue, and boosting mental recall and concentration.

- Maintain an even blood-sugar level that keeps fuel flowing to your brain and muscles by eating small, regular helpings. Avoid a large meal when you need to be alert.

- Go for complex carbohydrates—fruit or crackers. They will keep you going longer than lollies.

- Drink caffeine in moderation. It can improve mental performance, but excessive amounts don't increase mental alertness beyond the effects of the original dose.

3 Eat smart.

A well-balanced diet is one thing; but if you don't have good eating habits as well, sooner or later you will do yourself a good deal of damage. So don't skip breakfast, and make sure it's a healthy one. Don't miss lunch, or rush it, or eat it on the run; but eat light meals. And watch those during-the-day snacks—often they're loaded with fat, salt, caffeine, and sugar.

Exercise regularly.

Get an energy boost by doing something you enjoy. How about 30 to 45 minutes of brisk walking four to five times a week before breakfast? Or 30 minutes of more vigorous activity, such as jogging or aerobics, three or four times a week? A short walk after lunch brushes away early-afternoon cobwebs. Remember, too, that a short exercise break, even a few stretching and breathing exercises in the office, will do more good for you than a caffeine break.

Get enough sleep.

Get the amount of sleep your body needs. Some people can do with less than others. Study yourself to learn how much sleep you require to feel rested and invigorated.

Get the best sleep by following a few simple preparations:

* Sleep naked or in loose clothes.
* Have good ventilation, fresh air being best.
* Sleep in a moderate temperature.
* Restrict noise.
* Buy the best mattress you can afford: firm and comfortable.
* Change your bed linen regularly.

And remember, if you can't sleep, the worst thing you can do is to worry about it. Just lie still, relax, and remember that resting is almost as restorative as sleep.

Identify and deal with those spirit zappers.

Though fatigue seems physical, it can also be a sign of mental distress—even depression and anger. Excessive tiredness and that run-down feeling should be viewed as danger signs.

Be alert to what's bothering you, whether it's a change in your life, a new boss, a domestic problem, or some other stressful situation. But do not suppress your feelings—that effort consumes energy. A much better alternative is to change how you view and deal with such events.

Learn from those who rely on energy.

Athletes can't afford fatigue when they're engaged in competition. One of their favourite 'energy-grabbers' is deep breathing. By taking three long, slow, deep breaths, pausing for long enough to let the air circulate, then exhaling slowly, pulling in their abdomens as they do, they're refuelled and ready to proceed. The technique can be used just as well when the 'competition' you're facing is a boss waiting for a report, an irate customer, or merely drowsiness.

Choose your company wisely.

Energy is catching—so too is a feeling of fatigue. Associate with people whose energy you can feed off. Similarly, stay away from negative people. Life is too short to go around with your battery half-charged and being continually drained by depressing colleagues.

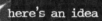 **here's an idea**

If you have trouble getting to sleep at night, and find that counting sheep doesn't work, try these sleep-inducing thoughts:

* Exploring rock pools
* A babbling brook through a fern gully
* Swinging in a hammock under a tree
* Cool fine sands slipping between your toes.

Sweet dreams.

here's an idea

Ever tried reading yourself to sleep in bed? The key is to catch the wave of sleepiness. As you read, you start to feel sleepy. It's then, when you feel the wave of sleepiness come, that you must go with it. If, however, you decide to keep on reading until, say, you finish the chapter, you may miss that wave and no longer feel sleepy. Catch the wave! When you feel sleepy, go to sleep!

here's an idea

Worry is thinking turned toxic. It leaves you in a state of mental exhaustion. When you worry, you go over the same ground endlessly and come out the same place you started. Thinking makes progress from one place to another; worry remains static. Thinking works its way through problems to conclusions and decisions; worry leaves you in a state of tensely suspended animation.

The solution? Change worry into thinking, and anxiety into creative action!

How to manage stress at work

Work stress is not necessarily a negative force. In fact, without a certain level of stress to challenge us, our jobs would be boring and unrewarding. Stress becomes a problem, however, when it reaches such an extreme that we are unable to cope with it. The solution to stress, therefore, is not to eliminate it altogether but to maintain it at a level where it remains a positive motivating force. Here are ten of the best simple strategies for keeping stress in check. They're easy to remember—and they work...

Create a pleasant work environment for yourself.

If you spend a great deal of time in your office, make it pleasant, without being self-indulgent. Convert your tired office into a place you can enjoy—with art pieces, rug, greenery, bookcase, paintings, and tapestries. And discipline yourself to keep that desk uncluttered.

Keep perfectionism in check.

Trying to be perfect in everything is not only self-defeating: it's also a major stress-generator. Learn what you are good at doing and perfect those skills.

Manage your time.

If you want to manage stress, you have to manage time. Of the stress faced by administrators, none is so pervasive as the stress of time. Forget about finding more hours in a day. Instead, use the existing hours more effectively. Set aside time for planning, contemplation, relaxation,

and problem-solving. Tackle the problems of drop-in visitors, the open door, telephone calls, and procrastination. Remember that time is the lit fuse of stress.

Avoid false guilt.

Be determined not to allow staff to make you feel guilty about something you or your organisation did. Be tolerant of your own mistakes: will anyone really care 100 years or 100 days from now? Try not to judge, criticise, or devalue yourself and your sense of adequacy. Be prepared to lose a few battles without feeling you are losing face. Learn to ignore that inner voice that tells you you should do this or should have done that. Becoming stressed about things beyond your control does little to resolve a problem.

Drive your own bus.

You can't allow everyone's problem to become yours. By all means provide a sympathetic ear—but remember that most people are capable of solving their own problems and will grow from the experience.

Nor is there a rule that says you must be available to everyone, or that you must never say 'no' to any request. You simply can't satisfy all demands. So, if you're the person in the driving seat, take charge of the controls.

Be selective about what you take on.

Resist the urge to take on everything. Remember that you're judged on the work you complete, not on the amount you take on. Slow down. Be selective. Learn to delegate duties and responsibilities. Say 'no' a little more often. Winning every round of the contest may not be necessary to succeed in the long term. Learn to discern what is worth being competitive about and what isn't. Focus on the things that really matter.

Plan and prioritise.

Stress often results from loss of direction. So, by establishing clear, detailed objectives and formulating plans and priorities to meet them, you will eradicate many ambiguities, eliminate confusion, and remove the anxiety that accompanies unplanned activity. Help to neutralise stress by achieving the sense of accomplishment that is associated with projects completed, deadlines met, and goals achieved.

Develop a support system for yourself.

Create an informal support network

that will enable you to let off steam, receive moral support, accept helpful advice, and share ideas and feelings in a leisure or social setting. The network might comprise mentors, professional colleagues, friends, or relatives. But make sure they're positive, trustworthy and enthusiastic—not prophets of doom and gloom.

Look after your body and soul.

You can go a long way towards managing personal stress at work by improving your own lifestyle. Consider these strategies:

- Take a short break every 90 minutes.
- Practise relaxation techniques daily.
- Eat only nutritious food.
- Commit yourself to exercise.
- Get enough sleep.
- Have an annual medical check-up.
- Avoid harbouring resentments.
- Have fun. Enjoy life outside work.
- Think positively.
- Develop a network of social support.
- Protect your leisure time: make time for play and hobbies.

Accept stress as a natural part of life.

Remember that you are not life's target, so don't react to stressful situations with 'why me'? Instead, have confidence in your ability to work through the potentially stressful periods and recognise that 'this too shall pass'. Stress goes with the territory; it comes with the job. Learn to manage it.

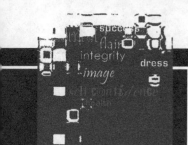

How to make the most of your mistakes

If only we lived in a world where we never made mistakes! We don't, of course, and managers are no different. As we do err, success will come to those who learn to turn their goofs into gold. The golden rule is *never ignore your mistakes*—if you do, you will probably repeat them. In short, it is no crime to err; the crime is not to learn from the mistake and not to improve as a result. Turn your goofs into gold by considering the following advice…

1 *Admit your mistake.*

Never ignore a mistake or try to cover it up. Confession can be good for the soul. In management, it can sometimes be a very effective strategy.

Unless the mistake is catastrophic, a manager has little to lose by admitting an error. In fact, you will gain the respect of staff. By admitting your error, you lend credibility to those occasions when you are right; and your staff will be less likely to challenge your judgement if they know you are honest and as demanding of yourself as you are of them.

As well, you demonstrate that you value truth above excuses, and truth is what you will get in turn from your staff. If they know that you know that everyone, including yourself, is human, they will do their best for you.

2 *Do not try to shift the blame.*

As the manager, you are ultimately responsible for the final decision and for the error. Your job now is to find ways to remedy the blunder, not to find someone to blame. If you side-step accountability by manufacturing excuses or by being defensive, you lose everyone's respect. Instead of becoming a learning opportunity, the mistake will simply become another exploding problem.

3 *Assess the damage.*

You cannot deal with a mistake intelligently unless you know how bad it is.

Consider first its *importance*—there is a great deal of difference between miscalculating product sales in one district and re-tooling a factory to produce a new product line with no customer appeal. Then consider its *cost*—there's a great difference between a $500 goof and a $50,000 blunder. Finally, consider its *implications* for you, your unit, or the organisation. The significance of the damage will determine the extent to which you must move into damage control.

❝ quotable quote

The best thing about mistakes is that they are gifts of opportunity. Mistakes are opportunities to learn, change, grow and improve. The key is not to see the mistake as the end result. It is a beginning. Accept that the mistake is an opportunity, even if at the outset this acceptance is in the form of an act of faith. If we learn from mistakes, we will never become chronic mistake-makers.[20]

💡 here's an idea

So you've made a mistake? To make the most of your error, explore ways to ensure your victim benefits.

It's not enough to correct your error. Ask yourself, 'What could I do for this poor soul so he or she will be *delighted* that I made the mistake?' Then do it, fast! In that way, your goof will become your gain.

❗ viewpoint

"You are going to make mistakes. In fact, you are going to fail repeatedly. So it's important to remember – failing doesn't make a failure. True failures are those who don't learn from their mistakes. Learn to fail forward."
– Ron Jenson

4 Determine the cause of the problem.

To learn from your mistake, you must find out why it happened. Only then can you take appropriate steps to prevent the mistake from recurring. Seek answers to such questions as:

How good was my planning? Did I allow enough time, enough money? Did I allocate the right equipment, material, and people? Were bottlenecks anticipated?

How good was my information? Was it incomplete, unreliable, out of date? Were my sources appropriate?

How good was my timing? Did I launch the plan or initiative on the wrong day, in the wrong week, month, or season?

How well was the plan supervised? Did I rely too much on others? Were they as committed as I was? Did I check progress adequately and often enough?

Was anyone else at fault? We're not always personally to blame. Was a supplier late? Did a supervisor take an unauthorised short cut? Did someone miss a deadline? You're not looking for a scapegoat, just a cause.

Did we run into unexpected problems? Did equipment break down? Did we encounter a maritime strike?

Were communications poor? …and so on.

In answering such questions, you should be able to pinpoint the cause of your mistake. You should then be in a position to cash in on what you have learned.

5 Prepare a plan of action to remedy the situation.

Any remedial action is usually dictated by the causes identified. Often, simple mistakes have simple remedies. If, for example, you underestimated costs, you must provide better budget estimates next time. For more complex resolutions, follow these steps:

- *Salvage what you can.* Isolate those components of your original plan that worked well. They're reusable. Now attend to those parts that did not work…
- *Explore new approaches.* Investigate new ideas and solutions through reading, consultation, and discussion; and get these new methods down on paper.
- *Look for flaws in the new plan*—don't replace your original mistake with one of a different kind.
- *Assign tasks and implement the new plan.*

Ask yourself: 'How much smarter am I for this experience?'

6 Encourage all staff to be alert for mistakes.

If you ensure that your staff understand that mistakes are opportunities for growth and that they can learn from everybody's blunders, you and your employees should be prepared to disclose errors as soon as they appear. Indeed, if members of your staff tell you that you have made a mistake, applaud them for it—for three reasons:

- They are probably right; if so, you'd better know about it.
- It helps staff get used to telling you unpleasant things quickly, so that you can put them right before they really go wrong.
- This way, you can learn from your own mistakes and show staff how to learn from the mistakes of others at the same time.

 smile & ponder

A lion, a fox, and a wild pig went hunting for rabbits. By the end of the day, they had a large pile of rabbits to split up.

The lion said to the wild pig, 'Pig, you divide the rabbits up among the three of us in a way that you think is fair.'

The pig divided the rabbits up into three equal piles, and said to the lion, 'There we are. One pile for each of us. How's that?'

The lion immediately sprang at the wild pig and killed him. Then, the lion threw all the rabbits into one big pile again. He turned to the fox. 'Well now, Mr Fox, why don't *you* divide the rabbits between the two of us in a way that you think is fair.'

The fox walked over to the pile of rabbits, took the smallest one for himself, and left the rest in a big pile. 'This one rabbit is for me, Mr Lion, and that big pile is for you,' said the fox.

At that point, the lion said, 'Where did you learn to divide so evenly, Mr Fox?'

And Mr Fox replied, 'The wild pig taught me.'

■ Smart managers not only learn from their own mistakes – they pay attention to the mistakes of others and learn valuable lessons there as well.

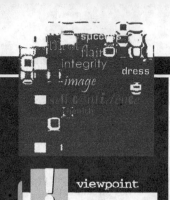

How to get rid of your bad habits

here's an idea

Having isolated the habit you wish to eliminate, it should become a focus of your attention each day. This approach will help:

- Set aside 5-10 minutes each morning to plan what steps you'll be taking that day to combat the weakness.
- Set aside 5 minutes at lunch time to review your progress that day.
- Re-evaluate your progress at the end of the day.

Do this for 3-4 weeks and, with persistence and effort, you should have all but conquered your unwanted behaviour.

mini seminar

What is it that the world's most effective individuals have that sets them apart from the misdirected, the unproductive, and the counter-productive? The answer lies not in what they have, but in what they do. Is it all a matter of habit? [21] Discuss.

Habits get a 'bad' name when those dispositions to act in a certain way have negative effects on you and others. Consistently being late for meetings, for example, becomes a bad habit when your reputation is damaged and those with whom you are scheduled to meet are adversely affected. Getting rid of bad habits is rarely a straightforward process. If bad habits—smoking, procrastination, perfectionism, gambling, time-wasting, and the like—are getting in the way of the achievement of your life and career goals, here are some key considerations…

1 Decide which habits you seriously want to change.

Acknowledging that you have bad habits because others say so won't change you for the better in the long term. Through embarrassment, you may clean up your messy desk because your colleague comments on it, but it will soon get messy again unless you change your behaviour. Ultimately, *you* will be the one who has to decide whether or not you *want* to change, and you'll need dedication to the task. If commitment is lacking, the bad habit will persist.

2 Work on changing only one habit at a time.

From personal knowledge, together with feedback from colleagues, critics, and friends, you will doubtless know your bad habits—taking too long on the telephone, doing too many things at once, nail-biting, being reluctant to praise, speaking too quickly… Don't try to change too many bad habits at once. Adopt the one-thing-at-a-time approach and remember that 'the way to change begins with the first step'.

3 Analyse your bad habit and find your reasons for having it.

Removing some bad habits will involve considerable effort and is likely to require you to explore the issues related to the entrenched behaviour. Suppose, as an example, you have a reputation for 'never being on time for meetings'. To tackle this bad habit, you may need to:

- *Identify any patterns associated with your continued lateness:*
  Are you late for *all* meetings? Are you late only for those meetings you really don't want to attend? Are you late only for afternoon meetings?
- *Consider if you are personally responsible:*
  Do you give in to the temptation to take, or make, that extra phonecall before leaving for meetings? Do you back your meetings against each other with no adequate break between them? Do you always arrive late because you have long business lunches? Do you simply give yourself insufficient time to get to meetings?
- *Determine whether other people are always to blame:*
  Heavy traffic? transport problems? waiting for others? faulty alarm clock?

Such analyses will provide useful clues in tackling your problem.

Confront the enemy.

Gestalt psychologists talk about the paradoxical nature of change—that we cannot alter a condition, no matter how distressing, until we first totally accept it. What we run from clings to us like a second skin. But when we stop running and face up to our adversary, it transforms itself into an ally that empowers us. By confronting the enemy, we emerge with renewed commitment and strength.

Associated with this strategy is the danger of associating the elimination of bad habits with 'giving up'. Resolving to 'give up' smoking, getting angry, or using bad language succeeds only in empowering what we want to 'give up', thus making the task even more difficult. The language you use in confronting any change is, therefore, most important.

Try converting your 'bad' habits into 'good' habits.

Having confronted your bad habit and being careful not to empower it, you should use it as a catalyst for developing a good habit. With effort over time, for example:

- 'being continually late for meetings' can be overcome by 'being punctual'.
- 'interrupting others while they are speaking' can be replaced by 'becoming an active listener'.
- 'poor use of the telephone' can be overcome by 'setting aside a specific time for placing and receiving calls'.

New skills emerge from the removal of habitual blockages. Once you are aware of a particular bad habit, your efforts in eliminating or changing that habit can be rewarded by the acquisition of a new, good habit.

Give yourself time.

Most research recommends 21-day programs for making long-lasting and meaningful behavioural changes. The incremental nature of the process demands that you take regular, planned, specific actions to achieve your goal. The age-old wisdom that miracles do not happen overnight certainly applies to changing behaviour. If you're patient, continue to devote time to planning, and remain focused on your desired outcome, success will follow.

Obtain professional help.

You are unique; your bad habit is unlikely to be. There are websites, books, and trainers to make things easier for you. For more serious habits, professional help can open doors that might lead to learning more about behaviour modification techniques or self-help groups. Proactively pursue your own self-development path, and success will provide the motivation for you to eliminate the next bad habit on your list.

Persist.

A bad habit never disappears miraculously; it's an undo-it-yourself project. Persist, and remember that perseverance is not a long race—it is many short races, one after another, until the contest is won.

here's an idea

According to motivational guru Tom Hopkins, the key to eliminating a bad habit is what he calls *self-instruction* – deliberately repeated thoughts about yourself that you have decided to make come true. Write a short, vivid, emotional statement that describes and attacks the habit you want to destroy, and indicate what you intend doing about it; review it three times a day; and fight any thought of surrender for at least three weeks.

don't forget

It's all about discipline...

- Commit to an intense campaign against your old habits.
- Begin changing your behaviour as soon as you resolve to change.
- Refuse to tolerate exceptions until your new habit is firmly established.

read further

Self-Help Without the Hype, R. Epstein, Performance Management Publications, 1997.

Managing Everyday Problems, T.A. Brigham, Guilford Press, 1998.

Self-Directed Behaviour: Self-Modification for Personal Adjustment, D.L. Watson & R.G. Tharp, Cole Books, 1996.

How to cope with a personal setback

At some stage in our careers or personal lives, we all experience setbacks—the rejection of a proposal, the loss of a job, the failure to get a salary increase or promotion, the death of a partner. The key in overcoming any setback is to understand the range of emotions that accompany such incidents, and to cope with them, using our knowledge of these emotional stages to guide in a positive way our behaviour, and to return once more to a state of normality. In essence, overcoming setbacks means motivating oneself after having successfully negotiated an unpleasant period of demotivation…

Know that we all react differently to setbacks.

A setback is an incident that checks our progress and brings our momentum to a grinding and usually disappointing halt. Our self-esteem can deflate; our confidence and motivation hit rock bottom. People respond differently. Some fall apart; others get back to work immediately; some turn to drink, become depressive, withdrawn, angry, and non-productive, the setback affecting all areas of their lives for some time. One's degree of maturity, particularly in terms of emotional intelligence, becomes a vital factor in successfully overcoming the personal impact of a major disappointment.

Work through the stages of emotional turmoil after a setback.

US psychologist Hendrie Weisinger identifies seven sequential post-setback stages common to most people.[22] He says that, following a setback, 'you need to experience and manage each stage, successfully moving through each one. Failure to do so keeps you stuck in a particular stage and therefore that much further from your comeback.'

The sequence of stages is not set in stone. You might experience several at once; you might flip-flop between stages; you might return to one already passed. But, says Weisinger, it is essential that you work thoroughly through each stage…

1. Disbelief – *overcome it.*
The first reaction has been likened to a lull before an emotional storm. 'This isn't really happening to me. I can't believe this.' It is a buffer between the shock of learning and the flood of powerful emotions that follow. The first productive step in making a comeback is to acknowledge gently the reality of the setback, assess the situation accurately, and know the feelings you will normally experience as a consequence…

2. Anger – *deal with it.*
An anger feedback loop that feeds on itself begins to form , making you feel worse as the reality of the setback sets in. 'It's so unfair. I'm really annoyed. I hate Jack and the way he treats my

proposals.' You complain, feel bitter, and often expect others' support and sympathy. Know that this is a natural emotion at this stage and try to defuse it through some kind of physical activity —e.g. write a mock letter to Jack, telling him it's the worst decision you've come across, and what's wrong with the company…then burn it. Or undertake other forms of anger-dissipation such as vigorous exercise.

3. Yearning for the good old days
– *which won't get you far.*
Nostalgic thoughts of yesteryear are usually the next phase. They help you to feel good; but this desire to turn back time is only a mechanism preventing you from facing reality. Acknowledge this stage and deal with it in the only way possible: accept that it's impossible to turn back time.

4. Depression – *fight it.*
Often, after a setback you'll feel like going to bed and pulling the covers over your head. Many do. Others shun friends, wishing to suffer alone, incapable of doing anything. Some find it hard to sleep and become exhausted during the day. Depression is the major hurdle in making a comeback: you slump into despondency and despair, depressing thoughts, and feelings of gloom.

On the brighter side, this stage is also the turning point: once you've passed it, you're on your way to returning to normal. Seek the support and advice of family and friends; use positive self-statements; try problem-solving techniques. Once resolved to look positively at your current situation, you are ready to move on.

5. Acceptance – *face the new challenge.*
Your confidence and motivation are now beginning to return. You've weathered the worst of the setback.

You finally acknowledge that your old situation no longer exists and that you are prepared to face the new one. Focus positively on new goals and desires, and adopt a strategy to realise them.

6. New hope – *embrace it.*
Optimism has returned. You now have meaningful goals, thought through the steps to achieve them, and are reasonably confident of doing so. Hope has aroused you sufficiently to get you to the final stage…

7. Positive activity – *undertake it enthusiastically.*
Your motivation is nearly back, and you feel encouraged, energised, and ready to do whatever it takes to follow the new course. Hold on to this new attitude by breaking down your tasks into achievable minitasks, monitoring your behaviour from time to time, embracing the support and advice of others, and using problem-solving skills to generate new effective responses to any obstacles you might encounter on the way.

Remember the 'Comeback Toolkit'.
In essence, Hendrie Weisinger proposes that, to help grapple with our setbacks, we should make use of a 'Comeback Toolkit'. He lists the following actions among its basic components:

- Tune in to your feelings and interpretations.
- Use motivational self-statements and constructive internal dialogues.
- Keep your sense of humour.
- Practise relaxation.
- Engage in physical activity.
- Use problem-solving techniques.
- Draw from your support team.
- Reassess your goals and set new ones.

don't forget

You're never alone when it comes to setbacks…

Writing was a painful process for Scottish historian Thomas Carlyle, but in 1835 he had completed his magnum opus *The History of the French Revolution* – 167 handwritten sheets crammed with 600 words per page.

Carlyle gave the manuscript to his friend John Stuart Mill to read, who in turn lent it to his future wife Mrs Harriet Taylor. She read late into the night, leaving the document on a table.

In the morning her maid spotted the messy heap of papers and, assuming it was rubbish, she lit the fire – with *The History of the French Revolution*! Mill was devastated.

But imagine how Carlyle would have felt – he had not earned a penny from writing for two years and did not possess a single note on the book he'd written.

After struggling through the despair of his setback, he began again from scratch, rereading the staggering amount of research.

By 1837, though the task 'had nearly choked the life out of me', version 2 was complete – and hailed a dazzling masterpiece.

How to overcome the fear of failure

How often have you avoided tackling a job because you were afraid of not doing it well, or backed off a new initiative because you feared it might not succeed, or not accepted a speaking engagement because you were afraid of embarrassing yourself? Fear of failure is surprisingly common. But it is a fear that can be conquered, especially when you realise that it isn't failure that counts in life: it's what you can learn from the experience that matters. Heed this advice to help overcome your fear of failure...

1 Try not to be hard on yourself.

If your company's aim was to make an annual profit of $100,000 and you managed a profit of only $78,000—is that *really* failure? Failure is a relative term, depending on who is doing the measuring.

2 Set your own standards of success or failure.

Success, or failure, is in many instances only a matter of opinion. If your spouse has always wanted you to become managing director of the company, just remember that you don't have to be if you don't want to. In the long run, it's your choice. Don't allow your life's goals to be set by others. It's better to succeed in doing your best than to fail by doing nothing.

3 Don't confuse 'success' with 'excellence'.

Why do we always think we have to win or achieve excellence in everything we do to be successful? There's nothing wrong with a par round of golf, just as there's nothing wrong with an ordinary game of tennis—provided we have fun doing it and do it as well as we can.

4 Stop seeing everything in black-and-white terms.

Why must everything we do be seen in terms of success or failure? In future, if you set yourself a goal, try judging your performance in terms of degrees of success.

5 Consider the worst case scenario.

Next time you're fearful about biting the bullet, ask yourself, 'What's the worst that can happen if I fail?' If your answer is something you can live with, why not give it a go? Remember, too, that fear of failure is the father of failure.

6 Accept that you're not alone.

If you analyse the performance of your work colleagues, you will quickly find that they all have strengths, weaknesses, successes, and failures—unless you are working with fail-proof robots. This is the human condition. So, by acknowledging that others around you are also capable of failing—and sometimes do, you may be better prepared to fail once or twice yourself.

7 Stop trying to be a perfectionist.

Being a perfectionist is laudable, if not essential, for such people as brain surgeons or aircraft maintenance personnel. But, for the rest of us, the quest for perfection is demanding, frustrating, even futile. What's important is that we display a willingness to try and not be put off by failure. Remember the adage: 'Those who are not trying and failing are either stagnant or dead'.

8 View failure for what it is— a learning experience.

Failure is only an opportunity to begin again, more intelligently. If you perceive it as part of the growing process, then failure becomes something positive, a contribution to future success, and not something to be feared. So your recent speech to your trade association was disappointing? Never mind. You can always learn more from your failures than from your successes—a good thing to remember. As Josh Billings once said: 'It ain't no disgrace for a man to fall, but to lay there and grunt is.'

Or, as Robert Schuller, in *Tough Times Never Last, But Tough People Do*, writes:

- Failure doesn't mean you are a failure… It does mean you haven't succeeded yet.
- Failure doesn't mean you have accom-

plished nothing… It does mean you have learned something.
- Failure doesn't mean you have been a fool… It does mean you had a lot of faith.
- Failure doesn't mean you have been disgraced… It does mean you were willing to try.
- Failure doesn't mean you don't have it… It does mean you have to do something in a different way.
- Failure doesn't mean you are inferior… It does mean you are not perfect.
- Failure doesn't mean you've wasted your time… It does mean you've a reason to start afresh.
- Failure doesn't mean you should give up… It does mean you should try harder.
- Failure doesn't mean you'll never make it… It does mean it will take a little longer.

9 Talk about your fears with others.

Discuss your campaign of courage with a close friend or colleague. Talking about your fear of fouling-up can be helpful if you have a friend who is understanding and supportive. Meet regularly to analyse the risks you have recently taken, to determine their 'success' rate, and to set specific targets for the future.

10 Plunge right in!

The purpose of fear is to warn us of danger, not to make us afraid to face it. So, next time you fear trying something, throw caution to the winds and do it! If you're concerned about the danger, first set a safety net—but do it! Even if you achieve only partial success, you'll be doing what you really want to do, and that's a good feeling. And even if you do stumble, remember that a worm is about the only thing that doesn't fall down.

here's an idea

Salespeople can't afford to throw in the towel when they get rejected. Like the best salespeople, to keep yourself in the right frame of mind at work, remember the letters SW-SW-SW-N. They stand for an old saying in sales: Some Will, Some Won't, So What . . . Next! If someone says no and won't budge, deal with the rejection, put it behind you, and move on to the next prospect.

See success for what it is; see knockbacks, even failures, as learning experiences.

viewpoint

"Fear is the darkroom where negatives are developed."
– Zig Ziglar

here's an idea

Turn failure into advantage. If a project flops, sit down and, rather than assign blame to yourself or someone else, explore the real reasons for the failure. Search for the cause – Were the resources insufficient? Were they faulty? Was the timing poor? Was the planning inadequate? Was the data erroneous? Did failure reside in a personality trait – perhaps a tendency to jump to conclusions, or to rely on ambiguous data? Only then can you address the problem at its root.

It's what we learn from the experience of failure that matters.

How to become a leader

Leadership is not an exclusive club for those who are 'born with it'. Although leadership relies on some inherited characteristics, it also depends on training and experience. Indeed, many of the traits and abilities that are the raw materials of leadership can be acquired. If you link those traits with an essential desire to achieve, nothing can keep you from becoming a leader. You may even become a great leader. This ten-point program will get you started...

Believe that you can become a leader.

Leadership is a function; it is something that a person does, a set of skills—and any skill can be learned, strengthened, and enhanced. Not all leaders are 'born leaders'; and leadership is certainly not just a group of personality traits. The leader lives within each of us. So acknowledge that leadership begins with your own belief in yourself.

Be sure you have a burning desire to lead.

Are you 'fired-up' and enthusiastic enough to get something done? Leaders must have a desire to serve, to achieve a goal, and to leave things better than they were when they found them. Remember, leaders need causes and causes need leaders. So make sure you have a clear sense of mission, a focus, a band-wagon to leap on—and a passion to achieve.

Study the qualities of recognised leaders.

What distinguishes leaders from others in the group or organisation? Interview, observe, read about and study leaders you admire. Buy or borrow biographies of leaders you respect; and explore what makes them exemplars of the art of leadership.

Be clear about what leadership entails.

Know what it means to lead. According to Kouzes & Posner[24] you must be able to:

Challenge the status quo: seek out challenging opportunities to change, grow, innovate, improve, experiment, and take risks.

Inspire a shared vision: envisage an uplifting and ennobling future; enlist others to share the vision by appealing to their values, interests, hopes, and dreams.

Empower others to act: foster collaboration by promoting cooperative goals and building trust; strengthen people by giving power away, providing choice, developing competence, assigning critical tasks, and offering visible support.

Model the way: set an example by behaving in ways consistent with shared values; achieve small wins that promote consistent progress; build commitment.

---

it's a fact

Do you know why geese fly in that characteristic V-formation, honking their way over thousands of kilometres to a warmer destination? Consider these fascinating observations – which can have meaning for perceptive leaders:

■ Leadership upfront is rotated. When the lead goose gets tired, it swaps the point position with a goose in the V-formation.

■ By flying as a team, the geese help each other by creating an upward air current for one another. Each flap of the wings literally creates an uplift for the bird immediately following. In fact, someone has estimated that by helping each other in this way, the flock gets 71 per cent greater flying range than if each goose flew on its own.

■ When one goose becomes exhausted or gets wounded, two fall out of formation with it and follow it down to help and protect it. They stay with the straggler until it is able to fly again.

■ The geese at the rear of the formation are the ones who do the honking. Perhaps they're announcing to the leaders up front that they're following and all is well. Certainly the repeated honks encourage those upfront to hang in there till the destination is reached.

It's fascinating the things leaders can learn from geese.

Encourage the heart: recognise individual contributions; celebrate team accomplishments regularly.

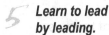

Learn to lead by leading.

The more opportunities you have to serve in leadership roles, the more likely it is that you'll develop the skills to lead. Warren Bennis writes that 'effective leaders learn by leading'—and they learn from failures as well as from successes.

Volunteer for leadership roles.

Find ways to broaden your base of leadership experience by looking beyond the workplace. Remember that there are many opportunities to develop, practise, and sharpen your leadership skills and talents, e.g.

- Volunteer for leadership roles in community groups and professional associations. Such organisations always need good people and they provide broad avenues to learn leading skills.
- Seek tougher assignments. They usually involve greater risk, but have a greater pay-off in terms of your leadership development (and promotional prospects).

Learn from your experiences.

Take time to reflect on what you've learned from life's successes and failures. Think back over one of your leadership episodes; review the experience by asking:

- Where and when did the episode take place? Who was involved? Who initiated it? Why did I get involved? How did I challenge myself and others?
- What did I hope to achieve? How did I generate enthusiasm in others?
- How did I involve others? How did I encourage collaboration? How did I foster trust and respect?
- What principles and values guided me and others? How did I set an example? What strategies and structures did I apply? How did I progress from one milestone to the next?
- How did I acknowledge the work of others? How did we celebrate success?
- What lessons did I learn from that experience about myself and about leadership?

Study yourself.

What are your strong and weak points? What should you be doing to strengthen the former and eliminate the latter? Ask for feedback from people you know. Make your own list of developmental needs—in public speaking, understanding the change process, handling people, motivating others, and so on.

Learn as much as you can about group action.

Make sure you understand the dynamics of your group. We no longer motivate our teams with a whip; we give them a dream and help them reach it—*that's* leadership.

Develop a plan of learning.

Effective leaders are constantly learning. Devise a plan to improve your leadership, including formal study, and work to your plan. Leadership is a capacity that doesn't just happen for most people. It needs to be worked at.

viewpoint

"I demonstrate the art of leadership with a simple piece of string placed on a table. Pull the string, and it will follow wherever you wish. Push it and it will go nowhere at all. It's just that way when it comes to leading people."
– Dwight D. Eisenhower

quotable quote

Each one of us, in large or small ways, is a leader. Some have an official title for their roles as leaders, while others may lead their brothers, sisters, or friends. Leadership is a state of mind – what you do to yourself, not what you do to others.[25]

viewpoint

"Leaders will be those who empower others... Empowering leadership means bringing out the energy and capabilities people have and getting them to work together in a way they wouldn't do otherwise."
– Bill Gates in *Entrepreneur*

quotable quote

A manager can make a good team work well. A good manager can make an average team work well. A true leader can change the whole attitude, philosophy, and spirit of any group of people.[26]

How to release the leader within you

it's a fact

Manager is derived from the French term 'ménagerer', meaning 'to mind the horses behind the field of battle'.

Leader is derived from the Norse term 'löder'. It means, literally, the one person on a Viking raiding ship who knew how to read the 'lodestone', which was a crude compass.

viewpoint

"A person might be a brilliant leader in one situation and hopeless in another. General George Patton was a very effective combat tank division commander, but I think he'd have trouble leading my local school's Parent Teacher Association. And a good PTA chair might not make a good tank division commander!"
– Fred Fiedler

There is nothing elusive about leadership. Although great leaders may be as rare as great runners, great painters, or great actors, everyone has leadership potential—just as everyone has some ability at running, painting, and acting. Unfortunately, there is no simple formula, no foolproof handbook, that leads inexorably to successful leadership. But don't despair, for if you can draw on the following essential leadership qualities, you'll be well on the way to displaying the features of a great leader…

1 Make a commitment to work hard.

Nothing of worth comes easily. Most great leaders thrived on hard work, their main motivator being their desire to meet their own high standards. You'll find that a combination of self-discipline and a desire to make a difference will provide the necessary commitment to succeed.

2 Show confidence.

Overwhelming confidence in your own ability is essential. If you don't believe in yourself, others can't be expected to believe in you. Confidence can be acquired through experience, skill, and positive affirmation. People will 'buy into' the leader before they 'buy into' his or her leadership.

3 Display integrity.

Integrity is a quality you must develop. It helps to build trust, allows you to influence others, sets and maintains high standards, and builds your reputation as one who can be relied on. Socrates told us that 'the first key to greatness is to be in reality what we appear to be'. In today's terminology it's known as congruence… Followers are acutely aware of any difference between what you say and what you do.

4 Demonstrate extraordinary persistence.

Researchers have identified three major opportunities for learning to lead—trial and error, observation of others, and education. All three require 'stickability'—seeing tasks through despite the setbacks and learning from your mistakes. Success is experienced only by those who are prepared to persist.

5 Be responsive.

Responsiveness is giving customers or employees what they want—courteously, when they want it, at a price that matches their expectations. You will be remembered not for the number of tasks you take on but for those you complete successfully. Your level of responsiveness will be the quality you will be recognised for.

 Bring out the best in others.

Leadership doesn't occur in a vacuum. Invariably it involves working with others—selling them your dream, instilling in them a desire to achieve, motivating, cajoling, even coercing them. Your ability to influence is a key leadership factor. Be tolerant of those less competent than yourself, providing they are willing to make the effort to perform to the best of their ability.

 Demonstrate a high degree of energy.

Often actions speak louder than words. Be prepared to share the load; roll up your sleeves and mix it with others; apply yourself longer; and give that little bit extra. To that end, maintain a level of fitness that ensures you are physically capable of leading by example.

 Back your judgement.

Boldness and courage are two key leadership qualities. You need to demonstrate a willingness to take chances, to experiment, and to display a level of optimism that rejects any prospect of failure. Any failure is viewed as an opportunity to begin again, better prepared than before.

 Develop humility.

Learn to recognise your place in the scheme of things. Demonstrate high ideals, a strong sense of personal morality, and avoid the 'sand-pit behaviour' so reminiscent of child's play.

 Get your timing right.

Seizing the moment is the key to any successful endeavour, so make sure you get your timing right when taking action and making decisions. Timing is a combination of alertness, foresight, and imagination.

 Develop a winning attitude.

It's not what happens to you; it's what you do about it that counts—and your attitude will determine your response. As John Maxwell writes in *Developing the Leader Within You*, 'The pessimist complains about the wind. The optimist expects it to change. The leader adjusts the sails'. Resolve now to start thinking and acting like a leader.

 And finally, focus on the 10 C's of leadership…

Bear in mind Michael Pegg's 10 C's, the characteristics of compelling leadership. You'll need to be…

1. Charismatic
2. Caring
3. Committed
4. Crystal-clear
5. Communicative
6. Consistent
7. Creative
8. Competent
9. Courageous
10. Crazy (well, just a little) to think that you really can make a difference.

How to prepare yourself for a brilliant career

Climbing the management ladder to success is not something to be left to chance. Unfortunately, there is no magic formula. In fact, no two management consultants would agree completely on any certain recipe for reaching the top job. They would agree, however, that, if you are ambitious to reach the top, then the best person to help you get there is yourself. So here are a few guidelines to help you on your way…

1 Be prepared.

There are no better candidates for advancement than those who, while handling their own jobs in exemplary fashion, have also prepared themselves for the job above theirs. Keep close to the people whose job you want, for they often have much to say about their successors.

2 Attend seminars and courses regularly.

The sharpening of management skills through continuing education is essential for effective managers. Additionally, exposure to other managers at seminars and conferences is stimulating.

3 Build your own management library.

Exposure to the literature of management is vital to one who would manage. Management is a profession that can be taught, read about, and learned. Build up a personal management library—and use it.

4 Subscribe to at least one top management journal.

A good management journal is the primary source of new ideas and information and is an essential tool for managers who need to be up to date with the latest in the field.

5 Join at least one professional association.

Such associations provide the opportunity to 'get a fix' on the job; to mix with others facing similar problems and seeking similar answers; to break the daily routine; to hear professionals present topics of managerial interest.

6 Be seen.

Become visible and known by name—through networking, attending conferences and seminars, writing for professional journals and newsletters, joining committees and taskforces, being active in professional associations, and attending company social get-togethers.

quotable quote

People used to have a career master plan: get a degree, get a job, get a gold watch when you retire… To survive today, you have to learn to manage your career and your life in a changing workplace.[1]

here's an idea

According to management consultant Brian Tracy, everyone works eight hours a day for survival. The time spent *beyond* eight hours, he adds, allows one to become excellent in one's field.

By simply spending one extra hour a day developing a special area of expertise, it is possible to rise to the top three per cent in one's field within three years, he says.

So, career advancement could well depend on disciplining yourself to set aside that extra hour each day.

don't forget

It's an old saying…

Success is only a matter of luck – just ask any failure!

7 Develop a questioning mind.

A questioning mind is alert to change, is constantly in search of facts, relates facts to situations and projects them into future possibilities, views interruptions as opportunities, and seeks and explores relationships among facts, situations, and people.

8 Lead from the front.

Support the efforts of your subordinates. By helping their careers, you ensure strong loyalty. Build a strong team around you to complement your skills, and undertake team tasks crucial to your organisation's success. Publicise the results.

9 Dedicate yourself to the organisation.

Show your interest and dedication to the organisation. Take on new assignments. Tackle existing tasks in different ways. Talk shop with your colleagues.

10 Build a reputation as a forward-looking manager.

Broad-mindedness, appreciation of innovation, creativity—all have a place in the portfolio of a modern manager. Experiment with applying new approaches to executive problems and routine tasks.

11 Be aware of the company culture.

If you want to climb the company ladder, be aware of the company culture. If others wear white shirts and ties, don't wear turtlenecks; if others work twelve-hour days, don't arrive at 9.00 and leave at 4.30; if others work as a team, don't hog the spotlight. On the other hand, if you want to be nonconformist, start by outperforming the others.

12 See yourself as a winner.

Understand the politics of your organisation and the values of each level within it and match your achievements to them. Be ready to make firm, sometimes unpopular, decisions. Be loyal, but don't jeopardise your career. Use talented people to cover your weaknesses. Be realistic about your strengths, weaknesses, and ambitions.

13 Remember also...

- Review your performance continually. Spend 15 minutes at the end of each week considering your successes and mistakes, and learn from them.

- Be determined to improve. Experience alone will not bring improvement. Welcome constructive criticism.

- Find a nonjudgmental mentor who will help you by providing feedback, suggestions, challenges, and support.

- Ask yourself continually, 'How can I proactively determine my own destiny?'

smile & ponder

In his day Gary Player won more international golf tournaments than anyone else and later went on winning on the Seniors circuit. One day someone commented to him: 'I'd give anything if I could hit the ball just like you.'

Player's response was: 'No you wouldn't. You'd give anything to hit a golf ball like me if it was easy. You know what you've got to do to hit a golf ball like me? You've got to get up at five o'clock in the morning every day, go out on the course, and hit one thousand golf balls. Your hand starts bleeding, you walk up to the clubhouse, wash the blood off your hand, slap a bandage on it, and go out and hit another one thousand golf balls. That's what it takes to hit a golf ball like me.'

▪ And there are many successful people at the top of their profession who would endorse the words of Gary Player.

here's an idea

Look for new "ah ha" ideas all the time. Keep an 'Ideas File' – a ring binder or notebook in which you record all new ideas. At least once a week, in a standing appointment with yourself, review your ideas.

41

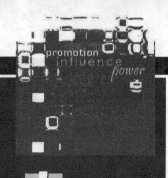

How to prepare a résumé that promotes you to best advantage

A résumé is a vital first step in achieving your next promotion. It is, in essence, your personal advertisement, a short document encapsulating your qualifications and experience, a door-opener to that all-important next step, the job interview. The following check list is designed to help you to prepare and present a winning résumé…

Format

Résumés can be prepared in various formats, the most common being:

- *Chronological*: your experience and information are listed in reverse chronological order, present job being cited first. This format clearly shows your growth and development.
- *Functional*: your work experience is arranged in categories such as project management, leadership, personnel administration, stock control, community relations, and finance.

Burdette Bostwick (*Résumé Writing*, John Wiley, NY, 1990) details ten varieties of formats; Richard Beatty (*The Résumé Kit*, John Wiley, NY, 1991) focuses on three. Serious résumé writers should consult such books, which are rich in sample résumés and covering letters.

Process

The résumé writing process involves the following steps:

1. Assemble the information on yourself.
2. Select information relevant to the position advertised.
3. Decide on résumé section headings.
4. Prepare a first draft.
5. Allow an 'incubation' period.
6. Revise your draft.
7. Review it with others—then rework it.
8. Use a high-quality secretarial service.

Content

Remember that *résumé* comes from the French word meaning *summary*—so your text and headings must be concise, to the point. The document must convey your potential by telling *briefly* what you have already accomplished.

- ☐ Reveal your abilities, your potential, and what you can offer the employer by citing past experience as proof.
- ☐ Link your experience and skills to the relevant job objectives.
- ☐ Emphasise your achievements rather than simply describe your responsibilities. They are not the same.
- ☐ Use section headings, such as Personal Directory (name, address, contact), Qualifications, Work History, Achievements, Honours, Professional Affiliations, and References.
- ☐ Avoid gaps in employment in your

Work History section. A gap in work history is a red rag to employers, and could get your résumé discarded.

- Don't make the employer read the entire résumé to realise that you're the perfect candidate. Hit a home run with strong statements up-front under 'Summary of Qualifications'.
- Your résumé should clearly indicate how capable you are of performing rather than leave this important information to conjecture.

Style

Style relates to the way you express your content. A sloppy, dull style could cost you that all-important interview.

- Use bullets to set off responsibilities or achievements.
- Use action verbs— *led, initiated, prepared, reviewed,* or *headed*—to describe your achievements or responsibilities e.g.
    - *Addressed delays in mail-sorting procedures by introducing a program which…*
- Minimise the use of personal pronouns such as *I, me, my, myself.*
- Avoid long paragraphs. They're too difficult to read.
- Avoid narratives and descriptions.
- Check, and double-check, for typos, misspellings, and poor grammar.

Presentation

Your résumé *must* be visually inviting:

- Pay particular attention to the components of appearance—typing, layout, margins, typefaces, headlines, bullets, centring, and spacing. Poorly done, they can wreck a good résumé; well done, they can enhance a poor one. When in doubt, use a reputable secretarial service.
- Do not use borders, artwork, or decoration; and never attempt to be cute or gimmicky.
- Do not cram the pages. Clutter distracts the reader. Leave plenty of white space.
- Keep at least a 2cm margin on every edge of your paper.
- Leave space between paragraphs.
- Consistency counts: ensure that all headings, indents, margins, typesize, capitals, italics, etc. are uniform.
- Type or print your résumé on one side of good quality A4 white, cream or light grey paper, preferably via a quality laser printer or top-of-the-line photocopier.

Other matters

Also check out these points:

- Limit your résumé to two or three pages, plus a one-page covering letter.
- The laws on equal opportunity employment prevent an employer from discriminating by reason of age, race, disability, health, weight, religion, marital status, and sex. Judge for yourself whether to include such data in your résumé.
- Do not date your résumé. Your covering letter indicates its currency.
- File a copy of your résumé in a safe place. Update the document regularly.
- Know your résumé backwards before attending an interview.
- Take a couple of copies to your interview—just in case they're needed.
- Make sure your referees have copies.
- Be aware of résumé readers' major criticisms of these documents: 'too long, too short, too condensed, too wordy, too smart, too amateurish, misspellings and poor grammar, poorly presented, dishonest, lacking information, poorly expressed'.
- If you do not value yourself highly, others will not value you highly. The way you feel about yourself will show through your résumé.
- If you post it, don't fold it.

! viewpoint

"There *is* no perfect résumé. Each résumé reader (who gives you only an instant of attention) brings his/her own prejudices and viewpoint to what is written. In short, if that piece of paper does not make you look as if you fit the recipe that Human Resources/Personnel has been given, you are screened out.

So why write a résumé at all? Because it orders your thinking and helps you sell yourself more effectively. And, well done, it can be that verification of your professionalism, as much a part of your image as the good-looking suit, polished shoes, quiet hair, and portfolio."

– Eleanor Baldwin
300 New Ways to Get a Better Job

How to prepare a professional portfolio

In today's competitive environment, you need to develop a range of effective and eye-catching strategies that can give you the edge over your colleagues when promotional opportunities arise. A well-presented résumé and letter of application, and a successful interview, are of course very important; but a carefully prepared professional portfolio can also help you showcase your skills, experience, and accomplishments. Gain that extra advantage by considering these helpful ideas...

don't forget

Times have changed...

Careerwise, begin to develop your contingency plans today. Nothing will ever again be certain in organisational life. No longer is there any such thing as job security.

The ongoing compilation of a professional portfolio will help you to develop an inner sense of self-preservation, personal security, confidence and control, and provide you with an important personal and professional showcase – just in case.

here's an idea

Consider compiling your professional portfolio on CD or as a personal website.

Understand the purpose of a portfolio.

A portfolio is a tool that allows you to 'prove' your experience, skills, and achievement in the tough competition for management positions—as architects, designers, and similar professionals have found over the years. But, as well, the very act of compiling your professional portfolio:

- allows you to evaluate your work and reflect on what you have accomplished, how others have responded, what you have learned, and what gaps there are in your professional experience
- demonstrates an approach to problem-solving and decision-making that research suggests are essential assets of a highly effective administrator
- encourages you to survey the big picture of your personal professional development over a long period of time
- permits you to develop a fairly accurate representation of yourself as a manager. Do you like what you see? If not, how can you change for the better?

In turn, an interview panel should find clear evidence to support your application for promotion, including:

- examples and illustrations of your accomplishments in abbreviated form
- the breadth and depth of your experience
- proof of your ability to perform as a manager
- a high level of personal organisation and presentation
- evidence that you know how to select the appropriate materials for a particular purpose.

Devise a suitable structure for content.

Consider how you can give structure to your content and logically present your documentation. For example, you may decide to divide your portfolio into, say, five sections:

a. Personal development
b. Knowledge of, and competence in, management
c. Professional development
d. Community service
e. Notes and acknowledgements.

The search for content can then begin.

Assemble your content materials.

Begin by including everything you

can think of in each section, e.g.

Personal Development: Résumé; a short autobiography revealing how your professional life has developed to the point where pursuit of a career in management is a logical step; a list of short- and long-term goals; a statement that describes your values and beliefs; a statement of leadership style…

Knowledge and competence: Documents that provide evidence of experience in management tasks and initiatives such as committee leadership or membership; participation in interviews; samples of professional letters, newsletters, or reports; central- or regional-level involvement; projects initiated; proof of having collected data and made decisions based on analyses of data…

Professional development: Samples of writing for journals, newspapers, newsletters, reports, submissions; a conference presentation; abstract of research or study completed; evidence of attendance at conferences, workshops, or study groups…

Community service: Evidence of awards and honours; memos requesting your services; news clippings; descriptions of voluntary actions; certificates of appreciation from agencies or community groups; proof of professional involvement in activities beyond the company—for religious, service, or community groups…

From this weighty collection, delete material that is not relevant to the overall picture you wish to present. On the other hand, if your collection is a little thin, it's vital to begin the process *now* and to add to the portfolio over time. A good portfolio is not compiled overnight.

 Attend to its presentation.

A portfolio is not a scrapbook filled with thank-you letters, memos, and newsletters. It should reflect a successful career. It should be a well organised, attractively presented collection of professional material of which the possessor is proud. One suggestion is to present the portfolio as a solid, white ring-binder with transparent sleeves for insertion of your material. These page protectors keep the material clean, eliminate the need to punch holes in precious documents, and allow for easy additions and deletions.

 Know when to use it.

Consider this manager's approach :

"I carried the portfolio with me to the interview and placed it on the table next to me. I did not refer to it until the end of the session, when I was asked whether I had any questions or additional comments to make. Explaining that I had brought along my portfolio and would like to leave it for a few days, I said, 'If you have any questions, or want more information about me, it is all in the portfolio.' This strategy also gave me the chance to return to the office in a few days to claim the portfolio and touch base again."

It's important to be subtle and strategic. And remember, the same collection of materials may not always be appropriate for every interview. Include only those items that best represent your qualifications for the position you are applying for at the time.

Update the content regularly.

The challenge now is to maintain and update your portfolio. But you'll find it easier once you have the foundation in place.

 it's a fact

The idea of a portfolio is historically rooted in the traditions of the visual arts, where one's portfolio consists of a carefully selected sample of one's work.

 don't forget

These legal aspects…

- Make sure the samples presented are your own work, not someone else's, pinched by you to create a false impression of your competence, experience, and abilities.

- Never falsely put your own name as the author of someone else's work. This may be more than plagiarism; it may also constitute a serious breach of copyright.

- The truth often comes out because the checking of credentials and claimed achievements has now become a routine procedure in the appointment process of many organisations.

- There can be severe legal penalties for falsification of your portfolio.

 **viewpoint**

"I will study and prepare myself and one day my chance will come."
– Abraham Lincoln

How to face your next job interview with confidence

In applying for a new job, you may indeed be experienced and well qualified, and you may have submitted a wonderful letter of application and a perfect résumé. But today, more than ever, it's that face-to-face interview that really counts. To gain the advantage, you'll need to project a confident image, as the following strategies suggest...

Do your homework.

If you've done your research and preparation thoroughly, it will come across confidently and naturally during an interview. So,

- *Know your résumé thoroughly.* Be able to elaborate on each item and to discuss strengths and weaknesses confidently, positively, and honestly.

- *Assemble your résumé, other documentation, and examples of previous work* as support material for use when appropriate during the interview.

- *Familiarise yourself with the company and the position you have applied for.* You needn't be an expert, but take note of a few important facts. Try to make some global observations based on the content of printed materials you examine (company publications, local newspapers, or annual reports) or the people you speak with beforehand. Be able to talk about the organisation's successes, and emphasise what strengths you can now bring to the company or the specific position.

- *Prepare your responses—but don't overdo it.* By all means prepare thoroughly for the questions you expect to get at the interview, but don't be so thorough as to be unprepared for those you don't

expect. And don't be so intent on giving your prepared responses that you answer questions you were never asked.

- *Be ready to ask some intelligent questions of your own.* Interviewers often give you that opportunity.

Rehearse.

The best way to build confidence and manage uncertainty is to practise beforehand. So rehearse questions related to each of the selection criteria and other fundamental questions such as these:

Why did you apply for this position? What have been your major achievements? Which of these relate most closely to the position you are seeking? How well are you going to be able to perform in the role? What is your potential? Why should we choose you? What are your special qualities that set you apart from the other applicants? Why are you the best person for the job? How will it fit in with your career plans?

Practise your responses aloud (running them through your mind is not the same). Engage in mental imaging: actually see yourself performing well; hear the certainty in your voice.

Visualise the introductions, your final statement to the panel, and your exit. Remember Don Clayton's advice in *Up the Ladder without Snakes*:

'Most of us tend to make rehearsal a half-hearted affair and we are rewarded (or punished) for this when we walk into the room and feel our minds melt into mush.'

3 Pay attention to first impressions.

First impressions count a great deal:

- Look the part. Dress appropriately.
- Make sure you arrive ten minutes early —ample time to psych yourself up. Never arrive late. Ensure you don't feel rushed. Breathe in deeply; exhale slowly.
- Walk in confidently and be sure to smile, make direct eye-contact, and introduce yourself. Carry your materials in your left hand, so that you are ready to return a handshake firmly without fumbling.
- Relax. Try to give the impression that you are approaching the interview confidently and calmly.

4 Use these proven interviewee tactics.

Be familiar with and use the following techniques during the interview itself:

- Support your answers with examples.
- Think before you open your mouth. Take a few seconds before responding.
- Make your answers long enough to cover the topic and short enough to hold interest.
- Gauge how the panel is reacting (tired, alert, interested, bored?). Respond accordingly.
- Remember: most people hear only about 10 per cent of what you say. The rest is *how* you say it—your tone of voice,

body language, facial expressions.
- A winning vocabulary is essential. Judiciously use buzzwords that emphasise your commitment, awareness, effectiveness, and knowledge— e.g. empower, excellence, mission, participate, initiate, collaborate, accountable, cooperative learning, lead, performance-based, etc.
- Speak positively of past experience. Emphasise the positive aspects of your previous positions. Acknowledge the contributions of colleagues to show you're a team player.
- Listen attentively during the session.
- Don't try to answer questions you don't understand. Request clarification.
- If you are interview number three or more for the day, the panel could well be in a daze by the time it's your turn. You'll need to revive interest—a non-routine answer, some appropriate humour, a novel solution—nothing out of character, just enthusiasm and pizzazz to set you apart from the pack.
- Watch your body language: don't deliver your lines from behind a tangle of crossed legs, folded arms, or slumped shoulders. Sit erect and try to mirror the body language of the interviewer.
- Answer questions truthfully. Misrepresentations could return to haunt you.

5 Leave a good impression.

Interviewers forget 85 per cent of what you have said an hour after you've gone. You need to impress positively in the final phases of the interview. The panel should remember you as confident, enthusiastic, energetic, and dependable. End as you began— with a smile, direct eye-contact, firm handshake, and a few positive words.

 smile & ponder

A candidate I once interviewed for a secretarial position could type 90 words per minute and take short-hand at 120 words per minute.

She was presentable and had good references …but in addition to showing up ten minutes late, she called me 'Mr *Melody*' (instead of Medley!) throughout the interview. The two main things I remembered about her were that she had kept me waiting and that she had constantly mispronounced my name. I finally offered the job to someone whose typing and shorthand skills were not nearly as good.

■ My message? More often than not, it is the little things that occur in an interview that spell the difference between getting a position and being rejected.[6]

research says

Research has found that applicants who engage in more eye contact at interview are seen as more confident, alert, dependable, and responsible. In another study, only applicants who used an above-average amount of eye contact (accompanied by a high-energy level, speech fluency, and voice modulation) were invited back a second time.[7]

How to prepare yourself before taking up that new position

So you have been appointed to a new management position. Congratulations! Obviously, you will want to get off to the best possible start—that's important for your own self-confidence and for the impression you make on your colleagues. Often, however, some people feel inadequate in those first few weeks, particularly if they're coming from outside the organisation. So, to assist you to overcome any initial uncertainty and to help you feel secure when you take over your new job, here is some useful advice…

1 Take time to plan and prepare for the move.

Time spent in planning and preparing in advance for your new job will pay dividends. Usually you will have several weeks at least between the date of appointment and taking up your new position. Get yourself organised immediately and start thinking about your new role.

2 Brief yourself as fully as possible.

Make contact with your new boss and obtain as much printed material as you can about your new organisation or position. This material will include mission statements, strategic plans, annual reports, organisational diagrams, projects in progress, productivity statements, policy handbooks, and the like.

Examine the material to become generally acquainted with the company—especially the part for which you will be responsible. Check out the qualifications and responsibilities of staff. Sort through the information provided, listing items about which you might need additional information.

3 Visit the organisation.

If possible, take time out to visit the premises of your new organisation, preferably when no-one else is there. Walk around the buildings and environs. Visit empty offices or workrooms; read the bulletin boards. Browse and observe—not to be critical but to familiarise yourself with the surroundings. First impressions can be important later on, so take notes. In time, these notes can be very revealing.

4 Spend time with your predecessor.

If possible, try to have a long discussion with your predecessor. You will not, of course, be committed to continuing your predecessor's policies; but you want as much inside information about the position and the organisation as possible, so the present incumbent is the best source.

Ask for any information not

previously forwarded to you to help determine current practices and details about staff, products, policies, and procedures. Be a good listener but don't pursue issues which appear to be sensitive.

 Meet your staff.

It is much easier to begin at your new job if the rest of your team are not complete strangers. Explore the possibility of meeting with them informally for a brief chat over coffee or lunch. It may not be possible to meet with all staff at this early stage, but at least target the key players in your team.

 Clarify your role.

If you are head of a department or work group, it is a useful strategy to talk over your responsibilities in the organisation with your new boss. You won't want to discover anything unexpected on your first day! And if your position was recently created, find out why.

 Plan your priorities.

Having assembled a great deal of information about your new position and its environment and gained some preliminary impressions of the organisation's strengths and weaknesses, you can now begin to list some preliminary thoughts about short- and longer-term priorities for action.

In determining your plans for the future, these points should be

considered:

- Do not attempt to be master of all aspects of your new position.

- You do not have to do everything on your first day, or even your first week, or even your first month.

- Make a habit of consulting your colleagues before doing anything drastic.

- Avoid making snap judgements. Keep an open mind early on and make your final judgements later.

- Your first staff meeting will be an important one: you will establish your level of leadership and lay the foundation for your tenure in the position. So think long and hard about making it a success.

- You shouldn't have to establish your authority aggressively.

- Decide how you intend to establish two-way channels of communication.

- Consider how you intend in those early days to become more familiar with the people and the operations.

- Don't form alliances too quickly.

- Don't adopt a policy of wait-and-see. Show some initiative. What you do in those first few weeks will be setting the pattern for your leadership.

- Heed the native American advice: 'Don't push the river'.

- Read Richard Koch's *The Successful Boss's First 100 Days: The Official Guide for the New Boss*, Pitman & Institute of Management, London, 1998.

 quotable quote

You will have your own personal aims and needs as a manager. But remember that those who work with you have also entered into a contract with the organisation. They will give a lot if handled correctly. They will want something in return. They, too, seek meaning in what they do. They must be nurtured *by* the organisation *through* you.[8]

viewpoint

Some managers start planning what to do in their new job on day one. Too early, you may think. Well, you'd be wrong. It is far too late, actually...

"If you don't walk into your new empire with at least a rough idea of what you want to achieve, what the main things going for you are, and what are the main obstacles you are likely to encounter, you will get knocked on the head by unreasonable reality before you get into your stride. Then it will be too late to plan: there will never be time to get round to it; and you will be at the mercy of circumstances.

Working out what you want to do, before you arrive, will take time and introspection."

– Richard Koch in *The Successful Boss's First 100 Days*

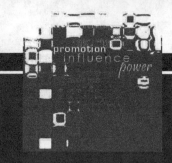

How to position yourself in your new job

When you take up a new management position—actually sit in the manager's chair—it is natural to feel some pangs of uncertainty in the new environment. The following guidelines will help you overcome the initial insecurity of these early days in the job…

don't forget

Make these adjustments…

When moving from the workface to a management position, you'll need to make these important adjustments:

- Expand and raise your own sights and become aware of new responsibilities which entail seeing things from a new perspective.
- Leave the world of specifics and details and be ready to deal with the unknown.
- Shift interest from 'things' to 'people' and make decisions affecting them.
- Realise that you are dependent more than ever before on the work of others.
- Accept responsibility for those whose work you cannot know and often cannot do or even control yourself.

1 Avoid becoming too visible too soon.

In the early days, many people will be eager to see what your approach will be, particularly in terms of changes to 'the way things are done around here'. Let there be a touch of mystery about your presence in these early stages. Just as you will go out to meet your staff, let some of them come to you. Don't show your hand until you are ready. Use this period to gather information and plan.

2 Focus on the important things first.

Don't try to master all aspects of your new position. Ask your superior to list the three or four most important responsibilities of your job, and make every effort in these early days to master them first.

3 Avoid making snap judgements.

Don't fall into the trap of making snap judgements about who's important, who's going to be your ally, who's the most impressive operator, and so

on. It's smart not to form set opinions about people until you know them well and have seen them interacting with others. Similarly, be wary of those negative stories about who's out to get whom, who's about to get fired, who's cheating, and so on. Keep an open mind and make your own judgements much later.

4 Peruse the files.

Company files will provide you with essential background information about the organisation and help you find out what's important to the organisation, how things have been done in the past, and what the current issues are.

5 Become familiar with the way the organisation works.

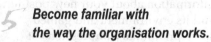

Familiarise yourself with the regular routine of the organisation, its communication networks, and the mechanics of daily life in the workplace. If necessary, fill your briefcase each night with reading matter that will help you, through home study, become acquainted with the organisation and, in particular, with that part of the business for which you are now responsible. Such documents would include annual reports, handbooks, newsletters, procedures manuals, and company prospectuses and brochures.

 Get to know your staff.

Seek out or compile an organisation chart showing staff positions and responsibilities. Over the following weeks, as you obtain any missing information, the chart will become more detailed; your knowledge of the organisation will grow. Get to know your people by name and be able to talk to them about their areas of interest both inside and outside the workplace. Focus your efforts on such questions as these:

What do you do and why? Who and what do you depend on to do a good job? What would enable you to do a better job? Are there things you do that could be done more quickly, or not at all, with little or no loss of value? What would you like to spend more time doing? Would that activity help the team and our customers? Are you fully stretched? Could some of the things you do be delegated to a lower cost resource without serious loss of quality? How can you best help me to help the team? If you were in my position, what other steps would you take to improve the team's overall performance and morale?

 Endear yourself to your boss's secretary.

Entrepreneur and manager Mark McCormack offers the following advice to all new managers, urging them to be aware of the importance of communicating upstairs: 'Most people either fail to appreciate the power of the boss's secretary as gatekeeper to the executive suite or neglect to turn that, through a warm personal comment, to their advantage. I'm convinced that my secretary could persuade me to see anyone—or, conversely, prevent me from hearing his or her name—depending on the impression that person has made.' The boss's personal assistant can become a valuable ally in getting your future ideas through the system. Cultivate the relationship.

 Avoid the whingers.

Gripe sessions about other people are common practice in most organisations. There'll be those who will want to ingratiate themselves to you in the early days by downgrading the worth of others. Their remarks are often misleading, so try to stay clear of these encounters. Remember, if you are too receptive to such people, you may acquire the kind of reputation you don't want.

If necessary, restrict your social life.

For the first few weeks at least, you should try to keep your outside social life to a minimum. After at least nine hours of intense concentration learning the ins and outs of your new position, you should be exhausted anyway, and will need time to recover overnight. Besides, the new job should be the focus of your attention in these early days.

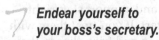
51

How to build on the successful start in your new job

A manager who has succeeded in making a successful start at a new job needs to consolidate the benefits gained in those first few weeks. To maintain that momentum, here are some further suggestions…

Seek out a mentor.

Ask for or identify a superior or colleague who can 'show you the ropes' and assist you through the first few months. Stay in contact with this mentor and take the opportunity to learn. Your mentor will acknowledge your enthusiasm, recognise your ability, and be eager to continue this working relationship.

Listen to what others have to say.

It's been said that listening is 50 per cent of our education—so listen more and talk less. Use speech to post winners, not to attract attention. Accumulate information and use it to your advantage. Your aim should be to ask smart questions to find out what you want rather than let everyone know how much you think you know.

Adapt to the working style of those around you.

Without compromising your personal and professional standards, you should fit in with your new colleagues and staff, at least in the early days in your new position. If, after observing your new organisation during the first few months, you find a change of style is necessary, you can bring about the change in an appropriate way.

Specialise.

Stay out of other people's patches; let your staff members get on with their jobs without necessarily involving you. Being a manager does not mean that you must neglect your own talents. Create winning ideas in your area of expertise. Use your talents to become recognised as an expert in your field of interest.

Respect the efforts of your support staff.

Get on the good side of your secretarial and support staff right from the start. If you treat them with consideration and friendliness, they will always be eager to help you. Do not make unrealistic demands on them; don't harp on clerical errors; and don't demand impossible deadlines. Remember, the receptionist may one day be able to give you the most important piece of information of your life; and that new junior clerk in the back office may one day be your boss.

Pick the brains of your peers.

Your fellow managers may hold many of the parts missing from a full understanding of your new position. Get to know them informally and socially. Ask for their help to learn how the organisation works. If you make your peers understand that you need their assistance, that you know less about the organisation than they do but need to know more to become a good team member, you'll find that they will help. They won't mind you, as the new guy, asking for information.

Focus on developing your management skills.

Developing, honing, and using the essential skills of management should remain foremost in your mind as you settle into your new position. The key areas include these:

- *Communicating:* expressing yourself concisely, clearly, regularly, and persuasively.
- *Decision-making:* developing the confidence and analytical skills to make timely, incisive judgements.
- *Motivating:* knowing what your staff can do, making it clear what you expect from them, enthusing them to maximum effort, and rewarding them according to their contributions.
- *Problem-solving:* adopting a logical and creative approach to dealing with the problems that will confront you daily.

- *Listening:* listening to ideas, acting on them, hearing what others say, showing interest, letting people feel they have made important contributions.
- *Self-managing:* achieving control over your day by managing time, handling paper, simplifying the workload, and coping with the stress that shadows the managerial role.

Strive for an early success.

People make judgements on first impressions and early successes. So, choose an area that will clearly qualify as a 'success', with the minimum amount of team effort and little risk of failure—something never previously attained that would make the team feel good. Make it a modest objective, something that could come to the attention of people who are important to your unit, both inside and outside the organisation—for example, launch a new product successfully; remedy a costly mistake inherited from your predecessor; hit a higher level of monthly sales; improve the quality of service in an important and measurable way…

Take your time—be patient.

Unless you've been instructed to bring about change overnight, demonstrate your capabilities over time rather than try to hit full pace on the first day or during the first week. Tread lightly, one step at a time, and maintain a good sense of humour. Take all the time you need to get all the knowledge you need—about the business, your employees, your work, and the jobs you have to delegate. Only then can you give your people the time and attention they need to work well.

don't forget

Drucker's Six Deadly Sins

Management's elder statesman, Peter Drucker, identified six frailties which he advised those who take on new managerial and leadership roles in any organisation to guard against:

1. Having lofty objectives that can't possibly be met.
2. Trying to do several things at once. Splintering of efforts guarantees non-results.
3. Believing that 'fat is beautiful'. For example, overstaffing makes non-performance somewhere in the organisation a certainty.
4. Failing to experiment.
5. Making sure you cannot learn from experience.
6. Refusing to abandon. Everything outlives its usefulness and the belief that it won't will ensure that it will. [12]

Committing two or more of these sins, said Drucker, will guarantee that a manager will perform poorly – so keep them in mind when you take on that new management position.

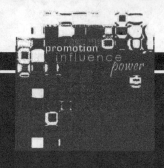

How to prepare for your own performance appraisal

It's hard to like performance appraisals, whether they're the traditional type or the 360⁰ version. At one extreme, they're an annual ritual at which bosses or their nominees list a litany of your flaws and then send you away to reduce or eliminate them. At the other extreme, however, they're a wonderful opportunity to discuss openly your job performance with your boss. If *you* show some initiative, you'll get a great deal from an appraisal interview, as the following points reveal...

ask yourself

The end of the first year in a new position can be a major milestone. It is, therefore, an appropriate time to re-read the CV and letter of application you submitted for the job. Use these documents to evaluate your progress as a manager, focussing on such areas as:

- Have I begun to achieve what I set out to do?
- What factors have helped or hindered my progress?
- How accurate was my reading of the situation and culture of which I am now a part?
- What do I know now that I wish I had known before?
- How can I use this knowledge constructively?
- How closely has my practice reflected my beliefs?
- What would I write now if I were to re-apply for my own position for next year?

1 Become a participant rather than a target.

Resolve to take an active part in any appraisal, preparation being the key. Begin by accumulating evidence of your own performance throughout the year. For example, you might decide to:

- Keep 'hard' copies of your contributions, accomplishments, awards, and so on. File cards can be completed daily or weekly to help you to maintain an up-to-date record.

- Regularly update a computer data base set up specifically for that purpose. A scanner will eliminate the need to accumulate hard-copy samples of your work.

- Compile a professional portfolio (see page 44) and a personal achievement list (see page 64).

- Use a copy of the appraisal form to help structure your presentation. Include an agenda and support materials.

The quality of your preparation will convey the right message to the person conducting the appraisal.

2 Talk to others about their interviews.

Colleagues and workmates will prove to be valuable sources of information to help in your preparation. You might ask them about:

- their impressions of their appraisal interviews—procedures, outcomes, and questions
- the boss's level of preparedness and specific agenda items
- issues discussed
- follow-up items
- suggested improvements for future interviews.

3 Be prepared to assert your position.

To participate successfully as an equal partner in the discussion, you must assert yourself rather than act submissively. Your assertion skills will be improved if you give some thought to the types of questions you will be asked and practise your responses aloud. You can disagree if you think the boss is wrong, but take issue with the facts, not the boss's judgement. Be prepared to look on any criticisms as opportunities for improvement.

 Get your documentation right.

Documentation to support your case is important. It should include a variety of data, supported by examples wherever possible, that will help you to lead the discussion and respond to any queries. If salary increases are linked to performance appraisals, your prepared argument and supporting evidence should lead to acknowledgement of your worth. The effort that goes into your preparation may help make your job secure; and the accumulated data will serve as a valuable addition to your résumé and portfolio in interviews for further promotions. Offer to leave any relevant material with the boss.

 Rehearse.

The boss may not know the details of your job, and probably will not want to—that's what *you* are paid for. The one key quality you need to convey, however, is confidence. All your actions and words must reinforce your boss's confidence in you. Practise your entry and exit. Give some thought to the layout of the room where the interview will be conducted and plan accordingly. Remember, most meaning is communicated nonverbally. For example, your bearing and the tempo (rhythm) of your voice are important factors; so prepare by reaffirming

that 'When I'm at the interview I'll be calm, confident, and relaxed'. You'll be impressed by the result.

 Confirm the interview.

The interview is about you and your future, so make sure it proceeds as planned. Confirm the time, place, and duration. If you've followed these suggestions you may decide to provide in advance a copy of your agenda and any documentation you have prepared. That forethought will not only help the boss's preparation but also demonstrate the importance to you of the meeting.

 And finally...

- Listen carefully.
- Ask questions if you need clarification.
- Focus on outcomes.
- Emphasise the future, not the past.
- Thank your boss and make a commitment to follow up.
- Review the goals you discussed with your boss and take steps to implement them. If professional development was an issue, sign up for a seminar. If you're supposed to make more decisions, make them...
- Prepare for the future now. Don't wait for the appraisal process to discuss your performance with your boss. Arrange for regularly scheduled progress reports. Short, focused sessions ensure that you're well prepared for the next appraisal session.

 ask yourself

■ How do you feel you have performed in your job, during the period under review?
■ What difficulties (if any) have you encountered relating to aspects of the job which are within, and outside, your control?

 here's an idea

Managers have room for improvement – even those who think they're perfect...

You may be in for a surprise. Do *you* really know what your staff think about your accessibility and willingness to listen? your supportiveness of their efforts in the workplace? the way you run your staff meetings? your handling of crisis situations?

To find out, why not design a report card for yourself, one that gives your staff the opportunity to reflect on your effectiveness?

A simple, non-threatening form consists of but three statements – *Do more...*, *Do less...*, and *Continue to...*, and a space after each for staff input. Distribute the blank forms to staff and ensure responses are anonymous to guarantee honest input.

Share the results with staff. You might even want to draw up a plan of action in response to their input and share that plan with them.

Managers should risk evaluation by subordinates – if only to see themselves as others see them.

How to improve your chances of getting promoted

To get promoted, you must build what management consultant Daniel Johnson has called 'career equity', in that way establishing your 'professional net worth'. Career equity is achieved by developing, improving, and strengthening each of eight specific assets that will enhance your professional value in the management marketplace...

1 Improve your knowledge and skills.

To progress in your career, you need to assess your knowledge and skills to uncover any deficiencies. Work purposefully to remedy these weaknesses. Continue to learn. Participate in training and updating programs. Attend seminars and conferences to increase your knowledge, to inform yourself of new trends, and to meet influential people in your field. Read regularly the books and journals of your profession. Creative ideas can be nurtured only by broad, up-to-date knowledge.

2 Strengthen your credentials.

Most employers still value highly credentials earned through formal post-school education. This asset can also be strengthened through active membership of professional associations and committees, and through involvement in community service organisations and clubs. Distinctions and honours gained through formal education, and through service to the profession and the community, will also gain for you important credit points.

3 Enhance your reputation.

Your reputation focuses on your overall image within the organisation and beyond. It is based on what people think of you and your accomplishments. The development of your credibility in terms of honesty, integrity, hard work, and consideration for others will strengthen this asset immensely.

4 Build up your relationships.

It's been said before: 'It's not *what* you know, it's *whom* you know.' Here's where mentoring and networking come in. A mentor can provide career information and opportunities for you. Similarly, developing a network of professional contacts is also a positive career-strengthening strategy. Talk with senior people in your field; ask how they started and progressed. Try to develop a relationship with your immediate superior and discuss career options together. Become visible and known by name. Get to know strategic people in the system by participating in relevant committees, and making worthwhile suggestions for consideration at higher levels. Working actively with others in professional associations can later lead to career advantages as well.

Remember, too, that it's important to get along with people at *all* levels: if you can't get on with others, you won't get on promotion-wise.

 ### Nurture your track record.

To build up this asset, you need to be a proven performer at each stage of your career: a listing of your achievements over time will provide evidence of your track record. By developing expertise in a particular area, you also embellish your routine accomplishments and make a name for yourself in the wider business community.

Finally, don't hide your light under a bushel: make sure others know of your successes, but be subtle about it.

 ### Consider your tenure.

How tenure affects career equity varies greatly from profession to profession. In some organisations still, however, the longer an employee's tenure, the greater the respect accorded. Increasingly, though, in an age of rapid change, effectiveness on the job is often far more important than tenure.

 ### Weigh up your life-balance.

Your career will be greatly enhanced if your life as a whole is in balance. Work towards establishing harmony between your job and the following important life areas: health, spiritual and mental well-being, finances, social-recreation, and family-lifestyle.

 ### Focus on your effectiveness.

In your quest to build career equity, effectiveness depends on all the other assets. It also encompasses a wide range of components of your job including, for example, self-management, interpersonal communication skills, leadership style, motivational skills, time management, public speaking, chairing of meetings, and so on. And remember…

A successful year is the sum of successful months.
A successful month is the sum of successful weeks.
A successful week is the sum of successful days.
A successful day is the sum of successful hours.
A successful hour is the sum of successful habits.
In the end, successful habits provide the foundation for promotion.

Take time to analyse your assets in each of the eight categories listed, and then search for ways to improve in each one. In a year's time, not only will your effectiveness have been increased, but your career equity and promotional prospects will have been boosted as well.

research says

A New Zealand survey found that employers place emphasis on personal qualities more so than expertise or qualifications. The most coveted attribute in an employee was reliability with a 76% rating in importance, followed closely by motivation (73%) and the ability to work as part of a team (70%). Confidence rated 56% and qualifications 38%.[15]

here's an idea

For those seeking promotion, mastery of the language is important – and here's a good way to increase your vocabulary skills… *use a paperclip!*

When you come across an unknown word, look it up in the dictionary, highlight it, and place a paperclip on that page. The next time you use the dictionary, repeat the process, but this time check to see if you remember the previous word. If you do, remove its paperclip.

ask yourself

In today's hectic business environment, your supervisors often don't have time to notice what you are doing. You have to tell them – and show them. You need to become your own public relations person. Ask yourself – *how?*

How to choose the best course for further study

Advancement in most professions these days requires continuing self-development through formal coursework at recognised educational institutions. Such courses can be very expensive—sometimes running into tens of thousands of dollars. They are also very demanding in terms of your hopes, energy, and time. Drop-out rates can be as high as 30 per cent. Many students persevere even though they admit they made the wrong choice. Further study is a major investment, so you would be wise to consider the following advice before choosing your program…

Focus on your own qualities.

Consider first your personal motivations and hopes. Are you the type of individual who finds formal study hard work, or do you get enjoyment from such activity? Are you seeking specific understanding and skills to boost your future employment prospects, or will study be simply a way of keeping youself up to date, giving you a chance to catch up with what's new and interesting? To what extent are you motivated to learn?

Consider your personal circumstances.

Examine your current personal situation. Can you, for example, afford the tuition fees, textbooks, additional travelling, residential workshops, laptop computer, or other requisite tools? Will the demands of home life and work allow you enough time and energy to undertake the course? Will your current employers acknowledge, reward, or appreciate your acquisition of additional skills or qualifications? Just how realistic are your hopes?

Analyse the big picture.

Always try to begin with the entire menu of courses that interest you. Never enrol in a course or institution simply because you happen to have heard of it. Obtain a copy of such publications as *The Australian Good Universities Guide* or TAFE handbooks, which usually list all available courses in detail. Begin with a process of elimination—rule out those courses that you can't afford, can't reach, or can't get into. Arrive at a short list of viable options after also considering whether you want to study full-time or part-time, on campus or off campus, course duration, assessment methods, and whether the offerings are too specific or too general for your purposes.

Explore the quality of your short-listed courses.

Having isolated several possible programs or courses, your process of elimination can become even more specific. Ask such questions as these:

- How experienced and qualified are the teaching staff?
- Who are the other students in the course likely to be?
- Will those students have backgrounds that I will find helpful or interesting?
- Is the program or course too big or too small for my requirements?
- How employable are the graduates of this program?
- What are their starting salaries?

You will find the answers to such questions in the range of Australian Good Universities Guides currently available—e.g. *The Australian Good Universities Guide to Business and Management*—and in material provided by the institutions themselves.

5 Focus on your chosen course of study.

Once you have eliminated all but one or two likely programs, you should begin first-hand research. This process may seem like hard work but, because of the amount of time, energy, and money you will eventually be allocating to your final choice, now is the time to be certain of your selection.

Approach the course coordinator. Explain your hopes and background, and discuss the appropriateness of the course for someone in your position.

Seek evidence. Ask the coordinator for evidence from student evaluations and course reviews, as well as labour market research on graduate employability, salaries, and career success. In an age of high competitiveness, most reputable institutions have such data readily available.

Approach previous students. The coordinator should be able to provide you with the names of graduates— and drop-outs. Ask graduates how the course affected their skills, outlook, and careers. Inquire about course basics—the quality of lectures, tutorials, assignments, staff assistance, and so on. Would they hire a graduate from the course? Have they heard of similar or better programs offered elsewhere?

Check gender issues. Women might be interested in the extent to which gender issues are addressed in the program, the number of female students and staff, and the degree to which the course is female-friendly.

Consider the on-line possibilities. Increasingly, for those with heavy family, work, and other commitments, tertiary institutions are offering online study opportunities for busy students. Investigate this possibility in your areas of interest.

6 Don't be fooled by the glossy literature.

In competing for students today, educational institutions have become increasingly market-wise. Their brochures, handbooks, and websites can contain plenty of hype and gloss, and only after having penetrated this sometimes superficial material and conducted your own thorough research into all available offerings can you afford to fill out your application form with confidence.

---

viewpoint

"You will have your own reasons and possibly your own set of anxieties for returning to study. Your reasons may be bound up with career advancement, or with a need to prove to yourself that 'you can do it', or with competition with colleagues, or it may be that your employer feels you need more qualifications. On the other hand, it may mean that you have quite simply always wanted to engage in further study but have, for one reason or another, never had a chance…

Whatever your reasons, returning to study, whether full-time or part-time, is by no means easy… But many have found that, in the face of new and potentially conflicting demands, it helps to be very clear about the reasons for accepting the challenge of further study."
– Stuart Powell in *Returning to Study*

it's a fact

For increasing numbers of students unable to attend a campus, e-learning – delivered through the Internet – is fast becoming a viable option. But self-management is a major factor in e-learning – which is why most courses in this area are developed at post-graduate level where students display greater maturity.

How to make the most of your professional reading

To remain fully effective, managers can usually turn to a variety of sources for personal and professional growth—courses, conferences, networking, discussions, professional associations, workshops, and so on. But of all these avenues, research shows that independent reading of professional books and journals continues to be efficient, reliable, accessible, and indispensable. Leaders simply must be readers…

quotable quote

Good readers aren't primarily readers at all. They are detectives, explorers, scientists, critics and editors – all active, seeking roles. The effective reader wants information – and uses reading as a searching technique to get what is wanted. Reading is a kind of treasure hunt. The trick is to find one's way to the gold nuggets in the most direct fashion, and in the shortest possible time.[17]

it's a fact

Did you know that a recent weekend edition of *The New York Times* weighed 3.5 kilos, and contained 10 million words in its 1600 pages? Did you also know that, on any day of the week, there is more information contained in a copy of *The New York Times* than a person living in the mid-Eighteenth Century would have been exposed to in a lifetime?

Our bookshelves bend under their burden. Clearly we need to grapple with the never-ending flood of reading material that currently swamps the management marketplace. It's vital for us to become selective about what we read. We need to make much better use of our reading time.

Accept this fact: If you're not reading, you shouldn't be leading.

The American Association of School Administrators supports this message.

Reading is *the* most fundamental, reliable, and efficient resource for leaders. It is the purpose of professional reading to equip the leader for independent creative thinking. It is through the literature that executives live, learn, and think about their swiftly moving and complex profession.

Set aside time to read.

The problem for busy executives is not finding something to read; it's finding the time! The key is to discipline yourself: set aside a specific part of each day for concentrated reading—say 10 or 20 minutes. In this way you're saying: 'I value reading. There's a time and place for everything. This time belongs to reading.' Alternatively, develop the productive habit of reading in snatches—on the train, between

meetings, before breakfast. (Evangelist John Wesley did most of his reading on horseback.) Use precious time wisely by becoming a more efficient reader…

Become more selective in what you read.

For busy managers, the secret to tackling professional reading is to do less, better, rather than to do more faster. If you can't find enough time to read, you must eliminate all the unwanted and unnecessary reading matter that swamps the marketplace. Reduce your reading load by determining the areas in which you *must* keep up to date; and select only those books and journals that currently best serve your particular areas of interest.

Adopt reading strategies that work for you.

To get value from your reading time, consider the following strategies:

- *Always scan a book before spending time on it*—the jacket, table of contents, preface, index, author's credentials, content, and structure. Weigh up these features, know what you want from the book; and only then decide whether it's worth spending valuable time on it.

- *Always read with a purpose.* Go in and find the meaning. Search for answers and key ideas. Feel free to skip irrelevant sentences, paragraphs, and chapters.

- *Resist the temptation to flick through the pages of a journal* if time is of the essence; you'll inevitably be distracted by the advertisements and peripheral material. Work from the contents page.

- *Learn to skim.* Peruse the first one or two sentences of a paragraph to see whether the information in the paragraph is pertinent to your immediate quest. If not, pass on.

- *Pause to reflect.* After each session, sit back for a few minutes to reflect on, criticise, or summarise the author's message. By so doing, you substantially increase your comprehension and retention.

- *Use what you have read.* The reason for reading is to recall a useful idea later, when you need it. Underline; make notes in the margin; jot usable ideas on index cards; start a file of valuable points or articles. Impress your colleagues: be able to cite one or two key points from each item you've read.

- *Develop a sound working relationship with a good professional library*—such as the local Institute of Management.

- *Consider speed-reading courses.* These can significantly improve the reading effectiveness of some people.

- *Set yourself an achievable goal for the year.* Try beginning with a modest one book and two journals per month—that alone becomes an impressive 12 books and 24 journals annually!

 Don't allow your reading to accumulate.

Professional literature can very quickly choke your in-basket. Resolve to read material by a certain date—or discard it. Keeping informed or up to date doesn't mean reading last year's or last month's journal today. As Michael LeBoeuf advises in *Working Smart*:

> Think of professional reading material much as you would think of a movie playing at a local theatre. After a certain date it's gone, but if it's truly spectacular it will be around again.

 Delegate reading when appropriate.

Reading can be delegated to your staff if you yourself don't have enough time to read. They in turn can underline key points, summarise, or make brief presentations to staff meetings, thus keeping you and themselves informed.

Don't feel guilty about reading.

Many managers feel guilty if they spend ten minutes at their desks reading professional journals: they erroneously feel they are not 'doing something', and fear others may think they are not being productive. This is short-term thinking. As J.J.McCarthy reminds us in *Why Managers Fail*:

> Managers must realise that their organisation's continued progress will be based, in part, on their ability, and that of their colleagues to increase their knowledge and skills and to keep pace with progress and change—through the professional literature!

Be assertive. Promote the importance of reading professional literature at staff meetings and by example.

 here's an idea

By underlining passages in books and journals you can locate important information easily when you come back to it. That's an old trick. But it's important not to underline *while* you are reading. Wait until you've finished reading an entire section or chapter, then go back and highlight the key points. This is because most of us tend to underline too many words and usually we don't really understand the key points until we've finished the passage.

 here's an idea

Have you thought about forming a reading co-operative? Find another three or four colleagues who each agree to read their share of the journals, articles or books. Then, once a month, hold a meeting where each member has, say, 20 minutes to disclose the worthwhile items each has read. It may take a while for the membership of your cooperative to stabilise but it is worth the effort – in time saved alone.

 viewpoint

"Just 15 minutes a day would enable the average reader to complete 15 books each year. Reading is a good way to use your spare time, to really get ahead in your career."
– Zig Ziglar

61

How to get the most out of a conference, seminar, or workshop

To stay on top of your career and ahead of your competition, you have to make learning a lifelong, ongoing process. Conferences, seminars, and workshops are acknowledged forms of training, information-gathering, and networking. They are usually short, practical, and up to the minute. But such events must be more than just a day away from the office. If you want to take full advantage of these opportunities to invest in yourself, you'll need to be aware of the following advice…

 Prepare yourself beforehand.

Your attendance and participation are investments in yourself, so don't leave preparation to the last minute or allow 'emergencies' to limit your pre-event preparation…

- Study the agenda, and focus on what you want to get out of the event.
- Talk to your boss about the program and find out whether there is information you should concentrate on.
- Do any pre-reading, recommended or otherwise, that will increase your knowledge and understanding of the topic. If the presenter or facilitator is the author of a particular book related to the event, read it. Take notes; list follow-up items and possible discussion points.
- Consider and contact others attending from your organisation. Discuss with them thoughts and ideas triggered by your pre-work to date. You may consider still others who should be going and recommend their attendance—either to them or to their bosses. You might consider contacting those from other organisations who may be interested. Your actions will be appreciated.

- Make a 'learning contract' with yourself by listing what *you* want from the event and will actively seek out.

Be determined to maximise outcomes.

Your attendance and participation deserve maximum results, so resolve to behave in ways that deliver those outcomes. Your list of resolutions might include these:

- Be on time so that you don't miss parts of sessions.
- Avoid internal and external distractions.
- Take risks and try some new behaviours.
- Raise issues of concern to you.
- Disagree with an opinion you think is wrong.
- Be open to ideas or approaches you would normally reject.
- Ask the speaker the questions that are on your mind.
- Start conversations with strangers during the breaks.
- Stay attentive and avoid the temptation to daydream.
- Be optimistic that a problem you have can be solved at the conference.

here's an idea

So you have trouble keeping up with the speaker at a conference or seminar when trying to take written notes of what is being said? Why not get into the habit of speed writing where you lv out unwntd vwls & consnts & smply abrev whn poss & dvlp shrt cts.

here's an idea

Think back to the last time you attended a seminar, read a book, or talked to a colleague… a time when you got a bright idea and decided you wanted to do something – but not straight away.

Why not keep a 'perhaps list' – a list of things you may do…or maybe not. These goals become fodder for future action, so file them in a place where you can access them when their time has come.

Arrive early and network.

Look on your attendance as an opportunity to spread your network of contacts. Tom Peters in *In Search of Excellence* says that 'meeting your colleagues and friends is the most important aspect of a convention'. After registering, select a position near the door or the coffee service area where you can see and acknowledge most others attending. A mix of familiar and new faces will add variety to your networking. Don't forget to include a presenter or facilitator on your list of networking contacts. Remember, the one topic that most people enjoy discussing is 'themselves'. Exchange business cards and, if necessary, arrange follow-up meetings. Jot on the back of the cards points about the contact and where you met. Don't leave it too late to take a seat at or near the front of the room.

 Participate, listen, and learn.

Introduce yourself to those seated near you. Seize this opportunity to be proactive in the interests of your learning. Take notes, but be careful not to let your note-taking interfere with the act of learning. Remember, too, that people tend to record points with which they agree rather than those with which they disagree. Why not try writing down what you're going to do with what the presenter is saying? Keep asking yourself: 'How can I use this information to improve my job or my life?' As well, jot down questions to ask at the end of the talk or at an informal gathering.

 Share information on your return to the job.

Avoid post-conference paralysis. What can you implement in the workplace? What can you change for the better? Consider also ways to disseminate information about the event within forty-eight hours of your return to work. You may decide to include your summary as an agenda item at an appropriate meeting, assemble a group with an interest in the outcomes, send an email, circulate a hard copy of your notes, or report outcomes individually. Use this opportunity to show how committed you are to your own professional growth. Others will be interested to see how you apply the information you acquired, so don't disappoint them.

Set specific requirements if you send an employee.

Before the event, inform those you're sending that you will require a succinct written report within forty-eight hours of their return to work. The report could include responses to the following questions:

- How can the organisation directly benefit from your attendance?
- Will it be possible for the organisation to recoup the cost of your attendance?
- Would you recommend that other staff attend the event if it is repeated?
- What immediate action should be taken to commit the organisation to an improvement process based on what you have learned?

 here's an idea

Every time your staff go to a conference, it's a chance for *you* to learn too. Make sure they know that, on their return, you will be asking them to sit down with you for a 'debriefing'. Develop a list of questions: e.g.

- what industry trends were people talking about?
- the hottest topic?
- the most crowded sessions? (indicating high-interest)
- new/outdated techniques or practices? and so on.

This simple tactic allows *you* to 'go' to many conferences every year.

ask yourself

A conference or seminar can be quite an enjoyable experience for you and your staff, but just *how* valuable was the experience? To find out, after returning from your next conference, you should try to answer the following questions:

- Was the level of instruction satisfactory?
- Did I ask any questions or take part in discussions?
- Did I network with other colleagues?
- Did I learn anything that will make my job easier and more effective? What exactly?
- Did I learn anything what would help my relations with colleagues in the workplace?
- What am I able to pass on to my colleagues and how will I do that?

How to accomplish more through the use of a personal achievement list

Too often managers modestly, and often unjustly or even unwittingly, hide their successes from others—and indeed from themselves. They fail to understand that the simple strategy of recording personal successes can motivate, increase self-productivity, and support career advancement. The compilation of a personal achievement list can have a considerable effect on a manager's professional life...

viewpoint

"I long to accomplish a great and noble task, but it is my chief duty to accomplish all tasks as though they were great and noble. The world is moved along, not only by the mighty shoves of its heroes, but also by the aggregate of the tiny pushes of each honest worker."

– Helen Keller

don't forget

It's all about attitude...

The only thing that limits our achievements is the thought that we can't achieve. When it all boils down, people who say they can, can, and people who say they can't, can't.

Or, as Henry Ford said: 'If you think you can or you think you can't, you are probably right.'

Which is one reason why, to motivate oneself and to record progress, a personal achievement list is well worth considering.

1 Acknowledge your achievements to date.

Most managers see themselves as 'modest achievers'. They're so accustomed to doing what they do and what is expected of them that they rarely, if ever, class any of their accomplishments as 'achievements'. Indeed, when people are impressed with something they've done—something that perhaps seems rather ordinary to them—they're surprised.

As a manager, you can use your past achievements more positively to motivate you to greater heights. To shrug off those achievements modestly, as most professionals are prone to do, or to forget about them, will just make adding further successes to your repertoire harder. Acknowledge your achievements. With a little planning and persistence, you'll be able to build on them and motivate yourself to strive towards greater successes.

2 Appreciate how achievement-motivated you really are.

If you are achievement-motivated, you'll be able to answer these questions positively...

- Do you want to accomplish something significant?
- Do you like to set your own goals?
- Do you like doing your own thing, rather than being told what to do?
- Are you self-motivated?
- Do you prefer to select moderate, practical, achievable goals for yourself?
- Do you like immediate feedback on how you are progressing towards your goals?
- Do you want full responsibility for attaining your goals?

If you are very low in, or completely bereft of, achievement motivation, you may find your work and your life empty of vitality and vigour.

Start a Personal Achievement List.

You'll be surprised how much you achieve as a manager in a year. Systematically listing your achievements is the only way to keep track. So keep a list of your successes in chronological order, month by month, over a year— initiatives, milestones, articles, talks, interviews, books read, awards, and similar things signifying that you've accomplished something.

Use your Personal Achievement List.

The benefits of keeping and reviewing your list soon become obvious, e.g.

- *for gauging progress.* Seeing your achievements all in one place, in chronological order, helps you determine whether you're making the kind of professional and personal progress you have in mind for yourself. Do the successes support your goals? Or do they simply consume time and energy?

- *for getting the attention of others.* You can promote yourself well at interviews and meetings only when you know yourself well.

- *for supporting your documentation.* The process of putting together your résumé is streamlined when you have already listed your successes.

- *for motivating yourself.* Use the stimulation of success to accomplish even more.

Begin a Projected Personal Achievement List.

Once you have mastered the process

of putting your achievements in writing, it makes sense to project achievements into the future to guide your progress. The achievements that go into this list are the ones you can realistically accomplish, again month by month, in support of your overall goals.

 Be realistic when compiling your list.

In determining your future achievements, be realistic. Don't just list everything you think you'd like to accomplish. Instead, stick to those items that you feel you have a reasonable chance of accomplishing. But don't 'hedge your bets' by developing a very short list that includes only safe items and few of the achievements you would really have to strive to complete. The list should act as an incentive to spur you on and keep you on track.

Make your list a 'living' document.

An advocate of personal achievement lists, American management authority Jeffrey Davidson, says:

> Ensure that your projected list is a 'living' document: it will require continual revision as achievements occur. It is important to revise your goals and the steps you will take to achieve them, rather than just include what you know for sure will happen. In this way, you will be in charge of a logical pattern of accomplishments; and it will be more likely that they will bear a concrete relationship to your own goals.[19]

 research says

Research into achievement motivation by Harvard's David C. McClelland reveals that:

- Achievers have a deep interest in their work, and seek success and the feeling of having done something well.

- They prefer situations in which they can take personal responsibility for their performance.

- They like to get feedback as to how well they are doing and they respond to such feedback.

- They like to have control over their work and require measurements to know how well they are doing, so that they can bask in the joy of accomplishment.[20]

A personal achievement list is a useful tool in this regard.

 don't forget

Wise words for achievers...

If your list is to have a significant effect on your own productivity as a manager and achiever, then remember:

- If what you did yesterday still looks significant to you, then you mightn't have done much today.

- Unless you undertake more than you possibly can do, you will never do all that you can.

- It isn't how much you know, but what you get done that the world rewards and remembers.

65

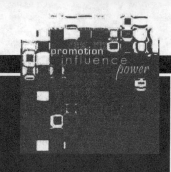

How to survive and thrive in the politics of your organisation

In every organisation, people will play politics for personal gain or sectional interests. On the darker side, more organisations are diseased by internal politics than their bosses dare to admit. But internal politics need not be characterised by dirty tricks, back-stabbing, manoeuvring, and skulduggery. Indeed, it is possible to survive and thrive by legitimate and acceptable means. The following suggestions will help you to become a politically astute manager...

1 Assume that political undercurrents run through your organisation.

Political behaviour exists in all organisations because of the presence of hierarchical structures, power, influence, and human beings. Indeed, whenever we do something to affect other people's perceptions of us and our work, or to gain power and credibility in the organisation, we act politically. Politics is all-pervasive, working constantly beneath the surface. Learn to play the game, or you'll be left behind.

2 Know what it means to play politics.

You become politically astute when you become skilled at working your way up the promotional ladder and gaining power within the organisation. You display your political ingenuity when you hold influence, have many loyal followers, and can get your ideas, views, actions, and yourself recognised and accepted. This ingenuity can take either of two forms—one manipulative and devious, the other legitimate and acceptable to the majority.

- *The dirty face of organisational politics* is the scheming and self-seeking that advances one's career or sectional interests regardless of what's best for the organisation. It is characterised by back-biting, white-anting, self-interest, lip-service, cheating, misinformation, lying, crawling, point-scoring, treachery, and back-stabbing. Only unprincipled people adopt these behaviours and in such an organisational culture, an overall climate of mistrust develops.

- *The acceptable face of internal politics* is the struggle between individuals and groups who all have the best interests of the organisation at heart, but disagree on what those interests are and how they might best be served.

Organisational politics is often equated with self-serving actions that can hurt others and the company. But it *can* operate both ethically and appropriately. It is a personal choice.

3 Listen, observe, and learn how to play the game.

Develop political awareness by seeing and hearing what happens in your

organisation. Ask yourself:
- What gets people promoted?
- Who's in the 'in' crowd and who's 'out'?
- Who's got the *real* power?
- Who are the opinion leaders?
- Who supports whom, and why?
- Who are the fence-sitters?
- Who is the competition—their age? experience? background? attitudes? abilities? prospects?
- Who are the ideas people, the cautious people, the risk-takers, and the blockers?
- Who makes the decisions?

By being observant and patient, you can learn to recognise and use behaviour politically advantageous in your workplace.

 Be subtle.

If you blatantly try to gain power or to influence others, you will meet with resistance. Subtlety makes political behaviour successful. For example, you'll have more success in promoting a pet project by lobbying in the corridors and exchanging positive comments about it over coffee than by trying to bludgeon it through a staff meeting. Subtlety is always more persuasive than blatant use of power.

 Lay the foundation by working hard.

If you can't justify your claim to power, no amount of politicking will help. You earn your spurs by showing that you can work hard, help others, and accept unpleasant tasks; that you are tolerant, principled, trustworthy, courteous, and caring. People who

lack these qualities usually resort to character assassination, skulduggery, nepotism, and treachery—and sooner or later their sins catch up with them. Until then, they're for ever looking over their shoulders. Competence alone won't guarantee advancement, but it's essential in the long run.

 Build relationships.

Politically astute managers build alliances according to the principle of reciprocal favours. Maxims such as 'one good turn deserves another' illustrate the ethic of political reciprocity. Build healthy relationships with supervisors and colleagues, and treat subordinates with respect and fairness to foster loyalty and support.

 Learn to negotiate.

Knowing when to make concessions, when to compromise, and when to hold out is part of the political process. Negotiation involves subtle attempts to influence others to achieve a goal or to gain power.

 Keep the power brokers on side.

It is political suicide to alienate those in power. Never disagree with them in public; find ways to make them look good; follow the chain of command; be a team player; don't create problems that make them look bad. But you need not argue with everything they say: *that* would damage your credibility. You must, though, support and remain loyal to those who can help you most.

Avoid being against anything. Instead, be *for* something. For example, instead of being against company proposals to move into the outsourcing of services, be for it – so you can focus on improving outsourcing. Instead of being *against* your company policy on purchasing, be *for* an improved policy.

What happens, according to Wayne Dyer in *You'll See It When You Believe It* is that, whatever you are against works *against you*. You begin fighting it and become part of the problem. But when you state what you are for, you begin focusing on the potential for positive change – and, in the process, get a reputation for progress rather than for negativity.

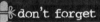

Advice for when things get rough...

- Arranging for the presence of a witness to some conversations can be an effective self-protective measure.
- Keep good records, as legal proof, for when recollection fades.
- Comprehensive diaries and minutes of meetings are important records of places, dates and decisions.
- If you are aware of an offence, report it. Don't use it to advance your own position. Blackmail is a criminal act.

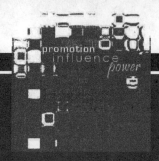

How to gain power and influence

Enthusiastic and committed managers strive to get things done by exerting influence, a process that involves the use of power. If you have power, you can influence the behaviour of others and get people to do what you want them to do. Normally power should come with the job; but you can gain it by other means. Here are some of the ways in which you can accumulate power in your organisation…

1 Gain control by moving into a position of power.

Seek promotion. Power and influence are normally part and parcel of the formal authority vested in a senior managerial position. But remember that, as well as using your recognised title and role in the organisation, you may need to bolster this legitimate coercive power with other forces to increase your influence over others…

2 Gain control over resources.

You will gain additional power over others if you are in a position to approve their requests for essential resources such as money, equipment, space, staffing, transportation, or facilities.

3 Gain control over the flow of information.

People rely on access to information to do their jobs; so the more you know about what's going on, the better you can decide how to use that information to influence others. Find out what is going on through formal channels and through your own informal network. Get yourself on to the right committees and distribution lists. And if you know what's going on behind the scenes by accumulating privileged information, all the better: you can act far more effectively than those who are not in the know.

4 Gain power by possessing knowledge.

Expert power can be yours when others choose to act as you suggest because they acknowledge that you know more than they do. So build your knowledge of matters technical or professional, or of the running of the organisation, so that others rely on your expertise and defer to your judgement.

5 Gain power by establishing credibility.

You can build up the trust of your employees and colleagues and, in time, their dependence, by earning a reputation as a performer, one who delivers, and who keeps promises.

6 Gain power by doing others a favour or two.

Get others to feel obligated to you in some way so that gratitude is a natural consequence. Good managers can do so without any sinister Mafia-type underpinnings—because it's good business and makes sense. Usually the organisation benefits from such favours, but remember that you can also gain influence over others by doing them a good turn or two.

7 Develop strong links with other people with power.

One of the smart organisational strategies is to get to know the boss's personal assistant well—because that person has the boss's ear and is, for that reason alone, in a position of power. Why? Power comes from having direct access to someone with power. Proximity or a direct line to the powerful obviously gives you more scope to exert influence, direct or perceived. So develop close links yourself by

- identifying your organisation's opinion leaders and power brokers—and they're not all higher level people. What would these people welcome in terms of 'favours' (help with a project, more resources, respect, etc.)?

- providing such favours if doing so is not being unethical or disloyal to colleagues.

- antagonising no one unless some greater purpose is at stake.

8 Gain influence through the power of your personality.

If you have a powerful physique or a deep and resonant voice that unnerves or even intimidates others, you are well on the way to having others defer to your wishes. But nature has blessed few of us in that way. You can influence others, however, if you possess or develop some kind of charisma or self-confidence or sense of mission that persuades colleagues and employees to agree with you. Try to make yourself personally compatible with people at all levels in your organisation. And, if necessary, create the illusion of power by attending to the way you look, dress, and furbish your office. The company you keep is also important.

Do some thinking...

- List the sources of power in your organisation—don't merely study an organisation chart—and find ways of tapping into that reservoir.

- Think about using some of the power you already have to accumulate more.

- Consider joining unofficial networks (such as clubs or social groups) in your organisation so that, through involvement, you can build a personal support base.

 viewpoint

"Despite the bad odour that clings to the very notion of power because of the misuses to which is has been put, power in itself is neither good nor bad. It is an inescapable aspect of every human relation-ship, and it influences everything from our sexual relations to the jobs we hold, the cars we drive, the television we watch, the hopes we pursue. To a greater degree than most imagine, we are the products of power."

– Alvin Tofler
in *Powershift*

❝ quotable quote

Influencing others isn't about manipulation or the misuse of power.

When you establish and maintain good working relationships so that other people will be receptive to your ideas and willing to consider your suggestions, you are using influencing skills. When you present your concepts logically and persuasively (and truthfully) so that people can understand and appreciate the value of your proposals, you are also using influencing skills.[24]

smile & ponder

Any time you think you have power and influence, try ordering around someone else's dog.

69

How to use power appropriately

All managers have power. It comes with the position. Some use it well; some use it poorly; and some let it slip from their grasp. The challenge for managers is how to use power to enhance the organisation they serve and their own reputations as well. If they abuse their power, the odds are that they and the organisation will suffer. Power used well, however, can lead to growth, better service, greater efficiency, higher quality—and more power…

1 Know how you feel personally about using power.

If you seek power, then you must know why you want it and what you're going to do with it. Determine your motives for wanting power: only by analysing and understanding these motives can you develop a positive and clear picture of what it means to you. Most importantly, decide whether you're prepared to use it appropriately.

2 Be aware of the darker side of power.

Sometimes power is perceived as evil, and is associated with self-seeking and scheming individuals. This dark side of power is apparent when someone uses such tactics as:

- withholding information from others who need it
- empire-building
- pursuing personal vendettas
- blocking other people's legitimate work plans and proposals for one's own benefit
- inventing new rules and procedures to obstruct other people
- passing off other people's ideas as one's own
- blackmail, sabotage, slanderous gossip, even threats of violence
- forming cliques, and fostering a climate of 'us' and 'them'
- pursuing personal advancement unfairly or at the expense of the organisation and others.

3 Stay within acceptable limits of fair play.

Remember Watergate. Driving ambition and the quest for power that ignores the greater good can be self-destructive. Outfox and outmanoeuvre other people by all means; but avoid cheating, lying, or breaking your word. In power struggles, chickens have an uncanny tendency to come home to roost.

4 Do not overuse power.

If you become blatant in your use of power, you're likely to create resistance in the ranks. So managers who regularly make unilateral decisions and arbitrarily mandate new procedures and rules often get complaints, refusals, even sabotage, from employees. Those who gradually and subtly persuade staff members to see the value of a new procedure will often gain ready acceptance and support. An oppressive display of power is a sure way to lose it.

Vary the way you influence others.

Flexibility in your use of power will always be important; what works in one setting may be less successful in another. Your choice will vary from direct methods (face-to-face, confrontationist, or collaborative) to indirect methods (controlling such items as work schedules, meeting agendas, and memos). Build up a selection of both approaches and use them to achieve the outcomes you want.

Understand people in your organisation.

Employees will always want to protect their self-interest, so you must be able to define those interests and behaviour styles if you are to become skilled in dealing with and influencing them. You need to be aware of the different types of power to which others respond. Experts, for example, respect expertise. So power will be afforded you by experts if you are seen as a genuine expert in your field—and you live up to that reputation. As well, when you appeal to individuals' preferred power

types, they get satisfaction from their imagined influence over you.

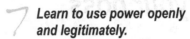

Learn to use power openly and legitimately.

Gain a reputation for exerting your influence in a mature and self-controlled way. Resist the impulsive use of power and don't use it for your own aggrandisement. Create a healthy balance between your own personal goals and those of your organisation. Commitment to your organisation generates personal power, which leads to increased service, which in turn attracts more power, and so on.

Don't abuse power.

When *Fortune* magazine listed its 'Ten Toughest Bosses', their portraits were pretty unpleasant. They were variously described as 'ridiculing, aloof, strident, obnoxious, brutal, egocentric, autocratic'…even 'unpopular'. Not surprisingly perhaps. They might have been very effective in their jobs, but the ways in which they were described suggest ways in which managers can abuse their power.

Mitchell Posner in *Executive Essentials* has written:

> 'Power is healthy. It is the misuse of power that is not. Everyone has power to some degree. Most people handle it well. But it's the abuses that make headlines.' [25]

So the bottom line is—stay out of the headlines. Use power appropriately.

? ask yourself

There is no end to the tricks people get up to when exercising power in the workplace, particularly when their purposes are dubious ones.

Which of the following power tactics have you seen being used by people in your organisation?

- Pretending to have less power than they do
- Pretending to have more power than they do
- Keeping back information from people who need it
- Distorting information
- Circulating slanderous gossip
- Passing off other people's ideas as their own
- Working to rule (e.g. go-slows)
- Inventing new rules to restrict other people
- Reinterpreting existing rules to ease their own freedom of action
- Empire-building
- Espionage and infiltration of other groups
- Fostering a climate of 'them' versus 'us'
- Forming temporary cliques to squash other people's plans
- Blackmailing people
- Sabotaging other people's work or ideas
- Physical violence (or threats of).

'Understanding who exercises what kind of power, for what purposes, and through what tactics may be your first step to deciding whether it is in the best interests of yourself, your section and the organisation to go along with them or to fight back.' [27]

How to win the support of your boss

The art of management requires that you spread your influence upwards through the organisation, as well as downwards. If you want to achieve results and get on, you will need to gain the support of your superior. Most bosses can quickly detect flattery and manipulation—but there are other more acceptable strategies that will enhance your upward influence and win for you the continued backing of your superiors...

1 Support your boss at all times.

If you give your boss loyalty and support, you can normally expect such support in return. You can make your support obvious in various ways, and page 118 provides details. Remember: in the wash-up, you exist to support your boss.

2 Take a long-term view.

To prove that you're worthy of your boss's support, you'll need to win that support over time. It will require your continuing efforts to develop a positive working relationship. Be persistent and patient in working towards that goal.

3 Make sure your boss notices what you do.

Find ways to show your boss your strengths, your abilities, and your willingness to accept responsibility. Being recognised as being very good at what you do is the best way to stand out from the crowd and win the support of your boss. Think about how you sell your ideas, present information at meetings, collect and collate information, interact with your boss and others, and so on. What differentiates you from your colleagues? And is your boss noticing? Consider providing your boss with a monthly one-page report of your achievements. Keep copies of those reports to use at performance appraisal time.

4 Try making your ideas your boss's ideas.

Present your proposals in such a way that your boss can contribute to them and thus feel some 'ownership' of them. Management consultant Derek Rowntree offers this advice:

- Show your boss how to gain something of value from what you are proposing.
- If your boss makes suggestions that are at all practicable, incorporate them into your proposal.
- If they are not practicable, get your boss talking about the implications until it is obvious to everyone they are not.

- If your boss offers a better proposal altogether, praise it; and *you* be the one to offer suggestions.
- If the only way of getting your ideas adopted is to let your boss get the credit for them, you may sometimes decide to do so for the sake of the proposal.

The key is to win over your boss by working *with* him or her. Gain your boss's confidence in your ability to create and develop your worthwhile proposals cooperatively. Let your boss appear to have played the major part.

 Tackle conflict constructively.

From time to time, conflict with your boss is inevitable. By all means disagree if you have a case, but don't dispute authority (the ultimate decision rests with the boss) or incite confrontation in the presence of others. It's smarter to retire to fight another day. Never beat your boss into the ground. If your boss loses face, *you'll* end up losing more. Remember, 'in the end, the boss is always right'.

 Gain a reputation for solving problems.

Keep minor problems off your boss's desk; solve these yourself. If your boss must hear about problems you're having, make sure the news comes from you first. Never let your boss be embarrassed by having to admit ignorance of a problem or crisis in your area. Whenever something is seriously wrong, tell your boss and indicate what you're doing to remedy

the situation. Make it clear that you have learned from the experience and that the error is unlikely to happen again.

 Be open, frank and honest.

Your boss needs to rely on you, to believe in you, if you are to gain his or her support. The faintest suspicion that you are not being perfectly honest will cause the boss to have doubts about trusting you again. Gain a reputation for honesty and straight-shooting.

 And remember...

- Don't wait for your ship to come in; swim out and meet it. Look for opportunities to impress your boss and win support.
- Learn to play office politics. If you find such games disagreeable, remember that those who play them well may soon be your superiors.
- When your boss makes a mistake, tread lightly.
- Observe the chain of command. Never go over your boss's head.
- You'll gain your boss's respect if you refrain from spreading gossip or put-downs about colleagues.
- Help your boss look good if you want to win real support.
- Finally, heed James Cribbin's advice: 'Avoid crying on their shoulders, stepping on their toes, twisting their arms, and breaking their hearts.'

 here's an idea

We all need to be told that our work is appreciated – yet how often do we praise our bosses? They're people, too.

When was the last time you praised your boss? If your boss has been extra supportive of you, tell him or her that you appreciate it. Be honest, however. A phony attempt can be detected immediately.

don't forget

Consider this useful advice...

■ Know what your boss needs – both work needs and emotional needs. When they're legitimate needs such as loyalty, feedback and support, provide them without having to be coached. Never criticise your boss in front of others. Never under-estimate him or her.

■ Share your expertise, innovation and creativity with your boss. Your boss can learn from you, too, and relies upon you as a problem solver and a source of ideas and skills.

■ When problems arise, be straightforward in dealing with them. Develop the confidence and skills to discuss problems with your boss and, if necessary, how you expect your boss's behaviour to change. Stay objective, concise, professional and calm.[30]

How to stay at the top once you've got there

Success, we're told, consists of three things: knowing where you are; knowing where you want to be; and each day, in some way, moving towards that goal. That's why success is often referred to as a journey rather than merely a destination. And that journey can be considerably easier if you heed the advice of those who have travelled that path previously. Here's what they'd probably tell you...

Demonstrate humility.

The journey to the top of your tree does not need to be a race. Even if it were, it would, by definition, be a race without a finish line. Your main competitor is yourself. Flaunting your tertiary qualifications, for example, ends up being an acknowledgement of what you *don't know*. In fact, admitting you don't know is often viewed by others as a positive personality trait. Remember, humility is not a sign of weakness or compliance. Quite the contrary, in fact; people who are humble are often assertive and demonstrate 'strong' characters.

Be generous with your support.

One of the many celebrities to entertain American troops during the Korean War was Frank Sinatra. Notable among Sinatra's behaviours was this: he refused to move the piano—his job was to sing. Few of us can afford such a luxury as being detached from many of the seemingly mundane issues—we're often required to shift our own pianos. Demonstrate your willingness to contribute in any way possible. True leaders roll up their sleeves and contribute to the task at hand. And they're noticed.

Keep your nose clean.

Business may be, as Tom Peters says, a series of relationships between people; but it's important that those relationships present you in the best possible way. Never give others an opportunity to suggest any unethical behaviour on your part. Stay out of gossip by letting the person feeding the grapevine know that you're not interested. Always keep your boss informed of projects you are involved in and use memos to keep others up to speed. Ensure that the outcomes of important meetings are accurately reported in the minutes.

Let others share the credits.

The ancient Chinese philosopher Lao Tzu was one of the first people in recorded history to advocate ownership by everyone involved in a project. He said that leaders were most effective when others participating in projects believed that their contributions had made the difference. By spreading the credit around, leaders look much stronger than those who take all the credit themselves. Practices like empowerment, delegation, and collaborative decision-making are just some of the ways in which ownership can be maximised.

Move on.

One of your key qualities should be that you are progressive—you don't dwell on the past. The story of two Buddhist monks illustrates this point:

> As two monks approached a flooded river, they were asked by a young woman if they could carry her across the stream. The older monk obliged, even though contact with women was taboo. When the three reached the other side and the older monk had put the woman down safely, the two monks proceeded on their journey. Several hours later the young monk, still disturbed, said to his travelling companion, 'You know, that woman you carried back there…'
>
> The old monk responded, 'Are you still carrying her? I let her down hours ago.'

Carrying around old baggage not only weighs you down but also hinders your career.

Learn to like people.

You can learn any behaviour—even learn to like people you don't like.

We all have idiosyncrasies that may upset others. When you find that one of your behaviours may upset others, refrain from using it in their presence. Remember, the one behaviour you have control over is your own. Let your actions demonstrate that self-control and flexibility help you to work productively with the most difficult of people.

Beware of 'small talk'.

Communicating by interrogating is a definite 'no-no'. If asking a series of inane questions is the best technique you have to find out about the other person, you've probably not done your homework. Avoid topics that do not interest others—like your salary, or your political or religious beliefs. Effective communicators will want to lead the conversation into a discussion about the other person, not themselves. As the saying goes, 'Gossips talk about others; bores talk about themselves; and the perfect communicator talks about me'.

Seek others' involvement.

Although you may consider that no one else could do a job better than you can—and you may be right—you just can't afford to operate that way. By asking others for help, not only are you inviting participation and ownership but you are also demonstrating your humility, fallibility, and desire to work collaboratively. People who try to accomplish everything single-handedly inevitably set themselves up for a 'fall'.

How to guarantee your employability over the coming decades

As managers continue to speculate about the challenges, opportunities, and uncertainties associated with the new millennium, thriving and surviving—even remaining relevant—will become a major concern for many. Maintaining your employability will continue to be an ongoing challenge—and it will be your responsibility. To prepare yourself for the uncertain times ahead, consider the following advice...

1 Try to understand what's coming.

You'll have more control over your future if you stay at the cutting edge. Read all you can. Speak with others. Reflect. But be aware of emerging trends—such as these:

- Managers are likely to change their jobs several times during their careers.
- Technology will eliminate old jobs and create new ones.
- Computers and machines will become smarter—and people will need to do the same.
- Staff will have more flexible working arrangements.
- Companies will become 'virtual' through outsourcing, telecommuting, and staff working at home.
- Those who cannot adapt to new technologies will find themselves working harder and achieving less.
- Lifelong learning will be essential.
- People who learn skills quickly will be highly valued in a fast-changing world.
- Training will be delivered 'on demand', whenever people need it, using a variety of technologies.
- Organisations won't pay for the value of the job but for the value of the person.

- Employees will be more independent, moving from project to project within their organisations.
- We will continue to work well beyond the traditional age of retirement.

2 Become familiar with technology—now.

The three-step recipe for employability in the coming decades of rapid change is this—1. Prepare; 2. Prepare; 3. Prepare. The advance in technology in particular will be very dramatic. Indeed, unless we prepare ourselves by keeping up to date with technology—computers, the Internet, robotics, communications, etc.—we will ourselves become obsolete in the workplace.

3 Be prepared to be mobile.

In an increasingly global economy, supply and demand for managers will require that we adopt a mentality for mobility—a willingness to relocate as markets for our expertise shift. Be prepared for this—mentally, physically, and emotionally—for not only will such moves broaden your horizons, but in addition your expertise and experience will become more marketable.

4 Continue to develop your people skills.

Focus on the development of vital technology skills by all means, but not at the expense of people skills. Such skills will always be in demand. Learn to motivate staff, to deal with diverse groups, to get the most out of people, to communicate effectively, and so on.

5 Think globally.

The world will be shrunk by developments in transportation, technology, and communication. Worldwide mergermania will produce larger organisations employing fewer people. The global economy will become a reality. So think globally. Multiply your value to your employer by learning to understand cultural differences and etiquette. Become fluent in a foreign language or two— or at least embrace a few basics.

6 Develop an entrepreneurial streak.

Permanent employment cannot be guaranteed in the future, so try not to become too dependent on corporate employers. Be prepared to become a free agent, for employment in the future may mean employing yourself. So start planning for that possibility. Develop skills, contacts, and experience that will enable you to become a consultant, a freelance technical expert, or an independent operator. Nurture your network; survival may depend on your connections—peers, mentors, promising newcomers, retirees, clients, and customers.

7 Build a reputation as one who embraces the future.

In coming decades, employers will be eager to find people who visibly prepare themselves for an exciting future and embrace change willingly and enthusiastically. Don't be paralysed with fear or personal paranoia. Find ways to demonstrate your exuberance. Your attitude, more than your age, will determine your standing in the organisation. Remain marketable and employable as follows:

- Commit yourself to a program of lifelong learning.
- Develop a range of skills and competencies, for they will be valued more than depth of expertise in a single area.
- Demonstrate your versatility, which will become a key factor in determining employee value—with strategic planning, leadership, problem-solving, technology, and people skills close behind.
- Associate with winners and distance yourself from malcontents.
- Become active in trade and professional associations.
- Be visible—the more people know about you, the less likely that you'll be lost in the shuffle or overlooked in times of transition.
- Develop your computer skills.
- Become known as a valuable team player, with strong problem-solving and decision-making skills.
- Make it happen—your future isn't a matter of fate, circumstance, or good luck. It's up to you. So start now!

> ❝ **quotable quote**
>
> The secrets to success and survival in the new century are simply to make friends with change, to build on existing strengths, to maximise options, and to become fanatic about continuous growth and development. This is exactly what good supervisors have always done. That's why they always tend to land on their feet no matter what happens. A new millenium won't change that.[33]

> ❝ **quotable quote**
>
> Make change your ally. Understand that nothing can remain static. Go with the change but prepare yourself for the future. We must take care of our own career needs and speak up for ourselves. There is no longer a single-company career track. Know there are some things you cannot change and work you cannot achieve. While you may never find your *perfect* career, you can be sure that you can find your *right* career for now at least.[34]

> ❗ **viewpoint**
>
> "My interest in the future is because I am going to spend the rest of my life there."
>
> – Charles F. Kettering

How to ask for a raise

 don't forget

Three key principles...

- To be successful, a salary negotiation should leave both parties feeling as though they have won something – you, a satisfactory raise; your boss, a contented, productive manager.

- Job relevancy is important, but personal achievement is better.

- There's a right way and a wrong way – once you find the right way, stick with it!

In some organisations, pay increases are tied automatically to levels and years of experience. In others, regular salary reviews are held with individual employees. Elsewhere, little will happen unless the employee takes the initiative. If you are in this position, and you want to remain with your existing employer, here is essential advice for getting that next pay increase—and the importance of preparation cannot be overstated...

1 Make sure you deserve it.

Are you really earning the money you currently receive? Do you work hard at your job? Do you carry your own weight in the organisation? How valuable are you to the firm? The first requirement in gaining a raise is to be worth more than you're earning now.

2 Keep tabs on your own performance.

Constantly monitor your performance, particularly in those areas your superiors view as important. Work hard to meet your bottom lines—your budget, your performance standards, your sales targets, your deadlines.

3 Keep a record of your achievements.

Particularly if you have no formal reporting requirement, record your accomplishments regularly. You will need these files later to help justify your case for a salary increase. Such records, of course, serve a double purpose: they are also vital for

building your personal portfolio if you apply for another job in your organisation or elsewhere.

4 Promote yourself.

Subtle self-promotion is essential if you intend to progress in the organisation. Make sure you keep your mentor or superior up to date with your achievements. To do so without sounding boastful, compliment your staff on their (and your) success. Don't fish for compliments; but when someone thanks you for doing something extraordinary, ask him or her to tell your boss as well.

5 Hold regular meetings with your boss.

Never assume you are performing well, or, if you are, that everyone knows you are. If it is not already part of workplace procedure, try to have time set aside regularly—say every three months— to discuss your performance with your superior. Indicate that you believe you are doing a good job. Confirm that your boss continues to share your view. In this way you will be preparing the ground for a later meeting when you can press home your request for a raise.

6 Do your research.

Be sure you know your grade or level, salary ranges within those levels, any guidelines or timelines for salary reviews, and similar background information. Learn everything you can from the personnel section, your peers, and your superiors. Know what you normally might be entitled to. Find out what other organisations pay for positions similar to yours—talk to friends, search the 'positions vacant' columns, network at meetings and seminars, and read the industry magazines. Going into a meeting to discuss your salary requires you know exactly where you stand.

7 Put yourself in your boss's shoes.

After preparing, and before speaking with the boss, reflect on how your request might be viewed from his or her perspective. Do you and your work performance warrant the raise? How is the company performing at present? What will be the implications for others if you receive a raise? Think through the options, and how you can respond. For example, if the boss says: *"Now is not the time"* and you think you are being put off, be gracious and find out when will be the right time. Then, when you come back at the time your boss suggests, you will have the advantage. In fact, at that point, you should begin by

saying, 'Four months ago when I came to ask you for a raise, you suggested that this month would be the best time for us to talk about it', sounding as if you are only following orders.

If the boss says *"You don't deserve a raise"*, ask what you have to do to make yourself eligible. If it's worth it to you, you may want to improve your work performance and strengthen your case for next time.

If you still feel confident about asking for a raise, it's time to ask for a meeting to put your case.

8 Meet with your boss and make your request.

If you've put together a rational case with supporting evidence and done your research, you can feel confident in requesting a hearing. Be aware of the rules and ask for what you think is fair. Some bosses can feel threatened; but ask firmly, be decisive, and allow your superior time to think. Don't demand a decision there and then: you could well force a negative response. Above all, make it clear that this is a request—a strong request, certainly—but not a demand.

9 Don't despair if you're turned down this time.

A rejection can mean that your performance doesn't warrant a raise, that your boss cannot consent at this time, or that you have more serious problems than a pay increase. Find out why. The reason might help you to address problems you didn't realise you had. But if the reason had nothing to do with you, you might wish to try other options, such as a promotion, or training, allowances, travel, and the like, in lieu of the raise.

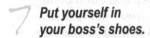

here's an idea

If you're going to get up enough courage to ask for a raise, you're going to have to get rid of any old programming that tells you that you are being selfish or money-grubbing. Such feelings stand in the way of your getting what you deserve.

How to make the best use of travelling time

Whether you are commuting to work by train, driving to a meeting, or catching a flight to visit clients and prospects, you must decide how best to use your travelling time. Are you going to waste it—or can you use it to catch up on your reading, your oral communication skills, or even your sleep? Whatever you decide, commuting time provides valuable opportunities to devote to personal development. Here are some ways to make the most of travelling time…

Develop a travelling time plan.

If your travel time (to and from work or meetings) amounts to several hours each week, you should consider a plan detailing how you can benefit from using that valuable time—or you'll lose it. The plan need not have a work focus: recreational and relaxation activities can be beneficial but will need planning, too. Your plan may embrace a variety of activities.

Choose the activity to match your mode of travel.

If you commute alone by car, there are safe, work-related activities such as listening to audiobooks. If your mode of travel makes reading an option, book summaries—or the real things—will prove an invaluable source of information. There's even value in talking to the person seated next to you—but make sure you have something meaningful to say. Communicating by interrogating (asking a barrage of questions) is a guaranteed turn-off.

If you decide to use your travel time for a particular purpose, other decisions you make will be affected. For example, a car pool might be an economical way to travel to and from work, but it may prove counter-productive if you want to use travel time to be alone and to reflect on aspects of your work or professional growth and development. Conversely, a car pool can be a way of getting to know people and build better relationships. You can organise activities that help to deliver the outcomes you want from your travel time.

Make use of available technologies.

Portable computers and Palm Pilots are great when you're commuting by train or flying. Even a small dictaphone is a useful tool for capturing those gems of wisdom or for dictating drafts of letters or memos to staff. At least keep a notepad and pen at the ready to ensure that valuable ideas and brainwaves aren't lost.

---

viewpoint

"My father gave me some great advice the day I became sixteen and received my driver's license. Climbing into the passenger side of the car, he placed a book in my glove compartment and said, 'Son, never be in a car without a book. Whenever you are delayed in traffic you can pull out this book and read.' Today my car also contains many tapes for me to listen to and a note pad to jot down thoughts. My car phone also allows me to make calls to people on the way to and from work.

Recently while driving I made several calls and saved hours of office time. Many times I drive staff to and from work with me; we discuss business and develop a closer relationship. I estimate that the average person could achieve eight additional hours of personal growth and work each week by using driving time wisely."

– John Maxwell in
Developing the Leader Within You

Use your time to adopt new habits.

Use your travelling time productively to develop good habits such as reading, communicating, exercising, and meditating. In exercising, for example, you might decide to walk to work or to a bus stop farther along the road than the usual one. A cycleway that takes you near your workplace could provide an ideal opportunity to cycle to the office—to get fit and avoid the traffic.

 Add variety to keep your travelling time productive and interesting.

Don't let your use of travelling time become just another wearisome task. Instead, build variety into your activities—sleeping, socialising, writing, reading, meditating, planning, etc. Brainstorm the possibilities. Every weekend, draft a plan for each day of the week… Work your way through a novel or management text you normally don't get time to read. Write a poem. Update your to-do list. Read short stories your child has written—the ones you said you'd read when you didn't really have the time. Do a crossword. Plan your case for a raise. Work on sections of your résumé. Build variety into your travelling plan—but get into the habit of drafting and working to a plan.

 Brainstorm ideas.

Some people say that they get their most creative ideas when they are flying, alone in a car, walking, or travelling by train. When you can't be interrrupted, you're free to focus your creative energies by brainstorming. For example, you could list perceived blockages to your current promotional aspirations. You can then focus on actions to eliminate or reduce them. Or you may have a problem—personal or professional. The solitude of travelling time will allow you to explore possible solutions.

 Catch up on correspondence.

It's been said that a sharp pencil is better than a dull mind. So keep a sharp pencil at the ready to respond to correspondence and to jot down memos and emails. You can even draft your responses to correspondence on a copy of the original. This technique saves you time and helps the recipient, who can see immediately the contents of his or her letter and your response.

 Expand the habit.

As you become increasingly aware of how you spend your time and the value you derive from the approaches you adopt, you can start applying that learning to other situations. For example, always keep a book in your briefcase so that, if your appointment is late, you can use the time to catch up on some reading. Or you might opt to read a chapter from a book instead of reading a newspaper or watching some irrelevant television program.

✔ **it's a fact**

Take advantage of the time you have travelling. Former US President Herbert Hoover wrote a book during the time he spent waiting in railroad stations. Noel Coward wrote his popular song, 'I'll See You Again', while caught in traffic.

? **ask yourself**

How many hours do you spend in travelling to and from work each day… each week… each month? Add them up. And how many hours each week do you spend travelling to meetings? How do you usually spend this time? You may be surprised at how extravagantly you're currently using this valuable time.

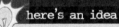 **here's an idea**

In recent years, institutions and other agencies have responded to the increased demands from commuters by providing a wide variety of personal- and professional-development programs on tape. Bookstores also stock books on tape.

So, while you are travelling to and from work each day, you could be engaged in self-improvement activities. Explore the possibilities.

How to plan for your overseas business trip

viewpoint

"Don't see business travel as a form of ego boost. It either helps you to do business or it doesn't. That's the bottom line."

– Mitchell J. Posner
US business advisor

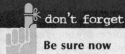

don't forget

Be sure now rather than sorry later.

Plan and prepare for the possibility that you may lose something:

- Make copies of essential documents. Keep them separate.
- Always carry your plane tickets securely and separately. They're tough to replace.
- Guard your passport. In some countries, you *are* your passport!
- Do you know what to do if your credit cards vanish?
- Heed the voice of experience when it comes to travellers cheques. Don't ignore the advice of the is-suer.
- Make sure your insur-ance policy covers everything you want covered.

Whether it's undertaken to negotiate a contract, to make contacts, or to buy, sell, or generate goodwill, an overseas business trip requires preparation and planning if it is to yield maximum results. You'll need to know how to get there with the minimum of fuss and expense, what to take, and what you'll be doing when you arrive. And, in addition to a need for vigilance in a world where personal security is increasingly under threat, there are several other important issues to consider in the planning stage—as the following reveals…

1 Be sure that the trip is really necessary.

Business travel can be one of the most exasperating and expensive aspects of executive life—so, with current advances in telcommunications technology, it is essential to ask 'Is this trip really necessary?' Consider viable options: teleconferencing, chat rooms, email, or video conferencing. Eliminate wasteful trips but, if one is imperative, make a good case for going —and adhere to the following advice.

2 Be smart when selecting your airline.

Here are a few handy hints for selecting an airline and booking your overseas tickets:

- *Travel agent.* To save time, money, and headaches, if you decide to use a travel agent, choose a good one—one that is looking to build repeat business.
- *Airline.* Larger airlines with frequent flights, appropriate backup, and good safety records are usually the most attractive.
- *When to fly.* It's usually cheaper and less congested to fly midweek than on weekends and Mondays and Fridays.

The best time to fly, to avoid delays and congestion, is first flight in the morning, late at night, or about midday.

- *Fares.* When are fares lowest? Not during holiday periods. Are round-trip tickets cheaper than two one-ways? Are Internet bookings cheaper? Are there special rate structures? What about stop-overs? Check out package deals—there are always strings attached. Shop around. Make your reservations as early as possible, and confirm your bookings and details before the day of departure.

3 Plan your itinerary in advance.

Before you set out…

- Plan your route and itinerary in detail.
- Where possible, combine several visits in the same region or country.
- Compile a precise daily schedule with contact details, and leave a copy at the office before departing.
- Assemble all documents required for meetings during the trip.
- Confirm all meetings before leaving in case of cancellations or reschedulings.
- Gather essential business and other information you will need during the trip.
- Include several fax cover sheets; and be confident you know how to send email through any laptop computer you may take.

Consider your wardrobe.

Traditionally, conservative attire is the best for business anywhere in the world. Base your wardrobe on a single colour-scheme so that all outfits work with the same accessories. Image consultant Susan Bixler advises:

For a man, the selection is easy, even for a relatively long trip. You can rotate two suits (or sportscoats) for days if you pack a supply of shirts and ties. For a woman, the coordination requires some additional planning. Select one solid-colour dark suit – perhaps with matching pants – in a wrinkle-resistant fabric. Add an alternate skirt to wear with the solid jacket and an alternate jacket to wear with the solid bottoms. Several bright blouses (and perhaps scarves) change the basic look. Include a fine-gauge silk sweater as a blouse alternative.[36]

Depending on the length of your trip and your location, and to eliminate the risk of lost or delayed luggage, if everything can fit into one piece of carry-on luggage or a garment bag, all the better. If not, pack efficiently.

 Know what to take.

In addition to medical requirements, you might consider what 'take-alongs' you might need, including these:

- An alarm clock to avoid hotel wake-up-call foul-ups.
- A supply of company letterheads, fax cover sheets, with-compliments slips, business cards, etc. to keep your correspondence professional.
- Ear-plugs for the flight or a noisy hotel.
- A dictaphone to record oral notes and comments.
- A spare pair of eyeglasses or contacts.
- A small screw-top container for pins, safety pins, needle and thread, etc.

- A small fold-away umbrella.
- A few muesli or energy bars for late nights in your hotel room.
- Copies of crucial things you could need to get home if the originals are lost or stolen on the trip—credit cards and IDs, travellers' cheque numbers, phone numbers—and store them separately.

 Visit your doctor.

Depending on the length of your visit and your destination, consult your doctor before leaving for advice on any vaccination requirements and on any medication you should carry—such as decongestants, antibiotics, analgesics, vitamins, antihistamines, etc. Know your medical basics—e.g. your blood group, eyeglass prescription, any allergic reactions to drugs, and medical insurance details.

 Consider these useful tips.

Seasoned travellers adopt the following guidelines:

- Start packing a week or so in advance.
- Suitcases seem to get heavier on the trip. Luggage on rollers is recommended.
- Be prepared for climatic changes such as temperature variations and rain.
- Know how to handle any protocol or cultural expectations you may encounter. Do your homework.
- Do you need a haircut before you depart? Or a visit to your dentist?
- Will you need to present a gift or two at your destination? If so, select and wrap them before embarking.
- Take work to do in an airport lounge in case of flight delays.
- Make sure you have essentials in your carry-on bag in case your luggage goes astray—e.g. toiletries and change of underwear.

here's an idea

A tracksuit or jumpsuit is a useful addition to your travel wardrobe because it can fill a variety of roles:
- for exercising in the hotel gym or for jogging/walking
- for lounging about in your hotel room
- for hotel wear – dropping down to the newsagent
- as pyjamas
- as a cover-up when using the hotel swimming pool.

viewpoint

"I choose my airlines carefully. I make a point of knowing which ones in which cities have the most flights, the most non-stops, the most delays, and the most backup planes; which ones are closest to baggage claim; which ones have more than one-class carriage; even which ones are lenient about carry-on luggage."

– Mark McCormack, sports management entrepreneur

 quotable quote

Dress professionally for your flight. You're the ambassador for your company and you never know whom you will encounter on the way. A long flight can also take its toll on your clothing... This is important especially if your host is meeting you at the airport.[37]

How to ensure you have trouble-free air travel on business

When you have to travel overseas on business, it is smart to make the flight as trouble-free as possible. You can accomplish this by attending to some important matters at the airport and minimising the effects of air sickness and jet lag during the flight. And it pays also to know what to do in an emergency— just in case...

Become travel-smart.

Consider the following advice:

- *Arrive early rather than late for your flight.* Why endure the discomfort of negotiating peak-hour traffic wondering whether you'll make it on time? Play it safe: for international flights, be at the airport two hours in advance. Besides, you can arrange a better seat if you arrive early and ensure that your baggage is safely tagged and booked in.

- *Double-check your connections.* If you have to make a connection or two before reaching your final destination, know your scheduled arrival time and the departure time of each connecting flight.

- *Allow the airline to help.* If you travel often, get to know the customer relations people. In so doing, in an age of competition, you won't need to be a movie star or a politician to get a better seat, an upgrade, or other special services. Airlines want to help. Let them.

- *Join a VIP club.* Particularly for frequent flyers, VIP airport clubs are handy if you arrive early or your flight is delayed. Enjoy the free refreshments; relax; work; use the office facilities or showers; or conduct a meeting.

- *Don't do in the air what you can better do on the ground*—advice from experienced business flyer Mark McCormack, who continues: 'I used to catch up on reading and paperwork during flights. But I soon realised I could do this more productively on the ground. Now I catch up on sleep because there are no phones or email and few interruptions 30,000 feet in the air. As a result, I'm more awake on the ground.'

- *In the air, set your watch to destination time.*

- *Dress the part.* You'll get better service from airline personnel if you're well dressed; and your seating companion may prove to be a useful new contact— provided you don't have to explain why you're wearing a track suit or jeans.

- *Take work to do in an airport lounge in case the flight is delayed.*

Take care with your baggage.

Your baggage will arrive safely with you if you take it on board as carry-on items—but that is not always possible. So consider these points:

- *Identify your bags clearly.* Use a concealed ID tag and attach brightly coloured tape so that your luggage stands out from the rest. Inside, include details of your itinerary and addresses.

- *Address your bags prudently.* Never put your home address on your luggage, announcing to would-be thieves that you're not at home. List your business address or the name of your travel agent. Similarly, a prestigious title is a tip-off that your bag might contain valuables.
- *Allow enough time.* Arrive early to check in your luggage without being rushed.
- *Make sure the counter clerk tags your bags correctly.* Ensure that they're labelled with the correct destination. Keep your claim stubs in a secure place: you may need them if your luggage goes astray.
- *Be aware of airline and customs restrictions on baggage and its contents.*
- *Know what to do if you lose your baggage.* File a claim at once: baggage can usually be traced and recovered within a day. If you delay your claim, the recovery becomes more difficult.

3 Combat air sickness and jet lag.

With improvements to aircraft, air sickness is rarer these days; but jet lag still remains a problem. Long flights across time zones can cause disruption to your body's natural rhythms and cycles; you can get to your destination exhausted, even distressed. Reduce the discomfort by taking this advice:

- *Prepare in advance:* change your eating and sleeping habits to match the time zone of your destination.
- *Choose your flight carefully,* to avoid lengthy stopovers or to leave in the morning and arrive when it's time to sleep.
- *Try to get as much space on the plane as you can.* Fly first class, choose the emergency exit seat where the leg-space is greater, or stretch across an empty seat if possible.
- *Avoid travelling alone.* Jet lag can lessen when you travel with others.
- *Keep fresh.* Use toothpaste and toothbrush, deodorant, mouthwash, razor, after-shave, and moisturiser.
- *Don't drink alcohol*—or at least drink moderately. Drink water.
- *Exercise.* Take a walk. Stretch. Combat deep vein thrombosis.
- *Eat less; eat right; or don't eat at all.* Schedule your eating according to the time zone of your destination. Eat nothing exotic in flight.
- *Sleep, or don't sleep.* Again, keep the time zone of your destination in mind and adjust your sleep pattern accordingly.
- *Avoid prolonged flights.* Excessive cabin dryness and accumulated sleep debt can wreak havoc on your body.

4 Know the basics of an air emergency.

To be prepared, contemplate the unthinkable. Most air crashes occur on take off or landing, and most people die because they don't know how to survive the impact and evacuate the aircraft as quickly as possible. Be prepared:

- *Read the safety card* in the aircraft and heed the preflight take off instructions.
- *Know the location of flotation gear*—have you ever seen it under the seat?
- *Be alert during take offs and landings.*
- *Follow instructions to survive an impact.* At any sign of fire, twisting, or breaking metal, or abrupt change in altitude, assume the brace position. It gives protection against debris and shock.
- *Get out as quickly as you can.* Leave everything behind and head for the exit—inflatable slide, window over wing, or stairs. Remember: planes are designed for easy evacuation within 90 seconds.
- *If there is smoke—the real killer—crawl to the exit* on all fours, but not with your head right down (toxic gas hugs the floor).
- *Get away from the plane quickly,* a safe distance—but stay around for a headcount.

quotable quote

Your daily life is governed by an internal body clock which regulates sleep patterns. Jet lag occurs when you travel through different time zones and disrupt this clock.

If you are travelling to a time zone with a 2- or 3-hour difference from your own, try going to bed when it is time to sleep at your destination on the day before you travel. This allows your body to adopt the new sleep pattern. For places with a larger time difference, ensure you are well rested before you travel and allow for rest time upon arrival.[39]

read further

Check the Internet for the latest advice on what to take and packing tips at such locations as www.oratory.com/travel; and for travel advice and warnings relating to travel in countries from Albania to Zambia on www.smartraveller.gov.au.

viewpoint

"The rule for travelling abroad is to take your common sense with you, and leave your prejudices behind."
– William Hazlitt

How to avoid hassles while at your overseas business destination

On your next overseas business trip, the less affected you are by problems that could upset your schedule, health, accommodation, or performance, the better. Through experience, seasoned travellers learn to avoid or eliminate the hassles of living in another country for a short time. Others never quite manage to cope. For newcomers, an overseas trip can even be frightening. To 'travel smart' in a foreign land on business, the following advice may be useful…

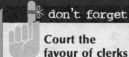

Court the favour of clerks and others…

Much-travelled sports entrepreneur Mark McCormack advises travellers to 'appreciate how important the face on the other side of the counter' can be.

Ticket agents, waiters, maître d's and hotel clerks have a great deal of discretionary power within their narrow field of influence. He suggests:

- *Flatter them* – even if you're tired, harried and behind schedule. Show an interest in them and defer to their judgement – and you'll elevate their opinion of you, and you'll get them on your side.
- *Let them display their power* in your favour – and they'll go out of their way to prove it.
- *Make them negotiate*, particularly in Mediterranean and South-East Asian countries. In fact, you'll lose some respect if you don't bargain with them.

McCormack concludes: 'These people can be the most important people in the world as far as your comfort and sanity are concerned.' [40]

1 Do your homework.

Before embarking, familiarise yourself with the customs, negotiating styles, and any potential pitfalls of doing business in your targeted country. The serious business person will consult trade journals, international business dailies, websites, the international business department at the local university, the bank, the government's trade department, and any colleagues who have visited the country previously. Know, in particular:

- the purpose of your visit and your planned itinerary
- the corporate culture and how meetings and transactions are conducted
- how deals are done
- the culture of doing business—e.g. gift-giving, introductions and other formalities, and the social component of business, if any
- the importance or otherwise of punctuality
- how humour is received, if at all
- cultural nuances—e.g. in Japan, the place of bowing, and the fact that 'yes' means 'I understand', not necessarily 'I agree with you'.

2 Attend to personal safety.

At most airports, theft is prevalent. Robbery and violence can occur even in the finest hotels. Be alert and take such precautions as these:

- Keep the door of your hotel room double-locked.
- Know how to escape your hotel room in case of fire.
- Request a room near the lift to avoid being followed while walking down long corridors.
- If the hotel clerk announces your room number so loudly that others can hear, ask for a different one.
- Do not leave valuables unattended in your hotel room.
- Ask how safe it is to walk the streets at night.
- Keep separate copies of valuable documents—e.g. credit card details, ID, insurance, and airline tickets.
- Keep a low profile and remain alert in countries with a high personal security risk. Obtain guidance on safety precautions before you leave.

3 Watch what you eat and drink.

Take care when eating and drinking in overseas countries. Although this precaution may not be necessary in the larger industrialised countries, you can easily become ill in others.

Tap water is often safe in many developing countries, but if in doubt drink bottled water—making sure that you are the one to break the seal. Be wary of fruit and vegetables washed in local water, and be careful when brushing your teeth.

Food-related sickness results from food that has been left in the open, poor hygiene in food-preparation areas, contaminated food (seafood from polluted waters, undercooked meat, or fruit with broken skin), and poor judgement when sampling exotic fare.

Take care with your communication skills.

Language and communication can be formidable barriers in some countries, which is why cultural understanding becomes so important. Be aware of the following:

- Make an effort to speak at least the minimum courtesies and salutations in the foreign language. Even if you stumble, you'll gain points for trying.
- Observe 'personal space'. Keep the appropriate distance as demanded in a host country—e.g. Latins tend to huddle; others keep their distance.
- Mirror the behaviour and body language of your hosts.
- Be familiar with business etiquette: greetings, handshakes, introductions, and behaviour at social functions.

Consider your wardrobe.

If in doubt, dress conservatively when doing business. Do not take risks. Dress as if you were to meet the most important person in your own company. You wouldn't want to look too flashy, just impressive and professional.

Avoid overseas medical treatment if possible.

If overseas for a short time, particularly in a developing country, avoid medical treatment if possible—thus avoiding the possibility of infection, complications, and inappropriate follow-up. On a longer visit, you may have little choice. So get a referral to a doctor who can be trusted. If you can, ask your embassy for advice.

It is also wise to get a medical checkup on your return from the tropics or a developing country, or after a long absence.

Remember also...

While you are away, remember to:

- Keep in contact with your office, update staff as required, and tell them of developments that might affect your plans.
- Travel at off-peak times if possible to avoid the stress of having to battle with local rush-hour commuters.
- When appropriate, try combining business meetings with meals to save time and to create a more relaxed working environment.
- Respect punctuality—although acceptable punctuality varies from country to country. Five minutes late in New York might be acceptable, as might one hour in Spain. Learn about the culture.
- Make full use of your dictaphone for notes and memos, and your laptop for recording notes and sending to your email address (as a backup copy).

don't forget

Reduce the risks in high-risk locations...

Personal security is important when doing business in high-risk countries:

- Stay alert.
- Vary the patterns of your movements and habits.
- Keep a low profile.
- Dress like the locals.
- Don't leave valuables around.
- Limit information concerning your movements.
- Use your eyes and your ears.
- Stay in touch with home regularly.
- Check your destination's security status, e.g. at www.smartraveller.gov.au.

quotable quote

When meeting people for the first time, we struggle initially to find common ground. We do this through language, dress, manners, humour, mutual acquaintances, opinions – and we aim to relate to each other as quickly as we can. Hence, if we don't speak the language at all, dress inappropriately, use offensive behaviour, manners or humour, voice contrary opinions, are of a different age or sex, then communication becomes a herculean task, if not an impossible one.[41]

How to put some fun into your role as a manager

Just because you're a manager, you don't have to be all buttoned-down and grim. In fact, bringing a little levity to your role as a manager can make you and those around you more relaxed and effective. The best managers in any organisation aren't afraid to show the world that they have a sense of humour they enjoy using. Nor should you be. Humour is good for your career and for your health…

Know the value of humour to your own well-being.

Many managers often underestimate the value of humour. Research has shown that it not only offers a most effective tool for engaging and relating to staff, but can also relieve stress, defuse a situation, promote trust and team bonding, restore our equilibrium, deflate our pomposity, reveal our essential humanity, offer us new perspectives, and help us to soar above the mundane in our job. It has been shown that people with a sense of humour do a better job, are more creative, less rigid, and more willing to try new ideas and methods. As one commentator writes:

> Humour must come into your work, because a lot of what happens stops at your door—you deal in crisis management mode all day. And unless you can hit back with humour and a bit of light-heartedness, you'll find the job extremely depressing. It's your pressure valve… Humour is the ability to celebrate, to enjoy something that's a little out of the ordinary. And the fact that you can take delight in it, and celebrate it by laughing and sharing it with others—that is humour.[42]

In short, humour can help you and others to cope. What more could a busy manager ask for?

Look for humour around you.

It's everywhere—in the newspaper, as you commute, in the staffroom, in the office or factory—and recognising it can make your days less dour. You have at your fingertips a gold-mine of humorous anecdotes from your own workplace—like the factory supervisor who asked a worker everyone called 'Slow Joe' why it was he always carried only one box while all his co-workers carried two. 'I guess they're just too lazy to make two trips like I do,' Joe replied.

Find a model.

Think of people who have a great sense of humour—colleagues, relatives, personal friends, or even well-known comedians. Then, when faced with a stressful situation, think of how these people would react. Remember Rodney Dangerfield's motto, 'Look out for Number One, but don't step in Number Two'. It's a good rule for managers—and a sure stress-buster.

 Start a 'funny' file.

Save funny cartoons, clippings, quotations, and anecdotes. You can draw on them for meetings, speeches, and memos—or when you need a chuckle. When a manager anticipated a budget shortfall recently, he paraphrased Woody Allen: 'When you're at a cross-roads in life, one road leads to unhappiness and despair, and the other leads to total destruction. Pray we choose the right road.' Have a couple of similar wisecracks up your sleeve when you have to release the tension of a situation.

 Get your life and your job in perspective.

When you're under stress, it can be impossible to find anything amusing. But, later, try to stand back and ask yourself, 'What could be funny about this?' You'll get a new perspective and feel a greater sense of control over the event if you can laugh at it later on.

 Get support.

Form a network of friends who help you laugh at situations—and at yourself. Rely on each other when pressures mount. Go out for dinner with your staff a couple of times each year . Have a good laugh. The fun and laughs and enjoyment will help to weld you together as a team.

 Work on your surroundings.

Use humorous items in your

workplace: stationery, buttons, cards, notices, photocopies. They can make you seem more human to the rest of the staff, and they can keep you from taking yourself too seriously.

 Swap anecdotes.

Encourage staff to tell their funny stories; tell your own at staff meetings or informally. Many things that staff, co-workers, or relatives say and do are amusing.

 Develop a humour bulletin board.

Have a place in the staffroom where your staff can post a cartoon or clipping worth a good chuckle or two.

 Laugh with, not at, someone.

Humour must be used as a constructive tool, not a destructive weapon. If humour is contrived or hurtful, it is not humour. The essence of humour is laughing 'with'—the sharing of a joke or seeing the funny side of a situation. Above all, a sense of humour should never be confused with sarcasm. If you must laugh at someone, you'd better make it yourself!

 Don't go overboard.

Finally, a word of caution about all this: You don't have to be a stand-up comedian—nor should you try to be. Too many jokes can damage your credibility and take time away from the important decisions and activities that should make up your day.

So, go ahead. Lighten up a bit today.

smile & ponder

A pilot on one of the major airlines would wait until the going got bumpy, then stroll through the cabin with a book under his arm. The title, which he kept prominently displayed, was *How to Fly in 20 Easy Lessons.*

■ A little humour can often relieve stress and defuse a tricky situation, whatever the workplace.

research says

In a survey of 329 company executives, 97% agreed that humour is valuable in business, and 60% felt that a sense of humour can be a deciding factor in determining how successful a person can be in the business world. Over 84% of personnel directors said that staff with a sense of humour do better work.[43]

smile & ponder

'Having a sense of humour has done wonders for your effectiveness as a manager Ms Boswart. However… '

How to attract the headhunter

Headhunters are specialised corporate recruiters employed by businesses to find top management talent for new jobs. Many managers dream of being phoned by a headhunter seeking an appointment or luncheon meeting to canvass interest in a too-good-to-refuse offer to join another organisation. Seldom, however, do dreams come true without planning and preparation…

Know how the headhunter finds a candidate.

Headhunters stalk their prey by word of mouth, through data banks, in current business directories, by compiling press clipping files on any newsworthy high-flier, and by keeping tabs on all sorts of industry sources that might turn up the names of likely candidates. The best candidate is often an executive who is not only employed, but happily employed and not even thinking about leaving.

Take your first step to being hunted.

If you want to attract the attention of a headhunter, you will need to identify what you want to gain a reputation for—setting up new companies, cost-cutting, planning mergers, strategic planning, troubleshooting, and so on. The best thing you can have going for you is to be acknowledged by your peers as being good at what you do.

Assess demand for your skills.

The familiar supply and demand concept applies to headhunting. If you can satisfy a demand or create a new one for your services, you are in the box seat and have progressed a long way toward attracting an offer.

Keep a check on your track record.

Results, not ego, will gain for you the reputation you want. Stay focused on what you want to achieve. Remember, success requires just three things: knowing where you are now, knowing where you want to be, and—each day in some way—progressing along the path to where you want to be.

Maintain quality networks.

Whom you know, or more importantly who knows you, *does* make a difference. All decisions ultimately come down to subjective assessments… Do I like this person? Is he respected by his peers? Does she get on well with others? Could I rely on her in a crisis? Such issues as these are why the network is so essential.

You need not rush out and join every club or professional association, but you must find rewarding ways to associate with individuals and groups who can help you to achieve your career aspirations. The word will soon get around the network.

 Be prepared—always.

In front of every talented person there must be a vacancy somewhere—and there's sure to be one in front of you at some time. So be ready for when that opening occurs. Remain up to date with developments in your field; keep your slate clean; keep your CV current. And don't despair: Pope John XXXIII accepted the top position in the world's largest organisation at age 76 and made one of the greatest contributions in the history of the Papacy. So be ready for when your moment of glory arrives.

 Make things happen.

You'll just grow old if you simply wait around, hoping for that call. Your actions will make the difference. Stay focused; don't expect anything of others; drive your own bus; and tell others only what you want made public.

　　Importantly, make yourself visible. You must attract the attention of the headhunter. Try these strategies…

- Publish in trade journals and the press.
- Work on your public speaking skills so that when you make a presentation you make it well.
- Speak at public meetings, service clubs, and trade conferences.
- Make a good name for yourself by

being newsworthy and active in social, professional, and community affairs.
- Think, on behalf of your company, of public relations ideas that will indirectly have you quoted in newspapers or trade journals as the author of those ideas.
- Keep doing a good job.
- Cultivate professional contacts. Headhunters always listen to the corporate grapevine.

 Establish your own 'home page'.

The Internet offers a great opportunity to promote yourself to a much larger audience. Talk to your existing website guru about designing for you a home page that will present you to the national and international business community. But be prepared to respond to requests for more information by having your self-promotional pack ready as email or hard copy.

 And, as a last resort…

Still no phone call? As a last resort, introduce yourself to a headhunter. Send a résumé; wait a week; then phone for an interview. If you are lucky enough to get an interview— and you just may if a vacancy exists in your area—follow-up with a thank-you note and a short reiteration of your current situation. Do not follow up with a phone call. Remember, headhunters work for client organisations, not for you.

　　Even if you miss out, the headhunter may be impressed enough to call on you the next time a position falls vacant.

don't forget

Remember that honesty is the only policy…

Headhunters have, through experience, become suspicious persons, a result of their not infrequent uncovering of false credentials during previous consultancies.

　　In serving their client's best interests, they will normally check and crosscheck the claims which you make in your self-promotional package. Accordingly:

- make sure your claimed credentials and qualifications are genuine.
- make sure your résumé is truthful.
- make sure you have not falsified your portfolio.

If you stretch the facts and produce a glossy but undeserving image in an attempt to boost your chances, you take the real risk of being found out, thereby gaining a blacklisting and even running the risk of legal action against you.

ask yourself

　　Before you ever approach a headhunter, ask yourself:

- Have I evaluated my present and past achievements?
- Do I know my strengths and weaknesses?
- Am I willing to relocate?
- Am I willing to travel?
- Do I have clear short- and long-term goals?

How to kick those irritating supervisory habits that employees complain about

Like most people, managers are rarely perfect. They allow themselves to acquire a range of personal quirks and annoying habits that can become extremely irritating to their staff members. Over time, there is a danger that these mannerisms will ossify and become integral and unattractive parts of their personalities and managerial styles. You can guard against the most irritating and frustrating of these habits by heeding the following advice…

1. Do not skimp on praise.

"You rarely compliment me on a job I think I've done well." Everyone responds well to praise. One or two compliments won't take much of your time but will do wonders for an employee's morale. Why not make a quick visit to the workroom or office or send a short note to a staff member who deserves praise for a job well done?

2. Be decisive when decisions are required.

"You avoid making decisions." First, clarify the real problem: Is it your poor decision-making ability or simply procrastination? If it's the former, read the literature on decision-making; and also make sure that your staff clearly understand where your decision-making responsibility ends and theirs begins. If it's procrastination, a problem is sometimes best attacked after you have spent time thinking about it. In other cases, a lack of action will only inflame the issue. As a supervisor, you are expected to make timely decisions based on the available evidence and information.

3. Be available when needed.

"You're always too inaccessible." Schedule regular staff or department meetings. Make yourself available for urgent matters and at least be accessible by appointment for non-urgent issues. Don't go overboard, however—an open-door policy can become very time-consuming.

4. Listen.

"You never seem to be listening to what I say." To listen attentively and patiently is a skill that requires great effort. We don't always hear what others are saying to us: we fidget, look elsewhere, shuffle paper—all visual clues indicating that you are paying less attention to the speaker than perhaps you should be. Working to improve this irritating habit is well worth the effort.

Stand by what you say.

"You say something—and then deny it later." Honesty and integrity are crucial to a manager's reputation. To ensure that your statements are not misinterpreted, keep notes of meetings and ensure that all participants get copies of relevant minutes.

Hold those calls.

"You always take telephone calls during our meetings." Either have all your calls held until after the meeting or hold your meetings away from the office. Accept incoming calls only in emergencies. Show your colleagues that you consider any discussion with you important.

Let them get on with the job.

"You won't let me do my job—you're always interfering." Encourage your staff to complain to you when they feel you're interfering, but use the occasion to discuss the reasons for your involvement. Implement, and foster an understanding of, a staff appraisal system to ensure that you become an integral and valued part of an employee's life, rather than purely an 'interruption'.

Do not play favourites.

"You play favourites." There is no quicker way of lowering staff morale than to show favouritism in your daily relationships with staff. Of course, some employees are brighter, more dependable, and more personable than others; but you must guard against any display of personal bias. It is perfectly proper to assign a task to an employee who is better equipped than others to handle it; it is improper to overdo such delegation or to deny others the opportunity to develop their talents and skills.

Keep in touch with what's going on.

"You're out of touch with what's going on in the workplace." With a heavy workload, managers often find it difficult to remain abreast of day-to-day action in the workplace or office. Try to schedule at least a few periods a month at the workface: your credibility as a supervisor will be enhanced.

Be open to employees' ideas.

"You always pooh-pooh our ideas." Do you kill a staff member's idea simply because it challenges the status quo? If an idea is obviously poor, do you enjoy shooting down the originator's kite—or do you haul it down with tact? Creativity is not the exclusive province of the talented few. Everyone has creative qualities that lie dormant and untapped, waiting to be released. By word and deed, you must allow creativity to flourish in the workplace.

Finally, take heart from the advice of Churchill's aunt...

Before introducing him, Sir Winston Churchill's aunt reminded a man applying for the job as his private secretary: "Remember, you will see all of Winston's faults in the first few hours. It will take you longer to discover his virtues."

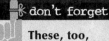 **don't forget**

These, too, are irritating habits:

Talk behind their back. In any organisation, if you say something behind someone's back, s/he is sure to hear about it.

'People are saying that you…' This variation of talking behind someone's back is never appreciated by your colleague who will normally treat you as if you started the rumour – whether you did or not.

Public humiliation. Failing to give credit, correcting facts, interrupting, etc. can push people's buttons the wrong way when you do this in front of a group.

Pull rank. There are more subtle ways of exerting your authority and getting a job done.

Minimise experience. If you imply, by words or actions, that you know more about doing other people's jobs than they do, it will surely infuriate them.

Call someone into your office. Don't do this when everyone knows the only reason you call people in is to chew them out.

Imply dishonesty or moral turpitude. If you set universal policies to control the worst of your employees, you'll anger your best who resent the implication that they too are lazy, dishonest or disloyal.[46]

How to overcome boredom on the job

Boredom is most frequently linked to a wide variety of feelings associated with monotony, repetition, even insecurity and stress. Some people say they are bored at their jobs; others are bored in their leisure time. For some, immersing themselves in a task can be boring; for others, completing a task can be the most boring part of a job. Still others find meetings dull, 'ho-hum', 'a big yawn', boring. Although there can be no one prescription for overcoming boredom, some considerations will help you to deal with this modern-day ailment...

Do things differently.

Start by identifying possible contributors to your feeling of boredom—and change them. Doing the same thing is often identified as a contributor. If so, change the task. A solution may be as simple as having a sleep-in on weekends to break out of the rut of rushing to arrive at work on time. If you're bored replying to emails, you might write letters instead.

Do the same things in a different way.

If you cannot postpone a task, you can vary the way you do things. Just as you can telephone someone instead of sending an email, you can devise different ways of doing the same thing. A change of scenery can also help. Dan Sullivan, strategic coach to successful entrepreneurs, found the environment in coffee shops such an inspiration for his creative thought that he established his own close to his training rooms. If you're feeling bored doing things in a particular way; do anything but continue that way of doing things.

Change the order of tasks.

Accomplishing your goals need not limit involvement in other pursuits. You might find that going for a brisk walk or jog can actually help you to complete a task without any associated feelings of boredom. This approach may also indicate that you could be taking on too many tasks that provide little opportunity for savouring your successes.

Reward yourself.

If you have so many tasks to complete that, as soon as you successfully finish one, there is another awaiting your attention, you need to build in a reward system for yourself. Give yourself a lift—take a walk in the park or see a movie. We are usually critical of others when they do not recognise our contributions and accomplishments, yet we're prepared to accept similar behaviour from ourselves.

Take time out.

Researchers recommend that we take short breaks—of 10 minutes, say—every 90 to 120 minutes. This practice, we're told, helps to replenish energy, enabling us to return to the task refreshed. Although most people have experienced the benefits to be derived from such a practice, the majority continue to work through the barrier—which can lead inevitably to boredom.

Feelings of boredom could also be brought on by tiredness or fatigue. The message here could be to take a break—a long weekend, perhaps.

 Get to know yourself better.

Some describe themselves as 'morning' people; others 'evening' people. Generally, these are descriptions of when people consider they are most productive. Try to allocate tasks that fit your feelings or perceptions. Be careful, of course, that you don't fall into the trap of spending significantly more time on tasks that you enjoy but that do not contribute to important bottom-line results. Schedule the most important tasks to coincide with the time when you're feeling at your most productive.

 Identify possible causes.

Sometimes saying 'No' can help to reduce boredom. If you're finding yourself overworked, you could be the recipient of other people's monkeys. Remember, there are a variety of ways to say 'No'. (See page 162.) Critically assess your timetable to determine whether all of the tasks you are currently engaged in are really necessary—and are really yours.

 Investigate delegation.

If you are not delegating enough tasks, you might be being swamped by having to complete things below your station. And a task that you find boring could be one that someone else finds challenging. In fact, your decision could be a real win-win. You win because you've taken positive action to reduce a feeling of boredom. The delegatee wins because successful completion of the task is an extra opportunity to impress key people.

 Remove busy-ness.

Every job has its busy periods and its quiet times. But some people hope to avoid confronting issues that they fear—like being bored—by always being busy (or pretending to be). When used as an escape, busy-ness can be unproductive. A far better alternative is to confront any perceived fear by asking, 'What is it about being bored that causes me such concern?' Probably you'll find that your fears weren't justified. View long-term busy-ness for what it really is—an unproductive excuse for avoiding getting to know the 'real' you.

95

How to resign

In an increasingly mobile population, you will probably change jobs—if not careers—several times during your working life. Some say more than five times. Whether you're 'headhunted' or you've been on the lookout for yourself, you're going to have to resign from your current position. And, like most things, there's a right and a wrong way to approach this task. Here's some useful advice to help you take this important step…

ask yourself

Are you thinking of resigning? It's possible you will be doing so for one of the following reasons. You…

- do not get along with your colleagues or supervisors
- believe you could make a stronger contribution if you were given the freedom to do so
- believe you are not being paid enough or receiving enough recognition for your contributions
- feel you are personally stagnating and not being challenged
- feel you don't have control over your own future
- disagree with the direction the organisation is taking
- believe the organisation has not determined its priorities (You are asked to do one thing today; the exact opposite tomorrow.)
- are frustrated by the amount of red tape you have to cut through
- feel you're working in the dark and lack resources needed to perform your job
- perceive that you are not working in a fun environment
- simply cannot turn down that better offer.

…which, be warned, can be among the reasons why your staff might also be contemplating quitting!

1 Be convinced you're ready to resign.

People resign for many reasons:

Have you peaked too early in the company? Do you face a long wait before further advancement? Have recent successes enhanced your market value? Do you feel you are not getting enough recognition? Is the company falling behind competitively? Can't you persuade it to change? Has a reorganisation left your career plan in tatters?

If you've made up your mind, do not delay your decision to leave too long. It is better to change than to stagnate.

2 Keep your decision to resign under wraps.

News on the office grapevine can travel at an alarming speed, so you can't afford details of your decision to resign reaching your boss before you have a chance to break the news yourself. To avoid embarrassment, keep things quiet. Reserve the news only for those who must know of your plans, and whose help you will need, now and in the future. If the grapevine news reaches your boss before you do, your best-laid plans for an organised and supported exit will be thwarted. An additional bonus for you will be the respect of those who normally rely on the grapevine for their news. They should first hear of your resignation via memo or other official communiqué.

3 Pow-wow with the boss, first.

Don't delay. Having decided to resign, make an appointment to see your boss promptly. The boss will want to hear your news first-hand and will value being told of your plans. Reach agreement on the story each of you will tell in public. After all, it is in your interests and those of the organisation for everyone to hear the same message. Be prepared for an exit interview in which your suggestions for organisational improvement will be sought. View that interview as a quid-pro-quo from which both you and the organisation can benefit significantly.

4 Resist counter offers.

Some bosses will try to offer you

an inducement to stay—increased salary, more entitlements, and so on. As attractive as they may sound, you must refuse. If you have *really* given your initial decision the attention it deserves, counter offers are little more than ego-enhancements. By accepting, you will indicate that you can be bought. Your credibility will plummet. So simply thank the boss for the offer and reaffirm your decision. Remember, too, that those who attempt to play one employer off against another often end up losing both.

Ask how you can help.

Organising your transition can be a stressful time for you and your boss. What happens to your project commitments? Offer to work together to plan your transition. Agree on what you will complete before you leave the organisation, and when and how news of your resignation will be communicated to staff. Your involvement and cooperation in this process will reveal you as a true professional.

Ask for a testimonial or reference.

Always obtain a testimonial or reference from your employer. Written testimonials must be on the organisation's stationery and, ideally, signed in blue ink so that readers can identify the reference as an original. Depending on your relationship with your boss, you might prefer telephone referrals; and you should agree on the overall message to be communicated.

Many executives prefer this latter approach: written references tend to be more generalised, even evasive.

Dot 'I's and cross 'T's.

It is essential that your reputation remain intact. Decide with your boss what needs to be finalised before you leave. Even check that any obligations to the social club and colleagues have been met. Never give others an opportunity to suggest that your honesty and integrity are anything but first-class.

Move on.

Once you have decided to leave the organisation, that's it. All baggage should remain in the organisation. Move on with a fresh outlook; make a clean break. Whether or not you retain contact with former colleagues is your decision, but make it clear that happenings in the organisation are as interesting as reading yesterday's newspapers. Your main interest must be the next stage of your life and career.

Maintain irregular contact.

Once you have established yourself in your new position, give your former boss a call to update your progress for dissemination to colleagues and other staff. And if necessary, your boss can canvass your opinion on a residue issue or a loose end. The response your call receives will let you know whether or not a future call will be appreciated.

How to use your retrenchment to advantage

Technology advancements, restructuring, downsizing, and other forms of cost-cutting inevitably mean that some jobs just won't exist any more. One unfortunate outcome of the remarkable changes in today's workplace is redundancy—termination of a worker's employment because that worker is now surplus to company requirements. But your redundancy need not be bad news—providing, of course, you're prepared to make the most of the opportunities...

Keep your ear to the ground.

Retrenchment should rarely come as a surprise. By keeping yourself informed about developments inside and outside your organisation, you will have a pretty good idea about how the organisation is travelling and about your prospects. Current management literature, the media, the office grapevine—all are sources of information. These days, you should be preparing yourself long before the news breaks.

 See retrenchment positively.

As one door closes, another invariably opens. Being retrenched can provide the encouragement you need to make a break—even pursue a new career path that you may not have considered previously. Remember, whether you see any event positively or negatively is your choice. Career changes are the same. As the ancient sages taught us, our interpretation of 'good news' or 'bad news' often depends on the way we view it. View a redundancy in a positive light.

Pull yourself together.

Psychologist Karen Nixon urges us to tackle the fear of losing our jobs. To avoid fear by trying to push it away only gives it more power. Fear should not be repressed, she adds, and feeling our fears is the best way to control them. So, if you notice that you feel anxious, be courageous enough to allow yourself to 'feel the fear' or anxiety until it dissipates.

Nixon advocates the following in fighting the fear of losing your job:

- Imagine losing your job.
- Allow yourself to feel the anxiety this generates.
- When the feeling subsides, make a contingency plan and take action as required (e.g. learn new skills).
- Focus on what you have to offer.
- List what you really need to live.
- Notice the precious things around you that money can't buy (sunsets, children, rainbows, songbirds).
- Practise feeling fortunate and grateful for what you have.

It's not a nice feeling to lose your job, but you'll gain little by indulging your emotions. Self-pity will not get you another job or help pay the grocery bill. By the time of your exit interview, you should have already begun to take positive action.

4 Be prepared for your exit interview.

In-house or contracted outplacement services are becoming more common. Find out in advance about the outplacement services provided by your organisation. In addition to helping you finalise your payout, the services may also include assistance with your résumé, interview coaching, career advice, counselling, advice on superannuation and financial planning, and temporary work accommodation. As well, you'll need to agree with the organisation about any public statement that will be made about your career change. You can't afford to have mixed messages communicated—particularly at your expense.

5 Negotiate fair severance compensation.

You have a right to be compensated fairly and to negotiate the best severance arrangement for your situation. Become fully versed in your organisation's severance policies and be firm in any negotiations.

6 Adopt a positive position and stick to it.

Redundancy is an opportunity to show some of your real qualities. Avoid complaining, whingeing, or carrying on a 'poor-me campaign'. Realise that 70 per cent don't care, and that the other 30 per cent enjoy the entertainment. If you want to let off steam, save it for a select, trusted few; better still, hit a golf ball, go for a run, meditate, or find some other form of relaxation. People will think the better of you if you adopt a rational approach.

7 Resist moving immediately into a similar position.

A common and predictable response from people who fear change and crave security is to seek out a position similar to the one they have just left. A better approach is to take time, to play it cool, to consider your options, and to decide rationally what you *really* want to do. After all, you only get one chance at life; so make sure you get the best from it.

8 Resist burning bridges.

Business is a series of relationships between people, so, if possible, try to maintain existing relationships: you never know what the future holds. Wish your former employer and colleagues every success and move on to the next chapter in your life.

9 Think and act strategically.

Panic will get you nowhere. Plan your next life transition; consider how you want to spend the next phase in your life, the names of others who may be able to help you, and how you are going to go about letting people know that you are on the market. Professional outplacement support services can help you to do so.

Redundancy can be tough on the ego, but that's all the more reason to attack the job market energetically. Develop your job search strategy and follow it through.

here's an idea

If you are being laid off, don't hesitate to ask your boss for leads to decision makers, telephone calls on your behalf, and letters of recommendation. If you are a good employee, but the project has ended or your company simply is eliminating your position, then you should feel comfortable asking for help from every source. What better person to start with than the person who knows your work best and can sell you better than you could possibly do on your own?

viewpoint

Don't fool yourself into thinking that the organisation will fall completely apart when you leave. It won't. Take the case of an upper-level manager in a large national enterprise who later admitted:

"When I was made redundant I didn't think they could make it without me. But somehow they did, of course. Now the only person who remembers me after my 28 years' service with the company is the finance officer who, as part of my parting package, sends me a regular cheque every month – and damned if he isn't an IBM machine! My advice to you is to get on with life."

How to ready yourself for re-entry to the work force

Life is full of transitions, and one of them is career change that inevitably involves starting a new job. Many women, for example, take time out of paid employment to have a family, care for relatives, learn new skills, or reassess their futures. When the time comes to re-enter the work force, they need to be ready and ensure that they optimise their potential. So, too, do people changing jobs. Here's how to get yourself ready to thrive from this challenging experience…

Build a positive self-image.

Becoming as good as you know you are demands a positive self-image. You need to value yourself and your contributions if you expect others to do so. You can't not have a self-image. It is evident in the way you present yourself in everything you do—and it is best accompanied by self-confidence and a positive mental attitude. The bookshops contain self-help literature, audiobooks, and CDs.

Conduct your own SWOT analysis.

Know yourself. SWOT—Strengths, Weaknesses, Opportunities, Threats—is a process of looking inwardly and outwardly. Using this process, you can consider your main strengths (what you can offer an employer) and your weaknesses (those qualities or defects that may require additional attention). You also examine the opportunities that exist in your area of expertise or in the marketplace; and you explore threats that may prevent you from achieving your goals.

Be positive and honest about your assessment so that you have a clear picture of your current situation and what actions are required. Don't sell yourself short. If you're returning from home duties, for example, remember that managing a home and a family requires skill in controlling time, projects, and finances—skills that are valuable in any workplace.

Develop an action plan.

Your personal SWOT analysis will have helped you identify what needs to be done. List specific actions you need to take and the completion time for each. Successful accomplishment of each action will require specific steps.

If one of those steps involves training, do it! In this way, each day in every way, you will progress closer to your goals. Goal achievement, you will find, will be a constant contributor to your positive self-image and success.

Make a list of contacts.

Networking is one of the essential practices for most people in business. Your networking should involve two actions. First, list the people you know who may be able to help you in your quest for, or in starting, a new job. Contact those people. Second, start attending meetings of groups whose members have similar or complementary interests to your own.

 Understand the lay of the land.

An essential part of your preparation is building your awareness of the marketplace you will be rejoining. Networks will provide some information. So, too, will the daily business papers, selected current affairs programs, and the Internet. By becoming more conversant with the market you hope to join, you will feel more confident and able to engage in discussions on current issues during interviews and other conversations.

 Construct a résumé— and keep it current.

Even if you have found employment, you should keep your résumé up to date at all times. Keeping a copy on your computer will simplify this task. Your résumé is your sales document. Often, the quality of that document will gain you an interview. Ensure that it is written with the reader in mind. Your prospective employer will not want to wade through pages and pages of irrelevant material in the hope of 'discovering' the real you.

 Begin the search.

What you focus on grows. If finding the job you want or re-entering the work force is your principal goal and you devote attention to it, in time an opportunity will present itself. You will find that the search drives your networking, motivates visits to your local job agencies, encourages you to check out the local newspapers, and so on. Once you've made a commitment to action, you've overcome the greatest hurdle.

 Rehearse.

Spend time in front of the mirror, seeing what others see. Practise entering an interview room. Enlist the support of trusted others to provide honest and open feedback on your presentation. A dry run of a job interview will help you to be calm, relaxed, and in control when the real event happens. Remember that one of the key qualities you are selling to your prospective employer is confidence. You need to make the interviewer feel confident that you are just what he or she is looking for.

 Know what you need to know.

Whatever your situation, there will be questions you will need to ask any interviewer. A woman with family responsibilities, for example, may need to know about flexible leave arrangements, equal employment opportunities, childcare facilities, and policy on working from home. Clarify all issues that are important to you.

 don't forget

The rules of the job hunt:

The rules of the job hunt are easy to master, because they are the same for those re-entering the world of work as they are for everyone else…

• Know your skills.

• Know what kind of work you want.

• Talk to people who are doing it.

• Find out how they like the work, and how they found their job.

• Do some research in your chosen geographical area, on organisations which interest you, to find out what they do and what kind of problems they and their industry are wrestling with.

• Identify and seek out the person who actually has the power to hire you there, for the job you want; use your contacts to get in to see him or her.

• Show the person with the power to hire you how you can help them with their problems; and how you would stand out as 'one employee in a hundred'.[51]

 read further

What Color is Your Parachute? A Practical Manual for Job-Hunters and Career-Changers by Richard Nelson Boles, Ten Speed Press, Berkeley Cal., 2002.

101

How to go it alone and establish your own consultancy

 don't forget

The traps for newcomers...

Having made the decision to begin your own consultancy, it's vital to be aware of the traps which can bring about your downfall...

- Overcommitting your time.
- Failing to recognise changes in the field.
- Miscalculating the fee structure.
- Giving away ideas and expertise for free.
- Having the wrong attitude towards clients.
- Failing to market your services.
- Being poorly organised.
- Failing to keep killer overheads in check.

More and more managers are abandoning the safety of company careers to become consultants in their chosen fields. They cite a number of reasons—a need to pursue their vision, a desire for increased independence, the lack of a meaningful future in a large organisation, or the reality of redundancy. If you're contemplating such a move, here are some important actions you might take...

Identify existing demand.

Successful businesses provide services that people want and are prepared to pay for—the concept of supply and demand. Demand will result either from providing different services or from providing those services differently. As very few consultants have different products or services, they usually attempt to differentiate their services in other ways, such as targeting niche markets, being increasingly responsive, and so on. One indicator of demand will be that you have potential customers lined up before you start, so that, before making the jump, you can tell existing clients of your plans and secure their continuing support before.

Get your networks established.

Abraham Lincoln said, 'Good things come to those who wait—but only that left by those who hustle'. Networking is an important means of hustling, so use your existing contacts to make new ones. Hustle at business breakfasts and lunches, industry seminars, and other events conducted by professional associations; have your work published in industry journals or in the local media. Then, when potential clients need the types of services you provide, they will associate your name immediately with their needs. Hustle also in directory listings and Yellow Pages. Try starting a newsletter. Create a website. Even approach former employers. Hustle for work.

Get a mentor and a coach.

A mentor will be someone who has succeeded in your field or in another field and who is prepared to nurture your development by taking you under his or her wing, offering guidance and advice. Mentors are role models and valuable sources of advice in such areas as getting started, providing services, finding niche markets, and advertising. Coaching differs from mentoring in that it focuses on providing specific assistance with a specific problem.

A coach, for example, may teach you and help you to improve your public presentation skills so that you can, for example, increase demand for your services as a conference speaker.

 Choose your business name wisely.

Time spent on choosing a company name and logo is time well spent. You'll want a name that helps to distinguish you and your services from the competition—and one that provides credibility. Do not add 'and Associates'. In business, 'and Associates' often means 'small', usually a one-person operation trying to sound 'big' by inventing associates. Register your chosen name with the relevant authority.

 Establish essential support.

Develop a sound working relationship with those whose support you will need—for example, an accountant, a banker, and a solicitor. Initially, you may employ part-time accounting or bookkeeping support, seek income protection and other professional insurance, use a graphic designer to design your logo and present your reports and tenders professionally, an office supplier to provide everything from furniture to stationery, and even a fashion consultant to keep you looking the part.

 Know what it takes.

Being a consultant and being outstanding are two different things. Top consultants possess a bedside manner or a capacity to get along with clients, an ability to diagnose problems and find their solutions, technical expertise and knowledge, communication skills, self-marketing and selling skills, management skills, a willingness to work erratic hours…

 Ask: 'Do I really need that…?'

It can be tempting to want at once all the 'trimmings' often associated with a successful business—for example:

- A fancy office. Most consultants go to their clients, not the other way around—so use technology and save on rentals.
- A bank loan. Some would say that if you can't set up a consultancy without a loan, don't do it.
- Elaborate professional marketing and advertising. You should know your own business best. Keep these experts on tap, but never on top.
- Partners. By joining forces with other consultants you can offer a broader base of skills, target a wider range of market niches, and reduce overheads. Informal partnerships are often preferred.

 Stay focused on the bottom line.

In the establishment phase of your business, expenses will probably exceed income. Don't panic. Just keep overheads low without skimping. You'll need the best equipment you can afford, but the Mercedes can wait until you're well established.

don't forget

The qualities needed…

For success as a consultant you'll need to:

- *Know the business environment.* You must be worldly, plugged in, and fully understand new developments and policies in your field.
- *Be a trend spotter.* You must ride the waves of change, recognise the trends and get in first.
- *Be self-motivated.* You must be a self-starter with a get-up-and-go attitude and lots of ideas.
- *Be willing to work long hours.*
- *Be results-oriented.* You must stick to the promises you make, must not overcommit, and have good time management and organisational skills.
- *Have the ability to write well.* You must be good at identifying the client's needs and writing to the client's satisfaction.
- *Have a customer focus.* You must possess good listening skills, patience and the tolerance to work within a wide range of client idiosyncrasies.
- *Be willing to sell yourself.* You must be confident and charismatic and believe that your skills can make a difference.[53]

103

How to reap the rewards of working from home

Increasing numbers of people are working for themselves. In 1996, management guru Peter Drucker predicted that, by 2004, more than half of the working population in the United States would be self-employed. Others, for a variety of reasons, would establish home offices but continue to work for the company—but from home. Working from home, therefore, will continue to be the preferred option for more and more people. Here's the information that will help you to make and benefit from that decision…

Weigh up the pros and cons.

The decision to work from home has four main advantages:

- You are in the driver's seat in terms of focus, short- and long-term priorities, and how you spend your time.
- You will save time commuting, and avoid peak-hour traffic and getting caught up in endless office meetings.
- You will save money in a variety of areas like rental, travel, and parking costs.
- You will have increased flexibility ranging from the number of hours you need to put in to the way you manage short-and long-term projects.

On the other side, three of the main disadvantages include these:

- You can be interrupted or distracted by the everyday life in a home.
- You may be tempted to overwork and rob yourself of relaxation.
- You can become less visible in your business community.

 ### Manage yourself.

Your self-motivation, planning, and preparation are the keys to maximising the benefits of working from home. Self-motivation will come from the picture or vision you have for your future—what you want to become or the way you see yourself operating in, say, five years' time. Planning means translating your vision into actions supported by reasonable time lines. Preparation entails activities leading to the achievement of those plans. You will find plenty of tools to support these three essentials. Your aim will be to find the ones that best suit your operating style.

 ### Manage your time.

Dan Sullivan proposes an innovative approach to time management— *Free days, Focus days,* and *Buffer days*.[54] Adopt it, says Sullivan, and your productivity will experience exponential growth:

Free days are when you take total time out from what you are doing. This full twenty-four hour period should be free from any work-related information or activities, giving you time to recharge and come up with a fresh perspective on things. Free days become your reward for successful task completion.

Focus days occur on about one hundred days a year and are periods set aside for completion of one or more particular tasks. Sullivan advocates 80 per cent focus on these days with minimal interruptions. Focus days will be your main fee-generation days.

Buffer days are when you do a little of this and a little of that—a little free time, a little focus time. Buffer days are essential for focus days to happen. Tasks can be delegated, staff know what is required of them, and you tidy up a myriad issues requiring your attention.

Others will soon learn your habits associated with free, focus, and buffer time, allowing you to reap the benefits of this simple but effective time management technique.

 ### Overcome feelings of guilt.

Self-discipline is rarely a problem for people working for themselves. Many, however, feel guilty if they are playing a round of golf or engaging in some other form of relaxation when office-workers are heading off to work. Free days, focus days, and buffer days happen according to demand. There is no need to feel guilty if a free day occurs when others are at work. Remember that you have chosen this lifestyle for the added benefits it can provide. One of those benefits may be not having to queue before teeing off.

 ### Maintain your business networks.

Make a conscious effort to retain business networks. Continue to attend industry meetings, lunches, and other events that will keep you in the public eye. Use the telephone, fax, and email to maintain regular contact with your clients. Remember those important marketing maxims:

- Talk to every client at least once every 90 days.
- Your telephone will ring only if you make it.
- Don't just sit there: phone someone.

 ### Continue to project a high-quality image.

Wherever you are, image remains a key quality. Your personal appearance, the appearance of your office and your stationery, the way your phone is answered, the appearance of your car—all will be just as vital now as they were before. Working from home may have been a life-quality choice but should not detract from the image you project. The quality of the company you keep will always provide an insight into you and your operations.

 ### Become your own best friend.

At times, working from home can leave you feeling a little isolated. Recognition and rewards are most frequently identified as what people miss most of all. Rather than rely on others to provide those essentials, you can use this experience to out-grow the need for continued recognition. Find ways to reward yourself. One example of a reward could be additional free days to celebrate the successful completion of an important project.

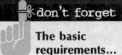
105

How to reduce the risk when establishing your own business

Most people, at one time or another, have a job, their time and effort being rewarded with wages or salaries. An increasing number of people, however, are becoming dissatisfied with that time-and-effort economy and seek the greater rewards that a results-economy can provide. This change inevitably means establishing their own businesses, working for themselves, and—if necessary—employing others. This transition from a time-and-effort to a results-economy is a major personal growth experience that can occur with the minimum of risk if you heed this important advice...

Know what it takes to succeed.

People who succeed in a results-economy believe two things—that they are prepared to rely only on their own ability to achieve financial security; and that they will never get any opportunity in life unless they have first created value for someone else. Those two considerations identify entrepreneurial behaviour, which applies to any structure—sole trader, partnership, franchise, or limited company.

Try to be different.

Most business strategy comes down to one of two things: either doing things differently or doing different things. Few businesses have the luxury of being the only player in a market, so doing things differently will be the only way to differentiate themselves from others in the field. Identifying that area of uniqueness leads to planning and strategic action. Most people recall first and second placegetters in a class and, after that, only those that differ in some way. Few people starting out in business can be number one or two: most have to rely on being recognised for their differences.

Investigate your market.

Market and competitor intelligence is vital if you are going to differ meaningfully from the opposition. So get to know as much as you can about those competing in your market. This process must be reviewed constantly: competitors quickly match those characteristics that previously differentiated your product or service from theirs. Change, therefore, is a constant for any business that realises the need to stand out from the rest.

Get the best resources.

People, planning, and equipment make up the important resources you will require. Your accountant, financial planner, and legal adviser will have the information you need on taxation, insurance, investment, and other legal issues like tenancy agreements and restrictions on business activities. A business plan will not only be an invaluable tool for yourself but also a requirement of banks and other fund providers. The quality of your office equipment must help to deliver the services you advertise. Quick turn-round time on tasks and projects demands the right equipment and expertise.

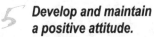

Develop and maintain a positive attitude.

A positive mental attitude is an essential life quality—especially when establishing a new business. 'I will', therefore, continues to have a greater effect on the success of businesses than 'IQ'. Stories of those who have succeeded in their chosen fields identify desire and focus—'I will' behaviour—above education and giftedness or IQ. This 'fire-in-the-belly-behaviour' leads ultimately to

- loving what you are doing
- learning new things
- gaining extra energy.

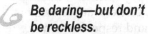

Be daring—but don't be reckless.

People with entrepreneurial flair who leave the security of employment to venture into their own businesses are sometimes labelled as daring risk-takers. In truth, studies show that successful entrepreneurs avoid high-risk situations. They do choose challenging goals, but they do everything they can to reduce the

risks. They usually enter their new venture with an advantage—they are experienced in the business they intend to start. They are aware of, and seek information on, the risks and potential problems. They remain open to feedback, both positive and negative. They have confidence in themselves and in their ability to make their new ventures work somehow, even if things don't happen as they hope. They work to minimise risk within the confines of their basic aim: meet challenging but not impossible objectives.

Heed your own advice.

'The best advice you can take is your own' is the best advice you'll ever receive. Although listening to the advice of respected others is important, the one person with a better understanding of the entire context in which your business operates is *you*. For various reasons, many people underestimate the value of their own contributions and place greater emphasis on the views of others.

Do it!

The most important four letters for people in business are 'Do it'. Having the best plans, the best advice, and the best intentions are essential qualities; but if you never do anything, nothing will happen. Yet gaining a reputation as a 'do-er' is easy—just do it!

don't forget

The four types of risks...

Some small firms are endangered by owner-managers being too impetuous and taking risks that the firm can't afford to take. Many others suffer from owner-manager attitudes to risk which paralyse them by making them afraid to take any risks at all. Being in business involves some risk; so does driving a car and getting married.

Astute owner-managers must be able to calculate or estimate whether the risk of doing something new and different is one that the firm can afford to take, or one that the firm *cannot* afford to take.

Sometimes, when survival depends on doing something different (e.g. changing to a new location, adding a new branch, or taking on a new product), that may be a risk that the firm *cannot afford not* to take! Doing nothing is often more risky than doing something new and different.

In a nutshell, then, understand that there are four types of risks...

- the risk of being in business
- the risk we can afford to take
- the risk we cannot afford to take
- the risk we cannot afford *not* to take.[56]

How to get on well with other people

We all want to be accepted and well liked by our staff and colleagues, if for no other reason than that it makes our task as managers so much easier. Managers should be easy to get along with and understand other people. If you want to win friends within your organisation, here are some well-proven principles for you to consider...

1 Always be open and honest.

Gain a reputation for being a straight-shooter. To be open with people, you will need three qualities:

- Expressing your own views openly and accepting responsibility for your own actions.
- Reacting honestly to incoming information. Indeed, where an important decision is required from you, disagreement is often better than indifference.
- Making sure that other people are quite clear where you stand on a particular issue.

2 Empathise with other people.

If we make a practice of putting ourselves into the shoes of other people, we will understand far better the feelings of our staff members and colleagues. Although we can't 'own' another person's feelings, we can say that we understand how we'd feel under the same circumstances. We win points for empathising with others.

3 Be known as one who espouses equality.

Do all you can to ensure that your work place recognises that everyone is worthwhile and valuable, and has something important to contribute to the organisation's success.

4 Listen to what people are saying.

People will know if you're really concerned about their welfare. Showing an interest in what they're saying is one clear indicator of this concern. So pay attention, maintain eye contact, concentrate on what is being said, and respond warmly.

5 Try not to impose your expectations on others.

One of the most common causes of tension in any relationship is other people's failure to meet or satisfy our expectations. If you have particular expectations of others— expectations important to you and the organisation, make certain you share them with your staff. You can only ask them to do their best.

Gain a reputation for being supportive.

People work best in a non-threatening environment, one in which they feel free to say what they think rather than what they think you want them to say. They need to feel that your relationship with them is openly supportive. When you offer this support, they will make every attempt not to let you down.

Be positive.

A positive attitude will affect all those with whom you come in contact. Here are three steps you can take right now:

- Think positively about yourself. Believe that you're OK. Others will respond to you in the same way.

- Get others to feel good about themselves too.

- Encourage a favourable exchange of communication among all those with whom you come in contact.

Embrace these classic principles for gaining the esteem of others.

For over half a century, the advice of Norman Vincent Peale has worked for many people. There is no reason that it wouldn't work for you, too…

☐ Learn to remember names. Laziness in this area may indicate that you are not sincerely interested in other people. Names are very important to some people.

☐ Be a comfortable person so that there is no strain in being with you. Be an 'old shoe' kind of individual.

☐ Become relaxed and easy-going. Don't let things ruffle you.

☐ Don't be egotistical. Guard against being a know-all. Be natural and humble.

☐ Cultivate the quality of being stimulating and interesting so that people will want to be with you and to get something from you.

☐ Determine and eliminate the abrasive elements from your personality.

☐ Sincerely attempt to heal every misunderstanding you have had or now have. Drain off your grievances.

☐ Practise liking people until you learn to do so genuinely. Will Rogers said, 'I never met a man I didn't like.' Try to be that way.

☐ Never miss an opportunity to congratulate anyone on achievement, or express sympathy in disappointment.

☐ Listen more than you speak; smile more than you frown; laugh with, rather than at, others; and watch your manners whether you feel chipper or not.

☐ Finally, remember that 'there is a curious quirk in human nature: some people just naturally won't like you'.[2]

here's an idea

Think of the most boring people you know. Aren't they always talking about themselves? *You* don't have to be a bore. Instead, encourage people to talk about themselves. Acknowledge their expertise and draw on it. 'Grace, you're good at this – what do you think?'
Remember…'you' is always better than 'I'.

here's an idea

Don't flash an immediate smile when you greet someone, as though anyone who walked into your line of sight would be the beneficiary. Instead, writes Leil Lowndes in *How to Talk to Anyone*, look at the other person's face for a second. Pause. Soak in their persona. Then let a big, warm, responsive smile flood over your face and overflow into your eyes. It will engulf the recipient like a warm wave. The split second delay, he says, convinces people your flooding smile is genuine and only for them.

here's an idea

Try this simple trick to help you project a good impression whenever you meet someone for the first time: Take note of the colour of the person's eyes as you shake hands. In this way, you'll gain that strong eye contact that's so important first up, and at the same time indicate that you're interested in the person and in what s/he has to say.

How to get on with people you don't like

People behave the way they do for two main reasons—they don't know any other way of behaving or they believe that that behaviour gets the outcomes they want. Managers are likely to come across at least one employee whose behaviour they don't like, with whom they don't see eye to eye, or whom they dislike for some other reason. The challenge resides with managers. Are they flexible enough to bring about desired changes in the employee and the relationship? Here are a few considerations…

1 Try to be tolerant.

The fact that you don't like certain employees should not be allowed to affect the way you relate to them. You have to be tolerant and positive in your attitude toward such people. Try to adopt a relaxed, confident, easygoing style to demonstrate that you are not put off by people who can be hard to get on with.

2 Practise liking people.

Will Rogers adopted the famous line 'I never met a man I didn't like' as his way of getting on with people. Other successful ways include these:

- Create opportunities to recognise an individual's achievements.

- Remember people's names.

- Treat all people with respect.

- Concentrate only on the work context.

- Focus on the person's good points; don't be too critical. Remember Richard Burton's description of

Elizabeth Taylor: 'Her arms are too fat, her legs are too short, she is too big in the bust, she has an incipient double chin, and she has a slight pot belly'. He still married her—twice.

3 Be flexible about how you respond to the behaviour of others.

If you learn to be flexible in the way you react to difficult people, you'll learn to live with their unpleasantness. The secret is to choose an appropriate response to particular behaviours. For example,

- If the person always reacts aggressively, give responsibility and encourage ownership.

- If the person carries a personal grudge, avoid discussions about pet peeves.

- If the person never admits being in the wrong, avoid direct criticism, sarcasm, and ridicule. Deal with the problem in private.

- If the person is argumentative, stay

calm and cite hard facts and figures to present an alternative position.

- If the person is overtalkative, have someone 'interrupt' you at a prescribed time, or plead another appointment, or start to move away.
- Practise tact—the ability to rub out another's faults instead of rubbing them in.
- For additional examples and advice, consult 'How to deal with difficult people' on page 122.

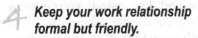

Keep your work relationship formal but friendly.

Being formal does not mean avoiding the employee altogether. It means that you confine your interest in that person to work-related matters. In fact, by dealing with the employee in this way, interactions will be kept to a minimum and will not interfere with work outcomes. Let the employee make the first move to discuss any matters not specifically related to the job.

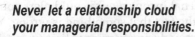

Never let a relationship cloud your managerial responsibilities.

Do not let testy relationships with difficult people inhibit your managerial style. Indeed, you should try extra hard to involve such people by delegating appropriate tasks and inviting them to participate in committees, working parties, and other essential activities. Managers who set out to be liked by everyone all the time are heading for problems—just as those who do not attempt to patch up differences will inherit a similar batch of managerial headaches.

 Talk to the employee.

Life is too short to get trapped into playing games such as 'I don't like you' or 'I'm not talking to you'. If there's a problem with an employee, discuss it maturely and non-threateningly. You will have taken the first step to a possible resolution of any conflict.

 Make changes.

As a result of talking over the matter with the employee, you may be able to recommend some changes. If you are in the wrong in any way, admit it and resolve to do something about it. If the employee is in the wrong, reach agreement about particular changes to be made. Let the person see that you are eager to operate in a friendlier way than in the past.

 Develop coping skills.

Your desire to get on with all behavioural types will require that you improve some existing skills and take on new ones. By your actions you will demonstrate your intention to get on with all people—even those you don't like.

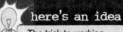 **here's an idea**

The trick to working with someone you don't like is to make an effort to find something about the person that you *can* like – for example, their job skills, sense of humour, their sporting prowess, or a personality trait. Focus on the good point/s and, hopefully, you'll soon forget the intangible factor/s that generated your dislike.

 don't forget

There are legal implications...

- Don't seek support or sympathy from other people, by back-stabbing the person you don't like. Therein lies the legal possibility of a defamation action against you.
- Don't indulge in workplace bullying of those you don't like. You can be sued.
- Take care if you contemplate termination of the person's employment. Ensure you have adequate grounds and that you follow legally correct procedures.

 read further

Dealing With People You Can't Stand by Brinkman & Kirschner, McGraw-Hill, 2002.

How to establish rapport

Rapport—an harmonious relationship of trust and confidence—is the essential ingredient in any meaningful communication. Where rapport does not exist, most efforts to communicate effectively will be in vain. Managers, therefore, need to be skilled in establishing rapport with individuals or groups. Although there is no single technique for building rapport, some general principles need to be observed...

Know what outcomes you want.

All behaviour is outcome-related—people act as they do to get what they want. So, before entering into conversation or a meeting, you need to know what *you* want, and you'll need the flexibility to adopt the appropriate behaviours to achieve that outcome by building confidence and trust in your colleagues.

Encourage conversation.

In the early stages of most conversations, get-togethers, or meetings, some people can be reluctant starters. The best approach is to get them talking—the topic or content is not important (though we do know that most people like talking about themselves). Talk and laughter help to establish a breathing pattern that helps to relax people, making them feel more at ease in the situation. So that's your initial agenda: maintain eye contact, listen attentively, nod intermittently to match the tempo of the other person's voice, and demonstrate your interest with an occasional 'a-hum' or 'a-ha' to match voice tone. Your encouraging behaviour will be appreciated.

Listen and observe.

Most meaning is transmitted non-verbally—more than 80 per cent, according to some experts. We are particularly aware of incongruence—that is, when there is a conflict between what people say and what their body language communicates. That incongruence could alert you to the fact that something is wrong. You may decide to pursue that uncertainty further by asking appropriate questions.

Use getting-to-know-you activities if necessary.

In groups, brief, well-structured ice-breaking activities can establish rapport. The right activity can help to remove any inhibitions people may have about participating actively in a group. It can also focus attention on the task at hand. If you decide to develop your own icebreaker, rather than select from a plethora of commercially available ones, focus on three main points:

- The activity has to be simple, straightforward, and fun, encouraging people to participate.
- Activity involving interaction among group members is required.
- The activity can be linked in some way to the main purpose for assembling the group in the first place.

Examples of simple ice-breakers include these:

☐ *This is me!* Participants in turn give their names, where they're from, and one other brief fact about themselves. The facilitator suggests what this third fact might be—a recent accomplishment, their most embarrassing moment, their finest hour…

☐ *Round the Circle.* To help remember people's names, sit people in a circle, the first person saying, 'Hello, I'm…(name)'. The next person says, 'Hello, I'm… and that's…'. And so on around the circle, all introducing themselves and all those who have gone before. A fun, rather than a competitive, activity.

☐ *Pairs.* People form pairs of strangers. Person A interviews Person B for three minutes—name, origins, interests, strengths, and so on. Person B then interviews A. Using the information gathered, they then introduce each other to the re-assembled group.

☐ *Biographical Name Tags.* People are given name tags or cards on which they write their names and several other facts that can be fun things—favourite food, film, resort, book, sport, or items relevant to the meeting. People then mill around looking at each other's tags and talking to people as they wish.

5 **Test and re-test for rapport.**

The main indicator that rapport is being established is 'feel'. Instinctively, you will know when a feeling of trust and confidence exists between you and another, or among people in a group. That feeling is the precursor to the main business.

Occasionally, particularly in a group, you will need to re-test for rapport. If you are operating didactically, for example, pause and ask the group, 'How am I going?' Encourage, and listen to, their feedback. Another approach is to involve the group in an energiser—a brief, high-energy activity designed to stimulate and re-focus attention.

6 **Act 'as if'.**

When working in a group, show that there is nothing that can happen that you can't handle. Your actions will then instil confidence in others. And that confidence is easily achieved. By acting 'as if' you are in control, you gain control. So start behaving 'as if' establishing and maintaining rapport is one of your special abilities.

 viewpoint

"Rapport is something we do with a person, not to a person."

– Kris Cole in *Crystal Clear Communication*

smile & ponder

Rapport is like money – when you're short of it, it increases in importance.

 don't forget

Why rapport is important

Without rapport, you reduce your chances of getting:

- full commitment from others
- unconditional agreement in relation to your ideas and suggestions
- business
- promotion
- friends…

 quotable quote

Creating rapport doesn't depend on saying just the right words and smiling all the time. You generate rapport largely through nonverbal behaviours such as facial expressions, tone of voice, posture, gesture, and so on.[7]

113

How to remember people's names

A good memory for people's names is not only an important social asset: it's a basic requirement for successful managers. Remember people's names and what they're interested in, and you'll flatter them and get them on side immediately. But forget their names, and the things important to them, and you're telling them you don't consider them important. If you want to avoid the embarrassment of forgetting the names of people you meet, here are some suggestions for you to consider...

1 Get the name clearly.

The most common problem in remembering the names of people we meet is not paying attention during the introduction. Whether we're self-conscious about meeting a new person or we feel out of place—whatever the reason, we tend to focus instead on the *How do you do*'s and the *Nice to meet you*'s.

What's more important, as the person is being introduced to you, is to listen for the name. Pay more attention to it than to anything else being said. If you don't pick it up, ask for it to be repeated. Be in no doubt about the pronunciation or spelling. Taking such care shows that the name and the person mean something to you.

2 Repeat the name to the person.

Take a second to repeat the name when you are introduced. Indeed, find an excuse for the name to be repeated (and reinforced): 'Hello, Mike. I'm sorry, I missed your last name...' Then, follow up with: 'Mike Buckman! It's nice to meet you, Mike.' The process of retention has begun. During later conversation, try to repeat the name—'Mike' or 'Mr Buckman'. That technique will not only strengthen goodwill but get your memory into gear as well.

3 If possible, focus on the derivation of the name.

A useful suggestion, especially if the name is unusual, is to ask about its origins. Many people enjoy talking about the derivation and history of their name—particularly if it's unusual. And what they have to say might make them more memorable for you.

4 Look for a memory hook.

The literature usually recommends that we establish 'mental filing systems' or 'memory hooks' that will instantly attach a name to a familiar face. Such hooks may, or may not, work for you.

The tactic of linking names to

images need not make sense to anyone but yourself. At first the process may seem cumbersome—but anything is probably better than trying to remember names just by repeating them. Five options may be considered:

- *Try to put a name to the face.* Perhaps Mr Baldwin is bald, Mr Bigge has a large body, and Ms Sharpe has a sharp nose.

- *Check whether the name has a meaning in itself.* Meaningful names are valuable aids to memory—like animals such as Wolff, cities such as York or Washington, celebrities such as Monroe or Kennedy, or adjectives such as Strong or Little. Create a vivid mental image—Mr Strong as a weightlifter.

- *Find a word substitute.* If the name has no meaning, substitute a meaningful word that comes close in sound to the name in question—e.g. Buckman could be bucket or buckle, creating a mental picture… But be warned, there is a hazard: don't go calling Mr Buckman Mr Bucket!

- *Link the mental picture with the location.* To remember where you first met the person, create your image at the location—picture Mr Strong waltzing through the Hyatt Regency ballroom with a bar-bell held high over his head.

- *Link the mental picture to the person's interests.* To remember Mr Buckman's interest in sailing, imagine him bailing out his sinking yacht with a bucket!

The literature says that the sillier the image, the better we will retain the information.

 Repeat the name to yourself.

After the initial encounter, look back at the person a few times to reinforce the episode. Repetition is the means to a good memory. The more often you say the name to yourself, in association with the memory hook you may have devised, the more entrenched your mental image will become, and the harder it will be to forget that person's name.

 Use pen and paper.

By writing information down, you increase the chance of committing it to memory. Exchange business cards if possible. As soon as the opportunity arises, jot down the name with a line or two of details. Include when and where you met, any memory hooks you have created, and what common interests you found. Later you might transfer this data to index cards for regular review, taking time to recall the person's appearance. If you adopt this strategy, you'll soon earn a reputation for having a terrific memory for names.

Work on it.

The best way to remember a name is to tell yourself firmly to do so. Most people need to apply discipline and effort. But, to be an effective manager of others, you have to get to know them by name. The effort will be worth it, however, for you will be rewarded—by winning friends instead of just nodding acquaintances.

 quotable quote

There are courses and books on the topic of remembering names. One problem is that the skill is similar to speed reading. When you come out of the course, or put down the book, you're impressive enough to appear on the Tonight Show – but if you don't practise, the skill fades. Still, it's a great, and imperative, ability for managers.[8]

 it's a fact

Throughout history, great accomplishment has often walked hand in hand with a great memory.

According to *Fortune* magazine, a blind John Milton composed *Paradise Lost* in his mind, 40 majestic lines at a time, and then recited them to a scribe. Conductor Arturo Toscanini knew every note of more than 400 scores, from Bach to Wagner. Winston Churchill could recall so much Shakespeare that he would mouth the bard's words from the audience, much to the distraction of the actors on stage.

Memory can be a wonderful thing.

Today Microsoft chairman Bill Gates can still remember hundreds of lines of source code from his original Basic programming language – but Gates, no doubt like his eminent forerunners, has a soft spot… he admits to being terrible when it comes to remembering names!

How to build other people's confidence in you

Confidence has long been recognised as a desirable—if not essential—life quality. A recent study in the United States, for example, identified 'confidence' as the one quality women found most attractive in men. A great deal of research and writing, therefore, has been devoted to identifying ways of building self-confidence. But attention also needs to be devoted to how to build others' confidence in you—your effectiveness and success rely on it. Here's how to help others to become confident in you...

1 *Focus on building relationships.*

Tom Peters is attributed with saying 'Business is a series of relationships between people'. In fact, relationship building has become a key value-adding activity—the better the relationships, the better the business. To build and maintain the desired relationships, four behaviours are essential:

1. Arrive on time (or earlier).
2. Do as you say you will.
3. Finish what you start.
4. Say 'please' and 'thank you'.

Failure to adhere to any *one* of these behaviours leads to a decline in, or dissolution of, the relationship.

Robyn Henderson says that to build relationships, you must gain the respect of...

- *Your work colleagues* – pull your weight; acknowledge the contribution of others; don't be afraid to ask for help; be positive; and don't gossip about others.
- *Your superiors* – treat them as you would your colleagues; work to deadlines; stay calm in a crisis; be organised and efficient; be a problem-solver; think creatively; be articulate; keep up with trends in business; and

relate well to customers or clients.

- *Your customers or clients* – be polite and helpful; be pleasant on the phone; solve problems; know your products; offer advice and creative solutions; get action; meet deadlines; follow up; return calls; and show a genuine interest in people.[9]

Note that most of this advice boils down to being organised and polite, and being an expert on the procedures, products, and services you offer.

2 *Observe established communicative know-how.*

Years of investigations and observations have helped to increase our understanding of the effect our behaviour has on others. We know, for example, that:

- the first four minutes is a most important period in any interaction.
- more than 70 per cent of information is communicated nonverbally.
- voice tempo communicates much more information than either volume or tone.
- remembering and using people's names, and knowing what they're interested in, gets them on side immediately.

- people appreciate those who listen more than they speak and smile more than they frown.

Your awareness and application of this information enhances relationships and builds confidence.

3 Help others to see things differently.

Often, the greatest barriers to achievements are self-created, brought on by a limited view of the world. The way you question others' assumptions, make suggestions, and challenge established views helps to increase your value to people who more confidently see merit in developing their relationship with you.

4 Reinforce what others are good at.

For people to feel confident about others and move forward, they must first feel confident about themselves and their strengths. By helping others to identify and build on their strengths, you are promoting their self-confidence, forging even stronger relationships with them, and increasing their confidence in you. An ideal starting point, therefore, is to help people identify—tell them if necessary—what they have already accomplished. As they become aware of those accomplishments, they will not only value your encouragement but also look to you to provide any missing qualities.

5 Increase others' sense of certainty.

One of the most important aspects of building others' confidence is to increase the amount of certainty they feel about working with you. Your achievements, knowledge, resources, and capabilities play an important part: others feel they are gaining a great deal through their association with you. It is important, therefore, that you let people know—subtly—about your achievements, knowledge, and capabilities. The letters after your name, your certificates and degrees displayed on your office wall, club and association memberships, resources and backing you have access to, all help to build a sense of certainty in others.

6 Identify and develop 'your unique process'.

Everyone is famous for something. Or, as Dan Sullivan says, 'Everyone in life seeks out other people who have translated their unique skills and knowledge into a unique process.' Only a few people, however, make the effort to name what that 'something' or 'unique process' is.

The first step, of course, is to realise that you do have a unique process. Then you need to put a name to your process or special something that differentiates you from the rest. When you have done so and devoted time to its continued development, you will find that you can give enormous confidence to everyone you deal with—staff, colleagues, suppliers, customers, and prospects. After all, if this skill or quality is unique to you, there will be only one place where others can confidently obtain it.

don't forget

Be a builder of bridges.

A small boy was taking a long journey and, in the course of the day, his train crossed a number of raging rivers.

The water seen in advance always awakened doubts and fears in the child. He could not understand how it could be safely crossed. As they drew near each river, however, a bridge appeared and provided the way over. Several times the same thing happened and, finally, the youngster leaned back with a long breath of relief and confidence: 'Someone has put bridges for us all the way.'

quotable quote

You are no more than the composite picture of all your thoughts and actions. In your relationships with others, there's a basic and critically important rule: 'If you want to be loved, be lovable. If you want respect, set a respectable example. If you want people to be confident in you, exude confidence yourself!'

You can't change heredity or the early environment you were dealt. But you certainly can change your attitude toward them and learn how to respond to life in a healthier, happier, and more worthwhile manner.[12]

117

How to support your boss

Your career prospects often rely on how effectively you interact with and support your boss or others farther up the organisational ladder. In front of every competent person there will eventually be a vacant chair; and your boss will have a major voice in determining who gets to sit in it. Often, your success will depend on your boss's success, so he or she will need your continuing support. Keep these suggestions in mind if you want to support your boss...

Get to know your boss.

Find out all you can about your boss—likes and dislikes, quirks, expectations, interests, and prejudices. By observing and by asking others, get to know how your boss likes things done. Learn your boss's style of writing, for example. Is a succinct proposal on one sheet of paper preferred, or a detailed argument? Find out what's really important to him or her and make sure that's what you deliver. Or, as James Cribbin suggests, 'Study them to understand what catches their minds, stimulates their souls, and turns their stomachs.'

Keep your boss informed.

Keep your boss up to date on all matters you are responsible for, as well as other items that you find are needed. In other words, always anticipate your boss's information needs and questions. Press clippings and media releases can provide valuable data. Be sure to include a 'with compliments' slip with your signed, personal, but business-like message. Never let your boss hear good or bad news from others when it's your job to provide it.

Find out when and where your boss is most approachable.

If your boss is an early starter, morning may be the best time to meet for discussions. If your boss takes some time to warm up, the end of the day might be a better time. Learn to read changes of mood. The boss's personal assistant is often a valuable ally: timing can be vital.

And is it best to tackle your boss in the office, or over lunch, after work, or even at home?

Deliver the goods.

When your boss gives you a task, do you see it through to completion—or do you turn in a half-finished job with all the tricky bits left for your boss to tidy up? If you're asked to do something, do you do it promptly and thoroughly?

Successful people are usually

quotable quote

By learning to manage your boss, you can earn more job satisfaction, bring more motivation to the job and have more fun. To do this your relationship with your boss must meet your needs. You and s/he must work together in a way that complements both your styles. In an atmosphere of mutual respect, you should be able to communicate clearly your expectations of one another. You need to be able to trust one another and to be honest with one another... Your boss has a great influence on your job satisfaction. The steps you take to improve the way you are managed are part of your personal pursuit of happiness.[14]

here's an idea

What loyalty do you owe your boss? Like most managerial questions, this evokes both a simple and a complex answer. The simple and logical answer is 'as much as your boss shows you in return and your common-sense tells you is right'.

Most good bosses inspire loyalty. If you work for a good boss, the question of loyalty should never come up. You will act loyally simply because you feel there is no other way to act.

busy: they agree to take on tasks that others find too challenging or too demanding of their time. If attracting the attention and respect of your boss is a priority, manage your time to give these additional tasks the priority they deserve.

Don't offer promises: just deliver. Don't make excuses when something goes wrong; just deliver next time. Be a tough self-critic, and always deliver the goods promptly and well.

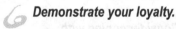

Focus on solutions— not problems.

Henry Ford is supposed to have said, 'Don't give me a problem; give me a solution'. You should also adopt this approach. Make it a personal rule to provide solutions, or at least options for consideration—never problems for the boss to solve. Bosses don't need messengers conveying bad news; they want to hear what you've done about any problem. So gain a reputation for being a 'doer', not a 'gonna'.

Demonstrate your loyalty.

Be as loyal to your superiors as you would wish them to be to you. When you honestly can, speak well of your boss to other people. Offer protection when necessary; serve as a buffer and absorb some of the shocks when you can prudently do so. Always help your boss 'to be right' without yourself being subservient. And, if you are fortunate enough to have one who deserves it, don't be too proud to express admiration for your boss. (Remember, however, to show equal loyalty to and openness about your colleagues as well, so that you don't

earn a reputation as the boss's pet or the office crawler.)

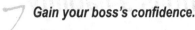

Gain your boss's confidence.

If you're determined to support your boss, you should show that you can be relied on—not only to do your own job but also to help your boss to do his. So, whenever the opportunity arises, you should try to convey some of these messages :

- I'm happy to have you talk to me about your concerns and problems.
- I'm keen to be allowed to take some of the load off your shoulders.
- I have certain strengths that you can use.
- I'm always available.

Match strengths and weaknesses.

Have a good grasp of your own strengths and weaknesses as well as your boss's. You'll then know where you two complement each other, where you conflict, and where you need help. In other words:

Some of the finest collaborations, whether in business or the arts, come about because the individuals involved complement each other: the writer helping the speaker, the detail-thinker supporting the big-picture person, the late-night person spelling the early riser. If you are strong where your boss is weak and vice versa, the resulting team can be far more effective than either of you could be alone... A good working relationship with your superior is the foundation of being a successful manager.[13]

? ask yourself

How well do you know your boss? To develop a worthwhile working relationship, you need to ask yourself:

- Is s/he ambitious or concerned with protecting him/herself from harm and criticism?
- What are his/her values?
- Who are the people s/he admires?
- Is s/he autocratic, expecting me to do as s/he says, or intuitive, expecting me to follow broad informal indicators or signs?
- Do his/her goals and values match mine?
- If not, can I live with the resulting differences?
- Is s/he quick to see essentials, keen to resolve issues?
- Does s/he need time and lengthy explanations?
- Does s/he contribute good ideas and practical solutions? Or does s/he rely on me for that?
- Does s/he enjoy conflict and handle it well, or does s/he seek to avoid it?
- Does s/he prefer written reports, or oral briefings?
- Does s/he prefer formal meetings with agendas, and preparatory memos?
- What are the pressures on him/her?
- What is expected of him/her?
- How am I contributing to what s/he is trying to achieve?
- How do peers view him/her?

Attempt to complement your boss's strengths and weaknesses.[15]

How to deal with a boss who is a liability

Although a great deal of a manager's time can be devoted to improving the performance of staff, bosses can also be difficult to work with. Like many other people, they too can be lazy, incompetent, bullying, or arrogant. Coming up with successful ways of coping with poor-performing bosses can tax the resources of the most talented managers. Here are some suggestions that will help you handle a boss you have a problem working for…

Recognise the problem.

There are a few perfect bosses in this world, but many are not great performers. If you have trouble with your boss, you can try to tackle the problem only if you know exactly what your problem is. For example, bosses can be:

Inconsistent—warm, supportive, and encouraging one day; aloof, rigid, and uncompromising the next

Inflexible—unable, or unprepared, to change when it is obvious to everyone that a new direction is required

Closed—reluctant to provide oral feedback, leaving others to translate a mix of non-verbal messages

Manipulative—getting people to 'perform' by resorting to carrot-and-stick approaches, and by making promises that they have no intention of keeping

Exploitative—continuing to assign tasks to those who never complain

Inactive—demonstrating a lack of control over people and over projects; even lazy.

In *Never Work for a Jerk!*, Patricia King identified the really difficult bosses: scoundrels and liars, slave-drivers and bullies, ignoramuses and incompetents, cheapskates and skinflints, blowhards and egomaniacs. Can you identify the problem (if there is one) with your boss's behaviour?

Take your choice.

If you have a boss who's a liability, you have three choices: cope with the situation; try to improve the way you're managed; or look for another job. The choice is yours…

Consider coping with the current situation.

You can handle the current situation in two ways—by moaning and complaining or becoming stressed, even ill, and a martyr to the cause; or by making the most of the situation by being positive and using the following approaches:

- *Keep things in perspective.* Make it a practice not to take things personally. Remember, in the wash-up, your boss has the problem, not you.
- *Keep your cool.* Others, too, are likely to be affected by your boss's actions, so let your responses to the boss's actions set

an example for others to follow.

- *Learn from your boss.* Problem behaviours will identify for you the way *not* to do things, thus saving you from falling into similar traps.
- *Get as much satisfaction out of your job as you can* by doing your job well. Find other competent people in your organisation and work with them to try to absorb and cope with the most destructive influences of your boss.
- *Learn to play the game the boss's way*—grin and bear it, but take a stance against unethical or rude behaviour, harassment, or bullying.

4 Consider trying to improve the situation.

Some bosses may be unaware of any problem. Most would be eager to address their faults if they knew about them. If you have the kind of boss who's approachable, however, do so. But remember, you must focus on the behaviour, not the person. Describe the problem as you see it, indicate its effect on others—including customers—and on productivity. Bosses who are committed to the organisation and its goals will welcome your concerns and respond positively. Offer to help if you can. If the boss is not prepared to change, talk to other managers likely to be experiencing similar problems. Even talk to the boss's boss if confidentiality can be assured.

If the upfront approach is inappropriate in your situation, consider ways of changing your boss's behaviour over time in small ways:

- *Make the most of your relationship* with your boss by concentrating on common aims and mutual gains.
- *Understand your boss.* Compare the way you like to work with your boss's style of management and find workable links.
- *Help your boss achieve common goals* by focusing on each other's assets and finding a mutually acceptable style of interacting.
- *Strengthen your people skills.* Your ability to get along with others, including the boss, should be one of your most important qualities.
- *Take a more active role to make up for the boss's inadequacies*—but always work through your boss so that your actions are not seen as undermining.
- *Be diplomatic.* Don't say: 'You never invite me to Monday morning management meetings.' Say: 'I'd like to come to the Monday morning management meetings because with my financial background I think I can make a useful contribution to group discussions…'
- *Record everything*—especially if your boss is the type who denies or distorts what you have discussed.
- *If your boss lets you down,* let him or her know that you feel let down and why.
- *Discuss strategies with fellow managers* on how to deal with your boss's undesirable behaviour.
- *Consider any machinery* that exists for lodging an official complaint.

5 Consider looking for another job.

Always keep your options open. But, if your situation is intolerable and unlikely to change, get yourself another job—either a transfer within the company or a new job elsewhere. Having made that decision, regard your current state as temporary. Once you have made the decision to go, make sure that your energies are focused on your next step.

smile & ponder

'When you said the boss had been riding you lately, I had no idea...'

How to deal with difficult people

According to Napoleon, the driving force behind behaviour is either self-interest (people doing what they do principally in their own interests) or fear (doing what they do because they fear the consequences, perceived or otherwise, of not doing it). That's what makes managing others a unique activity: outward expressions of such basic drives differ from person to person. Most people are easy to get on with, but some difficult individuals will require that we dig deep into our people-skills bag…

1 Know why some people are difficult.

If Napoleon is to be believed, the main motivation of difficult people is fear—fear of loss, embarrassment, ignorance, inadequacy, etc. Although fear is a natural phenomenon, you are not to know its cause—what it is that individuals are fearful of. To complicate the matter further, individual behaviour changes according to context: an aggressive person at work may be a gentle, loving parent at home, or a person you find shy may be open and outgoing in the company of others.

So, when people display behaviours you identify as difficult, ask yourself these questions:

- What is that person afraid of?
- Where did he or she learn that behaviour?
- What response do I need to achieve the outcomes I want?

2 Be familiar with difficult behaviour types.

Most organisations have difficult employees in varying numbers and degrees, but the most common types include these:

Hyper-sensitives—desiring their own space, rarely taking risks.

Fusspots—taking an eternity to produce top-quality results.

Excuse-makers—using any reason to account for their poor performance.

Deadline-missers—leaving things until (after) the last minute.

Can't-doers—insisting 'we've always done it this way' to avoid change.

Careless-cavaliers—believing that near enough is good enough.

Loafers—doing just enough to get by.

Pig-heads—resisting change by insisting on one way of doing things.

Thin-skins—overreacting to anything that sounds like criticism.

Shrinking violets—avoiding social contact at all costs.

Bullies—seeking power by throwing their weight around.

Grim-reapers—expressing dissatisfaction with people and the environment.

Nit-pickers—finding fault, no matter what.

Cross-examiners—questioning everything.

Chatterboxes—talking about little or nothing to anyone who can be cornered.

Know-it-alls—being closed to others' expertise.

Snail, *mule*, and *clown* metaphors may be used to describe other types.

The list is limited only by your experience in dealing with people.

Sexual harassment and *substance abuse* also pose difficulties and are dealt with separately.

 Embrace key behaviours.

Different types often require different responses from management, but some useful management maxims are common to most behaviours…

- Behaviour that is reinforced, rewarded, and recognised is likely to be repeated.
- Behaviour that is not reinforced, rewarded, or recognised is likely to diminish gradually.
- You don't have to be liked by everyone; don't let your ego get the better of you.
- Make sure people are aware of acceptable standards—not all customers will want a 'Rolls Royce' version.
- Performance should be clearly monitored; employees should know when you expect greater effort.
- Pressure brings out the worst in people. Control the flow of work, or employees will feel snowed under and react accordingly.
- You must keep your promises and follow up on theirs.
- Ensure communications are clear, open, and available to everyone.
- Acknowledge contributions in ways valued by the individual.

 Avoid the pitfalls.

There are definite 'no-nos' in dealing with difficult types. If people are…

Aggressive, don't argue. Encourage them to study a proposal from both sides.

Shy, don't force them into things. Get to know them so that they feel comfortable in your presence.

Slow, don't be overbearing. Be more patient and negotiate tighter deadlines.

Negative, don't get involved in discussions with them. Show reasonable optimism by asking for a worst-case scenario or using a lesser-of-two-evils argument.

Obsessed with detail, don't get into a debate about quality. Emphasise overall objectives and suggest a logical, step-by-step approach.

Lazy, don't give them more work. Instead, assign them more challenging tasks and monitor progress.

 Identify new behaviours and skills you'll need.

The one behaviour you have most control over is your own. So, to become more skilled in dealing with different types of people, you'll need to increase your flexibility. Some of your new skills may be patience, assertiveness, authoritativeness, self-confidence, reframing, and listening. When you're in control of your actions, your level of personal power greatly increases; so reduce the nature and number of difficulties confronting you.

 here's an idea

It's a fact of life: People are bothered by other people. Whether it's the colleague who always stops by your office uninvited 'to chat' and ends up stealing 30 minutes of your time, or the person who doodles while you're talking. If you let these things get to you, they'll drive you to distraction and affect your productivity. Here are four things to remember when dealing with annoying colleagues:

■ *Ask yourself, 'Is it really that big a deal?'* Often, we let things build up over time, and they take on more significance than they should. Get things in perspective. While irritating, some things just aren't worth getting worked up over.

■ *If you can't beat 'em, join 'em.* Get to know the people you work with – outside of work. Often, after you get to know someone, a quality you once found irritating becomes merely quirky, and easily ignored.

■ *Don't try to get along perfectly with everyone.* Accept the fact that even in your best relationships, there are going to be difficulties.

■ *If you're desperate, and having trouble approaching your colleague to say something – try writing it instead.* That way, you can take several cracks at it, until you say it just the way you want to. Keep the note brief. And try to point out some positive elements of the person as well as the negative ones you want corrected.

123

How to get the most out of networking

Networking is a process that exposes you to new people, new ideas, and new ways of looking at things. Importantly, it can increase your visibility and advance your career prospects. But the creation of this structure of valuable personal interrelationships won't just happen. You have to develop this network of organisational contacts for yourself— and here's how you can do so...

here's an idea

One of the hardest things to do at a conference or workshop is to start talking to people you've never met before. Here's a strategy for making this easier:

The coffee or lunch queue is a good place to begin. Usually there are at least half a dozen people waiting in line. Strike up a conversation with someone in the line, and then continue that conversation when you leave the queue. But, importantly, talk to the person *behind* you in the line, so that you can wait for that person after you get served. If you start talking to the person *ahead* of you, s/he might get their coffee and move away while you're still being served.

1 Be aware of the benefits of networking.

Although networking can be a very time-consuming activity, its benefits can be very rewarding to you professionally. It can:

- help you learn from an increasing range of contacts with whom you can share ideas, advice, and strategies.
- provide you with referrals for a variety of needs. A good network will always know somebody who can help you.
- supply you with a sounding board to test your ideas, provide feedback, let off steam, or discuss problems.
- promote your career as you become known, aware, and involved.
- lessen your professional isolation, particularly if your organisation is located in a remote area.
- be enjoyable by giving you the chance to meet new colleagues, socialise, and expand your professional horizons.

2 Work to develop areas of personal expertise.

Networking presumes that members have competence and expertise, so develop your own skills and knowledge. Become a recognised authority on something, someone worth getting to know, so that you can become a vital member of the network.

3 Analyse your current network of contacts.

Examine your current network's viability. Check your address book, business cards, correspondence files, professional association contacts, and phone index. Create an up-to-date, flexible card index or computer database on which to build.

4 Establish your own networking goals.

Aim at revitalising your network file over the next year. Set yourself such achievable goals as these:

- Meet at least two new professional contacts each month.
- Attend two major conferences this year.
- Join an organisation comprising local business or community leaders.

- Submit two articles to a professional journal during the coming year.
- Contact at least four colleagues on the network file every month…

Get out there, promote yourself, make contact.

The key to networking is to raise your visibility. Attend meetings, serve on committees, write for journals, speak to gatherings, become a spokesperson. Meet as many people as you can. If you meet a potential network contact, widen the conversation and find out all you can about that person. The longest journey always begins with a first step, so find out and file all you can about people you meet.

Sell networking to others.

Encourage colleagues to network. Talk it over with them. Your own network will get stronger if all those in it develop active networks of their own.

Make sure networking benefits all parties.

As John Naisbitt wrote in *Megatrends*, 'In the network environment, rewards come by empowering others, not by climbing over them.' Networking is a two-way street. Self-centredness becomes quite transparent to network contacts. The more you can help your contacts, the more they will want to help you. As Robyn Henderson says in *Networking for Success*, networking is 'giving without hooks'.

Be an advocate of others.

Talk regularly to members in your network and, if someone has a need you cannot fulfil, offer to share a contact. You'll be doing both a favour, fulfilling the needs of one while providing the opportunity of another contact for the other. And you'll be strengthening the network itself.

Consider these important points also…

- *Keep up-to-date notes* about the people you meet, so that you can refer to those notes later.
- *Grade your contacts A, B, or C* so that you can prioritise your time in following through. Focus on those people with whom regular contact will be most mutually beneficial.
- *Touch base regularly with your contacts*—through phone calls, letters, swapping articles of interest, socialising, meetings, and so on. Do so often enough to maintain the relationship.
- *Don't expect instant miracles.* Positive outcomes are often not immediately apparent. Rewarding professional relationships, formed through networking, develop over a period of time.
- *The key word is ASK.* If people can't help you, ask whether they can refer you to someone who might be able to help.
- *Swap business cards at every opportunity.* Jot down useful information about your new contacts on the back of their business cards.
- *Set up meetings and organise other people.* Make things happen.
- *Thank everyone who helps you.* A written note of thanks will strengthen links and encourage others to think of you in future.

smile & ponder

I didn't catch your name.

Networkers in action

here's an idea

A common mistake many managers make at networking events (seminars, meetings, conferences) is to try to talk to too many people – in an attempt to 'really get their money's worth'.

Harvey Mackay, in his book *Dig Your Well Before You're Thirsty*, tells managers to spend time with fewer people at such functions. One or two meaningful dialogues are infinitely more valuable than time spent flitting from one person to another. The aim is to build meaningful relation-ships – not just see how many people you can meet.

read me

Networking Magic by Robyn Henderson, Networking to Win, Coogee, NSW, 1999.

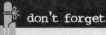

don't forget

The usefulness or utility of a network equals the square of the number of its users.
– Metcalfe's Law

How to use a business lunch to your advantage

There's no such thing as a free lunch—or any other meal for that matter, so be prepared to pay in some way. Whether you're the guest or the host, mealtime meetings are the business of doing business. And with today's hectic schedules and work loads, combined meetings and mealtimes can be productive and enjoyable. All you need to do is choose the type of meeting that will deliver the outcomes you want. Here's what's required to get the most from your next mealtime meeting...

Plan your meeting carefully.

Mealtime meetings must achieve the results you're looking for—in furthering business relationships and social contacts, or improving your business. Without a plan, the meeting might become little more than a social get-together. If you're the guest, think about the likely reasons for the invitation; but set *your* goals anyway. If you think the meeting may go over time, and you don't want to be delayed unnecessarily, plan your exit in advance—perhaps have a colleague phone you at a predetermined time.

Create the right impressions.

If it's an important meeting and you are the host, make contact with the restaurant beforehand. Find out the name of the waiter who will be responsible for your table. Introduce yourself and explain the importance of the meeting and that *you* will be settling the account. Tell the waiter how you would like to be addressed and provide some general details about your guest or guests that will assist positive recognition. If necessary, discuss special meals and seating arrangements. You may consider offering to pay an additional amount, say 10 per cent, for very personal attention. This planning will create the atmosphere of a 'club' of which you are a valued patron.

Dine—to your advantage.

The meeting must make the best use of everyone's time. If the invitee is reluctant to have a business lunch, provide some options—breakfast, dinner, coffee. Perhaps the other person may prefer a brief office meeting with lunch being brought in. If you're the host (or guest), try to suggest the time and place for the meeting that best suits *your* purpose.

Select the appropriate mealtime meeting.

Your goals and your guest's availability will generally determine the type of mealtime meeting you will choose. Consider the following:

Breakfast meetings can be held in a restaurant or at your office. Their purpose is primarily to talk business. Their advantages are these:

- you're fresh and wide awake
- a simple menu and quick service should suffice
- there is no temptation to drink anything stronger than coffee
- there is a work-imposed time for ending the meeting.

Luncheon meetings, either in-house or at a restaurant, provide for a high degree of flexibility in timing and location. If you want a serious meeting, and privacy, have it in your office. You may even consider having the meeting first, then going to lunch. Luncheon meetings provide:

- a chance to impress with good food, responsive service, and a quiet atmosphere
- a convenient and pleasant way to talk business
- an opportunity to be seen in a business/social environment.

Dinner meetings are more social events to 'wine and dine' important clients. Very few big deals are ever closed over dinner, but you can set a specific date for an office appointment or another less social meeting at which you can get down to business.

Other options.

- Try a coffee break: it feels good to take a break and get out of the office for a little while.
- Order in: if you're lunching with a colleague co-worker, why go out at all?
- Pay your own: discuss ideas and plan areas of mutual interest—and share the bill.
- Let your hair down: provide a night on the town for clients and their partners.

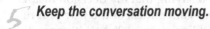 **Keep the conversation moving.**

Intersperse the conversation with issues of common interest—family, mutual friends, issues peripheral to your industry, sport, or some other interest. Never lose sight of your objective, however. Encourage your guests to talk about themselves, their business, their goals, and their aspirations. Remember the old saying, 'Bores talk about themselves, gossips talk about others, perfect conversationalists talk about me'.

 Play your cards slowly.

Get to the point of the meeting by letting your guests see your position step by step. Encourage discussion, and make sure they're listening. Try to have your guests study your proposals and arrive by themselves at the conclusion you favour—as if it were their idea.

 Use a note pad to jot down important issues.

Even a blunt pencil can help a sharp mind. Don't be embarrassed to jot down some notes to act as memory joggers. Always have business cards and brochures on hand just in case. After the luncheon, immediately write a brief note of appreciation and make diary notes on the outcome of the meeting, including dates and future deadlines.

 Stay focused.

You're not in the business of buying people meals; you're in business to do business. If the other person seems reluctant to schedule a follow-up meeting after your lunch meeting, he or she is probably not interested in doing business with you.

 here's an idea

Realistically, it's hard to talk business over dinner. People are trying to eat, restaurants are often noisy, and you keep getting interrupted. That's why, when you set up a business lunch or dinner, you should try to arrange to meet in the restaurant bar, if possible. Set the meeting time for 45 minutes before your reservations. Then, try to conduct as much business as possible before you sit down to eat. Use the time while you're actually eating to engage in small talk, and get to know your counterpart better – just as you would during a non-business dinner.

 don't forget

Here's some good advice...

- Pick a restaurant near where the majority of meeting attendees are coming from, to cut down on travel time.
- Ask for an early reservation – you'll get quicker service and less noise.
- Limit alcohol, as it shortens the attention span and lengthens the meeting.

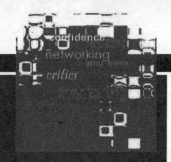

How to handle your critics constructively

How should you react to criticism of yourself or your organisation? Ignoring the criticism may be one way—but that approach often solves nothing. If you can build a co-operative, supportive environment in which criticism can be given and received with little pain, however, you'll be perceived as an effective communicator and a highly effective manager. One of the hallmarks of success is being able to react to criticism constructively—and here are a few ideas that may help...

1 Acknowledge that you will be criticised.

Recognise that you, as a leader, will have faults. Someone will always be out to put you on the defensive—it's a hazard of your position. Awareness of this will make criticism easier to accept. Remember the saying: 'They who shrink from criticism cannot be showered safely with praise.'

2 Face your criticism as soon as possible.

Criticism is often the result of faulty communication. Whether you believe the criticism is fair or unfair, it's important if possible to make personal contact with your critic. Open communication will prevent the build-up of resentment and help defuse a potentially damaging situation.

3 Listen to the criticism with an open mind.

Let your critic criticise openly. Resist the temptation to interrupt with defensive counter-arguments. Don't let your emotions block your listening. Weigh the words as you hear them. Be courteous. Angry critics in particular need to be listened to before they will be prepared to hear your point of view.

4 Keep your cool.

Don't raise your voice and wave your arms about. There are other occasions when you can do so, but dealing with criticism is not one of them. The way you visibly respond to criticism will be remembered more vividly later than the argument you present in reply.

5 Clarify the criticism.

To understand your critic's perspective fully, seek further details if necessary. 'What exactly is it about my decision that bothers you?' 'Are you saying that my decision means that I am critical of the way you're tackling your job?' And it's sometimes sobering to consider whether you, in your critic's place, would not have responded similarly.

Find any hidden causes for the criticism.

Analyse the credentials, identity, and motives of your critics. Are they just passing the buck to save themselves from criticism? Are they criticising merely to compensate for their own faults or to vent their rage? Is this one criticising from a genuine desire to help you improve your performance? Is that one a chronic complainer? Answers to such questions will help you to frame your response.

Encourage your critic to offer a solution.

How might you have better handled the situation that generated the criticism? Invite your critics to work with you to find a workable compromise. Ask what they are prepared to contribute towards it. Often such discussion can clarify roles, change the priorities of certain activities, and cause responsibilities to be shared.

Take appropriate action by responding positively.

Admit to shortcomings without self-castigation. Being able to wear a mistake is enormously stress-reducing for you and your organisation. As Robert Browning once said: 'When a man's fight begins with himself, he is worth something.'

The ability to offer a simple, 'Yes, perhaps I could have done that differently', reduces staff defensiveness and creates goodwill

all round. But, in admitting your shortcomings, it is also appropriate to set limits: indicate perhaps that you cannot be everywhere at once and that problem-solving requires others to take responsibility as well.

So, if the criticism is justified, tell your critics what you intend to do to remedy the situation. But if the complaint is unjustified, be calm and firm in telling your critic just that; explain why nothing can be done and why.

Acknowledge criticism with courtesy.

Thank your critics for pointing out the aspects of your behaviour that upset them. Don't sulk: view justified criticism as a way of improving your performance. As Andrew Sherwood, author of *Breakpoints,* advises: 'Treat all criticism as friendly and well intended. This professional outlook will enable you to recognise the value of legitimate criticism and ignore the rest. By conceding the critic's goodwill, you can turn an attacker into a friend; and, as you climb the career ladder, all friends are welcome.'

Follow up.

If your critics' grievances or suggestions were valid and helped you perform better, let them know about it—because criticism often does improve overall efficiency.

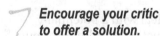

And you thought a few critical comments about *your* performance in the workplace were hard to take!

■ Critic Gary Griffith commenting on a performance of *Tosca,* in which a substitute soprano took over the leading role: "She left something to be desired – like my money back!"

■ Columnist Jack O'Brien: "Andy Warhol's latest movie is titled *Trash,* which at least is truth in packaging."

■ *New York Times* critic Clive Barnes hammered the playwright: "The plot of his play crawls across the stage as if in search of a last line to put it out of its misery."

here's an idea

It's so easy to get upset when we're criticised. It's important we don't. Madelyn Burley-Allen in *Managing Assertively,* lists several factors that lead to us handling criticism emotionally, rather than effectively:

• Taking the criticism personally instead of seeing it as corrective feedback.
• Failing to separate founded from unfounded criticism.
• Reading into the criticism a message that isn't there.
• Seeing the criticism as an invitation to get angry or to judge oneself harshly or punitively.
• Failing to get specifics and examples of what is being criticised.
• Believing that expressing criticism is bad or wrong.

How to apologise

In his 'Essay on Criticism', Alexander Pope assured us 'to err is human'. Mastering the art of apologising, therefore, became an essential life skill. Whatever your position on the social and corporate ladders, there will inevitably be times when you will have to say you're sorry (but not necessarily admit you're wrong). The ability to apologise is an admirable trait: it takes a 'big' person to say they're sorry, which can be a powerful management technique. Here's how you can master this art...

Recognise the two types of apology.

The most common form of apology is an admission that you're wrong—just as Pope's famous line suggests. A second type, however, is an apology for your actions—such as when laying down the law to a staff member who submits a report several days late. In doing so you point out that any repetition will lead to a severe reprimand. You not only apply pressure to improve the staff member's performance but also, in apologising, you defuse the employee's possible anger at what might be perceived initially as your bullying.

Forget ego and admit you've erred.

If a disagreement between two people is to end, one of them needs to 'carry the can', accept responsibility, and apologise. From a management perspective, it really makes little difference who is right and who is wrong. Your apology will be seen as a strength: logic, rather than emotion, is used to deal with a potentially difficult situation. In addition, your admission and apology will help to establish a 'standard' by which people can acknowledge their mistakes, learn from the experience, and focus on issues important for achieving objectives.

Adhere to the rules of apologising.

Despite your best intentions to offer a sincere and meaningful apology, a great deal of its effect can be lost if you ignore any, or all, of these rules:

- *Don't wait to be asked to apologise.* Sometimes you won't know you've made a mistake. Then, when the error is drawn to your attention, apologise with grace. More often, however, you'll know you've erred. It's galling if people come to you and ask for an apology.

- *Make your apology unconditional.* 'I'm sorry, but...'—it's what comes after the 'but' that people will remember most. Indeed, 'but' is a signal that your apology is shallow.

- *Apologise as soon as possible after the event.*
  Don't delay—or apologising will get harder.

- *Make your apology meaningful.*
  Be clear why you're apologising—for example: 'I'm really sorry for rescheduling the staff meeting without asking you. I'll make sure I don't do it again.'

- *Apologise once and leave it at that.*
  Don't keep repeating your apology.

4 Let them have their say before apologising.

People who are feeling aggrieved will become even more upset if you don't give them a chance to express their concerns or anger. Any apology from you *before* they have finished is likely to be seen as an attempt by you to get off the hook. Listen to what they have to say. Acknowledge their anger—then apologise and tell them what you are going to do to ensure that the cause of their concern is not repeated.

5 Sharpen the skill.

Apologising effectively is a skill; like any other skill, it can be learnt. If you're the boss, you will find that this skill will help to inspire extraordinary efforts among your staff. Your actions will demonstrate what staff know—that the 'buck stops with you'. An apology can be a powerful management tool: only honest,

straightforward people prepared to acknowledge their mistakes and correct them are big enough to say they're sorry.

If you have to apologise to your boss, explain what happened and accept responsibility. Be prepared, however. Your boss will probably want to know what you've done to rectify the situation and to ensure that the mistake is not repeated. Indeed, your skilful handling of this situation could even further enhance your position in the organisation.

6 Avoid cover-ups.

Psychologists tell us response is meaning—that is, people's responses demonstrate the meaning they attach to the message conveyed. Even though you might not have considered your actions offensive, the recipient might have done so—in which case an apology is required. Trying to back out of apologising or any attempt to cover up will only act against you in the long run. Apologise. Acknowledge your error. Ask how you can rectify any misunderstanding caused. Focus on strengthening the relationship.

No foul-up is worse than the mess you can get into by trying to cover up. Remember Nixon and Watergate, Clinton and Lewinsky? If you've dropped the ball, admit it—and apologise.

! viewpoint

"Managers who never apologise are diminished. Employees know that no one is perfect and lose respect for managers who can't accept that. As one employee asked about her boss: 'Is it that he doesn't know when he screws up, that he's too dumb to know, or that he's too big a coward to admit it?'"

– Rob Rosner, syndicated US columnist

here's an idea

When a foul-up occurs in your workplace, you should ask yourself if it were possible that you may have, in some way, contributed to the problem. Perhaps you did nothing. Check it out anyway – it's a good way to keep yourself honest. And if you were responsible in any way, admit it and apologise.

! viewpoint

"An apology is the superglue of life. It can repair just about everything."

"An ounce of apology is worth a pound of loneliness."

"An apology is a good way to have the last word."[24]

How to take people under your wing

The term 'mentor' is derived from Homer's classic, *The Iliad*. Before Odysseus, king of Ithaca, left his family and went to fight in the Trojan War, he asked an old and trusted friend, Mentor, to raise his son, Telemachus, to succeed him as a wise and good ruler. To do so, Mentor had to become a father figure, teacher, role model, trusted adviser, challenger, encourager, and counsellor. Individuals will need to be 'mentored' in your organisation—nurtured in growth and development. This advice will help…

viewpoint

"The best way to really train people is with an experienced mentor, and on the job."
– Tom Peters

here's an idea

Fortune magazine (11 November 2002) introduced several of Warren Buffett's protégés who provided insights into 'the Oracle of Omaha's' mentoring skills. Their list included:

- regular one-on-one communication
- availability to act as a sounding board for new ideas
- clearly stated expectations
- continuing support.

don't forget

The four questions

The best mentors do *not* solve problems for their protégés. They help the protégés solve the problem themselves by asking them four questions:

1. What is the cause of the problem?
2. What are your going to do to fix it?
3. How will you know when you've fixed it?
4. In what way can I help?

1 Understand why mentoring is required.

Try to see mentoring not as a program but as a way of life. Mentors can play a variety of roles. They can:

- help new staff members to feel part of the organisation.
- provide information about the way the organisation 'really' works.
- help protégés set goals, plan careers, and develop the skills necessary for career advancement.
- listen to problems, calm fears, provide feedback, and boost the confidence of their protégés.
- provide a role model for protégés to observe and emulate.

Although you may act as the mentor, you can still enlist the support of others (workmates—'buddies', if you prefer) in helping to provide general support.

2 Consider the needs of newcomers.

Mentoring should be a consideration when a new employee is set to join your organisation. But remember, *you* can't possibly act in that role for every newcomer. Before a new employee

arrives, you (or the designated mentor) should:

- make contact with the employee, complete introductions, and generally make the employee feel welcome. Don't forget, one of the most common reasons for people leaving an organisation is that they feel they do not fit.
- arrange a meeting to determine any particular needs the new employee may have, provide any preliminary reading that may be of assistance, and explain the mentoring function. If you're involved in these preliminaries but are not going to be the mentor, tell the employee who will be.
- do everything you can to make the employee feel part of the organisation during the first two weeks. (see page 364).
- remain available for questions while encouraging independence, and take an active interest in the new employee's work, reading, etc.

3 Identify and encourage rising stars.

Though your open management style will encourage most employees, some will have qualities and potential that impress you more than others. Such people have a great deal to offer the organisation if their talents are nurtured and developed. They will be the ones you are more likely to take under your wing.

Distinguish between buddies and mentors.

Mentors often appoint buddies to provide on-the-job support for their protégé. The buddy will probably be a peer with similar academic and work backgrounds, have at least two years in the organisation, be a recognised good performer, be a good listener, present the desired image of the organisation, and have the maturity to suspend personal judgement and prejudice. Buddies, therefore, can be used to exemplify and reinforce important messages about day-to-day life in your organisation.

Promote individuality.

One of the potential downsides of mentoring can be the desire to 'make' protégés resemble the mentor. Such outcomes are counterproductive. Experienced mentors will work at building a relationship but maintain their individuality and their protégés'. Mentors' expectations can be explicit without dominating the behaviour of their protégés.

Realise how the process can benefit the mentor.

The practice of mentoring has stood the test of time: it is a win-win for the mentors and the protégés. Mentors experience a high degree of personal satisfaction as they see their protégés 'grow'. Protégés often bring to a position fresh insights that can provide challenges and motivation. In addition to being encouraged to consider different perspectives, protégés can help to keep you abreast of new developments and new skills. Protégés can also become walking advertisements for their mentors. Not only does the protégé speak highly of the mentor in discussions with others in the organisation, but the mentor also gets to bask in the glow of the protégé's success.

And, finally...

- Although some people mentor for the personal satisfaction of contributing to the organisation, some organisations formalise the process by providing perks, funding for pet projects, and recognition dinners for those who take on mentoring.

- Organisations benefit from the process: socialisation occurs faster, protégés learn more quickly, potential is realised faster, youthful talent is tapped, and mentors' skills and motivation are maintained.

- Relationships should not be forced but evolve naturally over time.

- Mentors should guard against discriminating, often unintentionally, against other people on their team.

- If the mentor and protégé are of different sexes, recognise that professionalism, discretion, and decorum are paramount. People talk—so make sure they have nothing to talk about.

viewpoint

"Conscripting people into mentorship partnerships usually doesn't work. Generally the best mentors are people who want to share their time and their knowledge. They don't regard the role as a time-consuming burden, but as an opportunity to make a meaningful contribution to the organisation and to maximise their own professional development."

– Lisa Davis in *Shortcuts for Smart Managers*

quotable quote

Mentors need a good understanding of the organisation, its objectives, and its culture. They need effective communication skills, patience, and the ability to establish and maintain good working relationships. Good mentors are motivational and inspirational, and they serve as a role model for their protégés. They understand the importance of the mentoring partnership, take their responsibilities seriously, keep partnership confidences, maintain integrity, and act with the utmost professionalism at all times.[25]

quotable quote

Two are better than one; for if they fall, the one will lift up his fellow; but woe on him that is alone when he falleth, and hath not another to lift him up.[26]

133

How to help your staff with their personal problems

Staff members with a personal dilemma usually work at their problem and it goes away. But sometimes the problem is not easy to cope with. As an effective and sympathetic manager, you will frequently be approached by people with problems that might be affecting their work, or home life, or both – and they will ask you for help or advice. Here are some useful suggestions to assist you to improve your counselling skills...

quotable quote

Y ou will often need to give people clear guidance and advice when you are counselling them. You may even need to take action to solve someone's problem – say by separating two workmates who are not getting on together. Such a 'directive' approach is not always appropriate. Much in favour nowadays is the so-called 'non-directive' approach. Instead of telling the person how you think they should solve their problem you let them talk it through, come to terms with it and find their own solution. In many cases the person will be unable to 'own' and implement a solution unless it is the one they feel they have arrived at for themselves.

You will need to decide which approach is the more appropriate to the problem of the particular person you are counselling.[27]

viewpoint

"When a team leader 'counsels' an associate, it's more analogous to a coach of an athletic team counselling a player than to a psychotherapist counselling a patient. Professional counselling should be done by trained specialists."

– Dr Arthur Pell in
Managing People

1 Set aside time for the counselling session.

Once the need for a counselling session has been identified, you have to create the right conditions—private, unhurried, and free from interruption. Put the employee at ease by offering coffee and assurances of confidentiality. Make the setting relaxed by getting out from behind your desk; sit next to the employee. Take time to establish rapport early: the success of the session will depend on it.

2 Encourage your colleague to talk.

Use the early stages of the session to let your colleague talk. Often all anyone needs is someone who will take the time to listen. Here are some techniques to encourage your colleague to unwind:

- **Listen actively**. Show that, at the moment, your colleague is the only person who matters. Maintain eye-to-eye contact. Demonstrate that you're listening by making 'listening' noises ('yes' and 'uh

huh'), and by rephrasing and summarising.

- **Be reassuring**. Be supportive. Show that you are not being critical or disapproving... 'Yes, I can see how that would get you down...'

- **Ask questions**. Relevant, open-ended questions will make it easier for your colleague to open up, to disclose feelings, and to begin exploring and clarifying the problem... When did you first become aware of the problem? How does the problem affect you? When do you tend to get angriest? Why do you think the problem has arisen? Who else is involved?... Such questions should emerge gradually as natural stepping stones during the session.

At this stage your behaviour is the key to a successful session. Encourage your colleague to talk freely; be empathetic, non-judgemental, and supportive.

3 Observe.

Your colleague's oral communication

will provide you with other useful insights into the person and the problem. His or her speech will be full of hidden meanings. Take particular note of tone, expression, mannerisms, and body language.

 Isolate the problem.

Having now worked your way through the web of emotions and detail, and having extracted the facts of the case through listening and questioning, you can now identify the core of the problem and its possible cause. The one person who has the answer to the current problem is the person you are counselling. It is up to you to assist your colleague to identify the true problem—not just the symptoms—and to analyse the situation.

 Work towards a solution.

Remember: the aim is for your colleague to solve the problem personally. Consider these approaches:

- Ask questions to solicit ideas and explore various ways of solving the problem—e.g. 'So what are the options?', 'How can we improve the situation?'
- Make your suggestions tentative— e.g. 'I guess one option might be...'. 'What about trying this...?'
- Make encouraging noises but avoid specifically approving or disapproving anything.
- Get your colleague to work through the pros and cons and decide

without your help, on the best course of action.

- Your aim is to help and support your colleague, so accept his or her solution even if you have misgivings. The solution must be seen as your colleague's own.

 Follow-up if necessary.

If your colleague asks for specific help with implementation, agree to give it. Later, if the problem does not appear to be resolved, another meeting may be warranted.

 And finally...

These points should also be considered:

- If you feel insecure as a counsellor, don't try to give advice. Suggest that your colleague approach a better qualified person.
- Counselling, to be effective, must be conducted carefully and sensitively.
- Never betray a confidence; otherwise your colleague will never trust you again.
- While you are counselling a colleague, you must suspend your professional authority.
- Always stay calm and do not show any dismay at what is revealed.
- A 30-minute counselling session should be adequate. A longer interview could be protracted and purposeless.
- Obtain professional help if necessary.

here's an idea

Smart managers take employee problems seriously, and here's one tactic you can use to tell your staff that their concerns are your concerns.

Every time an employee comes to your office with what they say is a 'very important' question or concern, get out of your seat, leave the office, and say, 'Let's go somewhere where we won't be interrupted.'

Staying in the office is begging to be interrupted – by the phone, by another employee, by your boss, etc. Getting up and taking a walk to an empty hallway, or the water cooler, allows you to listen uninterrupted – and sends the message that you care about the employee's concerns.

quotable quote

If an employee is having problems with a project, these may be caused by personal matters... Be an empathetic listener. Your role as counsellor is to give team members an opportunity to unload their problems. Encourage them by asking questions. Don't criticise, argue the point, or make a judgement. Act as a sounding board to help release the pressures causing the problem. Help the person clarify the situation... Of course, there are many areas in which you just can't help and you might need to suggest the person see a professional counsellor (medical doctor, psychiatrist, psychologist, marriage counsellor, financial advisor...)[28]

135

How to comfort a grieving employee

The death of a close relative or news of a terminal illness in the immediate family can be the source of considerable emotional strain for an employee, whose work habits and performance are usually affected. It is also a difficult time for an employee's manager and co-workers. But a manager can provide support and help the employee through this difficult period by considering the following points...

 Discuss any crisis in private.

It is important that the employee feel at ease and able to talk openly and frankly with you, so choose a comfortable and non-threatening setting for any conversation.

Be empathetic.

The effects of a personal loss can be traumatic. An employee can exhibit a range of emotions—shock, disbelief, numbness, disorientation, denial, helplessness, guilt, anxiety, fear, anger, or a sense of futility. In all discussions, you must be aware of such possibilities. Listen attentively, repeat and reflect the emotions revealed to you, and ensure that the employee feels free to ventilate any built-up emotions in your presence. Empathy fosters openness and trust. Help the person identify and express feelings. Reassure him or her that those feelings are natural and will ease with time; and help the employee remember how he or she coped before the loss, trauma, or onset of the terminal disease.

 Demonstrate your support.

With your staff member, discuss strategies for providing support at this critical time. For example,

- explain how you might be able to bend the rules for the employee during these difficult days.

- list ways of accommodating any problems during this time. 'Forget about your project while you're away. We'll take care of it.' or 'Would you like me to call anyone for you?' or 'We'll ease your work load for the next few weeks by sharing it around the office.' Such expressions may be all that the employee needs to hear from you.

- with any particular difficulties, a problem-solving approach is a useful counselling technique; your organisational and decision-making skills will prove useful here.

- obtain the views of the employee. Ask him or her what levels of performance you can expect at work during this period. Find time to discuss special needs.

4 Provide advice on available resources.

Where necessary, refer the employee to specialised counsellors and supporting agencies within your organisation and the community. Make the employee aware of your company's policy on compassionate leave and the like.

5 Seek progress reports.

From time to time (when appropriate), show your interest, concern, and support by asking how the patient is progressing and how the employee is coping. In so doing, you are also gathering information that reveals how the employee is handling his or her work and what other action you might need to take in the workplace.

6 Don't be afraid to raise the subject.

There is a tendency for fellow staff-members to avoid the grieving employee during this difficult time. Often, however, the employee would prefer the opposite. So, if the opportunity arises, don't be reluctant to mention the name of the ill or deceased person to the employee. Be prepared to listen to personal stories about the loved one, even though you may have heard them before.

7 Keep other employees informed.

Within the constraints of confidentiality, keep other appropriate staff members informed. Your staff are perceptive and will notice if you are supportive, sincere, and caring. Your sensitivity will foster positive feelings and loyalty among employees.

8 Expect grieving to be a long and difficult process.

The scope of 'normal' grieving behaviours is wide; people grieve in different ways. If the loss is significant, rebuilding one's life will usually be a long and painful process. Even with considerable support during those first few weeks, the healing process can take years. It is important, therefore, to accept that grieving can be a slow process and that during that time a wide range of behaviours, symptomatic of grief, can be considered normal. But if the individual is particularly or persistently distressed—for example, displaying severe depression, agitation, fear, guilt, memory gaps, disorientation, self-neglect, disturbed sleep, inability to function normally, and drastic personality changes—or does not have a strong emotional support network, then referral to specialist counselling or a support group may be of assistance.

don't forget

Sound advice...

Following a death, to help grieving friends or colleagues, counsellor Kate Minogue advises:

- Give them the space to grieve in their own way.
- Understand that grieving can take a long time, at least several years, and that certain occasions like birthdays, Christmas, or the anniversary of a death can be particularly difficult.
- Allow them to go over the death and its circumstances many times if they feel the need to.
- Let them talk about the guilt they may be feeling.
- It's important to ask direct questions. Instead of saying 'How are you?', try asking 'I'm wondering how you're getting on since your wife died?'
- Be a good listener; don't give advice.
- Encourage them to do physical activity.
- Encourage them to allow themselves to be distracted at times and listen to music, go for a walk, work, or go to the movies.

viewpoint

"*Sympathy* is when someone hits his thumb with a hammer and you say, 'Oh, I'm so sorry.' *Empathy* is when someone hits his thumb with a hammer and you say, 'Ouch!' You feel with the other person."

137

How to develop your emotional intelligence: *(a) increasing your self-awareness*

The Road to Emotional Intelligence

1920s – Psychologists and social scientists explore the concept 'social intelligence'.

1980 – Psychologist Reuven Bar-On, studying 'personal intelligence' and 'emotional factors', coins the phrase 'emotional quotient'.

1990 – John Mayer and Peter Salovey coin and define the phrase 'emotional intelligence'.

1995 – Daniel Goleman's bestseller *Emotional Intelligence* popularises the concept.

1997 – *The Bar-On EQ-i* published: 'the only scientifically based and validated measurement of emotional intelligence' (www.mhs.com).

read further

Emotional Intelligence by Daniel Goleman, Bantam, 1995.

Working with Emotional Intelligence by Daniel Goleman, Bantam, 1998.

Emotional Intelligence at Work by Hendrie Weisinger, Jossey-Bass, NY, 2000.

The EQ Edge by Steven Stein and Howard Book, Stoddart, 2000.

Our emotions provide us with valuable information about ourselves, others, and situations. From frustration to contentment, from anger to elation, we confront these varying emotions daily in the workplace. The key is to use our emotions intelligently—by being aware of their presence and intentionally using them to guide our behaviour to enhance our situation. This process comprises two elements[30]—first (considered here), we need to understand our emotions and develop self-awareness and, second, we must know how to manage those emotions to best advantage in the workplace.

1 Understand the meaning of emotional intelligence.

Emotional intelligence is 'the ability to monitor one's own and other people's feelings and emotions, to discriminate among them, and to use this information to guide one's thinking and action'.[125] For example, if a client drives you crazy to the point of anger, do you shout at him? Or, knowing that you can derail your relationship with the client if you don't keep your emotions in check, do you put a lid on your anger, and use your emotions more appropriately? How you manage this situation is a measure of your emotional intelligence.

2 Understand self-awareness.

Because you are at the centre of your universe, you must understand what it is that makes you do what you do before you can begin to alter your behaviour for better results. You must understand what is important to you, how you experience things, what you want, how you feel, and how you come across to others.

Without self-awareness, your effectiveness in the workplace will be stunted. According to US psychologist Hendrie Weisinger, to increase your self-awareness, you need 'some serious thoughtfulness and the courage to explore how to react to the people and events in your worklife'. To sharpen your self-awareness system, he says you must focus on five areas…

3 Work towards increasing your self-awareness.

In all situations, try to meet the following five demands:[30]

(a) *Engage in positive inner dialogue and appraisal.*

Hundreds of times each day, we talk to ourselves in the form of an inner dialogue comprising judgemental thoughts. These 'silent appraisals' are the impressions, interpretations, evaluations, and expectations we have about ourselves, other people, and situations. Once we become aware that these thoughts can influence our feelings, we can alter them to handle our situation and relationships better.

Look for patterns in your inner

dialogue. Perhaps it always reflects insecurity, raises doubts, or suggests uncertainty. Perhaps your thoughts are invariably optimistic or critical of others and yourself. By seeing patterns, you can find out whether your inner dialogue works for or against you in the workplace.

(b) *Tune in to your senses.*

Our senses—seeing, hearing, tasting, smelling, and touching—provide us with data about the world, ourselves, other people, and situations. Frequently this data is filtered and transformed by our inner dialogue or silent appraisals.

But it's easy to misinterpret sensory data—a frown does not always indicate anger, nor a tapping foot impatience—but, with a high degree of self-awareness, by consciously tuning into our senses, we can double-check, clarify, and amend our thinking to provide more accurate appraisals.

(c) *Get in touch with your feelings.*

Our feelings are our spontaneous emotional responses to the interpretations we make and the expectations we have. Like sensory data, they provide important information that helps us understand why we do what we do.

Tuning into feelings does not come easily for most of us—although physical and behavioural evidence will often help. For example, a warm flush in your face can signal embarrassment, a stirring stomach can indicate nervousness, clenching the arm of your chair can mean anger, or tapping your pencil anxiety or impatience.

By ignoring or denying our emotions, we deny ourselves the ability to work through them. Negative feelings can often fester—which is why high self-awareness will enable us to acknowledge their presence, manage them, and move on.

(d) *Know what your intentions are.*

Intentions refer primarily to our immediate desires—what we would like to accomplish in a specific situation. It's important to be fully aware of our intentions: we can use that information to adopt better strategies. Weisinger provides an example:

> Your intention may appear to be that you want to get promoted to a vice presidency. But your hidden agenda might be that you want your parents, who always thought you wouldn't amount to anything, to be impressed with your success.[31]

High self-awareness means that you recognise the *true* intention of your actions.

(e) *Pay attention to your actions.*

Our actions are physical, so other people observe them. If we want our actions to work better for us, we should be aware of the signals they give out. For example, you sit slumped in your chair at a meeting because your back hurts (but others think you're uninterested in the discussion); or you keep interrupting because you have lots of ideas and are eager to have your comments heard (others think you're simply rude and don't care what other people say). Monitor such actions—speech patterns, body language, nonverbal behaviour. They can have others judging you inaccurately.

4 Put it all together.

Self-awareness means becoming fully aware of the wealth of information you have about who you are. By tuning in to all five components, you can step back and observe yourself in a particular situation and be better able to choose the most effective course of action.

---

mini seminar

Here is a workplace example of the five self-awareness components at work:

'I walked down to John's office to ask him a question [INTENTION]. I saw him typing fast and furiously at his computer [SENSES] and figured he must be very keen to complete the report I had given him [APPRAISAL]. I was very happy [FEELINGS] he was working so hard. I didn't want to disturb his concentration [INTENTION], so I quietly slipped out of his office [ACTIONS].

Analyse a similar situation in your workplace to clarify your understanding of the five self-awareness elements.

---

 quotable quote

To effectively navigate your work world, to know what course you are to follow and how to stay on it, you need a gyroscope. Think of your emotional self-awareness that way: it helps keep you centred and immediately alerts you when you are tilting off course.[32]

---

quotable quote

Emotional Intelligence is the ability to use your emotions in a positive and constructive way in relationships with others.[33]

How to develop your emotional intelligence: *(b) managing your emotions*

US psychologist Hendrie Weisinger reminds us that our emotional responses are driven—*not* by someone else's actions or an external event—but by our own thoughts, bodily arousals, and behaviours. So, after an outburst by a short-tempered colleague, your pounding heart and your clenched fist cause you to feel angry. Knowing this, you can appreciate that the power to manage your anger, and indeed all your other emotions, rests with *you*—not with your nasty colleague or anyone else. Managing your emotions means *you* can stay on top of them— and here, Weisinger[30] suggests, is how...

Keep your thoughts in check.

Our internal conversations, inner dialogues, or appraisals play a vital role in defining and shaping our emotional experiences. So...

(a) *Beware of spontaneous thoughts.* The thoughts that automatically spring to mind after an incident are different from internal dialogues or appraisals, which usually entail some deliberation. Spontaneous thoughts tend to be irrational ('I could kill him'), initially believable ('He's always hyper-critical of me'), cryptic ('I'm history!'), and often trigger other inappropriate spontaneous thoughts. Beware of such knee-jerk reactions.

(b) *Avoid distorted thinking.* Spontaneous thoughts lead to distorted thinking that can muddy our perception of reality. To distance yourself from this trap, try not to overgeneralise ('She never listens to me'), avoid destructive labelling ('He's a jerk!'), eliminate mind-reading ('The boss probably thinks I should be fired'), avoid rule-making ('He ought to have apologised to me'), and don't inflate the significance of an incident ('This will cost me that promotion').

(c) *Develop constructive inner dialogues.* Eliminate destructive spontaneous thoughts and distorted thinking before they gain a foothold on your emotions.

Think constructively to defuse the effect of distressful events. Focus on problem-solving techniques; ask relevant questions; make reassuring statements about yourself, your boss, your situation and your future. Think positively.

Manage your arousal.

Physiological changes or arousal are those sensations that often accompany an incident and lead to an emotional response—racing heartbeat (fear), warm cheeks (anger), sweaty palms (nervousness). The key is to use them as cues that it's time to calm yourself enough to think and act effectively. So...

(a) *Learn to identify shifts in arousal levels.* By failing to tune in to the changes in your arousal level, you run the risk of acting impulsively. So, after an unsettling event, be alert to the warning signs—increased heart rate, beading perspiration, flushed cheeks, jittery stomach, sweaty palms. It's easier to act at this point to prevent yourself from getting anxious, angry, frustrated, fearful, or vengeful than to try to stop these emotions once they have taken over.

(b) *Use relaxation techniques.* Diminish arousal as soon as you identify it. Relaxing is the most effective way of doing so. When you relax, you slow down your bodily activity and restore your body to its normal state, giving you time to determine the best course of action, rather than act impulsively. Try counting to ten, taking a walk, deep breathing, meditation, yoga, music, or calming images. Once you can condition yourself to relax at will, you can short-circuit any change in arousal.

3 Take control of your behavioural patterns.

Behavioural patterns are actions we often involuntarily take in response to a particular situation—tap a pencil when angry, fidget when nervous, or yell when angry. To keep our emotions in check, we need to recognise and act on these signals. So…

(a) *Learn to identify your behaviours.* Certain behaviours are generally linked with specific emotions; if those behaviours remain unchecked, they perpetuate the emotion. For example, if you continue to fidget, your anxiety will persist. Remember, too, that not all behaviours are physical—you may habitually resort to sarcasm if you don't get your own way; colleagues may avoid you if you're a show-off. Consciously monitor your emotions; look for patterns; ask other people for their observations. Awareness will lead to elimination.

(b) *Eliminate counterproductive behaviours.* Having identified behaviours that work against you, take steps to eliminate them. Use constructive inner dialogue to take charge of your thoughts and actions. Try deep breathing to slow youself down and regain control.

4 Develop good problem-solving skills.

Problem-solving can manage not only staff and projects, but also your emotions. A distressful emotion is caused by a problem situation. Why did you get angry? Why does your

assistant make you feel frustrated? Why does your client leave you depressed? To manage your emotions effectively, you need to develop your problem-solving skills (see page 266). The key is to reframe your thoughts about the situation in emotional terms and to see the issue afresh—e.g.

- 'The real problem isn't what's done that bothers me; the problem is how I feel.'
- 'The real problem isn't why it happened; the real problem is why I responded the way I did.'
- 'The real problem isn't that my job drives me crazy, but that I haven't found an effective way of handling it.'
- 'The real problem isn't that my boss keeps giving me more and more work, but that I haven't found a way to get help with it.'

5 Seek alternative ways of managing your emotions.

Also consider using these three techniques to manage your emotions:

(a) *Humour.* Laughter is the best medicine —and there is a scientific basis for this belief: laughter causes your body to produce its own painkillers (endorphins). They have a healthy effect on such negative emotions as anxiety, anger, sadness, and depression. So don't take work too seriously; look for the whimsical; take humour meditation breaks; and encourage fun in the workplace (see page 88).

(b) *Redirection.* Instead of fidgeting, brooding, or feeling depressed or angry about a situation, take on some busywork to get your mind off the issue.

(c) *Time out.* Taking a break from an emotionally taxing situation can slow down your emotional responses. The short break can give you the moment you need to keep yourself from saying something you might later regret. If necessary, walk away from the situation until you become more rational.

smile & ponder

Socrates's injunction 'Know thyself' provides a keystone of emotional intelligence: awareness of one's own feelings as they occur – in much the same way as is illustrated in this old Japanese tale:

Once upon a time, a samurai challenged a Zen master to explain the concept of heaven and hell. But the monk replied with scorn, 'You're nothing but a lout – I can't waste my time with the likes of you!'

His very honour attacked, the samurai flew into a rage and, pulling his sword from his scabbard yelled, 'I could kill you for your impertinence.'

'That,' the monk calmly replied, 'is hell.'

Startled at seeing the truth in what the master pointed out about the fury that had him in its grip, the samurai calmed down, sheathed his sword, and bowed, thanking the monk for the insight.

'And that,' said the monk, 'is heaven.'

viewpoint

"Emotional Intelligence is the capacity for recognizing our own feelings and those of others, for motivating ourselves, and for managing emotions well in ourselves and in our relationships."[36]

– Daniel Goleman

How to help your staff improve their emotional intelligence

A healthy organisation relies on the healthy interaction of its employees. In the context of emotional intelligence, the members of such an organisation help each other to manage their emotions, communicate effectively, solve their own problems and those of others, are supportive listeners, and resolve conflicts readily. Imagine what it might be like to work in a company where everyone freely communicates with understanding and respect. Here's how you can help to create such an organisation…

1 Ask if you want an emotionally intelligent organisation.

Do you want an organisation in which all employees take responsibility for increasing their own emotional intelligence by developing self-awareness and managing their emotions? Do you want a company whose staff know how to conduct themselves and how to relate to others? Do you want staff using their emotions to enhance, rather than sabotage, their own performance and relationships at work? You should.

2 Know the basics of emotional intelligence.

Emotional intelligence (EI) is 'the ability to monitor one's own and other people's feelings and emotions, to discriminate among them, and to use this information to guide one's thinking and action'.[37] According to Israeli psychologist Reuven Bar-On, there are five broad areas of emotional intelligence: intrapersonal, interpersonal, adaptability, stress management, and general mood (see accompanying side panel). Your

employees will possess strengths and weaknesses in the range of EI areas; no-one is equally strong in all. To help your staff increase their emotional intelligence, you will need an understanding of these areas. See www.mhs.com for starters.

3 Determine which areas require the focus of your organisation.

Analyse the five areas that define emotional intelligence and decide which are the most relevant for the people in your organisation. For example, interpersonal skills are more important for salespeople than for assembly-line workers; and problem-solving skills are needed more by architects than by house-painters. Few workers will require strengths in all the five areas or the 15 subsections.

4 Assess the needs of your employees.

Having identified the appropriate EI areas for specific jobs in your organisation, you can now assess your staff either informally or formally.

(a) *Informally.* An informal approach

demands that you adopt a watching brief: monitor your employees at work to determine whether they need help. For example, how well do airport counter staff handle the stress of the peak-hour rush—delayed or cancelled flights, several customers talking at once, customers shouting to be served, customers complaining, and so on? Gather anecdotal and individual case study data for discussion with the staff member.

(b) *Formal.* A more formal approach would be to administer a test instrument such as the Bar-On Emotional Quotient Inventory *(EQ-i)* to individuals or groups. This tool not only identifies areas for personal improvement but also provides a benchmark against which progress can be measured.

With formal testing instruments, remember that it's important to

- follow the test developer's guidelines
- keep each candidate's scores confidential, although summary statements of overall strengths and weaknesses within the organisation can be provided more widely
- ensure that the test does not invade any employee's privacy, or disclose protected details of a person's physical or mental health
- ensure that the instrument is work-related and validated, and tests what it is supposed to test.

5 Help employees sharpen their identified areas of weakness.

Through mentoring or coaching (see pages 132 and 366), reinforce and hone appropriate skills you have

targeted to raise your employees' emotional intelligence.

Focus on specific rather than generic work-related behaviours. For example, don't simply suggest that employees be 'more flexible' when handling customer complaints. Rather, explain what 'being flexible' means in their jobs and why it is important. Use concrete examples. In particular, use learning opportunities as they arise in the workplace and take the time to discuss how any difficult situation might be better handled.

Remember that emotional intelligence can be learnt, nurtured, developed, and augmented. It isn't a trait that one either has or doesn't have. Importantly, also, emotional intelligence can't be imposed. So don't force the issue.

6 Provide feedback.

Watch for improvement in individual employees and reward those who make the effort. Raising the level of one's emotional intelligence is not always easy: behaviour can be an ingrained quality. But, as one commentator writes, EI's potential for personal and organisational success is significant:

> It gives you the awareness you need to analyse your relationships; it enables you to manage your emotions so that encounters at all levels of communication are as productive as possible; and it gives you the communication skills—from self-disclosure to dynamic listening and assertiveness—that allow you to connect with another person meaningfully and appropriately.[38]

Measuring Emotional Intelligence

Emotional Intelligence, according to Dr Reuven Bar-On, is 'an array of non cognitive capabilities, competencies and skills that influence one's ability to succeed in coping with daily environment demands and pressures and helps predict one's success in life, including personal and professional pursuits'.

Recent research suggests that emotional intelligence, measured by Emotional Quotient (EQ), is possibly a better predictor of 'success' than more traditional measures of cognitive intelligence (IQ).[35]

The *Bar-On EQ-i* instrument explores emotional intelligence in five areas, with 15 subsections or scales:

Intrapersonal
Emotional self-awareness
Assertiveness
Self-regard
Self-actualization
Independence

Interpersonal
Interpersonal relationships
Empathy
Social responsibility

Adaptability
Problem solving
Reality testing
Flexibility

Stress Management
Stress tolerance
Impulse control

General Mood
Happiness
Optimism

For details: www.mhs.com

143

How to communicate effectively

The term 'communication' now includes many activities associated with everyday organisational life—oral, face-to-face, formal, informal, personal, interpersonal, nonverbal, and written—which is why so many organisational headaches are attributed to 'communication problems'. Indeed, a common finding of organisational reviews is that 'communication needs to be improved'. We spend so much time 'communicating', but so few of us give much thought to the essentials of this key management activity…

1 Always work to establish rapport.

Without the trust and confidence of others with whom you are communicating, much of what you say will be lost. It is imperative, therefore, that you take time to establish and build rapport. Knowing your audience is a vital part of this process. See page 112 for suggestions in this important area.

2 Attract the attention of your target audience.

It's not *what* you communicate but *how* you do it. People are being bombarded with information and have become very selective. If your message is going to penetrate today's highly critical market, you'll need to make it stand out from the rest. Make your communications short, sharp, and customised to capture the attention of your target groups.

3 Demonstrate confidence.

A key quality in any communication is confidence. Research reveals that, if you sound and look confident, others are more likely agree to what you might propose. The converse also applies.

4 Give people your full attention.

Not everyone who communicates with you necessarily wants *your* response. For example, he or she, may be using you as a sounding board from which to develop a proposition in more detail. For this reason:

- ask questions instead of giving answers
- focus on what the other person is saying, not what you'll say next
- focus on what you can learn instead of what you can teach
- ask how you can help.

5 Opt for clarity.

The way others respond is a useful measure of the effectiveness of your communication. The messages we communicate must be specific, straightforward, unambiguous, consistent, and complete. The amount of information you communicate will depend on the recipients' abilities to interpret and act on it.

 ### Match saying and doing.

When communicating, there is a close link between what you say and what you do—which is why you can communicate personal values, ethics, and credibility. Messages go unnoticed if the messenger can't be believed. So make sure you walk the talk and, when you don't, explain why.

 ### Be aware of your nonverbal communication.

Most meaning is communicated non-verbally. Although a long list can be found on page 158, the essentials are to stand or sit erect, look directly at your listener, make constant eye-contact, and adopt an enthusiastic tone of voice. Learning to observe body language is also a skill; so keep your eyes, ears, and other senses attuned to nonverbal messages signalled by others.

 ### Learn to listen.

Effective communication is a two-way process, which demands that you hear other people's messages. Listening, therefore, is an essential and most demanding skill. In ancient times Zeno of Citium observed that we have two ears and one mouth to encourage us to listen much more than we speak. Others have emphasised that we learn more when we're listening than when we're speaking. The bottom line is that if employees think you're a poor listener, they'll stop talking to you. Suggestions to develop this important skill are presented on page 148.

 ### Invite feedback.

Before obtaining the views of others, make sure that you can rely on them to provide honest feedback and that you can handle the truth when it is presented. Winston Churchill established a group whom he trusted to provide a balanced assessment of events – *especially* any 'bad' news. On the other hand, Saddam Hussein is alleged to have shot one of his generals for giving feedback that he didn't want to hear. When people know that you appreciate feedback and are prepared to act on it, they will keep you well informed.

 ### Ask the right questions.

Charles Darwin assured us that solving the mystery of evolution was a straightforward process once he knew the right questions to ask. Effective questioning is an essential problem-solving skill that can be used to help others solve their problems, too. Check this skill on page 150.

 ### Capitalise on informal communication.

The grapevine, that informal network that carries information faster than any known technology, survives and thrives in every organisation. Learn how you can use this means of communicating for the organisation's benefit. For suggestions, see page 170.

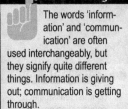 **don't forget**

The words 'inform-ation' and 'commun-ication' are often used interchangeably, but they signify quite different things. Information is giving out; communication is getting through.

66 quotable quote

A good communicator takes responsibility for the flow of communication, whether speaking or listening. Don't rely on people to accommodate themselves to you. *You* are in charge of every commun-ication situation you're in.[1]

viewpoint

"The most important thing in communication is to hear what isn't being said."
– Peter Drucker

66 quotable quote

Of all the activities and functions performed by a manager, none takes up more time than communication ... If it is hampered, the entire organisation suffers; when it is accurate, thorough and timely, only then can the organisation move effectively towards goal achievement.[2]

 read further

Communication Gaps and How to Close Them by Naomi Carten, Dorset House, London, 2002.

How to get the most out of a conversation with an employee

Face-to-face communication remains the most important form of communicating—whether it occurs formally, as in a scheduled interview or disciplinary situation, or informally, as in a chance meeting in the car park or corridor. Cordial, cooperative discussions with employees ensure that their opinions are heard and provide a very effective means of obtaining information that will make your job much easier. The following approaches are worth considering…

Build trust and confidence.

Your initial aim must be to establish rapport by making employees feel comfortable in your presence and converse freely with you. Although there is no magic formula for creating that situation, authenticity and empathy are essential qualities—it's OK to be yourself (apart from the fact that people are very quick to recognise incongruence, where physical and verbal messages contradict each other). A good starting point for any conversation is to get people talking about the most important persons in their lives—themselves.

Listen and be listened to.

Listening actively is hard work and is more than just not talking. Not only must you hear what the other person says but you must also convey understanding and interest through clarifying, summarising, paraphrasing, and reflecting feelings. Consider tailoring your conversations to your employees' preferences—are they listeners or readers? 'Listeners' won't *read* long written reports—they prefer to hear about them and the details, making a brief note to remind them if necessary. On the other hand, 'readers' have difficulty following a great deal of oral detail—they prefer to see it in black and white. So tell them the bare facts and leave your detailed message written out for digestion later.

 Follow a successful formula.

The key to conducting a fruitful conversation involves the following:

- Get to the point.
- Get all the facts before reaching any conclusion.
- Avoid using too much direct questioning; don't cross-examine.
- Don't use verbal or facial cues that alert the listener to what is coming.
- Keep your conversation factual and objective.
- Confront issues, not people.
- Slow down; instil confidence.

Practise conversation skills.

If you're alert, you learn something new from every conversation if you practise these skills:

- Call people by their names; it's the word they most like to hear.
- Ask questions; show interest; listen attentively.
- Develop techniques for bringing conversations to a close: 'Thanks again, Joan. I've enjoyed our chat. I'll see you on Friday at 3.30.'
- Maintain eye contact, but don't stare. Research indicates that in a conversation the less assertive person often disengages eye contact first, usually after only a few seconds.
- Use nonverbal invitations to encourage talking—nodding, eye contact, leaning forward, narrowing physical distance. It isn't only *what* you say that registers but also *how* you say it.

 Use clear, straightforward communication.

Clear, effective oral communication is more than not talking down to people. You must also:

- eliminate space fillers like 'um' and 'er' and catchphrases like 'you know', 'basically', 'in actual fact', and 'sort of thing'.
- slow down, watching for signs

of uncertainty and checking for understanding.

- not talk too much. Even when you're giving information, the other person needs at least 20 per cent of the air time. In other conversations do less than 50 per cent of the talking.

 Keep the conversation going.

Use motivational phrases like 'We're here to solve this problem together', 'I'm concerned. I care about what happens to you' and 'I'm finding this chat very helpful' to keep the conversation moving. Phrases like 'Can you add anything else?', 'I'd like to hear more about that', and 'Do you see any problems with any of that?' help to steer the conversation. Remaining silent is another way of keeping the conversation flowing.

 Organise your thoughts.

Abraham Lincoln once said of an acquaintance, 'He can compress the most words into the smallest ideas of any man I ever met'. So know what you want to say and say it. Keep a small notebook with you at all times, indexed with key persons' names. In the notebook, jot down subjects you want to discuss with any of these people. Those jottings will act as memory joggers and others will be impressed by your knowledge and attention to detail. Make a note of the outcome of any discussion to remind you of any necessary follow-up.

 smile & ponder

Dale Carnegie, author of the classic bestseller *How to Win Friends and Influence People,* was once invited to a party at which he knew few people. During the course of the evening, relates success-trainer Tom Hopkins, he spoke with several new acquaintances. The following day, the host of the party received several compliments on the new guest – specific- ally, that he was a wonderful conversation- alist.

Now you probably picture Dale Carnegie in the middle of a group of people, spouting hilarious stories and imparting interesting facts. Not so, says Hopkins.

All Carnegie did was invest a little time with several people one on one. When introduced to them, he asked them each a question about their backgrounds. The guests, of course, obliged with discourses in varying lengths about their lives. Whenever they paused, Carnegie asked another question or encouraged them simply by saying, 'Go on'.

Carnegie actually spoke very little the entire evening, yet he was thought of highly by the others as a great 'conversationalist'.

How to listen actively

Listening accounts for well over half of a manager's communication time, and it is unquestionably the weakest link in the communication chain. We simply don't listen well enough. The failure is not in the hearing, but in our ability to attend to what we hear. Listening is hard work. It's so easy to 'switch off'. If only we listened attentively and with empathy, we would eliminate so many misunderstandings, arguments, delays, and mistakes. Become a better listener by adhering to the following advice...

1 Commit yourself to each individual act of listening.

Whenever you need to hear everything someone is saying, commit yourself—really commit yourself—to do so. Say to yourself, 'The most important thing in my life at this moment is to understand this person's feelings and views.' Accordingly, focus *all* of your listening capacity on the speaker for the next five, fifteen, or fifty minutes. Actually *want* to listen better. It's a small investment of your time that can pay enormous dividends.

2 Really concentrate on what is being said.

When listening, listen. Listening is not a passive activity. Unless you're concentrating solely on what is being said, you're not listening. If you've heard it all before, hear it again. Fight the 'switch-off' syndrome. The more you work at concentrating while listening, the more your powers of concentration will develop and the easier listening will become.

3 Neutralise your biases.

Don't let your personal biases turn you off, despite what you may feel about the speaker's voice, character, appearance, or reputation, or the subject being discussed. Don't let your feelings distort the real message. Stay calm; don't get upset; and keep an open mind.

4 Encourage the speaker.

Show the speaker you're listening by nodding, facing him or her, maintaining eye contact, leaning forward slightly, smiling, and repeating (silently) key words or points. Don't interrupt with a response until the speaker has finished. Remember, as Austrian pianist Alfred Brendel once observed: The word 'listen' contains the same letters as the word 'silent'.

5 Ignore all distractions.

Particularly if the speaker or the topic

is dull, or once we get a rough idea of what is being said, we readily allow distractions to interfere with our listening—noises, ringing telephones, our own thoughts, the speaker's mannerisms, daydreaming, passing employees, a memo you're working on… Giving in to distractions is a bad habit that could have you not hearing something worthwhile or vital.

Focus on the main ideas.

Good listening involves separating the verbal grain from the chaff. Learn to identify the major points to which the facts point: good listeners are concept listeners rather than fact listeners. Finally, search for the implications of what is being said.

Test your understanding.

Ensure that you really understand what the speaker is saying. Ask for repetition, clarification, amplification, and examples. Summarise from time to time. By doing so, you will also indicate to the speaker that you are really listening.

Delay formulating your arguments.

Since brain speed works at about 90 times the rate of the speed of speech, we sometimes allow our minds to soar ahead of what we're hearing, and we begin working on our response. While doing this, we don't hear what is being said. So try not to let your attention wander too soon to formulate a reply.

Suspend judgement.

Listening is a separate task from interpreting and evaluating, both of which can hamper the listening process. Make sure you comprehend before you judge the message, so resist the temptation to debate the message mentally and prematurely instead of listening. Your time would be better spent checking and rechecking the information by questioning. Delay the processing until later.

Don't talk too much.

You can't talk and listen at the same time. If you want information, you shouldn't say much—you already know what *you* think. You should be more interested in what the other person has to say. So let him or her dominate the discussion, so that you can stay focused—listening.

Remember: listening is a key to personal success.

Recognise that listening is something you do if you want to succeed. But you should not only listen: you need to strike a balance… or as Oliver Wendell Holmes Jr said: 'It is the privilege of wisdom to listen and the province of knowledge to speak.'

Listening earns you power and respect, and gets you the information you need to be an effective manager. But listening is a sophisticated skill. It requires self-discipline, and you'll need to work on it.

don't forget

Consider this handy advice…

■ Listening often means not saying anything, even when a speaker doesn't get right to the point. Cultivate patience.

■ Be aware that, while your mouth may be silent, your body may be speaking volumes. If you're fidgeting or not focusing on the speaker, you probably aren't really listening.

■ Emulate the body language of the speaker. Adopt alert posture and maintain eye contact. Let your body show you're interested.

■ Keep an open mind. If your staff sense that you're unwilling to listen to their ideas, they won't tell you about them.

■ Don't judge ideas by the way they're delivered. Many people have good ideas but can't express them well.

■ Be willing to listen to all your staff, not just your senior people.[5]

here's an idea

Become a better listener by stepping up the Listening Ladder:

L: Look at the person speaking to you.
A: Ask questions.
D: Don't interrupt.
D: Don't change the subject.
E: Empathise.
R: Respond verbally and nonverbally.[6]

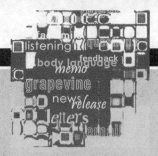

How to ask questions

The best way to solve a problem is to ask the person who has the key to its solution. Asking the right people the right questions is the pathway to real information—about your workplace, your employees, and your customers. So whether you're solving problems, establishing a better working relationship, shaping your vision, motivating, interviewing, or negotiating, asking the right questions is a vital management technique. Here are the essentials of effective questioning...

1 Understand the purpose of questions.

Questions are used for a variety of purposes:

- to get information
- to clarify a point
- to keep discussions going
- to communicate feelings
- to make another person feel good
- to gain insight.

Your task is to understand the purpose of your questioning, then to use the types of questions that will deliver the desired outcome. Remember, the more senior your position within the organisation, the more questions you should ask. By asking questions— rather than by attempting to provide answers—you help to keep your organisation 'open', tap into others' accumulated wisdom and insights, and conceal your own agenda.

2 Use the right type of question.

The type of question you ask can influence the response; in the hands of a skilled interviewer, a question can be a powerful tool. For example:

Open-ended questions (Why? How?) These explore opinions and attitudes, encourage others to keep talking, and avoid a yes-no response.

Closed or *yes-no* questions ('Did you see…?') These establish specific fact, elicit a pattern of agreement, or force an unambiguous response.

Leading questions ('Don't you think…?') These suggest the required answers.

Reflective/probing questions ('Are you saying that…?') These restate or reflect what you've heard and invite the disclosure of other information.

Rhetorical questions ('Have you ever wondered why…?') These are used for effect; you do not expect an answer.

Directive questions ('So you agree that…?') These focus on desired outcomes.

'Dumb' questions ('I don't follow. Could you go over it again, please?') These test the rationale of why things have always been done in a certain way.

Summary questions ('So what you're saying is…?') These check understanding and confirm your interest.

Keep your questions simple and direct.

Good questions are direct and to the point, worded so that the listener has no difficulty in understanding exactly what the questioner wants. If the response to your question is 'I'm not quite sure what you're asking…', your question was not simple nor direct.

Ask questions that are focused.

Questions should emphasise only one point at a time. Avoid complex, double-barrelled questions. If you keep your questions concise and brief, you'll not cause confusion and you'll get the answer you're looking for.

Move from general to specific.

Whenever you want detailed information, if you get too direct too soon you run the risk of creating a defensive attitude rather than encouraging open communication. Start with the general issues and gradually focus on specifics. If you start with difficult or delicate questions, you will only cause the other person discomfort. A person at ease will respond openly and without animosity.

Ask the question; then pause.

There's nothing wrong with silence. It places the onus to respond on the other person. So, after you ask a question, pause, and use your body language to let the person know that you're waiting for a reply. By nodding your head and minimising your verbal response by using 'mm' or 'yes', you can encourage the other person to keep talking.

Don't telegraph an answer.

Don't be bluffed by an answer. Remember, sometimes we inadvertently word our questions so that listeners can guess what answer will satisfy us; they give it to us and we are happy. Be alert when asking your question. You need an answer based on facts and information, not on guesswork.

Refuse to accept inadequate answers.

Be persistent when answers are vague. Seek out the specifics until you are satisfied with the information provided. Remember that powerful word *why*. If a response is a simple 'yes' or 'no', ask 'why?' This three-letter follow-up is very potent and often elicits information that leads to better decision-making.

Don't baulk at unsettling responses.

When seeking information or when interviewing, avoid evaluating answers and showing your disapproval, verbally or nonverbally, when someone responds incorrectly or displeasingly. In fact, such answers can help to identify gaps in your knowledge, or indicate to you specific areas where further probing is warranted.

! viewpoint

"When you are managing people, one of the greatest timesavers is asking questions – more specifically, asking the *right* questions. In behavioural psychology we learn that everything is a result of something else. And when a problem arises, it is usually a clue that a deeper problem lies beneath the surface. The best way to get to the bottom of things is not to jump to conclusions but to ask questions.

– Jim Rohn in *Seven Strategies for Wealth and Happiness*

---

here's an idea

Questioning, writes Allan Pease in *Talk Language*, can be the lifeblood of a good conversation – if the questions are asked effectively. But, in questioning, we often make mistakes – for example:

Asking questions that are too open-ended. Very open-ended questions require so much effort and time to answer properly that most people give up without even trying. e.g. 'What have you been up to lately?' and 'What's new?'

Beginning with difficult questions. Always start with simple questions about topics which others are likely to be interested in or familiar with.

Asking leading questions. Such closed questions only invite agreement on your personal opinion. e.g. 'You don't want the last cake, do you?' or 'It's 8.30. Shouldn't we stay home tonight?'

151

How to make a good impression on the telephone

Often, the only impression a customer or client gains of your organisation is the one generated by your staff on the telephone. Research has shown that poor telephone etiquette can result in poor public relations and millions of dollars in lost revenue. Having invested large sums of money in equipment to improve communications with customers, some organisations simply forget to invest in the human skills. First, consider the following advice…

1 Know what really frustrates your callers.

Organisations have suffered in recent years through staff failure to use the telephone appropriately. Recent research reveals that the main frustrations customers or clients experience today in dealing with organisations by telephone are these:

- taking too long to answer
- being put 'on hold' and forgotten
- being transferred and having to repeat the inquiry
- being answered by voice mail and other 'machines'
- not having calls returned
- music on hold, rudeness, perceived indifference, not getting to the point…

If you can do something about these frustrations, then you'll restore the telephone to a position as your organisation's most valuable communications tool.

2 Be familiar with new technology.

First make sure you and your staff become expert in dealing with the equipment. If you have the technology, it's foolish not to be fully familiar with the advantages it can provide. Do you know how to…

- transfer a call
- park a call
- discern a distinctive ring tone
- redirect calls in your absence
- place calls on hold
- set up 'automatic callback'
- operate the PABX
- use the conference phone facility?

Don't test your caller's patience while you bumble your way through the technology at your end.

 Pick up the handset—consciously.

Remember the saying: 'You never get a second chance to make a first impression'. So be conscious of that advice whenever you pick up the phone. Consider these pointers:

- Answer promptly. If possible, pick up the handset before the third ring ends.
- Quickly finish off any office conversation before lifting the handset so that the caller doesn't hear any irrelevant discussion.
- Put a smile in your voice. It may sound silly, but your voice actually has a more

pleasant tone when you're smiling. So, answer the phone with a smile.

- When answering, say 'Good morning' or 'Good afternoon', then identify your organisation and yourself.

 Be organised.

By being organised you will minimise caller frustration:

- No caller likes to wait for you to 'find a scrap of paper to write on'. Always have message pads and pens on hand.
- Minimise screening questions. It may be justifiable for staff to screen your calls, but make sure they don't turn the call into an interrogation.
- Listen carefully for how callers pronounce their names—phonetically spell tricky names on any message slip.
- Make sure your assistant has a copy of your schedule in case a caller requests an appointment or wishes to call back.
- Keep your internal telephone directory up to date for accurate call transfers.
- Ensure your phones are never left unattended during lunch breaks, holiday periods, and staff absences. A continuously ringing phone advertises a slack organisation.

 Take pride in the quality of your conversation.

Train your employees (and yourself) to be concerned, interested, and efficient on the phone. In particular:

- Sound confident, knowledgeable, and unrushed.
- Take enough time to establish the caller's needs clearly.
- Try to eliminate verbal pauses, abrupt or garbled speech habits, 'ums', 'ahs', 'you knows', and other sloppy talk.
- Speak slowly and distinctly. The information being sought may be routine to you but it's not to most callers. Make the caller feel important.

Repeat the information if necessary. Leave the caller happy.

- Don't smoke, chew, slouch, shout, or whisper when on the phone.
- Cover the mouthpiece if you must talk to another staff member. Be warned, however, the caller can probably still hear what you are saying.
- When leaving voice mail or answering machine messages, try not to speak in a mad rush as if you are about to be cut off. Enunciate clearly, especially your name and number.

 Put yourself in the caller's place.

Empathise with the person on the other end of the phone. Treat callers as you'd like to be treated—be courteous and helpful:

- Don't keep your caller on hold for any inordinate time.
- Give callers the option of holding, speaking to someone else, leaving a message, or having their calls returned.
- Avoid terse, unfriendly phrases such as 'Hold on ...'.
- Never answer a question with 'I don't know'. Instead, say: 'I'm not sure—but I'll find out and get back to you before close of business.'
- If you promise to return a call, do so—promptly—even if merely to say you're still working on the caller's request.
- Respond promptly. If the caller wanted an answer next week, you would have been sent a letter, not a phonecall!
- Check that your message distribution procedures are efficient.
- Use your caller's name. It replaces the eye contact you normally give when face to face.
- Ensure your staff know how to handle complaints and irate callers, and how to terminate long-winded calls courteously.
- Don't forget: The telephone hides your face but not your attitude.

153

How to sell your new idea to other people

As a manager, you'll often have to persuade people to believe in your views and to accept your ideas. If you're good at selling your ideas to employees and colleagues, you'll go further, faster, in your career. Unfortunately, good ideas must first be sold to staff and, if you can't get your proposals across as you envisaged, they may well go the way of many other good ideas—into oblivion. So here are some simple rules that will help you sell your ideas more effectively in the future...

quotable quote

Nothing turns off enthusiasm faster than consistently watching ideas get shot down, either by active objectors and/or passive resisters. The main reason that ideas aren't accepted –assuming they're practical to start with – is that little thought is given to the selling effort involved.[10]

ask yourself

Before tabling your idea, run it through the following checklist to be clear on its...

Viability – Can we easily carry out the idea? What are its risks and benefits? Can we market it?

Impact – What waves would the idea create in our organisation? And beyond?

Cost – How much money do we need to find to carry out this idea, and can we afford that? Can we lower the cost?

Effectiveness – How well does the idea mesh with our goal or goals? Is now the right time for this idea? Can we simplify it?

Intuition – Do we feel this is the right idea for us? Does it appear to be the best idea for us? Is now the time?

– *Communication Briefings*

1 *Know what you want—exactly.*

Don't present a vague fuzzy shadow of an idea and then grow angry when you fail to get it across to others. Pretest your idea for clarity: put it on paper. If it can't be written down— goal, numbers, key players, deadlines, budgets—it isn't a fully developed idea. The very act of finding the appropriate words with which to express an idea compels you to think it through.

2 *Double-check everything.*

Make sure that all the necessary research and validation has been done to support your idea and that you have all the facts and figures readily available. You'll need them later.

3 *Consider current circumstances.*

Ensure that the idea suits the current climate of your organisation. For example, you wouldn't want to suggest a costly idea if little money were available in your organisation's coffers.

4 *Highlight the benefits.*

The key to persuasion is to see your proposition from other people's points of view. Their questions (to themselves, usually) will be: 'How does this affect me?' and 'What do I stand to gain or lose?' So make sure you can clearly demonstrate the specific benefits to be gained by others if they adopt your idea—and keep these benefits foremost in your mind, *and theirs*, during your presentations and subsequent discussions.

5 *Be prepared for the objections.*

People are always suspicious of new ideas; most prefer the *status quo*. Anticipate their objections before-hand by consciously and diligently examining your idea for flaws. List potential objections and prepare yourself to tackle them with data, not emotion. Of course, the surest way to squash an objection is to incorporate both the objection and its solution into your presentation. Another useful strategy is to overcome people's objections not by showing them the error of their logic but by reiterating what's in it for them.

Make your idea their idea.

A great way of gaining support is to give away the credit for an idea. By skilfully making suggestions, you can often get people to adopt, and commit themselves to, your ideas as if they were their own. It's amazing how much you can achieve if you don't mind who gets the credit! As well, it's important for you to sow the seeds of ownership by getting others, if possible, to contribute in some way to the idea.

Get some kind of 'yes' early on in the process.

Good salespeople know that it always pays to start their sales pitch on a point—however minor, even irrelevant—with which your audience can agree. In other words, find some common ground quickly to start off with agreement of some kind.

Solicit the support of colleagues.

Discuss the idea in advance with your close colleagues and opinion leaders in your organisation. Their support and agreement can then be called on at the meeting at which you present your idea for consideration.

Prepare a simple and effective presentation.

Your presentation should take two forms: written and oral. Writing adds weight to an idea by indicating that the ideas are less likely to be half-baked or lacking in commitment. Keep your written proposal to a graphic, simply expressed, concise page or two.

Your oral presentation should simply convey the main points of your proposal and its benefits and costs. Avoid being drawn into too much detail. You cannot be accused of hiding or concealing something if you also bring out the disadvantages—before shooting them down yourself. Be convincing and enthusiastic in your summing-up.

The effectiveness of your presentation will also depend largely on how well you have prepared for it, having your facts and figures straight, deciding what you are going to say in what order, and how you are going to say it. It's wise to rehearse your presentation.

Check timing and sequence.

Determine precisely when you should present your idea. Make sure your timing is appropriate, and thus give your idea a greater chance of being accepted.

Check your fallback position.

If your proposal is not entirely acceptable to your audience, make sure you have a fallback position with which you're comfortable, so that, if your first idea is defeated, you are not left with nothing. Don't let your planning inhibit flexibility.

here's an idea

To become more persuasive in the workplace, always get into the habit of using the words 'if' and 'then'. Whether you're trying to sell a new idea or a new car, the message that works is 'If you will take this action, then you'll get this reward....'

So, next time you're planning to try to persuade someone, think about using these two words to get what you want.

here's an idea

If you want a novel way to gain support for an idea you're presenting, consider this useful technique for a meeting:

Write 'good questions' on palm cards. Put each question in an envelope and, before the meeting, tape these randomly under chairs in the meeting room. If necessary, number the envelopes in logical order according to the question they contain. Make some questions humorous and some obvious. After you've delivered your basic message, ask those attending to reach under the chair and read their question aloud. The strategy clarifies your message and responses like 'Gee, that's a great question' and 'I'm glad you asked that' keep the presentation light-hearted.

viewpoint

"Great ideas need landing gear as well as wings."
– C.D. Jackson

155

How to lead others to your way of thinking

Verbal brawling shows a lack of control and an inability to use those vital skills of persuasion. Managers must be able to present their particular point of view or to express an opinion on an issue without being too emotional or engaging in a bout of verbal fisticuffs. Here's a peaceful way of persuading people to accept your line of thinking and ideas...

1 Avoid arguing with extremists.

Until you are shown otherwise, you must assume that others have some fairly good reasons for taking the position they do in any debate or argument. Indeed, most people are rational, so you can always hope to persuade them to accept your point of view. However, remember that, if someone is a fanatic to a cause, you'll be unlikely to convince them.

2 Analyse your stance before you get involved.

Be convinced that the subject or issue is worth arguing about. Will you be going on the defensive or the offensive? Will it be worth the emotional effort?

3 Prepare your case in advance if you can.

If the opportunity arises, make ready for the discussion by considering the following:

• Understand the issue clearly. If you don't, you're disadvantaged from the start.

• Reflect on the issue and clarify your side of the argument.

• Organise your thoughts. Tease out the issue. Jot down salient points.

• Consider your opponent's possible argument; build up ammunition to counter such views rationally.

• Rehearse.

4 Listen to what the other person has to say.

Speed of reply counts very little in an argument, so let your opponent express an opinion without interruption. Besides, how can you reply cogently if you don't know what's been said? So listen carefully while having your own case ready. If you really listen, you'll be able to refute the faulty points in your opponent's argument.

5 Give the impression of giving the other side a fair go.

Don't signal your impatience by responding too quickly. Pause and reflect. Give the impression that at least you are interested in your opponent's point of view and that you are considering his or her opinions. A rational opponent will return your courtesy—and that's important if you want to win the day.

Keep your cool and present your case logically and calmly.

Calmly stated facts are more effective weapons than intimidation, raised voices, immoderate language, and table thumping. If you allow the debate to degenerate into emotional out-pourings and name-calling, a satisfactory conclusion is unlikely. If your opponent resorts to such statements as 'Nonsense!', 'Ridiculous!' or 'That's crazy!', insist on knowing why. Make your opponents destroy your line of reasoning logically. If they can't, your case is almost won.

Consider these valuable weapons in winning your case.

- If you can, make use of a third person to state or support your side of the debate. After all, that's what lawyers do in court.
- Resist attacking the conclusions of your opponents. Instead, attack the reasoning that got them there. You have to erode the foundations on which their conclusions are built.
- Concentrate. In this way you will not only generate more intensity, but also be able to argue more forcefully.

- Establish and keep in mind the basic principles that underlie both your argument and your opponent's. Defend yours. Attack theirs.
- If you attack your opponent's character or name-call, you've all but lost the debate.

Let your opponents retire gracefully.

If you sense it is hard for your opponents to admit defeat, give them the chance to save face. For example, say: 'As you didn't have all the information at your fingertips, I can see why you felt the way you did…'

Move on.

Eventually, the situation will result in your
- convincing the others that your position is right or worthy of adoption
- becoming convinced that the other person is right
- arriving at a compromise
- arriving at an impasse.

Whatever the result, it is vital that the discussion not degenerate into a verbal brawl.

Don't dwell on your victories…or your opponents may dwell on their defeats—and vice versa. If you've won the day, your next challenge will be to work with your former adversaries. Having persuaded others that your ideas are best, it's now time to lead on.

don't forget

When it all boils down, persuasion is all about:
- attracting attention
- holding attention
- providing motivation
- instilling belief
- stimulating action.

here's an idea

In presenting your case, stay SHARP…

Supercool
Honest
Assertive
Realistic
Prepared

viewpoint

"To persuade other people to feel or react as you do, you will need to…
- Set a good mood and give them sufficient reason to sit and listen to you
- Convince them that your interests and needs are similar to theirs
- Help them to see the magnitude of the problem or project
- State your intentions and objectives so they do not feel they are being manipulated
- Avoid distorting facts or suppressing key information." [12]

– Linda Swink in *Friendly Persuasion*

157

How to use body language to improve your communication

According to researchers, it's possible to 'read' bodies. We all have mannerisms that we're not even aware of, and they can send out messages to other people. Gestures, posture, head and eye movement, facial expressions, voice qualities—all provide important cues. Body language speaks volumes. Understanding the body language of other people—and being aware of your own nonverbal cues—can make you a better communicator...

Face the facts.

Effective communication depends more on *how* we send and receive rather than *what*. Although words are important, we are told that they convey only about 7 per cent of the meaning of the messages we communicate. The rate and inflection of our speech accounts for about 38 per cent of the exchange; our gestures and body signals, often unconsciously account for about 55 per cent. These nonverbal messages serve either to reinforce or contradict the message we want to send, for that reason, they deserve our attention.

Be aware of posture.

Posture can indicate boredom, interest, or even fear. If seated, sit up straight and don't cross your legs. Crossed legs and arms could be interpreted as being closed to others' ideas; both feet should be flat on the floor. Slouching can indicate low self-esteem. If standing, try not to shift body weight from one foot to the

other. When listening, lean forward slightly. Though leaning back may be a sign that you're relaxed, it also may be interpreted as disrespectful—that you are not giving the speaker your full attention. Leaning back with your hands behind your head can convey contemplation or scepticism.

Keep control of hand and arm movements.

Pay attention to your arms and hands. Arms folded across the chest can suggest that you are feeling defensive rather than receptive. Clasping your hands in your lap gives the impression that you are in control and making critical evaluations. Don't fidget, or finger your jewellery, hair, or clothing while someone else is speaking. Such actions can convey impatience, boredom, or discomfort with the subject being discussed. Never point at your listener. Pointing may indicate hostility and aggressiveness. And keep your hands off your hips or risk being seen as arrogant. If you finger your watch, squirm in your chair, or turn to face the exit, you're conveying a wish to terminate the discussion.

Avoid using flamboyant gestures.

Using your hands to emphasise a point can be effective; but, generally, hand movements should be confined to an area about the width of your body. Excessive gestures can be distracting or give the impression that you are out of control.

Make eye contact.

Eye contact suggests that you are paying attention and are at ease with the topic. Don't stare, however; staring may be interpreted as being hostile or aggressive. If you nod your head from time to time, you acknowledge you are actively listening. Note, however, that men and women interpret this body cue differently. For women, nodding means 'I'm paying attention'; for men, it usually indicates agreement.

Aristotle Onassis once admitted that he normally wore dark glasses when negotiating so that his inner thoughts would not be revealed. Indeed, researchers tell us that eyes reveal a great deal:

- Darting eyes can convey anxiousness or lack of confidence.
- A slow blink can communicate that you don't enjoy being there.
- Glancing to top right can indicate that you are imagining or making up information.

Face the listener directly.

Don't sit at an angle or face away from the other person—unless you want to appear indifferent or rude. If you're wearing glasses and look at the listener over the rim, you could be interpreted as evaluative or sceptical. A smile, of course, will show your enjoyment and pleasure.

Keep your distance.

When speaking, don't get too close; otherwise the listener may feel threatened and become defensive. Of course, that technique is all right if your intention is to intimidate. Maintain a distance that allows you to observe the listener's body language.

Use voice volume, tone, and tempo to effect.

Avoid monotone by changing the rate of speech for emphasis throughout the conversation. Also use inflection and moderate changes in pitch and volume to engage the listener's attention. An incident at the fish market, involving British writer G. K. Chesterton, illustrates the power of voice qualities. In a low, endearing voice, he told a woman waiting on him, 'You are a noun, a verb, and a preposition.' The woman blushed. After buying the fish, Chesterton said in a lecherous tone, 'And you're an adjective, an adverb, and a conjunction as well!' The woman slapped him with a flounder.

here's an idea

Just because someone is drumming their fingers on the table or tapping their foot on the floor doesn't mean they're impatient; they could simply be beating out the latest tune. The key to reading body language is: *Always think about the context in which the body language occurs and observe clusters of signals, not solitary signals.*[14] So...

Boredom is given away by a combination of crossed legs with a foot swinging, doodling, a blank stare, drumming fingers, taking deep breaths, or putting head in hands.

Disagreement might be revealed by crossed arms, accompanied by avoiding eye contact, tapping a foot, and occasionally shaking of the head (while someone whose crossed arms are accompanied by rubbing of upper arms, hunched shoulders, and stomping feet is probably just cold!).

here's an idea

Nonverbally increase your status and power by incorporating some nonverbal gymnastics into your office...

- Have a slim briefcase.
- Make sure the height of the back of your chair is higher than your visitor's.
- Have your chair higher off the floor than your visitor's.
- Leave some red folders on the desk marked 'Strictly Confidential'.
- Cover a wall with your awards or qualifications.

How to say thank you

Saying 'thank you' has been called the neglected art. Indeed, there is a reluctance among some managers to express adequate appreciation for a job well done. A few simple, well-placed thanks, however, can do wonders to improve the performance of your staff. To maximise the benefits of this powerful word, here are a few useful suggestions…

 Speak up.

Silent gratitude isn't much use to anyone; you should never mistake your warm feelings and beaming smiles for the art itself. If you express your gratitude to a colleague, though, don't cheapen the value of the well-earned thanks by mumbling the words or by being embarrassed. Think about what you're going to say and how you're going to say it. Even a simple thanks sometimes requires preparation.

 Say it—and mean it.

Every time we express sincere appreciation, we give value to the other person. Our words say, 'You are important to me and to our organisation.' Remember:

> They who thank with the lips
> Thank others but in part;
> The full, the true thanksgiving
> Comes from deep within the heart.

So say it as if you mean it—not just because you're expected to. Routine and ritualised expressions of thanks often lack any real effect.

Be specific.

A vague, sweeping 'thank you' is not nearly as effective or as flattering as a clear-cut: 'Thanks for drafting that letter to Joe Thompson, Judith. The reply was spot-on and it saved me heaps of time.' Don't leave people confused about what you're thanking them for.

Avoid implied compliments.

A salesman stitched up a major contract on which his company was not the lowest bidder. When he returned to his office, his boss expressed pleasant surprise, saying that this was the first public bid in his memory by which the company won the contract without being the lowest bidder. This implied 'thank you' only left the salesman disappointed and let down; he felt that his performance was under-valued.

Make eye-to-eye contact.

Look directly at the person you're thanking if you're serious about what you're doing. You might like to reinforce your appreciation with a casual pat on the elbow or shoulder.

 ### Thank them by name.

A generalised 'thank you, everyone' carries little weight. Be generous and thank people individually whenever possible.

 ### Surprise them.

Top managers everywhere practise daily the winning art of appreciation. They do it in offices, corridors, canteens, and carparks; over the telephone and in writing. And what they find is that thanks has much greater effect if it is given when least expected. A small surprise gift and an accompanying 'thank you' from the manager makes an employee feel appreciated.

 ### Thank them in writing.

It was Lee Iacocca who said: 'When I must criticise somebody, I do it orally; when I thank somebody, I put it in writing.'

Thanks is even more effective in writing: oral praise fades away; a letter or brief note endures.

Consider producing sets of folded 'thank-you cards' on which the words *Thank You* are printed on the front, with space on the inside for your comments. Whenever a colleague or employee warrants your gratitude, write a brief note expressing your appreciation. Certificates of appreciation or plaques are other alternatives of lasting value to an employee.

 ### Do it in public.

People usually appreciate the thanks if you acknowledge their individual efforts in front of their colleagues. When people feel they matter, morale is high. When extra effort is recognised publicly, self-esteem soars.

 ### Know the person.

With experience, you will get to know the different ways your various staff members like to be thanked. Some like public appreciation; others don't. Some appreciate flowers or chocolates; others prefer a written note of thanks. Consider your options; consider your people.

 ### Be creative.

The ways in which you can thank someone are limited only by your imagination. Saying thanks can be just as much fun for you as it is for the recipient of your gratitude.

161

How to say no

In difficult times, managers are often called on to exercise their powers of veto. Saying 'yes' is so much easier—it's certainly so much less confrontationalist and unpleasant. But managers often have to say 'no'—to proposed expenditures, to the call for extra staff, and to new ideas and other proposals from staff. There is a right way to say 'no' and to minimise the rejection or disappointment that may result...

Know when to say no.

No is a powerful word. Here's when you might want to use it, suggests motivational writer John Milne...

☐ *Say* No *to allow you to define your priorities.* Consider international speaker Dr James Dobson. He had to say no to hundreds of speaking invitations that were taking him away from his family.

☐ *Say* No *to take control of your time.* Control this precious resource by saying a selective, definite no to those meetings and invitations that consume your valuable time but produce little.

☐ *Say* No *to maintain integrity.* Men and women of integrity have to say no to temptations that threaten their personal or professional beliefs or codes of ethics.

☐ *Say* No *if the cost or risk is too high.* You might need courage to say no in meetings where ideas involving unacceptable risks or imposing too high a price are presented.

☐ *Say* No *to allow you to say* Yes. By having the courage to say no to some things, you allow yourself the benefits of saying yes to finer, more productive, more lasting activities and experiences.

☐ *Say* No *to provide breathing space.* Saying no to an idea or proposal can provide a constructive 'waiting period' for timing or conditions to be more opportune.

'No can be a gloriously positive word,' says Milne, 'as well as a negative retort. And don't forget that there are many circumstances when it's important to remember that No *isn't forever!'* [17]

Be courteous in considering a request.

If you want to maintain your dignity and to prevent the discussion from degenerating into a shouting match, remember to be polite, pleasant, and courteous throughout the conversation. As a rule, if you are courteous and polite, most people will copy your behaviour.

Listen to the proposal.

People expect their views to be heard and considered. If you refuse to listen, even if you are familiar with the arguments, you'll be asking for trouble. If you ignore what people are saying to you and off-handedly dismiss their request, you will only create animosity.

Do not procrastinate.

A delayed decision can only increase the chances of disappointment and resentment. You should try to make a quick decision. By delaying, you allow people to think you will be saying yes. So if you know what your response will be, answers such as 'I'm not sure yet' and 'Let me think about it' only get people's hopes up. And then it's even more devastating when you finally say no.

 Say no; then explain.

There's nothing wrong with saying no —but say it politely, having based the decision on a just consideration of the facts. Explain why you decided as you did. Outline the supporting inform- ation that affected the decision, and make it very clear that all the options were carefully taken into account.

 Never argue.

The disappointment or rejection can sometimes lead to heated debate, allowing people to force their views on you again rather than accept your decision. Firmly tell people that your decision is final—that you have weighed up all the facts and given justifiable reasons. And there the matter should rest.

By all means allow people to discuss your decision with you rationally, perhaps exploring alternatives; but limit their speaking time. Be fair, but always be firm. Ultimately your decision is still going to be no.

 Don't apologise.

Easier said than done, but try. You have done nothing that warrants an apology; so, having made your decision after considering all aspects, you can confidently live with the outcome. Be sympathetic, but point out that your decision was made for the good of the organisation.

 Offer a counter-proposal.

If you think it's appropriate and the request is valid, you may consider offering a counter-proposal. For example: 'I have a lot of work on my plate, Gordon, so – no – I can't sit in for you at this afternoon's meeting. But I'll be happy to answer your telephone while you're out.' Such an approach can soften your refusal.

 Follow-up.

When your refusal is accepted, don't assume that the episode is over. Depending on the degree of disappointment, you must rebuild the bridges between you and your staff member. This rebuilding helps to relieve any lingering tensions and to strengthen your hand on the next occasion.

 And, don't forget...

Expect to say no several times a day. This is your right as a manager. Then, when it happens, you shouldn't be too upset or feel guilty: you've already come to terms with this responsibility.

How to encourage feedback from your staff

Feedback provides managers with the information they need for sound decision-making. Indeed, it's important for bosses to stay in touch with their employees—that's where many winning ideas come from. As well, feedback acts as a kind of early warning system about potential problems and grievances. Unfortunately, many managers don't realise that achieving this form of upward communication requires a good deal of intelligent activity on their part…

1 Know why you need feedback from your staff.

Feedback from employees alerts you to what may be going wrong, to discrepancies between how your staff see their jobs and how you see them, to conflicts, to inadequate workflow, to deficiencies in supervision, to low morale, and to other emotional staff issues… And just as importantly, feedback lets you hear about what you're doing right, so that you can then continue in or refine these areas.

2 Tell people you want feedback and be prepared to get it.

Tell staff in various ways that you value their feedback. If necessary, specify where information is required for the good of the organisation. Your task then is to make it easy for employees to gain access to you. An 'open door policy' is one approach. Visibility and accessibility are important; so some managers prefer management-by-walking-around (MBWA). The best way to understand what's happening in the workplace is to be part of it, they argue.

3 Provide regular avenues for feedback.

More formal feedback strategies require structure, planning, and effort. Some organisations set aside certain times when top executives are available for phonecalls or visits from employees on any topic. Others train facilitators in the mechanics of information-gathering and presentation. Elsewhere, staff meetings are used for the delivery of regular oral or written status reports. Formal exit interviews with employees who resign or retire are also revealing, as are employee-opinion surveys and questionnaires. Many employees are sceptical of the value of suggestion boxes.

4 Try informal get-togethers to encourage feedback.

From time to time, informal gatherings—staff breakfasts, morning coffee conferences, parties, barbecues, dinners, and picnics—can be used effectively to stimulate the free flow of communication on work-related matters.

Show that you're serious.

Whatever strategy you adopt, a positive and interested response from you will guarantee staff acceptance and determine the quality and frequency of future feedback. So you should:

- *Listen.* Give the employee your undivided attention and the clear impression that you *are* interested in what he or she is saying.

- *Take notes.* Use a palm card or diary to take immediate notes.

- *Promote understanding through questions.* If an issue requires clarification, ask such questions as 'What did you mean when you said…?' or 'Is this what you mean…?'.

- *Encourage elaboration.* By using such leads as 'Tell me more about…', 'Tell me what you think about…' and following up with statements such as 'As I understand it, this is what you are saying…', you clarify important issues and show your interest.

- *Never react badly when you hear something amiss.* Try not to 'kill' the bearer of bad tidings. Tell staff that the only bad news is the news that is *not* communicated upwards. You need to hear both the good news *and* the bad.

- *Thank people for their feedback.*

 Obtain as much specific information as possible.

People usually tend to offer vague responses or comments. The more specific the information provided, the more useful it will be. If you intend to use the feedback to make changes to your organisation's performance or program, it will normally need to be detailed and specific.

 Communicate results.

Employees don't expect that every one of their suggestions will be adopted, but they do expect that, at some stage, you will give reasonable consideration to their comments. If employees' suggestions *are* acted on, let them know—and such feedback will be more effective if made publicly in the presence of colleagues. As well, commendation is a powerful motivator for encouraging feedback from others.

 Stay clear of unprofessional issues.

At times, you will no doubt receive feedback through the company grapevine. When this feedback takes the form of malicious gossip, indicate that you do not want to become involved in unprofessional issues and unproductive behaviour. Your assertive stance may encourage employees to reassess the quality of grapevine communications.

 don't forget

How feedback should be given…

Do your staff members know how and when to give you feedback – particularly how and when to let you know if something's gone wrong in the organisation?

If brought to the attention of your staff, the following guidelines from the US Bureau of Business Practice will make your life easier:

• *Report the problem promptly.* Telling me right away will often allow me to solve the problem before it gets worse.

• *Give me only the necessary facts.* Overstating the problem could make it look worse than it is. Think it through before you report and be ready to explain exactly and objectively what happened.

• *Use tact.* Don't say 'We've got a terrible problem on our hands'. Instead, say something like 'Here's something I thought you should know about'.

• *Offer a solution.* Don't just tell me we've got a problem. Recommend a way to correct a mistake or an error in judgement or a predicament, and provide suggestions on how you'll prevent it from happening again.

• *Don't deliver only bad news.* Pass along the good news as well. That way, when you do have bad news, I'll take it better and your suggestions for improvement will have more impact.[21]

165

How to give feedback

Feedback is a powerful management process. If used effectively, it will maintain or improve your employees' output and, in turn, improve the overall performance of the organisation. Employees want feedback because it helps them learn about themselves and their performance. To provide effective feedback—positive or negative—consider these guidelines…

research says

Research shows that effective feedback leads to increased employee performance. Feedback can help subordinates set and achieve goals. Adequate provision of feedback from a trusted superior also seems to be related to the level of communication satisfaction and workplace commitment felt by employees.[22]

don't forget

Four feedback tips…

■ The more immediate the feedback, the better. Choose the shortest practical interval – daily if possible – but no longer than a week.

■ Individual feedback is more effective than group feedback. If you can't get data on each person's performance, at least get data for the smallest possible group.

■ Acknowledge group performance publicly, for example on notice boards. This increases reinforcement amongst members of the group and encourages positive remarks from outsiders.

■ Resist the temptation to compare one performer with another.[23]

1 Provide feedback continually.

Whether informal, on-the-run comments or formal performance reviews, feedback will be less traumatic and more effective if it is given continually. Continuity of reporting is essential.

2 Provide immediate feedback if possible.

Feedback will have maximum effect if given while the behaviour is fresh in the minds of both parties. The most powerful feedback is given when you actually catch someone doing the right or wrong thing. Delayed feedback should occur only if it would embarrass the employee in front of others or if you require further information.

3 Be specific.

The more specific you can be with examples, the more telling the feedback will be. For instance, it would be inadequate to tell an employee that 'Your manners leave a lot to be desired'. But if the person was told, 'I was disappointed at this morning's committee meeting when you kept talking while I was speaking', the person could take some purposeful action to correct that behaviour.

4 Be descriptive, not evaluative.

Describe behaviour in observable terms, rather than use emotional, judgemental language. Refer to the observable fact that the employee 'missed four deadlines last month'. Don't use words like 'lazy, slack, and irresponsible' (even though you might like to). Labelling and character attacks only inflame the situation. Such judgements are merely your opinion anyway—you might be wrong!

5 Focus only on things that can be changed.

Some things about an employee can't be changed—such as personality, or physical features, intelligence, speech impediments, shyness, left-handedness, and poor complexion. So don't focus on such aspects unless they are somehow affecting the work environment. Concentrate instead on those areas where change can be brought about—output, writing style, dress, untidiness in the workplace, or behaviour.

Adjust feedback to individual needs.

Individual employees differ in their approach to feedback. Most people appreciate positive feedback; high performers usually like a good deal of it. Some employees are scarred for life by negative feedback; others simply reject all feedback if any of it is negative. You must learn to match the content and timing of feedback to the individual and the situation.

Try not to mix positive and negative messages.

When you have negative feedback to impart, do not sandwich it between positive introductory comments and glowing statements of appreciation at the end. This technique only dilutes the importance of the negative message and sometimes sends a mixed and confusing signal to the employee.

Ensure feedback is always constructive.

When used as a weapon rather than as a tool for improving performance, feedback can be very destructive. Both parties should see negative feedback as an important component of performance improvement and the ongoing review process. Here, the concept of 'feedforward' is gaining

new life as a performance review tool. Unlike feedback, which assesses staff by past performances, feedforward involves helping employers to anticipate potential situations and problems.[24]

 And don't forget...

■ See feedback as encouragement. Whether you're giving constructive criticism or positive reinforcement, your message should be: 'I know you can do better and that you want to do better—and I know I can help you do better.' In this way, every time staff hear from you, especially if your feedback indicates progress and growth, they will be motivated and encouraged.

■ Make sure the employee is actually listening. Feedback not heeded is feedback wasted.

■ Make sure the feedback is understood. If necessary, check for understanding.

■ Guard against any hint of the 'I am better than you' syndrome which communicates your superiority in knowledge, wisdom, or power.

■ Be alert for an employee asking for feedback. It's easier to feed a hungry person.

■ Feedback calls for objectivity. Don't communicate if you're upset, angry, or hurt.

■ Give the employee the opportunity to discuss the issue and to explore how the behaviour might be further modified. After all, feedback should be part of the employee's learning experience.

■ Use the giving process as an opportunity to seek feedback yourself. The process is facilitated if you demonstrate that *you* are open to feedback.

How to set up an employee suggestion scheme

More than anyone else, your employees have ideas on how to improve your services, processes, and products, and the way your organisation is run. The trick is to get them to speak up and to accept that management cares and is prepared to listen to, and indeed reward, good ideas that might increase productivity, cut costs, or improve working conditions. If you want to install a workable employee suggestion program, consider the following advice...

1 Consider the value of a suggestion scheme.

A well-implemented staff suggestion scheme can not only encourage staff involvement, leading to improved motivation and morale, but also result in greater efficiency and cost savings throughout the organisation. The scheme can create a workplace in which innovation and creativity flourish. It can allow staff at all levels, who often see problems and solutions that management does not, to feel valued in helping to improve the way the organisation is run.

2 Review the merits of proven schemes.

Larger organisations should identify and consider the merits of successful schemes elsewhere before deciding on a workable approach to adopt or adapt. For example:

■ Com-Corp Industries has installed 'Screw-up Boxes' to encourage staff to tell management when something's wrong. Comments, complaints, and questions are posted on bulletin boards together with management's responses.

■ On its annual Ideas Day, staff at the US Department of Energy in Washington examine ways to improve customer service, streamline work processes, and enhance the working environment. Recently, 2,134 ideas were gathered—and 68 per cent of them were implemented.

■ A few years ago, Rosenbluth International sought ideas as part of 'Operation Brainstorm'. Over 400 cost-saving ideas were received—and they saved the company from laying off staff.

■ Freightliner Corp supplies staff with yellow and blue preprinted Post-it note pads. Any employee with a workplace problem fills out a yellow note describing the issue and posts it on one of the special boards throughout the plant. Anyone with a suggestion for solving the problem fills out a blue note and places it on a board in response.

■ Valeo Autoparts expects each employee to make 10 suggestions each year, guaranteeing that each will be responded to within 10 days. Annually, 250,000 suggestions are received!

3 Decide on a few basics.

In setting up a scheme, give some thought to the following:

• Give the scheme a name—it will help in publicising the initiative.

- Decide whether this is to be an ongoing activity, or limited to certain periods.
- Determine the format of the scheme—suggestion boxes, formal face-to-face meetings, noticeboard strategies, etc.
- Devise a strategy for assessing ideas and rewarding staff appropriately.
- Consider testing the procedures by using a small pilot scheme.

4 Publicise the scheme.

Publicise the scheme fully before it starts, and keep it fresh in every employee's mind through periodic reminders. Initial publicity should spell out the advantages for staff and the organisation and dispel any reluctance staff may have to become involved. Include details of the scheme as part of staff induction; use posters or leaflets on noticeboards, and articles in newsletters, including details of 'winners' and ideas implemented.

Make it clear that any idea is welcome and that employees need not worry about the fine details of implementation, which will be considered when the panel weighs up the merits of the suggestion.

By all means publicise the formal system, but remember that some employees won't take the time to fill out official forms; others may be more comfortable calling at a superior's office to present an idea in person. Tell staff that ideas will be accepted anytime, anywhere, in any form.

5 Develop workable assessment procedures.

Establish a small representative panel drawn from all levels to oversee the scheme and to assess each suggestion. In this regard:

- Compile a set of assessment guidelines on such issues as the originality of the idea, the ease of its introduction, an estimate of its implementation costs, the benefits to the organisation, and so on.
- Weed out bad ideas early. Be sure that those left are not only 'good' ideas, but also 'do-able'.
- The panel coordinator should review each suggestion first. You don't want the panel to debate the merits of an idea if it's not worthy of debate.
- The panel can then promptly explore each feasible idea before finally recommending implementation, or briefly explaining why it can't be done.
- Insist that all ideas submitted be individually acknowledged, even those that can't be used, so that your staff will know their efforts are appreciated.
- Publicise widely any idea used and its positive effect on the organisation.

6 Recognise and reward good suggestions.

If an idea saves money or generates increased profits, give the employee whose idea it was a slice of the profits. Eastman Kodak in New York, for example, gave out $3 million each year to staff members for suggestions used. Alternatively, provide gifts or awards, even a prestigous 'Suggestion of the Year Award'.

7 Evaluate the scheme.

Over time, evaluate the scheme by examining such items as:

number of suggestions made, types of ideas offered, number taken up and implemented, costs incurred, savings made, increases in efficiency, rewards offered, awards made, problems evident, staff reaction, etc.

Make improvements accordingly.

169

How to make best use of the grapevine

Rumours and gossip are an inevitable part of everyday life at work. Your organisation's informal communication network, the grapevine, draws groups together because of their common interests, fears, and shared beliefs. Indeed, it is a perfectly natural organisational phenomenon that fulfils the members' desire to be 'in the know'. If left unattended, however, malicious rumours on the grapevine can be very destructive. Conversely, properly managed, the grapevine can be used to your advantage...

1 Understand why rumours begin.

Your organisation's grapevine is very active and carries large amounts of information, at times inaccurate, with amazing speed. To deal with it, you must first know the conditions in your organisation fostering the spread of rumours:

- lack of information and news
- anxiety
- faulty information
- prolonged delays in decision-making
- a feeling by staff that they cannot control circumstances
- serious problems in the organisation
- personal antagonisms.

2 Assess the importance of any rumour.

Before planning counter-measures, assess first the potential damage a particular rumour might cause. Often it is best ignored. Ask: 'What would happen if I did nothing?' If the spreading rumour is damaging, however, confer with the people primarily affected by it; assure them of your concern; and reveal your plans to combat the story. Move quickly to debunk the rumour by presenting the facts.

3 Combat misinformation— call a meeting.

It's always best to communicate face to face if possible. Written messages or those relayed by a third party aren't always understood. Conduct small-group meetings with staff or the community if necessary. Present the facts. This candid approach also provides instant feedback and an opportunity to clarify the situation immediately through questions and answers.

4 Adopt a positive stance.

Don't risk reinforcing the rumour by restating it. Try to avoid references to it when disseminating the facts. Never be defensive. Most people can sense when someone is masking the truth or clouding an issue in an attempt to dissipate a problem simply because it is unpleasant. Respond calmly and reasonably with details to destroy the credibility of those who would make irresponsible statements regardless of consequences. Hide nothing if you have nothing to hide.

Encourage people to call you.

If staff hear something injurious to the organisation or a departure from its policy, encourage them, through your newsletters and staff meetings, to contact you immediately.

Keep key players on side.

Stay in constant touch with key subordinates and opinion-leaders. Their friendship can be valuable when people are needed to support your position in a crisis. On such occasions, meet with those people and solicit their assistance to spread the truth via the grapevine.

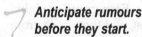

Anticipate rumours before they start.

Probable staff, customer, or client concerns should be anticipated and defused *before* they ever become a hot grapevine item. Meet with key people; give them the real story; and guide their thinking. They can then spread the facts before anyone else can spread the rumours.

Communicate.

Very few of your staff think they get all the information they need.

The grapevine is most active when information is scarce and demand for it is high. But when people believe that they are being kept informed of every detail of your organisation's operation—maybe even more than they want—the thirst for additional data from others is quenched.

Learn to use the grapevine yourself.

Alert leaders acknowledge the grapevine's existence and try to take advantage of it. For example:

- Tune in to it and learn what people are thinking and feeling.
- Feed it yourself using trusted colleagues, opinion leaders, and company advocates.
- Mention some planned change in company routine; then wait to see what reaction occurs.
- Feed good news into the system before it is officially released. This way you get a double effect: first, a good rumour increases morale; later, the official confirmation provides another boost.

Learn to live with the grapevine.

Don't try to kill the rumour mill—that's futile. It will always exist. Devote your energy instead to knowing what's on it, taking appropriate action, and fostering conditions within your company which do not fuel the fire of rumour-mongering.

---

here's an idea

Use the grapevine for a good purpose. A compliment a person hears is never as exciting as the one s/he *overhears*. A great way to praise is not via the telephone or even face-to-face, but rather via *tell-a-friend*. This way you escape possible criticism that you're a back-scratching sycophant trying to win brownie points. You also leave the recipient with the happy fantasy that you're telling the whole world about their greatness.

research says

If yours is a large organisation, and if you worry about staff gossips and the vitality of your grapevine, then may be you shouldn't.

According to researchers at Goldsmith's College at London University, having 'a good old gossip' about colleagues and bosses can relieve tension or anxiety and boost morale in the workplace. Idle chatter often makes staff feel better about their job and those they work with, especially in organisations undergoing change or upheaval.

What is important for leaders, however, is that they have strategies for dealing with such grapevines when they become malicious or outlandish.

How to conduct a gripe session

don't forget

There is a difference

A *gripe* is an informal complaint, which, if not dealt with appropriately, may soon become a grievance.

A *grievance* is a formal complaint which usually is based upon the violation of company policy.

here's an idea

So you have chronic gripers on staff? The best way to minimise their annoying and time-consuming activities is to pay more attention to them. Often, they simply crave to be the centre of attention. Talk to them, ask for their opinion, praise their work – and you will usually satisfy their need for attention and give them less reason to complain.

Griping occurs in most groups at various times, but its existence in your organisation should not necessarily be interpreted as a personal criticism of your management style. Constant complaining indicates the likelihood of perceived problems, the presence of negative energy that needs to be redirected and refocused, and opportunities to use those gripes to bring about meaningful changes. Here's how you can derive maximum benefit by having your staff air their gripes...

 Learn to capitalise on complaints.

Gripes can be blessings in disguise, alerting you to existing and potential (and imagined) problem areas. If particular kinds of gripes are common among your employees, some company procedures or practices may need changing; or they may be precursors to other gripes. Regard all complaints—including employees' gripes—as springboards to better performance. You will probably become so sensitive to employees' needs that you will know their complaints almost before they make them.

 Adopt a structured approach.

Gripes can indicate the existence of group problems that can inhibit organisational development. Never try to apply a bandaid or cover up. Instead, embrace a proactive, structured strategy by, first, assembling a group comprising those with gripes and any others with an interest in hearing and acting on them.

 List the gripes.

In a group situation, have people work alone and compile lists of gripes. Then have individuals form pairs and compile combined lists. Similar gripes are rewritten to form descriptions satisfying both people. Pairs then form into fours and continue the process. Fours then become eights. Each group of eight presents its list, and the whole group then produces one list representing all contributions. Number each item for ease of reference.

Categorise the list.

Classify the list into four categories based on the control the group has over individual complaints. A useful classification is this:

- *Acts of God*—those over which we have no control and will have to learn to live with.

- *Acts of lesser gods*—those we will probably have to live with. But at least we can let those gods know the group's feeling.
- *Shared issues*—those we share with others (organisations, divisions, or departments) and can resolve in cooperation with them.
- *Individual issues*—those that are ours alone and that can be remedied immediately.

Save time by listing numbers against the items in each category.

Address each category.

Have the group assign actions to each complaint in each category:

- *For the 'God given' category*, write statements in the form of, 'Learning to live with...'. Acknowledging the problem is all anyone can do about it.
- *For the 'lesser gods' category*, the group might decide to draft a letter or memo to be signed by all members and directed to the persons responsible. They will have alerted others to the problem; the ball is then in the others' court.
- *For 'shared issues'*, the group decides which of those it wants to address. Meetings with the identified 'others' are arranged for a time when each party can devote full attention to solving the problems. So this step might have to be postponed until the fourth-category issues have been addressed.
- *For individual issues*, the focus

is on those items that the group considers it can work on independently. By using a simple voting procedure to establish priority (see page 270), the group can work its way down the list. In the process, actions should be assigned to individuals.

Develop plans for action.

Action plans are best constructed in matrix form listing goals, timetables, expense allocation, individual responsibilities, and support persons. The action plans should be reviewed regularly and individuals held accountable for their completion. Ensure that members are satisfied that all items on the list have been adequately addressed. The first draft of the plans should be returned to participants within three days of the workshop. Encourage a 24-hour turnaround on corrections so that completed plans can be delivered to participants the next day. For credibility, strike while the iron is hot.

And don't forget...

Don't limit your handling of employee gripes to group sessions alone. As a manager, it's easy to forget about employees who do not have any complaints; they may be silent for a reason. If you have employees who never complain, make a point of meeting with them once a month to review their workloads and any workplace concerns they might have.

How to criticise other people constructively

No-one likes to be criticised—even justified criticism has the potential to demoralise. But sometimes managers have no other choice; indeed, not critising errant behaviour is often worse than criticising it. But you can criticise staff so that they actually feel good when you've finished. It's a very complex management skill that can be learned, particularly if you view criticism as an investment in a colleague's future...

1 Know when and where to criticise.

Criticism should follow errant behaviour as soon as possible, while the experience is fresh in the transgressor's mind and before anxieties begin to fester or the mistake is repeated. Except in emergencies, such as when a factory worker endangers the life of others, criticise in private, where interruptions can be minimised. If possible, allow for a second contact later in the day, when you can show by your amicability that your regard for the individual has not diminished.

2 Know why you are criticising.

Before confronting the person, know the real reasons for your criticism and make sure they're valid. Are you criticising to let off steam, to put people in their place, or to show someone who's boss? Or are you criticising for valid reasons—to motivate to greater effort, to indicate how performance is being judged, or to prevent the recurrence of a particular behaviour?

3 Get to the root of the problem... but first gather your facts.

Find out what went wrong, when and how, before you talk to the person. If you are sure of your facts before you criticise, your criticism will be more convincing. And don't forget to investigate the 'why' and the 'who': it might not be the fault of the person you think is to blame. Or the fault may be shared.

4 Be prepared to criticise the act, not the person.

If you get personal and accuse someone of 'having a poor attitude towards work' or of 'being an irresponsible and lazy employee', he or she can take offence and become defensive; you could buy into a heated argument. Instead, stick to the *facts* and the *evidence* of the behaviour you want to change—lateness for work, rudeness to customers, failure to meet deadlines, and so on. People can more easily change their behaviour than their personalities, so they will be more responsive to your message if you focus on the facts.

State your concerns as you see them.

Confront the person and share, from your perspective, all information relevant to your criticism. Listen to the other side of the story... but you can't go any further until you both agree that a problem exists and you are sure that the person understands clearly what you find objectionable.

 Make your expectations clear.

Although some mistakes are stupid and sometimes you have to make a superhuman effort to avoid sarcasm or invective, the only valid purposes of criticism are positive. Having both agreed that a problem exists, you now can show that you want to help the person you're criticising. Seek his or her own ideas for improvement. Discuss what can be done to rectify the errant behaviour. Don't leave the person confused about what action is required.

 Provide back-up support.

Providing support is a way of re-establishing your confidence in the person and that person's confidence in you. You need not re-open the topic (unless it is raised again by your colleague); nor should you nag. Simply keep in touch and be available to help if needed.

 And remember...

Here are a few more important suggestions to keep in mind when next you must criticise another person:

- Do not use humour; too often it is mistaken for sarcasm.

- Never criticise personal matters, such as drinking habits or home life. Relate such transgressions only to the effect they may be having on performance in the workplace.

- Never criticise when you're angry: you need to be calm, rational, and objective. Never act in haste. Never raise your voice. Never let the discussion turn into an old-fashioned chewing-out or tongue-lashing—which simply crushes egos, creates tension, triggers hostility, and generates aggression.

- Try to create a climate of reasonableness in which your colleague will be encouraged to work with you against the common foe: a fault.

- Commend before you criticise. By prefacing your criticism with an honest compliment, you are assuring your colleague that you still think highly of him or her, and you indicate that you view the errant act as an atypical departure from the norm. With this implied assurance, your colleague is likely to be more receptive to what you say.

- You'll make the criticism much easier for the other person to accept if you share at least some of the responsibility for the mistake.

- View criticism as an opportunity for you to learn as well, for you may indeed be part of the problem.

- Finally, never forget that the act of criticism often strips the tree of both caterpillars and blossoms.

 smile & ponder

Two taxidermists stopped before a shop window in which an owl was displayed.

They immediately began to criticise the way it was mounted. Its eyes were not natural; its wings were not in proportion with its head; its beak was too pointed; its feathers were not neatly arranged; and its feet were too small...

When they had finished with their criticism, the owl turned its head – and winked at them.

◼ Until we know all, we should not pass judgement at all. As Benjamin Disraeli once said: It's so much easier to be critical than to be correct.

 here's an idea

If criticism isn't constructive, it will do more harm than good – the employee will resent your comments and you, as the manager, will lose a valuable opportunity to teach the employee something.

For this reason, every time you have to criticise a staff member, write down at least two suggestions on how that employee might fix the problem at hand or improve performance. Take those ideas with you to the meeting and focus your attention on them, rather than the criticism itself.

How to communicate with someone who doesn't speak your language well

here's an idea

Depending on the nature of your workplace, if you've taken on an employee who doesn't speak or read your language, that employee's safety should be a major legal concern.

If training is to be given in safe use of work tools, work equipment, lifting, and dangerous substances, then the use of multi-language posters and instruction booklets, internationally recognised safety language, and the use of bi-lingual workmates and interpreters for instruction and follow-up evaluation, is a must. By not implementing these measures, you may be breaching your legal duty of care.

Yours could be a dangerous work environment for employees who lack fluency in the base language. A risk audit could be a good starting point.

As managers increasingly employ people from diverse cultural backgrounds and pursue global markets, they will inevitably be required to communicate across language barriers. Learning to speak the languages of one or two other countries would certainly help but would never eliminate the problem. Here are some helpful hints to increase your flexibility when having to communicate with someone from a foreign culture…

Do your homework.

If you have advance warning of an important meeting, find out all you can about expected attendees—their cultures, their languages, their companies. No one expects you to be an expert, but you could buy a book on the culture and language of the other country. You will impress your guests or hosts when they see that you have made the effort. Although interpreters may be available, think carefully about introducing a third party—particularly without the consent of the people you are planning to meet.

Test for understanding.

The people you are meeting may have developed 'survival skills' and may use common phrases in your language. Ask them whether they do—either in your language or theirs. You can, of course, create a favourable impression if you at least attempt to use their language, even in the most elementary way. Many books are available containing the most commonly used sentences and phrases.

Be patient.

Meeting and communicating will be equally as challenging for the other person, so progress slowly to avoid confusion and frustration. Remember, most meaning will be communicated nonverbally; impatience will be easily detected. The speed at which you progress will be dictated by the other person, and you will become aware of that speed if you're patient.

Note the responses.

The response to your communication will indicate the meaning the other person attaches to what you've said. If the response is not what you expect, your message has probably not been understood. Begin again, speaking slowly and clearly, making certain that you do not raise your voice.

Avoid jokes.

An attempt at humour may be misunderstood; it may even be taken as a joke at the expense of the other person. Seek eye contact with him or her, smile, use open-hand gestures, mirror posture, but never attempt to provide comedy. When in doubt—don't.

 Chunk-down.

Break instructions into smaller, more manageable pieces. Provide the information slowly enough for it to be understood. It is far better to get your communication right the first time than to have to repeat it.

 Seek feedback.

Don't be afraid to stop occasionally and ask, 'Do you understand what I am saying?' or 'Is what I am saying clear?' A blank response will convey information about the meaning attached to your communication efforts. Remember, response is meaning.

 Be aware of your nonverbal messages.

You can't not communicate, so ensure that your nonverbal messages—gestures, eye contact, use of space—harmonise with your message. All people are acutely aware of incongruence between what is said and what is communicated non-verbally. Remember too that, in some Asian countries, making eye contact could be considered disrespectful.

Staring or pointing could also be regarded as offensive. And in some countries, our simple thumbs-up signal for 'A-OK' is an obscene gesture. Be aware!

 Avoid the no-no's.

If you've done your homework, you will be aware of some of the 'no-nos' for particular cultural groups. Avoid our jargon and slang, and certain topics of conversation—religion, politics, and personal issues.

As well, interaction can be difficult. We can sometimes be seen as rude, pushy, assertive, and impatient. In other cultures, people may prefer to hint at what they mean, will not communicate bad news or rejection, and will tell you what they think you want to hear rather than what they actually believe. Competition is valued in some cultures, collaboration in others. It is difficult to encourage people to behave in ways that contradict their cultural conditioning. Be prepared to learn, adapt, and adjust.

 Consider taking lessons.

If you find that expanding business interests require you to hold frequent meetings with business people whose first language is different from yours, or if many of your employees are from another country, consider learning their language and their culture. You will be pleasantly surprised at the developments that have occurred in language teaching—even since your school days. So try it.

 quotable quote

Instead of examining people's external characteristics (where they come from and what they look like), we need to explore their underlying values because the real reward in diversity is learning to work effectively with people who think differently than we do…

As managers we're encouraged to be straight-forward and offer constructive criticism. Well, if we're managing people with that same value, there is no problem. But suppose we're managing people who value indirectness. To them, saving face can be very important; straightforward criticism, even politely offered, can be humiliating…

Understanding those values and observing the behaviour that reflects them will make you a better manager.[30]

 don't forget

Do's and Don'ts

If a non-English speaking person cannot understand your words or your accent:

- Do be patient.
- Do speak more slowly than normal, use simple words and avoid slang.
- Don't try to imitate the other person's limited use of the language (e.g. by speaking 'broken English').
- Don't raise your voice and speak louder, as if the other person is disabled.[31]

How to handle a media interview

The press and broadcasting media can offer great opportunities to publicise a positive aspect of your organisation. They can also cause problems and create embarrassment when they find that something has gone wrong. These are the two sides of the media coin—and you must be prepared for both. So you could find yourself talking to journalists when you send out a press release and the media respond to it, or when the media themselves have nosed out a story about your company. Are you prepared to cope with such interviews? The following suggestions will help…

Know the medium.

When providing an interview for any medium, it's important to know its peculiarities. Newspapers cover stories in greater depth, need more background material, and seek human-interest items with local angles. Television newsrooms rarely send crews on good-news stories without first making an appointment; but they can disconcertingly arrive unannounced when something more sensational breaks. Television is an immediate visual medium. Radio news does not have the visual impact of television but commands a larger audience. Radio interviews take various forms—a notebook interview (information sought for a story to be read on air), tape-recorded (for replay later), or talkback (live to air).

Be clear about the purpose of the interview.

When invited to be interviewed, ask about the context—What is the issue? Why ask me?—and about the format. Will the interview be live or recorded?

For news or for a magazine feature or program? Studio-based or on the run? If time permits, study the style of the interviewer. Is it likely to be a relaxed, entertaining, or difficult session? What will be its duration? Know what you are letting yourself in for so that you can prepare adequately.

Do your homework.

Preparation is the key to performing well. Never go into an interview without thinking about what you might say. If necessary, tell a radio interviewer that you'll ring back in ten minutes; or ask a TV journalist for a few moments to think the issue through before the camera rolls. Focus on three or four main points and how you intend to make them simply and clearly. Check your facts and figures: it's too late after the event.

Get your message across.

Most encounters with the media should be pleasant, even exhilarating.

The important thing is to appear confident, positive, friendly, and interesting—whether you are promoting a success story or dealing with controversy. Consider these points:

- Be helpful and informative, never dismissive or patronising, if dealing with a reporter whose knowledge of the issue seems less than adequate.
- Keep it simple. Stick to the three or four points you want to make and, if the interviewer is not asking the right questions, lead him or her back to your points.
- For radio or TV, find out the first question in advance so that you can prepare a crisp initial response.
- Remember, radio and TV programs don't have time for lengthy statements. Keep your answers short, relevant, and to the point. Practise giving a 30-second grab; make your points in that time.
- Don't be hoodwinked into accepting views that you do not hold. Don't be bluffed, intimidated, or bullied; remain polite, firm, and cool.
- Be prepared for the curly question. If you are concerned that the interview might stray into delicate areas, make the interview conditional on the reporter's keeping within agreed parameters.

5 Look and act the part.

Expect to be a little nervous in radio or television interview situations. Breathe slowly and deeply to relax. Speak clearly and confidently but naturally. Avoid 'ums' and 'ahs' and other annoying vocal mannerisms. Check your appearance for television—you should be neat,

tidy, and conservatively dressed. Focus on the interviewer and forget the microphone, camera, and lights— they're someone else's problem. But remember, microphones can pick up anything—rustling papers, moving chairs, dropped pencils, and whispered asides.

6 Beware of the traps of defamation and litigation.

Take the utmost care when making statements about other people or organisations. If you utter a defamatory statement that appears in any form, you, as well as the media outlet, can be sued. If there is any chance of an official enquiry or litigation, be careful what you say in public. Obtain advice beforehand if necessary.

7 Consider your options if something goes wrong.

Often, your story will not be reported in the media as you expected. You might be misinterpreted, misquoted, or taken out of context. Try not to nitpick. But if it's a serious mistake, damaging to you or the company, contact the editor of the publication or the station involved. Consider your options: an apology, a printed retraction, or a follow-up story to remedy the first. Seek an harmonious solution.

8 Foster sound relations with the media.

Work to cultivate cordial and co-operative relations with the media. They can do much to enhance your public image and your organisation's.

> **❝ quotable quote**
>
> The essence of gaining the best coverage from any situation – positive or negative, planned or unexpected – is to know what to expect, anticipate the questions, and then control the interview. In addition, identifying the many potential pitfalls and how to neatly sidestep them, will give you a better chance of getting your message across – not necessarily the angle the media may be pursuing.[33]

💡 here's an idea

American Speaker provides this advice for when you face the video camera:

■ *Always use makeup.* A camera balances all the shades, hues and intensities of colour and lighting on the set. That means your face may look washed out, lines emphasised and dark spots under your eyes exaggerated.

■ *Control your expressions and movements.* Much of the time you're on camera, all the audience will see is your face, so your expressions are emphasised.

■ *Use your gestures to good advantage.* Gestures can enliven your appearance on TV. But a small gesture goes a long way.

■ *Exude energy and enthusiasm.* It may seem like an impossible mission with all that's going on around you, but energy can do wonders to make you more interesting to watch.

179

How to become a better writer

The ability to express oneself clearly on paper and to write effective reports, memos, letters, and other business documents is one of a manager's most important skills. But some managers find it difficult to write clearly, concisely, and convincingly. Others take far longer than necessary to complete a written assignment. No matter whether your task is a letter, memo, report or novel, you can become a better writer if you follow this advice...

1 Prepare yourself.

Before you begin to write, consider these three key issues:

☐ *Know precisely the purpose of your writing task.*
You must first be clear about the purpose of your task. Ask yourself: What do I want the reader to think, do, or know? The more specific you can be with your answers, the easier it will be for you to plan your writing.

☐ *Know your reader.*
Reading is a solo activity, so you must imagine you are writing to one reader at a time. Strike an appropriate balance between the formal and the casual approach. No matter how impressive your writing may seem to you, your reader will be the final judge.

☐ *Know the image you want to project personally.*
Are you trying to be helpful, formal, objective, appreciative, apologetic, caring, confident...? Try to be whatever you want to be.

2 Plan your approach.

Organise your thoughts, ideas, and information before choosing words and constructing sentences. If you spend time planning and drafting an outline, particularly if you have to write something lengthy, you will eventually save considerable time and energy. So it's essential first to assemble your ideas into a logical structure before attempting to clothe your ideas in words.

3 Write your first draft.

Having formed a clear picture of your reader, your purpose, and the initial outline of your document, you can now begin your first draft. It's important to get something written as soon as possible, even though you might scrap it later. So don't feel you must start at the beginning—if you find the beginning difficult, start somewhere else. The important thing at this stage is to get words on paper (or a computer screen). Focus here on *what* is said, not on *how* it is being said. Most people are too critical of themselves at this stage, and that criticism becomes a major obstacle. Trust the writing process more: it does not have to start out right, only end that way—and the next step helps to achieve that objective.

 Polish your product.

Under no circumstances should you consider the first draft of your document to be the final version. Even the best of writers rework and revise their written material. The number of times you do so depends on your skill as a writer and the importance of the document. The more times you revisit your work, the tighter, more polished, and more effective it should become. Remember, good writing is really rewriting.

Here, then, are the strategies to help polish your draft to perfection:

- *Leave the draft for a while* before revising it. Revisiting the material 'cold' will help you see it from a reader's perspective.

- *Underline the main points* to check that you have actually said everything you intended to say. You may well change the order of ideas once you see how they appear to the reader.

- *Read it aloud*. Anything you find awkward or tedious to speak will be equally so for your readers to read.

- *Check the big words:* if they're not precise in meaning, replace them with shorter, clearer ones. Check

every sentence: if it's possible for a reader to get lost in one, break it down into shorter sentences. Check spelling, grammar, and punctuation.

- *Criticise the content severely.* Are the facts correct? Are they relevant? Do the conclusions follow logically? Can anything be left out? Have you countered any likely objections?

- *Obtain criticism from a colleague* if the task is important and if time permits.

 Develop your own style.

Over time, you will refine your methods and create variations that make your style unique, as distinctive as your own personality. But you will do well to remember these basics:

- Be concise. Eliminate the unnecessary. Make every word count. Get to the point.

- Vary sentence length, structure, and beginnings. As a rule, keep sentences short.

- Use familiar, concrete words. Write to express, not impress.

- Write naturally, using the words you typically use when speaking.

- Convert sentences from passive to active voice.

- Use transition words to link ideas and increase readability— 'In addition…', 'Thus…', 'Conversely…', 'Therefore'…

- Write for your reader, not for yourself.

 here's an idea

If you're at your computer (or you're staring at a sheet of blank paper) and can't seem to put thoughts into words, try this: Talk to a colleague or call a friend and simply explain what you're writing about. You'll be surprised at how easily the words will spill off your lips when you're not obsessed with proper style. Then get back to writing.

 here's an idea

■ In all your written work, whether it be a letter, article, or essay, say something meaningful in the very first sentence.
■ Distil each paragraph into one sentence. Include that sentence in the paragraph.

 read further

One of the most common problems facing writers of books, letters, or reports is choosing the right words… Is it *affect* or *effect, that* or *which, will* or *shall, imply* or *infer, lend* or *loan, instil* or *instill?*

Do you have access to the latest editions of such basic references as:

The Penguin Dictionary of Troublesome Words (Penguin)

The Macquarie Dictionary (Macquarie Library)

Usage and Abusage (Penguin)

Roget's Thesaurus

Style Manual for Authors, Editors and Printers (AGPS)

How to write a better letter

Letter-writing is an important managerial skill; managers are often judged by the quality of the letters they write. The problem is that most of us usually become expert letter-writers after years of trial and error. If you would like to cut the process short, here is a proven strategy and several important points for you to consider…

Take your time.

Letter-writing is not something to do in a hurry. Routine business letters may require only a few minutes of thinking about phrasing and sequencing, but more important letters can require many hours of planning and drafting and passing through several versions before completion.

Assemble all relevant data.

Gather all the data you will need to prepare the letter, including previous correspondence, company files, and policy handbooks. Extract the details necessary for your first draft.

Group and sequence your material.

Know roughly what you want to say. Collate all the relevant pieces of information under headings, arranging the material in a logical sequence. If your letter is being written in response to someone else's, know exactly what is expected of you—information, opinion, clarification, instructions… and make sure your letter does what it should do. It is often useful to underline the points to be answered. Make brief marginal notes on these items.

Prepare a first draft.

Convert your grouped and sequenced information into a first draft. Precision and polish need not be your concern at this stage. Refer to the original correspondence in your first paragraph and provide the response required. If yours is an originating letter, state its aim, provide explanation, and close by saying what action you expect. The important thing at this stage is to get your words down in a rough but logical sequence.

Revise your draft letter.

Rework your first effort, rephrasing unclear and ambiguous statements, removing unnecessary words and phrases, deleting unnecessary information, and simplifying and sharpening your argument.

Polish your revised version.

As you write your final document, make improvements. Your final version should be succinct, crisp, and courteous. Attend to presentation and layout, paying particular attention to proofreading, paper and envelope quality, generous margins, balanced blocks of type—all of which help make a favourable impression.

Consider using a P.S. to reinforce your main message.

Letter-reading research reveals that people look first at the salutation, then at the signature. Then they scan the P.S. if there is one, and afterwards they return to the first paragraph. So, use the P.S. to drive home the point of your letter or to sell your message. Consider these points:

- Long postscripts can work. Successful postscripts can contain as many as five sentences.
- Make your postscript stand out. Use underlining, boldface, italics, a second colour, or legible handwriting to highlight your postscript.
- Whenever possible, include a 'call to action' to give the reader all the necessary information to act—for example:

    '**P.S.** Remember, our discounted offer ends on Friday. Phone the hotline on 9876 5432 *NOW*. We're waiting to book your special place at the function.'

 Remember these important points...

For good business letter writing:

- Put yourself in your reader's place.

Adjust your language to what is most meaningful to your reader.

- Keep your writing simple, natural, and concise.
- As a general rule, use short words, short sentences, and short paragraphs.
- Avoid technical terms and jargon or you could confuse your reader.
- Always be courteous and polite. How do *you* feel when you receive an abrupt, curt letter?
- Remember that, to many people you deal with, your letters *are* you. Those people may never see you, shake your hand, or speak to you. They must size you up from what you say in your correspondence and how you say it.
- Take care with special letters. In replying to letters of complaint, for example, explain why something happened and what you're going to do about it. Promote goodwill. Solve the problem; don't exacerbate it. Or, if writing a letter of refusal, do so without causing offence. Say no plainly, giving reasons; and convey your appreciation of the writer's interest or concern.
- Always apply the CATS test to your final letter:
    Content – Is what you're saying clear, concise, correct, and to the point?
    Accuracy – Are grammar and spelling perfect?
    Type – Does the typeface look conservatively professional?
    Shape – Does the letter appear attractive and balanced on the page?

183

How to write a good memo

Semantic sludge—that's how many of the memorandums that filter up, down, and across our organisations can be described. Most people would prefer to receive clear memos—on paper or by email—saying exactly what you mean. No doubt, you would prefer to receive the same. Often, however, an examination of these management communications often shows them to be ill-conceived, poorly expressed, and ineffective. Memo-writing is a skill you can master by following this advice…

1 Know when to write a memo.

Memos should be written only if

- you must avoid personal contact
- any other means would be too slow
- the material needs to be kept for future reference
- you need proof that you have taken action.

2 Be brief and to the point.

If you have nothing to say, don't write a memo. If you have something to say, keep it short—short paragraphs, short sentences, short words. Keep your memo as short and as simple as you can. A one-paragraph memo is sometimes all that's required.

The first objective is to express, not impress; so write simply and clearly. Weigh every word against your reader's time and attention span. And get to the point early. If you're asking for a new computer, say so at once; then provide the supporting argument.

3 Collect your thoughts.

For a memo longer than one paragraph, assemble your main points in advance. When you begin the structuring process, you'll have a complete set of ideas to work from. A rambling memo will reflect muddy thinking, laziness, or a failure to organise your thoughts.

4 Talk your ideas through to yourself.

In essence, a memo is a written statement whose content is sequenced appropriately. So, having isolated your main points, talk your ideas through to yourself. This process helps you decide the main point and frame the supporting arguments that hang off it. An outline then begins to take shape.

5 Focus on your audience.

Although you may be writing to a staff of 20 or 200, focus your written statement on one person. By speaking to that individual, you'll answer everyone else's questions.

 Structure your memo.

Consider adopting a standard structure for your longer proposals. Use headings such as these:

> To:
> From:
> Date:
> Subject:
> Background:
> Proposal:
> Recommendation:
> If approved:

Numbered paragraphs also make the memo easier to write, to read, and to refer to. You are forced to unravel your thoughts, to break your complicated idea down into its component parts, and to develop your message sequentially. For larger memos, subheadings and bullets are also useful.

 Be selective.

Rarely do readers want a blow-by-blow description of the issue. So state your ideas early, clearly, directly, and briefly. Include only information the reader needs to know. Avoid literary flourishes; in most memos, the main villain is pomposity. Stick to your main points and keep each idea simple.

 Review and revise.

Re-read what you've written. Ask yourself, 'Can I say this any more clearly?' Ensure that the final version is clear and crisp. Check that the memo is not arrogant, demeaning, or abrupt. Polish to perfection—and remember, neatness counts. Sloppy managers send out sloppy memos. Set an example: you'll want perfect grammar, correct spelling, and a neat presentation. Even if your proposals are rejected, you will at least gain credibility by displaying professionalism and courtesy to the reader.

 Check your subject heading carefully.

From the title of the memo, the reader should be able immediately to focus on the topic. Avoid murky, vague headings. For example, instead of writing, 'Subject: Computer', write: 'Subject: Proposal to purchase additional computer for personnel department'.

 Compliment good memo writers.

Praise reinforces good writing skills in your staff members. Set the example by gaining a reputation as a good memo writer yourself. Only then can you wage war on muddled memos. Express appreciation to good memo writers. When murky, rambling memos no longer are seen as models for staff to follow, all of your office messages will begin to improve.

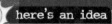 **here's an idea**

There are three areas in your memo or report where readers will immediately notice an error: The headline; a title; and the first line of copy. Unfortunately, those are also the three places where you're most likely to miss an error when proofreading your writing. So if the report is important – and important people are going to read it – take a few minutes after your normal proofreading to double-check all headlines, titles, and first lines on pages.

here's an idea

To keep your memos short and sweet, consider this technique: Try limiting your memos to three sentences.

The first sentence should explain why you're writing. 'I'd like you to provide me with some advice in relation to the Donnelly project.'

The next sentence indicates exactly what help you need, and why you're asking the memo recipient for assistance. For example: 'I'm bogged down on the marketing end of the project, and I know you've done some work in that area recently for the Bradley people.'

Finally, the third sentence asks for action. State what you want the person to do.

You may not be able to do it all in three sentences, but by practising this technique, you'll keep your memos as short as possible.

How to write a news release

The news media—newspapers, magazines, radio, television—can play a major role in your public relations program. News releases are normally used to make initial contact. Often, however, they are poorly written, and long-winded, containing little that is newsworthy. If you want to get valuable and accurate media coverage of news about your organisation, these important guidelines should be followed...

1 Prepare the release for the appropriate medium.

Unless you package your news release for a particular medium, you may be wasting your time and other people's. For example, a television station will be interested if you highlight visual aspects of the event involving movement and colour. A local newspaper will be more interested if the event features local identities and issues.

2 Make it timely.

Your news release must be sent before the event, not after it. The media want news as it happens, and are rarely interested in history. Stale news is no news. But if yours is an old event or story, you might just be able to resurrect it as news if you give it a topical new angle.

3 Find an angle for your story.

Whatever the medium, your news must be something that is new, unusual, even sensational, up-to-the-minute, affecting many people, and in the public interest. So it's important to lead with something about your event to catch the attention of the news editor, something that will make interesting reading or viewing or listening. Find an angle that is innovative, creative, beneficial, funny, or out of the ordinary.

4 Follow the established rules of release writing.

Here are the important points to remember when drafting your release:

- It must be composed in journalistic style, which is quite different from essay writing.
- A short headline should encapsulate the story in a few simple words.
- The opening paragraph must summarise the whole story. Indeed, if no more were printed, this single paragraph would tell the whole story in a nutshell. This paragraph can make all the difference between acceptance and rejection. It should include information based on the

angle you have chosen: what is to happen, where it will take place, why, how, when, and to whom.

- Write the remaining information in descending order of importance (the inverted pyramid style), allowing the journalist to cut details from the bottom up while still retaining the sense of the story.

- Keep it simple; use familiar words and short sentences; and avoid jargon. Each sentence should form one paragraph.

- Include original, simple, and strong quotations from an important company spokesperson or community member.

- Avoid judgements, opinions, or superlatives, unless they appear as quotations.

- Accuracy in all aspects is essential.

- Have a secretary, janitor, or clerk check your draft news release for ease of understanding.

5 Pay attention to how you present the release.

A release must have a professional look that pleases the eye of the editor, and save him or her the trouble of having to correct or rewrite it. Adhere to these guidelines:

- Always type your releases, double-spaced, on one side of A4 paper (preferably your organisation's letterhead) boldly marked 'NEWS RELEASE'.

- To make your news releases more professional and more recognisable, always use the same headings, paragraph indentations, and wide margins.

- Put the date of issue at the top of the page.

- Underline nothing, and do not hyphenate at the end of a line.

- Limit your release to one page if possible and type the word 'ENDS' at the end.

- If a second sheet is necessary, write 'more…' at the end of the first page. Do not break a paragraph at the end of a page. Number the pages.

- Provide a contact name (or two) and telephone numbers (business and after hours) at the bottom of the page.

6 Follow it up.

You may write a number of high-quality news releases and never see any of them in print (or on the television or radio news)—unless you follow up each release with a phone call. Here's how:

1. Introduce yourself.
2. Ask whether the release has been received.
3. Ask whether it is of interest.
4. Ask whether you can provide any clarification or elaboration.
5. Ask whether any good photographs are required.
6. Invite the reporter to call or visit to follow up the item in detail.
7. Prepare the way for future contacts.

viewpoint

"Puffery must be avoided, however enthusiastic one feels about the subject. Eulogies kill stories. A news release is not an advertisement. It must present bare facts only, without superlatives, self-praise, or comment. It is the editor's privilege to praise or criticise.

Of course, marketing, management, and advertising people are apt to criticise drafts of news releases because they do not boost the organisation or product. But you are not writing advertisement copy or propaganda: you are writing *news* and the difference is immense. This requires eliminating or avoiding superlatives and cliches such as 'brand leader', 'world famous', 'renowned', 'leading', 'foremost', 'unique' and other advertising expressions."
– Frank Jefkins in *The Practice of Public Relations*

here's an idea

Whenever you submit an article to the press it's more likely to be published if it is accompanied by a good photograph. When taking photographs, remember…

- Avoid large group pictures.
- Take more than one photo.
- Keep subjects close together.
- Identify everyone using correct spelling
- Caption each photo.

187

How to make the best use of social media in your business

Today, the social media afford you or your organisation opportunities to build and maintain relationships among people who share the same interests, activities, or personal contacts. Not only is the take-up of this media exponential but it's also increasing. Facebook US, for example, gained 100 million users from January 2009 to 2010, which represented a 145 percent growth rate in one year. By 2012, that number had increased to 300 million. Here are some of the ways that you can make the best use of what social media sites can offer your organisation...

1 Embrace social media – it's here to stay.

Social media is not a fad. And it affects all areas. Take, for example, politics. In 2012, President Barack Obama was seeking re-election as U.S. President. At that time, he had 25 million Facebook fans. His challenger, Mitt Romney, had 1.46 million Facebook supporters. At the time, *Forbes Magazine* said that Romney needed to improve his voter engagement via his Facebook page and in his use of social media, in general. And, as an indication of the 'spread' of social media, a 2011 study claimed that stay-at-home mums in Australia spent 70 percent of their time online, usually in social media. In whatever area you operate or function, the message is clear: when done right, social media can grow your business faster than any other means. In the world of social media, it's not *what* you know or *who* you know, but *who knows you*.

2 Get started.

Before jumping-in, heed the advice of Lon Safko in his bestselling book, *The Social Media Bible: Tactics, Tools, and Strategies for Business Success.* Safko recommended answering several questions as part of establishing a social networking strategy, including:

1. What are my *needs*, and how can social media apply to my business?
2. What am I planning to use the site for? Clarify *goals*.
3. Whose *attention* am I trying to get? Facebook has millions of users, so you'll need to target specific groups.

Safko then recommended considering answers to these questions:

1. Which sites do I want to be involved in?
2. Who's going to manage my page? Will I have the resources available to manage the page.
3. Who will have access to my page?
4. Who's going to be the personality of my page? Who will be representing my brand and will remain with the organisation.

3 Choose a site.

It's time then to choose which social networking site/s would best fulfill the requirements of your strategy. Most sites can be categorized according to the different purposes they serve. There are 'social sites', 'professional sites', and 'industry-specific sites'. Check-out how others use chosen sites.

Sign-up.

Read the rules of your chosen site and take note of the provider's commitments to privacy: restrict spamming. Employees become key advocates, so be sure to inform and include them wherever possible.

Combine and save.

Save time, energy, and reinforce your message. What appears on your Facebook page, for example, can be adapted to become a blog, newsletter, and a tweet – and feature on your website. Time-efficiency acknowledges your's and your followers' limited time.

Post updates.

Your targeted audience ('friends', eventually) is going to check out whether or not they want to follow you, so make sure you have content that encourages them to follow. Your selected social media can provide the ideal vehicle to stay in touch with selected and potential clients. Keep in mind that creating and growing a tribe takes time and ongoing commitment.

Convert followers into dollars.

Organisations that successfully convert followers into dollars are those that interact most with the users by posting content of interest to

recipients. Social media sites cater for this facility, so be sure to spend time exploring and familiarizing with the necessary how-to information and strategies.

Find and engage friends and followers.

Use your chosen site to stay in touch, keep people informed, build trust, target specific groups, and engage with potential customers. For example:

- On Facebook, share friends' and followers' links on your wall and / or comment on them. And birthdays are big on Facebook. Why not offer a discount coupon for a birthday treat via Facebook?

- On Twitter, retweet friends' and followers' stories and comment on them. Reply to each and every message. Keep the conversation going. Build trust.

- On Google+, create circles of certain people you want to target for different reasons. It makes it easier to post certain promotions to one group over another.

- On LinkedIn, engage with potential customers by joining industry groups and starting group discussions.

Use your site to promote company or product.

As your confidence in using these media grows, use your networking site / s to promote your company or product. Try to make any promotion benefit-based. Talk about new or uncommon features and how they can be used. Include details of discounts or savings or limited-time offers that invariably attract customer attention.

How to make the best use of email

Email is a powerful communication tool. More and more people in business rely on desktop and handheld technologies to communicate with colleagues, clients and others. Knowing email etiquette is vital to maintaining a healthy electronic business relationship, however, and an email policy could be essential if employees are not to abuse the many privileges which email bestows. Consider these suggestions…

1 Be aware of these basic guidelines.

Email will work for everybody if the following basic rules are followed:

- **Watch your words.** Remember that words can be misconstrued, so be concise and get to the point if you want to eliminate the need for follow-up emails to clarify earlier messages.

- **Keep paragraphs short.** Long chunks of text are difficult to read on-screen. Write short sentences, short paragraphs and short email messages if you want a quick response. Conciseness is always desirable. And only use abbreviations that the recipient understands.

- **Stick to one topic per message.** The more topics in your message, the more likely that the reader will be confused and delay a response.

- **Minimise your 'CC's.** It's easy, with the simple click of a button, to add people to your email's distribution list. But send messages only to people who need, or want, to see it.

- **Remember: Once you click 'send', your message can't be retrieved.** So be sure you won't regret what you've written.

- **Don't forget: Nothing is private.**

Even when a message is deleted, many software programs and online services can readily access it on the hard drive. Emails can easily be re-sent, intentionally or unintentionally, beyond your intended circulation list. Put nothing in an email you might later regret.

2 Follow the email etiquette rules.

By adhering to email etiquette, you will become a better email user and make life easier for recipients:

- **Avoid angering someone.** If your email contains antagonistic or critical comments (cyberspeak calls it 'flaming someone'), it can hurt and create problems. Keep your emails free of negative comments. Resolve problems face to face or by phone.

- **Sign each email.** Never assume people can identify you from your email address. Always sign off at the bottom of your message, giving your name and position.

- **Never CAPITALISE sentences.** Slabs of text in capital letters makes your message harder to read.

- **Think twice about sending unsolicited emails.** Ensure your emails have value for the recipient. If they don't, they'll be viewed as junk mail, and deleted as soon as they're listed.

- **Minimise attachments.** These take longer to download and eat up the recipient's computer memory. Mail lengthy documents, or explore the use of YouSendIt, SendThisFile and similar file transfer protocols.

- **Respect your chain of command.** Email allows us to jump over our immediate supervisors and get straight to the top. Consider the consequences of such action.

- **Don't forward others' emails without their permission.** Assume that the sender wanted only you to see it. Always check before you send someone's message to you elsewhere.

- **Use a meaningful subject line**—'New item for Ajax meeting agenda' is more meaningful than 'Re: your email of 6th July'.

- **If you attach files**, specify in the text what they are so that the reader can ensure they are received.

- **Read and proofread the message before you send it.** Sloppy emailers soon gain a reputation for carelessness.

- **Follow your email up with a phone call** if your email is an important one, to make sure it was received and understood.

 Be creative in your use of email.

Apart from using email for handing out assignments, checking progress, and passing on information, you'll be wasting a valuable tool if you don't creatively explore its potential. For example:

- **Try using email to brainstorm.** Email is great for brainstorming staff in

different locations. Outline the objective and email the challenge, together with a routing list, to the first person on that list who provides input and emails the next person. As the last person on the routing list, you can collate the accumulated responses.

- **Try using email to improve morale and motivate:**

  Offer help. If an employee is struggling with a problem, send an email expressing your concern and offering support.

  Show appreciation. Send selected employees little notes to let them know you appreciate their efforts.

  Go over their heads. If someone helps you, send a short note to his or her boss, outlining the contribution. Send a copy to the employee.

  Share the credit. At day's end, identify something good that happened to you. Send a thank-you email to a staffer who helped make it happen.

 Develop an email policy for your organisation.

Consider adopting an email policy to streamline its use and prevent its abuse—and potential lawsuits...

- **Clarify ownership.** Computer systems and email traffic on them are the property of the company.

- **Warn of monitoring rights.** Tell staff that the company might monitor the use of its computer systems by intercepting and reading emails.

- **Ban inappropriate emails.** Warn employees that they will be disciplined for sending insulting, harassing, or defamatory messages.

- **Promote work-only emails.** Reinforce the message that 'private' emails should be sent by other means.

- **Set timely response guidelines.** Could all inhouse emails be responded to by the end of the following day?

How to prevent employee abuse of email and telephone

Most people will be tempted to use their organisations' emails and telephones for personal reasons, and infrequent use of those resources is usually tolerated. In fact, any attempt to eliminate this practice is likely to meet with both overt and covert resistance. When employees abuse that privilege, however, action is required. Lost productivity, costs incurred, and the potential for legal intervention demand that you become involved. Here are some prevention and intervention suggestions…

Involve employees in developing a policy.

Ideally, every organisation should have a policy on email and telephone usage. Involving employees in developing that policy will encourage their support and make monitoring much easier.

The difficult task is specifying which activities are permitted and which are forbidden. Australian Government guidelines pinpoint the issue as follows:

It is a matter for each organisation to determine what it considers to be appropriate usage of its system. However, for a company to simply say that all activity must be 'work-related' may not provide sufficient clarity. There may be scope for guidelines outlining what type or level of personal use of email, both within the organisation and to other organisations, is appropriate. Obviously, some activities should be specifically prohibited, for example, the use of email to harass, abuse, or defame, disclose information, or transmit pornography.

If an organisation determines that internet usage is to be work-related only, it should clearly spell out what it considers to be work-related and not work-related. The policy also needs to account for the fact that it may not be possible to tell whether a web page is relevant until it has been read, and links to other websites may be misleading.[40]

The challenge is to devise a policy that clearly establishes 'reasonable' usage of email and telephone.

Train employees.

Insist on regular 'housekeeping' of emails. Those no longer required should be 'binned'. Regular audits of the capacities of your organisation's PCs should be an important function of your IT staff. The need for regular email 'housekeeping' should feature at staff training sessions, as should telephone use and etiquette. Make your expectations clear to all employees so that there are no misunderstandings.

Advise employees of all monitoring procedures.

You have a legal obligation to ensure that emails are not used as vehicles for offensive materials and do not conflict with policies on sexual harassment and equal employment opportunities. Many options are available today to monitor both email and telephone use. New technologies appear almost daily. Many tools are available, for example, to scan the content of emails to filter out pornography, ethnic jokes, and language that could offend and lead to legal actions. Other practices could include charging staff for personal calls, recording outgoing and incoming calls and their destinations, and bluffing. Generally, however, you will find that telling your staff members that, as part of company policy, their calls may be regularly monitored will serve as an adequate deterrent.

 Stay visible.

Management-by-walking-around has many advantages—one being that you may appear when you're least expected. An employee's reaction will signal whether or not a business or personal call is in progress (some managers gain great enjoyment from observing those responses). Don't be in a hurry to move on. Wait until the call has ended. If it was a business-related call—and you will know from the employee's body language if it was—compliment the employee on one aspect of the call that you overheard. If the call was obviously personal, you might ask, 'Is everything OK?' This enquiry not only elicits a response but also reminds the employee that only important, personal issues would warrant such attention during office hours.

 Identify persistent offenders.

Despite your best attempts to have employees appreciate the importance of personal honesty and integrity, some might continue to flout company policy by overusing or misusing the telecommunications system. When you identify those people, you must be prepared to discipline them. Although they may not say so, those who have been adhering to company policy will support your actions. In fact, in the interests of staff morale, you can't afford *not* to take appropriate action.

 Ensure you comply with policy, too.

The informal communication network will keep staff informed of your own email and telephone practices. Of course, no one doubts that your management role is likely to involve considerably greater use of email and telephone. But you, too, must show your commitment to the agreed policy.

 Stay focused on results.

Don't lose sight of the reason for having email, telephones, facsimile machines, and other technical aids. If the use of these devices is not delivering results, the problem could possibly extend beyond that of staff misuse of the various technologies. But if you remain focussed on results, others will begin to model your behaviour, thus helping to keep things in perspective.

 don't forget

Towards an email policy

Your email policy should…

- be compiled in association with staff-users of the technology.

- refer to your organisation's computer security policy. Improper use of email may pose a threat to system security, the privacy of staff and others, and the organisation.

- detail, clearly, what is appropriate and what is inappropriate 'work-related' use of email and web.

- outline, in plain English, how the organisation intends to monitor or audit staff compliance with its rules relating to acceptable use of email and web browsing.

- clearly set out what information is logged, and who in the organisation has rights to access the logs and content of staff email and browsing activities.

- be reviewed regularly to keep pace with ongoing technological developments.

 here's an idea

To ensure your company's email and web policy is communicated to all staff, consider having the policy permanently linked from a screen that the users see when they log on to your organisation's network.

193

How to convey your message in print

As a manager, you frequently need to communicate with your staff, clients, customers, or general public through newsletters, brochures, leaflets, and other published materials. Unfortunately, however, although you might print and distribute a newsletter, you might not actually have succeeded in communicating with your readers. So, if you want to develop the ability to communicate effectively in print, consider these guidelines…

1 *Know your audience.*

Newsletters, brochures, and similar materials are effective and economical vehicles of communication—but only if they appeal to the people who are supposed to read them. If you are writing for a learned profession, your style will be different from what is required for a working-class community. In a nutshell, write from the vantage point of the reader, rather than from that of the manager.

2 *Determine what they want to know and provide it.*

Your readers usually want information about your organisation, its operation, programs, activities, products, services, and the decisions that affect them. Often they need to be persuaded as well as informed, thus requiring a different style of writing.

3 *Avoid jargon.*

In some organisations, when you spend most of your day talking to colleagues, it's easy to forget that your shop talk can be largely incomprehensible to an outsider. Don't let jargon sneak into your writing—ever. Convert your specialised language into everyday language for a wider readership.

4 *Keep it short, simple, and lively.*

Few people want to know as much about the subject as you think they should, so highlight the main points and go on to something else. Keep your writing punchy; use a journalistic style. And remember the three important rules of readability: be simple, specific, and brief.

5 *Make your points quickly and clearly.*

To capture the most readers, make your points quickly and clearly. Most readers are not waiting to devour every word. You must compete for their time. Remember the 30-3-30 rule… Many people skim—after 30 seconds, you've lost them; others will spend 3 minutes at most on your newsletter or brochure; your friends or the converted will probably be the only ones to spend up to 30 minutes on it. Remember the first two groups when you write.

If possible, write as you speak.

Newsletter-writing must be as simple, direct, and personal as speaking. Successful newsletters make readers feel they are hearing—not reading—information prepared just for them. Fancy or formal prose usually is discarded.

Write about people doing things.

Whenever you can, focus on people. Theorising, philosophising, or detailing mundane matters makes dull reading for most people.

Work hard on your writing.

Few of us are gifted with writing skill. Writing must be learnt and requires constant practice. Most good writers write, rewrite, and then rewrite again.

Ensure the layout emphasises the message.

Don't attempt to turn your newsletter or leaflet into a grotesque computer-generated masterpiece of decorative design. Concentrate on the words and visual simplicity.

Resist trying to cram in too much.

If your publication is formidable in both length and appearance, your readers will put it aside rather than read it. For this reason, a limited number of concise, well-written items, with white space making the page look less intimidating, will communicate a lot better.

Invest in a style guide.

Style guides—which provide information, rules, and advice for authors, editors, and printers—are essential tools for writing, editing, and preparing copy for printing. In Australia, the AGPS *Style Manual* is recommended.

And remember: appearance counts.

Pay attention also to your publication's appearance:

- Limit your line of copy to no more than two alphabets wide.
- Try to use a very short line at the end of each paragraph to make more white space.
- Don't crowd your text. Use ample margins around your copy.
- Avoid large tracts of italics.
- Do not put headlines in capitals.
- Avoid putting screens over italic or thin type; the words will be difficult to read.
- Make sure each page of your publication has a visual focus.
- Don't use large areas of reverse type on black backgrounds.
- Don't print over illustrations.
- Use action photographs rather than portraits.
- Use copy-breaking devices (photos, headings, advertisements, art, quotations, etc.) when you have large blocks of type.

How to conduct a successful video conference

One of the outcomes of the events of September 11, 2001, has been increased attention on video conferencing as a means of eliminating or reducing the need to travel. The issue of safety has been added to the previous cost-benefits of reduced travelling time and costs; time can be spent more productively. Increasingly, these benefits have made video conferencing more popular as a means of bringing people together— across the country and around the world. Here's how to make sure you derive maximum value from your next video conference...

1 Arrange service provision.

Video conferencing is a flexible medium facilitated by satellite, broadcast, or cable signals. In addition, web conferencing can be adapted to mini-conferencing by incorporating digital cameras. To choose the best option, obtain expert advice. Some larger organisations have in-house facilities and expertise, but you might need an external service provider. Contact the provider as soon as possible; discuss details, even asking for a copy of the video conference if necessary.

2 Allocate responsibilities to the facilitators.

A successful event needs a video conference manager, who will:
• appoint and communicate with facilitators at any other centres involved
• invite participants
• distribute an agenda
• communicate with the service provider
• obtain a list of the voice telephone numbers for each location.

During the conference, the manager's responsibilities will include:
• starting and finishing on time
• introducing all participants
• encouraging participants to direct questions appropriately
• adjusting the camera during the conference using zoom and pan to keep things interesting
• calling a break if necessary.

After the conference, the manager will coordinate any activities resulting from feedback and might also schedule the next conference.

Site facilitators will need to:
• work with the manager to coordinate service provision, facilities, and any site registration
• assemble equipment and make it work
• prepare materials for participants
• contact participants and keep them informed before the event
• coordinate interactive segments
• follow up if required.

3 Invite participants and provide a preliminary briefing.

Accompanying your RSVP invitation to participants should be a check list including some, or all, of the following:

- Essential details – venue, telephone number, time, goals, agenda, and their facilitator's details.
- Dress – blues or pastels, no busy patterns, minimal 'flashy' jewellery.
- Speech – clear, slow, natural.
- Visual cues – bold typeface (14+), landscape, and margin.
- Avoid – asides (use a mute button if you must chat off-camera), shuffling papers, tapping objects near the microphone, fidgeting, body movements that are too fast or lack expressiveness.
- Camera – remain focused on the camera; treat it as if it were another person, and be aware of transmission delays such as time lags.
- Conference etiquette – first identify yourself (give your name and location). Always address people by name and site. Humour can add sparkle.
- Arrival – 15 minutes before the conference starts.

4 Arrive early to ensure the facility is prepared.

The manager should arrange with site facilitators to arrive early at venues, before other participants arrive. This gives the coordinating team time to:

- become familiar with the rooms in which they will be speaking
- make the areas ready—to erect signs, arrange seating, and finalise room layout
- become familiar with the video conferencing equipment and practise using it
- learn and set the camera presets so that they will know exactly what happens when those preset buttons are pressed
- chat with the service provider
- preview all slides and charts on the document camera in the video room for clarity, type, and readability
- practise their presentation and videotape and review it if possible, taking note of mannerisms, dress, and voice volume
- introduce participants at their site to one another before the conference call is made
- run through the agenda with participants at their location before the conference begins.

5 Follow an established procedure during the event.

The video conference will need an assertive chairperson to:

- lead the discussion
- make sure everyone has a chance to speak
- keep the discussion on topic, interceding if necessary
- deal with conflict or impasse
- validate and confirm people's contributions
- complete the agenda items
- foster a friendly atmosphere.

The chairperson will:

- get the conference going by introducing participants—even if they know each other—beginning with his or her location, and moving the camera so that all participants can see the person being introduced. Facilitators at the other sites repeat the process.
- ask participants to alert him or her immediately if there are technical hitches, such as no audio or a frozen screen.
- establish ground rules. For example, when visual aids are used, participants will be given time to absorb the information; and how participants can interrupt when they have a question.
- end the conference on time (any decision to extend the time of the conference will need to be made about 15 minutes before the scheduled end-time so that the appropriate provider can be notified); ask participants for their feedback; summarise the main points; indicate any follow-up; and thank participants for their involvement.

here's an idea

Why not make Net Conferencing a regular feature of your communication? Internet conferencing can be the cheapest, fastest, and most flexible type of meeting. Participants merely have to log on to the provider's website to share a document for simultaneous discussion. Share your presentations with hundreds of participants while they listen to you on an accompanying conference call. The addition of digital cameras can add video conferencing capability.

it's a fact

The case for the adoption of video conferencing may be strengthened, given that nearly two-thirds of top executives say they suffer serious physical symptoms from business trips of 100 miles or more.[44]

read further

Videoconferencing by James Wilcox, CMP Books, Gilroy, Cal., 2000.

here's an idea

Video conferencing minimises the disadvantages of location. Begin exploring the possibilities for your organisation: to interview candidates, evaluate at a distance, deliver a speech to a larger audience, engage in small group discussions, discuss strategy, share ideas and materials, hold meetings, launch a project, deliver training…

197

How to get yourself organised —and save time

here's an idea

Sometimes you *can* do two things at once. Read a report while waiting for an appointment. Sign letters during a meeting. Exercise while watching the television news. Listen to an audiobook on leadership while driving. Do knee bends while brushing your teeth. Plan that overdue memo while having your morning shower. It's easy. Be creative and save time. What's important to remember is this: Any activity you can double up on saves you half the time.

Time is a constant. There are twenty-four hours in a day, no more, no less. The challenge is to maximise their use—and it's possible, provided you approach the issue methodically. All accomplishment in life, other than that which results by accident, passes through three stages—the goal, the plan, and the action. By maintaining this sequence, you can better organise yourself to squeeze more out of those twenty-four hours…

 Identify what is strategic— to you.

Know exactly why you're doing what you're doing. Identify strategic issues—the essentials of your job or the main reasons why you are employed in your current position— and isolate them from those that are non-strategic. An excessive number, more than six, say, indicates that you need to clarify your role description. Free yourself of the non-strategic issues: eliminate or reduce them significantly—usually by delegating.

Set goals and detail actions.

Having identified the issues strategic to your personal operations, you need to be quite clear about the goals associated with each issue. If you want to achieve those goals you will need to take specific actions within a reasonable time. Activities or blockages hampering the achievement of goals should be reduced or eliminated. You'll find many 'urgent' jobs now assume a different priority in your life.

 Plan your year, month, week, and day.

Planning how to make the best use of your time is a form of project management. And, of course, the parts of your project over which you'll have most control are those relating to today and the next twenty-four hours. So, while being aware of the overall picture, your diary for the next two days will require your immediate attention: it will be far more detailed than next month's diary. Though effective time management entails more than diaries and to-do lists, both play vital roles in keeping you focused on the key issues, being aware of the value of time—and being organised.

 Practise key management techniques.

If you are to become organised, you must become an effective time manager by making such strategies as these part of your daily operations:

- Prioritise your tasks; plan your time to deal with top-priority items

See also: 200, 202, 204, 206, 214, 312, 566, 568

when you are at your best.

- Learn to say 'No'.
- Establish and meet deadlines.
- Delegate non-strategic tasks.
- Avoid over-commitment by being realistic about what can be done in the time available to you.
- Bite the bullet rather than procrastinating.
- Avoid butterfly behaviour, flitting from one job to the next, often finishing up where you started.
- Tell people that a closed door means 'no interruptions'.
- Always keep an index card or notebook and pencil on hand.
- Take a speed-reading course.
- Find a hide-away area at home or at work where you can finish important jobs without interruption.

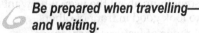

Use time-saving devices.

Keep yourself organised by keeping up with the technological and office management advances on offer. Devices such as laptops, smartphones and tablets, especially if synchronised with one another, provide opportunities for you to achieve more in less time. You can't afford not to be up to date with management technology.

Be prepared when travelling—and waiting.

Although new technologies such as laptops and audiobooks help to maximise the time available to you

when travelling and waiting, reading books, articles, and reports is still one of the most reliable means of getting information. Your time is too valuable to flip through 'old' news and irrelevant literature on planes and in reception areas. Organise yourself now—how will you use those idle moments while driving, travelling, or waiting? What reading matter will you put in your briefcase or glovebox—just in case?

 ### Organise your work space.

Time management researcher Merrill Douglass confessed that he logged two-and-a-half hours daily looking for information on the top of his desk! If you want to save time, a key is to keep your workplace organised. Pay attention to its location (to avoid interruptions), comfort, and space; have your work tools readily accessible; tidy that cluttered desk; establish a workable filing system; complete one project at a time and clear your desk of the rest; and get a large wastepaper basket.

 ### Don't worry.

Most of the things we worry about are unimportant, and we have little control over much of the rest. So focus your efforts on the few things you *can* do something about. Live a happier, more productive life by changing what you can and accepting what you can't. Think of the time you'll save!

How to use diaries and calendars effectively

In the pursuit of even better time management, and hopefully improved performance, every manager should use some form of time planner—diary, day book, appointment calendar, daily organiser or whatever. Although effective time management primarily depends on personal discipline and willpower, paper-based or electronic time planners can help you win that daily battle with time. Here are a few guidelines to get you thinking…

1 Know what a diary should be.

Pocket or desk diaries and calendars are the traditional 'appointment books', but they ought to be used for more than recording appointments. They require enough space to list one day's appointments and, on the same page (or screen if you're using a handheld device), enough room to comment on the planning or recording of the day's work: calls to make, reminders, meeting notes, goals, ideas, lists, events, etc. Your diary should become a written record of events, thoughts, and plans—a tool you will not want to be without.

2 Be aware of how a diary can help you.

If you have any doubts about the value of a diary, consider that it can:

- reduce your stress by reminding you of appointments, telephone messages, promises, and tasks to be completed.
- enable you to recall incidents / ideas.
- increase self-confidence and control, all the key aspects of your work being recorded in one handy place.

- remind you that time has both an economic *and* a spiritual value.

If you intend to become an effective time manager, you'll need a workable diary for regular reference.

3 Choose your diary thoughtfully.

A survey by the US magazine *Business Week* found that effective managers look for certain qualities in their diaries and calendars. They prefer:

- a 'planner' format to a simple diary. For them, a diary is more than an appointment book: it's a planning tool.
- a diary that lies flat. It should lie open on a desk without needing to be pressed flat. Electronic diaries should be easy to access.
- a diary with a time management section.
- a diary with aesthetic appeal. It says something about the user, who wants to look good in front of others.
- a range of features, including a double-ribbon bookmark to keep two places; quarter-hour time subdivisions; simple, uncluttered layout; and usable forward planning components.

Your diary or planner must satisfy your specific needs.

4 Investigate buying a commercial time management system.

Consider purchasing or adapting a commercial time planner (essentially a diary with enhancements). If used correctly, they literally organise your work life. In essence, you buy into a refined system of planning paraphernalia. You can customise your organiser using a variety of page formats—daily schedules, to-do lists, appointments, delegations, new ideas, project planners, meeting agendas, expense sheets, blank and lined pages, directories, forward planners, and so on. Various systems are available, e.g. FiloFax, Day-Timers, or Day Runner, each with its own advantages.

Quality organisers take time to set up and get used to. But, as Robert McGarvey writes in *As Time Goes By*:

Sift through the rigmarole associated with any organiser, and ultimately the indispensable key is to use it. Write down all appointments, phone calls that must be made, and chores—half of what any organiser provides is the freeing of your mind from the job of remembering little details that are better committed to paper and forgotten until needed. Do all this and, say users, the systems will shortly pay for themselves.

5 Make your diary work for you.

Your diary, planner, or calendar can become a powerful time management tool if you remember these points:

- At the beginning of the year, enter the important dates—e.g. staff meetings, product launches, conferences, and vacations.
- Always break activities into time blocks, with a start *and* an end. Time management problems are often caused by fuzzy end-times.
- Don't allow the entire day to be booked out. Leave some spare time to accommodate unexpected interruptions and thus reduce messy reschedulings.
- Avoid scheduling yourself too tightly. The pressure to finish one task or meeting in time to begin another reduces your effectiveness.
- Allow time for rest, lunch and relaxation. Error rates and stress increase with lack of rest.
- Block in time to complete important projects. Schedule enough time to build up momentum.
- Always allocate important tasks to the beginning of a day.
- Schedule long-winded callers at strategic times—just before lunch or closing time.
- Ensure that you can keep your diary with you at all times.

6 Explore electronic technology.

Today there is a wide range of electronic devices and apps that can help to increase your organisational and time management skills. By managing your time with these excellent apps, you can stay in control and on top of your work, and avoid the headaches that can come with a disorganised life.

 it's a fact

At first the term *calendar* did not relate to anything written down (there were originally no lists of dates), but to a herald's announcement!

Actually, the *calendar* is derived from the Latin, meaning 'to call out'. The beginning of each month was proclaimed by the head-priest or another appointed official.

No one knew beforehand when exactly the new month would start. It had to coincide with the appearance of the new moon and only when this had been duly observed could the official declaration be made. So it was that the first calendars merely referred to the *first* day of each month.

 quotable quote

A well maintained diary, given the nature of life and time, is anything but systematic or neat: it is full of tentative plans, plans replanned, crossings-out, scribbled ideas and items suddenly remembered. The only diary system worth having has simplicity and flexibility; even then, it will be no more than a tool of time management. More important by far is a realistic attitude to planning.[2]

 quotable quote

Want to know how to manage time well? Then start with this basic time management secret: We cannot manage time… It is ourselves and our situations we can manage, not our time![3]

How to tackle your priorities

Setting priorities is a decision-making process by which you rank in order of importance the tasks you or your staff members must do. By completing the tasks on your list in order, you will achieve your goals. It sounds easy—but it's not. In fact, priority-setting and sticking to the agreement you make with yourself will be major challenges for you as a manager. Here are several important suggestions to help you draw up a priority list—and make it work…

1 Address management problems first.

Give top priority to any problem on your list that is making you ineffective as a manager. If, for example, you have a personal conflict with your superior or your personal assistant, your effectiveness in dealing with other priorities could be seriously hampered. Face such problems immediately; get them out in the open; and devise solutions quickly.

2 Group your priorities meaningfully.

It is sometimes possible to prioritise your daily goals and save time and effort. For example, by postponing an inspection of new equipment in the factory block across the parking lot until after lunch, you might find that you can do so after a scheduled mid-afternoon meeting with the factory supervisor. You may even be able to accomplish a couple more of your goals for the day during that one trip.

Sensible planning brings its time-saving rewards.

3 Do it—or remove it.

Don't let an item become an irritation to you. If a task has been on your priority list for a long time, deal with it immediately or delete it from the list. If it has to be done, do it. If not, get rid of it; make room for something more important.

4 Resist chopping and changing.

Continually changing priorities will get you nowhere. If you start something and then switch to something else, you will soon lose motivation. If a task is near the top of your list, it's worth completing. Management consultant Ivy Lee's often repeated advice to US industrialist Charles Schwab is relevant here: 'Dig right in on priority job number one and stick to it until it's done. Tackle job number two in the same way; then number three; and so on. Don't worry if you finish only one or two by the end of the day—you'll be concentrating on the most urgent ones.'

Balance your priorities.

But by focusing on a major, very time-consuming task which you have placed at or near the top of your list, you can sometimes neglect others, causing further problems in the long run. Keep *all* your priorities in mind and avoid this confusion.

Ivy Lee's advice – to stick at priority number one until it's completed—may well be wise counsel for some managers, but it pays to be flexible when focusing on your top priorities.

 Reassign priorities when necessary.

When a task proves so difficult that an immediate solution is not possible, you may be compelled to take more time to consider the options. Move this item down the list where you can watch it but not forget it.

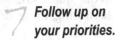 **Follow up on your priorities.**

Check daily to see that your priority tasks have in fact been completed and assess their outcome. Only when you're satisfied can you then confidently remove them from your list.

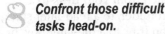 **Confront those difficult tasks head-on.**

Don't lower a high-priority task just because you're afraid to face it. Playing for time doesn't solve many problems. Your priority list will not serve you well unless you are honest with yourself and put the important (though difficult) things first. Once more, remind yourself of Ivy Lee's advice.

 Communicate all vital information.

If one of the tasks on your priority list requires communication throughout the workplace or office, for example, it should receive special treatment. Delaying such action could cause even more problems to be added to your list.

Treat your office like an operating room.

Surgeons don't get interrupted: they are required to focus all their attention on the task at hand. If you want to achieve your goals, you need to do the same thing. Develop the mindset that, during certain hours of the day, you are 'in surgery' and cannot be interrupted—no phone calls, no meetings, no drop-in visitors. During this time, focus 100 per cent on your high-priority tasks.

Accept that you will always have a priority list.

Whenever you complete a task, another will appear to take its place. As a manager, that's what your job is all about. If your list gets too short, you're simply not involved enough in the life of your organisation.

Finally, let your priorities determine your schedule. Don't let your schedule determine your priorities.

How to keep paperwork from accumulating

Does your desk sometimes look like a cluttered mailroom? Do you then go on a neatness spree—only to watch the untidy stacks of paper mount up again so that, in the following week or two, you have to clean up all over again? Some managers have a constant swirl of paper on their desks and assume that somehow the most important documents will float to the top. If you are being smothered by the paper avalanche, here are some useful ideas that may prove to be your salvation...

1 Adopt a system to process your paperwork.

The key to managing the paper war is to develop an effective processing strategy. It is essential to find a structured system that will work for you—and stick with it.

For example, the DRAFT system could be considered. Here, all incoming papers are sorted into one of the following five categories:

Delegation pile. Use routing or action slips to refer these items to staff members better equipped than you are to respond.

Reading pile. Put the journals, articles, and updates into a pile ready to grab when going to a dental appointment, or catching a bus, or taking off for the weekend.

Action pile. These items will require a personal response from you in the form of a written reply, an analysis, a draft report, or a decision. Subdivide this pile into 'top priority' and 'lower priority' tasks.

Filing pile. In a 'filing box', place all papers that need to be filed for future reference.

Toss pile. Junk mail and throw-away items are destined for the wastepaper basket. If you are unsure of what to dump, ask: What's the worst thing that would happen if I tossed it? Will someone be calling me later about this? Is there a duplicate elsewhere? If you feel it is impossible to decide on dumping immediately, keep the flyers and catalogues in a separate file to be browsed in one quick sitting each week before discarding, filing, or delegating.

2 Never handle a piece of paper twice.

Sort through all incoming papers as part of a regular daily routine. Handle each item only once—moving each from your desk to a delegation folder, to a read-later stack, to an action tray, to a file-later box, or to the wastepaper basket. (In reality, the goal should be to try to handle a document only twice at most—once on sorting it into the relevant pile, and, in some instances, once when resolving it.)

Enlist your assistant's help if possible.

Your secretary or clerk can save you much time by sorting your incoming paperwork for you, by handling the less important items routinely, by filing routine papers before they reach you, by highlighting the essential elements of the documents, and by routing the material appropriately after sorting.

 Develop skimming skills.

Move those papers across your desk promptly. Learn to skim background information to gain a general understanding of material without loitering. Consider a speed-reading course. Take time to read in detail only high-priority documents.

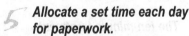 *Allocate a set time each day for paperwork.*

If possible, form the habit of processing paperwork at the same time every day. Such discipline combats procrastination and prevents your in-basket from overflowing. For example, 30 minutes of quiet time at the beginning of a day or after hours will send you home with a feeling of having accomplished much.

 Screen unnecessary paper.

Have your name removed from mailing lists that provide you only with junk mail. Cancel subscriptions to newsletters, magazines, and catalogues that no longer serve a useful purpose. Reduce photocopier use. Train your personal assistant to handle paper not requiring your personal attention. Work hard to stop the flow. Do you really need all those 'for your information' copies from staff?

 Focus on your action file.

Developing a workable paperflow system, like DRAFT, is essential; in the long run, it's your action file that counts. How can you ensure that you keep it to a manageable size? Here are a few tips:

- Use a priority list.
- Explore time-saving options: use form letters, form paragraphs, and with compliments slips, and tickler files…
- Use the telephone or email. It's faster and cheaper than mail.
- Make marginal notes on incoming mail and have your assistant draft your reply.
- Ask that every report over three pages in length include a summary on its cover page.
- Periodically check on the reports or bulletins you prepare—Who reads them? Are they of any use? Should you persist?
- Spotlight your tardiness. Mark a document with a red dot each time you handle it but fail to take action. Allow three dots—but no more.
- Don't put it down. Put it away.
- Learn the art of wastepaper-basketry. Take no prisoners!

205

BUILDING ESSENTIAL SKILLS

How to end procrastination

quotable quote

The key to overcoming procrastination is to just get started. In fact, within a few minutes of working on a project, you generally get your second wind. Runners, for instance, know that the first mile is always harder than the second. Getting past the barrier to your second wind is what overcoming procrastination is all about, because that's when you're warmed up, you've found your rhythm and you're working at peak efficiency. [7]

viewpoint

"Procrastination involves you deciding that it is in your best interest to do something and you delay doing it – even though you can see the disadvantages in the delay. Procrastination seems a crazy thing to do. Bizarre!'

– Michael Bernard in *Procrastinate Later!*

it's a fact

Procrastination, from the Latin word for 'tomorrow', is the world's #1 time-waster.
'Banish it from your life if you want to become a better manager,' advises time management guru John Adair.

Procrastination is one of the main reasons we don't perform to our full potential. It is a comfortable human habit that is not easy to break. But if you allow procrastination to become deeply entrenched, it can wreck your personal effectiveness and, in turn, the effectiveness of your organisation. Here are a dozen simple techniques that people have successfully used over the years to beat procrastination. Through application, you can discover which will work best for you…

The priorities plan

If you are forced into procrastination beyond your control because there are just too many tasks and so little time, do the important things first. Prioritise and give greatest and immediate attention to the most pressing jobs.

The divide-and-conquer strategy

If you are procrastinating because of the sheer awesomeness of a task, the key is to break it up into smaller, more manageable components. Once you start accumulating small victories, you'll be well on your way. Edwin Bliss advocates this strategy, calling it the 'Salami Technique', by which you slice up the task like a salami. Alan Lakein prefers the 'Swiss Cheese Method', which punches small holes in a big job.

The killer-punch plan

The divide-and-conquer strategy won't work if your problem is that

you keep putting off a single task like returning a phone call, firing a worker, or writing a thank-you note. The killer punch is needed for a specific task that can only be accomplished in one hit. There *is* only one solution: get it off your plate immediately. Act now.

The ten-minute treatment

Take the task you've been procrastinating over and resolve to spend ten minutes a day on it. After your first ten whole-hearted minutes, reconsider. If you put it aside until tomorrow, OK. Probably, however, you'll realise that the job isn't so dreadful; you'll have gained enough momentum to go beyond the planned ten minutes.

The bribe-yourself technique

Promise yourself a reward for getting a job done by a certain deadline. Bribe yourself with new clothes, a night out, or a walk along the beach. But don't cheat yourself by accepting your bribe *before* you've finished for that will only reinforce your procrastination.

The post-a-sign strategy

Display a small or large sign at work or home with a message to remind you of the job to be done (preferably where it will annoy your colleague or spouse so that they can pressure you as well). Such a reminder will make the 'out of sight, out of mind' principle harder to operate.

The do-nothing method

Do nothing for 15 minutes—nothing but stare at and think about the job at hand. According to Alan Lakein, 'you should become very uneasy—and after 10 minutes, you'll fire and be off and running'.

The see-it-all-done approach

We procrastinate when we cannot foresee achievement. Calano and Salzman recommend this exercise if you're having trouble getting started:

> Close your eyes and relax…
> Imagine that you have just finished your project, done a terrific job, and are basking in the good feeling of having achieved another goal. In your vision, focus on every process you went through to complete the task: the details, the hang-ups, the breakthroughs. Concentrate particularly on the elation of realising your reward.[7]

Such visualisation, they say, makes any task seem less intimidating.

The lock-away technique

Perhaps, as a busy manager, you simply need to isolate yourself from interruption for a couple of hours to get a difficult job done. If that's the case, tell people about your problem and lock yourself away from others for the required period.

The monitoring manoeuvre

For those lengthy and seemingly overwhelming tasks, take a colleague into your confidence—not to do the job for you but to have a trusted friend to talk over the task with, to provide support, to check on progress, and to nudge you gently, and often, towards the deadline.

The go-public tactic

Motivate yourself negatively by committing yourself publicly to a deadline—to avoid embarrassment, you'll get the job done, or lose face. And if you want either an incentive for reaching your goal or a penalty for falling short, make a $10 lottery ticket wager with a colleague.

The peak performance time routine

Do your toughest jobs at that time of day when you are most alert, rested, and energised. Or choose an unusual time for you—e.g. set the alarm for 4.30 a.m. and work for an hour drafting that difficult letter you keep putting off.

it's a fact

If you want to make an easy job seem mighty hard, then just keep putting off doing it.

smile & ponder

So you've got a couple of difficult jobs to do and you're having trouble getting started. Perhaps this awesome but apt advice may help:

If you've got to swallow a frog, don't spend a lot of time looking at it. And if you have to swallow several frogs, don't swallow the small one first.

read further

Eat that frog! by Brian Tracy, Berrett-Koehler, San Francisco, 2001.

smile & ponder

I am waiting for…
- Inspiration
- Permission
- Reassurance
- My turn
- More time
- A better time
- Someone to be watching
- An absence of risk
- Tomorrow
- My ship to come in
- My youth to return
- My suit to come back from the cleaners
- My boomerang to come back
- The wind to freshen
- Time to run out

Procrastination – the thief of time.

How to use the telephone effectively—and save time

The telephone is an essential tool of management. The phone means business. Even though it is one of the most effective time-saving tools, it is potentially one of the biggest time-wasters as well. So, to derive maximum benefit from the telephone, without becoming a slave to it, you'll need to gain control over it—and here's how you can...

quotable quote

The telephone has been described by a sociologist as the greatest nuisance among conveniences and the greatest convenience among nuisances.[8]

here's an idea

Trading phone calls with a business associate or prospect is one of the biggest time-wasters in business. You can eliminate this problem by leaving the right kind of message. Remember the Four Ws – Who, Why, What, and When – Who you are; Why you called; What you want the person to do; and When you'll be available for a return call. Make sure each of your messages has each of the four Ws, and on your outgoing voicemail message, ask callers to leave you the same information.

here's an idea

So you've spent valuable time on innumerable phone calls trying to reach someone? Get through to hard-to-reach people on the telephone with your photocopier and fax machine. Fill out a telephone message pad and use the photocopier to enlarge it. Then send it to that person. Your message will stand out from the rest.

Explore all available technologies.

Regularly review the technological advances made by the telecommunications industry. They provide opportunities to save you time while improving efficiency. Voicemail, message bank, fax, call redirection, conference calls, call waiting, email, and the Internet are just a few examples worth exploring. And the good news is that the competition among providers guarantees not only expanded technologies but also increasingly competitive rates for users.

 Adopt screening procedures.

Many incoming calls can be dealt with more effectively by others—your personal assistant, secretary, associate, or clerk. Appropriately trained personnel should follow procedures that:
* ascertain the purpose of the call
* decide who can best deal with it
* redirect the call where necessary
* promise a response in a specific time

if the required information is not immediately available.

Screening calls should not only save you time but also provide services more responsive to customers' needs.

Discipline yourself to keep calls brief.

Limit the length of your calls by considering the following techniques:
* Use an eggtimer to remind you of a three- or six-minute maximum limit.
* Stand up when you make a call; sit down only after you hang up.
* Use a stopwatch to help you measure time taken for individual calls—you'll soon find out who takes most of your time. Having done that, consider communicating with such people via a brief memo or email—you could save a good deal of time.
* Make your calls when people are less likely to chat, such as just before lunch or closing time.

 Plan your outgoing calls.

The following system puts you in control:

- List calls to be made during the day.
- Make the calls in priority order—at least you'll have completed the important ones if you run out of time.
- Write a brief outline for each call, including what you want to say or the information you need.
- Have any essential reference material near at hand.
- Set aside a specific period of the day for making the calls.
- Get to the point quickly, introducing yourself and the purpose for the call in the first sentence.
- Conclude the conversation promptly and courteously.

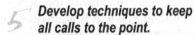

Develop techniques to keep all calls to the point.

Business calls are not the place for unnecessary chitchat.

- Your basic rule should be don't contribute to a conversation that's not going anywhere; the caller will soon get to the point. Make your business calls business calls.
- For incoming calls say 'Good morning, Sandy. How can I help you?' or 'Good afternoon, Sandy. I have three minutes before a scheduled meeting with my key staff. Go for it…'. In other words, make the caller get to the point quickly.
- For outgoing calls say 'Good morning, Sandy. If you have the time, I need two quick answers…' or 'Can we make a telephone date, Sandy? I have a break at 2.30 for ten minutes. I want to talk about…. Can I call you then?'
- Adopt courteous strategies for terminating long-winded callers. For example, interrupt to say you have people waiting at the door for a scheduled meeting starting in two minutes. Or, when you're desperate, hang up in mid-sentence—while *you* are talking.

Use your head when returning calls.

Your assistant, voicemail, or message bank will have calls that must be answered. Allowing calls to accumulate for several hours before returning them is an efficient approach. Knowing the technologies adopted by the person whose call you are returning allows even greater flexibility. You may, for example, return a call to that person's voicemail after business hours. If you don't want people to call you back, leave complete messages. When you want your calls returned, leave messages that will encourage people to do so.

Don't play games on the phone.

Refuse to play ping-pong or tag over the phone. If you cannot reach clients, find out *when* they will be in—even make a telephone date to avoid further futile attempts. Or, if you return clients' calls when they are out, leave a message saying when you'll be available to take their calls.

Check that you're not causing calls.

Do your letters, brochures, etc. lack sufficient information—and thus prompt phone calls? People uncertain of whom to ring usually start at the top. So make the titles of your staff members available; and have them clearly reflect functions.

Organise a phone-free hour for yourself.

Organise your day so that you have an hour to work free from all interruptions—including phone calls!

 here's an idea

Did you know that more than half of all workplace communication these days is 'one-way', with little conversation really required? Despite this, over 50 % of the average business phone call is taken up with non-business talk.

That's one reason to begin each phone call with the prime purpose for your communication. Save the small talk to the end. That way, if the call is interrupted, you avoid wasting time by having to call back. You also leave the other party with some pleasant thoughts which may dilute any heavy work-focussed discussions.

 don't forget

Use your phone as a timesaver…

Business consultant Gary Lockwood says:

- An average manager spends 2.5 hours on the phone each day, and about 20 per cent of that time is wasted. *Plan every telephone call.*

- On average, an unplanned call takes 5 minutes longer than one that was planned. *Plan each of your calls – even if you only take 30 seconds to jot down a rough outline.*

- Around 68 per cent of incoming calls are less important than whatever they interrupt; so *if you're engaged in a high-priority project, don't pick up the phone.*

How to avoid playing 'telephone tag'

Trying to make a sales call or book an appointment to see someone? Despite the increasing number of ways to communicate with others—such as instant messaging, Facebook, emails and texting—a telephone call is often still the best way to get a response. However, some people can be very tricky to get hold of. You may find that after leaving numerous messages on voice mail or message bank, and engaging in numerous conversations with personal assistants and other gatekeepers, you finally get a response. But then *you* are unavailable. The game of 'telephone tag' has begun. Here's how to win at this frustrating game…

Know the rules of the game.

Telephone tag is a game likely to be played simultaneously with several people. It's a game of supply and demand. When demand for a product or service is created, people will want to make contact to obtain supply. The greater the demand, the more difficult it will probably be to make contact with the person concerned. You, too, are in a demand-creating market. If you increase demand for your products or services, you can expect an increasing number of other people to try to contact you.

Accept the challenge.

Trying to contact busy people can be frustrating. Busy people, by definition, *are* usually busy and unlikely to be sitting about waiting for your call. They're either creating demand or satisfying it. Making contact can be a real challenge requiring you to apply some of your most creative techniques. Remember that the best technique will be one

that works and will enhance the relationship you have with the person you're phoning. If a technique doesn't work, do anything except continue with it.

Do your homework.

Preparation means getting to know as much as possible about your targets—their habits, idiosyncrasies, and contact details. Habits might include a 7.00 a.m. start; an idiosyncrasy might be answering calls personally before 8.30 a.m. or before their personal assistants start work; contact details could include the person's direct and mobile numbers and email addresses. Plan an approach according to the results of your homework.

Make sure you attend to your answering system as well. If you're on the move daily, you might consider putting on a new message each day to tell callers of your whereabouts on that day and that you will return their calls the moment you have free time.

here's an idea

Telephone tag can involve fewer players if you identify your most frequent callers – clients, customers, family, and friends – and determine the level of functionality required to respond promptly to their calls. Reducing the numbers playing telephone tag can become a matter of identifying priorities.

here's an idea

Personal assistants, secretaries, and receptionists are key players in telephone tag. Time spent establishing rapport with them will be rewarded as you will enlist their support in reaching a satisfactory end to the game.

Be prepared for those message machines.

Before making a call, rehearse what your opening sentence will be: write it out, if necessary. In this way you'll have a clear, coherent message to leave if you're transferred to a machine. Start with your name and phone number; leave a message that will encourage a response; and repeat your number. As the sales and marketing gurus advocate, 'sell the sizzle, not the sausage'. If a personal assistant answers your call, leave a message that will encourage your call to be returned. Time spent talking to a personal assistant will not only reveal valuable information but also strengthen your relationship with this key gatekeeper. The one piece of information the personal assistant should be able to tell you is the best time to call back when your target person is likely to be available.

Demonstrate a positive self-image.

If you believe in yourself and your product or service, be persistent. After all, you're doing a real service by bringing what you have to offer to the attention of someone who may benefit. Use all media open to you. If your phone calls are not returned, use an email, a fax, even a letter. A very successful way of getting your call answered is to leave a message that you will be in the area on a particular day and will call in on the off-chance that the person will be available. Invariably you'll receive a call, either to confirm the meeting and the time, or to tell you that your arrangement

is not convenient. Then you can set a time that *is* mutually convenient. If a target person still does not return your calls, it could be because of pending retirement, transfer, or redundancy. It could, however, indicate a lack of demand for your product or service. The one person who can tell you is the person you're trying to contact, so persist until you get the answer.

 Avoid 'cold calls'.

Dan Sullivan, well-known coach to entrepreneurs, says that you should make only one cold call in your life (the first one); the remainder of your business should all be referrals. You can be certain that there is always someone who knows someone else. The well-known Six Degrees of Separation study found that any two people selected at random and who have never met are only five acquaintances away from knowing each other in some way. When you make contact, therefore, or leave a message, you should use your referee's name—one that is known to the person you're calling—for a guaranteed response.

Try reversing the role.

Often, the best advice to follow is your own. So when you're having difficulty contacting the person you're after, ask yourself how you would advise someone faced with a similar challenge. Then take your own advice!

 here's an idea

When your message is urgent – too important to leave on voice mail – wait for the instruction to be put through to a receptionist. You can then stress the importance of your message and enlist his or her support in having your call acted on.

quotable quote

Telephone tag has a simple solution. When leaving a message, think of it as setting a tentative appointment. Ask what time the person called is expected to be available, and say you will call back at that time. When you leave a message for the person to call you, leave a specific day and time when you will be at your desk to receive the call. And make sure that the message you leave will motivate the person to return your call.[10]

How to organise others —and save time

Time management invariably focuses on self—how you organise your day, your papers, your workload. But how well do your staff members use *their* time to benefit the organisation, you, and themselves? Do you really know whether they, and you, are getting full value? Your staff can save your time and theirs if *you* take the initiative and encourage them to be time-conscious...

Watch for the indicators of a disorganised staff.

Watch for messages indicating that the time of the human component in your organisation is not being used to best advantage:

• You are frequently interrupted by staff seeking assistance, instruction, or direction.

• Your staff practises reverse delegation —referring tasks back to you.

• Deadlines are often missed or postponed.

• Staff assignments often need to be redone because of their poor quality.

• Your action tray is overflowing and you seem to be taking home more and more work.

• Staff morale is low; work is no longer challenging.

• Employees seem to spend time off-task—chatting and socialising.

Find out how they spend their time.

Before staff can manage their time more effectively, it is important that they, and you, know how they are currently using their time. You might keep a time/task schedule, entering an employee's name, the task assigned, the date assigned, your estimate of the completion date, actual completion date, and comments on unexpected interruptions. Or have staff keep an accurate record in their diaries; or construct a simple matrix indicating times and tasks. All this is valuable information for future discussions with individual employees.

Help staff to organise their work areas.

By observing what staff do and how they do it, you can identify efficiencies that can be introduced. Consider office layout, for example. Proximity to essential equipment like photocopiers, computer printers, and telephones is important. If employees have to walk the length of the office to use a photocopier, you will have detected a real time-waster. Office landscaping, too, improves productivity by not only enhancing visual appeal, but by reducing distractions as well.

Compile a skills index for staff.

A skills index for staff can be easily calculated using the many commercially available measuring tools—or you may prefer to construct your own. You may find, for example, that clerical staff use their word-processing package to only 40 per cent of its capability. Training in that area will significantly improve individuals' confidence and productivity. Employees with the skills necessary to complete their jobs will be less likely to interrupt others by asking for help.

 Provide the right mix of resources.

The right mix of people and other resources is essential if staff are to complete the jobs assigned to them. Allocating too few resources not only reduces productivity and profitability but also means that idle people use their spare time to interrupt others.

 Implement procedures and work instructions.

ISO 9000 certification will ensure that you adopt procedures for all work practices. Because staff will be involved in the certification process, ISO 9000 and its associated training will help staff to become organised. Documented procedures and work instructions will serve as common sources of reference for all staff.

 Teach staff time-saving techniques.

Never assume that 'everyone knows that' about time-saving techniques. Teach staff about your time-savers,

which might include:

- allocating tasks for periods when you'll be most productive
- setting daily priorities and sticking to them
- handling each piece of paper only once
- continuing to ask, 'What is the best use of my time, right now?'.

 Make sure you're not part of the problem.

Compile a list of time-wasters identified by employees. If 'the boss' appears on that list, find out what aspects of your behaviour need attention. It could be that you need to:

- communicate more clearly or more frequently
- avoid interrupting staff unnecessarily
- ensure that staff are not kept waiting for an appointment with you
- stop being indecisive…

 And don't forget to...

- *Set deadlines for staff.* Without them, projects tend to take more time than is really necessary.
- *Keep their work challenging*—then employees will be enthusiastic and time-conscious.
- *Build interdependencies.* When employees rely on colleagues, they realise that their actions affect others. Time-wasters (the office gossip) and time-wasting habits (arriving late or leaving early) are soon brought under control by peers.
- *Keep communication lines open.* Blocked channels or slow-flowing information can waste valuable staff time.
- *Set an example.* By your actions, demonstrate that you disapprove of time-wasting.

213

How to handle drop-in visitors —and save time

As a manager, you might adopt an open-door policy—a noble objective. Total accessibility, however, can be counterproductive and waste your valuable time. Unless you are prepared to control the extent to which unexpected visitors take up your time, your efficiency as a manager will suffer. Limiting the time taken up by drop-in visitors demands courtesy, good judgement, and tact. Here's some advice to help you minimise the debilitating effects of those often trivial and time-consuming drop-in visits...

1 Have your assistant intercept all visitors.

Your personal assistant, if you have one, should discreetly screen all visitors. Most routine problems can be handled in this way. If not, three strategies are possible:

- Determine the purpose of the visit and make an appointment.
- The assistant might say 'The manager is busy now. Can I contact you when the manager's free?'
- Or the assistant might say 'The manager is busy at the moment. Is the matter serious enough for me to interrupt?'

2 Appraise your office furniture.

Eye contact often invites passers-by to enter your office. Preferably position your desk so that it is not visible from the door. Or turn your desk so that your back is to the door: most corridor socialites will not interrupt you if they see you are busy.

As well, your office should not be too cosy—straight-backed chairs, a bit hard, not plush. Remove excess seating. In fact, chairs are for scheduled guests. Think twice about offering a chair to a drop-in visitor.

3 Set a time limit for each visit.

Be forthright with drop-ins. In response to 'Got a minute?', say 'I'm busy right now. Can you come back at 11.15?' Or, tell the visitor, 'I can spare only five minutes now. Is that enough?' If not, make an appointment for later. Or, can the matter wait until tomorrow's staff meeting?

4 Hold the meeting outside your office.

You can prevent drop-ins from planting themselves firmly in your office by:

- meeting the unexpected visitor in the outer office or corridor.
- suggesting the meeting be held in the visitor's own office or workplace, where *you* would have control over the length of the visit.
- asking the drop-in to walk with you on your way to another meeting or location, thus limiting

the meeting with the drop-in caller to the length of the journey.

Hold your meeting standing up.

When unwelcome drop-ins arrive, get on your feet, get out from behind your desk, greet them, and stay standing. You can then decide on the importance of the interruption and whether to offer a chair. Otherwise, work your way to the door. Stand-up meetings rarely last long.

Be available at certain times only.

Being accessible is essential for managers, but can often waste time. Consider being available for drop-ins at certain times only—for an hour before work is scheduled to commence, from 9.00 to 11.00, and so on. For sanity, you must put limits on an open-door policy.

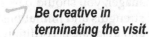 Be creative in terminating the visit.

You can control the length of a drop-in's visit in several ways:

- Say little. Don't contribute to a needless conversation and there won't be one.
- Say 'I'm afraid I'm expecting a rather tricky phone call any minute, so I won't ask you to sit down.'
- Say 'I'm sorry I don't have any more time, but I'm rushed this morning.'
- Say 'You've caught me in the middle of getting ready for an important meeting later today. I can spare two minutes.'
- Your assistant can remind you after

a few minutes that you have another matter (real or imagined) to attend to. You respond: 'That's OK. We'll be finished in two minutes.' Then stand.

- For a drifting conversation, *you* suggest what you believe is on the visitor's mind. If you're right, you've focused the discussion; if you're wrong, you will make the drop-in get to the point.

And consider these useful strategies. . .

- Let staff know that, before they drop in, you require a brief written summary of the problem for discussion with at least two possible solutions. Often the need for a drop-in meeting dissipates.
- Keep a clock in full view of yourself and the visitor.
- Drop-in visits by staff can be largely eliminated if you hold regular staff meetings, or department planning meetings or have your lunch with staff.
- Make it known that, whenever your door is closed, you do not want to be interrupted. Justify your unavailability on the grounds that you are 'at a meeting' (with yourself!).
- Simply learn to say 'no' or 'later' if you have something important to do.
- Keep a visitor log for a month. When you know who your main interrupters are, you will be better able to devise a strategy for minimising their effects.
- Plan your day to accommodate those inevitable drop-in visitors.

 smile & ponder

It was a classic case of the drop-in visitor. Samuel Taylor Coleridge explained that his famous 54-line poem 'Kubla Khan' was but a mere fragment of the glorious vision inspired by an opium dream he had just experienced. Unfortunately, the dream had been shattered by a drop-in visitor and the rest of the magnificent poem was lost to us forever.

While staying at a lonely Exmoor farmhouse, Coleridge had taken two grains of opium for medicinal purposes (he was, we are told, an addict). On waking from his drug-induced dream, he began writing down the poem in a frenzy of inspiration.

When he got to the lines

For he on honey dew has fed,
And drunk the milk of
*   Paradise...*

he was interrupted at the door by an unwelcome drop-in visitor, an insurance salesman from the nearby town. Try as he might, the poet was unable to recapture his vision of the legendary world of Xanadu – and the loss to literature remains to this day.

■ Even today, the drop-in visitor is still able to cause random havoc to our daily efficiency in the workplace.

How to delegate

Managers get things done through other people. They delegate primarily because it makes their job easier. If they try to do everything themselves, they become unnecessarily burdened; their performance and health deteriorate; they fail to develop their staff adequately; and, in time, the organisation will suffer. Indeed, many writers believe that the ability to delegate is the main distinguishing feature between good and bad managers. Knowing how to delegate is a crucial management and leadership skill...

1 From your prioritised jobs, select one to delegate.

List in priority order those tasks you might consider delegating. To qualify for this list, a task should be taking too much of your time, be not strictly related to your key role, be rather routine, be appropriate and challenging for another staff member, or be better undertaken by someone with more appropriate skills or know-how than yours. The purpose of delegating is not just to dodge work or to unload unrewarding, tedious, or difficult tasks—nor should you retain only the jobs you enjoy. Select a task that could and should be delegated.

2 Define clearly for yourself the task to be delegated.

Clarify in your own mind the task to be delegated. Think through the task so that you can outline it clearly. For example, be able to provide details of:

• the expected results or product
• how the task might be approached
• sub-tasks within the overall task
• the limits of authority

• the necessary timelines
• how you will know the task is done
• what resources will be required
• what training might be necessary.

Understand the task fully yourself so that you will later be able to brief a staff member thoroughly.

3 Select the right person for the job.

As a good manager, you should be aware of the strengths and limitations of your staff and delegate accordingly. Ideally, the person you choose should have the ability, knowledge, skills, enthusiasm, talent, and time needed to get the job done. Unfortunately, such qualities are not always found in the one person. So, before selecting someone, ask yourself:

• Who has the necessary skills?
• Who would be most challenged?
• Who would learn most? Who would benefit least?
• Does the task require previous experience? Will training be needed?
• What particular personal qualities are needed? Who has them?
• Who can be trusted to do the job?

- What other workloads does that person have?
- Is more than one person needed? If so, can they work together successfully?
- Who would enjoy a job like this? How will others react?

Delegation to the right person should improve skills, morale, and esteem.

 ### Conduct a thorough briefing.

In handing over the assignment, be prepared to set aside adequate time in private to communicate clearly:

- the scope of the task
- the specific results required
- the time schedule and deadlines
- the available resources
- the authority needed to carry out the job
- how performance can be measured
- sensitive or risky aspects of the task
- reporting procedures
- your confidence in the person you select.

Ask for feedback and encourage questions to eliminate any confusion.

 ### Delegate appropriate authority.

When you give people a job, make sure you tell them how much authority you are handing over. For example:

- 'Look into the problem; suggest three solutions; and I'll choose the best.'; or
- 'Look into the problem; tell me how you plan to solve it; and do so unless I tell you otherwise.'; or
- 'Solve the problem and tell me when you're finished.'

Set parameters and establish controls to ensure this authority and the accompanying power will be properly used. If necessary, inform other relevant staff.

 ### Keep lines of communication open.

When you delegate, you do not abdicate responsibility: you must maintain some control over the project. At least, agree to have your delegate inform you only when things are *not* going according to plan. Be accessible but not meddlesome. The delegate should make the first contact.

 ### Monitor progress unobtrusively.

Keep an eye on your delegate's progress without intruding. If necessary, confirm in advance how often progress is to be reported. As the delegate gains confidence, tactfully withdraw—but remain alert for problems. Help if asked to do so.

 ### Reward performance.

Appreciate a job well done by recognising good work privately and publicly. Sincere recognition will increase your effectiveness in working with others.

 ### Delegate as part of a master plan.

Review the project on its completion to make sure your delegate has also gained from the task. See delegation as part of the planned growth of your staff. Through delegation, they grow in confidence; and they—and your organisation—will benefit in the long run.

 smile & ponder

One day in 1898, a printer brought to Edwin Booth the proof of a new poster, which introduced the famous American actor as 'the very eminent tragedian, Edwin Booth'.

Said Booth: 'No, no. That's too much. Here's something I want you to do. I want you to leave off that 'eminent tragedian' stuff. I want it to be a simple 'Edwin Booth'.

'Very good, sir,' agreed the printer.

The following week a modest Mr Booth went for a walk and found the town plastered with large posters announcing the forthcoming appearance of 'A Simple Edwin Booth'.

■ The point of the story is that it is important, when delegating a task, for you to make sure, among other things, that your instructions are clearly understood.

viewpoint

"Willingness to delegate is one of the hallmarks of leadership, but delegation is difficult to exercise effectively. This is chiefly because it entails getting work done in a way that suits the person to whom the task is assigned – not you."

– Arthur Young in *The Manager's Handbook*

How to keep delegating

! **viewpoint**

"Delegation is paradoxical: you must do it in order to free yourself to manage; having done it, you enslave yourself in a higher order of tension and anxiety. It makes life difficult, but like any difficult game, it has its rewards."

– Roger Black in *Getting Things Done*

Some managers still believe that the best way to get something done is to do it themselves. But, with this attitude, no matter how productive they think they are, at some point they will reach their limit. Beyond that point, their output will decrease and their stress level will increase. As well, the talent and potential of their staff will be ignored. In a nutshell, to ignore delegation is to mismanage. If you want to embrace delegation as a most effective management tool, consider these strategies...

1 Become delegation-conscious.

Have you really decided which of your tasks you could rightly delegate to your subordinates to complete? Spend a day or two considering what you do. Are there things only you can do? Are there things others could do? Who could do those? Would they need training? Sometimes your subordinates are better qualified than you are to answer these questions. You might be surprised how much of your own work can be delegated.

2 Stop postponing projects.

We all have tasks that we continually postpone or ignore for some reason— yet they will not go away. At some stage they have to be done. If you are in this predicament, you must learn to delegate such tasks to other people to complete and free yourself to get on with other things.

3 Stop taking work home.

All occupations have their peak periods when additional work loads necessitate your taking work home to complete. But, if you find yourself taking work home regularly, you need to question the effectiveness of your delegating skills.

4 Make sure you get your share of free time.

Those managers who are successful can maintain a hectic pace while they are at work, but they allow themselves regular periods for relaxation. If you find that you are missing out on this free time, then you probably need to delegate some of your work load to others.

5 Stop comparing the performance of others with your own.

Perhaps you withhold assignments from staff because you do not have faith in the quality of their work, or because you think you could do a better job. Or perhaps you feel insecure, fearing that your subordinate might do too well and outshine you as a delegator. If so, you have yet to grasp the value of delegation; or, as one writer has noted, 'if you are employed by the kind of company where you can delegate yourself out of a job, it's the best thing that could happen to you!'

 Attend to staff development.

Staff may be reluctant to offer to undertake some delegated tasks if they feel they lack the required skills. Perhaps the same reason also accounts for your hesitancy. If your staff are not taking personal responsibility for developing their skills, take the lead and arrange a program for them.

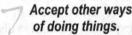 **Accept other ways of doing things.**

There is a difference between telling a subordinate to carry out a task according to your instructions, and true delegation. Until you understand that there is usually no single best way of tackling a task, you'll find delegation hard. Emphasise the result, not the process.

 Always be available for advice.

Employees feel secure if you make it clear that you are always there as a resource, ever ready to provide assistance and support if required. But resist the urge to be too helpful; instead, train yourself to return any problems to employees with some well-focused questions. Seldom should you accept the task back or provide an easy answer. Such action takes the growth out of the experience for the staff member.

 Intervene—but only if you must.

If you see that a delegated task is heading for disaster, you must intervene. In this case, Lisa Davis advises as follows:

Call an emergency meeting, put your cards on the table, ask questions, and listen to what the individual has to say. Provide clear guidance and assistance, encouragement and support. Steer the person back on course and then—and this is the hard part—step back and let the person continue. Unless the problem is really serious, resist the temptation to take the project away from the individual and do it yourself.[13]

 Develop healthy staff relationships.

Cooperation is the key to an effective organisation; where this cooperation exists, staff members will be eagerly awaiting the chance to participate even further. Work towards creating this healthy staff climate: you will find your employees keener to take on delegated responsibilities.

 Be prepared to share your ideas.

Your experience took years to acquire and is your most valuable resource. Don't let all your accumulated wisdom and knowledge remain hidden from others. Be prepared to demonstrate to others that you are happy to share your particular skills when necessary.

 here's an idea

- Don't underestimate your people – get close enough to every member of the team to know how much responsibility each can personally handle.
- Importantly, don't delegate only to high fliers.
- Some capable and ambitious people are naturally reserved – identify their potential and don't make them leave to achieve recognition elsewhere. For example, the low proportion of women in management, even now, is due partly to many women being non-assertive and their managers not recognising their potential.

 quotable quote

What you delegate and to whom are key issues. If you choose the right people for the job, brief them thoroughly, and monitor the situation regularly, you'll be able to delegate a wide range of tasks with confidence, knowing that they will be carried out the way you want them, and on time.

The amount of time you invest in preparing a delegation strategy will be repaid over and over again as your staff grows in competence and confidence, and you begin to feel more relaxed about the delegation process.[15]

219

How to overcome your reluctance to delegate

Even though there are very good reasons for delegating, there is sound evidence to suggest that delegation does not occur as often as it should. And why not? Because managers talk themselves out of it. In fact, they are capable of citing a whole array of 'reasons' why they are reluctant to delegate; but all such reasons can be discredited. If you are to be an effective manager, you simply must delegate. You must…

Find the time to delegate.

If you refuse to delegate because you are 'too busy to delegate', 'the project is too complicated to explain to someone else', you 'don't have the time to train someone', or 'the process takes too long', not only do you have a delegation problem, but you have a time management problem as well. Remember, skilful delegation saves time.

Admit that others can do it as well as you can.

The perfectionist thinks 'no one can do the job as well as I can'. If you think you can do the job better yourself and therefore do it yourself, then you'll find yourself doing *all* the work in future: nobody else has learned how to! In the long run, your ability and energy can hinder delegation and the development of your staff.

Accept that others might make mistakes.

So you think your subordinates might make a mess of the job? Everyone makes mistakes. Your staff must be allowed to also, and the cost must be regarded as a staff development expense. Through skills development training, counselling, detailed instructions, and so on, you can avoid repeated mistakes without discouraging delegation.

Put your ego second.

To receive personal credit from superiors, do you try to do all the important tasks yourself? Do you fear that your subordinate might do too well and outshine you? Do you fear that, by delegating the task to a subordinate, your promotional prospects may even lessen if that person succeeds? Ask yourself: 'If I can't get my subordinates promoted, should I be promoted myself?'

Give up the tasks you enjoy doing yourself.

Managers are usually promoted from the workface because they excel in—and enjoy—particular tasks.

Indeed, some managers thrive on hectic schedules and working around the clock; they feel a need to have their personal stamp on all projects. It's hard to hand over jobs you enjoy doing yourself, isn't it? But managers are paid to manage—and managing includes delegation.

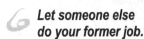

Let someone else do your former job.

As a promoted manager, do you like to continue making decisions associated with your former position? You must understand that you will contribute better to the organisation by concen-trating on current tasks and letting others do your former work.

Learn to trust your subordinates' abilities.

Perhaps you lack confidence in the ability of your staff to get the job done. This lack of trust is usually unwarranted. Familiarise yourself with each staff member's capabilities. You'll find that many people need only to be given a chance to prove themselves.

Become more receptive to the ideas of others.

You're not an obstruction in the system —or are you? Managers must not only be able to welcome the ideas of others eagerly but also must be prepared to plant their own ideas in the minds of staff and to compliment those staff members later on their ingenuity.

Suppress all fears that you'll lose control.

Only insecure managers fear that they'll lose control of their empire, even their position, if through delegation subordinates are trained to perform more duties . Such fears have no basis. If you hold back others for this reason, you are preventing them and the organisation from realising their true potential.

Believe that delegation is not a sign of weakness.

If you fear you'll be criticised for 'passing the buck' whenever you delegate, you have still to learn that managers face criticism of their style and reputation every day. That's part of a manager's baggage. You must overcome such fears if you are to delegate freely and effectively. Delegation is anything but a sign of weakness. In fact, not to delegate is to ignore one of management's most valuable assets.

Dispel any fear of being disliked because you hand out jobs.

The fear of being unpopular or resented by staff for passing too much work into the system looms large for some managers. US research has revealed that leaders whose staff rate them good or excellent are those who delegate most.

Your staff expect you to delegate— so do it. Indeed, most people want to feel that they are valued by their organisation; to make a contribution, they want to be given something meaningful to do. By not delegating to them, you could be even more likely to get them offside.

don't forget

The symptoms of poor delegators

- Need to know all the details
- 'I can do it better my-self' illusion
- Lack of experience in delegating
- Insecurity
- Poor planning
- Lack of objectives
- Slow decision-making
- Too large a span of control
- Believe delegating is a sign of weakness
- Fear of loss of control
- Constant pressure and confusion
- It doesn't occur to you
- 'My boss won't let me' syndrome
- Disinclined to develop team members
- Lack of organisational skills
- Fear of being disliked
- Too busy to delegate
- Lack of policy or too much policy
- Want to do it yourself
- Want to feel indispen-sable
- Perfectionism
- Lack of confidence in team members
- Fear of mistakes
- 'Workers don't want responsibility' fallacy
- 'No one has the experience' misconception.[17]

Are you exhibiting any of these symptoms now?

How to steer clear of delegation traps

The good delegator and the good golfer are very much alike—they both know how to avoid the traps. Unfortunately for you, as manager, the delegation fairway is lined with hazards. If you do not handle your management duties sensitively, you will spend much of your time digging your way out of these traps. So here are some words of wisdom to help the manager-delegator avoid the pitfalls...

1 Do not delegate tasks at random.

The art of delegation involves handing out tasks to those likely to be able to complete them successfully. This outcome will not be achieved by delegating tasks haphazardly.

2 Do not delegate only the unpleasant jobs.

Every company and every department has its share of 'boring' jobs—the tedious tasks that nobody wants to do. Try to do one or two of these per month yourself, rather than delegate them all to employees. If you make a commitment to do a couple each month, and your employees know about it, two things will happen: firstly, they'll appreciate your help; secondly, they'll be less inclined to grumble about the 'boring' jobs they themselves have to do.

In other words, delegation is not simply another word for dumping. Resist the temptation to offload only your unpleasant tasks. Delegate the good and the bad. A motivated staff member will soon become disgruntled if given only the boring, routine, or distasteful projects that you try to avoid.

3 Do not delegate without providing adequate information.

Spell out exactly what you want so that your intentions are complete and understood. Too little information means that the delegate will have to keep coming back to you or that the final product will be incomplete or inadequate. So ensure that the person is given access to the right tools, resources, people, and records.

4 Do not delegate too much for a person to handle.

Avoid falling into the trap of overloading the eager beaver, the upwardly mobile, or the highly competent employee. Staff members who are eager to please you may find that they have taken on more tasks than they can successfully complete. You not only overburden them, but your deadlines are missed.

5 Do not delegate responsibility without adequate authority.

Delegation means giving another person the authority to act in your place. Clearly define the limits of that authority. Where appropriate, let other people know what you've delegated to whom, and that you expect their assistance as required.

6 Do not delegate and then want things your own way.

When you delegate, you should be interested only in the final product. *How* your delegates do the job should be left to them—provided they understand the limits. If they have to check with you before every move, you not only undermine the trust that should accompany delegation, but also might as well do the job yourself. So by all means offer help, but let them do it their way—and they may well discover new and better ways to solve old problems.

7 Do not delegate and then expect an overnight response.

In delegating a task you formerly handled yourself, you might find that the delegate needs more time to achieve your level of performance. Be patient. In time, the task will be mastered. Do not expect error-free, independent performance overnight.

8 Do not delegate and then worry about foul-ups.

Assign tasks initially where success is probable: success is what builds self-confidence. Resist the temptation to dive in to obviate mistakes. And when a staff member makes a mistake

on a delegated job, don't make a big issue of it. Consider it all part of the learning process—for you and your employee. After all, the mistake may not be entirely the employee's fault. Perhaps you chose the wrong person for the job, or didn't inform, train, motivate, or monitor that person adequately.

9 Do not delegate without a periodic review.

Monitor your staff member's progress, but don't breathe hotly on the delegate's neck. Your employee will need a reasonable amount of freedom, independence, and trust to display real talent. Depending on his or her experience and ability, keep your ear to the ground without being obtrusive.

10 Do not delegate everything.

There are several areas and responsibilities for which delegation is not an option for line managers—counselling and morale problems, performance evaluation, disciplinary action, and confidential matters.

11 Do not delegate and then blame others for the outcome.

You're still the boss, irrespective of who performs a delegated task; so you must ultimately be prepared to carry the can for outcomes. If your staff know that you are likely to blame them for any unpopular decisions or outcome, then they will resist any future delegated responsibilities.

❝ quotable quote

When it comes to delegation, stop focusing on the unknown – on what disasters *might* occur. Instead, form a clear idea of *what* has to be done and *how* you can facilitate success.

For any project you will have three known goals. You want the job done (1) well, (2) on time, and (3) under your control.

Your job is to direct, guide, and oversee your employees' efforts – not do their work. You can make sure the job is done well by giving them clear, explicit instructions, sufficient time and resources, and motivation. And you keep your team on schedule by setting up many short-term deadlines that you personally supervise.[18]

---

here's an idea

ASAP – one of the most useless acronyms in time management. Think about it. What is *your* first reaction when someone asks you to do something 'as soon as possible'? Exactly. You drop it into your in-tray, and you'll get around to it – sometime.

If you *really* want something done, ask for it to be done by a certain date and time. In writing, be as specific as you can: 'Please have this on my desk by 3.15pm on Wednesday, 15 July'. Or in conversation: 'I need this by close of business on Thursday. Any problem with that?' If there is, negotiate an agreeable date.

When delegating, never yield to the temptation of the ineffective, unproductive, worthless ASAP.

How to use delegation to develop your staff

In a nutshell, managers need to delegate to get things done. But, if used wisely, delegation has additional advantages. It can enrich the work of your staff, develop their management skills, instil in them a sense of commitment to the organisation's goals, reveal to you their previously undisclosed talents, and prepare them for advancement. Delegation can indeed be a rewarding tool for staff development—provided you adhere to a number of important principles...

quotable quote

Delegation is difficult. It is perhaps the hardest thing that managers have to do. The problem is getting the balance right between delegating too much or too little and between over- or under-supervision. When you give someone something to do you have to make sure that it gets done. And you have to do that without breathing down his (or her) neck, wasting your time and his, and getting in the way. There has to be trust as well as guidance and supervision.[19]

here's an idea

Leadership skills are becoming more important in the workplace – and not just for managers. As organisational structures flatten and teams become more popular, employees need to learn and develop leadership skills as well. As a manager, you need to delegate to make sure every one of your employees gets a chance to hone such skills. Some methods for doing this: Have them chair a meeting; let them take the lead on a project; ask them to give a presentation; have four employees work on a report together, and put one of them in charge; create committees and appoint employees to lead them.

1 Try not to delegate only to the most capable people.

Resist the temptation to delegate only to the most capable staff members. Certainly the strong will get stronger—but the weak will only get weaker. By distributing assignments widely, you will be building a team of versatile performers and a handy group to have when emergencies arise.

When delegating to someone who has less than ideal experience, skills, or knowledge, select at least an individual willing to learn (with some help) how to do the job. In this way people develop, and staff development should be one of your major aims whenever you delegate.

2 Select assignments that will stretch your staff.

The purpose of developmental delegation is to build staff confidence in handling unfamiliar tasks, though the aim is ill-served if they fail on the first attempt. Delegate more than just 'jobs': motivate staff by delegating tasks that are interesting, and challenging—but not to breaking point.

3 Treat any foul-up as a learning experience.

An effective way to develop staff is to let them make mistakes on their own. If the consequences aren't too great, watch them do it wrong the first time; they'll appreciate the right way the next time. If they foul up an assignment, don't make a big issue of the failure. If you punish learning behaviour, you paralyse staff members and undermine their confidence. If they fear reprimands and criticism, they'll take fewer risks and ultimately perform poorly. To guard against foul-ups, remember to assign tasks only where success is probable, and always first take the time to check that your delegated assignment is clearly understood.

4 Recognise those teaching moments.

When staff members come to you with insightful questions or opinions, they are willing to expand their horizons and learn new skills. This is precisely when the teaching moment becomes the delegation moment. As Calano and Salzman write: 'Training and delegation are two sides of the coin. By developing a sensitivity to teaching moments, you will become a far more effective delegator—and leader.'

Know that you'll always be a role model.

Ensure that you function as an effective role model: your staff will normally follow your example. Research shows that staff initially learn how to organise, make decisions, manage time, deal with crises, run meetings, and handle problems by observing their managers.

Show confidence in the ability of your staff to carry out the assignment.

You must believe in, support, and help your subordinates succeed with their delegated assignments. If you trust staff enough to delegate projects in the first place, that trust must be continued until the project is complete. Display your trust by word and deed—by not continually looking over their shoulders, or interfering with their methods, or berating them when they stumble. In time, their confidence, sense of responsibility, and powers of judgement will grow, and you will be able to trust them with more demanding and responsible tasks.

Lay the foundations of success.

If you want to delegate to develop the managerial skills of your staff and to improve their performance and ability to carry out more responsible work, you must also adhere to certain key ground rules. Among them are the following:

- **Delegate the objective, not the procedure.**
  You are interested in the result, so let them do it their way, provided they are clear about the required outcome. Offer to help—but don't insist that they adopt your methods.

- **Delegate authority, not just responsibility.**
  Authority is needed to get a job done, but first set the limits—budget, deadlines, resources, and the other parameters of their authority.

- **Establish standards of performance.** The final result will reflect on you, so help yourself and the delegate by setting your standards beforehand.

- **Delegate but don't abdicate.**
  Remember that accountability rests with you. Monitor the task through periodic feedback. Offer help only if it is asked for or warranted.

- **Give credit for tasks well done.**
  You look good when a delegated task turns out well. So, by letting your staff shine, you and the organisation will both benefit.

here's an idea

Every manager has at least one employee who is constantly promising to get a job done: she'll finish the report a week early; next time, she's going to have to do extensive research before starting a project; next time, she's still learning the new software. And so on.

Rein in these promise-makers by starting a 'Promise File'. Keep track of everything they promise you. Then, if and when they renege, pull out the file and show them you're keeping track. At the very least, they'll learn not to throw promises around so lightly anymore. And who knows, if they know you're keeping tabs, they may start following through more often.

ask yourself

Many managers when delegating tend to over-manage their staff. Here's a strategy to make sure you're not doing this. Ask yourself these questions:

- How many things do I have to approve?
- How necessary is it that I am part of the approval process?
- When was the last time my input was absolutely crucial to a project's success or failure?

If you discover that you are too involved with too many projects, step back a little. Put more faith in your employees, and give them more power to make decisions.

How to follow-up

Most interventions end with an agreement to follow-up, that concluding action being an important part of a manager's role. Follow-up actions need to be more than *ad hoc* additions to daily routines. Effective follow-up discussions not only demonstrate to employees that you mean what you say—that you actually *do* follow up—but also show your interest in employees' progress. Here's how to make the best use of this important, though often neglected, aspect of management practice…

1 Review previous discussions.

Having set aside a time for a follow-up meeting, make sure it happens. Begin the meeting by briefly recapping any previous discussions, including any actions you both agreed on at that time. Be specific: highlight only important aspects of those discussions. Again, focus only on identified problems, not the person.

2 Arrive at an assessment.

If progress since the initial meeting has been made, encourage the employee to talk about the achievements. Take time to outline to the employee your assessment of his or her contributions and accomplishments. Express your pleasure at obvious progress. If you are satisfied with the improvements, proceed to point 7.

If, however, the problem has not been solved to your satisfaction, refer to specific data to show that the employee still has work to do, and continue to explore the issue…

3 Explore possible solutions.

In the case of insufficient improvement, suggest as many as possible different options to overcome the problem; but avoid demanding specific actions. People will work harder to solve their problems when they themselves have a voice in the strategy to be adopted. So let the employee decide on a suitable plan of action. You, of course, will need to agree on, and be prepared to support or disagree with, the proposed solution.

4 Clarify the consequences of continued lack of improvement.

This is a very sensitive part of the discussion. You will want the employee to understand what will happen if the problem isn't solved. You must not appear threatening or aggressive, nor will you want the employee to become defensive. Stress that you are on the employee's side and that the purpose of the discussion is to solve the problem. But you may need to broach the subject of consequences. In doing so, be specific and keep discussion focused on the facts.

Agree on actions to be taken.

If the plan is going to work, it will need the employee's commitment and your support. It must be seen as a cooperative effort, the end product being improvement in the staff member's performance in the workplace. To gain that commitment, agree on the specific actions to be taken, preferably using the employee's ideas and solutions. Support the plan that seems best.

Set a date for another follow-up meeting.

Agree to meet again at a later date to review progress. This requirement reinforces the fact that you're serious about solving the problem.

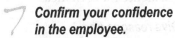

Confirm your confidence in the employee.

End on a positive note by acknowledging your confidence in the staff member. People are far more responsive when they know that you want them to succeed. Your demonstration of confidence and encouragement will contribute to a workable and lasting solution.

Record outcomes.

Whatever the outcome of the follow-up meeting, record all information immediately afterwards. This action signifies completion of another important management task; it also ensures that you have a permanent record of any further follow-up action required and that you have detailed comments for reference at the next meeting if required.

Stay in touch.

Remain 'visible' by maintaining regular contact with all employees. In that way you will be there to ensure essential follow-up action is taken.

Be aware of the legal implications.

As a follow-up activity, the outcomes of a range of important organisational activities must be recorded. Confirm agreements in writing; record meeting resolutions in minutes; enter contractual details into a written document rather than rely on memory or handshakes. In any later dispute, it's not what you know but what you can prove that counts. And if it comes to it, in any court proceedings, the side with the best and most complete evidence is usually the winner.

here's an idea

Explore appropriate computer software packages which incorporate features to help you follow-up. Some have reminder notes which pop on the screen when you start your program each day; some have alarms and other reminder capabilities. For those less computer-competent, time management diaries often have special follow-up features. At the minimum, reminder notes jotted on your desk calendar will help you keep track of follow-up demands.

viewpoint

"You can create excitement, you can do wonderful promotion and get all kinds of press, and you can throw in a little hyperbole. But if you don't deliver the goods, people will eventually catch on."

– Donald Trump in *The Art of the Deal*

smile & ponder

"I recall one of my early coaches who was frustrated with my lack of scoring in a vital game. As part of his usual game follow-up he got to me –and made his point – despite the way he put it: 'And you, Gretzky, you miss 100 per cent of the shots you never take!'"

– Wayne Gretzky, US hockey great

How to give orders

Not everyone can give orders that are clearly understood and carried out to the letter. If you've been frustrated by not having your orders (or 'requests' or 'suggestions') carried out, you may be overlooking the obvious—that in most cases the fault is yours, not that of your staff. Here are some suggestions to ensure that your orders are understood and obeyed...

1 Know exactly what you want.

Before delivering instructions, know exactly what you want and how you are going to communicate your requirements. What precisely is the result you have in mind?

2 Select the right person for the job.

Orders will be more effectively carried out when you select a person with the ability and desire to carry out the task, so get to know the capabilities of your staff. Make sure that the person you select for a particular job is capable of completing it.

3 Use your established chain of authority.

No matter how big or small the organisation, it should have a structured chain or line of authority through which orders, commands, or instructions are transmitted. If staff expect orders to come from their supervisors, make sure you communicate your orders via those people.

4 Use clear, concise, plain language.

Sequence your instructions clearly and logically. Use plain, concrete, and specific language, avoiding jargon if possible. Speak in the language of the receiver. Allow time for comprehension. Remember to be brief, accurate, and to the point; use short words and short sentences; and use one sentence for each idea.

5 Give reasons and explain significance.

Only when an employee has all relevant information, including the reasons for the task, can he or she make intelligent decisions, particularly if complications develop later when your orders are being carried out. Try to anticipate the employee's feelings, needs, and concerns. Remember what it felt like when you were given instructions and weren't sure why.

6 Check for understanding.

Be sure the employee remembers

the essentials. If possible, show employees what you want, or what things should look like when your order has been carried out. By repeating the order and by giving the employee the opportunity to ask questions (or, better still, by asking that your instructions be repeated), you will identify any areas of doubt or misunderstanding.

 ### Avoid overwhelming your staff.

Learn to anticipate reactions to an instruction and time its presentation accordingly. You can't afford to overwhelm people with orders. Try to have each task completed before assigning additional ones. Let employees know you'll remain accessible should problems or other questions arise.

 ### Respect individual experience.

The way you give orders will depend on the experience of individual employees and the particular situation or context. You can't expect inexperienced employees to understand as much as those who have worked with you for some time; you must be fair. If you invite feedback from experienced employees, afford that courtesy to others as well.

 ### Make sure you can enforce your order.

Assuming that you're sure the employee knows how to carry out your order, insist that your instructions be followed through.

Employees should know that you're prepared to take action against any refusals. Orders disguised as suggestions or requests, however, are preferable to any dictatorial approach.

 ### Distribute tasks evenly among staff members.

Don't overwork some employees merely because they will accept orders with less resistance than others. And don't give all the unpopular jobs to the same people all the time.

 ### Follow-up.

Check periodically to see that your directions are being carried out as you require within the agreed timeframe. Monitor progress and check on the final results to ensure they match what was requested. If appropriate, praise or thank the employees for their efforts.

 ### And remember...

- Always assume that the listener knows less than you do.
- Let people in on goals and priorities if you want them to use initiative.
- Always think of an order in terms of quality, quantity, time, why, how, and safety.
- Encourage note-taking.
- Don't be casual or off-handed; otherwise your order might not be taken seriously.
- Anticipate problems and suggest ways of handling them should they arise.
- When issuing the order, show confidence in the person. It's contagious.

229

How to prepare for a meeting

It was Hendrik van Loon who once said that a meeting would be successful only if it had three participants—one of whom is away sick and another who is absent. Organisational life is never so generous to managers, however. Meetings have become an unavoidable aspect of a manager's job. Fortunately, unnecessary meetings can be eliminated; others can be made more effective. Important ingredients are planning and preparation, as the following points reveal…

here's an idea

Never introduce an idea, strategy, plan, or concept for the first time in a meeting. Chances are, your staff will spend the whole meeting trying to grasp the concept – and that's not what a meeting is for. Give them detailed handouts, and other reading material well before the event, so that they have an idea of what's to be discussed. Then, make better use of the meeting time to expand, clarify, and improve the concept.

here's an idea

If you're planning to hold a meeting, particularly one where the roll up is voluntary and unpredictable, consider having fewer chairs in place. It gets around the embarrassment of speaking to a half empty meeting and, as well, if more people than anticipated arrive, the bringing of extra chairs into the room will make people marvel at the popularity of the cause.

1. Make sure you've called the meeting for a reason.

Meetings should never become rituals. They cost time and money, so it's important to call a meeting *only* when one is warranted—to solve a problem, to coordinate activities, to disseminate and discuss urgent information, to reach a consensus or decision, to build morale, or to reconcile conflicts. So don't ask people to attend a listening-session if you can send a newsletter or email instead.

2. Select the participants wisely.

Only those who need to attend should be invited to do so. Each non-essential attendee is wasting his or her time and costing your organisation money. As well, the more people attending, the more difficult it is to reach consensus. Consider inviting participants to be present at a particular time—that is, for the agenda item on which their personal contributions are required.

According to US communications specialist Milo Frank, unnecessary participants, like unnecessary meetings, are a waste of everyone's time. He suggests you consider six questions in deciding whom to invite:

1. Whom must you invite?
2. Who can give you what you want?
3. Who favours your objective?
4. Who will oppose your objective?
5. Who is sitting on the fence?
6. Who can cause trouble if not invited?

3. Prepare a benchmark of productivity.

Be clear on the purposes of the meeting and your hoped-for outcomes. How will you know when you have achieved them? By preparing a 'benchmark of productivity' for the meeting—a check list of what you want to accomplish, to refer to during the meeting, or to use later to compare the hoped-for outcomes with the actual ones.

4. Select the right time and place for the meeting.

Call a meeting only when you have the information required for decision-making and you can be assured that the appropriate people will attend. Ensure that the venue is accessible to all participants, but remote enough to prevent interruptions. Check out the venue—its location, seating, lighting, ventilation, whiteboards, electrical requirements, and other essentials; and book the facility if appropriate.

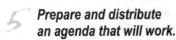

Prepare and distribute an agenda that will work.

The more care you take with an agenda, the more productive the meeting will be. The agenda should be more than merely a list of items handed out at the meeting. Key elements would include these:

- date, time, place, and duration of meeting
- a list of items to be discussed in sequence, detailing (for each item) who will lead the discussion, time allocated and, importantly, the objective (information sharing, discussion only, decision required, or problem to be solved, etc.).

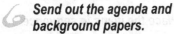

Send out the agenda and background papers.

By giving adequate advance notice and distributing the agenda and support documents, you will demonstrate your thoroughness and instil confidence in your leadership. (Remember, people being what people are, to allow time at the beginning of your meeting for 'reviewing' documents that may not have been read in advance.)

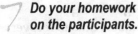

Do your homework on the participants.

If emotional or controversial issues, for example, are to be raised during the meeting, it is sometimes a good idea to discuss them with some of the key participants beforehand. Consider their reactions and how you might handle them during the meeting to achieve the desired outcomes.

Gather appropriate tools for the meeting.

Make sure you have considered the items frequently required during a meeting: notepaper, pens, a flip chart, a whiteboard, refreshments, an overhead projector, a telephone, and so on.

Be prepared—psychologically.

Mental preparation is also a vital consideration, so the following suggestions are offered:

- *Know the meeting process and your role as chairperson.* Understand the rules of the game before you play— whether they are formal rules of order involving motions, voting, adjournments, etc., or unofficial procedures developed by your own organisation.
- *Do your homework.* Be prepared and knowledgeable about the topics under discussion.
- *Believe you can lead.* If you have been called on to lead, someone believes you can do it. So be confident yourself that you can.
- *Seize the opportunity.* Responsibility requires extra effort. Give it—and grow.
- *Aim high.* Strive for excellence and set an example. Others will follow.

time management
negotiation
problem solving

speech making

How to compile a meeting agenda that really works

Call it a meeting plan or call it a simple list—but call it essential, because an agenda is the backbone of any successful meeting. The more care you take with its preparation, the more productive the meeting will be. So, if you want to gain a reputation as someone who conducts productive meetings, take the time to compile a workable agenda beforehand. Here's how…

quotable quote

Think of the agenda as a device to focus your meeting. A meeting with no agenda will have no focus and the results will be fuzzy. Too many side issues slip into consideration and, finally, like the famous Caucus Race witnessed by Alice in her Wonderland dream, all the attendees end up chasing each other around in circles.[24]

here's an idea

In your agenda, consider providing a SWEET objective for each topic under discussion – i.e.

Sensible – challenging, realistic, achievable
Written – providing a clear record of intent
Easy-to-understand – jargon-free, clear, precise
Easy-to-measure – you'll know when the agenda objective has been completed
Task related – expresses in clear terms the task that has to be done.

For example, if the topic is marketing, the objective may be 'to consider and discuss the presentations made by external consultants and to select the campaign we intend to use'.

In this way, participants will know what is expected of them and, at the end of the meeting, will be able to judge whether or not the objective has been achieved.[25]

1 Be aware of the need for an agenda.

An agenda is a written promise from the leader of a meeting to those attending. It is a commitment that, in the time allocated to the meeting, discussion will focus on the items listed. As well, the agenda is valuable because it provides the meeting with direction, purpose, confidence, and control. A meeting without an agenda is a meeting without an end.

2 Decide on the degree of formality required.

Some meetings are so small that a written agenda is inappropriate: the agenda is set in the first few minutes of discussion. Agendas are essential for larger gatherings, however. Formal meetings require formal agendas—including apologies, minutes of the last meeting, matters arising from those minutes, treasurer's report, etc. For less formal meetings, the chairperson usually has a free hand to list and order the items to achieve the aims of the meeting in the most stimulating way.

3 List the items.

At least a few days before the meeting, decide on the items for discussion. Participants might also be asked to contribute specific topics for the agenda. Often a pre-meeting discussion eliminates the need to put an item on the list. To restrict the length of the meeting, limit either the number of topics or the time to be spent on each.

4 Place the items in sequence.

The success or failure of a meeting can depend on the sequencing of its agenda items. Consider these points:

- If an item needs mental energy, clear heads, and bright ideas, put it high on the list.
- Hold back for a while any item of great interest to participants. Get some other useful work done first. Introduce the star item when attention begins to lag.
- To give members time to recover before the next tough topic, place less interesting items directly after

a very challenging one.

- If a participant must arrive late or leave early, ensure that an item requiring that person's input is placed on the agenda where those constraints are taken into account.

- Potentially controversial items can be dealt with later, when members have less energy to engage in conflict. Then again, problems are probably best tackled early when people are at their best. A tricky issue.

- Begin and end a meeting on a positive note with items uniting members.

 Structure the agenda.

An agenda should be more than just a list of topics. A good agenda includes these items:

- *Title, date, location,* and, possibly, a list of participants.

- *Definite start and finish times*—an essential courtesy for busy participants. Note also that few meetings remain productive after two hours unless adequate breaks are provided.

- *Topics, the names of people responsible for introducing or leading those topics, the objectives,* and *the time limits* set for those items (see accompanying box). Of course, the amount of time a topic will actually need can be unpredictable. But without some indication, the meeting could go well over time. Alternatively, some items might have to be postponed.

Topic	Person responsible	Objective	Time (mins)
1. Approve Agenda	Alan Fry	Decision	3
2. New information leaflets	Di Henty	Information	5
3. New requirements for leave requests	Alan Fry	Discussion	10
4. Changes to library	Phil Greer	Discussion	10
5. Increasing staff participation	Mary Gill	Problem-solutions	25

- When decisions need to be made, some chairpersons like to include (as a guide on the agenda) *the wording of the decisions expected.*

 Assemble any background papers.

The agenda should be accompanied by any necessary background material. Participants can then consider the topic carefully in advance and formulate useful questions.

 Distribute the agenda in advance.

Distribute the agenda and background papers at least two days before the meeting. If it is circulated too early, participants may forget it or lose it.

Use the agenda to monitor the meeting.

At the meeting, begin by agreeing on the agenda; then maintain the allocated order and times. Although temptation will arise, it's important to stay firmly with the agenda if you are to gain respect as a productive chairperson.

time management

negotiation

problem solving

speech making

How to conduct a successful meeting

Every manager needs to master the skill of chairing a meeting. Participants will leave a meeting chaired effectively with a sense of accomplishment and a clear understanding of future directions and tasks. If you want to chair successful meetings, follow these important steps...

quotable quote

Basically, there are three types of Chair: (1) the authoritarian, who conducts meetings like military drills and wonders why nothing very original is ever said or achieved in them; (2) the permissive, who lets the members run the meetings, and wonders why so many of them end in chaos; and (3) the majority, who are a little of both and who wonder why other people's meetings seem more effective than their own. This is because being an effective Chair does not come naturally. It requires certain skills, but the good news is that these skills can be learnt and they can be improved with practice. [27]

don't forget

Those first fifteen minutes

Studies have shown that meeting participants are more alert and creative during the first part of a meeting. As the meeting goes on, they become less and less attentive. So any problem that needs a creative solution, any information you really want employees to remember, and any important points that you want to drive home should be covered within the first fifteen minutes.

Start on time.

When you wait for latecomers, you penalise those who have arrived on time—and you inadvertently reward those who come late. Before long, everyone will arrive late. So how do you get people to your meetings on time? By starting on time! Always.

Get the meeting off to a business-like start.

Welcome and introduce yourself and the other participants and, if necessary, explain their roles. Clarify the objectives of the meeting, ensuring that each member understands the task at hand and is aware of the expertise available in the group. Be brisk and businesslike.

Preview and confirm the agenda.

Check that each member publicly agrees with the stated objective of each listed agenda item, thereby ensuring that all irrelevant and hidden agendas become redundant.

Indicate the criteria for a successful meeting and, in particular, how the group will decide or know when the outcomes are achieved. Other items might be suggested. After listing them under 'Other Business', close off the agenda.

Focus constantly on your objectives.

A meeting is held for a purpose—so keep its main objectives and desired outcomes clearly in mind at all times. Consider the following process:

- *Initiate discussion on each item* by setting the scene briefly and asking for responses. You may refer the matter first to a member who can make the best initial contribution.

- *Reinforce each item.* When moving on to a new agenda item, reiterate and clarify its purpose and objective.

- *Clarify issues.* If debate leads to confusion, it's your task to unravel the strands so that a decision can be reached.

- *Summarise regularly.* Particularly

during lengthy discussions, summarise progress periodically to maintain a sense of direction.

- *Clarify the decision-making process beforehand.* If people aren't sure about whether a decision has been made or, if it has, by what means, conflict and poor productivity will result.

- *Conclude discussion* of an item by summarising. When you sense consensus on major points, test it on the group, vote if necessary, and record the result. Resist the temptation to try to force people into agreement in order to tidy up discussions.

- *When a decision has been made*, be clear just what the decision is and how it will be implemented. Assign responsibilities and set deadlines for action.

- *If an issue can't be resolved*, find out why and appoint a task group or an individual to investigate and report to the next meeting.

5 End on a positive note —and on time.

Try to end on a positive note, even when there has been substantial disagreement during the meeting. Perhaps you could save for last an agenda item on which everyone can agree. Respect the plans of those who assumed that the meeting would end on time. Stop discussion about five minutes before the scheduled finishing time. Sum up the entire meeting; restate the outcomes; confirm allotted tasks and deadlines; and thank participants. Announce the time and date of the next meeting.

6 Review and analyse the success of your meeting.

While the meeting is still fresh in your mind, assess its effectiveness and review your own leadership style. Use that information to improve your next meeting.

You may, for example, raise with yourself such issues as these:

- ☐ Some people who should have been at the meeting were absent.
- ☐ People with important things to say were not given a proper hearing.
- ☐ The chairperson talked too much.
- ☐ Discussion was allowed to ramble on after a decision was made.
- ☐ The meeting ran out of time.
- ☐ Some topics failed to result in decisions.
- ☐ Too much time was spent on some topics; others were neglected or omitted.
- ☐ Some decisions were made on inadequate evidence.
- ☐ Several members came late and left early; others slipped in and out.
- ☐ The meeting went beyond the agreed finishing time.

7 Follow-up promptly.

Concise minutes, including a listing of decisions made, tasks assigned, and deadlines for action and follow-up, should be completed and distributed promptly. If necessary, inform other interested parties of outcomes as soon as possible after the meeting. Then, if possible, monitor the progress of assignments. At the next meeting, uncompleted assignments should be considered and unmet deadlines discussed. Such accountability helps ensure that the agreed outcomes of your meeting will have some meaning next time.

here's an idea

Do your meetings, which you call for, say, 2.00, usually start at '2.00-ish' – somewhere around 5 to 15 minutes late? And do they start later and later each time because everyone knows that everyone else is going to be late? You can attempt to solve this annoying problem by using the 'odd starting time' strategy.

For example, instead of scheduling a 2.00 start, specify 1.57 or 2.04. And when you're asked – as surely you will be – why you're being so specific, you reply: 'Because I mean it. That's precisely the time when the meeting must begin.' That's the key to the strategy's success. But you *must* start on time – at 1.57 precisely – even if all your staff aren't present.

Set the standard with your first odd-time meeting, and the credibility of the strategy will quickly establish itself.

here's an idea

If you want to run a smoother and more effective meeting, and help your staff to get involved as well, try this:

Firstly, it's essential that your staff members be prepared for meetings. Send them an agenda and any supporting documentation at least a day or two before the meeting is to take place. Then indicate when each person will be expected to contribute. For example: '3.35 p.m. to 3.45 p.m. Spare Parts report. John R. to summarise and answer questions on restocking strategy.'

time
management
negotiation
problem solving

speech
making

How to get the most out of meetings you chair

Good meetings are led; bad meetings are not. The success of a meeting will depend largely on your ability as chairperson to get things done efficiently and to reach group decisions in minimum time. The following strategies will help you conduct a successful meeting. Directly or indirectly, they all point to the one goal—ensuring that the meeting achieves its purpose…

1 Create a member-centred meeting.

A domineering chairperson will stifle a meeting. As chairperson, your primary job is to realise the expertise of the group. This means you should refrain from voicing your opinions until everyone else has had a chance to be heard. Good ideas are lost when participants are reluctant to contradict or disagree with a manager who has already stated an opinion. Know your own biases and be prepared to deal with contributions that may violate them. Be persuasive but not overly partisan. Be seen by all to have a balanced approach.

2 Encourage participation.

Make sure everyone has an equal chance to express a view. Allow no-one to monopolise. Avoid calling on the same speakers, even though they may be the most experienced, knowledgeable, and eloquent. Encourage different points of view. Defend the weak against the strong. Tactfully draw out the reticent members by asking them for their opinions or comments.

Tom Peters, in *In Search of Excellence*, writes:

> Why not strive to apply the essence of success in the school classroom to your meetings – drawing others out, getting them to share their knowledge, their hitherto hidden assumptions, to commit to one idea or another? Unfortunately, such commitment rarely occurs in adult group settings, even though most managers spend much of their working days in such settings.

3 Stimulate discussion and ideas.

A good meeting should be an exchange of ideas and information. The chairperson must foster this exchange by probing and asking open-ended questions:

- to clarify issues: 'Are you saying you can provide this material by the end of the week?'
- to restate certain points: 'So let's confirm this point…'
- to confront issues: 'Are we really prepared to…?'

- to question critically: 'What exactly do you mean by…?'
- to seek solutions: 'What should we do?' 'What do you think?' 'Why?'

 Ban those killer comments.

Crushing comments can kill enthusiasm and the flow of ideas. Treating a group member or a comment as uninformed, naive, or inferior will suppress discussion. Monitor and disallow such put-downs as 'That won't work', 'You're joking', and 'You'll learn in time'. Instead, encourage supportive comments: 'Let's follow that notion through a little…' 'Would anyone care to build on or refine that idea?' or 'I'd like to expand on that suggestion by considering it from another angle…'.

 Vary your style.

The key to chairing a meeting is flexibility. You will be a good chairperson if you assess the kind of leadership that the meeting requires and adjust your style accordingly. Respond to the mood of the meeting—know when to be relaxed, when to be firm, when to use humour, when to break. Each style exhibits effective leadership if it is right for the occasion.

 Keep the meeting on course.

Many meetings lose themselves through sidetracking or by getting bogged down on one issue. Some wandering may be useful, but frequently the group must be called back to the main topic at hand. Keep rambling speakers in check.

As well, watch for potential trouble. Deal with conflict, hostility, and tension when they begin to appear. Create harmony through mediation. Use humour, or call for a break at the right time to ease tension.

Watch the clock. Keep the meeting moving. Respect the participants' personal schedules: finish on time.

 Focus on the process.

Control the meeting by maintaining the agenda. Limit discussion times, but allow enough time to deal with complex issues. Stop and clarify issues if they become obscure. Summarise periodically to demonstrate progress. Monitor loss of attention. Watch for signs that an item has been adequately discussed; finalise it; and move to the next item. Divide the meeting into small groups if they can reach your outcomes more efficiently.

 And finally…

- Ensure that the meeting is not interrupted except in an emergency.
- Be first in the room. Then establish rapport with other early attendees.
- Start and finish on time.
- Thank members after they contribute, and at the end of the meeting.
- Always set an example. Be firm, polite, calm, businesslike, supportive, even-handed, and confident.

 here's an idea

Successful meetings require meaningful participation. Get into the habit of asking those people making comments (especially long comments) to summarise their two main points when they finish. This helps clarify the speaker's (and the other participants') thoughts and lets people know you always want to get to the bottom line.

 here's an idea

Here's a handy idea which helps keep meetings on task. Use two flipcharts. On one record ideas related specifically to the meeting's topic; the other is used to record all those ideas and issues which come up and usually tend to sidetrack discussions from the topic at hand. In this way you keep meetings focused, discourage repetition, and assure people with ideas that their unrelated topic will not be lost, but recorded for discussion at a later date.

 here's an idea

End every meeting with a stated conclusion. As the meeting draws to a close, use the final minutes to summarise key points, go over what you learned, and outline plans for action based on the meeting.

The bonus is that, by ending the meeting like this, participants will feel that it wasn't a waste of time – that they actually *did* accomplish something.

How to make a valuable contribution to a meeting

As a member of a committee or working party, or as a participant in a one-off meeting, you will have an excellent opportunity to influence decision-making and to make your talents known and available to the organisation. You can attend a meeting—or you can be a participant. Whether solving problems or pooling ideas, a meeting in which you are involved can be productive for you and the organisation, depending on how you act and what real contribution you make…

1 Understand why you have been asked to participate.

Ask yourself the following questions:

- Have I been brought in simply to fill a gap?
- Am I representing a department or section or specialist group?
- Have I been brought in to provide expertise or competence in a particular area?
- Am I here as the organisation's bright-young-person with ideas?
- Am I here as the voice of experience, the steadying influence?

When you can answer such questions, you can channel your efforts appropriately.

2 Know the other participants.

Find out all you can about the other participants—their likes and dislikes, strong and weak points, the powers they have, the way they operate, how they react to new ideas and proposals. Knowing all this, you can adopt effective tactics for dealing with them.

3 Arrive prepared.

Prepare yourself by studying the agenda and all working papers in advance. Focus on items for your particular attention and anticipate any needs the group will have for data you can supply. Prepare for your involvement by compiling handouts or charts, working up suggestions or recommendations, and making notes from which to speak if required. You may choose to canvass the views of influential participants beforehand. The amount of preparation you do will determine how others view you—as a passenger or as a valued participant. Plan in advance to make at least one specific contribution.

4 Arrive early and use the time wisely.

Arrive early and take the opportunity, if necessary, to introduce yourself to other participants. Use the waiting time profitably, perhaps learning their position on certain agenda items. If possible, get a seat close to

238

the chairperson—you'll get more involved and you'll be noticed.

 ### Talk up and get involved.

Don't hesitate to get into the act. A well-chosen question can often help to break the ice. Then you can enter into the discussion and speak freely. Research has shown that talkative participants usually contribute the most useful remarks, have the best ideas, and impress other members. The only drawback is that, in becoming influential, you also run the risk of becoming unpopular: some people can see productivity as a kind of control mechanism and therefore resent it.

 ### Make your presence felt.

Make your points clearly, succinctly, and positively. Remain silent when you have nothing useful to say. Listen, observe, and save your arguments until you can make a really telling point. Resist the urge to dominate the discussion.

The chairperson (and others) will recognise and appreciate your value to the group when you build on the ideas of others, pose 'what if?' questions, seek clarification of relevant issues, are supportive and make constructive comments, and are open-minded, willing to compromise, and respectful of others' contributions.

 ### Be an active listener.

Practise the skill of listening in meetings because it will lead to understanding and good questions. Often, many people try to talk at once; as a result there are too many interruptions. At other times, people are too busy thinking of what to say and fail to hear what others are saying. As well, animosity between participants often causes some not to listen or to disregard what's been said. Whatever the reason, failing to listen actively can cause meetings to fail.

 ### Be willing to learn.

Go into meetings prepared to learn. Effective participation in meetings doesn't always mean getting your own way. Rather, it means learning from others, accepting criticism, and incorporating the ideas of others into your own proposal.

 ### Volunteer to wrap-up the meeting.

Impress the chairperson, who is usually pleased to find someone willing to bring things together in a final summary, report, or action plan.

 ### Adhere to the rules of meeting etiquette.

Consider the following:

- Avoid interrupting.
- Refrain from distracting behaviour, such as pencil-tapping.
- Avoid side comments to your neighbour. If you have something to say, say it to the group.
- Always be pleasant, courteous, and tactful. If you must discredit another's proposal, expose its defects, not the person's.

 here's an idea

Being on time for an appointment shows respect for others and it's just plain good business. If you have trouble getting to meetings on time, then here are some useful ideas to contemplate:

- Never make promises you can't keep. Be realistic about making appointments and try not to overcommit yourself.
- Be precise about meeting times. 'Between 10 and 10.30' or 'around 2.15' is never good enough.
- Discipline yourself to end your previous appointments on time.
- Be aware of your environment. How long does it take by taxi? by bus? How easy is it to park? With rain, will it take longer to arrive?
- If you're going to be late, show courtesy by making a phone call.
- If you are late once, don't let it happen to the same party a second time.

here's an idea

Here's a three-part strategy for making your presence felt at meetings:

- State your position or idea on the topic being discussed.
- Support your position with appropriate facts and detail.
- And this is the component which most of us neglect: Ask the group what they think of your position or idea. This phase is vital because it adds weight to your comments by forcing the group to stop, to consider seriously what you've said, and to respond.

How to keep the minutes of a meeting

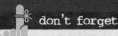
Every scheduled meeting of an organisation or committee is an important occasion. Such meetings make decisions that determine the daily business of the organisation. Was an issue discussed? Was it approved? Why and how was it approved? Who was present? The answers and outcomes of such questions as these must be recorded as minutes of the meeting. Minutes are an important decision-making record, so it is essential that the following points be considered...

1 Be aware of what minutes must be kept.

Minutes should be kept of all formal meetings of your organisation—of the governing board, the annual general meeting, any special general meeting, and any vital sub-committee meetings.

2 Know what the minutes must record.

The minutes should clearly indicate the following:

- the nature of the meeting—governing, annual, special, or sub-committee
- the place, date, and time of the meeting
- the name of the chairperson and the names of those present (for large meetings, names are unnecessary, but the number of people present should be recorded).
- the names of those who sent their apologies for being absent
- the time the meeting was begun
- the business of the meeting in chronological order—perhaps including:
  - a review and acceptance of the minutes of the previous meeting
  - a review and acceptance of the treasurer's report, including the passing of accounts for payment
  - a consideration of correspondence received and sent since the last meeting
  - any business arising from the previous minutes
  - any general business as listed on the agenda
- the place, time, and date of the next meeting
- the time the meeting closed.

The use of sub-headings and a numbering system for each item will allow for ready reference later. To make the minutes complete, add a copy of the notice of meeting, a copy of the treasurer's report, and the agenda issued prior to the meeting.

3 Be precise in recording decisions made.

During the meeting, participants will make proposals in the form of motions that, through the process of voting, will be accepted or rejected. For each item of business considered, the minutes must record this important procedure:

- the precise wording of the motion
- who submitted it
- a summary of discussion on the motion

- who moved it
- who seconded it
- whether it was carried or lost, and the result of the vote.

4 Record contentious matters carefully.

For those issues characterised by dissension and vigorous debate, it is important that the differing points of view be minuted—objectively and accurately. The minute writer must be careful not to reveal his or her own views, and must ensure that the views of all speakers are given appropriate space. The chairperson should later check that a balanced account of the issue has been recorded.

5 Write-up minutes promptly.

Unless the secretary can take short-hand, a rough copy of proceedings should be made during the meeting. As soon as possible afterwards, while memory is fresh, the minutes should be written out clearly or typed.

6 Distribute the minutes appropriately.

The chairperson should see a copy of the typed minutes before they are finalised to ensure that they are accurate. A master copy is then placed in a minute book or minutes file. Each committee member should have a copy of the minutes at or before the next meeting. Minutes, other than those of an annual general meeting, are not open to public viewing. Only AGM minutes are normally available on request for wider scrutiny.

7 Know the procedures for confirming minutes.

The first business of any meeting should be to confirm the minutes of the previous meeting as an accurate and true record of that meeting. If the participants have no objections, the minutes are confirmed and may be officially signed as a true record by the chairperson and secretary. Any objections or corrections should be discussed, agreed to, written in, and initialled by the chairperson before the document is signed.

If any business recorded in confirmed minutes is reopened at a later meeting and members feel that, in the light of further information or changed circumstances, the previous resolution should be changed, they can do so only if the meeting accepts and approves a resolution rescinding the earlier decision.

8 Maintain a high standard.

The key to providing a set of high-quality minutes is to make them accurate and concise, containing only facts (not the writer's views). Minutes should be set out so that they can be referred to easily and quickly when necessary. A good secretary keeps good minutes. Accurate, well-kept minutes are a sign of a well-managed organisation.

 don't forget

The qualities of a good minutes secretary

- be intelligent and clear-thinking
- have a good memory
- be good at, and enjoy, organising
- enjoy meetings
- be of the right status – not too junior nor too senior
- be of calm disposition
- be friendly
- have the right skills
- be a good listener
- be open-minded and fair
- be literate
- be well informed
- be able to think ahead and anticipate.

And when a secretary's role goes beyond mere minute-taking, to include planning for, organising, even 'running' the meeting, these qualities become even more important.[29]

 smile & ponder

Remember that although a committee is obliged to keep minutes, it also has the unfortunate ability to waste hours.

read further

The Secrets to Masterful Meetings: Ignite a Meeting Revolution! by Michael Wilkinson, Leadership Strategies Publishing, 2005.

241

How to reduce the number of time-consuming meetings

Meetings, whether they are one-on-one discussions or gatherings of five, ten, or twenty people, are an important part of working life—but they are time-consuming. And often they are criticised for being unproductive, costly, boring, and sometimes unnecessary. Are they always needed? And all of them? Check out these points, and you may find you'll be holding fewer meetings in future…

1 Be fully aware of the cost of your meetings.

Meetings consume valuable time. Often, time is wasted on rambling discussions, excessive socialising, political manoeuvring, special-interest conflicts, and travelling. Nor is time the only casualty. When did you last find out what your organisation's meetings were costing in salaries alone?

2 Consider why you hold so many meetings.

Meetings can be very useful tools for communicating ideas, clarifying information, solving problems, making decisions, and building teams. But they can also be held for the wrong reasons:

Do you meet simply because the day of the week traditionally calls for it? Do you meet (but primarily socialise) in the guise of work? Does your department meet once a week—only because another department does? Do you hold many meetings because you believe volume indicates 'busy-ness' and product-ivity of your organisation or yourself? Do you hold a meeting simply because you haven't the courage to make a decision yourself? Do you hold a meeting to decide something even though you've already made up your mind?

Spend some time thinking about *why* you hold regular or once-only meetings before considering the following strategies aimed at reducing unproductive meeting time…

3 Establish a workable review process.

Often, regular meetings outlive their usefulness. Try to set a termination date whenever you establish a committee—or, at least, review a committee's progress periodically and disband it if it is no longer productive.

4 Consolidate your meeting procedures.

One manager found she was spending hours each month in separate meetings with individual department heads, covering more or less the same topics. She now holds a monthly group meeting—which helps the department heads keep abreast of one another's activities and forges an *esprit de corps*. Are there any creative ways of consolidating your meeting times?

 Limit the number of participants.

Problem: The larger the crowd, the greater the discussion, the longer the meeting. Solution: Limit attendance to those concerned with topics on the agenda. Schedule some participants to attend only that part of the meeting to which they can contribute. Make sure key people are present.

 Define clearly the purpose of every meeting.

Have a definite reason for every meeting. Think 'reason' first, then 'meeting'. Legitimate reasons might include solving a problem or making a decision where group expertise is essential; obtaining information from participants before group discussion and clarification; motivating people with common goals; generating new ideas through brainstorming; exchanging viewpoints; announcing new policies or programs followed by a Q&A session to clarify the issues. Meetings are generally not an efficient way to dispense information; if that's the primary reason for the gathering, you should rethink the need for calling the meeting…

 Consider an alternative to a meeting.

Once you have specified the purpose of your meeting, consider whether another alternative might not be a

more efficient form of communication, e.g.

- Want feedback on a new proposal? Try a short survey or some quick phone calls.
- Need to disseminate information? Consider a memo, poster, or news sheet.
- Trying to get your staff to know each other better? Run a barbecue after hours or on Saturday.
- Want some ideas on an issue? Put a large 'graffiti sheet' in the staffroom.
- Need to hear about problems? Try ten-minute one-on-one meetings rather than tie up *all* staff for two hours.

If you can achieve some outcomes without calling meetings, you can save much time and the meetings you do call will become powerful, special events.

 And, as well…

- Occasionally cancel a regular meeting to test the need for it.
- Keep a folder of agenda items and, instead of having regularly scheduled meetings, call a meeting only when your folder has sufficient items. You'll find that many items will take care of themselves without a meeting!
- Question *every* item on an agenda. Could they be handled in other ways?
- To avoid losing production and time, work hard to make every meeting a very good one. As Peter Drucker reminds us, 'One either meets or one works—one cannot do both at the same time.'

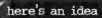 **viewpoint**

"If you had to identify in one word the reason why the human race has not achieved, and never will achieve, its full potential, that word would be 'meetings!'."
– Jim Mullen, *Paper* magazine

 here's an idea

US business consultant Gary Lockwood says that the typical manager spends 17 hours each week in meetings, plus another 6.3 hours preparing for those meetings. And nearly a third of that time is being wasted, he says – which means we're wasting nearly one 8-hour working day each week in useless meetings.

If you must have a meeting, get value for money: Have an agenda; stick to a firm time limit; accomplish your goals; do the follow-up work to make sure the time wasn't wasted – but evaluate whether you need to have a meeting in the first place. If you save even one hour a week, you're giving yourself the equivalent of two additional workdays each year.

quotable quote

There are many people who think that holding or attending a continuous string of meetings is a sign of their power and importance. The exact opposite is true. If meetings are merely routine or unnecessary, they are, in fact, a sure sign of bad management.[30]

How to overcome problems at meetings

As a manager, you are often required to chair meetings. To be successful, you will need to minimise your own involvement, foster interaction among the participants, and ensure that everyone makes a contribution. There are times, however, when awkward situations arise; and then you will need to draw on a repertoire of responses to maintain control. Here are some of the most common problems that arise in meetings and the strategies for handling them...

1. When the discussion becomes irrelevant...

Meetings sometimes get bogged down in time-consuming, irrelevant discussions that lead nowhere. To get the meeting back on course, you can:

- refocus the discussion by indicating that the group has strayed from its real objective.
- summarise the discussion to date and link progress to the objective.
- bring the discussion back into line by posing a question relating to the agenda topic.

2. When the participants begin to lose interest...

Often caused by lack of concrete short-term goals or successes, flagging enthusiasm can be revived in a number of ways:

- Propose a success-guaranteed, short-term task.
- List the achievements of the group so far.
- If the current topic lacks interest, introduce a related theme to encourage a more active response.
- If the group suspect that their recommendations will not be adopted, convince them that worthwhile ideas

might well gain acceptance.
- Check whether each participant still agrees with the group goals.
- If participants believe that a decision has already been made, assure them that solid arguments from an interested group could alter or reverse the decision.

3. When there is uneven participation...

Reluctant speakers can be brought into the discussion by asking questions that you know they can answer. Compliment them for their views. Or ask everyone, in turn, to express an opinion before anyone else can discuss or evaluate the issue further. Restrain the talkative participants tactfully.

4. When the meeting gets overheated...

Your task here will be 'to stop the warring parties shouting at each other from the mountain tops and to bring them to the valley floor again to talk'. To this end, here are some strategies:

- Summarise the hot issue, giving combatants a chance to calm down.

- Appeal to other members, thus using group pressure to restore order: 'Can anyone suggest a way of getting these two people out of their no-win situation?'
- Propose that the current issue be dropped for a while and another line of discussion followed.
- Call firmly for order, stating that progress is being hindered through lack of objective or reasoned discussion.
- Call for a short coffee-break.

When someone is distracting the group...

If you have pencil-tappers, paper-shufflers, or side-talkers, they're probably unaware of their disruptive action, or they've lost interest, or they don't feel included, or the issues being discussed are irrelevant to them. Try:

- looking directly at the offender
- calling the offender by name and asking relevant questions
- tackling them in public, indicating that they're making it hard for the group to get through the agenda items
- taking a coffee-break, and tackling the offenders in private.

When an argumentative person takes over...

Often, if a participant constantly argues over minor points, the group itself will show its impatience. Failing this, you could:

- indicate that, unless positive and helpful contributions are made by all present, nothing worthwhile will be achieved
- give the offender a job to do—taking minutes, recording on whiteboard, etc.
- break the meeting into small work-groups, giving the offender only a small group to distract

- speak with the offender outside the meeting or over coffee.

When a long-winded participant dominates...

Here are four suggestions to quieten the long-winded, repetitious speaker:

- Politely interrupt and suggest that it's now time to hear from other participants.
- Say: 'I think we've been over this before.'
- Fire a difficult question at the offender to halt the barrage of words.
- Announce that each speaker has only three minutes to speak. Be strict with the blabbermouth, flexible with the others.
- Discuss the problem in private with the talkative one.

When two people dominate discussion...

When two members engage in a back-and-forth contest, leaving others to look on, close the debate by:

- summarising their arguments: 'Is this what you two are saying?...'
- involving other participants: 'What do the rest of us think about this?...' 'So, everyone, is there some way all this helps us solve the problem at hand?...'

When a decision can't be reached...

Make it easier for participants to evaluate the pros and cons of the issue:

- Summarise the discussion so far.
- Restate the issue or question clearly.
- Reiterate the goals or decision criteria.
- Take a short break or postpone the decision until next meeting.

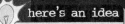 here's an idea

People who arrive late for meetings you have called can be a nuisance. Here are a few suggestions (some a little tough) to help you encourage these annoying people to change their ways...

- Don't wait for latecomers to arrive. Always start without them. In time, they'll learn, and soon get into the habit of arriving on time.
- Put items of interest to habitual latecomers at the top of the agenda.
- Make the last person to arrive take the minutes. (Ouch!)
- Pick and publicise an odd time for the meeting to begin. Instead of 3.30, try 3.28. It's surprising how people try to be there to witness the 3.28 start.
- Announce that a door prize will be awarded at precisely 3.29 – and the winner will need to be there to get the prize. An inexpensive novelty item is usually enough.
- Stop talking and create dead silence while any latecomer finds a seat.
- Make it a practice that any latecomer is required to 'volunteer' for any follow-up work from the meeting.

 quotable quote

Surroundings tend to affect the way we think and act and a poorly arranged and uncomfortable room is not likely to produce meeting results.[32]

How to deal with disruptive people at meetings

Meetings can be ruined by disruptive people who try to dominate proceedings at the expense of others. They frequently interrupt, emotionalise issues, sidetrack, challenge, complain, engage in repetitive speechmaking, threaten, discount the contributions of others, personalise issues, and in general throw a pall of gloom over the proceedings. Managers must minimise such disruptions and regain control over the meeting. Here are several strategies for handling disruptive people...

1 Create a smaller audience for them.

Give disruptive people only one or two people to influence. Break the meeting into smaller groups and instruct each group to generate statements by consensus, before reporting back to the full meeting.

2 Get a disruptive person to confront the issue.

Ignore the content of an individual's remarks and openly tackle the problem. For example, say: 'You seem particularly upset or disruptive today, John, especially when someone disagrees with you. Is there any way the rest of us can help you?' Alternatively, gain the support of the rest of the group by becoming a little emotional over the issue—by stating precisely how you feel about the situation. For example, say: 'As chair, I feel powerless to accomplish anything at present and I get upset when you try to take over the meeting and have your own way. John, how

can we get this meeting back on to an even keel?'

3 Attack the content.

Three strategies could be adopted here to force the person to focus on content rather than disruption:

- Turn the disruptive individual's questions, pessimistic asides, or veiled threats into statements. This procedure will force that person to take responsibility for expressing a point of view rather than block proceedings with questions or disparaging comments.

- If he or she continues to block the suggestions of other participants ('It just won't work!'), say something like 'OK, Bill, let's hear specifically why you think it won't work. Give us three good reasons.'

- Reduce the person's position to absurdity. Interrogate him or her to get to the bottom of the argument being put forward.

smile & ponder

The boss scheduled the weekly staff meeting for 4.30 on Fridays. When one of the employees finally got up the nerve to ask why, she explained: 'I'll tell you why – I've learned that's the only time when none of you seem to want to argue with me.'

don't forget

A root cause

If your staff are not adequately involved during a meeting in productive problem-solving and concensus-seeking, they are more likely to view the event as boring, unimportant, irrelevant, and manager-dominated – a situation which will cause some to be disinterested or disruptive.

4 Preplan the meeting and defuse the disruption.

Various tactics can be used if you know in advance that a disruptive individual will attend:

- Give the disruptive person a special task or role in the meeting, such as recording the views of others on the whiteboard, or taking the minutes.

- Structure the meeting to include frequent discussions of progress so far, thus giving others the opportunity to highlight the lack of progress due to this person's ongoing obstruction.

- Remove all vulnerable items from the agenda.

- Get others on side before the meeting by asking for their support in dealing with the expected disruption. For example, they can be asked to refuse to argue, or to confront the disruptive behaviour openly either verbally or through expressive nonverbal reactions.

- Request the cooperation of the disruptive individual beforehand. Ask him or her not to argue.

- List disruptive behaviour as an item for discussion early on the agenda.

5 Suggest a role reversal.

If the going gets tough during the meeting, try these suggestions:

- Invite the disruptive individual to argue the other side of the issue for a while.

- Have the disruptive person summarise proceedings to date.

- Offer to vacate the chair in favour of the difficult individual.

6 Listen—just in case.

Don't ignore altogether what is being said. A disruptive individual, despite the objectionable approach, might indeed have something useful to contribute to the outcome of the meeting.

7 Pull the plug.

When all else fails, and the meeting's real purposes are being thwarted, drastic measures may be called for:

- Indicate how the meeting has degenerated. Say that the only way out of the chaos is to adjourn the meeting.

- Leave the meeting, disavowing any responsibility for what has occurred—remembering, of course, that, if you are to retain your authority, you will have to take follow-through action.

Never threaten or bluff unless you are prepared to have your bluff challenged or exposed.

8 Remain calm and in control.

All these strategies demand that the chairperson adopt an unruffled, cool attitude. If you become angry, you give away power—and if that anger tactic becomes part of your routine style, you might prevent more timid participants from contributing to the meeting for fear of confrontation.

 here's an idea

If a meeting participant continues to dominate and interrupt, do not attempt to fight the battle alone. Use group pressure.

For example, thank the member in question for his contribution, then bring in the others. 'We've all heard what Bill has said, now I'd like to ask the rest of you for comments.'

Or 'I think we all understand Bill's point, but we have other matters to consider today and it's important we move on – if everyone agrees'. Rarely will members disagree, because they too have had to put up with Bill's disruptive behaviour.

here's an idea

When a disruptive individual dominates and undermines, a meeting is out of control. This is the time when you may need to defer to the strict procedures of conventional quasi-legal meeting rules. For example, use the chairperson's inherent powers to silence the trouble-maker and to record censures, reprimands, or other penalties.

A useful motion to silence disruptors is 'that the speaker be no longer heard'.

here's an idea

It may be impossible to reconcile differences during a meeting, but if you can cement agreement on items where there is agreement, you can lay foundations for future progress and cooperation.

BUILDING ESSENTIAL SKILLS

How to get results from a committee you appoint

Committees are frequently criticised for their inability to accomplish a great deal, for being costly and time-consuming, for being unable to reach decisions, and for often producing mediocre decisions. A committee's success or failure can often be traced back to the experience of the manager who appoints it and the extent to which the following guidelines are adhered to...

1 Be sure you really need that committee.

Sometimes the use of a committee is not the best means of tackling a particular task you have isolated. It might be wise *not* to use a committee if...

- you already have a solution, have made a decision, or will be hesitant about accepting the committee's recommendation. Remember, people resent spending valuable energy and time producing the axiomatic.

- there is not enough time or expertise available for the committee to operate effectively.

- the matter cannot be handled by group discussion. For example, policy formulation, problem solving, and planning are appropriate activities for a committee; managerial functions or research may be inappropriate.

In such cases, you might consider an alternative process, such as a survey, delegation, consultancy, or a task force.

2 Define the assignment specifically.

A committee must clearly know its purpose, as defined in written terms of reference, which in turn must be translated into a set of tasks or goals for completion within a set timeframe. Unless the committee's parameters and authority are specified, the members may not know whether they are responsible for a decision, a recommendation, or merely inconclusive deliberation. To whom will the committee be reporting? By when? How will it report? What resources are available?

Try to resolve such matters before the first meeting is held.

3 Choose your chairperson carefully.

The chairperson is the key to avoiding many of the criticisms of committee work. An effective chair plans for meetings, prepares and distributes agendas and supporting material, presents proposals for discussion and action, conducts meetings efficiently, and guides the thinking of committee members. A committee's success is clearly linked to the skill of its chairperson.

Appoint good committee members.

In selecting members for your committees, keep these points in mind:

- Seek voluntary membership preferably: willing workers provide for greater harmony and productivity in the long run.
- Appoint members according to the skills, strengths, energy, and commitment they will need to accomplish the task.
- Select members with a vested interest in completing the task.
- Attend to membership balance: consider age, sex, experience, and positive and negative views.
- Ensure that the members suitably represent the interests they are intended to serve and that they have the necessary authority.
- Select members able to perform well in groups.

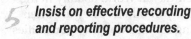

Insist on effective recording and reporting procedures.

Agendas and written minutes of meetings are fundamental to a committee's ongoing productivity. They stimulate members to reach conclusions, call for follow-up actions, and provide a permanent record for future reference.

Evaluate the effectiveness of your committees regularly.

An ongoing program of evaluation will show which committees are effective, which are not, how some could improve their operations, and when additional committees are needed. It is important to write an evaluation process into the life of all committees.

And don't forget...

- Monitor overlapping areas of focus: there is always the danger that one committee might need to discuss an item on the agenda of another. Take steps to avoid conflict. In such cases, propose joint meetings on the common issue; or refer the relevant recommendations of one committee to the other.
- Where possible, make your committees represent all organisational groups—clerical, professional, support staff, workers, even customers.
- Check that, with time, your committees don't become more concerned with maintenance rather than development.
- To preserve morale and to train the members in management thinking, provide feedback to the committee. Tell them how their deliberations were used, or how and why they were modified.
- Give credit where credit is due, even if a committee is having limited success.

quotable quote

Productivity in a committee comes through its being given urgent problems, the power to make decisions or recommendations, easy communication between the members, an orderly system of treating problems, a skilled chairperson, and the intelligence and originality of the group...[36]

smile & ponder

A committee...

- is like an easy chair – easy to get into but hard to get out of.
- is a group of people who individually can do nothing but, as a group, decide that nothing can be done.
- starts out considering two alternatives and quickly narrows them down to eight.
- is an avenue into which good ideas are lured and quietly strangled.
- is a collectivity where the ignorant come to pool nothing in the hope that they'll find someone who can produce something so that they can all take the credit for it.
- is a body that receives submissions and makes decisions in spite of them.
- of one gets things done.

Committees have such poor reputations – even more reason why it is imperative that managers should give much thought to their creation, their member-ship, their task, and their effectiveness.

How to motivate employees

From the lounge-chair sports expert to the company CEO, most people have definite views on what motivates others—and they're probably right, in part at least. Valiant attempts to convert theory into practice, however, have not always succeeded in getting people to give that little extra. The outcome often is a reversion to manipulative and kick-in-the-backside approaches. From the plethora of information and advice about motivation, here are the essential principles...

Understand motivation.

Ultimately, there are only two types of motivation—people do what they do either out of love or out of fear. Many go to work because they fear what will happen if they don't. Others go because they love it, the sense of achievement they get, the opportunity to meet with friends. Your challenge is to help employees love their work.

Focus on job enrichment.

Frederick Herzberg advocated enriching people's jobs as a principal motivator. By making the job more enjoyable, you will ensure that:

- it will provide challenges commensurate with the employee's skills
- the employee with more ability will be able to stand out and win promotion to higher-level jobs
- there will be long-term improvements in employee attitudes.

Though not all jobs can be enriched (nor do they need to be), through job enrichment big gains can be made.

Learn to like people.

From your own experience, you already know a good deal about motivation—so continue to:

- focus on individuals, showing a genuine interest in them
- get to know your employees, their families, and their interests
- listen to what they have to say
- take time to talk to them
- recognise their contributions
- promote a relaxed and trusting relationship.

Encourage genuine participation.

Most people spend a significant part of their day at work, usually in the company of others. They are often looking for additional opportunities to use their talents fully and to develop new ones. Wherever possible, then, you should:

- involve employees in decisions whose outcomes require their commitment
- seek employees' views
- provide opportunities for achievement through interesting, varied, relatively short, and challenging tasks or projects
- delegate tasks that help them to display particular talents

- build interdependencies among people thus fostering cohesiveness.

Provide open communication.

Open, two-way communication is vital, and feedback is an essential part of that process. People like to know how you think they're going and how they might improve even further. That's one reason why management-by-walking-around is so effective; employees receive first-hand feedback on performance and have a chance to discuss issues that are important to them.

Make work itself a motivator.

Work can be a motivator if you:
- give employees more scope to vary the methods, sequence, and pace of their work
- give people all the information needed to monitor their own performance
- encourage employee participation in planning and evaluating new techniques
- increase individual responsibility for achieving defined targets or standards.

Lead the way by example.

Nothing turns people off faster than those who don't practise what they preach. Motivators must be motivated, energetic, animated, with loads of zest and sparkle, striving to achieve new heights. You also need to convey confidence in others—people who are expected to succeed usually do. It's all part of a 'self-fulfilling prophecy'.

Instil a desire to win.

If it works in sport, why not in business? Managers often fail to exploit the benefits from competition and, as a result, employees don't extend themselves. Be aware, however, that the effect of this type of motivating decreases significantly immediately on the completion of an event.

Reward accomplishments.

People expect to be rewarded in some way. To make sure rewards match individual value systems, you should:
- spell out the relationship between effort and reward—payment by results, commissions, or bonuses
- set stretch targets that require that little extra effort
- tell people what they have to do to be rewarded
- place responsibility firmly with the individual
- give praise when praise is due.

Make sure your rewards unite (rather than divide) your team.

Provide opportunities.

Though the doors of opportunity are marked 'push', it's often managers who must show employees those doors. Motivate your staff by revealing to them the doors of opportunity in your organisation—for rewards, for achievement, for taking on additional responsibilities, for resolving problems, for sharing, for recognition, for advancement…

don't forget
The Five-Is of motivation

- *Interesting work.* Not every aspect of a job can be interesting, but smart managers make sure that every job has interesting components.
- *Information.* Tell staff how the company makes money, how they're doing at their jobs, and other information you can offer.
- *Involvement.* Let employees help make decisions.
- *Independence.* Give them a chance to work on their own, using a flexible schedule.
- *Increased responsibility.* More responsibility means more opportunities and more visibility in the company. All three motivate staff.[38]

here's an idea
Recognise employees who put in the extra effort by instituting *ABCD Awards* – 'Above and Beyond the Call of Duty'. When an employee does something extra (stays late to finish a project on deadline, cuts costs, etc.), give an ABCD Award. With the award (in the form of a certificate perhaps) could go a gift voucher for lunch or some other small item. Maybe allow employees to accumulate ABCD Awards and, when they have a certain number, they are entitled to a paid day off or a grander prize.[39]

How to use praise to motivate staff

Praising is a management skill that is simple, inexpensive, and inexhaustible. Praise rewards when reward is due. It builds a feeling of goodwill. It provides positive encouragement to continue good practice and creative endeavour. It has a ripple effect, providing deserved acknowledgement for the person who is performing well, and conveying to an entire staff that good work will be recognised. But it is important that the right kind of praise be given in the right way, at the right time, and for the right reasons...

1 Find something to praise in every staff member.

If a compliment can boost the spirit, lack of one from important people can hurt for a long time. People need praise. If you look hard enough, you'll catch even your borderline employees doing something right. Compliment them on that action right there and then. If you get into the habit of doing that, you'll see their performance improve.

2 Praise spontaneously and frequently, but only if warranted.

The sooner you praise people, the more it means to them. Spontaneous compliments are usually sincere; they reinforce the exhilaration the recipient feels in the first glow of success or accomplishment. But compliments can be short-lived. They tend to evaporate soon after they are received. That's why people need them often.

A word of warning, however. Undeserved praise rarely produces positive results. Not only do you lose credibility through its unjustified use, but over time your staff will begin to ask themselves, 'If my boss keeps saying I'm doing so well, then why should I try any harder?' A degree of rarity tends to increase the value of anything—even praise for a job well done.

3 Be specific with your praise.

Generalities are rarely as effective as specifics. Don't simply say, 'Well done!' Say instead, 'I'm really impressed with the way you led our discussions at today's staff meeting. You must have been putting a lot of thought into your suggestions on budgeting. A first rate job!' Tell people exactly what you liked about their work and, in that way, they're more likely to repeat the behaviours that pleased you.

4 Link your praise to skills requiring development.

You can help an employee develop a skill by focusing your compliments on the activity you want him or her to master. If you praise in small amounts and often, you'll be surprised at the cumulative effect this has on skill development.

Be sincere.

Nothing will backfire more quickly than phony flattery. As British essayist Richard Steele once wrote: 'When you praise, add your reasons for doing so; it is this which distinguishes the approbation of a man of sense from the flattery of the sycophants and admiration of fools.'

Praise effort, not just achievement.

By showing heartfelt appreciation to someone who has tried to reach a goal, you provide an incentive for that person to work harder. Praise for the genuine triers will motivate them to strive even further.

Praise initiative.

The office junior who quietly takes on the unpleasant tasks, the clerk who goes the extra mile without being asked, the assistant who accepts the unpopular assignment without complaining—these are the people, far too few in number, who deserve praise, recognition, and commendation …and often do not receive it.

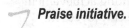 Praise individually and in public.

Offering praise for a group effort is fine in its place, but everyone craves individual recognition. Praise has a more lasting effect when you name the people involved.

And don't forget the adage, 'Praise in public, criticise in private'. People like receiving compliments from their boss in front of their colleagues or on other public occasions.

Show your appreciation in many ways.

In addition to complimentary asides and spontaneous acknowledgements, effective managers never forget the power of silent compliments, by using a variety of nonverbal gestures such as nods, smiles, and 'pats on the back'. As well, a short written note or a mention in the staff newsletter or at a staff meeting can have a dramatic effect. And nothing pleases employees more than learning of a manager's admiration of their work from other people: so occasionally express pride in your individual staff members to colleagues, the boss, or customers.

Don't use praise to sugar-coat a reprimand.

'You did good work on the Simpson project, Phil, but you came in over budget. You need to watch that.'

Sugar-coated reprimands are flawed: the employee won't remember the praise—only the criticism. Never try to soften criticism by wrapping a few items of praise around it. Keep praise and criticism for separate occasions or your staff member will become confused and suspicious of all future praise.

 research says

Praise can be a strong motivator, but many of us find it hard to handle. Research in the United States has shown for example that many people:

- want praise but can't and won't admit it.
- want to give it but don't know how.
- give praise for the wrong things – such as appearance or compliance – which usually causes the recipient to feel resentment, not pleasure.
- give praise to the wrong people – such as the flashy performer, the brassy participant, the con artist, the boss's pet, the self server, or the manipulator.
- give praise in the wrong way, too late, and too watered down.

quotable quote

Praise can be a powerful motivator. It can cost you very little but the rewards can be extraordinary… The old saying 'No news is good news' does not always ring true. Probably the worst action you can take is to withhold praise. Many simply see no news as no news – but some interpret it as bad news. Meaningful praise is one way of removing any uncertainty. Let people know what they are doing well. Reinforce the admirable qualities of their work. Meaningful praise makes a difference.[40]

How to gain staff commitment

High levels of staff commitment to individual projects or to the organisation as a whole are considered to be indicators of an organisation's success. Commitment, however, cannot be assumed. Rather, it requires continuing, credible, and confident actions that gain employees' trust and support. Although there is no single way of gaining commitment, there are some key considerations...

1 Be clear about what is required.

There are many examples in history of the lengths people are prepared to go in support of causes to which they are committed. You can't expect your employees to be committed to something that they, and perhaps you, don't understand. So before your staff commit their time and resources, they have every right to know exactly what it is they are letting themselves in for. And, of course, any confusion you have will soon be communicated to employees; so be clear about what you want.

2 Focus on action goals.

Assemble those employees whose commitment you are seeking; explain the situation as you see it; and describe the outcome/s envisaged. Explain any short-term goals and the specific actions needed for their achievement. Outline the benefits (what's in it for them) to be derived from successful accomplishment of those goals.

The noblest dream and the most appealing strategy are worthless until those involved make a commitment to achieve their objectives.

3 Adopt a problem-solving approach.

Use group facilitation skills (a force-field analysis, perhaps) to identify blockages preventing achievement of goals. Involve employees in planning for the elimination or reduction of those blockages. Allocate responsibilities for agreed actions and confirm individual commitment. Document all actions agreed on and circulate them to everyone involved.

4 Measure progress.

If possible, decide how goals and their progress can be measured. Rarely will employees be prepared to make or maintain a commitment when there are no measures of their progress and achievement. You will need to use measures as a means of assessing levels of commitment: if you can't measure it, you can't manage it.

Monitor staff response.

Employees will be waiting to see what you do. Even if they appear to show little interest towards your proposal or project, they will be keeping your subsequent actions under constant observation. Gaining and building commitment cannot be rushed and what *you* do will lead the way. Native Indians would have put it this way: 'You can't push the river'. If you find that commitment is not forthcoming, you will need to decide whether to persevere, to adopt another approach, or to scrap the idea.

 Foster interdependence among staff.

The development of strong links among employees benefits you and the organisation. One of those benefits, for example, is a decrease in absenteeism: staff realise how others are affected by their non-attendance. Interdependence helps to build ownership, trust, and commitment among employees as they see how their individual contributions affect, or are affected by, fellow workers.

 Develop a work environment where commitment grows.

Make your workplace one where employees want to be. An harmonious working environment brings out the best in people. They will be prepared to commit to a project or organisation they feel part of.

 Recognise achievements.

When employee commitment has resulted in goal achievement, provide rewards and other forms of recognition that individual employees value.

Recognition should cater for individuals, work groups, and even families. After all, the success of many projects depends, in part, on the support provided by life partners and other family members.

 Find reasons for declining commitment.

Sometimes on a new project, the initial exuberance and commitment of staff wane. Why? One of the following factors, or a combination, could be at the root of the problem:

- Did you take too long to get the project started after the planning phase? In the meantime, other demands might have intervened and 'cooled off' your staff.

- In the initial planning stage, did you account for any events or conditions that might distract your staff? Did you spend time trying to foresee and plan for such obstacles?

- Has the momentum slowed down because of vacation periods, Christmas holidays, or the shorter breaks? Timing is an essential ingredient in any new project.

- Did you set attainable objectives? Or were your staff like the greyhound chasing the rabbit at the dog track— always running but never able to catch the wretched thing!

- Are your staff having difficulty with some activity early in the program? They could drop their bundle.

- Did you plan periodic feedback sessions to identify and remedy any difficulties encountered? Feedback and evaluation keep commitment high.

 **quotable quote**

Successful organisations require the 3Cs – that's creativity, competition and commitment.[42]

smile & ponder

In his book *A Passion for Excellence*, business consultant Tom Peters tells a story about General Electric's CEO Jack Welch.

It seems Welch once asked some managers in his purchasing department to work on some tasks. He then met with them weeks later to review their progress.

To Welch's dismay, there was no progress to report – only weighty analyses and half-finished efforts at coordinating the projects with different departments.

Furious, Welch called an abrupt halt to the meeting and announced that it would reconvene four hours later – with the same purpose: to review progress.

This time, he got what he wanted. More was done in those four hours than had been done in the several weeks leading up to the initial meeting.

Tom Peters says this insistence on action versus lots of good logic and presentations is often what separates winners from losers in the corporate world.

How to reward staff for a job well done

People like to know that others appreciate their efforts and to receive recognition for a job done well. From management's point of view, it's a good practice to reinforce desired behaviour by acknowledging it with an appropriate reward. Rewards play an important part in job performance, motivation, and productivity. Now you can recognise employees' achievements and make your workplace a haven for high productivity by considering these suggestions…

1 Ensure performance and reward go hand in hand.

For your organisation's incentive scheme to be effective, your staff must see it as acknowledging good performance. If employees know that top performance, by individuals or teams, will be acknowledged in some way, then those rewards—and their efforts which earned them—will have meaning. In this regard consider such points as these:

- The size of the reward should reflect the size of the effort. An employee or team idea that generates a big return for the company should be rewarded accordingly.
- Rewards should be tied to one's contribution, not simply to the length of time with the organisation.
- Participants must be aware of the criteria being used to assess performance.

2 Devise a workable scheme.

Develop a set of principles that could form the basis of an employee reward system for your organisation. You might consider these points:

- To administer the scheme, establish a committee of innovative managers and, in time, previous award winners. Rotate membership to maintain the flow of fresh ideas.
- Ensure the scheme spreads the glory to all parts of your organisation and to all levels, from senior executives to back-room operatives.
- Avoid granting rewards at fixed intervals, such as at the end of the year or at performance appraisal time. Employees need to be motivated throughout the year.
- Recognise the achievements of teams as well as individuals—to heighten team spirit, downplay the nasty side of individual rivalry, and recognise the project-based nature of your organisational structure.
- Have supervisors nominate awardees in writing, documenting specific accomplishments.
- When designing your own incentive program, seek input from staff. Performance will peak if participants are involved in proposing their own rewards.
- Actively support the scheme, even participate in it—and this means the CEO and top managers as well.

Select rewards that employees value.

Different things motivate different people, so incentive schemes must provide a variety of rewards that staff value. For example, one researcher has identified those incentives which improve productivity most, including, in descending order of importance:

opportunities to advance, good pay, opportunities to develop new and old skills, pay on merit, recognition for good work, opportunities to be creative, interesting and challenging work, having a voice in decision-making, responsibility, fringe benefits, equal workload.

In other words, not all rewards need to be monetary or materialistic.

Brainstorm the types of rewards worth considering in your organisation—for example:

reduced working hours or nine-day fortnights, tickets to sporting events, company vehicles, praise, a weekend away, in-house fitness centres, housing loans, a trophy or certificate, choice of work hours, a feature article in the company newsletter, a week in the company villa, flowers or wine delivered home, a catered breakfast or lunch, a team 'conference' at a coastal resort, an overseas research trip, job security, movie tickets, permanent part-time work, a paid training course, promotion, a donation to a charity of the employee's choice, a letter of appreciation from the CEO, naming a space in the building after a winner, a restaurant dinner…

Variety is appreciated by most staff who will often choose particular endeavours for which they find the rewards most appealing.

Reward performance immediately.

We've all been brought up to want instant gratification. So, whether the reward is for individual excellence or team success, wherever possible give it immediately. Reward for performance long forgotten is of little value.

Make a big deal of the presentation.

Publicise winners widely, as well as the reasons for the choices. Ensure that the recognition is delivered personally and honestly. Avoid slick ceremonies: to some employees they seem artificial. Instead, consider tasteful alternatives such as lunch with the CEO, a brief presentation in the workplace, acknowledgement in the company newsletter, or a short ceremony at a senior staff meeting. Sincerity counts.

Explore model incentive schemes.

Consider initiatives introduced by others. For example, at Eastman Kodak in Rochester, New York, every time an employee suggested an idea to save the company money, he or she was given a financial reward. If the suggestion was adopted by the company, the employee received 15 per cent of the savings achieved in the first two years the suggestion was used. And if the idea led to a new product, the staffer was given 3 per cent of sales in the product's first year. Kodak was distributing about $3 million yearly to more than 30,000 of its creative staff.

A smart organisation understands that the more creative its employees are, the better off the company will be in the long run—and it rewards staff accordingly.

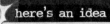

here's an idea

As a recognition-and-reward strategy, staff performance contests can present problems. When contests award expensive prizes (holidays, cars, trips), some employees will cheat, lie, even sabotage each other's performance, to win. Such contests motivate winners and alienate losers.

US management consultant Aubrey Daniels says a truly motivational contest should:

- Award small prizes and make bragging rights the main reward.
- Run for no longer than three months. Year-long contests put the reward too far from employees' behaviour. Even the best performers will tend to grow weary by the year's end.
- Be fun. Giving one or two large prizes instead of many small ones takes the fun out of it for most people.
- Allow an unlimited number of winners. Everyone who meets the criteria should walk off with a prize.

here's an idea

Choose symbolic, tangible rewards that anchor positive behaviours to success: A knife for being at the 'cutting edge', or a pair of scissors for 'cutting costs', or golf balls for being 'on the ball'.

Channel attention and enthusiasm toward reliving, discussing, and celebrating the accomplishment. Don't let the reward steal the show.

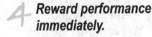

How to boost flagging morale

'Low morale' is what most managers don't want to hear when *esprit* among their employees is being discussed. Organisations whose morale is considered low usually lack achievement motivation and a sense of real purpose. As well, the turnover of their employees is usually high. Though reversing these trends will take time, you can be assured of success if you act on the following suggestions…

1 Become a morale missionary.

Morale is a group phenomenon but an individual matter. We speak of high morale in a group—meaning that most of the people in the group have a good sense of *esprit*. Group morale, however, depends on the morale of each individual in the group. Thus, improvement in *esprit de corps* can be achieved only by improving the morale of every person in the group. This is best achieved through the personal missionary work of the manager. Inspirational talks and group initiatives such as projects, services, and clubs can help; but unless the manager is there working with individual staff, group morale is not likely to improve.

2 Identify issues— not the outcome.

Morale is the outcome. Issues are the things contributing to that outcome. Employees may attribute the cause of low morale to the turn-round time on decision-making, the constant changing of priorities without

consultation, the lack of training, inflexible procedures, the incorrect mix of resources and people, or poor communications. Focus on identifying the issues; and you will have a much better chance of improving the situation and boosting morale.

3 Measure morale before trying to manage it.

You may decide to use commercially available tools to measure the effect that the issues have on productivity; or you may opt to design your own. Whatever your decision, it is best to use such instruments to get an accurate picture of the issues and the associated problems. As management experts tell us, 'If you can't measure it, you can't manage it'.

4 Build self-confidence and security.

Job security and a feeling of confidence in one's ability to handle the day-to-day incidents of life and work are key elements in good staff morale. You can provide this feeling—by training staff to do their jobs effectively, showing them the importance of their jobs to the organisation, and demonstrating your confidence in them.

 Set priorities—and be seen as supportive.

By establishing priorities, you help people make molehills out of mountains. Issues confronting staff will generally fall into three broad categories:

- those that they will not be able to influence at all
- those over which they have very little influence
- those that they can influence.

Help staff to live with what they cannot change, and take specific actions to remedy what they or you can change. Finally, communicate your feelings and those of your staff to the people who can change things that are out of your control.

 Establish work groups.

The essence of high morale is participation and the feeling of being wanted. The interdependencies created by people working in groups help to build bonds and enthusiasm among group members. In turn, other aspects of workplace life will be affected—absenteeism will reduce; cohesiveness will increase; and morale will improve.

 Encourage action.

Nothing succeeds like success, so get runs on the board as soon as possible. Empower groups to recommend

and act on a variety of issues. Not that you abrogate all responsibility to the groups; but if a group has been formed to deal with an issue, lend your support and acknowledge achievement.

 Keep people informed.

Communication is the lifeblood of any organisation, so make sure that employees have all the information they need to function effectively. An open, honest, and caring environment promotes *esprit de corps*.

 Remain alert to the morale factor.

Morale changes—sometimes daily— so you can't rest on your laurels when you think a crisis has been averted. Stay in touch with day-to-day events, and watch for changes in morale.

 And don't forget...

- Establish fair policies and administrative practices.
- Encourage staff members to discuss their problems.
- Help staff to guard against failure.
- Protect staff against unfair criticism.
- Develop a sense of purpose and solidarity.
- Keep jobs interesting, with new challenges, new authorities, and new responsibilities.
- Be friendly and appreciative of staff effort.
- Recognise the effect on morale of reassignments, redundancies, and dismissals.
- Encourage promotion from within.

How to develop staff cohesiveness

Cohesiveness holds a group together voluntarily. Staff will operate better as individuals if they consider themselves part of a well-functioning, supportive, and happy team. As committed participants in the group, they are more productive, communicative, trusting, motivated, and loyal. If you want to ensure your staff becomes a winning team, you should consider these suggestions to foster cohesiveness...

1 Be aware of the features of a cohesive team.

What are the characteristics of a team you are striving to establish? According to Douglas McGregor, the ideal team displays these features:

- The atmosphere is informal, comfortable, and relaxed.
- Everyone participates in discussions. Members listen to each other. Every idea is given an adequate airing.
- The goals of the group are understood and accepted by all.
- There is constructive disagreement. The group seeks resolution rather than domination of any dissenter.
- Decisions are reached by consensus.
- Criticism is frequent, frank, and comfortable. All members are free to express their personal feelings.
- When action is agreed on, clear tasks are assigned and willingly accepted.
- Members share beliefs and values, and benefit from each other's support and recognition.
- The group displays a united front.
- The leader does not dominate, nor does the group unduly defer to him or her.

2 Promote interaction between staff members.

Effective teamwork occurs when group members feel positive towards each other. Act as a catalyst to create and maintain a network of interpersonal relationships among group members. Arrange regular meetings that are either work-related or social. Organise an annual barbecue or similar function where colleagues can get to know each other better.

3 Set clear, attainable goals and priorities.

When everyone in the team knows 'where we are going and why', and helps to set those objectives, there is greater potential for cooperation and high morale.

4 Clarify and negotiate roles.

Just like a football team, your staff members need to know who is playing in what position and how to play together confidently and effectively. The way they play will be determined by their beliefs about the group, its members, and their place in the scheme of things.

To clarify such roles, have team members share this information:

- What I get from you that I want
- What I get from you that I don't want
- What I don't get from you that I want.

Then discuss individual contributions. Clarify and modify the roles and expectations until members are satisfied.

Using this technique, members will see that their own performance depends on the performance of others and this understanding creates a strong sense of unity, loyalty, and interdependence.

 Stress teamwork and ownership.

Show your commitment to the team principle at all times. 'I don't care who gets the credit as long as we achieve our goals' is the attitude to be fostered in the group. Talk about 'we', 'our company', 'what we hope to achieve'—positive suggestions that reflect a cohesive unit.

Provide leadership support to the team.

How can you increase and maintain each member's sense of personal worth and importance as a group member? Consider these strategies:

- Work with everyone. You may work very well with some people— but don't let this lead to the exclusion of others.
- Give everyone a piece of the action,

something they can be identifying with and recognised for.

- Keep the group informed.
- Look for opportunities to tap into the talents and develop the skills of each member.
- Explore ways to let everyone publicly share the glory of his or her achievement.
- Rotate jobs in the group (if possible) so that members identify with the team as a whole rather than with their own individual jobs.
- Ensure that all members are free to express their views to the group.

As team leader you must foster the trust and confidence of all members of your team. This may take time but, without this rapport, group cohesion might not materialise.

 Facilitate task accomplishment.

Ensure that team members are provided with the equipment, facilities, work methods, and time-table for accomplishing group goals. Focus also on solving any problems that interfere with goal achievement and the building of a team identity.

 Acknowledge good work.

Your task is to build a group of willing, cooperative people who work together in a climate of acceptance, support, and trust. Recognition and appreciation of every member's contribution are vitally important.

How to form work teams

There is no 'I' in 'T-E-A-M'. Teams are made up of people with complementary skills, committed to a common purpose and performance goals, and an approach for which they hold themselves mutually accountable. They may be established *ad hoc* as project teams or as more permanent work groups. Although most teams can outperform individual people, it's the 'people issues' that cause most of the problems. So when you believe a team is required in your workplace, consider these points…

 Establish clear, achievable goals.

One of the main reasons for the failure of teams is that they don't know where they're going or why they've been formed. A team works best when members clearly understand its purpose and its goals.

 Set a clear plan.

Having formed a team for a specific purpose and made that purpose clear, the next step in the process is to ensure that the team is not left to 'muddle through'. Help the team determine what advice, training, assistance, materials, and other resources it may need. Develop a flow chart setting out the steps of a project and the resources required, and list any training and budgetary considerations.

 Define roles clearly.

Effective teams empower members and require contributions; performance expectations are essential. Focus attention on 'who' is to do 'what'. Shared roles, too, need to be clearly stated. An added advantage of ensuring clearly defined roles is that it limits the possibility of the same people getting stuck with the same tedious tasks.

 Insist on clear communication.

An effective team is interdependent: each member makes significant contributions, and each depends on the other. In the team context, good discussions depend on how well information is shared by its members. Insist that members communicate clearly, listen actively, explore opportunities rather than debate them, and share all information.

 Encourage team behaviours.

'T-E-A-M' means 'Together Everyone Achieves More', so make sure the climate of your workplace encourages all members to use their skills to make work an even better place to be. Behaviours will include initiating, seeking information, suggesting procedures, clarifying, elaborating, summarising, compromising, and recognising the contributions of others. Collaboration replaces competition as the team's *modus operandi*. Set clear boundaries so that teams are aware of any limits to their autonomy.

 Agree on decision-making procedures.

Ultimately, a team will have to make decisions, and the way it goes about that will be an indicator of its effectiveness. (Group decision-making considerations are outlined on page 270.) Be prepared to intervene in any group process and provide the required leadership. You might even include yourself as a member of the team.

 Increase awareness of group processes.

If individuals are to become fully-functioning members of a team, they must be aware of group processes—how the team works together. You need to demonstrate the important role played by group dynamics, to draw attention to nonverbal messages, and be aware of changes in the group's behaviour.

 Expect participation.

Teams provide opportunities for people to be involved in problem-solving and decision-making—especially where the outcomes are likely to affect the members. Most

people are goal-directed, social beings; so all members should participate in discussions and decision-making. They should commit themselves to any project's completion; but participation will be balanced according to a variety of factors—such as knowledge about the topic under discussion, investment in the outcome, and the level of commitment a person is prepared to make. People who are not prepared to participate should not be considered for a team project or work team.

 Establish ground rules.

Have the team set rules or norms for what will, and will not, be tolerated in the group. It's too late to consider ground rules after the team has been operating for some time. For starters, teams should expect to encourage each other, listen well, share resources, pitch in, cooperate, take responsibility for their own actions—and have fun.

 Insist on the best available information.

Good data makes problem-solving and decision-making much easier; failure to find and use quality data will seriously compromise acceptable outcomes. Strong opinions—dominance even—are quelled by the presence of data. So opinions should be supported by, or at least defer to, such information. An added advantage is that reliable data will reduce the possibility of group disagreements.

don't forget

Why teams fail

Teams fail for many reasons, but the most frequent causes are:

- The team lacks visible support or commitment from management at the top.
- The team members lack self-discipline and are reluctant to take responsibility for their own actions.
- The members have received little or no training in team dynamics.
- The team has focused on the tasks – but not on the interpersonal relationships of members.
- There are too many people on the team and its structure is shaky.
- The team has been plagued by poor leadership.[48]

viewpoint

"In an effective team, team spirit has to be created so that the members work for the benefit of the group. To achieve its task the group needs each member, and so it is in the interests of the group to develop the skills of each member… Good individuals do not automatically make a good team until they learn to operate as one."

– David Trethowan in *Teamwork*

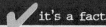

How to build and lead an effective executive team

People are your most valuable resource—a cliché perhaps, but true. To achieve what you want for your organisation, you will need to surround yourself at the top level with the best people—an effective management or executive team. The bonus is that having a good team is a very smart way of enhancing your own abilities. Here are a few ideas on how to assemble that team—then lead it…

1 Develop an inner circle.

Whatever your management situation, you need a trusted inner circle of colleagues; not people who always agree with you, but people who really contribute to the process and the end result. Smaller groups, often established on an *ad hoc* basis, are usually more productive than larger ones; entry to, or exit from, such groups depends on a person's talents, performance, and the specific task.

2 Select the best people.

For an executive team to be effective, you will need people who—

- can get things done
- have leadership qualities
- are able to create useful ideas
- analyse problems effectively
- are good at oral and written communication
- have technical expertise
- can control the work flow
- can think and evaluate logically.

Select or build a team with compensating strengths and weaknesses. If you inherit an existing team, reshuffle or reinforce it as required.

3 Stress the importance of the team's decision-making role.

People are often reluctant to make tough decisions; it's easy to postpone difficult decisions to another meeting. So when you assemble your executive group, see this as a major challenge. Set targets and make decisions—and don't let yourself be talked into extending deadlines. Your determination will gain the support of members tired of attending endless meetings that transfer agenda items to other occasions.

4 Keep it simple.

The old 'KISS' principle (Keep It Simple, Stupid) has been overdone, but simplicity *is* a key to achievement. Look critically at your decisions and their planned implementation. If the required actions are not straight-forward, complications often result, and additional work will be required.

Set goals that challenge.

Think in terms of S-T-R-E-T-C-H goals. Setting minimum standards for an executive team results only in that minimum becoming the accepted maximum. Hold your colleagues accountable for achieving those stretch goals. If people are to be recognised for their performances, often in the form of bonuses, make sure they earn that recognition.

 Maintain focus.

Remember the old saying, 'What you focus on, grows.' Once you have agreed on any action goals, stick with them until they have been achieved. Resist adding new ones until you have succeeded with the existing ones. Too many goals reduce the focus and stifle real achievement.

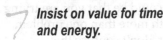 **Insist on value for time and energy.**

If you're having a meeting, insist on results—especially action in the form of decisions. Meetings are important, but every meeting does not have to involve onlookers or passengers. Only those who can contribute should be involved.

 Focus on the can-doers.

Quality people are sometimes hidden in organisations. Often such people may have chosen to avoid the game-playing and corporate politics. You can't afford not to identify, involve, and encourage them. At the same time, rid your team of the excuse-makers and the 'we've always done it this way-ers'. Surround yourself with those who can agree on what has to be done—then do it.

 Think 55.

The Rule of 55 states that, 'fifty per cent of an organisation's products usually produce only 5 per cent of its revenue and profits'. This means that half of your business represents only 5 per cent of your profitability! The challenge for you and your executive team is to identify that underperforming 50 per cent and apply the strategy made famous by Jack Welch, when the CEO at General Electric—find ways to fix your underperforming areas, sell them, or close them down.

 And remember…

- Executive team members must be very familiar with your organisation's goals and priorities.
- Members must know what is expected of them and what their responsibilities are in implementing team decisions.
- Members should be able to influence team decisions appropriately.
- Discussion is encouraged regardless of how critical it may be; views that differ are not taken as indications of a disloyal or uncooperative colleague.
- Members must be able to express ideas so that others clearly understand their intent.
- Members share equitably in the workload of the team.
- Members are able to present team decisions to client groups in a manner that generates understanding and support for implementation.

> ❝ **quotable quote**
>
> A team is not a self-contained motor that continues to whirr smoothly as long as you supply the fuel. A team is composed of individuals in a dynamic relationship, both with one another and with their immediate environment.[49]

> ? **ask yourself**
>
> Members of an executive team (or in any group for that matter) can be rated according to their participation in the group. To determine your value as a member of a group with a problem to solve, consider your own involvement and place a tick in the relevant box…
>
> ☐ I recognised the problem that needed a solution and I solved it.
>
> ☐ I recognised the problem and joined my colleagues in solving it.
>
> ☐ I recognised the problem but, not knowing how to solve it, I kept quiet and did nothing.
>
> ☐ I recognised the problem, felt no responsibility for it, and did as little as possible.
>
> ☐ I recognised the problem and solved only that part of it that helped me personally.
>
> ☐ I didn't recognise the problem and so I let someone else solve it.
>
> Of course, the only types of group members of any use are those in the first two categories. The rest are of little value.
>
> And, of course, you ticked one of the first two boxes… didn't you?

How to solve a major problem in your organisation

Managers are faced with a never-ending flow of problems—deviations from the norm. During the course of a week, hundreds of spontaneous, minor problems are usually tackled with the minimum of fuss, using years of accumulated knowledge and experience. At times, however, a major problem will arise. On such occasions, the wise manager uses a classic problem-solving strategy, one of which is outlined here. When you have a serious problem to grapple with, try following these nine steps...

smile & ponder

A young boy had a pair of squeaky black shoes. The noise drove him crazy. His father told him to soak the shoes all night long in a bucket of water. In the morning, the water was black and the shoes no longer squeaked. The young boy concluded that, by getting rid of the black, he got rid of the squeak.

■ The moral of the story is that, when trying to solve a problem, make sure you don't reach the wrong conclusion.

ask yourself

How do you handle problems? Do you *react* or *respond* to them? Do you get *bitter* or *better*?

1 *Identify the symptoms.*

When you sense that trouble is brewing in your organisation, it's usually the symptoms of a problem that surface first—bickering among employees, equipment breakdowns, changes in behaviour patterns, uneven performance, poor attendance at staff meetings, missing petty cash, litter… These symptoms can indicate a major problem lurking below the surface.

2 *Define the problem.*

You're aware of the symptoms—now try to define the problem. Be warned, however: it's not always easy to pinpoint.

For example, when two employees are continually bickering and cannot get along together, a supervisor might believe that he or she is confronted with a problem of conflicting personalities. After checking, the supervisor finds that the real problem is that he or she has never clearly outlined the functions and duties of each employee—where their duties begin and end. What appeared on the surface to be a problem of personality conflict was actually a problem of an organisational nature. Only after the true nature of the problem has been recognised can the supervisor do something about it.

Try to state the problem in a single sentence; this will help you to identify the actual nature of the problem. Indeed, it could be that you are trying to deal with more than one problem. Remember, don't confuse the symptoms, the causes, and the problem.

3 *Specify your objectives.*

Be clear about what you are setting out to achieve in tackling the problem. Compare the existing situation with the desired state: where you are now and where you would like to be. Then state the transformation necessary to move from one state to the other.

4 *Analyse the problem.*

First, get the facts. Ask questions of all parties; use your eyes and ears—without prejudice; and read for guidance in policy handbooks, precedent files, or the journals. You might never have *all* the facts but it is essential to have *enough* of them.

Second, order and simplify your information. Distill and reorder the material to get at the core of the issue, the real problem.

Third, check your facts for accuracy and relevance. Discard where necessary.

Finally, assess the data without prejudice, preconceived ideas, or emotion.

Generate alternative solutions.

Problem solving requires a choice of options. To find the best option, you must consider several possible solutions. By formulating many options, you will be less likely to overlook the best course of action. If necessary, use brainstorming and creative thinking techniques to foster the free flow of ideas.

Evaluate the various alternative solutions.

Evaluate the options you have now generated. List the advantages and disadvantages of each. Mentally test each option by imagining that each has already been put into effect. Think of the consequences—anticipated and unanticipated—of each alternative. Focus on the two or three that look most promising. The focus now shifts to decision making.

Choose the best solution.

You may now have come up with 34 ways to skin a cat—but you want the best way. In making your final selection, you could call upon previous experience, advice from others, intuition, experimentation, or such scientific tools as linear programming or simulation modelling. Compare your short listed options, perhaps even allocate values or points to each, and arrive at a final decision.

Remember, the best solution will normally be the one with the most advantages and the fewest disadvantages. Indeed, often the best solution will be the one that is least undesirable.

Take the necessary action.

Now is the time to plan carefully how best to implement your decision. You will need an action plan. Since most decisions affect or involve people, you should communicate and consult with those affected to gain their support. Decide on what has to be done, how, by whom, and when. What might go wrong? How will the results be reported or checked?

Monitor the results of your solution.

Routine follow-up checks will ensure that you have solved the problem. Check the symptoms again—have they disappeared or at least been reduced? Set up control measures to compare actual with planned results. Take corrective action where necessary. If the problem has in fact not been solved, you'll need to repeat the process, this time from a completely new perspective.

here's an idea

To get at the true cause of a problem, try asking 'why' up to five times. Example: A pump has burned out...*why?* There were metal filings in the bearings...*why?* The filter screen wasn't on the filter... *why?* Because it fell off and was at the bottom of the coolant basin... *why?* The repair man didn't put a lock nut on the filter...*why?* And there's the real problem.

One 'why' lets you take emergency and usually temporary corrective action. Five 'whys' help you isolate the real source of the problem and to solve it, permanently.

viewpoint

"The real problem is usually two or three questions deep. If you want to go after someone's problem, be aware that most people aren't going to reveal what the real problem is after the first question."

– Jim Rohn

here's an idea

Every now and again, every manager is faced with a problem for which there appears to be no solution. When faced with such a situation, try this tactic... Forget about the immediate problem. Instead, focus on how to make sure it never happens again. More often than not, looking at the problem from this angle will solve the immediate problem at hand as well.

How to become a better decision-maker

Decision-making is an inescapable task for managers. In the eyes of staff members, it is the managers who must take the final responsibility for decisions. Each year they make literally thousands of them, large and small. In the end, the quality of those decisions determines the success of a manager's efforts. If you want to become a quality decision maker, particularly when the 'big' decisions count, these guidelines will help...

1 Adopt a systematic approach.

Decision making is actually part of problem solving: there would be no decision to make if there were no problem to solve. Decision-making is that component of the problem-solving process that follows analysis of the problem and is followed, in turn, by action to carry out the decision. The problem-solving process outlined on page 266 could well be used in arriving at major decisions.

2 Focus on important decisions.

Try not to spend too much time on small matters. It's the important decisions that must receive your full attention. Deciding who should fill the hot water urn each morning is of less importance than a decision about the focus of the new marketing strategy. Importance is determined by asking such questions as: How close is the deadline? What are the consequences of a poor decision? Who is affected by the decision? Is the decision reversible? Answers to such questions will also help clarify the decision to be made.

3 Avoid making snap decisions.

Spur-of-the-moment decisions are often merely guesses. Quantity can be no substitute for quality. Impetuous decisions relating to major issues could later lead to a serious log jam of consequential problems. On the other hand...

4 Don't become a victim of analysis paralysis.

Limitations of time and resources do not allow for a thorough analysis of all issues every time. So don't drag your feet. By putting off a decision, you will only add to an already overflowing agenda of unfinished business.

5 Base your decision on facts.

A decision is no better than the data on which it is based. Have all the facts at your disposal. Improve your exploration of options by asking yourself such questions as: What facts do I have? What else do I need to know? Whom should I ask? What should I ask? What printed matter is available?

6 Don't be afraid of making the wrong decision.

There is a risk involved in every decision; no one is blessed with infinite wisdom. Ask yourself, what is the worst thing that can happen if I make the wrong choice? Rarely is a disaster the consequence! A readiness to risk failure is a quality that characterises all good decision-makers.

7 Learn from your mistakes.

If your decision is later shown to be the wrong one, find out where you went wrong. Seek advice from others. Did you neglect or under-emphasise any of the problem-solving steps listed on page 266?

8 Use your imagination.

A logical decision is not always the best answer in all situations. Be prepared to use brainstorming techniques, analogies, and lateral thinking in your search for a new approach to the problem at hand. Use the technique that best fits the problem.

9 Resist making decisions under stress.

When you have to make a decision under crisis conditions, stand back from the problem and consider the situation. For example, you may not have to make an immediate decision.

Use all the time available to ensure the best response. Avoid impulse decisions: if you are angry or upset, delay your response. Decisions made under stress can be faulty.

10 Make your decision, then move on.

US psychiatrist Leon Utterback says:

> The best way to make a decision is to do your worrying before you place your bet. In other words, do everything you can to first make sure the right decision is made. But once you've made that decision and execution is the order of the day, then stop worrying and fretting about the outcome.[52]

So, banish past decisions from your mind or you'll lose the capacity to give your full and undivided attention to the more pressing and important needs of the present.

11 And don't forget...

- View decision making as a valuable opportunity for your professional growth.
- Ask: What would someone else do in my circumstances? Seek help from others, journals, or reference books.
- Refer to existing policies whenever possible: decisions can often be straightforward and immediate.
- Periodically review the results of your decisions to check that they worked.
- Discuss with your colleagues decisions that will affect other people—but assume the responsibility yourself for the final decision.
- Every decision involves some risk.
- Time does not always improve a situation when it comes to decision-making.

viewpoint

"It's been estimated that 80% of workplace decisions you're faced with should be made on the spot, 15% need to mature, and 5% need not be made at all. Think about that when facing the many questions that cross your desk every day."

– Jimmy Calano and Jeff Salzman in *CareerTracking*

don't forget

Quick decisions are not always the best decisions. On the other hand, unhurried decisions are not always the best decisions either.

viewpoint

"A decision goes through a life cycle, from infancy to old age.

If you make the decision during its infancy, you don't have enough facts. If you wait until it is senile, you'll have little or no effect on the outcome.

So how do you know when a decision is ripe? How can you tell when an apple is ripe? You pick some, and learn. You have to practise decision making like any other activity."

– Don Paarlberg

How to help groups make decisions

Group decision making is an effective management practice that involves a group of people making a decision collectively. A major benefit is that the process increases the participants' ownership of and commitment to the decision. Helping groups reach those decisions, therefore, is a key management function that requires a working knowledge of the most popular decision-making tools...

1 Ensure the group knows when a decision is made.

There are five ways in which a group can make a decision. Agree early on which approach is to be adopted:

- Decision by unanimous agreement, with no dissenters.
- Decision by consensus. The decision has the support of the whole group and, while some may not agree with the decision, they have had their say and are happy to accept the will of the group.
- Decision by majority. The proposal attracting most votes is carried.
- Decision by minority. People agree, following their input, to allow those with greatest expertise or power, make the final decision.
- Decision by chairperson, following input from all in the group.

The approach adopted by the group usually depends on the situation or the significance of the decision. The following techniques will assist in working towards a decision based on agreement by the majority or by consensus—an ideal group result.

2 Avoid the traps of group decisions.

Busy managers can sometimes 'push' too hard for decisions and, in the process, create additional problems. So avoid such hazards as these...

- Interpreting silence as consent—making a decision by default.
- Settling for majority rules—believing that a win/lose result is better than no result.
- Letting minorities decide—'Trust us, we know what others want'.
- Believing that those who make the most noise are the most knowledgable.
- Accepting opinions as facts.

3 Select the best tool for your situation.

When decision making involves having to determine the relative importance of several different issues or priorities under discussion, a choice of techniques is available:

Brainstorming or Brainwriting.
Decisions can only be based on ideas and information. Brainstorming or its alternative, Brainwriting, is often the first step in group decision-making. It is

able to equalise involvement, generate excitement, and result in a range of ideas or items for addressing the problem in focus. See page 318 for details.

3 for and 3 against
This ensures that all sides of an issue are heard. When an issue is being discussed, the group is asked to give three reasons why the issue should be supported and then three reasons why it shouldn't.

Spend a Dollar
For prioritising a set of 5 to 15 issues, you need enough slips of paper for each participant to have one slip per issue. Distribute slips and have them write one issue on each slip. They have $1 to spend on the issues according to their relative importance. They must spend and record a minimum of 5c on each item. All spendings are recorded from the slips to a wall chart, and the totals, percentages and rankings can be calculated.

Multivoting
Number each item in the set requiring prioritising, then follow this procedure:
1. Choose one-third of the items on the list and discuss them.
2. After discussion, members vote by show of hands (or secret ballot) as each item is called out.
3. After voting, reduce this list by removing some items with fewest votes.
4. Repeat steps 1 to 3 on the remaining items and continue until only the most- voted-for items are left. If no clear favourite emerges by this time, repeat the process on the most-voted-for items.

Merging Priorities
The group breaks into pairs. Each pair discusses the set of items and agrees on the top two priorities. The pairs then join to form groups of four, which discuss the four priorities (although there could be overlap), and reduce the four items to

two. The fours join to make eights, and again agree on the top two priorities out of the accumulating set. Continue the process until you merge into one whole group with two surviving agreed-on priorities.

Nominal Group Technique
This is a fancy name for a simple procedure designed to involve all group members. Issue the following instructions to the group participants: Each person must think carefully about the set of items or issues requiring prioritising. From the set, each person must select the five most important items, and write them as a list on a sheet of paper. Put a 5 next to the item you think is most important. Put a 1 next to the item that is least important. Put a 4 against the item that is the second most important, then a 3 beside the next item of importance, and a 2 against the remaining item. Collect the sheets, shuffle, and tally the scores against a list of all items on a master chart. The group considers those items with the highest scores to be the most important.

Force Field Analysis
This technique helps groups to make decisions about change. It assumes that the current situation is the result of counteracting forces. One set is pushing the situation towards a more desired state (helping forces) and a second set is acting to restrain movement in the desired direction (hindering forces). Brainstorm to create two lists: 'helping forces' and 'hindering forces'. Examine each completed list to delete, add or integrate as required. Identify and underline those forces that are most important and most able to be influenced. For each underlined 'hindering force', think of a list of action steps that will reduce or eliminate the effect of the force. Repeat for the 'helpful forces'. Finally, develop a plan for action (see page 312).

 don't forget

The four rules for leaders

Intelligent, motivated people make superior decisions in groups *only* if managed with skill. Help your group make better decisions…

• Resist stating your own opinions early in the group's deliberations, because many group members will be afraid to offer their own, possibly good, ideas if they contradict you, the leader.

• Encourage the right kind of conflict within the group, and resolve it fully and fairly through debate and intelligence-gathering.

• Foster disagreement in the early stages of any group process. Then, as more facts and insights are gained, guide the group toward convergence on a final choice.

• If the decision process deadlocks, narrow the gap by separating factual issues from value issues.[54]

 quotable quote

Most business decisions are already far beyond the capability of single minds and single individuals. Decision making is increasingly a collective operation in which the ability to play as a team member, to listen, to build on the ideas of others and to make two and two equal five rather than three and a half is the key to success.[55]

How to take risks

If you're keen to display the qualities of true leadership, risk-taking must become part of your executive weaponry. Leaders must be disrupters of the status quo, which often requires them to take risks. Calculated risk-taking helps 'creative edge' organisations to thrive; and it earns an enviable reputation for individuals who deliver the positive results. But risk-taking requires courage and an awareness of the following advice...

1 Be aware of the pros and cons of risk taking.

Risk taking means moving from a situation of some security to another less secure position. But, to advance, there'll be times when you must place yourself, even your organisation, at risk. Courage is a basic requirement for risk taking, sometimes at great professional and personal cost. The alternative—choosing *not* to show leadership—will no doubt result in fewer risks and greater security, but it will also mean the loss of opportunity to bring about needed improvement in your organisation.

2 Confront fear first— then bite the bullet.

Fear is a demotivating factor in any situation. People don't do things because of fear—fear of the consequences of doing them (and vice versa). People who do not learn to confront their fears may go through life in the company of embarrassment, failure, rejection, disapproval, uncertainty, and myriad other doubts. Confronting fear is a precursor to taking risks. So, if you find yourself hesitating about taking a risk, ask: 'What am I *really* scared of?' Isolate that fear and face up to it; by weighing the disadvantages—and the advantages—you can decide whether the risk, the calculated risk, is worth taking.

3 Ensure the risk is justified.

Risk taking can be something of a gamble and one of the rules of gambling is never to risk more than you can afford to lose. Size up the odds, the rewards, and the risks. Don't risk a lot for a little, particularly useful advice when you're sticking your neck out only to take revenge, save face, or on a matter of principle.

4 Forget the rules.

The thing about risk taking is that there *are* no rules. In fact, risk taking often involves breaking or stretching any existing rules to breaking point.

Risk taking is all about change. And to bring about change, you can best assess the risks by becoming an observer of human and organisational behaviour. If you understand the way your superiors, peers, or subordinates work and think, you can venture a guess as to how they will react to any breathtaking initiative you undertake or propose.

Determine in advance just how far you can go.

Risk taking often involves threatening certain existing values, resources, and vested interests. Many people dislike change when it upsets their way of thinking, work style, or life pattern. So it's important to gauge at the start just how far you can push these boundaries. History is punctuated with stories of risk-takers who stepped where angels feared to tread. The difficulty for risk-takers, and for you, however, is to know when *not* to step over the line.

Know your limitations.

A long-shot is one thing; a no-win situation is quite another. So, if you figure you'll be outclassed, outfoxed, outranked, underresourced, or undermined, then don't be rash. Step back and rethink your strategy.

Prepare a contingency plan— just in case.

Suppose your risk doesn't pay off—how can you save face, cut your losses, or cash in your chips? Be prepared, by having in place a range of alternatives and contingencies that will allow you to reach a compromise by negotiating a mutually agreeable outcome.

Maximise the effect.

Once you've decided to take the risk, use whatever techniques are necessary to instil confidence in those around you and to keep your momentum going. It's not only what you say, it's how you say it—so be dramatic, stylish, and enthusiastic. The 'as if' philosophy is appropriate here; that is, if you want to succeed, begin by acting 'as if' you have.

Gain and remain in control.

You're taking the risk, so try to control as many variables as possible. Use power and influence—your own and your boss's—and, by your actions, earn the respect and support of other key players.

Learn to live to fight another day.

Fights are rarely won in the first round; the winner is the one still there at the end. So, unless it's a winner-take-all situation, don't be discouraged if your venture doesn't come off. The important thing is where you stand over the long haul. Always remember the turtle—it gets nowhere if it doesn't stick its neck out!

don't forget

How to minimise risk

1. *Always have a goal in mind when taking a risk* – otherwise, you won't know whether you're winning or losing. And if you list everything that might go wrong, you'll be aware of problems sooner because you'll be looking for them.

2. *Recognise that you'll always have problems involving risk.* Be serious about the risks you take, especially when the stakes are high, because if you don't intend to succeed, you intend to fail.

3. *Be realistic.* Some roadblocks you can hurdle, others you can't. And know that if you are looking for a totally safe risk, there is no such thing.

4. *Consider what is the best effort you are capable of making and don't plan on being able to do more than that.*

5. *Don't take a risk just to prove to yourself that you can succeed.* This is hazardous thinking and totally unnecessary.

6. *Don't take a risk because of anger, guilt, hurt, or depression.* It's dangerous to act out your feelings.

7. *Be decisive.* Once you've decided that the risk is worthy and the time is right, act. [58]

How to prepare your next speech

Managers are frequently called on to speak at professional
meetings, service clubs, and community groups, and to present
briefings or reports within their organisation. If a speech has
been well prepared, with a definite purpose, and well-rehearsed,
it will be successful. The most effective public speakers faithfully
observe several important steps when preparing for a speaking
engagement. As you prepare for your next speech, you might also
wish to adhere to these proven guidelines...

Understand clearly why you have been invited.

Before accepting an invitation to
speak, be sure you know why you
were invited and what the audience
wants to hear. Decline the invitation if
you feel you have little to contribute
on the topic.

Sketch out a brief plan of attack.

Three preliminary considerations
must be addressed before beginning:

First, clarify the purpose of your
speech—to persuade, inform,
amuse? What do you want your
audience to feel, think, or learn?

Second, what do you know about the
audience that will affect the way
you approach the speech? What are
their concerns, training, attitude,
background, knowledge, and
feelings towards you and the topic?

Third, focus on the subject. You know
the general theme so now you can
focus on a specific topic. Select
a working title and identify the
thrust of your message.

Research your topic.

Collect your facts and arguments:

• Brainstorm a list of random ideas
  relating to your central message.
• Look for natural clusters of ideas
  which gravitate around your main
  points.
• Isolate the main concepts you will
  present and collect further relevant
  data to support these key points.
• Check your facts.
• Roughly sequence your information.

Structure your speech.

A good structure is essential. It
provides continuity and balance,
makes your argument easy to follow,
and enables you to drive your
message home logically.

Your presentation will consist of
three parts:

The *introduction* must arouse your
audience's interest immediately.
Within 60 seconds you must have
answered their question: 'Why should
we listen to you?'

The *body* will present your main points

logically, simply, and interestingly. The *conclusion* should include a restatement of your objective, a reinforcement of what you presented, and a challenge for the audience. The conclusion is your big chance to leave a lasting impression—don't bomb it!

 ### Prepare your notes.

Even if you believe you are word-perfect, never speak without notes. Try to avoid a fully-scripted speech—the audience usually does not like being read to. Instead, use card-size hand-held notes that won't blow away.

On each card write a lead-in sentence to the point to be made, perhaps a few key words or phrases to jog your memory, as well as a brief reminder of an anecdote or quotation to be used while making the point.

Your introduction and conclusion should be on separate cards. Know them off pat, ensuring a confident start and a positive end to your presentation.

What are the images you want your audience to remember most? These become your visual aids—flip charts, OHTs, slides. Don't overdo them and keep them simple.

 ### Always remember the fundamentals.

If it 'reads' well, it doesn't necessarily 'listen' well. So focus on simplicity, brightness, concrete words, and declarative sentences. Avoid jargon and gobbledegook. Introduce your ideas little by little. Use anecdotes, real dialogue, personal stories, and humour to reinforce your message. Keep it clean—there's always

someone you'll offend. Don't bog down in detail. And keep it short! Few speakers can hold attention for much longer than 20-30 minutes.

 ### Rehearse.

Several practise runs will leave you more confident and at ease. Try this:

Imagine, in your mind's eye, every detail of the event. Actually see the room, the platform, the chairs. Visualise the room filling up with people and the chairperson rising to introduce you as speaker. See yourself rising, walking confidently to the lectern, and looking at the assembled listeners. Control your nerves. Imagine yourself beginning to speak. Work your way aloud through the speech. Don't try to be word perfect.

 ### Check the final arrangements.

Provide the chairperson with a brief introductory statement to read. Rather than just listing your accomplishments, however, use the opportunity to introduce the audience to the style and content of your presentation. Treat the introduction as if it's a part of the speech—put attention-grabbing, relevant material in there, so you catch the audience's interest before you even step up to the podium. Make sure you supply in advance a list of resources you will require on the day. Ensure your notes and visuals are in correct sequence. Arrive at the venue in time to check that your audio-visuals will all be seen clearly.

 here's an idea

The key to preparing a speech is to begin at the end. Write down what you will want the audience to do or feel as a result of having heard your speech. Keep this in perspective at all times as you structure and provide content in preparing the presentation.

How to deliver a memorable speech

here's an idea

Many amateur speakers make two mistakes:

• They skip their vision around the room, trying to make eye contact with everyone; and

• When coming to a break in thought, they fill in the gaps with 'um' or 'ah'.

Be aware of this. Make a conscious effort to look at people in the audience for at least five seconds before moving on. And, whenever you have the urge to say 'ah' or 'um', simply pause, and glance over your notes or take a drink of water.

read further

For further tips and techniques on speech-making check out:
www.wordnerds.com.au

From time to time, you may be required to speak to audiences of various sizes to inform, inspire, persuade, affect decisions, or stimulate action. Internally, you may find yourself speaking to a group of employees or colleagues; externally, you may address a community group, the press, or a service organisation. Of course, preparation is vital; but a poorly delivered speech can ruin weeks of careful groundwork. If you want to deliver an effective speech, then consider these key elements…

1 Try to control nervousness.

Top speakers are never free of nervous tension before their presentations—studies have shown that even pros like Bob Hope and Johnny Carson had increased heart rates just before they started their monologues; but those rates quickly returned to normal once the speakers were into their deliveries. Nerves are part of a good performance. Accept them. As well, learn to ease the tension through the process of auto-suggestion—the technique of imagining yourself in the speaking situation *before* the event. Having actually felt the natural anxiety beforehand, you are well on the way to controlling the ever-present jitters on the occasion.

2 Display confidence from the start.

When a speaker moves to the lectern, the audience will look, notice and listen. So start with energy and enthusiasm; smile; look pleased to be there; take your time; don't

get flustered; make introductory comments without referring to your notes; and project your voice to the back of the room. Look relaxed, confident, and in command.

3 Establish rapport with the audience immediately.

Show that you're glad to be up-front; that you like the people in attendance and appreciate the opportunity to speak to them. Establish and maintain good eye-contact with as many people as possible. You can't go wrong if you begin by complimenting those present—for their professionalism, or for their success in a project being undertaken, or for their attendance, and so on. Make them feel pleased that you're there.

4 Get your delivery right.

Vitality, enthusiasm, style, fluency, and tempo—all are important ingredients. Consider these important points as well:

• Imagine you are talking to people you know well. Be conversational. Try not to read your speech.

- Stand naturally and upright, project your voice to the last row, vary pitch and change tempo to keep your audience alert.
- Look at individuals in turn as you talk.
- Use a variety of gestures but not to distraction.
- Be light of touch and good humoured. Use jokes only if they are relevant (and funny).
- Don't preach or pontificate to your audience. Show sincerity and conviction, belief in your message, and enthusiasm in putting it across.
- Signpost important points—pause before making a key point, to highlight it, and again afterwards to allow it to sink in.
- Pace your delivery. Start in low gear and gradually build up in intensity.

 Avoid the common traps.

There are some things you should never do:

- Try not to read your talk or bury your head in your notes. Don't talk to the white board or your audiovisual aids; talk to faces.
- Never pace up and down, fidget or use other irritating mannerisms such as jingling keys or swaying.
- Never compete with distractions.
- Never compete with yourself. If you distribute an item to be looked at, stop talking until it has been examined by all.
- Never uncover your audiovisual aids until you need them. And put them away as soon as you've used them.
- Never 'um' or 'ah'. A moment's silence is preferable.
- Never overrun your time. As Mark Twain said: 'Few sinners are saved after the first 20 minutes of a sermon.'

 Drive home your key points.

It's important that you don't lose your audience. Summarise the main points regularly to help your listeners organise their thoughts and capture the ideas you present. Repetition and restatement are vital for effective communication.

 Keep a grip on your audience.

Watch your listeners. Be aware of how they're reacting to your speech. Are they getting your message—or are they yawning, doodling, reading, or cleaning fingernails? Watch for the nonverbal clues that provide valuable feedback. Adjust your style and modify your content or delivery accordingly. To keep your listeners attentive, use various strategies—questions, demonstrations, and illustrations.

 Finish conclusively.

Make sure you stop while your listeners are still with you. It's good to let them know when the end is in sight. Recap the key points. To strengthen the ideas presented, give your audience something specific to do or to think about in the days that follow—further reading, practice, follow-up, observations, or a challenge. Leave them with more than just a warm glow; leave them with a memorable idea or thought, or a dynamic closing sentence rehearsed until it is part of you. The last impression is the lasting impression.

 viewpoint

"Not many years ago, I began to play the cello. Most people would say that what I was doing was 'learning to play' the cello. But these words carry in our minds the strange idea that there exist two very different processes: (1) learning to play the cello and (2) playing the cello. They imply that I will do the first until I have complet-ed it, at which point I will stop the first process and begin the second.

In short, I will go on 'learning to play' until I have 'learned to play' and then I will begin to play. Of course, this is nonsense. There are not two processes, but one. We learn to do something by doing it. There is no other way.

So, too, with speech-making."

– John Holt

 don't forget

About speech notes...

- Reduce temptation. Keep your notes to a minimum. Use key words; avoid essays.
- Be familiar with your notes. Rehearse.
- Use your notes openly, but subtly.
- Never let your notes prevent you from speaking directly to your audience.

How to add sparkle to your speech-making

It's easy to spot a dull speaker—just count the number of nodding heads in the audience. You can add a little sizzle to your presentations by learning to deliver a palatable blend of facts, figures, philosophy, humour, and the unexpected. The result can be rewarding—happy audiences, rapt attention, and more support for your cause. Pep up your next presentation by considering this advice...

here's an idea

Develop your speech-making skills by having a few clever lines ready to 'roll casually off the tongue'...

Opening lines:
'It's nice to see so many smiling faces – and it's good to see the rest of you, too...'

Small turnout:
'I didn't expect such a small audience. Now I know how SBS feels.'

Having arrived late:
'Sorry I'm late. (The organiser) gave me directions to get here today but obviously she's heard me speak before.

After a break:
'It's a pleasure to see that so many of you have come back voluntarily.'

A joke nobody laughs at:
"That joke was designed to get a quiet laugh – and it did."

Question and answer:
'If anybody has a question, I've a few answers. With a little luck, maybe they'll match up.'

1 Use appropriate attention-grabbers.

Handouts, audiovisual aids, props, yarns, facts and figures, questions, show-of-hands, anecdotes, humour and demonstrations—all are capable of complementing your speech and of holding the attention of your audience. And all of those techniques are essential if you adhere to this basic principle for success: show them, don't tell them. If you illustrate your points with examples, demonstrations, or analogies that are visual or oral, you'll keep them interested.

2 Involve the audience.

Involvement keeps people from nodding off. Try asking questions and for a show of hands. Work in some role-play. Keep the audience active. Remember, you're up there to speak; they're out there to listen. If they finish before you do, you're in trouble.

3 Use props.

Anything your audience can *see* makes you and your message more memorable. Try using props—a football jersey (when talking about teamwork), an account book (when discussing spending), a large toy animal, and so on. But use props only if you feel comfortable in doing so, if they are compatible with your speaking style, and only if they are appropriate to your topic.

4 Do something unexpected.

The element of surprise can lift your performance. Why not break down that physical barrier your listeners expect between you and them? Desert the lectern and move out into the audience. Or at an appropriate moment, to illustrate a point, pull out an inflated balloon from beneath the lectern and explode it; or tear up and scatter a page from your speech.

5 Use technology.

Videos, computer graphics, audio, transparencies, slides, multi-media, and similar devices are all attention-

278

grabbers. They divert attention from your talking head, clarify your content, generate interest in the topic, increase retention, and help to reduce your stage fright. Make sure you know how to use each. But remember, *you're* still the most important audio-visual device in the room.

 Spin a yarn.

The best way to hold an audience's attention is to tell a story. Scatter anecdotes, real dialogue, and personal experiences throughout your speech to reinforce your message. Start a file of your favourite anecdotes and quotations. In your spare time, rummage through joke and quotation books, magazines, and the Internet; you'll find dozens of gems that can add sparkle to any topic.

Use humour, selectively.

Humour, used well, can reinforce your argument and keep your listeners wanting more. But don't forget these important points:
- *Make sure it's a funny story.* If you don't laugh when you first hear a story, chances are nobody else will either. So, don't tell it if it's not all that funny.
- *Avoid puns.* Puns almost always cause listeners to groan, rather than laugh.
- *Make it sound like the truth.* People are more active listeners if they think it's *your* story, about you or your acquaintances. Adapt stories to suit.
- *Make sure it's clean.* Never tell a story that can offend in any way. There's always someone who'll get upset.
- *Make sure it's relevant to your argument or the occasion.* Lead into it smoothly, making sure it fits into the logical

sequence of your speech.
- *Use a dual-purpose funny historical anecdote.* If the joke fails, at least the story still gets the point across.

 Use humour, skilfully.

Every speaker would love to be the life of the lectern, but humour can be hazardous if you ignore these warnings:
- *Make sure you learn the story.* Know it inside out. Memorise the punch line. A fumble can cost you the game.
- *Speak distinctly and with poise.* Every word must be heard. If the joke isn't heard, it won't raise a laugh.
- *Leave enough time for the laugh before proceeding.* Sometimes audiences react slowly, especially if the humour was unexpected.
- *Act out the story.* You're putting on a short show, so make it a good one—gesticulate, whisper, shout. Use appropriate facial expressions.
- *Keep it short.* Limit the extraneous matter; include only the details that relate directly to the punch line.
- *Enjoy it.* Spread good cheer. You're happy to be telling the story and you're enjoying yourself. If you look like you are, the audience will join in.
- *Talk to individuals out there in turn,* not to the audience in general and, in doing so, smile with your mouth and with your voice.
- *Carry on smoothly if the audience doesn't laugh.* People soon forget that you laid an egg if you remain confident and calm. Don't try to salvage the situation with an explanation or apology.
- *Avoid humour when speaking out of doors.* The laugh tends to get lost, leaving people with the feeling that the point wasn't funny at all.

How to handle a question-and-answer session after your next speech

Often your speech will be followed by a Q&A session. People may ask for clarification or more information or question the validity of your comments. Indeed, when you speak to persuade or to stimulate action, questioners might even challenge your assumptions, offer opposing views, or attempt to undermine your credibility. The Q&A session can be a trying ordeal for the inexperienced speaker, so it is important to become skilled in fielding questions by following these guidelines…

don't forget

Beware of a legal hazard

Don't try to match insults or criticisms with a trouble-making questioner – nor be provoked into forgetting the issues and making a personal attack upon a questioner. Therein lies the possibility of a costly defamation suit against you.

don't forget

An old Italian saying

A quick question often requires a slow answer.

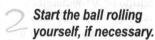

Display confidence from the start.

You can't afford to relax when your formal presentation is over; be prepared for a lively series of questions from your audience. Give the impression that you are looking forward to this session and, with self-assurance, ask: 'Now, who has the first question?'

Start the ball rolling yourself, if necessary.

If you have a reluctant or reticent audience, the first question is sometimes slow in coming. You may need to 'prime the pump' using such strategies as:

- Pose your own question: 'A question I'm usually asked is…' or 'Before the meeting, the chairperson posed an interesting question…'
- Before your speech, pass out index cards so listeners can jot down questions that arise during your speech. Ask for short questions, printed clearly, so that you can respond to them in turn from the lectern.
- Arrange with someone before the

speech to ask the first question; you don't have to provide the actual question.

Repeat the question.

For a large group, this allows everyone to hear the question. It also allows you to see if you really understand the question and provides you with a little time to frame your response.

Cover the entire room.

Try not to develop any blind spots as you look for questions. Let your eyes roam over the entire room. Keep eye-contact with the speaker when the question is being asked; look at the entire group when answering; return your gaze to the questioner as you complete your response—particularly if you want to give that person another opportunity to comment.

Be brief with your reply.

Q&A sessions should not be tedious

280

dialogues or debates but should provide a means for any listener to get quick clarification or additional information. So keep your answers short and to the point. Don't give another speech. If the question can't be answered in a minute or two, tell the person to see you after the session.

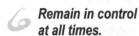

6 Remain in control at all times.

You hold the floor in this session so you can control the situation:

• *Answer only those questions you understand.* If you didn't hear the question, ask the speaker to repeat it. If you didn't understand the question, ask the speaker to explain it.

• *Anticipate questions.* Plan responses to questions you hope no one will ask. By considering common fears, assumptions, needs, or problems that listeners will experience, you can identify likely questions.

• *Keep your speech in focus.* Don't allow questions to divert you from your main thrust. Don't hesitate to say: 'You make an interesting point, but it's beyond the scope of my presentation…'.

• *Never dismiss a questioner.* If you think a question is foolish, keep your feelings to yourself. If the person is interested enough to ask, be flattered and provide a direct response.

• *Watch for several questions posing as one.* Don't try to tackle them all with one response. Treat them separately.

• *Discourage the long-winded questioner.* Give all listeners a chance to ask questions. If one questioner makes a speech instead of arriving at a question, interrupt when the opportunity arises with, 'You've raised some interesting points but, in the interest of time, we should move on to some other questions…'

• *Avoid entering into debate.* Sometimes a questioner is not satisfied with your answer and begins to engage in a debate. If this discussion is not fruitful, advise the questioner that you will be happy to continue the conversation after the session; then move quickly to the next question. Alternatively, have the debater rephrase his or her assertions as questions: never answer opinions—answer only questions.

• *Remain composed and polite.* Respond to challenges and objections with data, not emotion. Never lose control or show your frustration with a hot-headed questioner. Listeners will reject audience troublemakers and rally to your side; they appreciate good manners and fair play. Do not threaten, preach, blame, ridicule, or argue. Do not become hostile or defensive. Remain confident and in charge of your emotions.

7 Be honest: some questions can't be answered.

It's always more credible to admit you don't have an answer than to try to bluff your way through it. Graceful sidestepping requires considerable skill. So it's best to promise to follow up the question and to get back to the questioner at a later date—and do so.

8 Take charge at the end.

Whenever possible during a Q&A session, take the opportunity to repeat and reinforce the key elements of your speech. When you're ready, take control with a comment such as 'Before I make my concluding remarks, do we have one more question?' Then have your final say to end the session confidently.

here's an idea
Opinion-based questions – i.e. those which are preceded by the questioner's opinion – can be the most frustrating to deal with. The good news is that questions of this type rarely have a right-or-wrong response. Just tell yourself that everyone is entitled to his or her opinion and respond with your own view.

here's an idea
If you'd like more time to consider your answer to a question from the audience, say, 'That's a very interesting question and, before responding to it I'd be most interested to hear your views in that regard.'

smile & ponder
On concluding an exceedingly long and dull presentation in July 2001, the speaker announced, 'And now if anyone has a question, I'll be glad to try to answer it.'

A member of the audience stood up. 'I have a question,' he said. 'Is this still 2001?'

■ The moral of the story is, of course, that, when you're called upon to deliver a speech, 'Be sincere. Be brief. Be seated.'

speech making

How to handle a hostile audience

To be an effective manager, you need to be able to communicate in a variety of settings. Sooner or later, you may be in the difficult position of having to address an angry or hostile group of employees, customers, stockholders, or community representatives. Even one troublemaker in the audience can cause problems. The key is to neutralise the hostility using a range of strategies...

1 Stay relaxed and appear confident.

Prior to and during any introduction, sit confidently and in a relaxed manner before the audience. Act self-assuredly, but not arrogantly. Present a confident exterior by approaching the podium with assurance and composure and without any hint of cockiness. Be especially careful not to project any suggestion of animosity yourself.

2 Try to hose down the hostility at the very start.

If you're anticipating a hostile audience, or the nature of your subject is controversial and likely to arouse strong feelings, the secret is to address the disagreement before it addresses you. This can be accomplished in several ways:

- *Create rapport with your audience.* Do this as quickly as possible.

- *Express appreciation.* Thank the audience for being prepared to listen even though some of those present may hold ideas different from yours.

- *Advocate fair play.* Commend the spirit

of sportsmanship and fair play that gives everyone the right to disagree without being disagreeable and to object without being objectionable.

- *Set aside time for audience comments and questions—later.* If you allocate time for comments and questions after you have finished, you should hopefully be able to keep interruptions during your delivery to a minimum.

- *Explore common ground.* In your opening remarks, review the shared goals and important points of agreement between you and your audience. Establish mutual interests and concerns as quickly as possible.

- *Burst your opponents' balloon upfront.* Take the wind out of your opponents' sails by summarising their point of view early; even concede a few points. If you are the one who raises the issue, explain it in your own words and within the context of the view you are about to present. By stating their case for them, you'll take the sting out of their comments. And, in so doing, many in your audience will reflect on your evenhandedness and fairness.

3 Persuade people to your way of thinking.

The obvious strategy for coping with

hostile elements in your audience is to persuade the majority of those present to your way of thinking, thereby minimising the damage that troublemakers can cause. Set the scene by prefacing your comments with the following: 'For the next 20 minutes, I'm going to present a new concept to you. All I ask is that we just keep an open mind and hold our comments and questions until I finish. Is that all right?' Who could object to that reasonable invitation? Then, if troublemakers react during the session, you'll find the audience is prepared to put them down for not having an open mind or for not biding their time as requested. In the meantime, it's your opportunity to present your case.

4 Stay in control of yourself.

Avoid doing or saying anything to inflame your audience or to justify any abusive reaction. Keep your remarks strictly objective and impersonal. If possible, ignore hecklers and never personalise your comments or insult an angry group. If the audience *is* noisy, deliberately lower your voice and resist the natural temptation to raise it. By raising your voice, you are encouraging a corresponding increase in noise by the audience as well as suggesting that you are losing your composure.

5 Tackle the troublemakers with tact.

While remembering that negative comments or questions are not always hostile, you can defuse identified vocal troublemakers during or after your presentation, by considering such techniques as these:

- *Smother with facts.* You're the expert and you should have at your fingertips facts, figures, references, and quotes to combat any objections. Logical, intelligent argument will convince reasonable people anyday.

- *Answer a hostile question with a question.* For example, 'If you feel that way about the situation, then what do *you* think should be done about it?' The response is likely to be rambling, emotional, and illogical, a fact quickly picked up by the audience.

- *Seek clarification on emotionality.* Troublemakers often have hostile, emotional words embedded in their comments—like sneaky, stupid, hedging, rip-off, feeble… Defuse such comments by asking for clarification of such words. Never answer a question by repeating hostile words.

- *Meet me out the back later.* If all else fails, say 'It seems that we both have different views on this subject. I'm happy to discuss it with you in more detail after the meeting.' Invariably they fail to turn up— they're usually more interested in posturing in front of an audience.

- *Pull the plug graciously.* If the hostility is excessive, you may find it necessary to announce that, because it is impossible to continue, you find it necessary to end your talk; then quietly sit down.

! viewpoint

"Add a third certainty to death and taxes we can all count on. If you are a manager, sooner or later you will have to give a speech of some kind, perhaps to a less than sympathetic crowd… that simple fact of life can have a chilling effect."

– Allen Brown in *Just Smile and Speak Up*

✔ it's a fact

The shortest US inaugural address was George Washington's – just 125 words. The longest was William H. Harrison's in 1841. He delivered a two-hour, 9000-word speech into the teeth of a freezing northeast wind. The new President came down with a cold the next day and a month later died of pneumonia.
The moral? Be brief.

! viewpoint

"Public speaking can seem similar to bungee-jumping. The reaction can be: 'Oh, my God, who would really want to do that!'"

– Mitchell Osborn in *The American School Board Journal*

283

How to make special speeches:
(a) introducing a speaker (b) moving a vote of thanks

Managers usually get asked to make more short speeches than long speeches. Two short speeches that you may be called on to give will be to introduce a speaker or to move a vote of thanks at the end of a presentation. For such occasions, here are a few guidelines worth remembering...

quotable quote

The strength or weakness of an introduction will affect a speaker's task. A snappy, upbeat, interesting introduction clears the way for a quick takeoff. A dull, dreary introduction means that the guest speaker has to spend time on early damage control.

Introductions – short and simple though they usually are – really *do* matter. A good introduction should set the tone for the featured speaker. It should help bring speaker and audience closer together, establish a congenial climate, and build bonds of common interest.[64]

viewpoint

"Don't be nervous. Do just as I do. Whenever I get up to speak I always make a point of taking a good look around the audience. I say to myself, 'What a lot of silly fools.' And then I always feel better."

– Winston Churchill

smile & ponder

In conclusion – the phrase guaranteed to wake up your audience.

Introducing a speaker

 Follow this format...

To introduce a guest speaker, you'll need to do a little homework and then structure your speech as follows:

- Welcome the speaker and announce the title of the talk.
- Elaborate briefly on the relevance of the topic.
- Outline the speaker's qualifications and experience. Indicate any link the speaker might have with your organisation or the audience. Briefly describe the speaker's other interests, if relevant.
- Conclude with the following statement: 'Ladies and gentlemen, please welcome...', and lead the applause.

2 **Stay focused.**

Your introduction must prepare the audience for the speaker by concentrating the listeners' attention on the new presentation. Keep your comments compatible with the focus and tone of the talk.

3 **Be brief.**

Keep your introduction to two minutes' duration and don't indulge in your own pet views on the subject. Do not commit the speaker to any particular line of approach.

4 **Confirm if a Q&A session is warranted.**

Check beforehand to determine if the speaker is prepared to take questions from the audience at the end of the talk. Advise the audience in advance so that appropriate questions are forthcoming after the speech.

 And don't forget...

A good introduction must:

- provide a smooth transition linking speaker to program

- whet the audience's appetite
- throw out a welcome mat and mellow any audience resistance
- express gratitude to the speaker for sharing both time and knowledge with those present.

The vote of thanks

1 Be prepared to be spontaneous.

A vote of thanks is usually not the kind of speech you can prepare beforehand—unless you have a copy of your guest's talk in advance. So, as a rule, you'll need to be spontaneous.

2 Structure your response.

Listen carefully to the talk, and select and jot down two or three key points. Build your vote of thanks around these selected points. You might say: 'Madam Chair, ladies and gentlemen, our speaker tonight made two points which particularly appealed to me. First of all,... Secondly,... In conclusion, I found our speaker's presentation

to be informative, incisive, and entertaining, and so I am delighted to propose this vote of thanks. Please join with me in showing our appreciation...'

3 Remember these helpful suggestions...

- Be gracious, sincere—and brief. It is not the responsibility of the thanker to make another long speech.

- As a general rule, you should never voice your disagreement with the speaker, nor make corrections to the speech, nor use the occasion to push your views—no matter how much you might disagree with what was said.

- Stand in a position that gives you eye-contact with the entire audience. Occasionally turn towards the speaker.

- And if it's been a woeful speech? Make as little reference to the content of the speech as possible: focus on the effort and preparation involved, thanking the speaker for making the time available in a busy schedule. Be courteous and brief.

 don't forget

Speak with confidence

When Jennifer Denham, whose company, named appropriately *Speaking and Confidence*, was asked to list the key presentation skills for a speaker, she responded by listing the following fifteen...

S Smile! – and win your audience.

P Prepare thoroughly and rehearse your speech.

E Enthusiasm – you need it to persuade your audience.

A Audio – how do you sound?

K Knowledge – you must know your subject. Be the expert.

C Convince your audience with simple words and visuals.

O Organise your speech and equipment. Speak to time.

N Natural – be yourself.

F Funny – use humour to make your message fun and effective.

I Imagination – jump into the shoes of the audience. What do they want to know?

D Dress and Deportment – what do you look like?

E Experience – practice makes perfect, so volunteer to speak.

N Nerves – work at controlling them. Nervous energy is healthy.

C Contact the audience by using effective eye contact.

E Enjoy yourself!

How to make special speeches:
(a) presenting an award   (b) accepting an award

Speaking in public need no longer be something to be feared and avoided if you view those occasions as opportunities to be sought and prized. A public speech, no matter how brief, increases your visibility. So take advantage of the opportunity, for the podium can help pave your way to the executive suite once you learn the tricks of speech-making. Here are two more opportunities to help you make an impact...

Presenting an award

1 Give the background to the award.

Mention why people are gathered together for this presentation and provide, as appropriate, some background information relating to this particular award—its meaning, uses, history, previous winners, the selection process etc.

2 Elaborate on this person's achievements.

Provide details as to why this person has been selected for honour in this way. Support the selection with evidence of the person's accomplishments.

3 Punctuate your speech with appropriate attention-grabbers.

Do a little homework. Research a few books of 'quotable quotes' and drop one or two relevant quips into your presentation speech. For example,

couple the accomplishments of your awardee with such statements as—'It isn't how much you know, but what you get done that the world rewards and remembers' or 'The life of achievement is a life of hard work' or 'Footprints in the sands of time were not made by sitting down' or, as Helen Keller said, 'I long to accomplish a great and noble task, but it is my chief duty to accomplish *all* tasks as though they were great and noble. The world is moved along, not only by the mighty shoves of its heroes, but also by the aggregate of the tiny pushes of each honest worker'.

4 Make the formal presentation.

Conclude your comments with the statement: 'On behalf of ..., I'm delighted to present ... with this well-deserved award. Our sincere congratulations!' Shake the recipient's hand, step back, and allow the audience to hear the awardee's words of acceptance.

Accepting an award

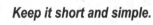

1 Keep it short and simple.

Unless you are in a very formal gathering, an acceptance speech any longer than one or two minutes is usually too long. So do your audience and yourself a favour: keep it genuine, simple, and as short as possible.

2 Express your sincere gratitude.

In one sentence, express your gratitude to, and respect for, the organisation presenting the award and for the kind wishes that accompany it.

3 Share the credit.

Acknowledge and voice your appreciation to others. Mention by name any colleagues or co-workers who helped you and then thank them specifically for their contributions. Where appropriate, also thank your family members for their support.

4 Speak of the significance of the award.

Why is the award important to you or your organisation and what does it mean to win the honour?

5 Praise the competition.

The more highly you speak of those you outperformed, the more meaningful your award becomes, and the more you come across as a good sport.

6 Indicate what you will do with the award.

Show the award to those present and refer to its attractiveness, usefulness etc. Indicate what you will be doing with it, and where in your office or building it will be placed for all to see.

7 Conclude with a final thank you.

Once more express your thanks: 'I/We shall cherish this award and what it stands for. Thank you.'

8 Remember: be humble.

Display a sense of humility. You will not only add to the lustre of the honour but also demonstrate your own modesty.

How to make special speeches:
(a) an impromptu speech (b) a retirement speech

How strange it is that, although we may be able to manage human, financial, and physical resources with complete confidence, we are fearful and trembling when called upon to 'say a few words'. Here are more suggestions to help you grapple with any such anxieties…

An impromptu speech

1 Acknowledge that an impromptu speech can be frightening.

You wouldn't be alone if you admitted that one of your greatest fears was to be asked to give an off-the-cuff speech at an important meeting. Impromptu presentations can be difficult to do as well. Speakers can easily ramble in a disjointed fashion and stumble; some literally go blank. But here is a helpful strategy to make the ordeal manageable…

2 Just remember the three-question trick.

The simplest way to handle the off-the-cuff speech is to compose, and then answer, three questions about the situation or topic you've been given.

For example, if you are invited at a meeting of associates to say a few words of farewell to a prominent colleague who is moving interstate, begin by asking three obvious questions, and then go back and provide an appropriate answer to each: 'What has been Diane's contribution to the organisation?', 'What incident will I remember most about Diane?' and 'How easy is it going to be for us to replace her as manager of personnel services?'

Remember the structure:

- state the topic
- pose your three questions
- go back and answer each one
- restate the topic.

So next time you're put on a spot and asked to make an impromptu presentation, you needn't be caught out.

After all, giving an excellent impromptu talk is no harder than asking and answering your own questions.

A retirement speech

Focus on the occasion.

Indicate that this is both a happy and a sad occasion—happy because everyone is here to congratulate your retiring colleague on his or her many years with the organisation, and sad because many people 'are sorry to lose you'.

Focus on length of service.

Mention the retiree's length of service, focusing in particular on his or her period with the organisation and the changes that have taken place during those years.

Outline the retiree's career.

Give a brief outline of the retiree's career in the service of your organisation. You'll need to do your homework.

Consider what made the retiree 'special'.

Highlight some of the retiree's outstanding achievements or contributions to the company. List also some of the personal things that have made him or her 'special'. One or two anecdotes to illustrate might also be appropriate.

Contemplate the future.

Give an indication of the retiree's intentions for retirement and how busy he or she will be in the years to come.

In a retirement speech, avoid any suggestion that this is the 'end of the road' for the guest of honour. In this regard, perhaps the thoughts of Oliver Wendell Holmes, US Supreme Court Justice on his 90th birthday are appropriate:

> The riders in a race do not stop short when they reach the goal. There is a little finishing canter before coming to a standstill. There is time to hear the kind voice of friends and to say to one's self: 'The work is done'. But just as one says that, the answer comes: 'The race is over, but the work is *never* done while the power of work remains.'

Conclude on a happy note.

Congratulate the retiree and make the presentation. Include, where appropriate in the speech, a couple of smart quips, e.g. 'Retirement takes all the fun out of Saturdays' or 'Retirement is the time when there is too much of it or not enough of it.'

negotiation

problem solving

speech making

How to prepare to negotiate

Negotiation—the process of arriving at mutual satisfaction through discussion and bargaining with another party—is an essential management skill. Managers negotiate to settle differences, to determine the value of services or products, or to vary terms or agreements. The smart manager enters negotiations with a clear strategy in mind. Planning for negotiation will improve its outcome for you; and the following advice will prove useful...

quotable quote

Successful negotiators will spend eighty per cent of their time preparing to negotiate and, perhaps, twenty per cent of their time actually conducting business. They know that facing an important or complex negotiation demands a high degree of detailed and thorough preparation. They will know everything there is to know about the other side; they will be clear about how far they are willing to compromise; and they will understand absolutely where to draw the bottom line.[66]

viewpoint

"Since every manager negotiates at some time, what are the ideal characteristics of a good negotiator? The main ones seem to be:

- a quick mind
- unlimited patience
- an ability to conceal one's position, opinions and facts without lying
- capacity to inspire trust in others
- to be self-effacing yet assertive at key moments
- possession of detailed knowledge of the issue under negotiation, yet able to see the wood for the trees."

– Andrew Leigh in
20 Ways to Manage Better

1 Identify the issues for negotiation.

Before you can negotiate anything effectively, first clarify what exactly the real issues for negotiation are. Identifying these issues is like separating the wood from the trees. For example, the focus of your negotiations could relate to staff health and safety (the trees). But what is the *specific* issue (the wood) in this topic about which you will be trying to negotiate the best deal for yourself or your team?

2 Set clear goals for the negotiation.

Knowing what you want out of any negotiation is most important. Your preparation needs to focus on your goals. Try to write them down. They may be as straightforward as 'To have improvements made to the community centre without any costs being incurred by the community'. Once you have identified your goals, you will then be able to decide on any fall back position you would be prepared to consider. For

example, your goal may be to get the improvements to the community centre carried out at someone's expense: your fall back may be to pay half of the costs.

3 Gather information about the other side.

If you have information about the other side at your fingertips, you strengthen your position at the negotiating table. What can you find out about your opponents?

What are their strengths and weaknesses?
What will be their concerns?
What is their financial position?
What's important to them?
What do they have that you badly need?
What do you have that they want?
How important is it for them to leave the negotiations with their reputation in place?

Have *facts* at your fingertips. Many negotiations fail to get the desired results because the negotiator deals, instead, in broad generalisations. The use of a phrase like 'It's the government's fault' is an example of a generalisation. You need to be able to name the person in the government so that some meaningful action can occur. It's important for you to impress (or bluff) your opponent with your level of preparation.

 Clarify your own position.

Be perfectly clear on the stance you are able to take. Be able to answer the following questions before you enter negotiations:

- What would be the best possible deal for us?
- What would be a realistic outcome for us?
- What would be the minimal acceptable outcome for us?
- What would be the worst possible outcome for us?
- What are the limits of our authority at the negotiating table? Are we free to negotiate cuts, increases, changes, add-ons, and new directions in the discussions?
- What concessions are we willing to offer our opponent?
- What concessions are we not allowed to propose?
- What is our opening offer (usually an exaggerated proposal) to get the negotiation ball rolling?

 Brush up on negotiating strategies.

Become aware in advance of the types of negotiating strategies that others may adopt in winning you over. For example:

- *The stampede tactic.* Don't be intimidated by displays of impatience or irritation by the other side. Patiently insist that your

concerns be addressed point by point.
- *The friendly tactic.* Here the other side assumes a level of friendship and intimacy that doesn't exist in reality. Don't be swayed to give away concessions simply because an atmosphere of goodwill exists.
- *The dismissive tactic.* Here they try to gloss over your concerns as being 'nothing to worry about'. Avoid being lulled into a false sense of security.
- *The threatening tactic.* Don't be frightened into submission. Stay calm and don't react. Negotiation is a process for cool heads.

And consider tactics *you* might adopt to win the day—see page 292 for *Play Dumb, Time Trap, Goodies and Baddies,* and *That's It.*

 Stay SHARP.

International management consultant Lisa Davis recommends that you stay SHARP as you enter negotiations. You'll need to be:

Supercool—Promise yourself to remain unruffled. Don't get angry, irritable, impatient, sarcastic, or upset. By controlling your emotions, you'll score valuable points at the table.

Honest—As part of the negotiating deal, never make promises you can't keep. Earn a reputation for honesty.

Assertive—Say what you mean, and mean what you say. Be neither passive nor aggressive, but be fair.

Realistic—Know what's achievable and what's not. Try to understand also what it's like to be sitting on the other side of the table.

Prepared—Do your homework before entering negotiations.

 don't forget

The basics of negotiation

Bear in mind the top ten tips for negotiating when preparing for the negotiation process:

■ *If you don't have to negotiate, don't.* Why do it if you needn't give anything away to get what you want?

■ *Be prepared.* Research thoroughly your position and the situation of the other party.

■ *Let the other side do the work, not you.* Make your demands early. Let the other party work hard to squeeze concessions out of you.

■ *Apply your power gently at first.* Build up your bargaining power early. Apply pressure by revealing any problems that could occur if the deal does not go your way.

■ *Make them compete.* Have them work hard to get your attention. If not, they could lose out to another party.

■ *Leave yourself room.* Leave space to manoeuvre. Ask for more than you expect and concede less than you would want to give willingly.

■ *Maintain your integrity.* Withhold if you must, but tell no lies. Be tough, cunning, even abrasive; but always trustworthy.

■ *Listen, don't talk.* The more they talk, the more they will reveal. Listen and learn.

■ *Keep contact with their hopes.* There is a limit to how much you can demand without causing deadlock.

■ *Give them time to get used to your big ideas.* Be patient. Give them time to come to terms with your demands.[69]

How to negotiate a better deal

Despite the best efforts of some of the world's best academics and practitioners to develop winning strategies, there is no universal set of irrefutable rules governing the complex process of negotiation. We do know, however, that good negotiators must be flexible. They must walk a fine line between domination and appeasement, embracing a range of proven behaviours including the following…

1 Know exactly what you want and draw two lines.

This is the key. Determine your bottom line position before beginning negotiation, by identifying your goal specifically, with dates, numbers, prices, and so on. Imagine yourself drawing this proverbial 'line in the sand' and then drawing a second line a few steps in advance of it. The second will be the line at which you begin negotiations. In this way, at worst, you'll be negotiated back to your first line in the sand.

2 Make sure this person can say yes.

Negotiation can be a long and protracted process. You don't really want to get into a situation where, after many hours of negotiation, the other party has to OK with a superior an agreement you have worked long and hard to negotiate.

So how do you know if this person can negotiate the deal? Just ask. Do whatever you can to negotiate directly with the person who *can* say yes.

3 Enter negotiations with a win-win attitude.

If you win at the expense of the other party, the deal will invariably return to haunt you. Continually adopt a win-win attitude because the only truly successful negotiation is one in which both parties believe their needs have been met.

4 Apply proven strategies.

Bearing in mind that you'll want to secure the best deal for yourself without making the other side feel that it has lost, consider these strategies for clinching the deal:

• Always allow yourself negotiating space by asking for more than you expect to get—you might just get it!
• Resist the first offer—you can't have the other side thinking they were too generous.
• Learn to flinch—your reaction, real or sham, will be noticed and perhaps encourage concessions.
• Be a reluctant seller—your perceived caution will encourage a higher offer.

- Look for ways of solving the other side's problems first—and then sit back and watch them meet your demands because they'll be wanting you to follow through on your end of the deal.
- Talk about the potential for future deals (or lack thereof)—by ensuring the other side sees the long-term benefits of sealing the deal *this* time.

5 Apply pressure by playing games.

A great deal of successful negotiation is game-playing. Try these games:

- *Play Dumb*—a game that allows you room and time to manoeuvre. You might indicate your agreement with the deal but state you will have to pass it by a higher authority. Return the next day with the news that the higher authority wants more concessions.
- *Time Trap*—a power game exploiting the fact that the closer you get to the deadline the greater the possibility of concessions being offered. When both sides are facing the same deadline, the least powerful side is going to feel the greater time pressure.
- *Goodies and Baddies*—a game that shifts the blame to another, leaving you smelling like roses. You indicate that you want to do the deal but your partner or boss won't buy it. Apologise and suggest concessions from the other side that may get the negotiations back on track.
- *That's It*—a game of bluff in which you walk away from a deal, either forever or to encourage the other side to make concessions. It is never a 'take it or leave it' ultimatum. Be prepared to say, 'I'm sorry, we won't be doing business after all.' And if they come back to you, don't drop everything to restart negotiations—over-eagerness could lose the day for you.

6 Make power your partner.

Negotiations are power games. Try using these five main sources of power, either separately or combined:

Legitimate or positional power—achieved through symbols like titles, address, physical presentation, and office setting. Exploit all of those symbols, but guard against falling for their's.

Reward power—achieved by the other side knowing what they will get from doing business with you. Make sure they know what's in it for them.

Coercive power—achieved by the other side knowing that they lose out by not doing business with you. Third-party testimonials can be extremely coercive.

Reverent power—achieved when others know that there are some things you will never deviate from—your core values, for example. You can always be relied upon to respond in a particular way.

Situation power—achieved when one side only has the power. Ever tried to get the attendant at the ticketing counter to provide you with a pre-booked ticket when you have no identification?

7 Remember also...

- Never make a concession without getting one in return.
- Focus on needs, not on personalities. Keep egos out of it.
- Never enter negotiations when everyone knows you have to pull off the deal—it's the worst possible time. If you don't have the luxury of negotiating well in advance, then at least feign a lack of urgency.
- Establish a clear and specific agreement that leaves no room for confusion or reneging.
- A deal is made, not won.

! viewpoint

"The worst thing you can possibly do in a deal is seem desperate to make it. That makes the other guy smell blood, and then you're dead. The best thing you can do is deal from strength, and leverage is the biggest strength you can have. Leverage is having something the other guy wants. Or better yet, needs. Or best of all, simply can't do without."
– Donald Trump

! viewpoint

"Negotiators are like two workers carrying the same burden: whether they like it or not, they are part of the same 'chain gang'. The negotiator who dislikes or is rude to the other side adds to the mutual burden instead of alleviating it. The better negotiator respects the other side."
– Janos Nyerges in *Negotiation Journal*

293

BUILDING ESSENTIAL SKILLS

How to begin each month on a positive note

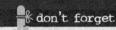
Things will happen to you over the next month. You can wait for them to happen, you can just let them happen or you can make them happen. If you want to change your professional or personal life for the better, you must start with resolve and determination. The following resolutions are provided to help you improve the way you function as a manager. Refer to them at the start of each month and decide which you will focus on. How determined are you to improve?

don't forget

The productivity misconceptions

In planning your month, always bear in mind these management *myths*:

- I procrastinate because I work better under pressure.
- The harder I work, the more work I get done.
- There's never enough time to finish what is really important.
- If there were more hours in a day, I'd finish what I need to do.
- It's better to do small tasks first and save the big ones for later in the day.
- When I'm most active I get the most work done.
- By doing them myself, tasks

1 Upgrade your professionalism.

Take responsibility for your own learning and development:

- ☐ Read two journals this month.
- ☐ Read one book this month.
- ☐ Contribute in some way to my professional association.
- ☐ Attend a seminar or course, and get involved.
- ☐ Improve my technology skills and know-how in some way.
- ☐ Write an item for a professional journal, newsletter, or newspaper.
- ☐

2 Improve the way you work.

When you can't work any harder or longer, working smarter is the only other option. Streamline the way you work:

- ☐ At the start of each week, set goals to be achieved by week's end.
- ☐ Plan each day by completing a daily to-do list.

- ☐ Keep each telephone call to a minimum.
- ☐ Make a determined effort to handle each piece of paper no more than twice.
- ☐ Be aware of any act of procrastination—and bite the bullet!
- ☐ Be on time for every meeting and prepare myself beforehand to make a worthwhile contribution.
- ☐ Ask myself often—'Is this the best use of my time and energy?'
- ☐ Become a better delegator—by doing it right.
- ☐ Be aware of every interruption. Can I do something about this?
- ☐ Focus on one thing each day that requires of me a special 110% effort.
- ☐

 ## *Improve your relationships.*

Do your best to get on well with other people and your managerial task will be much simpler:

- ☐ Make the effort to remember the name of each new person I meet.

- ☐ Catch at least three employees a day doing something right, and praise them accordingly.
- ☐ Work at eliminating a personal mannerism or habit that annoys others or hampers my effectiveness.
- ☐ Show a special interest in the work and life of three colleagues during the coming month.
- ☐ Act consistently in ways I believe to be fair and ethical.
- ☐ Say thank you more often.
- ☐ Defuse any grudge or hostility I have with a colleague or worker.
- ☐ Do one special thing this month to make this environment a better place for others to work in.
- ☐

4 Look after your own well-being.

Life and work are not to be endured, but enjoyed. You work to live, not live to work:

- ☐ Think about the need for balance in my life—work, family, friends, religion, community, self…
- ☐ Put aside the time to enjoy special activities with my family this month.
- ☐ Exercise daily—in what way?
- ☐ Make a few changes for the better in what I eat—in what way?
- ☐ Set aside time for myself each day—for reading, hobbies, or play.
- ☐ Give something back to the community this month—and enhance the company's image at the same time.
- ☐ What major task am I about to

complete? Is there a task over which I have been procrastinating? Finish it this month—and my reward will be………

- ☐

5 Make good use of your travelling/waiting time.

Travelling to and from work and waiting for appointments and meetings can be very time-consuming and inefficient. Do something about it:

- ☐ Read job-related documents, books, or journals.
- ☐ Reflect on three encouraging incidents that occur each day.
- ☐ List three tasks I felt most happy about accomplishing for the day.
- ☐ Listen to a management-related audiobook.
- ☐ Do some fresh thinking about a work-related problem requiring a solution.
- ☐

6 Add your own monthly resolutions...

- ☐
- ☐
- ☐
- ☐
- ☐
- ☐

 here's an idea

The management experts say you should put aside 30 minutes to plan your entire week in advance. How do you do it? One strategy is to follow the *OATS* formula:

O: Objectives. What results do you want to see by the end of the week? Write them down and rank them in priority order.

A: Activities. What do you have to do to achieve your goals? List the necessary activities, and put them in sequence.

T: Time. How much time will each activity require? To plan realisticially, allow yourself more time than you think you will actually need. This gives you flexibility if unexpected problems arise.

S: Schedule. Look at your calendar and decide when you can do each activity. Most people underestimate the power of a schedule, but you won't get anything accomplished if you don't set aside time to do it.

here's an idea

At the beginning of the month, spend 30 minutes with your monthly calendar. Write down all your deadline dates; when projects are due; important meetings; personal and business appointments; and other vital dates. Then, working backwards, estimate how much time you need to prepare for each event. For example, for a project due at the end of the month, you might have to start working on it on the 15th. Enter that 'start date' on the calendar *as well*.

295

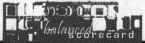
How to develop a mission statement

Leaders of today's organisations are faced with the challenge of transforming their companies and adapting to increased competition, deregulation, downsizing, and the globalisation of markets. The starting point for dealing effectively with such issues is the organisation's mission statement. By considering the following guidelines, you too can develop a mission statement that instils inspiration in your staff and truly reflects their dreams, hopes, aspirations, and reasons for being…

Understand the purpose of mission statements.

A mission statement is a key component of an organisation's entire planning process. It is more than a slogan or motto; it is the operational, ethical, and financial guiding light for an organisation. It articulates the goals, dreams, culture, behaviour, and desired future of a company. Strategically, it is a tool that defines a company's business and target market. Culturally, it serves as the 'glue' that binds the company together through shared values and standards of behaviour. It must inspire and stretch staff to higher levels of performance.

Form a task force to draft the mission.

Gathering the right words, setting the tone, and finding the main theme should involve individuals whose commitment to the final statement is expected. Establish a working party comprising representatives from various departments. Select wisely; people's hearts as well as their heads are required.

 ### Write a first draft.

Conduct a situation or SWOT analysis to identify where your organisation stands today, how it came to be where it is, what external forces will probably influence its future, and what it hopes to become. Be sure to get input from the CEO and other senior people. With this background, the working group can brainstorm to compile a collection of ideas that can be synthesised into a draft statement.

In preparing a first draft, bear in mind the following cardinal rules for writing a mission statement:

• *It can vary in length.* It can be very short (*Total customer satisfaction*—Motorola) or several paragraphs long, where the mission is supported by vision statements, values, objectives, principles or philosophies to provide guidance. Most mission statements would average 25 words in length.

• *It must be clearly articulated*. It should be easily understood, pithy and to the point, free of empty phrases and complex terms or jargon, espousing principles and values that will guide the stakeholders in their day-to-day and future activities. The mission of this US airline was succinct and readily understood: *The mission of Southwest Airlines is dedication to the highest quality of customer service delivered with a sense of warmth, friendliness, individual pride, and company spirit.*

• **It should be written in an inspiring tone.** It should encourage commitment and energise all staff towards achieving the mission. It should be elegant, positive, colourful, and inspiring. Consider Intel Corporation's mission: *Do a great job for our customers, employees and stockholders by being the preeminent building block supplier to the computing industry.*

• **It must be relevant and current.** It should echo your organisation's history, culture and shared values, focus on the present but look to an attainable future. But in an ever-changing, competitive environment the mission should be regularly reviewed and subject to revision to retain your company's current focus and direction.

• **It must reflect your organisation's uniqueness.** It should set your company apart from others, establishing your individuality. Consider the mission statement of Celestial Seasonings: *Our mission is to grow and dominate the US speciality tea market by exceeding consumer expectations with the best tasting, 100% natural hot and iced teas, packaged with Celestial art and philosophy, creating the most valued tea experience...*

• **It must be enduring.** Mission statements should guide and inspire for many years, challenging, yet just short of total achievement. Disneyland's mission, for example, will endure for as long as 'imagination' exists in the world.

• **It must cater for all audiences.** The statement must convey your message clearly, concisely and strikingly to all your stakeholders, who universally understand and accept its meaning.

4 Review, revise, validate, and seek acceptance.

A statement that is hurried, or does not reflect the input of those who must carry it as their standard into the community, will rarely inspire nor involve those whose input matters most. The process may take a few weeks, a few months—even a year. During that time you should circulate drafts to any who were not present at drafting meetings and whose commitment is required. Display the mission statement for employees to see, inviting them to add any minor finishing touches.

5 Operationalise the final version.

When you're confident that the mission statement has received and benefited from stakeholders' input, produce a final version. Hold meetings to gain commitment to the mission and to turn its message into reality. Agree on the other uses to be made of the mission—on posters, publications, business cards, T-shirts, coffee mugs, products, calendars...

6 Keep the mission under review.

Developing a mission statement is just the beginning. It must continue to have meaning for all employees. So, periodically, refer to it on the agenda at meetings of staff, Board, and other groups. An annual revisit should occur as part of the review of your organisation's strategic plan.

How to implement a mission statement

You've followed the suggestions provided on previous pages about developing a mission statement and are now ready to implement that mission. If you've used an inclusive process to develop the statement, your efforts will be rewarded in this implementation phase: you've demonstrated an understanding of the importance in development of acceptance, commitment, and ownership. Now, in implementation, you can benefit from your efforts thus far...

read further

The Mission Statement Book: 301 Corporate Mission Statements from America's Top Companies by Jeffrey Abrahams, Ten Speed Press, 2004.

The Mission Primer: Four Steps to an Effective Mission Statement by R. & D. O'Hallaron, Mission Incorporated, 2000.

1 Form an ad hoc committee.

Select a working party representative of all groups in the organisation—management and staff. This team, established for the specific purpose of successfully implementing the new mission, will be disbanded after this intention has been realised. By being expansive about committee membership, you will give every group an opportunity to be involved in the implementation process. Make sure that each working party member wants to be involved and, therefore, is prepared to give the task the priority it deserves and warrants.

2 Develop a shared meaning.

Before going public, the implementation working party must ensure that it will be communicating a message that is clear, straightforward, and embraced by its members. When people want answers to specific questions about implementation, it is vital that they receive a common message. If, for example, the mission is a 'kill-Darius statement'[3], there can be no confusion about the actions required.

3 Adopt an inclusive approach.

As part of the implementation process, the working party should provide opportunities for the organisation's staff *and* management to interact and get to know each other better. Some people will judge the importance of these events by who actually participates. For example, if the CEO or members of the executive team do not attend, this could be interpreted as an indication of the lack of priority attached to the mission and its implementation. Impress upon the working party team the need for them to motivate members of their own work groups to attend and to participate in the process.

4 Engage individuals and groups in discussions.

If people have been involved in the developmental phase of the mission statement, this step will be different from one in which people are seeing the plan for the first time. Give all staff adequate opportunities to express their views and speak their minds. The feedback and messages communicated will provide an indication about the ease with which the mission will be accepted and how it will be reflected in people's actions. If you have devoted time to developing an open climate, your efforts will be rewarded when people readily contribute their views during this implementation phase.

Assign responsibilities.

Assuming that you have discussed the mission and any associated actions required, you might decide to allocate specific tasks to groups and individual members. These tasks may be identified as 'immediate'(such as making contact with customers or clients), 'short-term' (conducting focus groups), 'long-term' (completing an environmental impact study), and 'deferred' (aspects of the organisation's capital works program). Individuals and groups will be expected to take responsibility for keeping everyone informed of progress.

Demonstrate your commitment.

Although 'outsiders', such as customers and community, can't be expected to elucidate your mission in specific terms, they should be able to come close to identifying it by observing the actions of you and your people. A mission that includes 'putting customers first' should be readily identifiable by customers. And, of course, as you personally set about 'living the mission', others will observe your commitment and, most likely, follow your example.

Celebrate accomplishments.

When Gordon Bethune was CEO of Continental Airlines, one of his management maxims was 'What you measure and reward is what you get'. This maxim can be applied to implementing a mission by celebrating accomplishments or milestones in the implementation process. The rewards can take the form of recognition such as thanking those responsible, providing special mention in in-house communication, and telling third-parties who you know will convey your message to the person concerned.

Keep the mission under review.

Remember: a mission statement alone cannot create a sense of mission. People must feel that they are part of the process, and will respond accordingly if they can understand it clearly, can relate to it, own it, and feel inspired by it. At both the development and implementation phases, include the mission on the agenda of in-house meetings. The mission should be the subject of continuing reference throughout the organisation. This will have the added thrust of communicating management's commitment to the mission.

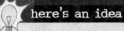

here's an idea

If you've kept your organisation's vision and mission statements concise, meaningful and action-oriented, implementation will be so much easier.

don't forget

Why mission statements fail to take root

■ *Lack of definition in the vision*
Failure to build full understanding effectively, or to manage organisational interpretations of the mission

■ *Lack of management commitment*
Cynicism, scepticism, uncertainty, and resistance impacting on all levels of the organisation

■ *Failure to actively enrol employees and the marketplace in support of the mission*
Ineffective communications based on all the above

■ *Lack of planning and focused implementation*
Seeing the work of bringing the mission to life as a 'task', or added burden, rather than as fundamental to the job

The one factor which is always present in a *successful* mission statement program is the active leadership and support of senior management on a continuing basis.[5]

How to conduct a SWOT analysis

A SWOT analysis is a management tool that helps you to isolate key issues and to facilitate a strategic approach by building on **S**trengths, minimising **W**eaknesses, seizing **O**pportunities, and counteracting **T**hreats. The technique can be used by a person constructing an accurate picture of a career, a business owner preparing a business plan, or a Board reviewing or developing a strategic plan. Once you are clear about your objective, the approach can be tailored to meet your particular situation. In a group situation, the steps could be as follows…

1 Invite contributors to participate in the SWOT analysis.

The best results are often achieved when contributors are given time to prepare by conducting their own SWOT in advance. With their invitations to participate, contributors receive a draft SWOT for completion before the planning session. The draft consists of a brief description with adequate space to record what they see as being strengths, weaknesses, opportunities, and threats. To do this, they could conduct discussions with, or survey, stakeholder colleagues who will not be attending the planning workshop.

2 Explain the process and establish ground rules.

When the group has been assembled, explain the process to be followed—documenting strengths, weaknesses, opportunities, and threats, prioritising those lists, and using that information as part of the strategic, business, or marketing plans. Explain that the SWOT is a cooperative exercise aimed at organisational improvement. It is not about allocating blame or passing the buck. Assure all participants that their contributions will be respected. Ground rules could include:

- Everyone's ideas are important.
- Every idea is a good idea.
- No one idea is better than another.
- Suggesting an idea does not mean that you will be expected to carry it out if it is accepted.
- Except in the case of an emergency, participants commit to remaining on task until completion.

3 List strengths.

First, consider your strengths…

Participants assemble their lists of strengths identified before the workshop. Invite them to form pairs and develop one list representative of each person's contributions. Pairs then combine to form fours and the process is repeated. Sets of four then combine to form eights and again the process is repeated. Each set of eight then presents its list. One list ('Strengths') is developed incorporating all contributions. The list is finalised by asking participants to reword any descriptions or include any additional strengths that they consider should appear on the list. Depending on your project, examples of strengths could include issues relating to personnel, location, pricing, and competitiveness.

don't forget
The purpose

The process of defining your strengths, weaknesses, opportunities and threats allows you to see, realistically, what factors are likely to work for or against you. This information will then help you when you are trying to identify the individual steps for achieving your goal.

don't forget
What is SWOT?

Strengths are what the team or organisation can offer that will propel you forward to success.

Weaknesses within the team or organisation are the things that may hold you back from success.

Opportunities are those things that are currently available, or likely to become available, which may assist you in achieving success.

Threats are those things your organisation or team may have to face while working towards success.

Identify weaknesses.

Next, consider weaknesses…

Repeat the process followed for 'strengths' to generate a list of weaknesses reflecting the participants' contributions. The list will also provide a useful indication of growth over a period—say, one year. When you review the list in a year's time, chances are you will notice that most of the identified weaknesses have disappeared. Even though other weaknesses will be identified, the disappearance of previous ones is an indicator of successful progress. Depending on your project, examples of weaknesses could include absence of new products or customers, staff absenteeism, declining market for new products, and distance to market.

 ### List opportunities and threats.

Next, consider opportunities and threats to your organisation…

Repeat the process followed for 'strengths' and 'weaknesses'. The focus now becomes external—as opposed to internal for strengths and weaknesses. Appreciate that opportunities and threats are not absolute: one person's threat can be another's opportunity. As the saying goes, 'A pessimist is a person who sees a calamity in an opportunity, and an optimist is one who sees an opportunity in a calamity.' Clearly, the same item or topic won't appear on both lists. Depending on your project, opportunities could include new technology, better training programs, diverse marketplace, and change of government. Threats could include increasing unemployment, higher interest rates, and environmental legislation.

 ### Establish priorities.

When you have completed the process, you will have four lists developed from everyone's input.

Ideally, these lists should be displayed side-by-side so that participants have an accurate and succinct picture of everyone's views of the current situation. Work your way through each list to establish a top-five priority using this process:

Draw participants' attention to each list, beginning with strengths. Depending on the size of the group, each person is given several votes (say, five). Establish a priority by inviting participants to assign a vote for their top-five topics from the list. Record the number of votes alongside each topic. The five topics with the most votes are listed on a separate sheet. If several topics attract the same number of votes, record all of those. Repeat the process for weaknesses, opportunities, and threats.

 ### Question each list.

Encourage group discussion about the four prioritised lists by asking:

1. How can we use our strengths to enable us to take advantage of the opportunities identified?
2. How can we use these strengths to overcome the threats identified?
3. What do we need to do to overcome the identified weaknesses in order to take advantage of the opportunities?
4. How will we minimise the weaknesses to overcome the identified threats?

 ### Prepare for the next step.

One option will be to use the four lists comprising about twenty topics to identify issues that are crucial to achieving the stated purpose of the business in which the company is involved. It is likely that you will be able to identify specific themes across all four lists. Try to restrict the number of themes or issues to about six.

 it's a fact

There are clear links between the principles of a SWOT analysis and the work of the military strategist Sun Tzu who, in about 400 BC, wrote *The Art of War*. Sun Tzu advocated looking internally and externally to help determine strategies.

 it's a fact

At first sighting, opportunities sometimes appear as a threat.

In the 1950s, for example, railroads in the United States refused to accept the idea that cars, planes, and trucks were here to stay. They viewed the new transportation as a threat not only to the railroads but also to the nation.

But a decade later, the railroads began to see the threat as an opportunity. The public would accept railroads dropping unprofitable lines and merging with other railroads thus allowing them to do what they did best – making long-haul deliveries.

 quotable quote

SWOT in and of itself will not give specific answers. Instead it is a way to organize information and assign probabilities to potential events – both good and bad – as the basis for developing business strategy and operational plans.[6]

How to articulate a vision for your organisation

It is so easy for an organisation to busy itself with daily activities that it can become oblivious to its future, without reflecting or envisaging what can happen, without a vision or a sense of direction. Your organisation may be active in the short term; but, without a vision of the future, it will lose direction, purpose, and control—those essential ingredients for success in the long term. Here is one way of articulating for your organisation a vision linking values, purpose, and mission...

don't forget

Why you need a vision...

In *Corporate Reputations*, Grahame Dowling writes that vision statements are useful to organisations because they can help to, for example:

* motivate and focus all employees on a common superordinate goal
* define the boundaries of the business
* provide an overall unifying theme for advertising and publicity
* help differentiate the organisation from its competitors.

It is important to list objectives such as these before setting out to design any vision statement.

 Get 'vision' in context.

Visionary organisations have two distinct, stand-out features—an enduring character that transcends all other things like products, bosses, management fads, and technological breakthroughs; and visible, vivid, real futures as yet unrealised. Vision helps to bring those two features to life. In *Leaders*, Warren Bennis and Bert Nanus defined an organisational vision as:

'A mental image of a possible and desirable state of the organisation... a view of a realistic, credible, attractive future for the organisation, a condition that is better in some important ways than what now exists.'

Understand the contributing factors.

In *Built to Last: Successful Habits of Visionary Companies*, James Collins and Jerry Porras identified three components that contribute to the articulation of a vision:

* *The core values*—the 3 to 5 guiding principles important to those in the organisation.
* *The core purpose*—the organisation's reason for being, its *raison d'être*.
* *A desired future* (or *mission*)—a clear, compelling, unifying and enduring statement that you believe distinguishes your organisation from others, a catalyst for team spirit.

By reflecting on these three areas, you will be well on the way to articulating your organisation's vision; that is, a vibrant, energising, and specific description of what it will be like to achieve your mission.

Isolate core values.

Only a few values can be considered as 'core'—those that define what you stand for—and are likely to be meaningful and inspirational only to those in the organisation. Ask a small selection of highly credible representatives from groups within your organisation such questions as these:

- If you were to start a new organisation in a different line of work, what core values would you build into the business regardless of the industry?
- If you won the lottery and decided to retire, what core values, held in our organisation, would you continue to live by?
- What would you tell your children are the core values that you hold at work and that you hope they will hold when they are working adults?

Identify core purpose.

Core purpose captures the soul of the organisation—why it exists. Though the purpose does not change, it inspires change. Walt Disney's core purpose, for example, is 'To make people happy'. 3M's is 'To solve unsolved problems innovatively'. Core purpose differs from a goal because purposes will never be totally fulfilled.

One way of identifying purpose is to ask selected, individual representatives what activity they are engaged in. To their response you ask, 'Why?' To their next response ask, 'Why?' After the fifth 'Why?' —the approach is called 'The five whys'—you are close to identifying the core purpose.

Picture a desired future— your mission.

This picture of the future serves as a unifying focal point of effort and acts as a catalyst for team spirit and inspiration. Though the mission needs to be visible, vivid, and real, it communicates unrealised dreams, hopes, and aspirations. The mission needs to stimulate and encourage forward momentum.

To arrive at this picture, you might ask your organisation's represent-atives: 'Imagine sitting here in twenty years time. What would we love to see? What should our organisation look like? If someone were to write an article for a major business magazine in twenty years, what would it say?' Would the picture painted raise a goose bump or two, and cries of 'aha!'?

Now articulate your vision.

Now is the time to paint a larger picture with words by bringing together all your reflections about core values, purpose, and the desired future, to create the vision—the big picture. As it describes what it will be like to achieve the mission, the description should attempt to be vibrant and energising, and capable of arousing passion and emotion.

Sony is a good example of a company with a clear vision that inspired the organisation over the decades that followed. In the 1950s, its vision read: 'Fifty years from now, our brand name will be as well known as any in the world… and will signify innovation and quality that rivals the most innovative companies anywhere… "Made in Japan" will mean something fine, not something shoddy'.

Will your vision inspire such achievement?

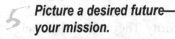

smile & ponder

Someone once said that doers get to the top of the oak tree by climbing it. Dreamers sit on an acorn.

While arriving at and articulating your vision requires more than simply dreaming, in the long run the vision will only become a reality through action – and that will require climbing, not sitting!

it's a fact

On 6 June 1844, George Williams and a group of his young friends met in a small room over a draper's shop in St Paul's Churchyard in London. They were very concerned about the welfare of others like themselves – shop assistants living away from home without any Christian influence. They had a vision, and they prayed and planned – and from that meeting the YMCA, the Young Men's Christian Association, was born.

Little did the visionary George Williams and his friends realise what they were about to create for other young men in the future. In the decades that followed, their unselfish work and great determination saw the YMCA establish itself throughout the world.

Everything worthwhile starts with a vision of an achievable future.

How to initiate a strategic plan

There's more to strategic planning than arranging for a select few to lock themselves away for a couple of days each year to develop a document they hope will lead their organisation to new levels of profitability. Preliminary deliberations and detailed preparation involving different people are required. Among the issues for your consideration during this preparatory phase are the following...

1 Be aware of strategy and what it has to offer.

In the organisational context, strategy is the design of integrated management systems to effectively serve the needs of carefully chosen sets of customers or clients. As you would expect, management strategists differ in their interpretations of strategy and how it applies to individual businesses. Strategy expert Michael Porter says strategy is choosing to do things that are different because, by making those changes, you can be uniquely good. Gary Hamel uses the 'revolution' metaphor urging that strategy be used to radically reinvent the industry. Adrian Slywotsky coined the phrase 'value migration' as the driving force associated with an entirely new way of doing business. David Maister, on the other hand, advocates a more conservative interpretation of strategy as it applies to professional service firms like lawyers and accountants.

2 Be sure your organisation is ready for it.

Drafting a unique and effective strategic plan takes effort, so be prepared for a busy and eventful time. One of your first considerations will be whether your organisational culture is one that is open to a detailed exploration of business opportunities. Exploring strategy must challenge the comfort zones of all members within your organisation —especially those at the top. If senior management is resistant to any change, its stay-put attitude will limit what can be achieved. If true commitment is lacking, gaining the necessary support will need to be at the top of your to-do list.

3 Gain the agreement of your key people.

Bottlenecks occur at the top of the bottle, so be prepared. Those with a vested interest in keeping things as they are have become experts at derailing threats to their comfort and security. They realise that their experience counts only if the future is the same as the past. Spend time with senior management and other key people to reach a shared view on strategy, what it involves, and what their contributions are expected to be.

 Involve stakeholders.

Your discussions will focus on:
- identifying areas of uniqueness for the organisation
- deciding on a strategic position to exploit that uniqueness
- considering trade-off areas that do not contribute to that difference
- constructing a fit among all parts of the organisational process.

The process must involve as many stakeholders as possible—usually long-serving, highly credible employees' representatives and perhaps selected clients. You may decide to conduct a series of group meetings designed specifically for that purpose. In this regard, two approaches might be:

- Ask the group to identify the 10 to 20 most fundamental beliefs that people in your business or industry share. In the hotel or hospitality industry, for example, one such belief may be that everyone checks out by 10 a.m.— even if they only checked in at 1 a.m. —and everyone pays the same price irrespective of the time they spend up to 24 hours. Have the group challenge those beliefs as a means of identifying new opportunities. Explore new horizons, such as late checkouts and variable rates, as opportunities to help improve services and profitability.

- Or, conduct a SWOT analysis (see page 300) of the organisation by having participants consider the organisation's internal *Strengths* and *Weaknesses*, and identify *Opportunities* and *Threats* external to the organisation. The compiled

lists can be used later in a planning workshop to determine issues crucial to the organisation.

There are other approaches, of course, like Slywotsky's 'radar screen', as a way of identifying as yet distant potential competitors. Having completed a preliminary audit of the organisation's operations, the group should be in a position to assemble its ideas about a suitable mission (refer to page 296). A first draft could be used at the subsequent planning workshop.

 Report outcomes to senior managers.

Either you deliver these documented preliminary deliberations from the group to management or have elected representatives meet for that purpose with top management, preferably somewhere other than the boardroom to avoid any feelings of intimidation. The documentation will form the basis of the next phase—a workshop to develop the strategic plan.

Document and disseminate results.

Share the outcomes of this preliminary process with all stakeholders who participated. Where possible, this should be done by re-assembling the groups. Indicate to contributors those suggestions you have taken on board and those you have not—and why not. Outline briefly the next steps in the planning process (see page 306) and how their contributions to that initiative will be sought. Make a commitment to report future outcomes in a similar way.

 don't forget

Wise words on strategy

- It's great to know where you're going. But if you don't know where you are, you'll find it difficult to reach the target.

- In strategic planning, analysis to determine the current situation is as important as a clear vision of the target.

- Strategic planning is about big ideas, about the one or two critical issues that will affect your future. So... think big! Don't waste time with the trivia; there are probably enough small thinkers around to worry about the small problems without your help.

- You don't need a crystal ball to look into the future. A small group of committed employees or friends will do the trick!

- If there's someone in the organisation with whom you're reluctant to share the strategic planning process, then it's doubtful if that person is relevant to the future you envisage. Are they relevant today? If so, might they not add something, however little, to your planning process?[8]

How to develop a strategic plan

If you have completed the preparation suggested on the previous pages, taking note of culture and context, and involving as many stakeholders as possible, you should now be able to develop and document a plan that will map out your organisation's future direction. The steps leading to the development of this plan, possibly conducted as a two-day workshop, are as follows...

1 Establish rapport and outline the program.

Get the group together, welcome participants, engage them in activities designed to build trust and confidence with fellow participants, then introduce the program outline (which follows), detailing areas to be covered with time estimates. Invite participants' comments, offer explanations, and make additions or deletions as necessary.

2 Articulate a vision.

Using information already compiled from the preliminary sessions and the expertise within the group, work through the following process which focuses on articulating a vision. This process, adapted from James Collins and Jerry Porras, and outlined on page 302, requires that you:

- isolate the 3 to 5 *core values* held in the organisation
- identify its *core purpose* or reason for being
- draft a *description of that future* in the form of a vision statement.

The process will also influence the development of a mission statement.

3 Consider existing and new opportunities.

Whichever approach you adopted under '4' on page 304, you need to encourage the group to consider the information compiled as a result of that preliminary exercise. If you used the SWOT approach, for example, consider the following:

- Invite participants to work alone to consider and record any additional strengths, weaknesses, opportunities, or threats not recorded. This encourages participation by everyone.
- Form into pairs to discuss individuals' lists and compile one list representing combined contributions.
- Repeat the process in groups of 'fours', then 'eights'.
- Group and categorise the final refined lists under broad headings such as 'production', 'marketing', 'communication', 'management or administration', and so on.

Considering various scenarios, either prepared previously or created by the group, can also be used to identify opportunities.

Your final list will contain those issues that are considered crucial to the organisation's growth and profitability over the ensuing period, the next few years, say.

 Develop a mission statement.

Using the information generated and refined thus far, you will now be in a position to develop a mission statement (see page 298). It is likely the result will be considered as a second draft (the first draft having being prepared already as part of the preparation for the workshop). A sub-committee could be formed to polish the draft for presentation to the group at a later date.

 Construct action matrices.

Now is the time to consider the specific actions that need to be taken. For each issue, develop action matrices detailing goals, necessary actions, individuals' responsibilities, timelines, and estimated costs. Not only does this activity outline the necessary actions, but it also instils ownership of those actions.

 Form think-tanks to overcome blockages.

If you find that discussion on a particular issue becomes bogged down, and goals and step-by-step actions are not forthcoming, you may decide to conduct a brief think-tank on the particular issue. By opening up the meeting for a brief (say, ten-minute) discussion on a specific topic, you will find that participants arrive at decisions and begin again feeling refreshed and ready to deal with the next issue.

 Link the plan to structure and budget.

It is generally accepted that strategy should inform structure. Analysing the structure of your organisation may take longer than the time available, so an appropriately briefed sub-committee may be formed for that purpose. The budget provides the funding necessary to convert plans into actions. It must be simple, straightforward, and workable. It, too, may be compiled by a sub-committee formed for that purpose.

 Document, disseminate, and implement.

A final plan should be produced within fourteen days of the workshop—any longer and the exercise will become a fading memory only. If possible, reassemble the group to distribute the document. Arrange meetings of other groups to communicate outcomes to all parties. You may decide that the completion of such an important document is worthy of a celebration involving all participants. Ensure that the plan becomes a living document by insisting that it is used, referred to, and reviewed regularly.

 quotable quote

A company can outperform rivals only if it can establish a difference that it can preserve... The essence of strategy is choosing to perform activities differently than rivals do.[10]

 don't forget

Publish your plan

- Exposing a dream, a vision of the future, can be daunting. It can lead to criticism and debate of both the dream and the dreamer. But if you won't expose your dream, how can others share it?

- Only published plans can be discussed and implemented.

- Confidential plans tend to breed distrust; not commitment.

- In planning, there is some justification for the cliché – publish or perish!

- It doesn't have to be a stapled bunch of duplicated papers. How about...

  ▸ a plan presented as a comic book?

  ▸ a plan summarised as a series of wall charts, and displayed at high-traffic places?

  ▸ a plan presented by video, with a copy for each branch office?

  ▸ progress reports against the plan from the CEO each quarter as a 'report card'?[8]

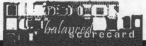

How to set achievable goals

Goal-setting has been described as 'the inner technology of success'. It is one of your organisation's most important activities. Unless taken seriously, this vital planning task will be futile, producing only a few high-sounding intentions that, for various reasons, are soon forgotten. So, if you want challenging and achievable goals, you should consider these basic principles...

1 Make sure your goals are realistic.

A goal that aims too high, or offers a great deal of risk, with little chance of achievement, leads to frustration and surrender. It's easy, for example, to say that a goal for the year is: 'To increase production by 150%'—but quite unrealistic with inadequate resources and uncommitted staff.

2 Keep your goals simple.

If goals are complex, it is unlikely they will be clear and specific enough to focus effort and marshal the necessary resources. Clear simple goals give staff an unmistakable vision of what needs to be done.

3 Develop your goals participatively.

When goals are imposed, rarely does anyone become committed to them. Develop goals with those who will be responsible for achieving them—your staff. The goals become a matter of record and, through personal involvement, everyone will be more motivated to work towards their attainment.

4 Know why you have set each goal.

For every goal you set down, ask *why* you believe that goal is important to the organisation. Be persistent in getting an answer. If reasons don't measure up to your expectations, revise the goal until it warrants inclusion—or get rid of it.

5 Make your goals specific and measurable.

Goals should be specific rather than vague, and quantitative rather than qualitative. For example, rather than proposing that you should 'become more visible' around the factory or office, it is more focused to state that 'I will spend at least one hour a day mixing with staff in the workplace' and 'I will meet weekly with floor supervisors'.

6 Write goals with accountability in mind.

The successful accomplishment of

goals usually depends on someone being held responsible for each goal. This often creates a sense of urgency and purpose, especially when personal reputation or career advancement is involved.

Make your goals timely.

There should be a time dimension that specifies when the goal is to be achieved. Tying a specific deadline to a goal along with individual accountability usually leads to a more proactive approach to its achievement.

Write your goals down.

By committing your goals to paper, and making them public, you not only convert dreams into tangible targets, but also work harder for their achievement—or risk losing face.

Align goals with the corporate mission.

Remember to link individual goals to group goals, which ultimately should be linked to organisational or corporate goals.

Publicise your goals.

The best way to accomplish anything is to set your goals—then publicise them widely. If you commit yourself publicly to a certain thing by a certain time, then it's very difficult to back out. If you do, you lose face—and most of us would rather get the job done than be judged as one who can't deliver the goods.

Review progress regularly.

Schedule regular meetings to review progress with colleagues. Be honest and forthright in your assessments and don't expect 100 per cent achievement. If you find that a specific goal is unreachable, that it was too ambitious, modify it to a degree that is attainable. It's a good idea to set and monitor sub-goals as a means of giving an ongoing sense of achievement and keeping people motivated along the way.

Make your goals challenging.

A goal that is too low, too easily reached, offers little challenge or interest. Add 'stretch' to encourage performance. Striving for our goals takes us out of our comfort zones and causes us to grow with each accomplishment. The best goals are beyond our grasp, but within our reach.

And remember also...

- Goals should focus not only on ends but also on means.
- People can attend to just so many written goals. Don't go overboard.
- The total set of goals should be mutually reinforcing—one goal should not have to be achieved at the expense of another.
- Face your goals with determination and resolve to never give up. Persistence is important for achievement.

ask yourself

Ask yourself these four questions about your goal...

- Is it **A**chievable?
- Is it **I**nspiring?
- Is it **M**easurable?
- Is it **S**hared with others?

Goals. They're all about AIMS.

viewpoint

"Goals are dreams with deadlines"
– Diana Hunt

don't forget

Zig Ziglar's 7 steps...

1. Identify what you want.
2. Clearly spell out why you want to reach that particular goal.
3. List the obstacles that stand between you and your goal.
4. Identify the growth process – the things you need to know – to get to your goal.
5. Identify the people you need to work with to reach your goal.
6. Develop a detailed plan of action to reach success.
7. Set a date on when you aim to reach that goal.

These seven specific steps, says Ziglar, will move you from a 'wish list' stage to an 'accomplishing' stage on your path to success.

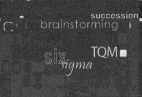

How to conduct a goal-setting session

Managers determine what they want to accomplish and how they plan to achieve it by setting goals—for individual projects, short- and long-term strategies, production, sales…. Owing to the importance of goal-setting, you will often be called on to conduct regular goal-setting sessions in which selected employees will take part. This process can be readily facilitated by adopting the steps suggested here…

 don't forget

How to set a goal

- Go for a short, clear and positive goal.
- Set a goal that is so clear that you will be able to keep it in the back of your mind.
- Make sure that achieving it is within your control.
- State it in specific terms.
- Make it achievable.
- Set a completion date.
- For a big or long-term goal, set targets or milestones along the way. Break it up into shorter and easily trackable action goals that are measurable and relatively easy to reach.[13]

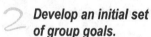 **Establish rapport.**

As with any individual or group process, gaining others' trust and confidence is essential. You may decide to use an icebreaking activity, engage participants in conversations about areas of individual interest, or use a more structured strategy. Whatever the approach, you should not proceed until you feel that rapport has been established.

Develop an initial set of group goals.

It is important that all participants contribute, so have individuals work alone to list two goals that are important to them. Work around the group recording first-choice goals on a whiteboard, then record others not previously listed.

List those affected by the goals.

Identify those people who will be affected by the goals. These stakeholders are likely to be either shareholders, customers, or colleagues—including members of the group. This action may require that some new goals be written taking into account this additional information.

 Identify the motivators.

Work down the list of goals identifying the motivations for each. What exactly is the purpose of each goal? Why has it been included? If no good reason can be given, it's doubtful if it should be retained. Consult with the person who contributed the goal in the first place regarding its continued inclusion.

 List constraints.

Constraints, sometimes called 'blocking forces', can inhibit the ultimate achievement of a goal. Such constraints may be rules, regulations, policies, or any other factor that may limit goal accomplishment. For example, inadequate funding or staffing may severely limit the extent to which a goal can be achieved. Seek suggestions regarding actions that will eliminate or reduce constraints. Explore briefly the tasks and timelines necessary for accomplishing each goal.

6 Revise and collapse the listed goals.

After taking into account the motivations, constraints and timelines, you may now need to revise your list of goals, re-write those that are considered similar, and collapse the list to a manageable number.

7 Distinguish between primary and secondary goals.

Primary goals typically relate to the products or services affecting profits. Secondary goals are achieved as a by-product of pursuing the primary goals and relate specifically to satisfaction and achievement. By differentiating between these two types, you will be better placed to take the necessary actions.

8 Collate a final statement of goals.

Record each goal statement to include both a primary and a secondary component. Each statement should be written so that as a primary goal is achieved a secondary one is accomplished as well.

9 Seek consensus for the listed goals.

Given the participative approach adopted, consensus can be expected. However, you still need to give participants an opportunity to suggest adjustments. Prioritise the final list.

10 Follow-up.

Arrange for participants to get a copy of the goals as soon as possible after the session. Indicate that any adjustments to the list can be made prior to the commencement of the next session when a plan for action—specific actions, timelines, and responsibilities—will be developed.

here's an idea

Sometimes, because your staff members are so absorbed in their individual jobs, they can't see beyond their own problems – which is why you will often have trouble getting them to buy into 'the big picture', your long-term goals.

You can overcome this reluctance with a goal-setting session, in which you...

• bring everyone in your team into the early stages of the planning process.

• discuss with your team the major points of your overall plan for the project etc.

• ask each person in turn to focus on and describe how he or she will be able to contribute to the big picture.

• have each person express their intentions as written goals.

In this way, you will break your long-term goal into bite-size pieces, allowing each person to see how their part of the project fits together with everybody elses.

it's a fact

After early setbacks, Lou Holtz soon realised that he would have to set goals if he was to reach his dreams. So he sat down and compiled a written list of 107 aspirations. They included scoring a hole in one, coaching football at Notre Dame University, and being US coach of the year. More than twenty years after setting them, Holtz had achieved 89 of those goals – including all of the above.[14]

311

How to develop a plan for action

Here is the situation: You have agreed on a solution to a particular management problem and you now want to convert that solution into a step-by-step approach for action. In simple terms, who is to do what by when? You will need to develop an action plan—and you can be assured of success if you follow these steps during an action-planning session...

1 Express your solution as a series of goals.

Having agreed on a solution to a particular problem within your organisation, you first need to define that solution in terms of a number of goals or objectives. For example, each goal could be expressed as follows: 'For us to..., we would need to...'. Record each goal at the top of a whiteboard or sheet of paper.

2 Generate a list of actions for each goal.

Use brainstorming to compile a list of actions to achieve a particular goal and record these below that goal. Arrange this list of suggested actions in sequential order.

3 Prepare a timeline.

Beginning with a time point labelled 'Now' and ending with a point labelled 'Goal achieved', build a timeline on which you allocate dates by which you intend to complete each of the sequential actions listed under a particular goal. It is important that you get both sequence and timing right if you are to reach 'Goal achieved' effectively.

4 Allocate resources.

Financial, physical, and human resources must be allocated to each action step. If resources are limited, or fall short of requirements at any stage, it may be necessary to return to an earlier step and revise the action plan.

5 Identify possible problems.

Consider all of the things that could go wrong in the process of achieving a particular goal. List these problems and identify causes and suitable actions to resolve them. If necessary, these actions might need to be added to appropriate slots on the timeline.

6 Develop strategies for monitoring progress.

List ways in which the progress of the action plan can be monitored. These monitoring stages should also be included on the timeline.

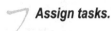 Assign tasks.

Take each point on the timeline in turn and ask: 'Who will do what, by the date set, to bring about the specified action?' Allocate these tasks to appropriate individuals or teams.

Estimate costs.

Give consideration to any expenditure required to complete the tasks. All costs will have to be taken into account when preparing a budget. If funds are not available, tasks will have to be reviewed and, where necessary, revised or eliminated.

Implement the plan.

Translate all your information to a clean copy, listing the actions required, the person responsible for a particular task, and when that task is to be completed. Having now finalised the plan for action in specific terms, this information can now be made available to all involved.

One sobering comment from Peter Drucker to put your action plan into perspective: 'Sooner or later,' he said, 'all the thinking and planning has to degenerate into work.'

Remember: It's not all over yet...

Les Bell, in *Managing Teams*, makes this relevant point:

'It has been said that if you do not know where you are going, any road will get you there, although it might well be asked how you will know that you have arrived. From the point of view of any organisation, planning is deciding where to go, how to get there and how to know when you have arrived…

Planning is also preparatory to action. Analytically at least, planning must be separated from implementation so that the major policy decisions can be taken and their implications understood prior to action.

Unfortunately this can lead to a situation in which vital revisions are not made because the planning process, mistakenly, is thought not only to be preparatory to action, but also to conclude once implementation commences.'[15]

Planning is a process which goes beyond the development of an action plan.

 don't forget

Requirements for your plan

■ It should be specific and explicit so there is less chance for it to be misinterpreted or misapplied. Clearly define all objectives and means.

■ It should distinguish between the known and the unknown so that both are given due consideration. Probable effects of the unknown should be estimated.

■ It should be based on facts, the more the better. If facts are not available, then reasonable, sound, intelligent judgements must be made.

■ It must be flexible and capable of being modified. No plan is infallible, nor can it cover all contingencies. Conditions change.

■ It must be acceptable to the persons who adopt it and who are affected by it. Acceptable implies that there is a willingness to cooperate in carrying it out and a willingness to take the consequences.

■ It should be devised by creative people with a good balance between optimism and pessimism and a practical as well as realistic viewpoint.

■ It must practical, logical and have a reasonable chance of being carried out.[16]

How to plan and manage a project

What makes a project different from your day-to-day work is that it has a beginning and an end. To get from one to the other, a project manager must follow a sequence of steps applicable to all tasks. Some projects can be highly complex activities, involving numerous sub-tasks, intricate scheduling, and detailed monitoring. They can range from planning a company conference to producing a video or building a factory. Here, then, are the steps to follow when tackling a new project...

1 Establish your objectives.

Define clearly, in concrete terms, the purpose of the project. Write down the project specifications or the criteria for a successful outcome and ensure that they are agreed to by all parties involved. These specifications define your objectives for the project.

2 Set a deadline.

Some projects must be completed by a certain date. Your planning will hinge on this final deadline. If you have not been given a completion date, set one for yourself.

3 Identify the tasks to be done.

List everything that needs to be done on the way to final completion. It could be a long list, but it must be a complete list. Ensure nothing is missing. If you are not sure of all the tasks, go to the experts for advice. If you do not have a complete breakdown of jobs, you will have difficulty organising the project's

timeline, developing a budget and handing out assignments.

4 Organise the tasks in sequence.

Arrange the tasks into their order of performance. What happens first? What comes next? Then what? Timing becomes a vital factor—projects can have a sequential line of development (do one job before moving on to the next), or a parallel line of development (several jobs can be taking place at once), or both. Understand the sequence clearly by creating a logic diagram—a PERT chart, a critical path network, or a work breakdown structural document (WBSD).

5 Allocate a time for each task.

Using your logic diagram, estimate how much time each task will take (try estimating an optimistic time, a pessimistic time, and then take the average). Factor in a little extra time to cover delays or problems.

Create a schedule.

Using this information, you can now place a target date for each task on to your logic diagram. It is sometimes wise to also set specific review dates to evaluate progress and to modify your course if necessary. Remember, if you have a definite completion date, it is often helpful to work backwards from that date, providing you with an indication of how much time compression must be applied to get the project finished in time.

The creation of a horizontal bar chart might also be useful at this stage. List the tasks sequentially down the side of the chart and appropriate calendar periods across the top. Create a bar of the calendar period that each task is expected to take.

 **Assign tasks.**

Delegate appropriate tasks to project members, not forgetting to allocate time to yourself for overall project management duties. Look for the full range of experience and expertise when putting your project team together. Ensure all team members are available at appropriate times, and are fully briefed as to their responsibilities and deadline dates.

The creation of a project team matrix might help you keep track of who's doing what, and to keep you from overloading some members. This matrix lists the tasks vertically, team members along the top, and responsibilities below each name.

 Establish a budget.

Project budgets are normally activity-oriented. Estimate all costs associated with each task and prepare a spreadsheet with tasks listed vertically and cost factors (expenses, labour, resources, etc.) listed horizontally, totalled at the right of each line.

 Monitor the project to completion.

Supervise the progress of the project, in particular…

- *keep track of progress.* Refer frequently to the project charts.
- *communicate regularly.* Keep on top of what's happening through status reports and formal and informal meetings with your team members.
- *become a troubleshooter.* Identify trouble spots and emerging gaps between scheduled and actual performance.
- *take corrective action.* When necessary, step in to develop alternative solutions, take remedial action, and follow-up to ensure your solution is effective.
- *use your managerial skills.* Check out those essential skills of motivation, conflict resolution, team leadership, meeting facilitation, persuasion, etc. You'll need them.
- *evaluate the project.* On completion, hold debriefings to review problems and successes, and make recommendations for future projects.

 don't forget

Maintain your project files

- For each project, keep a separate file containing all related documents.

- When assigned a project, write a project summary and attach it to the front inside cover of the file – project description, objectives, scope, deadline, summary of action steps in sequence and individual target dates.

- If unable to work on the project daily, write notes to yourself on what you've done and what you want to do next when you resume. Keep a 'follow-up action' list as well.

- When you finish a project, sort through its file and discard any duplicate and useless documents, then store for future reference.

- Once a project is complete, ask yourself (and your project team members) what you have learned from the exercise and how it can be applied to the next project. Keep these comments on file.[19]

 read further

Free resources – FAQs, booklets, fact sheets, interactive tools, project templates, guidelines…

www.egovernment.tas.gov.au/project_management

315

How to prevent things going wrong

Things go wrong in organisations for a number of reasons: people might do less than they are capable of, or misuse their resources, or choose an inappropriate time or place to act... We misread situations; we take the wrong actions; we're often out of tune and out of step. But things could be worse: what if our errors were tabulated and published every weekend like those of a football team? You can reduce the number of mistakes in your organisation by considering this advice...

1 Learn from your previous mistakes.

Mistakes will happen. Murphy had it right when he said that if anything can go wrong, it will. The worst mistake is to make the same mistake more than once. Learn to analyse what goes wrong, make notes on what to do and what not to do next time—and make sure you get it right in future.

2 Remember the basics of mistake minimisation.

(a) *Think ahead*.
Planning is the key to minimising mistakes. Think ahead, anticipate all eventualities, and make contingency plans to cover yourself. This might not make your initiative mistake-free, but at least you will be better prepared to handle any obstacles that arise.

(b) *Don't be over-confident*.
Many managers are so certain that everything is OK that they make no attempt to foresee any problems or be prepared for the unexpected. You certainly need confidence—but don't let it blind you or your staff.

(c) *Guard against carelessness*.
A simple act of carelessness, often the result of over-confidence, pressure, or the belief that a task is easier than we think, can destroy a project and damage a reputation. Check every fact and figure in every important report, letter, memo or email—and get someone else to check as well.

(d) *Tolerate no laziness*.
According to *Proverbs*, 'Hard work means prosperity; only a fool idles his time away'—basic advice for today's manager. Tolerate no fools, especially lazy fools, for they could cost your organisation time and money. All companies have lazy people. A few of them are lazy by nature. On the other hand, the manager may be at fault, for many employees are viewed as 'lazy' simply because they have been given inadequate leadership, insufficient supervision, or a poorly-defined role. Provided you have done your job, and if one of your staff is indeed indolent, then take action. Laziness cannot be tolerated.

(e) *Take a stand against incompetence*.
It is said in sporting circles that dropped catches lose matches. A dropped catch can be the sign of poor skill development in the athlete, and under-developed skills in the workplace can similarly lead to disaster. But incompetency can be minimised if you take steps to refine employee selection processes, monitor

and improve performance standards, and implement training and coaching aimed at correcting identified weaknesses in staff competencies.

(f) *Be disciplined when delegating to others.*

A poorly delegated job can have a disastrous outcome, so ensure you always select the right person for the task, conduct a thorough briefing, train as required, hand over authority, and monitor appropriately.

(g) *Supervise, supervise, supervise.*

Orders or instructions without follow-up or supervision court mistakes, even disaster. You can't be expected to check every detail of your employees' work personally, but supervisors and section heads can, and report progress to you.

3 Consider drafting a risk-management plan.

Since planning is a management priority, a risk-management plan will prove to be a valuable tool for minimising major mistakes. Corporate risk management applies commonsense to identifying, evaluating, measuring, and treating the broad range of risks confronting an organisation—especially its people, its assets, its profits, and its reputation. The risk management process consists of:

- identifying and evaluating the risk
- controlling that risk
- financing the process
- delegating responsibilities
- measuring results or benefits.

A typical risk-management plan may contain the following:

1. An overview, consisting of scope, objectives, evaluation criteria, and asset description
2. Risk identification and analysis
3. Risk assessment—risks to be accepted; unacceptable risks

4. Risk handling measures
   - List actions for reducing, avoiding, or transferring identified risks
   - Assign responsibilities for actions needed
   - Prepare a risk action timeline
5. A schedule for ongoing risk review and management.

Use of ISO certification and total quality management procedures will help put in place non-conformance reporting and preventative actions to eliminate, or significantly reduce, the chances of a problem recurring.

4 Finally, don't forget what Murphy said...

Murphy regaled us with several irrefutable laws of the universe (and of management) and we would do well not to forget his timely advice:

- If anything can go wrong, it will.
- Nothing is as easy as it first looks.
- If there is a possibility of several things going wrong, the one that will cause the most damage will be the one to go wrong.
- Left to themselves, things tend to go from bad to worse.
- Whenever you set out to do something, invariably something else will need to be done first.
- It is impossible to make anything foolproof because fools are so ingenious.
- Anytime things appear to be going better, you will have overlooked something.
- If you do everything right, nobody will notice. If you do something wrong, everyone will notice.

It's a pity Murphy is so often right. You'll need to do your best to prove him wrong.

317

How to generate creative ideas through brainstorming

If you're short on ideas or want a large number of ideas quickly, use the classic group process called 'brainstorming'. The process encourages divergent thinking among group members as they collectively address an issue confronting the organisation. Here are the steps to follow...

1 Explain the process to the group.

After familiarising yourself with the steps listed on these pages, outline broadly the brainstorming process to your group. If the approach is new to some participants, begin with a simple practical exercise. For example, 'To what other uses might a common house brick be put?' Encourage the group's creative input, with a recorder listing all the suggestions offered.

2 Discuss the rules for brainstorming.

The brainstorming process has five basic rules which can now be elicited from your group following the introductory exercise. These are:

- Keep an open mind—suspend criticism on anyone's idea.
- Let yourself go—'free-wheel' in terms of using your imagination. No discussion of any item is permitted in the process.
- Generate as many ideas as possible—all ideas are acceptable; quantity is encouraged.

- Try to build on the ideas of others by hitchhiking.
- All ideas are visible to everyone—upfront on a whiteboard or flipsheet.

3 Present the problem to the group.

Preliminaries over, you are now ready to generate ideas that focus on the problem at hand. Make sure that participants have a clear understanding of the issue to be addressed. If necessary, spend some time talking about the issue as you see it and encourage the views of others before moving into the idea-generating stage. 'Why', 'how' and 'what' questions are appropriate here.

4 Appoint a recorder.

Select a person to write down the ideas mentioned, preferably on a whiteboard or flipsheet that can be seen by everyone. By having someone else record the ideas, you are free to lead the process.

State the problem in clear terms and begin.

People often see an organisational problem through different eyes, so it is important to state the focus issue in terms that all participants understand clearly. List off various statements of the issue at hand before selecting the one that expresses the issue most succinctly. Display the selected statement in bold letters before the group. Give everyone a minute or two in silence to think about the question, before calling on the group to begin brainstorming ideas. All suggestions, no matter how 'off-beat', are recorded and numbered for ease of reference later. Allow no discussion at this point or the flood of ideas may be suppressed.

Synthesise similar ideas.

When the creativity of the group has been exhausted, have participants identify statements or ideas which are alike—for example, 'Numbers 4, 7, and 14'. Compile and record a new statement which incorporates these points and remove the superseded statements or ideas from the list.

Group the ideas.

In grouping the ideas listed, you will find they probably form into three groups:

- The impossible—those about which very little can be done (often these are the 'off-beat' ideas).
- The unlikely—those with little hope of implementation but which cannot be ruled out completely at this stage.
- The possible—those you can address and which can be given immediate attention.

Give priority to the best ideas.

When you have identified the 'possibles' and eliminated the 'unlikelies', place the ideas in priority order, using one of the techniques outlined on page 202 if necessary. Finally, develop an action plan to address the problem under review.

Consider the alternative— brainwriting.

If members of the group are shy or intimidated by the competitive or open nature of brainstorming, brainwriting is an alternative. Each member lists four ideas on a sheet of paper which is placed on a central table in exchange for another's completed sheet. Fresh ideas foster more ideas. Participants continue to add ideas to the sheet taken from the pool, exchanging it for a new sheet whenever additional stimulus is needed. All the sheets are later collected and processed as outlined in 6-8 above.

Or, to counter distance, use email to get the job done…. The project leader outlines the project, then emails that document, along with a routing list, to the first person on the list. That person provides input and sends it to the next person. The project leader is the last to receive the communication, at which time he or she collates the input and takes appropriate action.

 smile & ponder

Brainstorming is universally recognised as one of the most effective ways of generating ideas but, according to 'Stormin' Norman Schwarzkopf, Saddam Hussein had trouble understanding the rules of the game.

According to Schwarzkopf, the Iraqi dictator called together his think-tank of trusted advisers to come up with suggestions on how the long-running war with Iran could be ended. One of his closest friends and confidants was first to speak….

'Here's an idea,' he said. 'Seeing that the Iranians refuse to sign a peace treaty while you remain as President, why don't you stand down for six months until the treaty is in place? Then you can assume control after this time.'

Saddam Hussein was not impressed. He took his friend and adviser outside – and shot him!

At that point, we suspect, the really creative ideas from the President's advisers suddenly dried up.

Saddam Hussein would have done well to have brushed up on the techniques of brainstorming before scheduling his next meeting of advisers.

319

How to develop a business plan

A strategic plan is the 'where' of the planning process—where you plan to be at some point in the future. The 'how' is the business plan—how you are going to achieve the 'where' of the strategic plan. The business plan usually focuses on a 12 to 18 month period, setting out in operational terms what must be done. Again, the planning process and the commitment to it are the keys. Here are the main steps in the business-planning process...

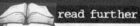

1 Consider adopting a strategic approach.

A useful strategic approach to adopt in drafting a business plan is to see the plan as comprising three main sections – the NOW analysis, the WHERE analysis, and the HOW elements of the plan...

- *The NOW analysis* outlines where the organisation is now and would consist of a business diagnostic or situational analysis.
- *The WHERE analysis* contains essential information linking where you are now and where you want to be.
- *The HOW analysis* details actions required to achieve desired outcomes.

Given that your plan will be read by organisational support persons like bankers and investors, give it a title page, a table of contents, an executive summary, and a general description of the business and its history. Supporting materials such as brochures, articles, research summaries may be included, but they must be brief.

2 Conduct a diagnostic—the NOW.

The diagnostic component involves coming to grips with the key issues in the organisation as it presently operates, referred to sometimes as an operational audit. In addition to your personal observations, you may decide to include in this analysis customer surveys, attitude surveys, questionnaires, and other information gained from staff interviews. A financial analysis will give an indication of how the business is travelling. A diagnostic may be run in parallel with the development of the strategic plan.

3 Investigate realistic futures— the WHERE.

Though the business plan is a 'how' document, your process must ensure that due consideration has been given to the 'where'. Here you will need to consider vision, mission, SWOT, and crucial issues, aspects which will no doubt be investigated in compiling strategic information for other components of the plan. Try to involve as many stakeholders as possible in this process. If people's commitment is required in implementing the plan, their involvement in its development should be encouraged.

Prepare action plans—the HOW.

Consideration has to be given to marketing, general operations, human resources, innovation, finance, and the actions required to convert ideas to actions. The action plans will indicate 'who' will do 'what' by 'when' and any costs associated with those actions. The inclusion of a financial component is essential to show the viability of the plans.

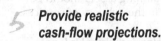

Provide realistic cash-flow projections.

The financials may include monthly cash-flow projections, quarterly or annual order projections, profit and loss projections, and capital expenditure projections. Cash-flow projections are based on the difference between the money that you expect to take in (your cash receipts) and the money you expect to spend (cash expenditures). In a start-up phase, cash flow will be negative but that number gives you and an investor an idea of the financial support you will need. Projections can never hope to be precise, so aim at raising 25 to 50 per cent more than what your projections indicate. But remember: excessively optimistic projections can ruin your credibility as a responsible business person. Be conservative, but don't use the word 'conservative'—

it's a tip-off that you actually think you'll do much better.

Consider adopting a more traditional approach.

The key to developing a business plan is to make it simple, yet businesslike in its approach. The alternative traditional structure comprises five sections:

- *Executive Summary.* An overview statement.
- *Product Profile.* A description of the product: what, where, how.
- *Organisational Structure.* Present and proposed venture structure and who is involved.
- *Operational Plan.* The strategy and basic financial forecasts.
- *Appendix.* Market research data, product brochures, CVs, assets and liabilities, competitive information…

Make sure the plan is usable.

Your business plan needs to be a working document and be kept under regular review. Its format should be simple and straightforward, contain essential information only, and have an in-built flexibility to respond to organisational and marketplace changes.

Maintain confidentiality.

The business plan is not for public display and should be kept in a secure place. As appropriate, your employees can be advised of the plan in broad terms, but it is not the kind of information you would want in the hands of your competitors.

quotable quote

Most business plans waste too much ink on numbers and devote too little to the information that really matters to intelligent investors – the people, the opportunities, the context, the risks and the rewards.[21]

---

viewpoint

"The actual *process* of business planning, which ends in the development of the product – the business plan, provides at least three-quarters of the benefit.

However, business planning is ongoing. By definition, as soon as it's done, it begins aging. The market changes. Competition responds to different strategies. We all become smarter about different ways to implement the written business plan. Soon, the plan we drafted just six months ago becomes obsolete. Nevertheless, that doesn't make the written plan any less useful. Further, the written document provides a base from which to revise the plan."

– Christopher Malburg in *All-In-One Business Planning Guide*

---

here's an idea

Are you planning to build a business website?… Make sure it's built into your business plan first.

321

How to develop a strategic asset management plan

Physical assets provide the platform from which an organisation delivers its services. Those assets have a life: they are planned and created, used and managed and (when no longer required) disposed of. The management framework through which that asset life cycle passes is strategic asset management—aligning physical assets with service demands, and promoting better practices at all stages of the journey. Consider these key points to help you improve your asset management...

1 Decide on a strategic approach to asset management.

In the past, asset management has been associated with 'accountant-speak' and policies governing purchases, disposals, periodic stocktakes, custody, physical security, maintenance, transfer of assets, and reporting losses.

A strategic approach, however, has much more to offer the long-term development of the organisation. The guiding principles are:

- Assets exist only to support the delivery of services.
- Asset planning is a key corporate activity that must be undertaken along with planning for human resources, information systems, knowledge creation and transfer, and finances.
- Non-asset solutions (enhanced technology, technological alternatives, reskilling), full life-cycle costs, risk and existing alternatives must be considered before investing in building assets.
- Responsibilities for assets should reside with the elements that control them.
- Asset management at the organisational development level should reflect the organisation's overall asset policy framework.
- Waste must be eliminated.
- The full cost of providing, operating, and maintaining assets should be reflected in the delivery of services.

2 Develop individual 'plans' leading to a strategic asset management plan.

The strategic asset management plan will consist of most or all of the following components:

Capital Development—applies to all capital 'built' assets including buildings, building services and plant, and the infrastructure necessary to support these assets.

Maintenance—applies to maintenance or restoration of non-current or capital physical assets to their original condition. Parts of this plan comprise: statutory maintenance (required by legislation), preventative maintenance (generally manufacturers' requirements), corrective maintenance (breakdowns, for example), and deferred and backlog maintenance. Deferred and backlog information is derived through a comprehensive facilities audit.

Facilities Management—aligns the physical workplace with the people and work of the organisation. Examples include energy management (lighting, air conditioning) and the management of other utilities, environmental management, cleaning, waste removal, and recycling, cleaning, Workplace Health and Safety, and training. The facilities management plan is the area most often associated with asset planning.

Organisational Management—ensures facilities management activities are aligned with the strategic direction of the organisation. It will be the organisation's culture and structure that ultimately determine the success of any facilities management.

Disposal/Adaptation—uses all assets to best support the mission of the organisation.

Apply a similar structure to those features.

The following structure could apply to each 'plan':

Definition—what you mean by 'maintenance' or 'facilities', etc.

Objective—what the plan hopes to achieve

Scope—what is covered by the plan

Benefits and Risks—benefits of having and the risks of not having the plan

Statutory Requirements—those that impact on the process

Responsibilities, Roles, and Functions—what is to be done, by whom

Performance Indicators—how you will measure the effectiveness and efficiency of the plan

Competencies and Training—what core competencies and associated training are required.

You will find a flow chart a valuable tool in illustrating how each element contributes to individual plans.

Compile an asset register.

Your asset register will be one of the outcomes of a comprehensive facilities audit. The register should provide some or all of the following details: location, original cost, current cost, insurance replacement cost, and any deferred maintenance. That register should be upgraded on a regular basis to incorporate new purchases, adaptations, and disposals. Labelling, bar coding, a simple numbering system, or similarly appropriate procedures should be used to ensure accountability and that the register remains current.

Prepare budgets, but...

A strategic asset management budget must be a working document affected by the direction set by the strategic plan—a good reason for including facilities managers in boardroom discussions. Remember:

- For many organisations the value of physical assets far exceeds the total annual operating budget, making decisions on only an annual budget impractical because you will be neglecting part of your assets.

- Effective facility management ensures that areas like energy and waste management are not interpreted as overheads but as manageable items. Waste management, for example, may include recycling, negotiating with suppliers like computer hardware providers to collect and dispose of packaging accompanying orders, or other innovative management approaches.

How to prepare to bring about change

Planning for change can occupy a great deal of a manager's time and energy, but it is not a process that can be left to chance: it can be tricky and disruptive if handled badly. Whether implementing a new job-rotation scheme, rearranging the office layout, introducing new technology, relocating your manufacturing operations, or anything else, a manager must use a preliminary, systematic planning approach to bring about successful change later...

1 Be convinced that change is necessary.

Are you sure that the intended change is sound and that there is every likelihood it will succeed? Is it practical, ethical, cost-effective? Will it solve more problems than it will create? Is it based on untested theory or speculation, on fashion, or a whim? Are the risks acceptable? Has it proven successful elsewhere? Can you specifically identify projected improvements in productivity? There is little to be gained from adopting a plan that is doomed to failure before it gets off the drawing board.

2 Analyse the change in terms of the present and the future.

Now would also be the time to question what might happen if you did nothing. Get a clear picture of your present organisation *without* the change in place. Then visualise the situation as it will be after the change is implemented. By visualising a future state, you're able to put a new perspective on the present, and be assured that the proposed change is worthy of support. Without a vision, change efforts dissolve into a list of time-consuming, incompatible, and confusing projects going in different directions—or nowhere at all.

3 Understand why the change might be resisted.

Resistance to change is a natural response because we usually prefer stability and feel comfortable and satisfied with habit and routine. If anything diverging from the norm is introduced into our environment, it will be seen as disruptive. As well, change is often resisted because of—

Self-interest: I will lose money, status, privileges, and authority. I will have added responsibility with no adequate recompense.

Fear: I don't have the skills and experience to adapt. I'll be worse off than I am now.

Uncertainty: I don't understand the specifics of the change. What does it all mean? How secure is my job? Will it mean more work?

External pressure: I resent external

interference and want to be in control of my own destiny. I have had little to say in the change.

Past experience: I've become too cynical about change. It's been too disruptive and ineffective in the past.

Consider how staff fears might be addressed.

As a manager, you must put yourself into the shoes of your employees and prepare yourself to tackle staff fears head-on by developing strategies to help in the implementation phase.

Begin by assembling facts and arguments to answer the concerns of employees and to dispel their fears. With a little creative thought, potential objections can be turned into advantages. Plan how to communicate your vision and this information, and how to offset any objectionable aspects of the change initiative which cannot be eliminated.

Develop a tentative but detailed plan.

Draft an outline plan by identifying and listing each task or element of the change. Arrange the elements into their proper sequence or parallel relationships for implementation, construct a tentative timetable, allocate responsibilities, where necessary undertake critical path scheduling, and consider resource requirements. Focus on the appropriate means of involving staff in the planning and implementation stages of the process.

Prepare to shake off complacency.

Change is a measure of life in progress; complacency is often what's holding it back. Consider how the following approaches might be used to reveal to your staff the need for change:

- Create a crisis or crises to shake staff out of their complacency.
- Introduce goals that require action rather than wishy-washy acquiescence.
- Benchmark your most successful competitor.
- Survey and report on dissatisfied customers' and shareholders' opinions.
- Restructure to remove the 'comfort-zone'.
- Raise performance standards for everyone.
- Visualise a lean and mean operation.
- Focus on opportunities, not on yesterday's successes.

Prepare for the involvement of others.

The key to successful change is for management to treat staff as part of the organisation, rather than as the opposition or target. For this reason, it will be essential to involve staff in the change process as soon as possible following this, your initial preliminary planning. How this is to be accomplished is considered on page 326.

> **❝ quotable quote**
>
> One of the biggest traps is the failure of organisational leaders to resist the temptation to rush through the planning process to get to the 'action stage'... A great portion of change effort fails because of a lack of understanding of what the process of change involves. Of course, when the manager lacks an appreciation of the complexity of the process, it is predictable that the emphasis will be on 'action' or results.[25]

> **❗ viewpoint**
>
> "Change takes place no matter what deters it... There must be measured laborious preparation for change to avoid chaos."
> – Plato

> **❝ quotable quote**
>
> Modern organisations are never static for long. Neither the local primary school, the country-wide chain of retail stores nor the multi-national corporation can shelter from the winds of change that are constantly blowing, soft or strong. Sometimes you will be introducing changes yourself; at other times you will have them thrust upon you by your bosses. Whether it's just that new equipment is needed in the typing pool or that Head Office has introduced a new accounting procedure, you will need to plan for and cope with the effects and repercussions.[26]

How to implement change

Change continues to be a feature of everyday organisational life—new technologies, new policies, organisational restructurings, downsizings, redundancies... Many employees are beginning to buckle under the weight of it all. Change might offer a promise of improvement, but it doesn't guarantee it. So many people now approach change with scepticism, fear, or frustration. How can a manager best introduce change in such an environment?

1 Note the basics of good change management.

The mere thought of change can be a real turn-off for many people and, if you ignore the following essential advice, you'll find the process of implementation even tougher:

• People will change when they see the need for change.
• People will change when they know how to change.
• People will change when they are involved actively in the change process.
• People will resist surprises.
• People will change when they are secure in changing.
• People resist being treated as things.
• People do not necessarily change on the basis of new knowledge alone—attitudes, feelings, and status are just as important.
• People change some attitudes slowly.

Keep these tenets in mind throughout the implementation phase.

2 Involve your staff in the process of change.

If your employees participate actively in the change process, they are more likely to feel ownership and less likely to resist it. In this regard:

• *Involve staff in the processes* of planning, implementation, and evaluation. They are more likely to see the initiative as their own, not as one imposed by outsiders.
• *Gain the support of opinion leaders* in the organisation. Others soon follow their lead, for people tend to model the behaviour of others, especially those they admire or trust.
• *Concentrate on the doers*, not the doubters; the risk-takers are more likely to support your efforts at change.

3 Ensure staff clearly understand why the change is necessary.

To alleviate staff anxiety and stress, you must explain fully the logic of the change, emphasising both the benefits and risks. New ideas are often misinterpreted, so make ample provision for discussion of reactions to ensure complete understanding and to alleviate any related concerns and fears. During implementation, chart the activities completed and those yet to be undertaken. Report periodically to all staff on progress to date. Upfront information and understanding help people feel more secure with the change.

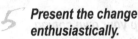

4 Sell the benefits.

How will the changes benefit me? my unit? the organisation? Will the change mean more satisfying work, greater security, an opportunity to show what I can do, less confusion, less fatigue, greater autonomy, improved communication? Motivate your staff to embrace the change by putting benefits on as personal a level as possible. It would be dishonest not to point out some of the difficulties and disadvantages as well.

5 Present the change enthusiastically.

Resistance to change is sometimes due to the fact that change is half-heartedly presented in the first place. Introduce and implement the change with enthusiasm. Enthusiasm is catching. Remember the saying: 'I cannot kindle a fire in others until it is burning in myself.'

6 Provide tools, resources, and support.

Give your staff the necessary implements and information so that they are able to feel confident with the change process. Remember:

- If you are unable to resource a new initiative, don't offer it.
- Train staff in the knowledge and skills needed to adapt to the change.
- Listen to frustrations and give time for them to be aired at meetings with staff.

- Arrange visits to locations where the change is operating successfully.
- Show that you understand the feelings and fears of those affected and take steps to relieve unnecessary concerns.
- Praise those who approach the change with a positive attitude. This will encourage others to follow.

7 Build a track record.

Concentrate on one project at a time and make it successful. Success, more than any other factor, will show those who might have a tendency to resist, that there is nothing to fear. Always be able to explain convincingly and without artificial justification why something new is necessary or desirable. If you develop a reputation for not leaping on every bandwagon, this too will add to your credibility as a change agent. You will be perceived as a thoughtful, deliberate manager so that when you do move in a new direction, there is confidence in your judgement.

8 Foster a supportive climate.

Stimulate an ongoing positive attitude to change by regularly discussing new ideas, initiatives, and issues with your staff. Celebrate the achievement of goals in the change process. Be flexible and experimental in your approach to the ideas of others, and encourage the risk-takers and innovators on staff. People constantly exposed to ideas and new practices are more likely to favour any call for change in the future.

How to live with change

As a manager, you can influence others. Take change, for example. The way you personally relate to change and cope with it will have a lasting effect on your employees. But before you can help others, you must be able to help yourself. When they see how effectively you cope with change, your staff, too, will see change for what it really is—an opportunity to lead a much fuller and productive life. Here's what you must do to survive and thrive in an age of ongoing change…

Look to the future.

It's futile trying to cling to the past—or the present, for that matter. The passage of time is inevitable. By trying to hold on to the past, you impair your ability to relate effectively to what is new and coming. And so you begin to feel anxious, fear the unknown, display ignorance, or desperately seek attachments. Moving forward is not a matter of giving up what you have, it's a matter of being free from any constraints in what you have. As the saying goes, 'all you'll get from looking back is a twisted neck'.

See change as opportunity.

All changes, even those you'd rather not have, contain the seeds of opportunity. Those opportunities can be ideas, relationships, points of view and new career directions. You'll see difficulties and obstacles until you absorb their wisdom and gather from them the essentials for further growth. Change is the price we must pay for growth, improvement, achievement and, finally, satisfaction and happiness. The way you grasp opportunities from change will help to inspire others to do the same.

Develop your own coping strategy.

You must be able to help yourself before you can hope to help others cope with change. Consider the following coping mechanisms. They may help you live through the next major change in your organisation…

Don't rush the change cycle. Be aware of the four phases through which you (and your staff) will pass, to varying degrees, in coping with sudden change:

Denial—the announcement is greeted with shock, and a refusal to accept that it's happening.

Resistance—acceptance is accompanied by personal distress, blame and complaining, even illness.

Exploration—after a period of struggle, you emerge from your negativity and move into a more positive, future-focused phase, attempting to find the

'best way' of coping.
Commitment—having weathered the storm and accepted the situation, you now focus on the new and pour your energies into it.

Think it through.
Isolate yourself in a relaxed environment and jot down answers to such questions as these:

What changes can I expect? How reliable are my sources of information? Can I find better sources? What's the best thing that could happen as a result of the anticipated change? The worst? What tasks will be removed from or added to my current responsibilities? How will the changes affect my staff?

Come to terms with yourself.
Now is the time to consider your future. Decide what you will be doing —staying, transferring, retraining, retiring, resigning… Your decision need not be permanent but, unless you are at peace with yourself, you'll enter the change process stressed and uncertain.

Shine in a time of uncertainty.
A period of high change can be very good for your career. During this uncertain time, if you do your job very well, you will shine while others around you fall apart at the seams. So plan ahead; organise yourself; set up new systems to cope with the changes; and motivate your staff to shine with you.

Discuss it with family and friends.
If the anticipated changes will mean extra work, stress, and anxiety for you, make sure your family members understand. They will feel more secure and better able to help you through a difficult time.

Take up stress-reducing activities.
Eat right, organise regular physical activity, take vitamin supplements, find a few spare minutes to relax each day, and do the things you enjoy and which boost your energy.

Remember your staff members.
What are the ramifications of the change for your employees? What information do you need and what must you do to help them cope with the changes?

Stay organised.
Draw up contingency plans for everything you can think of. Allow time for anticipated problems, for the unexpected will happen—although it will be easier to handle if you expect it.

4 Accept that nothing is permanent.

Your career (and life) is dynamic and fluid. How you cope with the dynamic process will not only affect your growth but also your ability as a manager to influence others. You need to demonstrate to yourself and others that you understand and accept why things must change. When there is no permanence, stay-put behaviour serves no purpose. Giving up a lifetime of judgemental behaviour, negative thinking, aggressive self-protection, or ego-driven striving isn't easy but, in one sense, it is inevitable if you are going to mature and grow. Your transition will be slow, incremental even. But that will give others a chance to observe how you live with change and allow them to learn from you.

✔ **it's a fact**

Early in the American Civil War, manufacturers created new rifles that were both easier and quicker to load than the standard muzzle-loading weapons of the time.

Strangely, the response from officers to these new guns was most unexpected. In fact, the new, more efficient weapons were never to be widely used in the war.

The military resisted changing rifles for two main reasons. Firstly, the easy-loading gun, the officers argued, would encourage soldiers to waste bullets. Secondly, the new weapon would enable soldiers to shoot lying down – they would refuse to stand up and fight, it was claimed.[30]

Back then, as today, some people found it difficult to accept and live with change.

---

66 **quotable quote**

The future is coming towards us like enormous waves of change. Set after set these waves are getting bigger and coming faster… Things will never get back to 'normal' because unpredictability and change are normal. There is no going back. Get used to it. Change will be followed by more change. That's one thing that isn't going to change. The waves in this ocean won't flatten out, they're only going to get bigger and come at us faster.[31]

How to introduce new technology

New and emerging technologies such as computers, printers, social media, laptops, tablets and smartphones are flooding into the business marketplace. But there's much more to introducing these technologies than simply purchasing the hardware and the supporting software. To avoid costly mistakes, remember that the success of any technology purchase in your organisation is directly proportional to the time and effort you spend on the planning you do before purchase and implementation...

1 Develop a rationale for the use of the new technology.

The first step in planning for the introduction of any new technology in your organisation has little to do with the equipment at all. Before considering hardware and software, spend time thinking about your organisation and what you want the technology to do, what software will help you meet those objectives, and what hardware will best run the software.

Here are some ideas to help in the process of developing that rationale:

- Do an audit. What technologies are currently being used, and for what reason, in such areas as: personnel, payroll, record keeping, library administration, word processing, scheduling, stock control, budget, communication networking, transport...
- How effective is current usage? What skills do staff currently possess? What staff development opportunities are available? What consultants are available? Who is responsible for the company's overall technology use?
- Verify the audit findings with the users.
- Formulate a plan which specifies how the new technology will facilitate more effective training, production, or administrative practice.
- Establish a reasonable timeframe for purchase and implementation.

Never purchase hardware and software before having identified clearly the purpose to which the technology will be put.

2 Build ownership among the key participants.

Any new initiative or purchase must be owned by and reflected in the beliefs and actions of the participants if it is to lead to altered professional behaviours. Without involvement and commitment, successful implementation will be difficult. Develop strategies for involving relevant staff members in the appropriate decision-making processes. Consider task forces, committees, regular communication, mentoring, and awareness sessions.

3 Examine fully all budgetary considerations.

Funding for technology initiatives

extends beyond the initial purchase costs of expensive hardware. Consider also maintenance, replacement and upgrading costs, as well as the costs of software, ancillary items, and training. Ideally, a 3-5 year fiscal plan should account for these costs and incorporate such alternative financial strategies as lease or buy-back agreements.

 Develop a staff training and professional development strategy.

Training and professional development are separate requirements when introducing a new equipment or a technological initiative. Training makes staff competent users of the technology, and users need training time to become familiar with the use of the new technological tools, such as copying files, adding graphics, crashing disks, losing files, and operating printers. Professional development allows staff to successfully incorporate the technology into the workplace environment or into administrative practice.

 Guarantee access to technical and professional support.

Staff require access to a range of support services that enable them to integrate the technology into the workplace environment. Without such support, the technology can become little more than another imposition on staff, rather than a catalyst for improving workplace performance. Explore the variety of opportunities: networking, journals, consultants,

professional or trade associations, and the technology suppliers themselves.

 Be sure, then purchase.

Before proceeding to purchase, therefore, make sure you answer satisfactorily the following questions:

- Will the new equipment fulfil an essential function?
- Is the equipment appropriate to the specific requirements of our company?
- Will it be effectively used by people who can be properly trained and are motivated to use it?
- Will it be genuinely cost effective?
- Has its use been fully discussed with those affected?
- Will its installation be non-disruptive to the environment in which it is placed?

If you can answer yes to each of these questions, then go ahead and purchase.

 Evaluate the initiative.

An evaluative process must accompany any new initiative in order to enhance further program decisions. In essence, did the initiative contribute to more effective workplace or administrative practices? What were the positives? What were the negatives?

 Appreciate the value of people.

Remember: a successful initiative depends on more than the mere injection of new technology into your organisation. It's the commitment, dedication, enthusiasm, skills, and knowledge of employees and other users that matter. Take steps to foster their involvement.

 quotable quote

Technology planning is not an isolated activity, but needs to be viewed in the context of the entire organisation. Planning is a people process which needs to involve the stakeholders... And just because technology *can* be used for an activity doesn't mean it *should* be used or even provides the best solution.[32]

 **it's a fact**

It's amazing how things are speeding up: Photography took 112 years from discovery to its development as a commercial product. The telephone took 56 years, radio 35, radar 15, and television 12. But it only took 6 years to develop a working atomic bomb and only 5 years for transistors to go from research lab to the marketplace. Today, a product can be conceived, produced, packaged, marketed and become obsolete – all in one year.[33]

smile & ponder

When 19th century US author Washington Irving lived in England, he went fishing one day. He had expensive tackle, yet he had no success. Along came a rather shabby little boy. He had a stick, a piece of string, and a 'vile earth worm'. Yet, in thirty minutes, the boy caught more fish than the American had done in hours.

The message? The best equipment does not always produce the best results if 'know-how' is missing.

How to apply the principles of succession planning

Research tells us that talented people choose to be associated with an organisation that considers both its employees' futures and the continued success of the organisation. In fact, the quality of an organisation's succession planning and its corporate image are closely linked. One of the success factors associated with those organisations that have developed and implemented effective succession plans is that they have identified and adhered to several key principles of succession planning...

Know what you're planning for.

Succession planning is an essential strategy for harnessing the substantial talents in your organisation. It is the process by which successors in your organisation are identified for key posts (or groups of similar key posts) and career development—and subsequent activities are planned accordingly. When you have created a workable succession plan for your organisation, you can then include in it various planned developmental activities for those identified for advancement.

Customise any plan to the needs of your organisation.

Although valuable ideas might be gained from perusing other organisations' plans, ultimately the one best suited to your situation will be the one you design yourself— tailored to *your* organisation's needs and demands including selection processes, reward systems, and management development. Suggestions to help with this process

can be found in *How to develop a succession plan* on page 334.

Involve top management in succession planning.

If top management isn't involved in, and supporting, the succession planning process, it just won't work. There are reasons for this. First, senior management should have its finger on the pulse of leadership talent within the organisation. Second, sustaining any broad-based succession plan involves substantial effort and requires a high priority among top management. If the bosses are not seen as owning the plan, why would others be expected to assume ownership?

Emphasise culture, values, and strategy.

The existing and desired culture of the organisation, its values, and future strategic direction will influence a succession plan. It is essential, in fact, that the plan is aligned with the organisation's future strategic direction. If that direction isn't clear, include succession planning as a crucial issue for discussion at your next planning workshop.

5 Focus on the development of successor candidates.

Succession planning is much more than selection: development is vital. Successor candidates can expect either to have their own individual career- and personal-development programs or to be involved with colleagues with perceived similar development needs. In both cases, candidates must accept responsibility for their contributions to such programs. Identified successor candidates can expect to have access to coaching and a senior person prepared to act as a mentor.

6 Develop a leadership team.

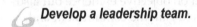

Succession can generally be expected to come from a strong talent pool of successor candidates. As pool members develop and take on more active roles in your organisation, individuals' leadership skills will increase. As these candidates develop, they will become members of a leadership team, and act as role models for others in your organisation.

7 Keep everyone informed.

Everyone in your organisation must know about the succession plan— even if they are not included on any list of successor candidates. You cannot afford to have the reputation and integrity of the plan be affected adversely by withholding information about it and the progress

of its participants. Consider including, in in-house communication media, details about criteria for identifying those aspiring to be included on the list of successor candidates. Potential selection as a successor candidate can act as a positive motivator.

8 See succession planning as a journey, not an event.

All aspects of an effective succession plan are inextricably linked to other parts of the organisation: succession planning can never be a stand-alone event. If it is ever allowed to become another ritual, you might as well resort to filling in boxes on an organisation chart.

9 Be aware of potential tensions for an anointed successor.

Leadership succession can bring with it an additional challenge. Some boards appoint a CEO's successor for a period—say, two years—before taking over the top position. This can be a time of excitement and promise for the anointed successor, but tensions can surface between the successor and the incumbent CEO. Ultimately, it is the successor's responsibility to defuse any problems. If you are the anointed, research[34] advises that you:

- Learn as much as possible about the CEO, professionally and personally, before signing on.
- Maintain regular and cordial communication with the CEO.
- Assemble and frequently confer with a balanced personal advice network consisting of other key persons in the organisation.
- Stay focused on the endgame.

don't forget

Why you need a succession plan

- You retain your best people.
- You cater purposefully for their training and development.
- You prepare your best people for future leadership positions.
- You increase staff commitment and satisfaction.
- You link your organisation's performance to the quality of your rising people.
- You enhance your organisation's corporate image.

read further

Effective Succession Planning by William J. Rothwell, AMACOM, NY, 4th edn, 2010.

How to develop a succession plan

Succession planning has come a long way from the days when it usually meant simply putting names in boxes on organisation charts. Effective succession planning has evolved to a process by which successors are identified for key positions, and career development and associated activities are planned accordingly. Here are the key steps in developing an effective succession plan...

1 Decide on the depth of your succession plan.

Although the most common model for corporate succession planning focuses on the most senior jobs in the organisation (the top two or three tiers), a broader-based model where a similar philosophy and processes are applied to a much larger population (managerial, professional, and administration) is becoming popular. Sustaining the devolved model will require continued support of a committed management, so that identified successors will embrace the priority given to this process.

2 Identify the specific qualities you seek in suitable candidates.

Whatever you call them—critical success factors, key leadership criteria, core competencies—you must spend time identifying the qualities you are looking for in staff and want to develop further. A suggested process is one of multiple dialogue which involves collecting views of selected individuals and groups, testing those views—focus groups

could be a useful tool here—and making any necessary amendments to the list. This approach will not only help to ensure that the view taken by the organisation of an individual is based on objective evidence but also helps to gain the commitment and ownership of those who are likely to be succession candidates. If you are having difficulty identifying those qualities, this could indicate you need to spend time defining the business you are in. Constantinos Markides in *All The Right Moves* outlines a straightforward and useful process to follow, providing a clearer picture to help identify the qualities required.

3 Identify high-potential candidates.

A previous decision about the depth of your plan will affect the nature and size of any list of succession candidates. If your plan is for a devolved model, the list must be sufficient to accom-modate predicted demands for a wide variety of positions that may become vacant, as well as any others needing extraordinary skills or qualities. Names on your list should also reflect your equal employment policy: succession planning can never be a stand-alone concept. In identifying a strong talent pool…

- Avoid the problem of incumbents choosing and developing successors who are much like themselves, thereby perpetuating the status quo and limiting diversity. A highly homogeneous organisation is susceptible to disease.
- Ensure candidates' values match closely those of the organisation. Jack Welch, when CEO of General Electric, said: 'Competencies are critical, but the company's values are even more central.'
- Ensure that all employees understand the identification process and how it works.

Work wisely to retain your stars.

Your retention plans must go further than dangling handsome financial packages. Research tells us that people who make career decisions based on money only will always be on the lookout for higher paying positions— they're liable to jump ship when someone offers them a better package. Your successor candidates should be given opportunities to participate in a rich variety of assignments with opportunities to display leadership skills, become increasingly visible in the organisation, gain and handle recognition for their contributions, and receive adequate coaching and mentoring. Share these mentoring and coaching roles among incumbent leaders with information generated about candidates being reviewed regularly. Ideally, discussion about performance and progress should focus on completed projects, so,

wherever possible, candidates should remain in their existing posts to see their individual projects through to successful completion. In 2002, the Board of the Australian Broadcasting Commission delayed appointing a new Managing Director, opting to give maximum time for a successor candidate to demonstrate his skills as Acting-Managing Director. His demonstrated success in this acting role resulted in his appointment to the top position.

5 Measure, reward, and review.

For a succession plan to be effective, it must be able to measure any performance improvements in its successor candidates. Successful candidates must then be rewarded in ways that are valued by individual candidates. Such rewards could vary from bonus compensation based on the extent to which they meet stated goals and objectives to an all-expenses-paid weekend for the candidates and their life partners. Any review must take into account the full process from identification, planned individual development, and eventual succession or job filling.

6 Act now.

Training and preparing candidates for key leadership positions cannot be rushed. A well-planned, structured succession strategy lays the foundation for your organisation's continued success, even when you're not there. Do not wait until it's too late to consider business succession— procrastination can paralyse.

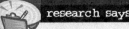

viewpoint

"From now on, choosing my successor is the most important decision I'll make. It occupies a considerable amount of thought almost every day."
– Jack Welch, CEO, General Electric, 1991 10 years before his actual retirement

research says

While most leaders who are selected internally are successful and stay in their positions, four in ten senior executives brought in from outside fail in the first eighteen months.[36]

viewpoint

"I start with the premise that the function of leadership is to produce more leaders, not more followers."
– US consumer advocate Ralph Nader

viewpoint

"My own successor is a matter of review by the Board at regular intervals. My own commitment is to pass the baton when the time comes cleanly and effectively to the Board's elected nominee."[36]
– Roger Corbett, CEO, Woolworths

How to prepare someone to take your place

At some time, you will need an assistant capable of slipping into your management position at a moment's notice. That person will probably come from the ranks of experienced employees you have identified as potential leaders. Indeed, your own promotion may well depend on having someone who can step immediately, in an acting or permanent capacity, into your role with minimum disruption. How can you find and prepare someone for this responsibility?

1 Be aware of the benefits of training a successor.

It is astute for a manager to select and develop a top assistant for a number of reasons. Consider the following:

- *There'll always be someone to take over when you're absent.* You might be absent through unexpected illness, accident, or vacation—but knowing that a well-trained replacement is in charge back at the workplace will provide you with peace of mind.

- *You'll have more time for other things.* A trained successor can take on some of your managerial duties during your busiest periods, and take care of some of those tasks you never seem to get around to.

- *You'll always be ready for promotion.* If you are given the opportunity to move up, you'll be able to guarantee there's a trained person capable of taking over your old job immediately.

- *You can devote more time to public relations activities.* Step out and improve the image of your company and yourself in the community, safe in the knowledge that there's someone capable of 'minding the store'.

2 Make the decision today.

For some managers, it can be a tough decision electing to hand over the reins of responsibility and authority for their organisation or department. But if you're in doubt, weigh the balance by making two lists. In the first, list those things that might happen if you *don't* train a successor; in the second, list those things that might happen if you *do* develop a replacement. Compare both lists—and you'll be convinced of the need to prepare for succession.

3 Know what you're looking for in a successor.

A capable assistant is most often the one whose strengths match your weaknesses rather than one whose strong points match yours: two dynamic and assertive individuals are apt to set the wrong kind of sparks flying. Make a list of the qualities you're seeking—for example, loyalty, a healthy attitude towards the job, the company and staff members, good communicator, relevant skills, experience, common sense, intelligence, a self-starter, ambition, energy, popular… With these qualities, plus initiative, your selection can readily be taught to cope with the additional authority and responsibility of your position.

4 Select the right person for the job.

The advantage of selecting an employee from within your organisation is that you have a knowledge of a possible successor's work over time, have access to personnel files and performance records, and you can test the person's potential on some trial assignments before making your final decision.

5 Develop your successor over time.

By working closely with your potential successor over many months or years, you will find the following suggestions useful:

- *Devise a program of development.* This could take the form of regular discussions, on-the-job practice in management, formal study, reading of trade and professional publications, frequent contact with suppliers, customers, colleagues and trade associations, and so on.
- *Outline what the job entails.* Outline what you do, and where your (and their) authority begins and ends.
- *Work with your successor on your job.* Tell about your plans, projects, progress, actions, decisions, and problems. Involve the person in the daily details of these activities.

- *Ease the person into the role.* Growth will come if the successor learns to handle the new responsibilities in small doses.
- *Don't stifle growth.* Hold a loose rein so that your successor can gain confidence. Constant checking on progress will inhibit initiative and development.
- *Provide appropriate authority.* Through delegation of relevant roles and tasks, your assistant will develop, but only if the necessary authority accompanies the responsibility.
- *Use tried-and-tested techniques.* Coaching, mentoring, delegation, project management, and decision making are among the many techniques treated in this volume that can be referred to and applied when working with your successor.

6 Make sure you don't lose your protégé.

There are those organisations, of course, that don't take the time to develop potential leaders, preferring instead to poach from those that do. Having trained a suitable successor, you must prepare for such corporate plunderers by letting your protégé know what his or her prospects are, and that your plans are to reward loyalty and effort as your company grows—with salary increases, opportunity to buy into the business, bonuses, stock options, junior partnership, and so on. If you don't take care of your successor, someone else might.

here's an idea

Are you so good at your job that it's actually hurting your career? It happens. There are managers who are so good at what they do that their boss is reluctant to promote them out of their current positions. To get around this, find and groom your replacement yourself. Tell your boss: 'I think Gail can step in and do my job. I'm going to be her mentor, and I want to be responsible for developing her.' Then, when Gail is ready, you can move up, and she can move in.

viewpoint

"Let me make one small suggestion on how to best pick the right person to succeed you, to be your assistant. I know s/he'll need to possess most of the same basic managerial abilities that you have. But you should try to find a person who complements you rather than one who reflects a mirror image of you.

If the two of you are exactly alike—if you have the same strengths and weaknesses—there'll be sparks flying in no time. The assistant who'll work best with you will be the one whose strengths match your weaknesses and whose weak points match your strong ones. That way, you'll mesh with each other rather than clash."

– Martin Block, Personnel Director, Sun Oil (US)

337

How to help your successor take over your position

How would you like to take up your new position, to arrive in your new office, and find that the only assistance offered by the departing manager was there in the middle of your desk—a bundle of unlabelled keys with a note on the company letterhead saying, 'Good luck!' Departing managers can easily avoid frustrating incoming managers. In the process, a departing manager can win a professional colleague for life simply by being considerate, collegial, and courteous. All he or she must do is undertake a few basic tasks before leaving…

1 Assemble essential information.

There are some items that will prove vital for the information of any incoming manager—staff lists, company handbooks, traditions, policies and procedures, project assignments, workplace committee lists, scheduled events, emergency evacuation plans, pending staff actions,…and so on. Gather such information into a clearly labelled tray and leave it on the new manager's desk with a sealed, personal memo detailing any critical or urgent matters.

2 Update the manager's computer files.

Sherlock Holmes would have trouble deciphering your computer files, and so may the incoming manager. Review your files, saving essential data and trashing the rest. And don't forget to leave a key to unlock the mysteries of your file labelling—for example, that 'bgt' means 'budget', that 'res' means 'resources', that 'dg' means 'delegated', and so on.

3 Organise essential references and filing.

On the most visible bookshelf, gather together the important references— company handbooks and policy manuals, current procedures and guidelines, relevant legislation, staff bulletins, budgets, annual reports, and other essential documentation. Organise vertical filing logically, grouping the material under as few categories as possible. If your files have been categorised in a more complex way, leave a roadmap if necessary to help the newcomer find relevant documents.

4 Use your wastepaper basket.

Throw out any material which you consider will be worthless to the incoming manager—ancient files that may have been left there when you arrived and were never referred to since, unwanted items from your cupboards, including out-of-date journals, folders, circulars, old coffee cups, and all that loose material at the bottom of your desk drawers.

Leave no important task incomplete.

The jobs you feel obliged to finish before leaving will depend on your date of departure. Never leave an important task incomplete. The later you leave the position, the greater your obligation to assist your replacement in terms of impending tasks and requirements.

 Tidy up your office.

In sorting, filing, and throwing out, you should also be taking the time to straighten out, reorganise and clean the new appointee's desk, cabinets and shelves. You'll be amazed at the volume of material you have accumulated over time which you now have set aside to take with you or to throw out. Finally, ensure that the office is thoroughly cleaned—windows, carpets, curtains, light fittings, shelves, and so on—prior to the arrival of your incoming colleague.

 Prepare transition plans.

If you know that your replacement will not be able to take up duty for some time after your departure, leave transition plans for key staff members. Set responsibilities and tasks for your office staff, janitor, and the executive team member who can handle anything requiring immediate attention.

Advise the newcomer that you're available.

No matter how much effort you put into preparing for your incoming colleague, in the early days there will inevitably be questions or issues requiring your input or advice. For this reason, be sure to leave your new location, phone, and email address.

 Offer to visit your replacement.

The incoming manager may seek the opportunity to meet with you during the transition period. Offer to do so if the request does not come. This gives you an opportunity to answer questions about projects, programs and procedures in general and specifically if requested. Accentuate the positive, the strengths and accomplishments. Avoid mentioning individual staff idiosyncrasies which you may have found annoying. Adopt the stance that everyone deserves a fresh start with the new manager. There will be exceptions, however, such as the employee whose personal behaviour continues to demand supervisory action.

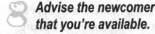 **Hand over responsibility.**

If you're remaining within the organisation, particularly if you're filling a seat above your successor, James Van Fleet offers this advice:

- Leave your successor with a complete and exact understanding of the job.
- Make sure all staff know your successor's exact status.
- Let your successor know what you're doing and how you want the work relationship to develop.
- Add responsibility gradually.
- Don't hold a tight rein on your successor. Let him or her grow with the job.
- Give your successor the authority needed to carry out the role.[39]

How to achieve operational effectiveness

Operational effectiveness means performing similar activities and practices better than your competitors and making the best use of your resources to do so. Effectiveness is achieved by focussing on quality assurance, cost management, and delivery systems; the aim is to foster continuous improvement and evaluation. But the key is to choose the appropriate tools or strategies that can help you retain an ongoing and sustainable competitive advantage. Here are some of those proven tools and techniques…

quotable quote

Differences in operational effectiveness among companies are pervasive. Some companies are able to get more out of their inputs than others because they eliminate wasted effort, employ more advanced technologies, motivate employees better, or have greater insight into managing particular activities or sets of activities. Such differences in operational effectiveness are an important source of differences in profitability among competitors.[43]

read further

When Gordon Bethune took control at Continental Airlines, he pursued operational effectiveness in a variety of areas – win market share by guaranteeing that passengers would arrive at destinations safely, on time, and with their luggage; and pay monthly bonuses to all employees who contributed to the successful achievement of this outcome. Bethune's continued pursuit of operational effectiveness helped take Continental from the brink of bankruptcy to one of America's most profitable airlines (according to pre-September 11 figures). For operational effectiveness in action read: From *Worst to First. Behind the Scenes of Continental's Remarkable Comeback* by Gordon Bethune, Wiley, NY, 1998.

1 *Embrace the spirit of kaizen.*

Kaizen focuses on the continuous improvement of current processes, most famously exemplified by the successful turnaround at Toyota Motor Company. The philosophy embraces ongoing improvement by all staff through the elimination of waste, working to new standards, and innovation. Kaizen uses a range of techniques such as small-group problem solving, suggestion schemes, brainstorming, work study, and statistics. Workers are inspired to participate for the satisfaction of using their creative skills to improve the operations they themselves perform and the goods or services they produce.

2 *Consider what TQM has to offer.*

Total Quality Management (TQM) is a management philosophy for focusing on process improvement. Each employee (as a supplier) in the organisation takes personal responsibility for delivering quality to the next employee (as a customer).

The end product is to maximise the satisfaction of the organisation's final consumer at the lowest possible price. TQM aims, through quality standards and awards, to get products and services right the first time rather than waiting for them to be finished before checking them for errors.

3 *Explore the possibilities of reengineering.*

Reengineering, also referred to as business process reengineering, is a process that challenges the operation and even existence of an organisation's fundamental processes. It is aimed at radically redesigning business processes in order to dramatically improve an organisation's competitiveness. Hammer and Champy first introduced reengineering in 1990 as a response to the failure of traditional business tools to make a positive impact on costs, quality, and service. Despite its offerings, reengineering has been criticised as the root cause of much business cost-cutting, downsizing and staff redundancies.

Focus on benchmarking.

Benchmarking involves isolating and implementing best practices. It is the continuous process of measuring your products, services, and practices against targeted competitors or those companies regarded as leaders in particular fields. Its goal is to reinvent operations to achieve significantly better performance and is best accomplished as part of a restructuring or reengineering process. Benchmarking's one main downside is that the more organisations benchmark one another, the more they come to look like each other. Rarely, therefore, does benchmarking provide any sustained advantage in a highly competitive environment.

 Consider outsourcing.

An increasing number of companies identify their areas of competitive advantage and focus on those. They outsource any remaining tasks or services. Outsourcing should provide access to specialist skills, free-up management time to focus on core business, and provide cost savings, improved service quality, and reduction in staffing. One of the problems with outsourcing is that the more rivals outsource activities to efficient third-parties (often the same ones), the more alike those activities become.

 Try time-based competition.

Time-based competition is a competitive strategy that seeks to compress the time required to propose, develop, manufacture, market, and deliver products. Though initially applied to manufacturing contexts, the approach has been successfully applied to non-manufacturing environments as well. Providing products or services in significantly less time can improve service quality and increase your organisation's profitability. Any reduction of product-cycle times by improving processes can have a significant effect on your organisation's performance.

Assess the benefits of Six Sigma.

Six Sigma is a data-driven process for achieving near perfect quality. It has a strong emphasis on statistical analysis, but the method implies more than simple quality control and statistics. It goes beyond the mere detection and correction of errors by providing specific approaches to recreate processes so that errors never arise in the first place.

Consider implementing the balanced scorecard.

The balanced scorecard is a tool that defines what management means by 'performance' and measures whether management is achieving the desired results. Measures typically include performance in the areas of finance, customer value, internal business, and learning and innovation. The scorecard reveals how these measures are interlinked and impact on each other, enabling the organisation's past, present, and potential performance to be tracked and managed.

it's a fact

When you think about quality and effectiveness, consider the impact of a 99.9 per cent error-free performance rate across all industries. Most of us would be extremely happy with a 99.9 per cent quality performance, wouldn't we? But would it mean universal excellence? Consider these US statistics... That 0.1 per cent would mean:

- 20,000 wrong drug prescriptions each year.
- Unsafe drinking water one hour per month.
- No electricity, heat, or water anywhere for 8.6 hours per year.
- Two short or long landings at major airports each day.
- Two thousand lost articles of mail per hour.[44]

viewpoint

"There can be no economy where there is no efficiency."

– Benjamin Disraeli

quotable quote

There's a fundamental difference between strategy and operational effectiveness. Strategy is about making choices and trade-offs. It's about deliberately choosing to be different. Operational effectiveness is about things that you really shouldn't have to make choices on; it's about what's good for everybody and about what every business should be doing.[45]

How to improve your organisation through total quality management

Total quality management (TQM) is a business philosophy devised by W. Edwards Deming and enthusiastically embraced worldwide. It helped Japanese industry to achieve world-class standards of quality. TQM is based on the belief that change for the better will occur through dedication to continuous improvement; everyone in the organisation must share constancy of purpose. Here's how you can put TQM to work in your organisation...

1 Rally your organisation around the quality banner.

The Deming philosophy requires that a strategy for pursuing quality be formulated collegiately throughout an organisation. Total quality requires a commitment to improvement by every-one in the organisation. It ends up as a dominant cultural value, becoming a part of 'how we do things around here'. TQM challenges managers to empower all participants to discover the joys of their labours, to improve continually, and to celebrate change that *they* devise and direct.

2 Focus on the process not the product.

Deming's hypothesis is that, if we focus solely on the product, we may never find out what is working or not working in the system. Rather, TQM focuses primarily on the quality of processes. For example, if we judge the success of an organisation solely on the price of its shares without looking at the quality of relationships, or morale, or professional development, then this is contrary to TQM principles. Managers must emphasise processes in their organisation—goal setting, communicating, decision making, image building, staff training and so on—not just the final product.

3 Commit your organisation to continuous improvement as a way of life.

One of TQM's tenets is that *kaizen* (Japanese for 'continuous improve-ment') must become ingrained as a value in the organisation's culture. Toyota used kaizen to become a leader in high-quality vehicle production. For Toyota, the term meant 'rapid inch-up'—small, ongoing improvements that eventually result in outdistancing the competition. Over time, the cumulative effect of endless small improvements will generate pride, commitment, and confidence in all stakeholders. As Philip Crosby in *Let's Talk Quality* says: 'The quality improvement process is progressive. One doesn't just go from awful to wonderful in one leap.'

4 Acknowledge the sovereignty of your customers.

One definition for quality in TQM terms is 'meeting or exceeding customer expectations'. Who are the 'customers' in your organisation? Does each employee have the same 'customer'? The storeperson? the clerk? the regional manager? the salesperson? the driver? In many cases, their customers are fellow employees. It's vital that all staff know who their customers really are and what their needs are. In TQM customer needs drive the organisation; they are seen as partners in an organisation's success.

5 Build in quality and then adjust as required.

It often costs more to fix a problem than to prevent one. TQM demands we constantly assess processes and adjust those that appear to be out-of-synchronisation. Be proactive rather than reactive. TQM means addressing quality at the mission and strategic planning stages. It may mean working to eliminate mistakes and waste—cutting back on those unnecessary emails, files and photocopying, or removing those time-consuming and superfluous meetings, or not mismatching staff to tasks.

6 Foster mutual respect and teamwork.

Fear, says Deming, creates an insurmountable obstacle to any improvements and it must be driven out of the organisation. There is no place for hierarchy-dominated structures where employees fear bosses and inflexible policies. This fear, he says, detracts from high-quality, collaborative work. The alternative is a system where the integrity of each person is respected, where the importance of each person's work is recognised and rewarded.

As Aubrey Daniels advises:

Don't focus on programs. Instead, concentrate on how people work together and use the present quality process. Correlate those behaviours to crucial measures of quality. If those measures aren't improving, you're reinforcing the wrong behaviours. Once you've focused human effort through positive reinforcement, it's only a matter of time before all the elements in the quality process are under control.[46]

7 Train and empower all stakeholders.

TQM stresses the importance of empowering the stakeholders by giving them more responsibility, autonomy, and participation in decision making. Encourage the generation of improvement ideas—and give the authority to carry them out. Provide opportunities for staff to undertake programs of self-development. TQM requires that managers become partners, mentors, coaches, and co-learners. It calls on them to recognise, nurture, and empower others to use their talents to maximise stakeholder satisfaction and to secure a competitive advantage.

don't forget

The rules for quality

According to Tom Peters in *Thriving on Chaos*:

- A reputation for quality must be earned.
- Quality must be measured. That measurement must be made by those directly concerned.
- Quality improvement must be rewarded.
- Quality improvement is the primary source of cost reduction.
- Almost all quality improvements come via simplification of design, processes and procedures.

viewpoint

"People forget how well you did it."

– Trainee manager

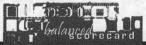
How to use benchmarking to improve the performance of your organisation

Benchmarking is a systematic process of measuring the products, services and practices of your toughest competitors (or of those regarded as leaders in a particular practice or business area) and improving your own on the basis of what you learn. The goal is to achieve significantly better performance and profitability, and is usually associated with changes in quality management, restructuring, or reengineering. Benchmarking can help you to become the best-of-the-best in your field. Here's how...

Identify what you want to benchmark.

Best practice benchmarking, the process of seeking out and studying the best internal practices that produce superior performance, can be traced back more than 30 years to Xerox Corporation, which at that time dismantled rival photocopiers to work out how they were built more cheaply. American Express has been recognised as providing a benchmark for effective and professional telephone services. Similarly, the Port Authority of Singapore provides a benchmark for similar organisations contemplating operational improvements. A high-achieving real estate agency in one State may be a valuable benchmark for another office interstate wanting to improve sales success. What you benchmark depends on the areas in which you want to excel.

Find out the leaders in that field.

The organisation identified as providing the benchmark need not be a competitor. In fact, it is possible that the organisation will be operating in a different field altogether—or even within your own organisation. You can identify leaders in your field of inquiry through observation, word-of-mouth, reading, or published surveys.

Set realistic targets.

Best-of-the-best or best-in-class are not absolutes. You need to:
* formulate criteria that define a 'class' of companies of interest
* define measures that can be used to compare companies to determine the 'best'
* find companies that meet your 'class' criteria and that appear to be the best performers to defined measures.

Collect the information.

Some organisations would be flattered to know that they have been selected as providing a benchmark and may invite you to send an individual or a small group on a fact-finding mission. Alternatively, the key people in those organisations identified may agree either to be interviewed or to respond to a simple survey or questionnaire. Whichever option you select, data will be required to make meaningful comparisons—and that information does not only apply to statistics or other 'hard' data.

Talk to customers.

Improving customer service, presumably, is one of the main reasons you have decided to benchmark; so don't neglect to seek customers' views about the services you are wanting to improve. You may even decide to ask the permission of the benchmark organisation to speak to its customers about the area of its business that interests you. Customers experience outcomes of processes, so their views are important.

Plan the process to overcome differences.

The key is to learn and discover why some operations are better, some are worse, and how both of them got that way. Having gathered your information, develop plans and decide on schedules to enable you to implement the best-of-the-best throughout your organisation by continuous improvement. Update your position and status constantly.

Do it quickly, or don't do it.

People, their positions, their interests, and the organisational context are all subject to constant change, so implement new-found practices promptly. You can help speed up the process by:
- allocating adequate resources
- using experts as required

- preparing well in advance
- biting off manageable chunks.

Manage the change.

Continuous improvement is essential for maintaining competitive advantage. The good thing about using a benchmark as the focus of the change process is that a successful working model already exists for you to emulate. Remember, benchmarking is a process, so keep stakeholders informed and supported throughout the process or you'll risk having your proposals collecting dust on the shelf. If indeed employees are having problems with change, act on those problems—perceived or actual—immediately.

Make measurement part of the process.

Selecting critical success factors—the things that must go right and can be measured—must be part of the process. These factors will influence the scope of the project, determine the key measures, help to identify benchmark partners, develop benchmark questions, and be valuable in your preparation of the final analysis and recommendations.

Set new benchmarks.

Continuous improvement means just that: once you have created the momentum, encourage employees to be on the lookout for winning ideas and organisations succeeding in particular practices. Always listen to what customers have to say; they will tell you other areas you need to be focusing on, too.

How to use what reengineering can offer your organisation

To compete in today's business world, you must provide customers with quality products and services. Otherwise they'll go elsewhere. To compete, you may have to abandon outdated notions about how your organisation does its work and start afresh. This is the essence of reengineering—a process of improving the old ways of doing business and creating new and better ways. Here's how your organisation can benefit from reengineering…

1 Consider 'reinventing' your business.

Look critically at the way things happen in your organisation. Ask yourself, 'If we were starting again from scratch, how would we do (what-ever we are doing)?' That's what reengineering encourages —redesigning selected processes to dramatically improve competitiveness and productivity. This may require making really tough decisions includ-ing selling-off, combining, or closing down areas of your business that don't fit with where you want to be.

2 Focus on processes.

Processes become your new basic building blocks. Improving processes or practices (what people do and how they do it) is the way to decrease turn-round time. By reducing turn-round time (and improving quality), you become increasingly competitive: more work-in-progress should mean greater profits. Remember, more than 85 per cent of problems in most organisations are process-related.

3 Emphasise and promote the need for change.

Reengineering reconstructs work into multi-task jobs, and that inevitably demands a fundamental shift in employees' perspectives. Your never-ending pursuit of best practices in the fields in which you operate provides an ideal catalyst for meaningful change. But one of your principal roles will also be to act in a 'gatekeeper' capacity, to control the introduction of change processes. Your challenge will be to build in a change process enabling staff to respond positively.

4 Gain the support of your employees.

Reengineering is about thinking big and bold. *You* may be the visionary with the big picture and the ideas about how to achieve best practice, but you won't be able to achieve your goals single-handedly. You'll need to enlist the support of your bosses and of your employees. And there is no rule to say how long this should take. What we do know is that you should hasten slowly until others share your vision of identifying the problem, redesigning the process, and fixing the problem.

Identify areas for improvement.

If you're tempted to take on too many areas at once, don't—your change initiatives may simply bog down. Initially, identify and select a few key areas for attention. If your company is involved in, for example, product development, manufacturing, sales and order fulfilment, develop process maps or flow charts of the existing processes followed in those areas. Let value adding be a key focus. Specific projects can then be identified to address process improvements. As processes improve, the boundaries—perceived or real—will disappear, heralding a more flexible and responsive organisation.

Create project teams.

Having identified specific projects, form project teams—one team per project—to research, report, and implement changes over an agreed time (usually between four and sixteen weeks). Include outsiders if necessary to inject fresh ideas. Early scores on the board are essential, so monitor the progress of project teams so that they achieve early successes. Remember to focus on business practices, aim for more than modest results, anticipate resistance, and spend time and money to make the new procedures work. The focus becomes results, not performing tasks.

Encourage employees to identify reengineering opportunities.

One measure of the success of a reengineering process will be that employees will identify new areas in need of attention. A reengineering culture encourages continual improvement to all parts of the organisation. Your efforts to reengineer the organisation are rewarded with the emergence of professional work groups who will pool their talents in the interests of organisational improvement.

Work to combat employee concerns.

Many employees associate job losses with reengineering—and this has been one of its severest criticisms as a management process. Assuring job security will need to be a consideration when you are attempting to enlist the support of staff in any reengineering initiative.

Check the legalities.

If labour cost-cutting is to be implemented as part of your organisation's reengineering process, ensure that the procedures used for retrench-ments and redundancies are lawful and litigation-proof, without discrimination, bias, or constructive dismissal arising from harassment and bullying. Scrutinise all employment contracts, union agreements, and relevant legislation to determine what room you have for legal manoeuvre. Seek expert advice where necessary.

You won't want any cost savings to be swallowed up by legal payouts for unlawful dismissal claims!

 read further

Reengineering the Corporation: A Manifesto for Business Revolution by Michael Hammer and James Champy, Nicholas Brealey, London, 1993.

viewpoint

"Michael Hammer and James Champy set the business world on fire in the early 1990s, selling two million copies of their manifesto, *Reengineering the Corporation*....

No one said reengineering would be easy. In fact, one critic has compared it to chemotherapy – a radical treatment that destroys a lot along the way.

Half-hearted attempts pretty much guarantee failure. And there have been plenty of failures, not to mention that companies used the idea to justify willy-nilly downsizing.

As the authors later acknowledged, they hadn't paid enough attention to the people."

– Ann Harrington, *Fortune*, 22 November 1999, p. 100

 here's an idea

When examining your processes, always start with the needs of your customers and redesign the process from the outside in.

347

How to apply the principles of best practice

In an age of increasing deregulation, technological change, and new competitive attitudes, organisations must become nationally—even internationally—competitive. To do so, it is essential to pursue 'best practices'—comprehensive, integrated, and cooperative approaches to the continuous improvement of all parts of an organisation's operations. Leading-edge companies achieve world-class standards of performance in this way. Here are the general principles of best practice. Consider adopting them…

1 *Develop a shared vision and strategic plan.*

Central to achieving best practice is a vision of world-class performance, shared by everyone in the organisation, translated into action through a strategic plan.

2 *Ensure that your bosses are committed.*

Committed bosses are essential to drive and support change processes. And one of their key roles is not only to provide leadership but also to recognise and encourage leadership at all levels of the organisation.

3 *Provide a flatter organisational structure.*

Competitive organisations respond to customers' needs in a time frame acceptable to the customer. Flatter organisational structures are better able to deliver a quick response. They are usually characterised by devolution of authority—particularly via team-based activities, empowerment of workers, and improved two-way communication strategies.

4 *Work towards a cooperative industrial relations environment.*

Best practice workplaces promote effective communication and consultation throughout their structures. Enterprise bargaining, for example, is an effective process for introducing and institutionalising best practices.

5 *Create a learning environment.*

Two key qualities of a learning organisation are its commitment to continuous improvement and a recognition of the contributions of everyone in the organisation.

6 *Develop and implement innovative human resource policies.*

Occupational health and safety, equal employment opportunities, career-path planning, new remuneration systems, flexible working hours, part-time work, work-based child-care, and literacy training are just a few examples of innovative workplace initiatives.

7 Focus on your customers.

Customers determine the success of any enterprise. Organisations responsive to customers' demands will profit in a variety of ways—increased market share, increased staff and customer satisfaction, and a reduction in the need for marketing.

8 Develop closer relationships with your suppliers.

Leading-edge organisations involve their suppliers as an integral part of their change processes. These links can cut inventories, create innovative opportunities, and ensure a higher quality of end product.

9 Pursue innovation in technology, products, and processes.

Market leaders have developed and employed integrated technology to ensure continuous improvement of production systems. Technology is not viewed in isolation, but as part of the whole system.

Use performance-measurement systems and benchmarking.

If you really want to compete, you will have to match and improve on the performance of the nation's or world's best. Benchmarking is a tool for organisations committed to achieving high standards of performance; so, too, are Six Sigma and the Balanced Scorecard.

11 Think 'green'.

Increasingly, the integration of environmental management to all operations is becoming a component of competitive strategy.

Develop external relationships.

Networks can enhance an organisation's competitive capabilities—through the sharing of information, by gaining access to services that individual organisations may not have been able to afford, in developing new technology or products, by exchanging staff to minimise costs associated with entering new markets, and so on. Networks can facilitate the pursuit of best practice programs.

---

66 quotable quote

The process of measuring best practices involves looking at various companies in order to discover basic principles of management that can be transferred to your own organisation.

A good example is GE's Best Practices Project, which asked the question "What's the secret of your success?" The answers from other companies were surprisingly similar.

Almost every company emphasised managing processes, not functions; that is, they focused less on the performance of individual departments than on how they work together as products move from one to the other.

They also outhustled their competitors in introducing new products and treated their suppliers as partners....

The implications of the Best Practices study were earth-shaking. GE realised it was managing and measuring the wrong things. The company was setting goals and keeping score; instead, 'we should have focused more on how things got done than on what got done...'

The findings were turned into a course that teaches three essential lessons: 'The first is that other companies have much to teach us at GE. Second is the value of continuously improving processes, even in small ways, rather than taking big jumps. The third lesson is that processes need owners – people whose responsibility and authority reach through the walls between departments.'[52]

How to compile and implement the balanced scorecard

Popularised by Robert Kaplan and David Norton, the Balanced Scorecard is a performance management tool that links strategic objectives to comprehensive indicators: financial performance, the contributions of customers, internal processes, and innovation and learning. The scorecard gives a more balanced view of organisational life than traditional financial measures alone. By measuring performance under each of these perspectives, all of the important areas can be addressed. Implemented effectively, the balanced scorecard can become a valuable management system. Here's how...

1 Be aware of these key points...

■ 'Balance' refers not only to the four perspectives listed above, but also to the relationship between:
  • the financial and the non-financial
  • the internal and the external
  • the current and future performance of the organisation.
Improvements in one area can be linked to those in another.

■ 'Scorecard' is a framework. It does not say what the specific measures should be. That's for you to decide.

2 Create the right environment.

Adopt a balanced scorecard as you would any major change. Preliminary activities will include the following:
• define the scope of the business to be measured
• link the initiative to other strategic initiatives
• identify those people whose support and commitment are required
• involve the entire senior management team
• outline the benefits of the scorecard
• time the introduction to fit in with

other initiatives
• appoint a project manager whose principal responsibilities will be the day-to-day running of the project during the start-up phase and liaising with any external providers.

3 Decide what to measure.

Perhaps *the* most important factor for the success of the balanced scorecard is ensuring that you are measuring the right things appropriately. Adopt a two-step approach:

■ First, identify the most important factors for creating success in your business. These factors may be apparent from your strategic plan. Alternatively, you might have to identify and analyse the needs of various stakeholders in your business. You must be sure of your customers' real needs, not just your perception or interpretation of them.

■ Second, with the needs of your stakeholders and the key objectives of your strategic plan in mind, draw up a set of objectives, outcomes, and measures under each of the four perspectives in the scorecard. Identify

---

! **viewpoint**

"The Balanced Scorecard is a framework for designing a set of measures for activities chosen by you as being the key drivers of your business. For the scorecard to be effective you will need to display these measures and manage the resultant actions to improve performance."

Understanding the Balanced Scorecard, M. and P. Bourne, Institute of Management, 2001

 read further

Balanced Scorecard Step by Step by Paul Niven, John Wiley, NY, 2002.

activities (no more than twenty) associated with those outcomes.

Design your measures carefully.

Measures accompany goals and should encourage desired behaviours. Key performance indicators (KPIs) accompany the measures and help to focus on them. Avoid over-measurement, but ensure that all data are collected consistently and support at least one of your key objectives. Devote enough time to analysing results, including how they relate to each other. Take precautions to ensure that individuals and teams can't manipulate the measures for their own ends, e.g. for recognition or rewards.

Display and use the results.

Teams' results should be collated regularly and presented to management, thus ensuring consistency among the teams. How you display and disseminate the measures will affect how seriously they are regarded and acted on. Whatever your approach, you must communicate meaning fully. You might consider briefings to discuss trends, correlate results, and agree on follow-up actions. For example, the measures might provide early indicators of trends and comparisons with earlier levels of performance, and reveal information on factors affecting your business—factors that otherwise might have gone undetected.

Learn from others' mistakes.

Others' experiences identify four main pitfalls:
- The process is time consuming; so, when deciding what to measure, ask yourself whether it is *really* necessary.
- Ensure that the results are used objectively—to improve the business not to allocate blame.
- Involve enough people in the process to ensure broad ownership and commitment.
- Avoid information overload—keep to measures you can really use.

Keep your scorecard relevant.

The balanced scorecard is a most effective tool for driving continuous improvement, but persistence is necessary. Successful implementation of the process outlined here may not result in instant success. To achieve the best results, be prepared
- to review and update your targets regularly
- to update the measures as your performance improves
- to change your measures according to your strategy
- to use the measures to monitor the success of that strategy.

Now read further...

In the space provided, only a brief outline of this concept is possible. Your next step should be to consult Robert Kaplan and David Norton's *The Balanced Scorecard: Translating Strategy into Action* (Boston, Harvard Business School Press, 1996).

here's an idea

As the scorecard is really a framework into which the organisation fits a set of measures most appropriate to its own activities, it can take a variety of forms and be adapted to fit many situations. You can, for example, have a team or a corporate card.

A team card records teams' commitment to established outcomes. A team could develop an outcome statement, test it against set criteria, and then consider how it will be measured.

A corporate card is used as the sum total of the individual team scorecards, with a few additional measures, to ensure achievement of strategic issues and, therefore, focus on the big picture. Reward and recognition can be linked to achievement.[54]

ask yourself

What does your company currently measure? Do you try to measure softer aspects of performance such as creativity and learning?

here's an idea

Innovative companies develop an initial Balanced Scorecard with fairly narrow objectives: to clarify, gain consensus, and focus on their strategy, and then to communicate that strategy throughout the organisation.

The real benefit comes when the scorecard is then transformed from a measurement system to a management system.

351

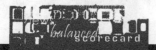
How to assess the benefits of Six Sigma

Some of the world's leading organisations, including General Electric, AlliedSignal, and Dupont, have reported impressive results using a process known as Six Sigma. Is the process suitable for your organisation? If its cost is prohibitive, you might consider using selected components of the strategy. At least you should be familiar with Six Sigma and what the concept has to offer. Here are some details and features to help your exploration…

Define Six Sigma.

Six Sigma is a business process that helps companies to improve their bottom lines by designing and monitoring daily business activities to minimise waste and resources. Its main objective is to improve customer satisfaction. Although it builds on the principles of kaizen, and the works of W. Edwards Deming and Joseph Juran, Six Sigma is more than simple quality control and statistics. It doesn't merely detect and correct errors: it provides specific methods for recreating processes so that errors never arise in the first place.

Understand the significance of sigma.

The sigma concept was created in the early 1980s. In 1994, it led to the forming of the Six Sigma Academy by Dr Mikel Harry and Richard Schroeder. Six Sigma assigns a sigma value to a process based on the number of defects per opportunity resulting from that process. Higher sigma values indicate better processes and products; lower values represent less desirable ones. Six Sigma (99.99966 per cent perfection) is far more desirable than three sigma (the level most organisations achieve). The higher the sigma level, the less likely the process will produce defects.

Work at reducing variations.

Six Sigma is based on a continuous reduction of process and product variations that indicate defects. In simple terms, this reduction is achieved by:

- defining the 'perfect' process
- measuring how the process performs
- identifying and analysing (using statistical techniques) the gap between current performance and the ideal, and then pinpointing the causes of defects in the process
- initiating new and better ways of improving the process, thus reducing the gap or variation.

Various tools—statistical and other—are available to assist.

Identify and train key people.

The individuals or groups who will help to drive and facilitate the Six Sigma process are key members of the infrastructure. Coloured belts are assigned according to mastery of the discipline in the same way that judo students are ranked:

Deployment Champions choose the projects and implement the strategies and tactics.

Master Black Belts, selected by the Deployment Champions, act as in-house experts devoting all their time to Six Sigma – training and coaching the Black Belts and Green Belts and communicating the overall progress and status of projects within their areas or businesses.

Black Belts focus on executing the Breakthrough Strategy and devote all their time to Six Sigma projects. They undergo extensive training in statistics and problem-solving techniques, and should pass that knowledge on by training Green Belts, of whom there could be a hundred in a large organisation.

Green Belts use Six Sigma and Six Sigma techniques as part of their overall jobs. They might also lead small improvement projects within their respective areas.

 Understand what Six Sigma is about.

Six Sigma focuses on several aspects:

It's about money – improving profitability. Each sigma shift provides a 10% net income improvement, a 20% margin improvement, and a 10-30% capital reduction.

It's about change. Achieving the desired level of profitability involves a daily commitment to ongoing, measured changes facilitated by stretch goals.

GE provided additional incentive by linking promotional opportunity to demonstrated involvement in Six Sigma. As for any major change, the organisational culture must be right for the initiative to succeed.

It's top down. Six Sigma is not a grassroots initiative. Picture an inverted pyramid illustrating how active, visible leadership provides the foundation and an infrastructure to support the customer, around whose expectations Six Sigma quality is built. The infrastructure consists of key people – champions, master black belts, black belts, and green belts – driving and facilitating the process.

It's process-oriented. Specific improvement goals are identified for every process.

It's about quality, the pursuit of which must influence people at every level.

It's about measurement, the tracking of progress of initiatives and indicating areas for improvement.

 Be prepared to spend money and effort.

Despite its impressive record, Six Sigma is not easily adopted, and is very expensive. General Electric's former CEO, Jack Welch, described Six Sigma as 'the most difficult stretch goal GE had undertaken'. In addition, Welch committed $US450 million in 1996 and 1997 for training and other support. Within a year, the investment began to pay off, leading to further investments both in processes and in intellectual capital.

Read Harry and Schroeder's book *Six Sigma*. The case studies provide valuable insights; all used specialist consultants, but the process could be adapted for use by well-trained, in-house personnel, under the guidance of an experienced third party.

How to implement the Six Sigma Breakthrough Strategy

You've done your homework, read the literature, thoroughly assessed the benefits of Six Sigma, and decided to implement the Breakthrough Strategy, wherever possible, using in-house resources. You have asked the essential questions; you've gained the necessary executive support for active, visible, top-down leadership; you've confirmed the considerable budget allocation; and you are now ready to proceed. These will be among the steps to consider…

1 Appoint a Deployment Champion.

A Deployment Champion will be a member of the key executive team whose principal responsibility will be to nurture Six Sigma throughout the organisation. He or she may be coached by a Six Sigma expert and may, in turn, appoint Project Champions. The Deployment Champion will be a major influence on choosing projects and implementing the strategies and tactics.

2 Assemble and train a Six Sigma team.

Ensure that you have the right people ready to lead the processes as part of overall projects. Before publicly announcing the introduction of Six Sigma, assemble a small team whose job it will be to coordinate the introduction with other organisational endeavours. Some employees, for example, may resist the change, seeing the introduction of Six Sigma as a further demand on their time. The coordinating team, led by the Deployment Champion and

supported by Project Champions, is likely to continue to monitor the success of the Breakthrough Strategy and will:

• recommend candidates for Black Belts and Green Belts (other Project Champions and Master Black Belts are already likely to be part of the coordinating team)
• arrange and monitor candidate training
• identify particular areas of focus, potential projects, and the criteria for selection and, if necessary, termination of those projects
• consider how to measure the success of those projects
• compare all costs with the budgeted allocation.

Three essential features of the team's training will involve:
• communicating with others involved in implementing Six Sigma
• developing the team's understanding of measurement tools
• studying relevant material—for example, Harry and Schroeder's *Six Sigma* and www.6-sigma.com

3 Communicate the decision to proceed.

Six Sigma is a major initiative, so proceed as you would for any major change initiative. When you are satisfied that your Six Sigma team is ready, conduct a meeting (or a series of meetings) with everyone in the organisation. The decision to proceed, communicated by the CEO and the Deployment Champion, should:

- outline the Six Sigma process: there are no Six Sigma companies, only Six Sigma processes
- introduce the Six Sigma team, who will provide the essential support –champions, master black belts, black belts, and green belts
- link Six Sigma commitment and competency to promotion and salary incentives
- allay any concerns about job security
- point out that another meeting of all concerned will be held (say, in ten days) to give people a chance to discuss the initiative with colleagues and return with any questions or suggestions for projects.

Ask customers.

Customer satisfaction is important in any Six Sigma process. So arrange a meeting with some of your best or biggest customers and tell them of your plans to invest a significant amount of time and money to improve your service. Ask the customers to identify any areas where they think the money would be best spent. One of the likely outcomes of this approach will be the identification of particular areas of focus or specific projects. You might even consider inviting customer representatives to be part of an *ad hoc* review team to monitor progress.

Involve employees in other meetings.

People will now be much better able to discuss Six Sigma issues. Customers' views will have also been considered. In addition to discussing the Six Sigma process, the key executive and Deployment Champion will indicate particular objectives and suggest possible projects. Include a brief overview of the Breakthrough Strategy (see panel, *right*).

Outline the Breakthrough Strategy.

The Breakthrough Strategy assumes that most organisations comprise three basic levels, and Six Sigma is used to improve the overall quality and profitability of these—Business, Operations, and Process. The Strategy changes the way every level of business is managed daily. Changes and improvements at one level affect other levels. The Strategy applies an eight-step process—recognise, define, measure, analyse, improve, control, standardise, and integrate—at each level.

Measure, analyse, improve, and control (MAIC) are the four core phases. Each step is subject to rigorous data-gathering and statistical analyses to pinpoint sources of error, and ways of eliminating errors.

As organisations learn the kinds of measures needed to improve their processes, they can gain new insights and develop new practices that can be adopted as standards within the organisation.

don't forget

How to apply the Six Sigma Breakthrough Strategy...

This Strategy requires that key players lead and facilitate the thinking of participants in considering the eight-step process listed in 6 *(left)*, as it relates to the three basic levels of organisational focus – Business, Operations, and Process.

At the Business Level: Key executives lead the projects that could include measurement of customer feedback and supplier quality. 'The business-level application of the Breakthrough Strategy focuses primarily on making significant improvements to the informational and economic systems used to 'steer' the business.'

At the Operations Level: Project champions focus on 'operational issues' which, in turn, can be broken down into interrelated problems that can be managed, resulting in planned positive actions to eliminate or significantly reduce contributing factors.

At the Process Level: Black Belts work to recognise poor processes that result in problems, additional costs, and eroded quality. 'Black Belts discover what methods correct problems, then standardise those methods to ensure that those problems don't reoccur.'

Actions associated with the eight steps for each level are outlined in detail in Harry & Schroeder's *Six Sigma*, pages 115 to 136.

How to prepare and use job descriptions

Job descriptions serve three main functions. They help organisations outline clearly the roles, responsibilities, and other specifications associated with particular positions. They help candidates and employees gain accurate ideas of jobs and their associated roles and responsibilities. They help recruiters—in-house or external—to match candidates with particular posts. If you're reviewing the effectiveness of your job description or starting from scratch, here are some essential considerations…

Conduct preliminary research.

Ideally, the best job descriptions will satisfy the needs of everyone involved in, or affected by, the description. For this reason, it is best to resist the temptation to copy one outright from another organisation. Instead, when you're preparing a job description, ask yourself—and others, where appropriate—three questions:

1. What does management want from the job?
2. (If the position exists already) What will the job holder *actually* do—as opposed to thinking what he or she will do?
3. (In addition to what may already be stated) What do workplace colleagues think the job holder should be doing?

Your responses to these questions will help you assemble information for use in preparing a draft description.

Compile the description's three key features.

Most job descriptions consist of three main parts—basic information, objectives of the job, and key areas of responsibility.

The *basic information* will include:

- the job title and description recorded in clear, straightforward language
- the main location—if this may change from time to time, say so
- reporting responsibilities; and to whom—manager, supervisor, mentor
- responsibilities for whom—employees and their reporting structure
- functional relationship—as represented on an organisation chart showing how the job relates to others and fits into the organisation as a whole.

The *objectives* of the job should be a clear, concise statement describing why the job exists—to ensure that…

Key areas of responsibility form the main part of the job description. Ideally, these activities should

- include no more than ten tasks. Restricting the list to ten or fewer encourages you to define clearly the areas of responsibility. A broad, open-ended statement preceding the list can be included to indicate that the list is not definitive. The statement might read: 'These

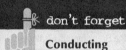

don't forget

Conducting a job analysis

In a nutshell, before you can prepare a job description, you must become thoroughly familiar with the duties and requirements of the job. To gain this familiarity, you will need to conduct a job analysis – by observing the incumbent at work, consulting previous job descriptions, talking with supervisors, even perhaps administering a questionnaire.

In performing the job analysis, you determine the duties, functions and responsibilities of the position (the job description) and the requirements for the successful performance of that job (the job specification).

duties are considered essential for undertaking this job effectively'.

- be put in some sort of order with each task described in a sentence or two explaining what is done and accompanied by any other relevant details. Begin each sentence with an action word; this leaves people in no doubt about what is required.
- be accompanied (where possible) by appropriate measures that are concrete, specific, easily understood, and attainable.

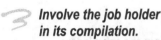
Involve the job holder in its compilation.

Make sure that the job description is a useful and well-used document. If the person is already acting in the position for which a description is being prepared, that person should be involved in the drafting process. Discuss issues such as:

- appropriate lines of authority
- appropriate reporting structures and numbers of people involved
- the different levels of authority
- the suitability of the existing structure
- current task allocation
- tasks for which responsibilities have not been allocated.

If a description is being prepared for a new position, involve the person who may have been previously fulfilling many of the tasks. Or if the description is for a new position on a team, invite input from members of that team.

Review regularly.

Job descriptions must be kept up to date. A review can occur as part of the annual performance appraisal,

or when the job falls vacant and you intend to advertise the vacancy. Another appropriate time is after a job holder has been in a position for a few months; here any significant changes in the job holder's duties can be considered as part of a probationary review.

Monitor its effectiveness.

Ineffective or dated job descriptions are capable of creating problems for your organisation by

- restricting the initiative of a job holder
- promoting a 'not-my-job' attitude among job holders
- stifling delegation.

If you observe any of these, it's a sure sign that now is the time to reassess your current job descriptions. Of course, when job descriptions are to be updated, make sure that those who will be affected by any changes are informed and consulted.

Maximise your use of job descriptions.

Having gone through the preparation process, you will identify a variety of ways in which the job descriptions can be used. In addition to its hiring function, you might consider using a job description as:

- a tool to help identify specific training needs
- a measure by which an employee can monitor his or her performance standards
- a touchstone document for use during staff performance appraisals
- an aid to structure project teams and various committees
- a reference to inform planning during an organisational restructuring.

---

here's an idea

Human resources consultant Arthur Pell offers four useful pieces of advice to compilers of job descriptions:

- In making a job analysis, be as diligent in determining the intangible factors as you do the tangible factors. The intangibles that make for success on a job are just as important as education, skills, and experience.
- Don't base your job specifications on your version of an ideal team member. That person exists only in your mind. Be realistic. Your specifications should reflect the factors the new member should bring to the job that will contribute to the team's successful performance.
- Don't clone your current team. When you set up specifications for a job, ask yourself, 'What must the applicant be able to do that I either can't or don't want to train him or her to do?'
- Keep in mind that your team will be stronger if it includes people with different but complementary skills (as opposed to a number of people who all have identical strengths, weaknesses, and capabilities).[1]

don't forget

By over-qualifying a job, you eliminate otherwise qualified people for the wrong reasons.

How to write a job advertisement that attracts the right applicants

If you decide to recruit your own staff, preparing an advertisement for display in the local or national press is important. Three groups will be attracted to your ad—recruitment agencies interested in referring their clients, competitors interested in your activities, and prospective employees interested in what you have to offer. Your ad will certainly be spotted, so it's important to get it right. Here's how...

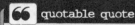
 Identify specifically what you want.

If you don't know what you're looking for, how will you know when you've found it? So, too, for people. For this reason, you'll need to take the time to construct the correct position profile before proceeding with the job advertisement. There are some simple, easy-to-use recruitment tools on the market that can help you construct that profile.

Grab the readers' attention.

When you're confident that you know the type of person you're looking for, find the up-front word or phrase that will attract that person. If it's simply an accountant, then say 'Accountant'. If you're looking for a person to fill a position that requires zest, initiative, and independence, your header may read, 'Put Yourself In The Driver's Seat'. Or for a design studio, 'Are you creative enough for us?' The header should match closely the 'cultural mores' of the position being advertised.

 Explain the job clearly.

You can eliminate many hassles later on by letting the reader know what the job entails. If they are expected to walk on water, be up-front about it. Interviews are not the place to introduce surprise information about jobs. If your expectations are realistic, the right person will be out there waiting to reply to your ad.

 Distinguish the job from others.

What is it about your job that helps to differentiate it from similar ones on offer? Why should the reader choose you and your organisation? Tell them. Often, it will be the little things that make the difference. That difference may be the human side of your business, the flexible hours, pleasant working conditions, great customers, good salary, overseas travel, the opportunity to be creative, and so on. Brainstorm for the attributes that make your organisation attractive. Current employees should be able to help you identify those qualities.

5 Explain your organisation's vision.

Attracting the right applicant can be as simple as saying something clear and honest about who you are, what you believe, and where you're heading—say, in the next five to ten years. You can't afford to have employees in your organisation who cannot share that vision. In addition, consider all those other interested readers (not necessarily job applicants) and use the advertisement to do a little public relations, by promoting your organisation's vision.

6 Tell them their next step.

Be specific about what you want applicants to do. If you want to screen applicants, you may request that they telephone you at a specific time to find out where to send their résumés. This will give you a chance to conduct a screening interview and to test their punctuality and voice presentation. If you want résumés only, make that clear in your ad, too. You should make a point of sticking to your request.

7 Disseminate copies of your ad.

Let others in your organisation who are likely to be affected by the ad know of its contents. The receptionist or any other person taking the initial calls will need to know so that they can be prepared for the resultant enquiries. Current employees who may be interested in applying for the position should also be afforded the courtesy of knowing about the position before it is made public.

8 Make sure the ad is well-presented.

A well-presented, attractive advertisement reflects well on your organisation. A poorly presented ad can have the opposite effect.

9 Choose the right time and place.

Ensure your ad is placed in the most appropriate newspaper or trade journal, on the most appropriate day, in the most appropriate section, at the most appropriate time of year. After all, you want to ensure that it receives maximum readership by the right audience, don't you?

10 Track your ads.

Count the number of responses that your ad generates. Ideally, that number should reveal a high level of competition for the position, a situation that will allow you to settle on a short-list of suitable applicants. If your ad does not encourage the desired response, review its contents before attempting a re-run.

don't forget

Focus on the basics

In preparing an advertisement to attract new employees, the advertising copy should be designed to explain as succinctly as possible:

- What the firm is
- What the job is
- Where the job is
- What job experience is needed
- What qualifications are (a) essential and (b) desirable
- What the salary etc. will be (if possible)
- What information is required in the response.[3]

here's an idea

If you're inviting applications for a vacant position in your organisation via email, suggest that résumés be included as part of the main text rather than as an attachment. This ensures that the email and the attachment aren't separated and as a minor protection against transmitting a virus.

If the résumé includes details of the candidate's personal website, a visit might contain additional information that could help your selection process.

How to hire the right person for the job

Think back to the last time you recruited someone. Were you quite confident then that you had selected the right person for the job? And has that person turned out to be a real winner? Hiring staff is a huge responsibility; it can arouse feelings of anxiety and hesitancy. In today's competitive world, however, the search for top-quality people is paramount. That's why your skills in hiring the right people must come to the fore. Here are some key considerations to help you with your selection process…

1 Get the job description right.

Examine the current job description thoroughly. Is it still appropriate? Consult with the position's immediate supervisor, even the present incumbent, and then revise the requirements in terms of title, purpose of job, key responsibilities and duties, skills, limits of authority, job relationships, special demands, and conditions of employment.

2 Create a picture of the ideal person.

Review and itemise the job description, personal attributes, and the specific expectations of the person sought to fill the position. The list could comprise over 30 items, and would include educational and professional qualifications, experience, special attributes and skills, ability to communicate, interpersonal skills, organisational skills, motivation, and so on. You will have created a picture of the ideal person. Rarely, however, will such a person exist. Therefore, break the list of requirements into three categories: must-have, should-have, and like-to-have.

3 Devise a standard evaluation form.

Prepare a standard data collection form for interviewers, to collect for each candidate as much high-quality information relating to credentials, experience, skills, and behaviour as possible, together with the interviewer's interpretative comments. This will later assist in reviewing the relevant merits of candidates.

4 Generate a battery of relevant questions.

Compile a list of searching questions in preparation for the interviews. These questions are designed to collect from each candidate as much information as possible on the behavioural specifications and personal attributes you have already targeted.

Begin the search.

Attracting suitable candidates is rarely a problem if you use advertisements, employment agencies, selection and search consultants, people you know, the grapevine, and your network to spread the word. Screen the résumés received; compile a list of 5-10 of the most promising candidates; send a thank-you letter to the remainder.

 Conduct first-round interviews.

The first-round of interviews are used to assess a candidate's compatibility and suitability in relation to future job performance. They enable you to gather and interpret the facts, so that you can compare all candidates against your picture of the ideal person. (See page 362 for guidelines on conducting these initial interviews, structured as follows: establish rapport; set the agenda; gather information; describe the job, organisation and conditions of employment; answer questions; and end the interview.) The purpose of the first round of interviews is to identify the most suitable candidates. Advise and thank unsuccessful interviewees.

 Conduct interviews of short-listed candidates.

You now have a short-list of the three most promising people. In second-round interviews you now ask in-depth questions about specifics. Don't accept candidates' accomplishments at face value since probing questions often reveal a great deal more than résumés or initial interviews disclose.

 Consider replacing 'gut feel' with a screening test.

It's important to hire someone whose personality fits your work culture and environment, and complements the personality of others they'll be working with. 'Gut feel' has traditionally been a reliable assessment tool; psychometric testing can also be used to provide helpful information. Tests are available to check most qualities. *Myers-Briggs Type Indicator, DISC* and *SPQ Gold* are popular examples.

 Review all data.

Analyse all the information collected on your short-listed candidates and assess individual strengths and weaknesses. Conduct a thorough check of qualifications and references. Talk to former bosses, peers, subordinates, and customers or clients if possible.

 Make a decision—and an offer.

Having followed the rigorous steps outlined above, you should be in a position to select the best person for the job. Confirm with the candidate the package on offer and follow up with official documentation within 48 hours; where required, make arrangements for the signing of an employment contract.

Finally, write and thank the unsuccessful short-listed candidates, remembering that they may well be worth considering for positions elsewhere in your organisation. Prepare an induction program for your new member of staff.

---

smile & ponder

Take care with those résumés and references!

In 1996, the résumé of the newly appointed Mexican Secretary of Education, Fausto Alzati, was challenged in the press. Alzati claimed to have a doctorate from Harvard. When the press questioned this and investigated, his office conceded that he had only a master's degree in public administration from Harvard.

But the press didn't let up, and one month later his office said that, actually, he didn't even have a bachelor's degree.

In January 1997, Alzati resigned, admitting that he was expelled for bad behaviour – from the second grade!

■ Before you hire new staff, check out their backgrounds to ensure they went to school where they said they went to college or university – because some people will try to fudge a little; and some people will try to fudge a lot.

---

 here's an idea

Ask referees for other referees. Remember that any person listed on a résumé as a reference has probably been prepped for your call. Ask that person if there are any other employees who worked with your candidate, and if you could speak to them. You'll get more candid responses this way.

How to improve your interviewing skills

Interviews have been defined as 'conversations with a purpose'. They are essential fact-finding management tools. Job interviews, discipline interviews, appraisal interviews, exit interviews... for managers, it is simply good sense to learn how to interview other people well. In the hands of an expert, an interview can be a short, straight path to the right answers. You can take that path by adopting the following proven practices...

1 Do your homework.

If you are unprepared for an interview, you'll make inefficient use of time, present a poor image, and struggle to obtain pertinent details. Don't try to start or muddle through an interview cold. Know exactly the purpose of the session, read and familiarise yourself with all relevant documentation, and prepare a set of questions or topics in advance.

2 Put the interviewee at ease.

Interviews can be stressful affairs. A relaxed setting, a warm welcome, and a few introductory pleasantries are enough to establish a friendly atmosphere. By doing all you can to reduce the intimidating aspects of the occasion and show genuine interest in the person, the more likely it is that you will get honest and detailed information—and, after all, that's the purpose of the exercise.

3 Remain focused on your objective.

Know in advance what facts and information you wish to obtain during the interview and frame your questions to get that data. Don't focus the session on yourself nor allow the interview to be sidetracked by irrelevancies.

4 Keep the initiative.

You are conducting the interview, so stay in control of the situation. Keep things moving by directing the flow of conversation along specific lines towards your desired goal and to cover your key topics. Your aim should be to maintain a pleasant atmosphere in which you encourage the interviewee to talk freely while you maintain an objective and impartial stance.

5 Ask the right questions.

Your questions should be framed in such a way that they get complete and detailed answers. Limit those questions which elicit yes or no responses. Avoid multiple questions: by asking two or three at once, you won't get satisfactory answers to any. Use follow-up questions to probe areas of uncertainty.

Keep the interviewee talking.

Your job is to encourage the interviewee to talk. Remember, you have a captive audience; the interviewee probably has no option but to sit and listen if *you* choose to do all the talking. So, always listen objectively and attentively. Don't worry about gaps in the conversation; if the interviewee stops talking, and you want to hear more on the same topic, just remain silent. Your silence will indicate you expect the other person to continue. The more the interviewee talks, the more will be revealed.

Be aware of legal issues.

It is illegal to ask questions that aren't related to a person's capacity to do a job. Avoid questions relating to marital status, child-care arrangements, religious practices, age, plans for having children, racial background, political beliefs, or physical disability.

Take notes.

As unobtrusively as possible, make notes during the interview, so that important points are captured. Where appropriate make use of check lists. For example, use a list of qualities you want to find in a job applicant, or a

list of topics you want to cover in an exit interview. These lists help you to focus the interview on pertinent matters and provide written data for analysis later.

Analyse and act on your information.

Immediately after the interview, take some time to elaborate on your notes, summarise answers, record factual information, and review the data. If you conduct several interviews in succession, e.g. job interviews, this process is essential; you'll find it difficult to associate information with particular candidates without the aid of detailed, objective notes on each person. As well, the time spent on this task will prove invaluable if you need to share your findings later with others.

Remember also...

- Ensure the interview session is free from interruption.
- Keep the interview going at an apparently unhurried pace. Don't keep looking at your watch—or you will unnecessarily make the interviewee feel unwanted or upset, on the edge of the chair ready for a hasty departure.
- Watch as well as listen.
- Don't let your feelings interfere with your judgement.
- Don't waste time repeating what is already known.
- Don't criticise or indicate disapproval.
- At the finish, invite questions about any issues not covered during the session and explain what the next step will be.
- Always end on a positive, friendly note.

research says

Recent research reveals just how inherently unreliable interviews can be:

- An average candidate who follows several poor candidates is invariably seen as particularly good.
- Physically attractive and well-groomed candidates are more likely to be appointed – even though they might not have been the best on paper.
- Even with highly structured selection procedures, the interview is often used to justify and explain the decision rather than guide it.
- Interviewers reach their decision about each candidate very early in the interview, according to one researcher within four minutes.
- Interviewers are poor at recalling information about the candidates.
- Most interviewers do not take adequate notes.
- In higher level interviews, e.g. for an executive position, more personal questions are asked than any other category.
- In making a final decision about higher level positions, selectors give more weight to personality and personal qualities than to job-related criteria.

Such findings confirm the notion that interviews should fill only a supporting role in any selection procedure.

How to make new staff members feel part of the organisation

For new employees, those early days in your organisation can be more of a test of survival than a time of growth and development. Often, new staff members are thrown into the workplace and expected to succeed with little support. It's no wonder that many of them become disillusioned. How newcomers progress depends on many variables, but research shows that the help they receive in the early days from management and colleagues makes all the difference...

1 Begin the familiarisation process immediately.

Instigate procedures that will enable new staff members to become familiar with important features of the organisation and its administration. For example, newcomers should:

- *undertake a guided tour of the company,* particularly those areas with which they will have most contact, such as the administration area, storeroom, staff facilities, reprographics room.
- *meet formally and socially with staff colleagues,* especially those with whom they will be working closely.
- *read relevant documents,* such as the staff handbook, policy guidelines, safety instructions, annual reports, and the like.
- *be briefed on procedures,* including office or factory routine, record-keeping, assessment, channels of communication, committee structures, and staff development.

These activities best take place before the newcomer officially takes up duty in the organisation.

2 Create a supportive atmosphere.

What is needed are managers and experienced staff members who are committed to being available to help newcomers as needed. Those who unite to meet the needs of beginners develop in that process structures of collegiality and collaboration that will also serve the organisation in other ways. Foster a warm climate of support.

3 Explain the job.

Outline the exact work to be done and how the work fits into the overall activities of the workplace. Do not make it sound too difficult at first and don't overburden the new arrival with too much information and too many rules. At the start, provide tasks that are readily accomplished to ease the recent arrival into the new job.

4 Appoint a mentor.

An experienced employee who is asked to serve as mentor or buddy for the new arrival provides the newcomer with friendship and open access to a colleague's expertise. Consider the support a mentor can provide:

- *Teaching* the newcomer about the job through coaching, conversations, and demonstrations.
- *Guiding* the newcomer through the unwritten rules of the organisation and in recognising group norms.
- *Advising* about the quality of expected work and the nuances of company policies and procedures.
- *Counselling* the newcomer if stressed, lonely, or in conflict with others.
- *Sponsoring* or giving stature to the newcomer in negotiations with others.
- *Role modelling* by providing an image of the effective professional or worker to which the newcomer can aspire.
- *Validating* over time the newcomer's goals and aspirations.
- *Protecting* the new arrival by being a buffer to the hazards of the company.
- *Motivating* by providing feedback and encouragement.
- *Communicating* openly with the newcomer so that all the other behaviours can be effective.

 Schedule visits to other areas of the workplace.

Once the employee has established reference points as to what it is like to be a worker in your organisation, structured visits to other departments can then be scheduled to enable the newcomer to observe how experienced employees handle specific issues and tasks.

 Visit the newcomer's workplace regularly.

Practical advice from experienced colleagues during the early days is best based on the newcomer's own experience. Therefore, arrange for regular visits with the aim of helping and working alongside, rather than judging or inspecting, the new employee. Give genuine feedback.

 Provide assistance in identified areas of need.

Research reveals that beginning employees commonly face similar problems in a new work environment. Work with your newcomers to pinpoint and remediate their specific areas of need, whether they be personal or professional in nature.

 Make them feel important.

Most newcomers feel uneasy, nervous, and out-of-place at first. Take time to greet them personally on their first day. Show an interest in them. Make them feel the company genuinely needs them. Ask questions and invite questions. Be sincere.

Provide opportunities for review and discussion.

Show interest in the employee's progress through, firstly, formal sessions to review progress and to address concerns and, secondly, through informal discussions in a relaxed setting. Be generous with your comments, supportive, honest and sensitive, and let newcomers know that their efforts are appreciated.

 here's an idea

Make sure new staff hit the ground running – have an 'employment package' ready and waiting for them. It should include any necessary personnel forms; any written policies or an employee handbook; safety information; information on the benefits plan; information on pay schedules, sick days, and vacation time; marketing materials that will help new employees learn about the company quickly; a list of local restaurants for lunch; an employee directory; contact names in HR or personnel; and any other information that will help ease new employees into their new jobs.

here's an idea

One organisation has fully embraced the concept of induction by asking some of its newly retired staff to return to help new members of staff to acclimatise. A retired staff association runs courses to help these retired staff members carry out effective induction and mentoring. This has a motivating effect on all staff, not the least of which the new recruits and those who are retired.[7]

 quotable quote

First impressions are the lasting ones. The induction and orientation period is an emotionally charged time for the new employee and those early experiences imprint lasting memories.[8]

How to improve employee performance through coaching

Managers have a two-fold role. They must correct their employees' performance problems and help them grow professionally and contribute to the organisation, at the same time advancing the employees' own careers. So, to be effective, managers must be coaches, employing face-to-face techniques to solve performance problems or correct skill deficiencies, and to help staff develop to their full potential. Here's one way to improve performance through the coaching process...

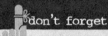

Know when to coach.

Coaching can be initiated by an employee who recognises the need for help; by you when you spot a need to intervene; or when you are delegating, giving instructions or encouraging an employee's growth and development. Normally, you'll be too busy to adopt a coaching stance every time an employee comes to you with a problem. So you'll need to be quite selective about when you use coaching. You may also decide to delegate the task to a colleague better qualified than you to help with the particular problem.

Decide if a formal remedial coaching session is warranted.

If you believe your intervention is required in a coaching capacity, confirm that such a session is really necessary by asking the following questions:

- Is there really a problem where an employee is not meeting a performance standard? Or is that employee simply not performing quite as well as another?
- If a problem exists, is the problem correctable? Have previous attempts failed with this employee?
- Is the problem beyond the control of the employee—i.e. faulty materials, late deliveries, lack of information, equipment failures, unrealistic deadlines?

Coaching is not the solution to all performance problems.

 ### Agree on a need for the session.

Whether the session has been at your instigation or at your employee's, you must first agree on the exact nature of the employee's problem or skill deficiency—because the staff member's understanding may differ from yours. Establish clearly the purpose and importance of the session, the learning objectives, procedures, measurable goals by which progress can be gauged, and a timeline. Remember, the best approach will be one in which the employee feels committed, because the learner and coach have an equal stake in success.

Prepare for the coaching session.

Advance planning is essential for a remedial coaching session: collect data, materials and records; structure the message to suit the needs and experience of the employee; consider the employee's learning style; anticipate possible outcomes and reactions; and select a time and place.

Begin the coaching session.

If you need to teach employees specific new skills, consider this three-step coaching method:

1. *You do, you say.* Sit down with the employee(s) and explain the task or skill—while you do it. This allows the employee to watch the task being done, and points out the proper way to do it. At each step of the process, explain what you are doing and why you are doing it.
2. *They do, you say.* The next step is to have the employee do the task—while you walk them through it step by step. Again, explain each step of the process as they do it.
3. *They do, they say.* The final step in the process is when the employee actually does the task, and explains each step of the process to you as they do it.[9]

During the session, encourage thoughtful employee participation:

- ask open-ended questions
- discuss the pros and cons of each step and explore the options
- anticipate potential hazards and blockages, and identify alternative strategies
- acknowledge employee suggestions but be prepared to disagree, with reasons, if justified.

- build on as many ideas from the employee as possible.

Anticipate potential problems, and watch and listen for signals that the employee might have missed something. End the session on a positive note.

Set up a program of review.

Establish and agree upon a schedule of review to ensure the skills have been mastered over time. Set follow-up dates to review progress and stress that you're willing to help if required. Follow up to make sure tasks are accomplished and remember to acknowledge achievement.

Avoid these common coaching traps.

- *Lecturing instead of coaching.* Coaching involves dialogue and shared decision-making.
- *Coaching only problem employees.* Coaching should not be seen as a short-term punitive measure for problem staff only. Remember to use long-term coaching to help all employees develop and grow.
- *Not being specific.* Avoid dealing in generalities. Provide examples, statistics, dates, and documentation to support your attempts to change employee behaviour.
- *Assuming too much.* Don't assume an employee is aware of the performance problem, or what is required; or will perform appropriately when agreement is reached; or even know when a good job has been done. Explain every step clearly.
- *Confusing a coaching session with a disciplinary session.* Coaching is a positive, non-threatening process.

ask yourself

- Has coaching been a serious consideration in our workplace? If not, why not?
- Is there an employee in our team who would benefit from coaching?
- Which skills or tasks would I be best at coaching?
- Which of my colleagues have skills which could be passed on to others through coaching?
- Have I ever been coached in the past? How effective was the process? How could it have been improved?

don't forget

Coaching is more than mere instruction. Successful coaching also depends on listening, questioning, observation, patience, and providing constructive feedback.

it's a fact

Coaching and mentoring are different techniques. In coaching, specific skills or tasks are passed on, mastered and measured; in mentoring, the longer-term progress of an employee is the focus. Coaching can be part of mentoring.

read further

Co-Active Coaching: Changing Business, Transforming Lives by Laura Whitworth et al., Nicholas Brealey Publishing, 3rd edn, 2011.

How to conduct a training needs analysis

Any problem, shortcoming, or gap preventing organisations or employees from achieving their objectives can usually be overcome, or at least minimised, through training and development activities. But how can such shortcomings be best identified and become the subject of training? The answer: conduct a training needs analysis or assessment, a process that every manager should be familiar with…

1 Adopt a framework for identifying needs.

Training needs can be identified at three levels:

- *The individual*—an employee lacks certain skills, understandings, or behaviours that limit performance, e.g. a discourteous receptionist.
- *The strata*—employees doing the same kind of work lack a certain skill, e.g. with the introduction of new computerised cash registers, the checkout people need training; drivers and storemen do not.
- *The organisation*—throughout the company a certain behaviour hinders achievement of a corporate goal, e.g. poor interpersonal skills are affecting staff and customer retention.

Consider that framework when deliberating on the need for training in your organisation.

2 Be aware of the work that may be involved.

Just as staff training does not simply happen, nor does its identification. The process of assessing the need for training demands time and energy in planning and analysis.

It demands the full involvement of staff in the discussion process, beyond the traditional approach where management decided what was best for staff. It demands co-ordination, allowing managers in all parts of the organisation to integrate common needs and priorities to avoid duplication of effort and cost.

3 Be ready to tackle any anticipated problems.

Be prepared to initiate training when a need is obvious—such as following, or before, the installation of new equipment in the workshop.

4 Be ready to tackle any unanticipated problems.

Keep on the lookout for the more difficult problems to identify. For example, you may have accepted for some time that the high turnover of staff in the accounts office was a result of the cramped, stuffy environment in that part of your building. It's a budgetary, not a training problem, you argued. But what if the real cause was poor selection of staff by the section head in the first place, or the poor interpersonal skills of the accounts office manager? In this case, training may well be required.

Use proven techniques to identify needs.

There is a strong case for ongoing, systematic monitoring. To identify training needs, or when problems arise, there are several instruments that may be used to locate the actual symptoms. Some of these needs assessment instruments are:

- *Literature research:* Scrutinise budget and quality control documents, goal statements, evaluation reports, staffing and scheduling reports, for problems.
- *Interviews:* Talk to supervisors, managers, employees, and customers.
- *Appraisal interviews:* Individual training needs will become apparent.
- *Observations:* Watch the job or task being performed.
- *Surveys:* Send out questionnaires.
- *Group discussions:* Involve employees and their supervisors.
- *Online monitoring:* Frequency of staff inquiries to in-house online resources.

Ask relevant questions.

Essential questions that you might need to ask to determine training needs would include:

- What are my employees doing that they shouldn't be doing?
- What specific things would I like to see my staff doing, but they don't?
- When I visualise my staff performing a job properly, what do I see them doing?
- What prevents them from performing a prescribed task to a set standard?
- Is that standard reasonable? Why not?
- If an employee could change one thing in the way current work is performed,

what would it be?
- What skill or behaviour would I like to see my staff trained in? Why?
- What would they like to be trained in?
- What new technology would benefit my staff the most in the performance of their work?
- What new technology would I like to see invented to help them with their work? Why?

Know the benefits of a systematic approach.

There are advantages in embracing an ongoing and systematic approach to identifying training needs. It's an essential requirement for improving performance, and a natural consequence of staff performance appraisals; staff morale, satisfaction, and motivation are enhanced when individuals and teams know that their development is a priority; and, importantly, it allows management to prioritise resources, in accordance with an effective organisational development plan.

Integrate training needs wherever possible.

To avoid duplication of effort and increasing costs, it is sensible for managers to aggregate training needs information and, whenever possible, to work towards integration of organisation-wide training activities.

Begin a training program.

Having identified needs, training can begin at the individual, strata, or organisational level. The bottom line is that no training should be arranged without first establishing that there is a clear need for it.

How to implement an on-the-job training program

When there is a gap between what an employee *can* do and what that employee *should* be able to do, training is needed. Most learning takes place on the job, and its success will depend largely on the effectiveness of the training method and the ability of the manager, or his or her nominee, to instruct the worker in that new skill. Here is a proven strategy to help you master the training process...

don't forget

Train for a purpose

Make sure that any skills acquired in training can be used by the employee directly in the job. This will overcome an all too common 're-entry' problem where the recently trained staffer, bursting with newly acquired knowledge, returns to the work-place to meet resistance when trying to implement the new-found knowledge and techniques.

The result... frustration and demotivation – to say nothing of a highly suspect training agenda.

read further

The Trainer's Pocketbook by John Townsend, Alresford, Hampshire. www.pocketbook.co.uk

1 Don't take the need for staff training lightly.

If you do not offer your staff the training they need to perform their jobs safely, you can be held liable for negligence. Lawyer Alan Levins elaborates:

> If you put a truck driver on the road without the training to keep him from being a hazard, you could be liable if he caused an accident. Similarly, an employee could file a claim if he were injured because a co-worker hadn't been trained to properly use equipment. Believe it or not, an employee can even claim he can't be terminated because the reason he caused $10 million in damage by forgetting to set the fire alarm at night was that he was not properly trained to do so![12]

2 Define the training need.

Be alert as to the need for training within your organisation. For example:

- Be aware of any plans for expansion or changes in technology which might require new skills within the organisation.

- Identify any operating problems, the outcome of inadequate performance, which would be corrected by training.
- Use job analysis and performance appraisal to identify individual training needs.

3 Prepare yourself for the training session.

Although you may be completely familiar with all aspects of a given job, it is essential to make adequate preparations before attempting to instruct others. For example, determine how much skill you want the trainees to acquire by what date; break the job down into its various components; isolate and write down the key points; have the right equipment and materials ready; and make sure the workplace is in order.

4 Prepare the trainees.

Some employees do not necessarily want to learn; others may even have a fear of learning. Hence, it is essential to put the trainees at ease and to foster an interest in the task by explaining the purpose of the training, what is going to be done and how the trainees and the organisation will benefit from it.

5 Find out what the trainees already know.

Check on what the employees can already do; you can then build upon that knowledge. You don't want to waste time teaching employees something they already know, but you cannot always assume that they *really* know what they say they know. Sometimes workers try to impress you by pretending.

6 Present the task step by step.

Explain and, wherever possible, demonstrate what has to be done and how. Instruct clearly, completely, and patiently. Pace your instruction carefully, one step at a time, and move on to the next step when you are sure each employee has absorbed what has been taught. Emphasise the key points. Encourage questions if something is not understood.

7 Check for understanding.

Having explained the task, let the trainees demonstrate the job to you, explaining each key point in turn. This is important. Unless they can tell you the key points as they proceed, you can never be sure they have grasped the message. If no errors are made—fine. If an error is

made, interrupt there and then, and patiently go over that point. Continue in this way until you are sure the employees have mastered the entire process.

8 Have the trainees practise the skill.

Practice will help to consolidate newly acquired skills. Under supervision, get the employees to practise each stage until the required standards of speed and accuracy are achieved. A progressive approach should be used. That is, when any two successive stages can be done separately at the required standard, have the employees practise them jointly until the desired standard for both steps is reached. Then the third step can be added, then the fourth, and so on until the entire task is mastered.

9 Put the trainees to work.

When you feel sure that the employees have mastered the skill, put them to work on their own. Designate to whom they go for help if required. Check progress frequently, particularly in the early stages. Retrain wherever necessary and be friendly and encouraging in your manner. As the workers become more sure of themselves, the need for coaching should diminish and finally the necessity to follow up on this task should cease completely.

Remember that, if the worker hasn't learnt, the instructor hasn't taught.

How to conduct a workshop

Workshops provide a forum for individuals and groups to explore areas of mutual interest or concern—skills, problems, or possibilities. And often the expectation is that you, as the manager, will lead and conduct the workshop, thus providing another opportunity for you to demonstrate your leadership and group skills—if you do it well. Here are some considerations to help you prepare for that next opportunity...

here's an idea

Four tips for keeping your participants interested...

Use your voice effectively. Ronald Reagan, for example, used to drink a glass of warm water before he presented. He believed that it helped him to relax and make his voice sound resonant.

Tell anecdotes. Anita Roddick of Body Shop fame claimed that it's story telling that makes the difference. Become a great storyteller.

Vary the pace of your presentation. We can hear at 325 words per minute and generally speak at about 170 words per minute. To maintain interest, all you need to do is vary the pace.

Incorporate participants' names into your presentation. The one word people love to hear most is their own name, so use it.[15]

Do the hard yards early —get prepared.

Preparation is essential. If you are not prepared, postpone the workshop until you are. Preliminary considerations should focus on:

- Timing—the topic must be relevant to the period and participants' needs.
- Establishing outcomes—fuzziness upfront will create problems later.
- Deciding on essential knowledge and skills—pre-workshop training may be required to ensure effective participation on the day.
- Identifying possible attendees—wall flowers are merely excess baggage.
- Developing materials to suit the audience—even the best materials will fail with the wrong audience.
- Liaising with any other providers—they'll be expecting to hear from you.
- Inviting participants, disseminating an agenda, arranging facilities, and providing directions if necessary.

 Plan the format.

Sequence activities to help achieve your desired outcomes. Adult learning techniques should guide the approaches you use (Kolb, for example, advocated a balance between activity, reflection, theory building, and consideration of any practical application). Ideally, the workshop should commence with an icebreaker to help the group relax, establish rapport, and help focus attention on the aim of the workshop. Plan to scatter energisers (short, sharp exercises or activities) throughout the session to help refocus attention on the tasks at hand.

 Arrive early.

You must be the first person to arrive at the venue. Check all equipment. Arrange seating to suit the purpose of the first session—e.g. theatre style, U-shape, or round tables. Greet people as they arrive. Direct people to refreshments. Introduce people to one another and generally make them feel welcome. The work done now will make your task much easier later. Housekeeping issues may be dealt with here rather than at the start of the workshop.

Start on time.

Never penalise those who arrive on time by waiting for stragglers. If a senior executive does not want to get things under way, you do it. Act and sound authoritative, but warm. Use an icebreaker, if necessary. Introduce yourself and ensure everyone knows each other's name, job, special skills, and what they want to get out of the workshop. Make the objectives of the program clear. Display them where they can be seen clearly. Review the agenda so people are aware of how you are aiming to achieve your objectives. Establish ground rules.

 Remain relaxed.

Adopt the attitude that there is nothing that can happen in the workshop that you can't handle. Your nonverbal and verbal responses will contribute substantially to the climate of the workshop. Be guided by these suggestions:

- If things don't go according to plan, there's no need to apologise. Move on.
- If you don't have an answer to a question, ask others. And if they don't have the answer, offer to get back to them later.
- Keep away from jargon. *Paradigms*, *parameters*, and other management mumbo-jumbo are a turn-off for many participants.
- Use visuals wherever possible; they're much more effective than verbal instructions.
- Make sure all material and language you use are culturally neutral. The need for cultural sensitivity cannot be overemphasised.
- Repeat or rephrase questions that are not heard by everyone in the audience.
- The attention span of most adults is about seven minutes, so vary your pace and presentation techniques accordingly.
- Cater for the anticipated 'slow time' after lunch. High activity will beat a video or lecture at these times.

Finally, remember that the word 'facilitator', with a Latin derivation, means 'one who makes things easy'.

 End on time— with the right message.

Stick to your committed finishing time. Begin the wrap-up about thirty minutes before then. Provide a summary of accomplishments. Invite others' input. Evaluate the workshop by distributing a short survey or use a less formal approach like handing out small cards and inviting a positive comment on one side and an improvement suggestion on the other. Thank participants and outline further follow-up.

 Review the workshop.

Use the planned outcomes, the feedback provided, and your own impressions to evaluate the success or otherwise of the workshop. Decide on your next step. Act promptly and program further meetings if required.

 Observe other workshop facilitators.

All presenters have their own unique styles. Watch other people conduct workshops and you will learn much. And by 'borrowing' ideas you can add to your repertoire of skills.

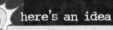

here's an idea

In many presentations today it's almost impossible to avoid using acronyms. By using an Acronym Chart you will not 'lose' your listeners…

The Acronym Chart is placed off to the side of your main presentation area. Each time an acronym is used during the session, record it on the chart in acronym form. Before and after each break, check participants' understand-ing of the meaning of the acronyms. This approach will ensure that participants can refer to and comprehend the meaning of the acronyms without letting your usage interfere with the flow of your presentation.

here's an idea

An effective and useful evaluation technique is to provide each participant with a blank sheet of paper or Post-it Note and a pen or pencil.

Ask them to record a '+' on the top right-hand corner of one side and a '-' on the other side. On the '+' side, ask participants to feedback one thing they particularly liked about the workshop or presentation. On the '-' side, ask them for an improvement suggestion that could have made the session even better.

This feedback will keep you focused on self-improvement.

 read further

How to Run Seminars and Workshops, Robert L. Jolles, John Wiley & Sons, 2005.

373

How to ensure that your next company conference is a success

Depending on the size of your organisation, when planning for your next major in-house gathering—conference, congress, symposium—remember that such events are what *you* make them. How do you assemble your brightest stars, integrate their contributions, structure the event, identify and explore opportunities, and focus on worthwhile outcomes? Successful conferences require time, money, and effort. Maximise returns on your investment and ensure that your next company event achieves the best possible outcomes by addressing these essential considerations...

1 Start preliminary planning early.

The best outcomes are achieved when you take plenty of time to consider what you want your event to accomplish. Consult with key people such as your CEO, MD or Chairman to identify goals and outcomes. Consider timing and processes to avoid clashes with other important company, state, and national events and demands.

2 Focus on a design that embraces the company culture.

The *Goldilocks Principle* (making sure that everything is 'just right') must guide your planning. When bringing your people together as participants, you need to consider issues as varied as selecting a conference venue, a conference theme, building ownership and commitment, involving delegates in pre-conference activities, capitalising on the use of technologies—and ensuring a cultural fit. A conference designed to reflect the overall company culture and direction, rather than a one-off event and an end in itself, is the more effective objective.

3 Assemble your planning group.

One of the most effective ways to ensure cultural fit is to form a small steering committee of 'thought-leaders'. This group is responsible for overall design, planning, conduct, and review of the event. For larger conferences, members of the steering committee could also chair subgroups, which focus on such areas as progam, social activities, venue, transportation, accommodation, budget, and publicity —and report progress to regular steering committee meetings.

4 Appoint a facilitator or conference organiser.

Smaller conferences use a facilitator; larger ones usually require an organiser. Whether you use an in-house or an external facilitator or organiser, he or she has five main tasks:

- to work with the steering committee to plan the complete experience for delegates—from arrival to departure
- to provide the necessary zest and sparkle in introducing, linking, and

summarising conference activities

- to keep the conference on track in terms of meeting protocols, agenda, and time allocations
- to be omnipresent to deal with the many issues that inevitably arise when talented people are involved in exploring opportunities and options
- to be involved in the evaluation process and to ensure follow-up tasks are seen to and next year's event is even better.

Consider all possibilities.

It's too late after the event to say 'We should have done....'. Planning design and facilitation should consider scores of questions including:

- What topics will be presented? Who will be invited to speak?
- How will speakers be briefed?
- Who will be invited, requested or required to attend?
- Will there be a conference website?
- How interactive will that site be?
- Will there be a daily conference newssheet or other technology to avoid time-consuming message-giving and to create a feeling of community?
- Will there be competitions conducted and company awards presented?
- Will technology be used to review the previous day and to introduce the next?
- Will there be a conference dinner and an after-dinner speaker?
- Will life partners be invited to attend and will a social program be needed to accommodate them?
- Will delegates receive a summary (print, CD, video, or downloadable from a website) of the conference?
- How will delegates be encouraged to evaluate the conference?

Maintain regular communication with delegates.

Resist the temptation to invite individuals to participate in the event until all the associated details are in place. Communications might include letters of invitation, information about pre-conference activities or tasks required of participants, details of video or teleconferencing, website access details, conference e-newsletter or newssheet, etc. Provide all the details needed to enable delegates to participate fully in pre- and in-conference activities.

Scrutinise venue and accommodation provisions.

Along with the program, the venue and accommodation demand special attention—people remember the good and bad points. Personally check a potential conference venue and accommodation via an anonymous visit, followed by a formal inspection with the venue executive. In a hotel, pay attention to its general condition and decor, housekeeping and food service, check-in and front-desk handling, staff attitude, room rates, and number, size and types of meeting rooms. And make sure your company VIPs get the VIP rooms—you won't want the CEO ending up trying to sleep in a room next to the bar!

Develop a checklist.

Compile a check list comprising a series of questions under such categories as: date, venue, program, participants, speakers, special guests, billing arrangements, meeting room needs, registration desk and procedure, AV requirements, food and beverage needs, social events, displays, signage, publicity, evaluation, follow-up...

don't forget

Let these be your goals...

For a highly successful in-house conference you should strive for...

- a plan that is outcomes-focused
- a design that adheres to the *Goldilocks Principle* of being 'just right' and culturally in sync
- tasks or topics that challenge, encourage, and inspire delegates to strive to reach new heights
- spot-on facilitation
- communications before, during, and after the conference that create an industry benchmark
- opportunities for delegates to network and pursue both professional and social agenda
- observable changes in delegates' behaviours as a result of participating in a unique event.

quotable quote

As a matter of principle it is strongly recommended that senior management make a showing at a company conference. The visit can be part social and part communication, but... a representative of top management (as senior as possible) should at least make a short presentation on the current business situation.[16]

How to get the most out of your next staff retreat

Retreats or getaways are an ideal way to get staff together in a relaxed and informal setting so that they'll feel good about each other and work together more effectively. Retreats are an excellent strategy for empowering staff and having them work together productively as colleagues. But this cooperation will only occur if careful attention is paid to organising the experience. So the following suggestions are offered...

quotable quote

Good things happen when co-workers get away from their pressure-filled environments. Business and industry have recognised for years that getaway days and retreats are useful for improving morale and organisational effectiveness... The retreat is an exciting vehicle for practising involvement, communication, and problem-solving strategies. It is probably the most complete procedure I know for enabling staffs to develop power and success in working together.[17]

it's a fact

A planning retreat is a meeting typically involving staff and management. It can be one to two days long, sometimes using a facilitator to help structure the process. Retreats are usually held away from the workplace or on weekends to ensure that participants can focus wholly on the issues at hand and are not distracted by the everyday office interruptions. Key stakeholders will sometimes be invited to join the retreat to strengthen the relationship between the stakeholder and the organisation or to educate individuals around certain organisational issues.

When used as part of the planning process, a retreat is a great opportunity for different elements of an organisation to work together to map the organisation's future.

1 Be convinced that a retreat is the answer.

An away-from-work retreat can provide a rewarding experience for staff in several ways:

- Longer blocks of time are available for in-depth discussions and problem-solving activities.
- The relaxed environment, with a minimum of disruption, fosters high responsiveness and involvement.
- Since status and authority roles are minimised, communication channels free up and problems are addressed on a more co-equal basis.
- Flexibility and creativity are more likely in this environment as a result of traditional organisational patterns and values being waived.
- The experience itself becomes the catalyst for individual and group commitment to action after the retreat.

In summary, a retreat is an ideal experience for team-building (the setting gets people feeling good about each other) and problem-solving (uninterrupted time allows work issues to receive focused attention).

2 Select an appropriate time.

Almost any time is a good time for a retreat—an evening, a weekend, a long weekend. What is more important, however, is to know why you're getting out of the workplace environment—to become re-acquainted as a staff, to grapple with a knotty work-related problem or two, to undertake specific training...

3 Select an appropriate location.

Venue selection is usually related to budget. Consider your needs in terms of participants, working areas, meals, recreational facilities, accommodation, travel, and your ability to finance the event. The location can range from an evening at a staff member's home to a week at a luxury hotel. In deciding, consider the facilities available from a variety of providers—universities, government, conference centres, local hotels, or religious institutions. Staff members may even make their homes or holiday houses available. Talk with colleagues who have been to retreats.

Consider who should attend.

In terms of whole-staff morale, the more participants the better, and that includes ancilliary staff. Specific work groups (production staff, accounts section, administrative or sales staff) may wish to plan their own retreats to address specific group problems. The general rule, however, is that the larger the group, the greater planning and leadership required. Indeed, sometimes a planning mini-retreat might need to precede the real thing! In some circumstances, e.g. for specific training or to ease staff tensions, outside consultants may be required.

Plan the program.

Retreats usually focus on staff working together to solve problems and to make specific plans to improve the organisation. A typical one-day program, depending on the time available, might feature:

- Late-afternoon arrival and an on-site briefing by the planning committee —registration, rooms assigned, housekeeping details, and draft agenda presented.
- Dinner, followed by an icebreaking activity and free time.
- Breakfast, followed by Workshop 1 (large and small groups focusing on identified issues and problems).
- Workshop 2 (problem-solving, group decision-making, and proposed action).
- Lunch, followed by Workshop 3 (action specifics—who, what, when, how?—and the development of action check lists).
- Evaluation and adjournment.

 Remember these key points for success...

For a memorable experience, make a note of these essential points:

- There never is enough time allocated in the program to the task. So resist the temptation to overload the agenda and, instead, focus on fewer issues and get maximum productivity through the use of appropriate group processes.
- Allow ample free time for informal conversation, mingling and the inevitable continuation of workshop discussion in the relaxed and unhurried environment of the site.
- Try not to set post-retreat goals too high. Realistic expectations will minimise or eliminate disappointment back at the workplace.

 Follow-up immediately back at work.

Most participants will return to work motivated and in high spirits. Capitalise on this euphoria as follows:

- Act promptly to implement some of the plans agreed to at the final retreat session. Advertise and celebrate this.
- To avoid 'us-and-them' alienation, advise the staff not present at the retreat that they were missed, of decisions made, and of the hope that they will be able to attend next time.
- Pin social photographs taken at the retreat on staff bulletin boards and follow-up with informal social events to reinforce *esprit de corps*. Include non-attendees in these events.
- In the weeks that follow, check that all action commitments agreed to at the retreat are kept.

How to unleash the creative potential of your staff

As a manager, you can increase the effectiveness, productivity, and competitiveness of your organisation if you establish a more creative working environment for your employees. In every organisation, creative people need a chance to display their talents. These people can be one of your greatest assets—but only if you know how to get the best from them. Here's how...

 Understand the creative process.

People won't be creative unless they want to be and work in an environment that encourages them to be. If people are given the opportunity to participate in planning their work and encouraged to make decisions about how it should be done, they will want to be involved. A positive attitude, ownership, and commitment are the key ingredients of creativity.

Creativity is a fluctuating process—there will be fallow periods during the incubation stage when little happens. Wise counsel will rekindle the creative spirit, so the manager must keep the communication lines open and provide a flexible, supportive environment.

Appreciate that all staff can contribute creatively.

Nobody has a monopoly on creativity. Good ideas can come from the receptionist or the managing director. The trick is to create an environment where everyone in your organisation is encouraged to have a say. Set in place procedures where the views of all staff members are welcome and considered.

Set the example yourself.

To foster a creative work environment, you need to be, in Douglas McGregor's terms, a 'Theory Y' manager—*you* see your staff as creative, imaginative, hardworking, and responsible. You need to favour informal organisational structures and encourage supervisors and employees to share ideas, resources, and information. You need to set the norm by occasionally coming up with a creative idea yourself. You need the ability to inspire, to 'work them up', to relax the controls, to demonstrate a positive attitude of confidence, and to offer praise and support.

React warmly and positively to all ideas.

Ideas are easier to tame down than to think up, so welcome those way-out ideas and toss them around;

Sidebar

here's an idea

If you want to solicit ideas from your team members, never present your own views first. Because of your position, what you say can often influence what others had planned to say. Listen instead. And with an open mind. Their comments may give you new insights into the problem and could even result in a better solution.

here's an idea

Put a bulletin board in a central area and encourage staff to use it to brainstorm ideas. Write a problem or theme on a coloured card and pin it in the centre of the bulletin board as the topic of the week. Provide a bundle of A5 sheets of paper on which your staff can jot down their ideas for posting on the board throughout the week. You'll find that, like most good brainstorming activities, people will build on the ideas of others as fresh postings are read daily.

here's an idea

Hold a monthly idea lottery. Every time a staff member comes up with a creative idea, give him/her a numbered ticket. At the end of each month, share all the ideas with the group, hold a draw, and give a prize to the person whose number is chosen.

378

often one idea will lead to others. Remember, criticism kills an idea faster than anything else—and creative people are usually very sensitive to criticism. So listen to yourself next time someone comes up with a new idea: Do you thunder 'No—that wouldn't work here!' or do you say 'Sounds promising. Let's see if we can do something with it'? If an idea warrants criticism, however, your objective should be to nourish, modify, and nudge the idea along—not kill it, and its originator's enthusiasm, outright.

5 Identify and encourage creative individuals.

Spend time with people; observe the quality of their work; talk to them about their views of things; and listen to what other staff and colleagues have to say. Words like 'risk-taker', 'leader', and 'exceptional' are variously used to describe people who are more creative than others; they are the ones who should be particularly nurtured:

- *Recognise that innovators on staff are apt to be 'different' and may need to be treated differently.*

- *Innovators should be free to associate with their opposite numbers in other organisations.* Enlightened managers see the value of an interchange of ideas among professionals working in the same field. Such people should be encouraged to network, to attend conferences, and to join professional associations.

- *Innovators should be allowed to select*

their own projects whenever possible. Creative people produce better results if they can identify with the project they are given to tackle.

- *Establish challenging assignments.* Creative individuals are too hamstrung when tied to tried-and-proven concepts. They thrive on adventure and experimentation.

- *Acknowledge individual achievement.* Many innovators are 'loners', rather than team players, and are often encouraged more by individual accolades rather than praise directed at a team's achievements.

6 Reward usable ideas.

3M stages its own annual Oscars night when, with considerable fanfare, several of its creative staff are honoured by peers. Devise strategies for acknowledging and rewarding your staff members for their creative contributions. In this way, others will also be encouraged to provide input.

7 Set aside time for creative thinking.

Remember that most ideas do not come in a flash of inspiration, but rather in a lather of perspiration. Focus meetings, brainstorming sessions, and think-tanks in relaxed settings—these are often the sources of the best creative ideas. As manager, you are in a position to remove the weight of everyday, routine duties and to set regular time aside for such creative activity.

✔ it's a fact

In 1853, George Crum, an American chef, was furious when his customers sent back his chips. They were 'too thick', they complained. In retaliation, the angry chef sliced them as thin as he possibly could and then returned them to the table. The customers loved them! The potato crisp was born!

In 1904, an American street-vendor, Anton Feuchtwanger, couldn't afford plates for his cooked frankfurters – so he stuck them in a breadroll instead and served them with a slash of sauce. The American hotdog was born!

■ There are innovative people everywhere, and often they need only to be gently nudged to display their creativity.

❝ quotable quote

William McKnight, who helped turn a failed corundum mine into a flourishing grinding-wheel business that grew into 3M [creators of such simple innovations as sticky tape, sandpaper, and those little yellow 'stick-it' slips], told his colleagues:

"Listen to anyone with an original idea, no matter how absurd it might sound at first. Encourage; don't nitpick. Let people run with an idea. Hire good people, and leave them alone. If you put fences around people, you get sheep. Give people the room that they need. Encourage experimental doodling. Give it a try – and quick." [18]

379

How to get staff to read material that matters

Research shows that independent reading of manuals, books, trade journals, and other professional literature remains the most fundamental, reliable, and efficient way of keeping up to date professionally. Unfortunately, many of us are reluctant readers. As a manager, you can use several strategies to promote systematic reading habits in your staff members. In so doing, you will contribute to their personal development and to the advancement of your organisation...

Work towards bringing about a change in attitude to reading.

Reading is essential for personal and professional development. Reading expands our interests; introduces new and challenging subjects; and exposes us to the latest ideas, trends, and issues in our field. As a manager, your main contribution will be to foster a positive attitude among staff towards reading for their own benefit and for the advancement of the organisation.

Encourage staff to set aside time for reading.

The time devoted to reading is a measure of its value to the employee and to the manager. The usual excuse for not doing more professional reading is that people simply 'don't have the time'. So the way around this is to make sure that appropriate reading material—journals, books, manuals, policy documents, handbooks, references—is readily accessible *and* that time is set aside for reading it. The question is whether you are able or sufficiently motivated,

to find ways of doing this.

Urge employees to be discriminating readers.

If your staff can't find the time to read sufficiently, a solution could be to trim from their reading focus the unwanted and unnecessary reading matter that currently swamps the marketplace. This selection process can be accomplished as follows:

1. Determine those areas of interest so important to the work task that these must, and can only, be explored in depth and thoughtfully.

2. Determine those developments and ideas that must be kept up with on a broad and less intensive basis.

3. Compile and consider two lists of journals and books which cater for your specified interests in 1 and 2 above.

4. Decide what *minimum* combination of those journals and books will best serve your needs in these two areas and focus on them only.

Establish a staff library.

Most employees, if left to their own initiative, are unlikely to purchase or subscribe personally to professional or trade literature. You can combat this reluctance by setting aside a small budget to maintain and upgrade a reading resource centre within your organisation.

 Adopt a variety of strategies.

Be proactive in your approach to fostering positive staff reading habits. Consider these ideas:

- Locate reading materials centrally.
- Establish a staff committee to select and purchase materials for the library.
- Scan items of interest to particular staff and distribute those.
- Display details of useful items on staff bulletin boards.
- Set aside time at staff meetings to discuss useful articles and ideas.
- Delegate some of your own essential reading to staff members to summarise and report back to you—or to a staff meeting.
- Acknowledge those staff members who initiate discussions on issues or topics of interest.

 Target the young employee.

Research reveals that young employees do not read the available literature as frequently as their older colleagues. Make a special effort to engender a respect for the literature in these younger employees.

 Advise publishers of your organisation's needs.

Many journals do not always give readers the information they want. Often we must read so much to find anything of real value that we end up turning away from the literature. Tell the publishers what you want. They want to know.

 Encourage staff to write for publications.

Encourage your staff members to get involved in writing for publications—even if it's only your company's newsletter. An enthusiastic involvement in this type of activity not only advances an employee's personal development and profile, but also raises the status of periodical literature in the eyes of the employee and his or her colleagues.

Set the example yourself.

Once upon a time there was a manager who had three basic rules for employees wishing to see him in his office. 'If I'm on the phone,' he declared, 'wait until you hear me put down the receiver, then come in. If I'm poring over paperwork, knock and enter. But if I've pulled out my bottom drawer, I've got my feet up, and I'm reading my latest trade journal, come back later!'

Here was a manager who valued (perhaps over-valued) the importance of keeping up to date through professional reading. In what ways do you indicate to your staff the value you place on professional or trade literature?

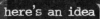 **quotable quote**

All professionals should be aware of the need for keeping up to date. We either progress or become obsolete. Growth is not easy; it takes work and discipline. Some people develop professionally by attending society meetings to learn the latest developments and to talk with able professionals. It is not practical, however, to attend all meetings of interest and there is not enough time to talk to all the capable top people in one's fields of interests. Therefore, through the ages, people have relied on studying the written word as input to growing knowledge. People must read to grow.[19]

here's an idea

Urge your staff to squeeze in a little professional reading each day. If they do but 15 minutes daily, it will make itself felt at the end of a year.

 don't forget

Why we read

Reading of the professional and trade literature is of no real value unless we translate what we read into the workplace itself.

viewpoint

"The worst thing about new books is that they keep us from reading the old ones."

– Joseph Joubert

How to retain your best people

As managers, we're only as good as the people who work for us. One way of assuring our continued success is to attract—and retain—good people. But competition for top talent is fierce these days. Just hiring the best people for your organisation can be tough enough—but keeping those employees can be even tougher. How can you keep your top talent happy and have them ignore your competitors' recruiters or headhunters?

Identify and focus on your real achievers.

Have you determined which people are the most valuable to your organisation? Who can you count on daily to follow through on projects and deliver results? Make a list, but consider these timely tips:

- *Don't confuse activity with performance.* Those constantly on the phone, at the keyboard, calling meetings, or dashing about aren't necessarily producing—they may not be your thinkers, problem-solvers, or decision-makers.
- *Consider performance, not noise.* The quiet ones are not necessarily daydreamers—they may be too busy getting things done to talk too much.
- *Remember, doers come in all shapes and sizes.* Don't fall for stereotypes—the wiry or muscular type may not necessarily be action-oriented.

According to the US organisation development company Linkage Inc., 'the top one-third of your employees should receive ninety per cent of your retention attention—managers don't have the time or resources to lavish attention on everyone'.

The secret is to spend time with these key people so that you know what are their 'satisfiers'—the things that make them happy. In this way, if they ever contemplate leaving, you'll know what buttons to push to retain them.

Know why top quality people leave.

Your best workers change jobs for a reason—and it's rarely only for more money, more perks, or better benefits. Often they leave because their satisfiers are not being met in the current job. Consider the following:

- *I'm not appreciated.* 'I make a valuable contribution and I get no thanks. My talent will be appreciated elsewhere.'
- *I'm bored.* 'I want to be challenged, stretched, and tested so I can show off my talents, experience, and skills.'
- *I have no career prospects here.* 'I'm a cut above the rest but I can see no opportunity for advancement. I want a career, not just a job.'
- *I'm just a small cog in the overall machine.* 'I seek a sense of purpose, of contributing to something bigger than myself, and a sense of belonging.'
- *I want to get better.* 'Here I have limited opportunities for growth and the

development of new and valued skills.'

- *I want to work with winners.* 'Here standards are low and sloppiness is tolerated.'
- *I want to work for an insightful manager.* 'As a prized worker, I respond positively to good supervision.'

3 Develop a retention plan for each top employee.

Once you identify your best people and recognise that they have different needs or satsifiers, you must develop a strategy to show that you are intensely interested in them and their future with your organisation. You need to consider what you are willing to do to retain each key person; and begin to prepare individual retention plans that will help tie each key employee to the organisation.

Talk to these people in turn, asking them what they want from the organisation in the short and long term—'What will it take to keep you motivated and part of our organisational family?' From this employee-focused conversation comes a vulnerability report which leads to a retention plan. Reach agreement with each key employee on how to approach their needs through a concrete strategy for the future.

4 Work proactively to retain your best employees.

Personnel management advisor Robert Ramsey suggests that, 'as a frontline manager, your goal should be to do everything you can to hang on to good workers for as long as you can'. To encourage your prized employees to stick around, he recommends the following strategies:

- *Set challenging goals and reasonable deadlines.* Outstanding workers thrive on pressure.
- *Raise the bar.* Hold high expectations and don't be surprised if your workers live up to them.
- *Promote from within.* It's a powerful morale-booster.
- *Give full credit for achievement and effort.* Recognition is a reward in itself for workers who take pride in what they do. Be quick with praise.
- *Delegate authority.* Encourage key staff to take on added responsibilities.
- *Pay attention.* Listen. Act on employee suggestions.
- *Let workers participate in making decisions* that directly affect them.
- *Be committed to excellence.* Don't accept second-rate workmanship.
- *Preach, teach and practise teamwork.* Celebrate each other's success.
- *Be open, honest, and up-front.* Keep key employees informed—what's going on and coming up… both good and bad.
- *Encourage risk-taking and innovation.* Allow failure once in a while.
- *Set your workers up for success.* Be their advocate. Fight to get whatever they need to do their best work. You won't always win, but you'll engender a lot of worker loyalty in the process.
- *Encourage experienced workers to become mentors* for newcomers.
- *Shred the policy manual if possible.* Keep workplace rules few and simple. Key workers need challenge, opportunity and a vote of confidence, not more rules and regulations.
- *Promote life-long learning.* Make continuous growth your catchcry.
- *Cultivate organisational culture.* Build workplace values of hard work, fair play, honesty, and mutual respect.
- *Have fun at work.* If no one ever laughs while you're in charge, you might soon be joining your best employees in looking for another job!

here's an idea

In *Keeping Good People* (McGraw Hill, NY), Roger Hermann offers over 125 proven strategies that have been successfully implemented to hold talented staff. They include:

■ *Environmental strategies* that provide flexibility in working hours, offer freedom of choice in break times, dress and vacations, provide for child-care services, maintain comfortable atmospheric conditions, guarantee workplace safety, and in general make life on the job more pleasant for everybody.

■ *Relationship strategies* that can help resolve conflicts, facilitate more open communication, provide people with freedom and flexibility, reduce stress, and help build self-esteem.

■ *Task-focused strategies* that offer employees exciting challenges, encourage initiative, inspire creativity and innovation, and empower individuals to work as a team.

■ *Compensation strategies* that link performance to rewards, encourage employee involvement with the company, and utilise a flexible system of benefits to accommodate the changing needs of today's workers.

■ *People-growing strategies* that provide incentives for both personal and professional growth. These include in-house training, outside seminars, company-supported education, and the assignment of special projects that teach valuable new skills.

How to encourage and keep innovative people

The trouble with having innovative or entrepreneurial people in your organisation is that they're often the hardest to keep. They get frustrated with all those organisational rules, controls, and restrictions that dampen their creativity. And such frustration often leads to their departure to set up their own businesses. Can you afford to lose such talent? What can you do to foster and keep these internal entrepreneurs—or *intrapreneurs* as Gifford Pinchot termed them? Try adopting the following strategies…

read further

Intrapreneuring: Why you don't have to leave the corporation to become an entrepreneur by Gifford Pinchot III, Harper & Row, NY, 1985.

 Let them select themselves.

Management cannot appoint an employee to become an intrapreneur, tell him or her to become passionately committed to an idea, and then expect success. Instead, look at every level for intrapreneurs with ideas—not just for ideas alone, because an idea without someone passionate about it becomes sterile. Find these people, then empower them to follow their dream. And if *you* have a bright idea, but not the time to carry it through, expose potential intrapreneurs to it and see who begins building on it and making it his or her own. In other words, it will pay to go the extra distance if you can locate self-appointed intrapreneurs.

 Keep them on the job from go to whoa.

Unfortunately, in many large organisations, new ideas are handed from group to group during the course of development. We often forget that intrapreneurs become dedicated to an idea and that this commitment is the primary force behind successful innovation. By all means involve other people, but remember, with each hand over, it is likely that a less dedicated person will become involved and the intrapreneur will drop a notch in enthusiasm. You must find ways of keeping your intrapreneur fired up, and on the job from start to finish.

 Let them get on with the job.

An intrapreneur's job is to create a vision of a new business reality and to make it happen. The major problem with many large organisations is not that they block the vision but, rather, they block the action. So, are the innovators in your organisation permitted to do the job in their own way, or are they constantly having to stop to explain their actions and ask for permission? Are you willing to allow them to make decisions and take action themselves? As Pinchot writes: 'To make intrapreneuring work, intrapreneurs need the power to make decisions and take action.'

Provide enough rope.

Company resources are usually committed to what is planned and nothing is left over for trying the unplannable. But innovation is inherently unplannable. Intrapreneurs need discretionary resources—funds, people, time, materials—to explore and develop their ideas. If you put a tight lid on the money bucket so that nothing is available for the new and unexpected, the result will be nothing new, and you'll end up with a creative and very frustrated employee.

 Be tolerant of risk-taking and failure.

You can't innovate if you don't take risks. In organisations that succeed with innovation—and retain their creative people—a tolerance for blunders, false starts, and failure is built deeply into the everyday activities of the company.

 Be patient.

One of the drawbacks of innovation is that it takes time. So, once you've decided to try something new, the challenge for you will be to stick with the experiment long enough to see if it will work, even when it may take several years and several false starts and many hiccups on the way. Intrapreneurs require more patient support than they generally receive.

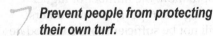 **Prevent people from protecting their own turf.**

Because new ideas almost always cross internal organisational boundaries—e.g. research, personnel, finance, marketing departments—the potential for people to protect their own interests and territory exists. 'Turfiness' blocks innovation. Pinchot elaborates:

> Innovation is not like a relay race in which an idea can be handed off from runner to runner. In many large organisations new ideas are handed from group to group during the course of development. It is a natural mistake. Systems of this kind almost never work for two reasons: one, a fact of human nature [The commitment and enthusiasm of the dedicated intrapreneur wanes with each hand over]; the other, a consequence of information theory [When an idea is handed off to someone else, most of the information the first intrapreneur has gathered is lost].[21]

Your challenge is to find ways to allow your intrapreneurs to travel with their ideas across territories, and to get everyone involved to value innovation more than politics.

 And remember...

To take full advantage of the innovative streak that may be lying dormant in your organisation:

- Make sure your company's vision for the future is clearly understood by all staff so that your intrapreneurs can work on creating innovative ideas that relate directly to the strategy of your company.
- Make it known that the greatest opportunity in your organisation lies in becoming an intrapreneur.
- Replace red tape with responsibility.
- Reward intrapreneurs with new career paths that fit their needs.
- Know your innovative people and nurture them—or lose them.

 viewpoint

"When all corporate resources are committed to what is planned, nothing is left for trying the unplannable. Yet innovation is inherently unplannable. Companies that successfully innovate empower their employees to use corporate resources in ways that cannot always be predicted or justified."

– Gifford Pinchot III in *Intrapreneuring*

❝❝ quotable quote

Intrapreneurs don't stand on ceremony or have standards about what sorts of work are beneath them. They do the mundane work that is part of every new project. Unlike managers, whose job is largely to delegate, intrapreneurs can often do things faster by doing them themselves. This tendency to prefer hands-on work gets the job done and helps intrapreneurs to stay quite literally in touch with all aspects of their intraprise. Their ability to make quick decisions and, when necessary, to consider sweeping changes of plan in terms of their impact on all aspects of the business depends on their being in touch.[23]

How to help an employee whose career has plateaued

Plateauing or coasting is a normal and familiar phase in many careers. Usually in mid-career, employees (and managers) can experience a levelling-out of their progress as a result of downsizing, restructuring, mergers, alliances, or plain boredom. Previously high-achievers seem to lose their zest, sparkle, and enthusiasm. They become disenchanted and frustrated. Over time, their morale and productivity decline. Here's how you can help to revitalise the career of an employee stuck in a rut …

1 Understand why people plateau.

Plateauing can occur for several reasons:

- There are too few jobs to satisfy the number of competitors for those jobs. Those who miss out feel 'dead-ended'.
- The employee's ability does not match the job—lack of skills and aptitude, or an inability to respond to changing job requirements.
- Some are faced with the so-called 'mid-life crisis'; or a sense of being trapped in an ill-chosen career choice.
- Some feel betrayed after having rejected other worthwhile life roles in favour of their current career.
- The extension—even abolition—of the mandatory retirement age results in some older workers becoming 'trapped' in upper-level positions.
- Increasing numbers of younger, highly-qualified employees progress too rapidly up the corporate ladder—only to be frustrated by a period of career stagnation.

Employees, too, can contribute to their own plateauing by:

- being less active than others in adapting to change
- displaying an inflated opinion of their actual work performance
- showing little interest in understanding their boss's problem
- being unwilling to improve their work performance.

2 Be aware of the social and economic impact.

Lay-offs, mergers, and other cutbacks in staff contribute to plateauing. High unemployment, too, has reduced outside options for employees: they become stay-put and plateaued. The two-income family may also mean that the employee may not be able to afford to transfer to other employment. Fewer jobs through the removal of layers of management through restructuring and downsizing has also resulted in more plateauing.

The 'baby boomers'—those born between 1946 and 1964—account for a major proportion of our working population; the number of higher management positions and others will not be sufficient to accommodate them. As a result, 'baby boomers' will have to adjust their expectation—

usually downwards. No longer will a university degree (or two) guarantee advancement—or even a job.

3. Be proactive in dealing with the phenomenon.

Although you may feel inadequate in dealing with this corporate phenomenon, ignoring it won't make it disappear. Alternatively, you can take a tough stance and demand greater productivity, an approach that will not work in most authentic cases. Or you can try to be understanding and offer assistance by considering one or more of the following options:

- *Help individual employees recognise that plateauing is a normal occurrence.* Honest feedback can send clear signals to employees that their activities are important and that you are prepared to provide support to assist them over this period.

- *Reduce the focus on promotion as a major indicator of success.* Where reduced promotional opportunities lie at the cause of employee plateauing, organisations can emphasise alternative ways by which success can be measured—
  - ☐ Provide opportunities for greater participation in setting goals and determining methods and procedures. Plateaued employees usually have a wealth of experience for the organisation to draw upon.
  - ☐ Assign the staffer to train new employees and bring others up to speed.
  - ☐ Devise a major project for the worker, with full autonomy, to show your trust and to provide

new zest.
  - ☐ Since plateaued employees are often bored, ensure they are given useful activities; avoid assigning duties and responsibilities that are clearly beneath them, just to keep them occupied.

- *Change the structure of the organisation.* Make modifications to create a more horizontal structure and establish additional responsible positions.

- *Consider lateral promotions.* If demoralised workers have little chance of promotion in your area, their skills and talents may be valuable in another area.

- *Seek the employee's input.* Explore with the individual how the current job can be made more stimulating, without overstepping current parameters.

- *Provide specialist, qualified counselling.* Where necessary, this will help them overcome individual crises associated with career plateauing.

4. Don't pamper the employee.

Maintain your high standards. By all means be supportive of the plateaued worker, but resist the temptation to let those employees coast for a while, hoping that they'll lift their game after the crisis passes. By ignoring the problem, you could be sending the message that you don't care whether a job is done well. This might translate into 'You have no future around here any more!' And that message will exacerbate the problem even further.

here's an idea

One approach to motivate plateaued personnel or coasters is to provide them with challenges – projects they can really 'sink their teeth into'.

Realistically, though, not everyone gets excited by challenges. Some people with a challenge, turn away from it – it's too much trouble. But for those who enjoy a challenging assignment, it can be a powerful motivator. For example:

- Make the coaster a mentor to a new team member.
- Assign special assignments, which frequently inject new enthusiasm that carries over into regular work.
- Involve them in the planning process.[25]

read further

Midlife Moves: Taking Charge of Your Future, Susie Linder-Pelz, Allen & Unwin, Sydney, 1993.

Understanding Men's Passages: Discovering The New Map Of Men's Lives, Gail Sheehy, Random House, 1996.

quotable quote

One of the features of a mid-life crisis is trouble in coming to grips with the new situation in which one finds oneself. The world we once knew is no longer there. As a result, our habitual ways of dealing with the world are no longer adequate.[26]

How to help older employees stay valuable

Older employees represent a valuable resource: they possess experience, know-how, and seasoned judgement. But many become less enthusiastic as their careers draw to a close. Indeed, they often feel threatened in an age of youth, technology, and redundancy. Age-discrimination protection measures, however, have forced most employers to be more aware of the issue. A few pointers will help you to consider your situation...

1 Review your attitude towards the older employee.

It's so easy to regard our older employees negatively—we stereotype them as less productive, less likely to keep up with new developments and technologies, less flexible, more difficult to supervise and train, more resistant to change, more likely to miss work for health reasons, less enthusiastic... Often we reinforce these attitudes by being indifferent towards them. But if you adopt this stance, you are in fact creating a liability your organisation cannot afford.

Indeed, research by Multi-Health Systems Inc. has found that older people are generally better able to cope with demands and pressures than younger people. Moreover, older people are:

- more independent in their thinking and actions
- more aware of others' feelings
- more socially responsible
- more adaptable
- better at sizing up the immediate situation and solving problems

- able to manage stress better than younger people.

The researchers concluded:

Our findings underscore that it is not only wrong to discriminate against older people in the workplace, but it doesn't make any sense as far as emotional intelligence is concerned.

Seniors *are* a valuable resource—if you treat them as such.

2 Explore a range of policies and practices.

According to Bob Rosner of Working Wounded, two-thirds of US companies say they are not actively recruiting older workers for regular jobs and almost half aren't trying to retain older workers. As well, 81 per cent aren't offering any provisions or benefits designed specifically with older workers in mind.

Rosner concludes: 'If older workers aren't being ignored, they're being discarded. And they're filing age discrimination suits in record numbers.'[27]

For this reason alone, ensure your company policy includes statements to the effect that older employees are valued members of your organisation. Adopt flexible working arrangements, such as job rotation, job sharing, part-time work, flexitime, or using older workers as independent consultants. These options to the working day of older employees can save you money by reducing turnover, and replacement and retraining costs— and help to re-enthuse older workers and maximise the use of their abilities.

3 Consider adding to the older worker's responsibilities.

Revitalise the motivation of older employees by dangling new challenges in front of them. Expand their work role. Provide them with new responsibilities and tasks. Often it will be in the area of leadership that they can shine. In general, older employees can be expected to assume control, delegate, and make the bulk of decisions themselves. In fact, it is not uncommon to find that Generation Xers and Yers appreciate such a take-charge attitude. Delegate, not abrogate, leadership responsibilities to this group.

4 Try changing the employee's job completely.

If given the choice of remaining in the same comfortable routine until retirement or of experiencing a completely new role, senior employees often prefer to go out in glory. A couple of years in a new position or on a special project where their experience and knowledge can be better used does wonders for their enthusiasm and self-esteem.

5 Use the employee's experience and knowledge.

Old-timers can always draw on their long experience with your organis-ation to become valuable members of task forces or committees. The stimulation and pressure of working with younger colleagues in such groups often enable your organisation to tap into a dormant goldmine.

6 Set goals with the employee.

A session with an older employee to set personal goals for his or her remaining few years can spur the senior to greater productivity. Ensure that the goals are practical and satisfy both the individual's and the company's needs; that they are specific within preset time limits; that they are attainable; and that they are challenging. Older workers should not be left to feel that they have been 'pushed aside'.

7 Prevent obsolescence through training.

It is short-sighted to see training as the sole province of younger workers. Training can enhance the older workers' productivity considerably, enabling the company to reap the benefits for several years to come.

8 Provide counselling.

As employees approach career's end, and you want to relieve their pre-retirement anxiety, offer to provide counselling on financial, health, social security, and recreational matters.

research says

According to PricewaterhouseCoopers, more and more people could be going back to work in their 60s and 70s, not because they need the money but because bosses will need staff. Employers will need to change their attitudes towards older workers.

Early baby boomers (post WWII babies) will begin leaving the workforce in large numbers in 2006 when they start turning 60. By 2010 they will all be over the age of 60, leaving a shrinking pool of taxpayers to subsidise the age pension and health care system. Accordingly, it is inevitable we'll see an increase in retirement age and/or a growing number of 60-somethings remaining or back in the workforce, whether it be in a full-time or part-time capacity.

it's a fact

In August 2002, one of Australia's largest banks recruited 900 'older' Australians as investment advisers who, according to the then CEO of the Bank of Melbourne (owned by Westpac) Ann Sherry, 'know the difference between good service and bad service.' Sherry indicated that she was inundated with inquiries about the jobs.[29]

How to manage the generations in your workplace

Organisations worldwide have become cross-generational workplaces with Baby Boomers (born 1946-64), a few older Veterans/Builders, Generation Xers (1965–80), Gen Yers (Millenials, 1981-96) and, increasingly, Generation Zers (1997-2009) all possibly represented. Managed well and without stereotyping, this generational diversity can enrich the workplace. But it can also challenge and frustrate managers striving to derive maximum productivity from all employees. Irrespective of your vintage, here are some suggestions to improve the approaches you adopt...

don't forget

How to nurture your generations...

In *Generations At Work*, Ron Zemke and others identified five common approaches (ACORN) that organisations must nurture in a generationally friendly and productive workplace:

Accommodate employee differences. Treat employees as you would customers. Find out everything you can about them, work to meet their specific needs, and serve them according to their unique preferences.

Create workplace choices. Shape the workplace around what it does, whom it serves, and the people it employs.

Operate from a sophisticated management style. Give those who report to you the big picture; specific goals and measures; empowerment to complete the task; and feedback, rewards, and recognition as warranted.

Respect competence and initiative. Assume the best of your people, treating everyone as if they have a great deal to offer and are motivated to do their best.

Nourish retention. Make your work environments a place where people want to be.[30]

Familiarise yourself with generations' characteristics.

Veterans. Although most of this group may have retired, their presence—particularly at the top of the corporate ladder and as customers—demands that you learn to work with them.

Baby Boomers. These are characterised by ambition, loyalty, and employment for life—usually in the one company. They believe in process: that there is a right way of doing things to achieve the desired outcome. Their attitudes toward the office, family, and themselves, have unquestionably shaped the workplace as we know it.

GenXers, the children of those who were too young to fight in World War II, were the first to experience the major consequences of the social revolution known as women's liberation. Xers 'work to live', not 'live to work'.

GenYers, (Millennials), born in the 1980s-90s and known as the Internet generation, have been surrounded by digital technologies. They require challenging work, flexibility, training and learning opportunities, and a low stress workplace.

 Communicate to all groups.

Ignoring generational difference will not work. Take time to communicate with the different groups, indicating your understanding of each generation's idiosyncrasies—values, icons, and language. This will involve considerable research on your part. There is no short cut. Xers, the major grouping, for example, have been brought up with email and respond positively to memos with bullet points. Xers usually see the most well-intentioned pep talks—the ones that can work so well for Baby Boomers—as insincere. Xers place value on office layout, the quality of technology, and more-relaxed dress codes.

 Earn their trust and respect.

Baby Boomers were taught to respect their elders. GenXers came of age during the scandals of Watergate, the Iran-Contra, and soaring divorce rates. GenYers were raised on the Clinton-Lewinsky 'soapie'. Xers have also observed that work is no guarantee of survival: termination can happen without warning, logic, or apology. Don't tell groups to respect you—give them reasons why they should.

Set clear expectations.

Many Xers were raised in single-parent households and have learnt to rely on themselves. Let them come to you with questions, rather than micromanaging them. *Forbes Magazine* labelled Gen X 'the most entrepreneurial generation in American history.' GenYers have received abundant encouragement to enable their achievement-orientation. Give them the task; explain the outcome you are seeking; provide the wherewithal required to achieve the outcome; then get out of the way and let them get on with it!

 Demonstrate flexibility in your workplace.

For GenXers and GenYers, flexibility is more than work hours, relaxed dress codes, and the right amount of supervision. It means you'll need to:

- Increase the levels of autonomy when people demonstrate their readiness for it.
- Vary your leadership style according to the situation.
- Rely more on personal power than positional power.
- Adapt or change policies when better options become clear.
- Manage individuals into teams for particular assignments.
- Demonstrate a balance between a concern for people and a concern for task.
- Work at gaining employees' trust.

 Ensure up-to-date technology.

GenXers and GenYers, reared on video games and computers, consider that having the best technology available on their desk is as good as having a corner office. GenYers are even more technically adept: technology has permeated their education and recreation.

 Provide consistent feedback.

All generational groups want honest, constructive feedback. For example, Xers want to hear from you almost daily about how they can do better—some authorities suggesting the lack of attention they received in their formative years as a reason for this.

 Provide appropriate recognition.

Many Xers resent the more visible, expensive recognition that Baby Boomers usually respond positively to. GenYers generally have greater idealism than Xers. Both groups value support for their personal and professional development, even if their personal development does not seem to be directly related to the work context.

 Remain in touch.

Research tells us that many Xers change jobs regularly. So if you're affected by such staff changes, don't burn any bridges. If (or when) a good Xer leaves, stay in touch. Send occasional emails, seek advice about issues of succession, and keep him or her informed about new positions you have available. The next time an Xer moves on, it could be back to your organisation. The single best source of good new employees can be former employees.

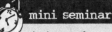 **mini seminar**

A picture often painted of Baby Boomers is of rebels, challenging society, willing to change, and to adapt. What has not been documented as much is that Baby Boomers could afford to do this because of the security blanket of full employment, guaranteed promotion, and a more secure family structure – the best of all possible worlds.

Is this interpretation accurate? How does it affect the way Gens X and Y relate to Baby Boomer workmates?

 research says

GenYers have been labelled as disloyal and non-committal workers, but leading demographers believe GenY may be the answer to the problems caused by the ageing Baby Boomer workplace. For advice on recruiting and retraining GenYers visit www.governmentnews.com.au and search in the search box for 'Managing Gen Y workforce'.

 read further

Bridging the Boomer-Xer Gap, Hank Karp, Connie Fuller, Danilo Sirias, Palo Alto, Davies-Black, 2002.

Generations At Work, Ron Zemke, Claire Raines, Bob Filipczak, Performance Research Associates, 2001.

Not Everyone Gets a Trophy: How to manage Generation Y, Bruce Tulgan, Jossey-Bass, 2009.

How to help your staff overcome complacency

Most people prefer things to continue the same old predictable way. If change is to take place, such people will probably argue that it should happen at some later date—when their routines will not be affected. Such complacency needs to be transformed into a sense of urgency. Otherwise your organisation will stagnate and you won't get the staff support you need to make changes. You can overcome staff complacency if you…

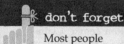
1 Set high performance standards.

Does your staff have enough to do? They may appear to be complacent, but it could simply be that they are content to cruise, given the amount of work they have. Never accept low performance standards. Set and check productivity, revenue, sales, and other performance targets, and set them so high that staff cannot afford to rest on their laurels. Goal-setting literature often places too much attention on words like 'achievable' and 'realistic'; these words have been interpreted by some employees as suggesting a 'softer' approach to performance standards. Your organisation's standards must encourage all employees to extend themselves.

2 Insist on S-T-R-E-T-C-H goals.

It's not hard for employees to accomplish goals expressed in easily 'achievable' terms—such as 'contact five new customers each day'. Avoid statements of *minimum* acceptable competence; these soon become accepted as *maximum* standards. Make sure that *you* have a say in what are acceptable goals. You will find that employees will appreciate your involvement.

3 Make employees accountable.

The success of the entire organisation should be the aim of all employees. Even if your staff have become used to focusing on their own individual divisions or departments—almost as if their area is all that matters—encourage them to think in terms of being accountable to the wider organisation. If the organisation prospers, they too will share in the recognition.

4 Share external feedback.

Employees need feedback of all kinds, not only from satisfied customers but also from dissatisfied clients, angry stockholders, and frustrated suppliers. If the only feedback they receive is 'good news', they may consider complacency acceptable behaviour.

Encourage honest discussion.

Employees sometimes fear that honest disclosure of information will not be well-received if the news is 'bad'. You can't afford *not* to encourage open and honest discussion of problems. You should come down heavily on those attempting to conceal such information.

 Adopt a 'What's next?' attitude.

Encourage your staff to be constantly on the lookout for opportunities. And if every opportunity is not grasped, or if things don't fall into place as one would hope, don't linger, lament, or engage in unproductive analysis. It is far better to ask, 'What's next?' and move on to the next opportunity.

 Go beyond a track record.

Don't use, or let your employees use, their past accomplishments or credentials to justify their current complacency. Often these are used by employees as an excuse to rest on their laurels and to continue to receive special treatment by the organisation. The only way you can justify special treatment is by rewarding current productivity, as measured by quantity and quality.

Be careful not to let the pursuit of quality blind you to a dip in quantity. Of course, this cannot be an ironclad rule, since occasionally staff may be working on an unusually complex task. But as a general rule insist that

goals and quotas be met—otherwise those employees who *are* producing a greater quantity of work may become resentful.

 Remove unhealthy messages.

If your organisation has all the outward signals of success—lavish parties, boardroom bashes, and other events that convey the wrong messages—employees can't be expected to be overly concerned about the organisation's future. Limit these obvious examples of excess. Communicate to employees instead the messages that will encourage them to lift their game.

 Find or invent a crisis.

If the organisation isn't losing money, or no lay-offs are on the horizon, employees don't see any visible threats—and thus might not feel any sense of urgency. If there isn't a crisis—create one, even a minor one. You'll find that crises help people to regain (or retain) their focus.

 Look to the future.

Focusing on past successes may serve some purpose, for example, when you're coping with a one-off rejection. You should not, however, dwell on past glories for too long. What you focus on grows; so concentrate on working towards the future and not on something that's history.

 here's an idea

Perhaps your employees are no longer quite clear about what you or the organisation expects of them. If so, and if it has been quite some time since you clarified your expectations and standards, maybe now is the time. In this way you attack the foundations of complacency by depriving employees of the excuse that they didn't know what you require of them.

 it's a fact

In the early 1980s, Coca-Cola's Robert Goizueta famously challenged his staff to stop thinking about Coke's 35% share of the soft-drink market, and to remember instead that people drank 64 fluid ounces of liquid a day – and only two of those were Coke.

Internal complacency has been identified as the main reason why companies stop growing.[32]

 viewpoint

"Management's principal job is to keep the herd heading roughly west."

– Peters & Waterman in *In Search of Excellence*

 don't forget

Even if you are on the right track, you will get run over if you just sit there.

393

How to improve the performance of your personal assistant

Your personal assistant—perhaps known as your professional assistant, or secretary, or executive assistant—can be the key operative in any manager's office. If highly trained in all aspects of office supervision, communication, human relations, and organisation, as well as in the basic skills of paper management and keyboarding, the personal assistant can be a true professional and your most valuable asset. To form a very effective team of two, consider the following…

Know what your assistant can and should do.

Today's top personal assistants must be as familiar with the management of people as they once were with paper and keyboard. Of course, core skills are still required—keyboarding, filing, telephone, screening of calls, mail and visitors, appointments and paperwork—but, the higher level assistants are called upon to display more sophisticated skills—composing letters, summarising reports and articles, supervising others and the office, scheduling your day, standing in for you at meetings, managing your calendar, tracking your jobs, and keeping you up to speed.

Good personal assistants are usually described as—helpful, hard-working, courteous, reliable, loyal, respectful, imaginative, level-headed, creative, resourceful, and efficient.

Do you really know where your personal assistant's strengths lie and what you want from the partnership? Take the time to sit with your assistant, to clarify expectations based on shared needs and goals, and to

determine what steps are required to forge a quality team of two.

Meet daily to plan your day.

To minimise interruptions throughout the day, set aside time each morning to organise the day for you both—checking assignments, appointments and priorities, clarifying tasks, processing paper, discussing problems. A five-minute wrap-up session at the end of the day is also useful to assist planning for the next day.

Keep your assistant—and yourself—informed.

The more your assistant knows what you're doing, where you're going, when you'll be back, what's behind this memo, why this is important, and what your plans, goals and projects are, the more they will be able to help you and handle their own priorities. By demonstrating confidence in your assistant in this way, you'll be surprised what you learn in return. Assistants, being hooked into the office grapevine, often know more about what's going on than their bosses do. Use them as sounding boards, and the feedback you get may prove invaluable.

4 Show you care about your assistant's welfare.

If you want to build trust and loyalty, cultivate a little sensitivity and thoughtfulness. Make the role easier by being organised yourself; when routine tasks pile up, or when the assistant is undertaking a time-consuming higher-level task, bring in a temp to help out; keep your assistant advised of your whereabouts; ask for suggestions on how you can help by becoming more effective yourself. Do something special whenever you can —cards, awards, lunch, or a surprise gift. Like all other key members of the team, personal assistants appreciate recognition and acknowledgement when jobs are well done.

5 Share the blame and the credit.

Shoulder the responsibility for a mistake or share it with your personal assistant. If the assistant is responsible for the problem, discuss it privately and offer positive suggestions for improvement. Never complain about performance or criticise in public. Always focus on what is right, rather than who is right. Your tact and support in times of crisis will be reciprocated down the track. Give credit where credit is due. Let everyone know when your assistant has done a job well or come up with that great idea. Bask in the reflected glory.

6 Work as a team.

Foster the belief that you are both working as a team to make the office, and the organisation, a more effective and efficient enterprise. Let others know that your assistant has your complete confidence and that it's likely they'll get a faster response by working directly with the assistant on routine matters. This is one reason why your early morning session to co-ordinate appointments, meetings, reminders, paperwork, and other matters is so important.

7 Help your personal assistant grow.

Managers are frequently guilty of over-management. Consider those jobs you currently handle which could just as effectively be undertaken by your personal assistant. Take time to train your assistant to do them— and then let go. Show an interest in the employee's further education. Encourage the undertaking of further studies and courses, and involvement in professional associations. Provide moral and financial support where possible.

8 Practise job enlargement.

Over time, by selectively and patiently adding to the raft of responsibilities, you will add greatly to your assistant's job satisfaction, especially as the need for those time-consuming, less skilful tasks reduces. But remember, greater responsibility also requires greater compensation.

don't forget

The importance of delegating…

Your administrative assistant can save you time in these key areas:

Information. Let your assistant, in charge of files, become your 'information manager', and pass it to and from you.

Mail. Let your assistant open it, record it, discard the worthless, answer the routine, and pass the rest on to you.

People. Let him/her make appointments and take messages.

Telephone calls. Have your assistant screen incoming calls and, if possible, handle routine calls on your behalf.

Meetings. Have him/her draft agendas, take and distribute minutes, and follow-up on tasks generated.

Correspondence. Your assistant can prepare routine correspondence for you.

Schedule. Let him/her take charge of your schedule. Let others make claims on your time through him/her.

Paper. Get paper off your desk and on to your assistant's.

Dollars. Allow your assistant to handle routine purchase requests, budget correspondence, and basic financial paperwork.[34]

395

How to get the most out of temps

Temps (temporary employees) have become regular features of today's workforce, filling in for permanent employees who might be unwell, on leave, attending to a family emergency, or involved in education or training. Most temps arrive and are expected to hit the ground running, causing minimal disruption to everyday operations. But rarely can they do so. Here's how you can get better value from your investment in temps…

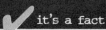
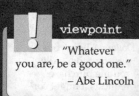
Prepare in advance.

If you know that the services of a temp will be required, start making enquiries so that a meeting can be arranged between the people involved. Consider this meeting as a one-on-one induction so that the temp will be able to hit the ground running on his or her first day. Arrange for the permanent employee to have uninterrupted time out with the temp. If a meeting between both people is not possible, ensure that the permanent employee leaves adequate descriptions of the tasks to be completed. If your organisation is IS9000 certified, procedures manuals and other relevant documents should be made available.

Delegate responsibility for employing temps.

It is unlikely that you will want to get involved in the process of appointing a temp. Ideally, the responsibility could be delegated to the person for whom the replacement is being organised or you may assign the responsibility for hiring temps to one person. If you use temps on a regular basis, it will be in your best interests to have a workable procedure in place for this activity.

Use an agency.

Unless you have an arrangement with a person who serves regularly as a temp in your organisation and with whom the organisation liaises directly, it is a sound practice to enlist the support of an agency. Those organisations have a larger pool to select from and have a replacement guarantee if you are not satisfied with a particular temp allocated. Any concerns you have about the temp can be communicated directly to the agency which, in turn, will inform the temp. In addition, if the temp needs to take time out for any reason, a replacement is forthcoming.

Select an agency that has relevant industry experience, understands your needs precisely, follows a code of conduct, provides ongoing support, and contracts its temps formally.

When you choose an agency carefully, the time saved by using their services will more than make up for the fee levied.

 Make it a habit to use temps.

Permanent staff do not object to filling in for colleagues for the occasional crisis. In fact, this practice can be morale-boosting as people pull together in the interests of the organisation. Employees, however, soon tire of regularly taking on the extra work load, such as when a colleague goes on annual leave. The person taking leave should not be made to feel that, by exercising his or her right to annual leave, it places additional burdens on colleagues. In addition, hiring a temp to fill in for someone going on leave is an outward sign of the importance you place on the employee and his or her position.

 Prepare a mini-induction.

If a more formal and relaxed induction is not possible before the temp arrives at work, have a mini-induction kit available. The kit might consist of:

- a signed letter of welcome
- a floor or office plan including kitchen, amenities, photocopying, emergency exits…
- copies of other documents – procedures manual, emergency evacuation procedures, emergency numbers, policies concerning office protocols, dress codes…
- a list of key internal extension numbers
- the names of those people with whom they can expect to be in regular contact.

In other words, give the temp all the need-to-know information but avoid overwhelming the new arrival with nice-to-know details. Set time aside later in the week for the temp to return with a list of questions he or she may have after spending time in the organisation.

 Emphasise the importance of customer service.

Your customers are not concerned about the status of the person with whom they are dealing. They expect the same high-quality standard of service from everyone associated with your organisation. So, for a temp with a customer contact role, pay particular attention to clarifying your expectations in this area. Keep in mind also that employees won't treat customers any better than they themselves are treated; do everything you can to make the temp feel a member of a fully functioning team.

 Consider temps as potential recruits.

Many temps, particularly those re-entering the workforce, use their positions to check out suitable places in which to seek permanency. Conversely, you can assess a temp's potential as a full-time employee. Having seen the way that a temp fits into your organisation, you might wish to broach the issue with the person before discussing the matter further with the employment agency. Clearly, temping is an arrangement that can have far-reaching benefits for all concerned.

 it's a fact

Temps are not put on your payroll. Your company pays the temp agency a fee for each employee, and the agency pays the workers. Although this fee is higher than the amount you would pay a regular employee, it is cost effective because you pay no benefits to temps and you also eliminate the high cost of recruiting for a short duration job. Because most temps are trained in office skills, the only training they need is to learn the specifics of your work assignment.[35]

 here's an idea

Temps talk. For this reason, they can become valuable sources of advertising in the marketplace – providing, of course, that you nurture your key message with them during their time with you.

here's an idea

It's not a bad idea to ask temps about other organisations in which they have worked. This serves a two-fold purpose. Firstly, the sort of information they provide will give you an indication of the detail and job instruction you, or your nominee, will need to provide while they are working in your employ. Secondly, their previous experience may furnish your organisation with some useful ideas on how to function more effectively.

How to weigh up the benefits of starting a volunteers' program

Most people have experience as volunteers—in social action groups, on school committees, with environment protection agencies, or emergency services groups, or community arts associations, or in major events such as the Olympic Games. With such personal experience, people often assume that all volunteer programs are successful and easy to manage and should feature more prominently in community and organisational life. Although many volunteer programs have impressive records, others are less successful. Before embarking on this potentially demanding management strategy, consider these points…

Dispel the myths about volunteering.

Be aware that there are certain beliefs about volunteers' programs and management which no longer apply:

■ *Volunteer management is a soft option when compared to the management of paid staff.* Wrong. The 'charity model', out of which many such programs developed, is no longer appropriate. Even the term 'volunteer' is less in vogue as a suitable descriptor of this particular group (one writer prefers the term 'Third Sector').

■ *Volunteers save you money.* Not necessarily. The infrastructure—office space, furniture, technology—and the management time required can be quite expensive. If you view volunteers as a source of free or cheap labour, think again.

■ *Volunteers adopt the three wise monkeys' approach—they see, hear, and speak no evil.* Wrong. Volunteers *are* aware of everyday life events in the organisation. Be aware that the volunteers' grapevine thrives as a means of informal (and sometimes inaccurate) communication. So keep them informed. Go public as early as possible about issues that are likely to affect them.

■ *Volunteers don't want to be involved in decisions.* No. Ownership of decisions is just as important to them as it is to paid staff.

■ *Volunteers are easy-going individuals.* Not necessarily. Some volunteers, particularly those with long work histories, can have entrenched views and resist change.

Consider the pitfalls.

Initiating a volunteer program may not be for you. In fact, some volunteer programs have been described as being more trouble than they're worth. Some of the most common reasons for this judgement are:

• Sustaining the work for volunteers requires considerable effort. Preparation is required and processes need to be in place to ensure timely and effective completion of tasks.

• The costs of providing appropriate infrastructure can be substantial. If you're not prepared to spend on such essentials as office space, furniture, and communication media, reconsider your decision to begin a volunteer program.

• Volunteers come from all walks of life. Making best use of their varied expertise is a challenge. If volunteers consider that their particular skills are not being utilised, they'll probably leave.

• Training is time-consuming, costly, and vital, for volunteers will be ambassadors of your organisation. Their word-of-mouth recommendations are likely to attract other volunteers.

- Turnover is likely to be high as some volunteers move to employment, or are dissatisfied with aspects of the program, or want to devote more time to travel and leisure.
- Volunteers can bring their own 'baggage'—family matters, ill-health, a need for companionship—that can be time consuming and a drain on already limited resources.
- A culture clash can occur. Routines can be disrupted, sometimes creating tensions between staff and volunteers. If your people have not worked with volunteers before, some preliminary educating might be required.

 Prepare to engage volunteers.

Volunteer management is rarely a straightforward, hassle-free process. Preparation is required in three areas.

In *relationship-building*, foster a healthy working relationship between staff and volunteers by:

- ensuring permanent staffs' job descriptions include the need to work with volunteers
- promote the volunteer program to existing staff using all media
- ensuring occupational health and safety, equal employment opportunities, and sexual harassment policies are up to date and adhered to
- implementing an induction program, appropriate training, and other support.

Essential *facilities* will include providing volunteers with suitable working accommodation with access to facilities such as telephone, copier, coffee-making facilities, secure storage for belongings, and in-trays for internal communication.

Assuring *quality* need not mean IS9000 certification, but many of the elements of that process can be utilised. Examples include developing

procedures, reporting and acting on areas of non-conformance, and document control.

 Identify the best volunteers.

Volunteers may choose your organisation—especially if others have provided positive word-of-mouth advertising. Other volunteers may have been referred to you by agencies or individuals, and still others may have responded to advertisements in various community bulletins. Ideally, candidates should be interviewed face-to-face, but telephone interviews can also be used. Records of interviews should be kept. Not all volunteers will be suitable, and you may find this out only after they join your team. So allow a two-month reflection or probation period to provide both parties with an opportunity to cancel any agreement or contract. Just because a person wants to volunteer does not mean that you have to accept the offer.

 Consider budgetary requirements.

In addition to the costs of providing infrastructure, there are other costs associated with volunteer management that will necessitate budgetary considerations. Expenditure could include membership of volunteer organisations, attendance at volunteer conferences and volunteer management programs, hospitality expenses, goodwill gestures, in-house training, relevant books, and subscriptions to volunteer magazines.

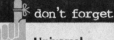 **don't forget**

Universal truths for dealing with volunteers...

- Good intentions are never enough. Untrained amateurs can be a disaster.
- Volunteers can make erratic and unreasonable demands on staff.
- Looking after volunteers can be very time-consuming.
- Some volunteers can be unreliable.
- Volunteers lack decisive action when important decisions must be made.

 viewpoint

"Volunteers need to be encouraged to participate. Publicising the opportunity is not enough. You have to sell the idea that voluntary work is a pleasure, even an honour, not a chore. And you have to make sure it is."

– Linda Vining, Director, Centre for Marketing Schools, Sydney

 don't forget

Volunteers need a focus

Volunteers do not commit their time to have it wasted in misdirected and unproductive activity.

399

How to develop a volunteers' program

You've weighed up the pros and cons of a volunteers' program and decided to proceed. You realise that a key factor in the success of any volunteers' program is how it is managed. Effective management of volunteers could be the difference between success or failure for your program. Here's how to build and manage a volunteers' program…

Develop a program structure.

Most volunteers shun a formalised structure resembling the workplace of paid employment, but they do insist that there be a structure with appropriate procedures that they understand and that are under constant review. They want organisations to derive the maximum benefits from their involvement so, ideally, the structure should facilitate continuity, quality, and clear communication.

Continuity is best achieved by:

- including volunteer management among the responsibilities of a permanent staff member
- allocating day-leader volunteers whose responsibilities include coordinating the activities of other volunteers.

Quality is assured by:

- putting in place procedures to ensure that all completed tasks are signed-off and incomplete ones are brought up for further actions
- recognising and eliminating areas that don't conform with these procedures.

Clear communication requires:

- conducting regular meetings among volunteers and between the volunteers'

manager and day-leaders
- continuing a commitment to face-to-face communication to build and enhance productive working relationships.

Appoint a volunteers' manager.

Ideally, a volunteers' manager needs to be a permanent employee who:

- works with you to develop appropriate policies outlining what specifically the program will do
- works with volunteers to develop appropriate procedures and quality-control mechanisms
- recruits suitable volunteers aiming at diversity rather than conformity (a highly homogeneous organisation is susceptible to disease)
- assigns a mentor or 'buddy' for each volunteer
- maintains a record or register of volunteers including skills, experience profiles, contracts, confidentiality agreements, insurance agreements, and current and potential projects
- monitors progress, maintains contact with volunteers, ensures their job satisfaction, provides support, and demonstrates effective people skills
- designs and modifies induction and training programs
- organises and facilitates meetings of

volunteers

- ensures that the program complies with union guidelines and requirements—e.g. volunteers must not be used as staff replacements and must not work in excess of fifteen hours per week
- prepares budgets for the program.

Assign day-leader volunteers.

Day-leader volunteers will be familiar with the day-to-day operations of the volunteers' program and will perform a type of supervisory role. They can:

- assist with policy development
- help develop job descriptions
- manage other volunteers within the workplace on a day-to-day basis
- arrange and provide suitable on-the-job training
- ensure suitable work space
- help volunteers and other staff to work together effectively.

Initiate recruitment procedures.

Ideally, you or your volunteers' manager need some form of recruitment procedures that could include all, or some, of the following:

- Record all enquiries.
- Send an information pack to the enquirer, including a covering letter, application form, statement of conditions, and program information.
- Process the volunteer's application form and contact referees if required.
- Conduct an interview with the candidate volunteer and, if possible, nominate a day-leader and mentor.
- Notify the applicant of the outcome of the interview.
- Arrange a commencement date.
- Try to have a volunteer and confidentiality agreement signed by the volunteer on or before the first day.
- Arrange for security pass or other relevant access and security details.

Conduct an induction program.

Depending on the number of volunteers, an induction program may be staggered to allow participation by all newcomers. Alternatively, induction programs may be conducted to meet demand. An induction plan could include:

- a welcome by the boss, volunteers' manager, or nominee
- a brief history of the organisation
- an outline of the business and structure
- an overview of the strategic plan
- a summary of the volunteers' program
- a presentation by a long-standing volunteer—a day-leader perhaps
- a tour of the office or plant
- brief presentations by others whom you consider could contribute.

An opportunity should be provided for inductees to ask questions about, or comment on, issues and any observations they may have made.

Recognise and reward contributions.

Obtaining public recognition for volunteers' contributions is not difficult. The media is always on the lookout for 'good-news' and community interest stories. Other forms of recognition valued by volunteers are:

- an award after satisfactory completion of a two-month probation
- occasional social functions
- a briefing on a particular aspect of the organisation's business
- an opportunity to participate in appropriate in-house training where this will assist in the performance of volunteer duties
- acknowledgement of volunteers' contributions in public documents.

here's an idea

Never allow your dedicated and hardworking core of volunteers to feel that they are being overused or that they are always the ones who end up doing everything. Burnout affects volunteers as well, so minimise the problem by spreading the load or by having a planned recruitment process in place.

here's an idea

Ensure that each volunteer has a well-defined area of responsibility that initially matches interests, talents, and availability. Meticulous people make good secretaries; good mixers make good social function organisers; some make excellent fund-raisers, others are best used behind the scenes; some are available one day a week, others three afternoons only. But be aware also: in the spirit of a learning organisation, provide the opportunity for your volunteers to learn new skills and take on new and unfamiliar tasks.

ask yourself

No matter how motivated and prepared volunteers are, the strength and quality of their involvement will be determined by the attitude and behaviour of your staff towards them.

What steps have you taken to ensure your staff is committed to a volunteer program?

401

How to conduct a performance appraisal interview

Most employees want to know: 'How am I doing?' Regular staff performance appraisals should fulfil that need and more. At least annually, staff member and manager review the employee's past and present performance and set future directions. The most effective sessions are simple; they encourage open dialogue between manager and employee. Here are some steps to follow when conducting a performance appraisal interview...

don't forget

Three points to note...

◼ Avoid apologising or becoming defensive if you've made a criticism in good faith. If you find yourself offering justifications and elaborate explanations for your opinions about the employee's performance, then you will have lost control over the meeting.

◼ Try not to pull your punches if punches are warranted. Most people hate unpleasant-ness and the prospect of hurting someone's feelings is abhorrent. So, instead, they hedge their comments and the end result is the people being appraised still do not know what the organisation thinks or expects of them.

◼ Take 'performance notes' on employees *throughout* the year, so that you can review staff members effectively when the time comes. If you don't, you're liable to base your reviews only on the month or two leading up to the review. Such recent information may be incomplete or misleading because some employees step up their production and perform wonderfully during the time just prior to a review – but only because they know they're about to be evaluated.

1 Allocate interview times for all employees.

Employees need to know well in advance the date and time for their performance appraisal interview. The meeting may occur during the month of the staffer's birthday or at some other mutually convenient time. This gives you and the staff member adequate time to prepare for the meeting.

2 Encourage the employee to prepare for the session.

With adequate forewarning, the job holder should be able to prepare for the session. The design of the interview form or an agenda can assist in this regard. Ask the employee to focus particularly on personal performance since the last meeting, comparing against goals previously agreed to.

3 Prepare yourself for the session.

As part of planning, assemble material relevant to achieving your outcomes. Review the records of the employee's past performance appraisal meetings

and decide if there are any other issues you wish to raise or emphasise. Arrange for a location where you will not be interrupted and ensure you both allocate sufficient time for the meeting.

4 Establish rapport.

Gaining the employee's trust and confidence is essential to successful outcomes. This process cannot be rushed and the interview should not proceed until you feel rapport has been successfully established.

5 Reach agreement on past and present performance.

Give the employee an opportunity up-front to describe personally how the job is progressing generally. Examine together how well the previously set goals in key result areas were achieved —were the standards met adequately? were they met on time? what improve-ment is needed? any problem areas? If both parties have completed their pre-meeting preparation, agreement can be reached by each person walking through their respective lists. Those lists will include positive items and others in need of attention.

Acknowledge employee successes.

Give full and generous acknowledgement for appropriate performance, and special emphasis to above average achievements. Indicate your intention to build upon these personal strengths.

Assess progress fairly.

When conducting performance appraisals, it's important to assess each employee fairly. Here's how:

Focus on facts. Discuss objective data—such as customer satisfaction scores, error rates, caseload volumes, etc. To arrive at an unbiased conclusion, always begin with facts rather than opinions.

Benchmark progress. Good reviews compare this year's work with last year's and against agreed-upon standards. Explore benchmarks to allow the worker to see what's been achieved and where he or she's going.

Balance details equitably. If you list examples of how Jack messed up, make sure you don't ignore the specifics of Ted's as well. Consider each worker's performance consistently by focusing on the same level of detail in each case.

Identify and agree on areas needing improvement.

Gain the employee's commitment to addressing those areas in need of attention. Focus particularly on no more than two or three areas. Explain why improvement is necessary, express improvement in measurable terms if possible, and record actions to be taken. This process should not be rushed and should involve considerable employee input: ownership of the issues is essential.

Stay focused.

If you are criticised or forced to defend your position at any stage, remain calm and focused on outcomes. Adopt the attitude that nothing can happen in the interview that you can't handle competently.

List future directions.

You'll gain little from dwelling in the past. Devote maximum time to discussing the employee's future. Reach agreement on the next stage and list the steps to be taken. Agree on new goals or standards together with an action plan to achieve them. How can you assist in any staff training that may be appropriate? Update the job description if necessary. Document the outcome and include it on the employee's file. A review of that list will form the basis for the next performance appraisal interview.

Close on a positive note.

Conclude the meeting by summarising what you think the appraisal interview has achieved. Ensure that the employee leaves in a positive frame of mind, feeling prepared to tackle the next stage with confidence. If required, set a date for a follow-up meeting.

Monitor outcomes.

Continue to look critically at the real results of your appraisal interviews and make changes accordingly. Those changes may even involve moving to a 360° appraisal system…

How to conduct a 360° appraisal

Multi-rater or 360° feedback refers to the process by which feedback on an employee's performance is collected from a full circle of viewpoints—peers, bosses, other staff, and customers. It was one of the most notable management innovations of the 1990s. A 360° feedback program gathers the information, usually through a questionnaire, and feeds that information back to the employee in a structured interview. Here's how to get the best value from this process…

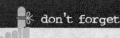

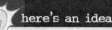

Get your design right.

A key feature of a 360° appraisal is a detailed questionnaire delivered to people who are familiar with the performance of the person being rated. The questionnaire items can be related to traits (e.g. 'unhurried', 'dependable'), behaviours ('praises people for a job well done'), attitudes or values ('believes in democratic participation in decision making'), and competencies ('manages quality customer service'). Whatever the focus, the issues must be:

- agreed on by senior management
- linked to performance criteria
- relevant to the job (or job family)
- clear and unambiguous
- valid at face value
- reliable
- able to reflect observable behaviours.

Remember, 360° feedback can be used at any level of the organisation so you need to be quite clear, in compiling the questionnaire, about what, and whom, you want to assess. It is also important to decide up-front about the key issue of confidentiality—who gets to see the results.

Promote the benefits of the process.

Like most initiatives, 360° feedback needs to be promoted to reach its full potential. Some of the key benefits to promote are that 360° appraisal provides:

- a more complete and accurate process than the traditional top-down appraisal system
- a broader perspective because of involvement by colleagues, boss, and customers
- enhanced self-development opportunities
- an opportunity for self-evaluation
- greater accuracy as reviewers have to defend their evaluations.

Of course, 360° feedback achieves the best results when conducted in a climate of trust, cooperation, and sharing. Results will improve if you communicate the benefits, involve, and prepare all those involved.

Involve the employees.

Participation by employees

will enhance significantly their commitment to the feedback process and, therefore, produce better results. For example, they could be involved in choosing colleagues to be invited to complete the questionnaire; and employees could also rate themselves against the criteria.

 ### Train the raters.

Raters need to be trained so they understand the 360° process, its importance, and their role in it. They must be clear about the performance criteria against which they will be rating the employee. By spending a small amount of time training the raters, you will improve significantly the quality of the feedback.

 ### Remain objective.

The principles of conducting a performance appraisement interview are dealt with on page 402. The principles for giving 360° feedback are identical. Remember, feedback should relate to the criteria listed and, where possible, be supported by examples that help to clarify meaning for and provide direction to the employee. Feedback may be provided in both written and oral forms.

 ### Convert the feedback into development goals.

To ensure action, it is essential that the feedback is converted into a few development goals supported by action steps to be taken. Avoid dictating step-by-step actions as though they are prescriptions to

solve problems. Be aware that the employee, too, may make valuable contributions. Whatever your approach, agree on actions and timelines for those actions to be completed. Always start with the goal that is easiest to achieve, before tackling the harder ones: success helps build confidence and determination to keep going. The need for additional coaching or counselling may be another outcome. And don't forget the development opportunities for employees by emphasising the link between feedback and training.

 ### Follow-up.

Despite an employee's best intentions of fulfilling commitments made, you will usually need to follow up regularly. By following up, you reveal your ongoing interest in the growth of the individual, and also guarantee that you keep in touch with all progress being made. This post-appraisal involvement will also ensure that 360° feedback continues to serve effectively the needs of your organisation.

 ### Aim for maximum benefits.

It is important that 360° feedback is seen as more than an individual performance management tool. If viewed in isolation, many of the opportunities associated with this valuable process can be lost; when used effectively, 360° feedback contributes to an overall performance management strategy. Consult 'How to maximise the value of 360° feedback' (page 406) in this regard.

smile & ponder

Once upon a time, the Emperor asked members of his court how he looked in his new clothes. Knowing the answer he wanted, his courtiers told him "superb" – in spite of the fact that he had on not a stitch of clothing.

The Emperor had just read about how people often tell others to their face what they *want* to hear rather than what they *need* to hear. The Emperor was anxious because he had scheduled a large parade, and would be wearing his new clothes in it. At the last moment, he asked those in his circle of influence – those he most trusted – to provide him with *anonymous* feedback about the look of his new suit. The anonymous feedback was unanimous: He was wearing only his birthday suit!

■ In this updated leadership tale, the Emperor used what is today called 360° feedback to overcome false information.

Imagine how many kings, presidents, prime ministers, generals, leaders, and other individuals have been influenced by information gathered in a manner that reinforced their false assumptions rather than told the truth. Honest input from others can overcome false self-conceptions, blind spots, and just plain ignorance. Candid feedback from relevant others may save careers, even help people avoid making stupid mistakes – like parading naked in public.

Candid feedback – that's what 360° feedback is all about.[39]

How to maximise the value of 360° feedback

360° feedback can be a powerful performance management tool. When used inappropriately, however, it can be quite threatening. Experts have found that 360° feedback should be used only as a tool to improve performance—not as a formal appraisal tool (although many managers are tempted to use it that way). It is most effective when employees and managers trust each other and are relatively open and honest with each other. To get the most value from this important process, consider these pointers…

Focus on positives; be aware of negatives.

Some of the advantages of this form of evaluation are important:

- 360° feedback is generally more complete, accurate, and objective than the traditional boss-down approach.
- Perspectives other than the boss's are taken into account.
- Self-development opportunities are enhanced.
- Self-evaluation generates discussions about individual strengths and weaknesses.
- The involvement of key others will increase accountability to a staffer's internal and external clients.
- An employee gets to understand the gaps between their intent and their impact.
- Greater accuracy is achieved.
- Comments are difficult to ignore when expressed by a number of colleagues.

Some of the drawbacks include:

- The process can be time-consuming.
- The raters can become fatigued and, having so many feedback reports to do, they may not think about the responses as carefully as they might.
- If not positioned properly time-wise, it can create unnecessary anxiety.
- Competition among staff can affect individual ratings.
- Employee-raters may rate their bosses high because the levels of trust are not high.
- Employees may be reluctant to contribute because of concerns about rocking the boat.
- Results can be difficult to interpret if too many appraisers are used.
- In companies where 360° feedback has been used formally—especially where results directly contribute to remuneration and reward decisions—ratings tend to be higher, generating data that is unreliable.

Reinforce organisational goals.

The bottom line about an individual's behaviour is that it will contribute to the organisations' competitive advantage. A great deal of time and effort is likely to have been expended on setting strategy, so it's important that the actions of individuals contribute to achievement of that strategy. The 360° feedback program will, therefore, serve as a valuable barometer for organisational change initiatives. Other effective uses can include identification of high potential employees, career planning, and succession planning.

3 Aim for a performance management system.

Consider using 360° feedbacks as building blocks or elements of an organisation-wide performance management system. This system will help your people focus on what's important and reinforce working relationships to ensure better business results are achieved through people. After all, if you are inviting colleagues' and customers' comments, it makes good sense to maximise the benefits of such data.

4 Involve customers and add value.

By involving customers or clients in the process, you will help to reinforce the important link between customers' needs and the long-term success of the organisation. In 1884, William Lever heard a customer ask for 'some of that stinking soap'. That comment motivated Lever to experiment with perfumed soap. By listening to his customers and adding value in that way, Lever became a household name, literally.

5 Create a continuous-learning culture.

The phrase 'learning organisation' is used to describe a situation in which everyone in an organisation is involved in increasing their value and contributions in a meaningful way to the organisation. 360° feedback helps people to develop skills and competencies and to progress along their career paths. As people see that accurate, constructive feedback contributes significantly to their personal development, a culture is created in which learning is valued and promoted by all.

6 Use the feedback.

Presenting information generated by the feedback process will not, alone, lead to improved performance, enhance working relationships, or result in a learning organisation. People are likely to need help in accepting and converting that information into goals within their own development plan. That's where formal development programs are important and can range from feedback meetings with the boss, to in-house and external training programs, to the introduction of coaching and mentoring.

7 Thank participants.

Customers' and employees' contributions should be recognised. This could be as simple as thanking them for their contributions. People will continue to be involved if they know that their contributions are appreciated, valued, and used in some way.

How to make best use of your 360° feedback report

If you have recently received a 360° appraisal report, you can use it to become more effective in your job, put your skills to better use, or prepare to take on added responsibilities. Or you can ignore it (at your peril). Ideally, your manager should work closely with you to review the results and help you make the most of the feedback. But your manager is often too busy to do so. Then you are left to your own resources. The following advice[41] will help you prepare for the feedback, extract the key themes from it, and make the most of it for your own personal development…

1 Remember that 360° feedback is different to normal feedback.

Unlike normal informal feedback, multi-rater feedback is packed with detailed information to sort through. The data has been provided by several people in addition to your manager, and focuses on on-the-job behaviour considered critical by the organisation to your effective performance. It is not feedback to be taken lightly.

2 Prepare to respond positively to negative feedback.

Most of us respond emotionally to criticism. We can get embarrassed or angry, or become withdrawn and defensive. Consider how you normally react. Be aware that 360° feedback can expose your weaknesses to the point of emotional pain—but you must stand prepared to counter this natural reaction with constructive effort. Your future success may depend on your resolution in this regard.

3 Analyse your feedback report.

After reading your report for the first time, you may feel unsettled or upset. Expect this, and be resolved to put such emotions aside. Analyse the document by asking such questions as: Any surprises? What are they? Do the raters' views vary? Why? Do your manager's views differ from other raters'? Why? Do your self-ratings differ from those of others? Why? Have you under-rated or over-rated yourself? Why? In which areas do you rate highly? And poorly? Why? Do any of the written comments provide clarification? Which items seem to belong together? Are any themes emerging?

It is vital that you thoroughly explore the content of your report before attempting to prepare a plan of action.

4 Prepare a plan of action.

How do you convert multi-rater data into goals for self-development? Consider this strategy…

• *Isolate common themes*. Rarely will single data points stand alone. They will link to related items, exposing more generalisable areas of strength or weakness. Scrutinise all items, consider written comments, inject your own concrete examples and feelings, and identify two or three common themes that stand out as areas in need of development. Turn each theme into an imperative, e.g. 'Become better at handling conflict situations', 'Confront employee performance problems', or 'Make more timely decisions'.

• *Select a theme to work on*. Consider your themes in terms of 'do-ability' and 'impact', rating as high-medium-low. In terms of 'do-ability', some will rate well (e.g. how to make more timely decisions or learning how to make better presentations). Others will rate 'low' or unrealistic (e.g. becoming a charismatic leader or a technology guru). In terms of 'impact', if you successfully execute your self-development plan, to what extent will it make you a more effective employee, or contribute to the success of your department? Select a theme to work on and get your manager's agreement.

• *Itemise the evidence that supports the need to focus on that theme*. Stating the problem is only half of the solution. To define your self-development needs, you must define and understand the theme clearly, sifting through the evidence identified in the feedback report, and including an honest self-evaluation of your situation. By listing hard evidence of your weakness, you'll have substance on which to base your development plan.

• *Specify how you will measure your progress*. To determine if your development plan is on track, you'll need to set up a few ways to measure your progress. For example, 'Make a daily tally of the number of times I give specific feedback to staff on their job performance' and 'Get weekly feedback from Bill and Sue about how appropriate my feedback to them is'.

• *Identify the resources you will need*. When preparing to make behavioural changes, you'll need access to certain resources to locate and develop the relevant concepts, techniques, principles and ideas. If time management is your theme focus, consider (a) seeking advice from books, colleagues, and courses, (b) devising 'scripts' or improvement

strategies to counter previous poor time management practices you admit to, and (c) workplace practice, when you put into effect your new behaviours. You may also need financial support (to undertake workshops and courses) or the help of a mentor.

• *Be aware of the obstacles you may encounter*. List any potential obstacles associated with your self-development plan and how you'll overcome them—lack of time, reluctance of colleagues to help (for a variety of reasons), resistance to change (if colleagues are uncomfortable with your changed behaviours)…

• *Define the workplace actions you will take*. Your new workplace behaviours should be specifically listed and defined. What exactly, are you going to do differently on the job? What new approaches or techniques will you be using? For example, 'When I disagree with someone's idea, I will first say what I like about the suggestion, then voice my reservations, and then ask for their help in overcoming my concerns.'

• *Develop a timeline*. Set specific deadlines to items listed under such headings as resources, workplace implementation, and measures. Transfer these to your diary or planning system.

5 Implement your plan.

Begin the self-development process. The quicker you tap your identified resources, and utilise any new behaviours in the workplace, the quicker improvement will be noticed by you and your colleagues.

6 Reflect upon your achievement.

Reflect and revise. What worked well? What didn't? What will you do as a result? What adjustments will you need to make in future planning?

don't forget

When you initially draft your self-development plan, you may not be able to list many work-place implementation strategies because some on-the-job actions only surface as a result of tapping into your resources. For example, you might be unfamiliar with the 9-step approach to problem solving until you read about it, or attend a workshop.

On the other hand, some very good on-the-job actions can come from your analysis of those past situations where the development need was evident and thinking about how you could have handled the situation more effectively.

quotable quote

Development, as distinct from appraisal, has to do with recognising the competencies required for a role, assessing the individual against them, and then offering learning programs to bridge any gaps. It offers a way forward for the individual and provides information about goals, rather than simply judging past performance.

In some companies, these action plans are staff-driven, so that the subjects of the assessment are enabled to make their own development decisions based on the areas for improvement that the 360° assessment highlights.[42]

409

How to maintain improved performance

Improving the performance of staff is hard enough; maintaining and building on that improvement present even greater challenges for managers. Most improvement processes consist of four stages—agreeing on the standards or expectations, monitoring progress, recognising achievement, and reviewing the performance displayed. Recognition and review will also feature prominently in any maintenance plan. To foster ongoing improvement in your staff, consider the following…

1 Link behaviour to outcomes.

Employees have to know what their improved performance—and the maintenance of that improvement—means to the organisation for two reasons. First, employees need to realise that, if the organisation prospers, so too do their opportunities for advancement and their job security is enhanced. Second, employees must understand that their actions affect others, thereby increasing interdependence and a desire to continue to improve.

2 Demonstrate your commitment to continuing improvement.

Schedule regular meetings with individual employees to talk about the importance of improved work performance—for the organisation and for them. At those meetings, demonstrate your knowledge of the employee's accomplishments by describing in specific terms what you have observed. Compliment them on their achievements and offer further appropriate encouragement. To maintain improved performance you have to be 'on the ball' at all times.

3 Reinforce desirable behaviours.

Recognition is a powerful motivating tool that helps to bring out the best in people by reinforcing observed improvements. A few well-chosen words at the right time can mean a lot to someone trying to do better. But that's only one example of how you can reinforce desirable behaviour. Positive reinforcement can also be traced to these four managerial behaviours:

- Create a work climate that is warm, supportive, trusting, and encouraging.
- Provide learning opportunities that let employees know that it's OK to fail.
- Be available to listen, even when you know it's news you'd rather not hear.
- Show that you know *what* employees are doing so that you can tell them *how* they're doing.

4 Encourage staff to blow their own horn.

When people are proud of their accomplishments, they will want to tell you how they did it. However, the majority are likely to be reluctant starters in self-promotion. So, provide opportunities for them to talk about their improvements and to bask in their moments of glory. Your actions will indicate that you consider their accomplishments to be important and, more particularly, that you value their extra efforts. When employees see that you understand and value their contributions, they will be inspired to give even more. And, of course, your active listening is helping to maintain improved performance.

5 Listen to what staff have to say.

If you've worked at building a positive and constructive climate, don't hesitate to ask employees for suggestions about how you can help them to maintain their improved performance. Together, you will come up with ideas to minimise, or eliminate, any problems that get in the way of continuing improvements. If you're able to grant a request or act on a suggestion, indicate what actions you are able to take, and when. If you're not sure, explain that you will have to look into the situation further and will respond by a certain date. Your actions will encourage

employees to be involved in future projects.

6 Encourage 'reflective structures'.

In the 1990s, when Warren Bennis interviewed eminent leaders from all walks of life, he found that they had a common way of staying in touch with what was important to them in life and business. They built into their lives what Bennis called 'reflective structures'—time and space for self-examination. Exercise, meditation, time-out, and prayer are just some of the practices that provide outlets for reflection—opportunities to get away from the demands of a job and to be with one's own thoughts. Your advocacy of this practice will encourage staff to contemplate the standard of their performance and the issues relating to its improvement.

7 Show your appreciation.

Thanking employees for improved performance reinforces any praise given earlier. The effectiveness of a simple 'thank you' is increased when it is the last thing the employee hears at the end of a conversation with you. Realistically, employees cannot expect that you can solve all of their problems, but they have every right to expect from you courteous and reinforcing behaviour.

---

here's an idea

Effective two-way communication is vital for improving and maintaining staff performance. Two basic communication strategies to consider might be:

Use a 'Friday Memo/Email' to update employees. Every Friday keep your staff updated by publishing a 'Friday Memo' in which you tell everyone what will be happening during the following week: meetings, anniversaries, birthdays, vacations, any changes in the department, information from head office, general announcements, production levels, on-call schedules, reminders, and any other information employees will find useful, motivational, and interesting.

Hold quick morning meetings. Weekly and monthly meetings are great, but daily communication with your team is vital. Try having a 15-minute meeting with key employees each morning. Use this time to discuss changes and progress within the department and answer employee questions. You'll be amazed how keeping everyone informed on a daily basis cuts down on the 'I didn't know' syndrome.

---

read further

Improving Employee Performance through Appraisal and Coaching by Donald Kirkpatrick, AMACOM, NY, 2nd edn, 2006.

How to improve employee performance on the run

Staff performance problems can occur at any time. When someone is under-producing or having difficulty meeting quality standards, immediate action is often required. The effective manager must be quick to act to effect a turnaround. Here's one approach for improving employee performance on the run, without having to resort to the formality of a discipline or performance appraisal interview…

Outline the problem in a friendly manner.

Meet with the employee—a discussion that will usually take place away from your office. Describe any apparent problem as specifically as possible, bearing in mind that most people have days when they do not perform at their best. So make sure that this is not just one of those days. Focus on the problem, not the employee. Refer to any available data that will help you show there is a problem. Leave discussions about attitude to a more formal, regular appraisal or discipline interview. Comments about attitude are likely to put the employee on the defensive and make it difficult to have a productive discussion at this time. Your intention should be to effect an immediate turnaround in inappropriate performance.

Ask for the employee's help to solve the problem.

You need the employee on your side so that you can work together to get performance back to an acceptable level. For this reason, telling a staff member what to do is unlikely to stand much chance of success, particularly if the employee doesn't want to improve performance. You can get commitment by simply asking for help in deciding what to do about the performance problem. In this way you are signalling that you value the employee's ideas. In most cases, your consultative approach will be appreciated and help to gain employee cooperation and commitment.

Discuss possible causes of the problem.

Remember, the discussion is about the person's performance problem, not the person's attitude or personality. Gather all the information you can by asking open-ended questions beginning with words such as 'when', 'what', 'who', and 'how'. The employee will not be threatened by these kinds of questions and will be encouraged to answer them. Listen, respond with empathy, and take notes if necessary. This is another way of demonstrating to the employee that you are interested in what is being said. Summarise the causes you have identified and make sure there is agreement about those.

Identify possible solutions.

Having identified the causes of the performance problem, you now want to correct them. Given that it is the employee's problem, ask for ideas and solutions. Discuss them. Perhaps write them down, listing as many ideas as you both can come up with. You will find that people are more committed to solving problems if they've had a say in the solution.

Decide on the specific action to be taken.

Now choose the best solution. At this point in the discussion, you should be ready to pinpoint exactly what must be done—by whom and by when—to correct the performance problem. Assign responsibilities for specific actions and write them down. Remember, support the employee's efforts to improve performance, but emphasise that the responsibility for improvement rests with the individual. Express confidence in the employee's ability to take the agreed actions.

Agree on a specific follow-up date.

By setting a date to meet again, you are sending a message that solving the performance problem is important to

you and that you will be available to assist in making sure the problem is addressed satisfactorily. A follow-up meeting encourages discussion of progress.

Record the details.

If the meeting is held away from your office, record the details of your discussion immediately on your return, using your notes as a guide and memory jogger. Enter any follow-up arrangements in your diary.

Be aware of the legal implications.

One motivation for improving employee performance 'on the run', or as a long-term process, is the fact that your organisation will probably have to shoulder responsibility for any injuries arising from employee negligence—that is, injuries to other employees as well as to customers or clients.

The legal principle is called 'vicarious liability', or second-hand liability. You employed the particular person, he or she is your 'servant' in the legal sense, and, if that employee carelessly injures someone, then the organisation is responsible, and almost certainly will be sued as a major defendant if any claim for compensation goes to court.

So, be on the lookout for inappropriate staff behaviour or procedures—and take immediate action.

smile & ponder

A senior manager briefed his boss on some major personnel changes – brought on by poor performance – that would involve several terminations.

The boss asked the manager how long he had been working with those people. 'Seven years,' came the reply.

'If you've been in charge of those people for seven years and their performance is still unsatisfactory, I think the issue is *your* performance,' said the boss.

don't forget

The biggest room in your building is the room for improvement.

here's an idea

For better performance, make people feel important.

quotable quote

A manager can think up a lot of excuses to keep from leaving his desk and going out into the actual work arena… but one of the most neglected areas in management is getting out, keeping an eye on the operation, helping staff in need, making sure the job is getting done – and done properly.[44]

413

How to recognise unsatisfactory job performance

One of the most important and demanding responsibilities facing a manager is evaluating the performance of staff. It should be an ongoing day-to-day activity: without such knowledge, a manager cannot make sound decisions on promotion, transfer, training, counselling, or even dismissal. Identifying poor employee performance is particularly important because it can indicate the need for remedial action. To identify unsatisfactory performance, consider the following…

Be alert for the signs.

When an employee's work perform-ance diminishes to an unsatisfactory level, the cost to both the employee and the organisation can be significant. From time to time, staff may exhibit one or more of the unsatisfactory indicators which are listed below and many of these can generally be addressed by the manager in consultation with the staff member.

For some of the more serious indicators, however, or when several signs recur in the same employee, a session with the organisation's employee adviser or counsellor may be warranted.

Assess the obvious signs of diminishing performance.

There are numerous outward signs of a poorly performing employee:

- excessive time required to complete work tasks
- missed deadlines
- untidiness in the workplace
- high accident rate
- decline in the quality of work

- complaints received from other staff and customers
- wasted materials
- indications of tiredness, loss of enthusiasm, and decline in concentration
- erratic performance
- lapses in fulfilling requests, tasks, and responsibilities
- increasing failure to attend to detail
- poor decision-making and judgement
- overall decline in standards.

Examine attendance patterns.

The factors indicating unsatisfactory attendance would include:

- consistent lateness
- early departure
- absences after weekends and paydays
- extended lunch breaks
- increased absenteeism
- frequent time off
- decline in organisation-related social activities.

A poor attendance record could be a symptom of more serious problems.

Investigate reasons for sick leave.

Poor job performance could be the result of real or feigned illness, or of more serious physical or emotional problems. Signs in this area would include:

- frequent excuses made for minor illnesses
- more frequent sickness than other employees, e.g. colds and flu.
- illnesses tend to recur
- more serious physical illnesses.

 Look for examples of deteriorating behaviour.

Behaviours indicating unsatisfactory performance, and requiring follow-up action, might include:

- mood changes
- trembling
- breath smelling of alcohol
- memory lapses
- increasingly dishevelled appearance
- speech difficulties
- increasing use of abusive language
- destruction of property
- hostile attitude towards others.

 Consider changes in personality.

The underlying causes of the following personality changes must be treated if performance at work is to be improved:

- undue emotion or aggression
- increased irritability
- increased moodiness and unpredictability
- inability to sustain effort
- disputes with others
- violence

- avoidance of work colleagues
- over-reaction to real or imagined criticism
- general withdrawal.

 Take appropriate action.

Knowledge of an employee's unsatisfactory performance and a pin-pointing of the outward signs of that diminished effort is one thing: what to do about it is another. A manager might consider a range of options— such as corrective action to bring the employee back to the required standard, re-training, coaching, counselling, mentoring, demotion, transfer, termination…

 And finally…

We must, of course, acknowledge that it's unrealistic to expect people to work at their maximum capacity all day, every day. As US consultants Ron Carr and Don Blohowiak remind us:

> You can try to limit your employee's periods of less-than-peak performance by creating conditions and an environment conducive to optimal performance but, even under the best circumstances, there will be times when people aren't performing at their best for whatever reason. As humans, we're all subject to mood swings and are influenced by the rhythms of life that can affect our work performance. Some days, and some hours of the day, are going to be less than peak. So, be reasonable in your expectations. Create conditions where people are encouraged to deliver their best work, while neither expecting nor demanding perfection.

viewpoint

"Your job is not to find fault, assign blame, or hold grudges. It's to analyse why people are behaving as they are, and change the consequences to get the behaviour you desire."

– Aubrey Daniels in *Bringing out the Best in People*

415

How to improve the performance of at-risk employees

If you have a staff member who is not performing to expectations, whose approach to the task is slipping, ineffective, even counterproductive, you need help that employee get back on track to improve performance and increase productivity. The following process of rehabilitation will help to isolate the cause of, and generate a possible solution to, the problem of this at-risk employee…

1 Ensure that action is necessary.

Everyone has an occasional off-day, but at-risk employees are those whose performance has been observed on several occasions to be in a state of decline. When you are certain you have identified at-risk performance, it is time to gather accurate information from a wide variety of sources.

2 Gather the facts.

Your information search should involve colleagues, supervisors, and others who have regular contact with the at-risk employee. The perceptions of those people can be compared with your own, thereby helping you to make a more informed judgement. Determine the relationship of this information to job performance, enabling you to omit information not specifically related to the issues under investigation. These information-gathering meetings will clear the air, establish the facts, help decide on possible actions, and suggest the types of assistance that can be offered.

3 Decide on appropriate actions— beforehand.

You should now have accumulated quality information to help you develop a plan of action. Remember, all this is done *before* you meet with the employee. The plan will list 'who' is to do 'what' by 'when' and 'how', and should consider the following strategies:

- *Make goals and standards specific and clear* in terms of what you expect and how you expect it. Spell this out clearly, in writing if necessary, so that the employee can't claim later that your requirements were vague.

- *Investigate ways of providing more challenging work.* It's often the case that at-risk employees are simply bored. If you can generate more challenging tasks, you may create a complete turnaround in that employee's attitude to work.

- *Plan a procedure to monitor the at-risk employee's performance.* How will you be able to get immediate feedback if there is no improvement or a significant lapse in performance? If the set goals haven't been met, why is this? A lack of immediate response from you will diminish your credibility and you'll lose whatever influence you might have.

Approach the staff member.

Raise the matter with the staff member, making your concerns quite clear and indicating that you both need to meet. The discussion is not whether a meeting will occur, but when. Make an appropriate time.

Hold a meeting and get right to the point.

Your meeting should cover the following points:

- *Express your disappointment* in your staff member's recent lacklustre performance. Play on the employee's pride by revealing that your esteem has not been lost as a result.
- *State the facts* as you see them.
- *Encourage a response.* Be prepared to listen to any reasons for poor or declining performance.
- *Create peer pressure* by stressing how the employee is letting colleagues down, forcing them to work harder to carry an additional share of the workload.
- *Offer assistance and present your draft action plan.* Agree on the actions to be taken. You've done the necessary research, you've done all you can to put in place a set of procedures to help the at-risk employee improve,

so it's now time to assert your position and insist on results in the future.

- *Ensure the employee is aware of the consequences of continued poor performance.*
- *End the meeting on an optimistic note.*
- *File a record of the meeting and actions taken.*

Set follow-up procedures in place.

At-risk employees can not be left too long without frequent reviews. Regular follow-up meetings should be a feature of the rescue package, thereby underscoring the priority you have placed on this matter. You might also decide to appoint a mentor or 'buddy' to provide additional support in the workplace.

Meet the challenge.

According to consultant Gary Bielous, improving marginal performers is no easy task. 'Yet,' he says, 'it is our responsibility to train or retrain our personnel properly and ensure everyone on the team is contributing towards the department's goals. This is where coaching comes into play. Effective coaching requires a knowledge of the subject, an ability to communicate it, a patience that will instill trust, and a will to follow up. As well, it requires courage—courage to be able to take the underachiever and 'mould' him or her into someone more productive. This shaping can only breed success throughout the department and ultimately the organisation.'

How to help reduce stress in employees

Stress goes with the job—most jobs. And the signals of stress include apathy, fatigue, tension, frustration, detachment, boredom, irritability, hopelessness, a sense of not being appreciated, deteriorating health, and absenteeism. Your staff are not immune from stress—in fact, you may well be the cause of it. But, as a manager, you can help to alleviate employee stress in a number of ways...

1 Be reasonable in your expectations.

Don't make unreasonable demands on employees. Extra duties take them away from core tasks and make their goals more difficult or impossible to achieve. Often we apply too much pressure on our staff to satisfy our own values or ambitions.

2 Be decisive, clear, and unambiguous.

When managers inappropriately delay making decisions or reverse previous decisions, employees report that they experience more stress than when firm, timely decisions are made. So collect relevant data, set achievable deadlines, and make decisions at the appropriate time. As well, lack of timely information about rules, standards, evaluative criteria, and goals causes confusion, uncertainty, and frustration. Effective communication is vital.

3 Create a supportive work environment.

Some work environments often isolate workers from one another and make it difficult for them to receive the encouragement and support of colleagues. Foster a supportive network to allow your staff to share problems and resources; colleagues' support softens the effects of stress on staff members' lives.

4 Be alert to the value of self-esteem.

Many workers suffer frustration from wondering how effective they are as practitioners. They report stress from lack of feedback, especially if they feel they do not get due recognition for any extra effort. Be liberal with meaningful praise and encouragement.

5 Communicate with each staff member.

Communication is the key to building trust, a healthy atmosphere, team spirit, and a sense of community within your organisation. Seek out your employees whenever possible and talk with them. Sponsor small group discussions or retreats away from the workplace. Use bulletin boards and in-house newsletters. Keep everyone informed of changes, however small those changes may be.

Plan ahead.

Stressful situations can be avoided with a little foresight and planning. Alert your staff to special events, projects, and meetings well ahead of time so they can plan their schedules accordingly.

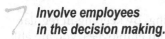
Involve employees in the decision making.

When staff are given the opportunity to participate in decisions affecting their work, they experience more clarity, fewer conflicts, and better relations with others. But don't ask for input and then ignore it!

Be consistent in disciplinary matters.

Be consistent in enforcing policies governing the conduct and performance of your staff.

Be an effective gatekeeper.

Protect your staff by controlling the rate of innovations entering the workplace. Some you will be unable to delay or exclude, but you can control your own initiatives. Protect staff from angry customers, and support staff when speaking with others.

Provide adequate resources.

Lack of supportive supplies, equipment, and facilities can be quite stressful for enthusiastic workers. Make every attempt to fund existing programs before allocating moneys to new programs or initiating activities for which employee commitment has not yet been secured.

Always follow through.

Implement only important innovations for which you can muster sufficient time, skills, resources, and commitment. Managers are often criticised for initiating new programs and then failing to follow them through adequately.

Provide variety in an employee's life.

Burnout can occur from a feeling of being locked into a routine job. Identify potentially exhausting jobs and wherever possible have your staff switch assignments, projects, and departments to find new challenges and a fresh environment.

Check your personal style for defects.

Your own managerial style may trigger feelings of anxiety among staff. So be alert to undesirable managerial behaviours—such as delegating too little or too much, blaming others, playing favourites, not delivering on promises, discouraging creative thinking and frankness, hogging credit, nit-picking, being cheap with praise, setting unreasonable deadlines, and showing lack of concern for others.

here's an idea

The simplest solution for overcoming job stress in the workplace is for employers to ask employees what could be done to improve their well-being at work – and to act on the advice.

here's an idea

Stress may have become a fact of life – but it need not become a way of life. There's a sports adage that says 'always work on a losing game' – so here are three strategies to assist you to help employees deal with the process of combatting stress:

- Encourage employees to say 'No', justifiably.
- Allow time-out. When people skip breaks their performance generally suffers.
- Promote leisure. People should not be made to feel guilty about their R & R.

viewpoint

"Although the push from the self-appointed motivational gurus these days is to eliminate stress from our lives and those of our employees, this is unrealistic.

Fear, anger, and stress can be healthy. You just have to find the balance, and the balance is different for everyone. Stress posing as adrenalin is good – it gives us a kick."

– Shirley Smith

419

How to deal with continuing absenteeism

It is not unusual to find that 10 per cent of employees account for 50 per cent or more of total absenteeism. Employees who continually let the team down by not turning up for work can cause real problems for management. Morale, productivity, and profits are affected; and absenteeism can also irritate managers called on to find temporary replacements for employees who fail to show. Here's how you can deal with the problem...

Focus on interdependence.

Research shows that the greater the reliance employees have on each other, the lower their absenteeism. Employees are less inclined to take time off if they know that workmates will be affected because of their actions. To foster interdependence, you might consider the following strategies:

- Use work teams to get employees involved.
- Involve employees in decisions on issues that affect them.
- Engage employees in project-based activities that require participation among colleagues.
- Encourage employees to tell you in advance when they will be absent.
- Build trust.

Be alert for the warning signs.

Most employees will have legitimate reasons for their absence. Others will absent themselves because they feel their jobs lack challenge, or are just plain boring. By keeping in regular contact with employees, you are able to nip problems in the bud and take corrective actions.

Look for patterns.

Errant employees are usually easily identified because their absenteeism often follows a pattern. It may be that their absenteeism coincides with major events or is tacked on to weekends. The employee often telephones in with an excuse, but you find it increasingly difficult to believe the excuse that is offered.

Keep accurate records.

People are less likely to be absent in companies in which absenteeism is recorded, monitored, and managed. Maintain a record of patterns of absence because that information will be essential if you choose to tackle the employee about the problem. Indeed, you will need such evidence to prove that you didn't discipline or terminate for discriminatory reasons.

Conduct post-absence interviews.

Don't let suspicious absences go by without an interview. Ask for a second explanation of the absence and subtly plant suspicion in the employee's mind that you are sceptical of the excuse offered earlier. More importantly, you want this discussion to convey the message that you are keeping an eye on the situation.

Be supportive of legitimate personal problems.

Before deciding on disciplinary actions, determine if the employee is experiencing personal problems—family crisis, genuine illness, low self-esteem, or a general wish to avoid problems at work, and so on. Show empathy for those who have a genuine problem. Offer help which might include counselling, additional skills training, or even paid leave to deal with a personal problem or domestic concern. Resolve the problem amicably and you'll generate long-term benefits for all parties.

Meet formally with the employee and act decisively.

If absenteeism does not improve and you are not convinced as to the legitimacy of the absenteeism, meet formally with the employee and reveal the evidence. Do you offer another chance to improve? Do you discipline or do you terminate? Whatever the identified cause of the absenteeism, take firm action to eliminate or significantly reduce the problem. If counselling or skills training is appropriate, schedule a

time immediately. If a warning is called for, make sure that you record that warning and notify the employee in writing. Have the employee sign your file copy of the letter if possible. If stern action is required, don't baulk at taking those steps either. Finally, feed the grapevine so that all staff become aware of management's firm stance on unwarranted absenteeism.

And also...

Consider the following strategies in the ongoing battle to improve attendance in the workplace:

- Establish attendance standards and communicate these to employees regularly.
- Make clear to staff the effect poor attendance has on work, peers, the organisation, and the individual.
- Reward good performance.
- Make jobs more interesting.
- Counsel poor attendees—absenteeism is often the symptom of other problems.
- Consider flexible working hours, child-care centres, fitness programs, accrued sick days, and incentives for good attendance.
- Does your organisation have a policy relating to longer-term, but legitimate, employee absence, e.g. in relation to the birth of a child? Do you, for example, continue to make an employee-mother feel part of the organisation even while she's on extended leave? 'Keep in touch': send flowers following a birth, mail or email internal staff newsletters, invite her to official staff functions, and offer some flexible work options after an appropriate period (part-time, job sharing, telecommuting).

How to help employees balance their work and home lives

The pursuit of a balanced lifestyle has a long and impressive history. Recorded interest in the topic dates back several thousand years. The concept of balance has received renewed attention more recently as people, often under stress, strive to juggle work and home commitments. Helping people balance their work and home life has become an additional expectation of managers who themselves are trying to balance their own. Here are some ways to help yourself and others achieve a balanced lifestyle...

Keep things in perspective.

In *Success: Full Living*, Justin Belitz provides a simple method of breaking down life's activities into seven categories which he calls the '7Fs'— Fun, Family, Friends (Social Life), Finances (Work), Fitness (Health), Faith, and Formal and informal education.[49] He stresses that his categories are only suggestive and can be added to or subtracted from depending on your belief system. It's the process that's the important thing. Balance is achieved by attending equally to each of the 7Fs. Conversely, when some are emphasised at the expense of others, imbalance occurs, requiring a review of life practices and a return to a more balanced lifestyle.

Appreciate diversity.

Workplaces have become more generational, ethnic, and culturally diverse. Veterans, Baby Boomers, Generations X and Y, and people from different ethnic groups contribute to a more heterogeneous and potentially stimulating workplace than in any other period in history. Another aspect of that diversity is the concept of 'family' that may, or may not, include children. Your attitude and behaviour must respect the choices people have made. Viva la difference!

Monitor behaviour— yours and others.

No one is expecting you to become a qualified psychologist or lifestyle counsellor. In your management role, however, you are likely to be able to help others lead a more balanced lifestyle. You are aware, for example, that people's behaviours have been learnt—from their upbringing, their schooling, and by modelling significant others. And some people can be oblivious to the detrimental effects that their behaviour can have on themselves and others. By people-watching in your organisation, you will come to realise those who lead a more balanced lifestyle than others and those for whom intervention could help. The ways that you manage these situations will influence your behaviour, too.

Be flexible.

It's not the amount of time that people spend at work that's important, but how effective they are while they are there. You will find that working hours can become more flexible when your focus is on outcomes. Parents often need this flexibility. No matter how well they think they have organised their time, something invariably happens to prove them wrong—children with flu, school meetings, or a family pet that needs to be taken to the vet. And unexpected demands on time are not confined to employees with children. Medical appointments, emergency dental care, and professional development activities are just some of the reasons why flexible working hours are worth considering. Show your preparedness to act in the best interests of your proven performers.

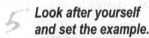 Look after yourself and set the example.

Others can forget that you, too, need help and encouragement to achieve balance in your life. The reality often is that you will be left to your own devices. If this is so, consider the advice offered in the side panel (*right*).

Accept that there will be emergencies.

Crises happen in everyone's life and workplace. Respond to such crises sensitively. Neither you nor your staff can be expected to leave 'the other

life' at the workplace door. The way that you respond to helping people cope with their work and domestic crises will help to reduce their levels of stress, promote a workplace where people want to be, and help to build your reputation as one on whom people can rely for help. People need your support, not your judgement. Be prepared to act always in your staff's best interests.

Don't leave your employees' children in the outer.

Most parents like talking about their children's academic, sporting, or musical achievements. If you're flexible as a manager, you will contribute to parent-employees' increased participation in their children's activities. When the situation allows it, include invitations for kids to attend social functions. Rarely will those employees without kids feel left out or neglected. You be the judge of an appropriate time to include children on the invitation.

Give people space and trust them.

People need room to move so that they don't feel 'fenced in' or 'tied down'. They are aware of their obligations and will respond positively to your efforts to empower them. Although you may think that you are the only one monitoring attendance, work hours, and time on the job, chances are that those involved will be doing that, too. People accept that autonomy brings with it increased responsibility.

 don't forget

Look after yourself

- Don't take things too seriously. Lighten up! Research tells us that we have control over less than ten per cent of things we worry about.
- Be prepared to laugh at yourself. In fact, adding more fun and laughter to your life is a great idea.
- Trust people. Focussing on negatives is a health hazard.
- Show genuine concern for others.
- If you're a Type A personality, take care. Type Bs live longer.
- Find out what individuals value most and talk to them about those particular interests. If you want people to become interested in you, first you must get them talking about themselves.
- Be the first to leave some days – for a few laps of the pool, or a round of golf, perhaps.
- Adjust your daily routine. Schedule a day working from home.
- Continue to develop good habits.
- Avoid mood swings.
- Talk less; listen more.

How to lay down the law to a staff member

Most employees act with their organisation's best interests at heart. Inevitably, however, managers sometimes have to take disciplinary action against an errant employee. It is then important that the disciplinary action achieve a positive response from the employee. Any retaliatory, get-even, disgruntled reaction is a clear indication that the manager did not handle the matter well. The following guidelines will better prepare you for reprimanding employees in future…

1 Make sure the rules are known and understood.

Not only must you be thoroughly familiar with the organisation's rules and policies, but you must also ensure that your employees know and understand them as well. Don't fall into the trap of assuming they know the rules because they once received a printed copy of them. You must make sure that employees are reminded of them from time to time.

2 Get the facts before you act.

Before you take any disciplinary action, make sure you know what happened and when, and why it happened and how. Never make a hasty decision. Be aware of the employee's past record and know how similar situations were handled in the past. Don't accept hearsay evidence or go on general impressions.

3 Know your authority and operate within it.

What actions can you take without checking with anyone higher up? What can you only recommend to higher authority? Can you send an employee home, with or without pay, while an investigation is carried out? Are there others who should be advised of any actions—your boss, an equal opportunity officer, or personnel officer. You should know these things before you take any action. And finally, remember the advice of General Norman Schwarzkopf—'Rule 13: When in command, take charge.'

4 Raise the issue in private.

Avoid open confrontation with the employee. If you censure a person in public, you can blow an issue out of all proportion and create unnecessary resentment.

So broach the subject with the employee in private, outlining your concerns and the problems created by the errant behaviour. Let the person know the general charge and the specific details of the offence. Reveal how you feel about the situation and invite an explanation of anything you might have misinterpreted.

Be calm, constructive, and consistent.

Discipline is not meant to be retaliatory; it should be constructive and consistent. Don't lose your cool. Be as objective as possible. If you're too emotional, postpone the confrontation until you regain your composure. What you say and how you will say it must influence the other person's response. The purpose of a disciplinary encounter is not simply to relieve your feelings of anger and frustration.

Act decisively and fairly.

Managers can't afford to be indecisive or wishy-washy; and risk paying the price for their inaction. Laying down the law implies leaving the employee in no doubt of your feelings, concerns, and disapproval, and that changes are required. The matter can be handled firmly but fairly by you, without any embarrassment and unpleasantness. The employee's dignity should be maintained at all times.

Offer assistance and end on a positive note.

The aim of a disciplinary action should be to teach, not to punish. If necessary, arrange for coaching and counselling. Set down what the employee should do differently in the future. Conclude by expressing your confidence that the employee

will make adjustments. Work towards the elimination of any feelings of resentment and bitterness. Motivate, encourage, and communicate optimism. Conclude with a clear understanding by both parties of what changes are required. Secure a commitment to future action.

Keep a written record.

Make notes on what happened and what you did about it. Even informal reprimands shouldn't be solely oral. You should keep a record of the incident; legal implications demand that you document any action that could later lead to serious disciplinary action that might culminate in probation, suspension, or dismissal.

Remember that Freedom of Information legislation allows access by individuals to any details recorded about them. For this reason alone, your records must be objective and not prejudicial in any way.

If possible, in serious cases, ask the employee to sign the record of the meeting. If he or she refuses, call in a colleague to witness the refusal and to attest to the response in writing if necessary.

Follow-up.

You must follow-up in a reasonable time to determine the success of your intervention and to discuss if necessary the results of any actions that may have been taken. An informal chat on a friendly, positive note is probably all that is required.

here's an idea

Always express a misdemeanour as a work-related problem. For example, 'Whenever you're late you place an undue burden on the other staff who must not only do their own work, but must also, unexpectedly, rearrange their responsibilities to handle the work they were assuming you would do.' Avoid personal attacks – 'lazy', 'irresponsible', 'sneaky', 'deceitful'…

don't forget

How to reprimand

■ Reprimand as soon as possible after the offence is committed.

■ Don't reprimand when you're angry. Calm down first.

■ Emphasise the what –not the who.

■ Begin by stating the problem – then ask a question about it.

■ Listen. Be attentive. Be open-minded. Get the whole story. Ask questions to clarify.

■ Encourage your staff member to suggest solutions.

■ If pertinent, suggest what you, or other staff members, can do to help solve the problem.

■ Establish a plan of action as to what will be done to resolve the issue.

■ End on a positive note. Reassure the staff member that you consider him or her a valuable employee.[52]

How to manage workplace romances

Most romantic relationships begin in the workplace. That practice will continue as people work longer hours in environments that encourage teamwork, openness, and familiarity. But sometimes those relationships can cause problems—particularly if they sour or go off the boil—contributing to reduced productivity or lower morale or even claims of sexual harassment. If you're faced with this tricky situation, here are some techniques to consider…

1 Understand the power of setting the example.

Office romances have occurred ever since men and women became co-workers, and have involved bosses and staff alike. A survey by the American Management Association found that 30 per cent of managers acknowledged having at least one office liaison of their own; 74 per cent approved dating co-workers, and 21 per cent approved of dating subordinates. One of the biggest influences on office romances, and the ways in which they are conducted, will emanate from the examples provided by those at the top of the organisation. In one prominent Australian professional services firm, a continuing affair involving two of its senior partners gave tacit approval to the practice. Irrespective of any policies espoused to the contrary, staff saw the partners' behaviour as approving workplace liaisons.

2 Respect individuals' rights.

Balancing individuals' rights to privacy with protecting employees from sexual harassment and the organisation from accusations of conflict of interest is fraught with complications. Indeed, it is the concern over claims of sexual harassment, usually after a romance has soured, that is a major concern about organisations' appropriate response to office romances. When you become aware of a blossoming relationship, you need to monitor the situation and try to pre-empt any problems. This could involve speaking to both people, together, right at the beginning. You may, for example, request that they refrain from public displays of affection. If, however, you don't consider that there could be a problem, stay out of it. It is a situation that calls for careful consideration, communication, and common sense.

3 Consider possible scenarios.

When in bloom, workplace relationships can take peoples' minds off the job causing productivity to suffer. Co-workers, too, can feel uneasy when associated in some ways with the romance; many informal communication networks are disrupted; break-ups can shatter more than one office relationship. And then there are the harassment claims that can result from those consensual relationships that go bad.

So there are three likely scenarios that should be considered. Your response to them is likely to influence your actions:

1. Will the relationship affect individuals' and organisational productivity?
2. Will the relationship affect the morale of co-workers?
3. Could the relationship lead to possible sexual harassment claims?

If you can live with your worst-case scenario, you may decide to take no further action. And conversely.

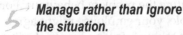 Know what doesn't work.

Anecdotal evidence suggests that various forms of 'legislation' to outlaw relationships in the office do not have a successful track record. Contracts of employment—sometimes dubbed 'love contracts'—are rarely legally binding. And asking romantically involved employees to sign legally binding agreements not to sue the company if the relationship breaks down is also a legal minefield.

Manage rather than ignore the situation.

Ideally, you'd like to manage the relationships in ways that maintain a productive, happy workforce on one hand, and not overly intrude

on the employees' private lives on the other. This approach is a much better alternative to the traditional double standard that officially forbad relationships, yet didn't interfere unless forced to do so. If your motives are in the best interests of the organisation, those involved will appreciate your considered need to bring your concerns to their attention. For the workplace to survive staff romances, you must take a deliberate, reasonable approach in defining what's acceptable and what's not.

Consider establishing a policy.

Although most organisations do not have written policies regarding office romances, this need not preclude you from involving your team in developing one. The main aim of such a policy is to deal with office romances while still maintaining a high level of office productivity. Remember, of course, you're creating policies regarding the private lives of adults, not lovesick adolescents. Ensure that

- you don't place yourself in the position of trying to enforce unrealistic rules
- practices are uniform and don't discriminate based on marital status
- the misuse of email is featured as part of this policy
- all guidelines and policies are reviewed by legal counsel to be sure they comply with relevant legislation
- confidentiality is assured.

Any policy should be brought to the attention of everyone in the organisation and be included as part of any induction program.

don't forget

If you're lovestruck...

- Try to predict the future. How will the relationship fit in with your life and career?
- Know the next step in the relationship. Where is it leading?
- If one of you has a history of other office romances, beware.
- If one of you is married, the probability of a successful relationship drops greatly.
- If you're having a relationship, you can be sure someone else knows or suspects. It's hard to cover up.
- Is one of you doing most of the giving? Lack of reciprocation is a negative sign.
- Check that you're not using the romance as medication to fight depression or burnout.
- Can you both be sure the romance is not affecting your productivity at work?

 quotable quote

Love is difficult to deal with rationally, but when it happens at work, it's especially important to let the cortex rule the courtship. The problem is that lovesick lizards are blind. In the early stages of infatuation, nearly every couple believes that this relationship is the Real Thing and, therefore, lies outside the rules of professional behaviour. It doesn't.[54]

427

How to help others to change their bad habits

No one is perfect: everyone is likely to have at least one bad habit. We also know that most undesirable habits take years to develop and won't be eliminated overnight. Some people don't want to change them anyway. But when people's habits begin to affect their performance—and that of others—and possibly their careers, your intervention is required. The flaws have to be eliminated or significantly reduced. Here's how you can help others to change their irritating behaviours...

1 Get the habit into perspective.

Bad habits generally fit into two types. There are the easy-to-deal-with compulsions—such as smoking in the workplace, bullying, and gossiping. Then there are the more complex habits —such as pessimism, rebelliousness, bulldozing, and pushing people too hard—that translate into consistently problematic behaviour. Both types can affect an individual's or a group's performance—the former being much easier to manage than the latter.

2 Ask yourself two questions.

Your possible involvement requires that you ask yourself two questions:

The first: *Is the effort required by me to help the person change worth it?* The person may not warrant the investment.

The second: *Am I the right person to help the employee change?* Perhaps your HR professional, executive coach, or a psychologist is a better choice. If this is the case, delegate the task to the appropriate person but insist on being kept informed of continuing developments.

3 Eliminate or reduce compulsive behaviours.

If you have decided to deal with the compulsive behaviour yourself, follow this established approach:

- plan the initial meeting; research the behaviour and the problems that it is causing; note issues you want to raise
- make sure you schedule enough time to discuss the situation thoroughly; avoid unnecessary interruptions
- express clearly your perceptions of the employee's behaviour – observed patterns, effects on others, etc.
- suggest specific ideas to help the person change the behaviour and enlisting his or her support in any process
- make time for a follow-up meeting soon after the initial discussion.

Be aware that a likely scenario could be that the person will make an effort to satisfy you without necessarily *eradicating* the problem behaviour. For example, your employee might agree to stop taking smoking breaks during work time, but may continue to do so when working away from the office. It is not unusual for compromises to be reached in this way.

4 Expose complex types of behaviour.

Understanding and dealing with more complex and habitual behaviours requires considerably more skill and persistence. A wide variety of behaviour types have been identified, however; these provide useful insights from which possible actions can be considered. One such list, for example, was identified by business psychologists Waldroop and Butler, who identified six types (see box, *right*) – the Hero, the Meritocrat, the Bulldozer, the Pessimist, the Rebel, The Home Run Hitter. The issue here is more the complex nature of the types rather than the specific types.

The inherent factors that negatively affect the types of employee classified by researchers Waldroop and Butler (and others) are usually:

- an inability to see the world from others' perspectives
- a failure to recognise when and how to use power
- a failure to come to terms with authority
- a negative self-image.

5 Meet with the person.

Even though there are individual idiosyncrasies that inevitably will need to be taken into account when managing any bad habits, there are commonalities that can help to provide the basis for your actions. Examples include:

• Express your appreciation of their loyalty. Most staff are usually loyal.

• Focus discussions on outcomes. With 'Heroes', for example, emphasise that winning the war is more important than trying to win every battle; for 'Bulldozers', show how they can get what they want without flattening people.

• Use analogies and stories to communicate your message.

• Emphasise the importance of being aware of others' body language and physical cues such as bags under the eyes, stifled yawns and their own body signals such as muscle tensions and sweaty palms. You might advise the person to 'lighten-up' if you think his or her intensity is contributing to the problem.

• Focus on the specifics of the habit. The hero could suffer burnout, the pessimist will experience others' avoidance.

• Be firm. If actions are damaging to morale, say so. Create crises if necessary. Ask the Bulldozer, 'Do you know how many enemies you have made?' Even deliver an ultimatum if you think that will work. For example, 'If you're not prepared to change, you must reconsider your position in this organisation'.

• Build a support mechanism in the workplace. After you have delivered your message offer ongoing support in overcoming the flaw.

• Give them a job—a high-profile task— that requires them to win the cooperation of others by applying their skills in a different way than they have in the past.

6 Demonstrate your control of the inherent factors.

Your attitude and behaviour will affect the success of any intervention. In discussions with the employee, remember that…

- Most types of behaviour have their strong points and the individuals whose behaviours are being questioned may be surprised to hear that their actions are causing concern.
- It is important to try to see things from others' perspectives. Sometimes, in order to change a bulldozer, for example, it is necessary to become one yourself.
- Positional power can be a valuable tool if it is needed.

! viewpoint

A typical classification of business behaviour types:

■ *The Hero* – always pushes too hard to do too much for too long.

■ *The Meritocrat* – ignores the politics inherent in most situations, believing that the best ideas can and will be determined objectively.

■ *The Bulldozer* – runs roughshod over others in a quest for power.

■ *The Pessimist* – focuses on the downside of everything, worrying about what can go wrong rather than considering how things could improve.

■ *The Rebel* – automatically fights against authority and convention.

■ *The Home Run Hitter* – tries to do too much too soon, swinging for the fences before learning to hit singles.[56]

---

don't forget

It's not easy…

Breaking staff members' bad habits involves changing behaviours, and that can prove very challenging. Most smokers, for example, acknowledge the health dangers and social unacceptability linked with this undesirable practice. Few, however, have the courage, willpower, and stick-ability to eliminate the habit. Some ingrained workplace practices are no less easy to eliminate.

How to negotiate and implement a collective workplace agreement

A collective workplace (enterprise) agreement is usually a result of consultation among management, employees, and unions (if they are on site or employees request their involvement). These agreements should increase productivity for the organisation through workplace reform, thus benefiting employees and customers as well. The process is best suited to companies with a good management-worker relationship and a high level of mutual trust. Here are the basics...

1 Decide what you can get out of a collective workplace agreement.

A collective agreement provides an ideal opportunity to look critically at your organisation to eliminate its inefficiencies and to increase its level of responsiveness to the benefit of all those associated with it. The collective agreement process integrates strategic workplace reform programs with the corporate planning process, so it will require the support of all key stakeholders—management, employees, and unions. Relationships at all levels, especially at the senior management level, will need to change from control- to commitment-driven.

2 Establish consultative structures.

Developing a collective agreement requires a highly consultative approach to replace the adversarial, stratified systems of industrial relations traditionally used to manage workplace change. Although, initially, you may opt for a top-down approach, a structure must be in place that allows for consultation among all stakeholders. Larger organisations may need to establish a joint sponsored project team made up of stakeholders' representatives. Consultation is a slow but essential process requiring the following steps:

- invite input from employees
- collate their feedback
- identify issues
- discuss those issues with stakeholders
- conduct workshops involving those affected
- present a draft agreement to all concerned
- produce a final agreement.

3 Build incentives into the agreement.

Opportunities exist for group and individual bonuses to be built into the agreement. By operating from a position that all salary increases are tied to achievement of key performance indicators, consultation among those directly involved will identify bonus opportunities. Employee gains would include:

- more interesting jobs with more responsibility
- more pay for more effort and skills
- the possibility of tailoring working hours more to their requirements
- job security for the term of the agreement
- increased voice in workplace issues.

Conditions and benefits for worker negotiation might include:

product and service discounts, child-care, health or recreation facilities, job redesign, flexitime, counselling, company cars, relocation or transfer expenses, parental leave, uniforms, training, job security, journal subscriptions, provision of tools, employee participation, insurance, multiskilling, expenses (telephone, power, travel), rostered days off, increased annual leave, membership of associations, superannuation or retirement benefits…

Employees need to know that, in return, such issues as these may affect them: pressure to keep improving productivity, some jobs may vanish, and changes to conditions of service, including hours of work, removal of restrictive work practices, no further claims clauses, and so on.

 Lodge the agreement.

In most jurisdictions it is a requirement that the agreement is lodged for approval with the relevant authority. In Australia, that authority is probably the Fair Work Commission—Section 185 of *The Fair Work Act* 2009 (FWA). A signed copy of the agreement and any declarations required under the procedural rules must accompany the application. Its approval requires passing the *Better-off Overall Test* (BOOT) in accordance with Section 193 of the FWA. The agreement must comply with Section 194 of the FWA and contain the mandatory clauses such as Individual Flexibility Arrangements and Consultation Provisions as prescribed in Division 5 of the FWA.

 Agree on the measures.

When the collective agreement is in place, the idea of a productivity scorecard, to record how well the reform process is progressing against agreed targets and to determine wage increases, is a useful measurement tool. Scorecard indicators may be customer service, employee satisfaction, and savings against budget. Like any other expenditure, wage increases must come from the budget. A more refined system of measurement could include key performance indicators applied to areas like service, quality, and costs. Targets must extend employees.

 Promote the benefits.

The normal employee response is initially 'What's in it for me?' If you make your collective agreement link productivity and efficiency improvements to a fair and equitable outcome-sharing model that can form the basis for wage determination, everyone profits from increased productivity. However, individuals vary in their response to organisational change, so there'll be some employees who will prefer to observe before committing themselves to the agreement. For this reason, it's important to have a support infrastructure in place to respond to employee queries and uncertainty—a telephone hotline, printed information, and trained facilitators.

 Implement the agreement.

The success of the agreement will be in its implementation. Increasing empowerment of employees commensurate with their skill development, their involvement in decision making, and ownership of organisational functions must be promoted as part of any strategy. As former General Electric CEO Jack Welch once said: 'If you give people the opportunity to spread their wings—and put compensation as a carrier behind them—you almost don't have to manage them.'

 Keep your agreement under constant review.

Keep your collective agreement under constant review relying on stakeholders' representatives to identify and act on problems before becoming major issues.

 it's a fact

In 2007 a change of government occurred in Australia. The new Labor government was quick to act to make changes to the industrial relations policies of the previous government. One of the immediate changes was the abolition of Australian Workplace Agreements (AWAs) to be replaced with Collective Workplace Agreements. Despite the controversy, particularly from many mining companies operating at the time in Western Australia, it was the view of the union movement that AWAs were an attempt to undermine the collective bargaining power of trade unions in the negotiation of pay and conditions of their members. The unions argued that the ordinary working person had little to no bargaining power by themselves to effectively negotiate an agreement with an employer, resulting in an inherently unequal bargaining power for the contract. And in other situations involving exceptional individuals and industries with labour shortages, the union movement argued that common law contracts were sufficient: fairness and equality of bargaining power remained. AWAs were abolished in favour of collective bargaining.

 read further

www.fairwork.gov.au provides a useful introduction to this topic. Consult local sources for requirements in your State.

How to terminate a person's employment

Termination—sometimes referred to as 'firing' or 'sacking'—is the act of ending a contract of employment. It can be an unpleasant task for a manager, compounded by the necessity of complying with relevant legislation. (In Australia, for employers covered by WorkChoices, it is the *Workplace Relations Act 1996*.) That Act aims to balance fairness to employees with the needs of employers to dismiss employees when there is a good reason. Here are some key considerations to ensure the process is handled competently...

? ask yourself

■ Did you give the employee advance warning of the consequences of the unacceptable conduct?

■ Did you conduct an in-depth investigation to determine if the employee did, in fact, violate the rule or procedure?

■ Has the company applied a similar penalty to other staff who have committed a similar offence in the past?

■ Is the employee's dismissal fair in light of years of service and record, the seriousness of the offence? Was progressive discipline used, if warranted, based on the offence, to try and correct such unacceptable behaviour in the past?

1 Make sure of your facts beforehand.

Termination can no longer be a matter of managerial whim. You must do your homework and make sure your actions satisfy the relevant legislative requirements of the day. In the Australian context, a person's employment may be terminated...

• by notice under an award, agreement, or other contractual provision. Adequate notice must be given: for example, 3-5 years continuous service requires 3 weeks' notice.
• by a contractual provision being fulfilled
• as a consequence of other events—death of employee, closure of business
• in cases of misconduct—assault, drugs, dishonesty, fraud, insubordination...
• through redundancy—usually retrenchment of a number of staff
• by resignation.

2 Ensure procedural fairness.

Unless you have exemption from unfair dismissal claims under the Act, it is not sufficient to dismiss an employee with only the requisite period of notice. The employee must be

• given a valid reason for the dismissal
• notified of the reason
• given a chance to reply to allegations

• warned previously in writing about his or her conduct
• given another opportunity to meet stated performance standards.

Where an applicant's termination is deemed to be unfair, the Courts may order reinstatement and payment of lost wages or other compensation.

Exemptions from unfair dismissal may cover WorkChoices employers with fewer than 100 employees, at the time of dismissal, or for employers with over 100 employees, the employee must meet a qualifying period of six months (agreed to in writing prior to commencement) before they can access unfair dismissal legislation.

3 Guard against unfair and unlawful dismissal.

Within 21 days of a dismissal, an employee may apply to the Australian Industrial Relations Commission alleging the dismissal was harsh, unjust, or unreasonable. The Commission will first attempt to conciliate the matter and the result of those efforts could lead to arbitration or a hearing. Generally, where unfairness is alleged, a claim will be heard by the Commission; the case for alleged unlawful dismissal will be heard in a Court of competent jurisdiction. Unlawful termination may occur in four different situations:

- Temporary absence due to illness or injury; union membership or non-membership; acting or having acted as an employee representative; filing a complaint or participating in proceedings against the employer involving an illegal violation of laws or regulations; discriminatory reasons; refusal to negotiate, sign, or otherwise be involved in a certified workplace agreement; and absence due to taking parental or maternity leave.
- Insufficient notice (or payment in lieu)
- Failure by the employer to comply with the Commission's order concerning severance allowance
- Where the employer dismisses 15 or more employees on the grounds of retrenchment or redundancy, and fails to notify Centrelink of the reasons, the number and categories of employees, and the period over which the termination will take place.

4 Arrange termination payment.

Termination payment should be prepared as part of the termination interview and is likely to include some, or all, of the following:

- Payment of work done to date
- Payment in lieu of notice
- Payment for accrued but untaken leave loading (at the ordinary rate of pay at the date of termination)
- Payment for fully accrued but untaken long service leave, or pro rata long service entitlement
- Job or employment protection payments, sometimes called 'severance pay', when an employee is dismissed as part of a retrenchment of employees caused by redundancy.

5 Meet with the employee.

Select an appropriate time for the meeting and a suitable private location

to allow you to call a halt to discussions if things become difficult.

If termination is the issue:
- Be brief, clear, firm, and to the point.
- Stick to the facts and information documented.
- Provide all necessary documentation— including termination payment.
- Empathise with the person, but stay firm and calm.
- Be precise as to the exact termination date—the sooner the better.

If retrenchment is the issue:
- Make it clear that the decision is non-negotiable, and that the decision was taken in view of the current financial circumstances in the organisation.
- Assure the employee that there is no implication of deficient performance.
- Communicate what severance will be paid and what outplacement support is offered. This should be made clear in a written letter handed to the employee at that time.

In both cases:
- Institute security procedures promptly —stop access to credit cards, purchase authorisations, computers, security numbers, keys to car park, building etc. Terminations should be escorted from the building and retrenchments given access only to those limited areas related to any task being completed.
- Provide the person with a way to save face by agreeing on a common story that will be communicated both internally and externally.
- Nip rumours in the bud. Inform all relevant staff but respect the employee and the confidentiality of the interview.

6 Document the event.

Following the interview, ensure that all data relevant to the dismissal is recorded, signed, and dated. If you have a concern that a dispute may arise, seek additional counsel from your professional association.

don't forget

Consider this useful advice

■ Every worker is entitled to be treated with dignity and allowed to retain his or her self-worth.

■ All workers strive for fair treatment.

■ How you terminate employees will have an effect on those workers who remain with you.

■ The termination process is a learning experience for both employee and employer; it is a two-way process.

■ Termination can be just as important as hiring, and is just one of many management tools.

■ When you hire an employee, be aware that termination is always a possibility later on. Keep that in mind, in fact, in dealing with all employees.

■ To avoid legal consequences, remember that ongoing communication is crucial, especially when a termination becomes a possibility.[58]

quotable quote

The law does not prevent employers from dismissing employees, providing the dismissal is dealt with in an appropriate manner – 'a fair go all round'.[59]

How to conduct an exit interview

Employees leave organisations for a variety of reasons— a desire to pursue other careers, offers too good to refuse, imposed retrenchments, or dissatisfaction with their current positions. Exit interviews are conducted just before an employee leaves. The meetings not only provide valuable information that can benefit the organisation but also attempt to end the relationship harmoniously...

here's an idea

To be as objective and as open as possible, the exit interview should be conducted by someone other than the employee's supervisor.

here's an idea

Employees who leave your organisation usually have deeper reasons for leaving than the one they give. Smart questioning will often reveal the real reasons.

1 Develop and implement an exit procedure.

Exit interviews are a valuable management practice that should occur for every employee leaving your organisation. The interviews offer a fleeting opportunity to gather information about your organisation that might otherwise be difficult to obtain, and provide a parting employee with the chance to be far more frank than he or she might normally be. It provides an excellent mechanism for taking a good hard look at your organisation.

Make sure that all employees know the importance you place on such interviews. Assign the responsibility to one person—the general manager, the human resource manager, or their nominee.

2 Plan for the interview.

An exit interview is more than an informal chit-chat. It allows an employee the opportunity to explain reasons for resigning or to reflect on the period of employment.

The interview procedure should focus on a detailed list of questions designed to get the information you consider relevant to organisational improvement. General headings might include 'leadership', 'my management', 'training', 'unfulfilled expectations', 'policies', 'morale', 'customer service', and 'salary'. The employee responses will provide valuable data for use in improving operational effectiveness.

3 Schedule the interview.

You want an open discussion, so the timing and the venue will be most important. For a senior employee, for example, you or your nominee may decide to conduct the meeting over lunch. During the last week is a good time for that meeting. Tell the departing employee that you intend to take notes so that you will consider and perhaps act on relevant comments. The number of times a similar item is recorded during other such interviews indicates a direction for your follow-up actions.

4. Assure confidentiality.

When people are leaving the organisation they are likely to be open about issues that may have affected their decision. Assure them that anything they have to say will be held in strict confidence.

 ### 5. Find out about the former employee's new job.

This topic will not only get the person talking but also provide useful information about reasons for leaving. You will gain valuable information about what is so attractive elsewhere as well as what is so unattractive about your organisation and what it has failed to offer.

 ### 6. Ask, ask, ask.

If there is something you want to know, ask. The exit interview allows you to be as probing as you like. That's why you should try to ask open-ended questions (those that do not encourage straight 'yes' or 'no' answers). And remember that examples help to communicate meaning, so ask, 'Can you give an example of that?'

7. Check feedback on outplacement services.

If you are paying for outplacement, ask for a summary of the value of assistance given thus far. The employee's satisfaction with the service will also provide a useful assessment of the service being offered by the contracted firm.

 ### 8. Settle money and security matters.

Be prepared to outline all the necessary arrangements regarding back pay, entitlements, references, and security matters. Err on the side of generosity if there are any doubts about any issues. If you are not the person to settle those matters, make sure the right person is available immediately after your meeting.

 ### 9. Offer to act as referee—but...

Guard against providing a reference carte blanche. Instead, offer to act as a referee by asking that you be contacted with specific details of any position being sought; you are communicating to the employee that you want to provide a reference of substance. You are also indicating that any 'general' reference the employee requests may be inappropriate: you'd prefer to link the person's qualities and experience to a specific position. Remember, you also have your reputation to consider and should not want to provide inappropriate information to any new employer. You can opt to provide a verbal reference when required.

 ### 10. End the interview positively.

Employees leaving your organisation can provide a source of positive advertising, so ensure the departing employee does so with the message your organisation hopes to communicate in public. Wish the employee well in any new career choices and make every attempt to part on a friendly basis.

 ### don't forget

The basics

- Prefer oral interviews to written surveys.
- Think carefully about the questions you want to ask before the interview.
- Work up to the tough stuff. Save the hardest questions to the end.
- Good questions would include: 'Why are you leaving', 'Under what conditions would you have stayed?', 'What did you like most (least) about your position?', and 'If you had a magic wand, what would you change?'
- Be prepared for some unexpected bombshells, which will happen, if anywhere, at an exit interview.
- Use an interviewer who listens well and is open-minded. The last thing you need is an argument with a parting employee.
- Try to find out if there were things the departing employee would suggest to improve conditions, production or morale.
- It's more important to listen than to write copiously. Take a few notes and provide the written detail later.
- Make use of the information gathered. If you do not use this new information, why do an interview? [61]

435

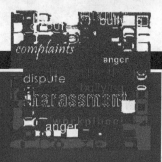

How to avoid causing conflict

don't forget

To minimise conflict...

- Say something good about another person or event before saying what you don't like.
- Recognise that, though a particular issue may seem critical at the time, in the overall scheme of life, it just may not be that monumental after all.
- Understand that feelings are not bad; only destructive behaviour is bad.
- A calm, reasoned response is always better than a hasty reaction.
- Accept others as they are, even all their shortcomings and annoying habits.[2]

Conflict is inevitable in any organisation. When handled properly, it can contribute significantly to personal and organisational health. It can improve understanding and produce innovative solutions to problems. When handled poorly, however, it leads to hurt feelings, damaged relationships, and low morale. Managers must be able to minimise hostility between themselves and their staff members; and the best way to manage harmful conflict is to prevent it from ever arising. Here are some suggestions...

1 Learn to be an effective communicator.

Communication is the lifeblood of an organisation. Conflict is often caused by people not listening to or understanding each other. Misunderstandings can result in accusations, blame, and personal attacks. At times, there is no real conflict, simply misinterpretation.

Work at improving your communication skills for listening and speaking so that you minimise misunderstanding. Convey the need for clarity in all your discussions.

2 Keep your staff informed.

By withholding information from all those it affects, you can create tension amongst staff, often causing some of them to react adversely and, in doing so, generate conflict situations.

3 Be honest and open with your staff.

When people feel threatened, they become defensive. The best way to discourage any fear of intimidation is for you to behave in a nonthreatening manner. Be open and honest with staff at all times. The more you are perceived as honest and forthright, and receptive and open to the feelings and opinions of others, the less inclined employees will be to go on the defensive. A climate of openness and honesty will prevent minor issues from blowing out into major catastrophes.

4 Avoid the use of threats, demands, and put-downs.

When you denigrate, moralise, threaten, or make demands of others, you are creating a conflict situation. Resist becoming involved in the conflict-generating games that people play.

Do not be hasty to judge others openly; never make personal attacks on people behind their backs or in public; never belittle others' achievements; rather, celebrate with them; and keep your pessimism to yourself.

Stay cool.

Don't let other people push your 'get angry' button. There are times when a show of anger may serve you well; there are times when it is smarter to keep your cool. Before over-reacting to anything, count to ten and check out the facts: perhaps you misunderstood, perhaps you misheard... Skirmishes can readily develop into battles.

 Criticise with caution.

You will be required from time to time to point out mistakes or critique the work of your staff. This should be undertaken in a spirit of support: never criticise anyone's work unless you can make practical suggestions for improvement.

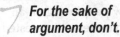 **For the sake of argument, don't.**

Arguing is a needless waste of energy and time. A battle between two closed minds only results in both parties clinging more tenaciously to their positions. It is far wiser to listen to the other point of view, understand the stance being taken, and attempt to guide the other party towards your point of view through negotiation.

 Try to be tolerant of others.

Be aware that rarely is anyone 'right', because all of us view situations through our own unique perceptual filters. Conflict arises when we refuse to respect or tolerate another person's values or opinions. Never condemn someone for failing to live up to your expectations, for such behaviour breeds hostility and frustration that is guaranteed to hurt your colleague—and you as well.

 Never play favourites.

The teacher's pet is often the cause of much resentment in the classroom. So too in the management situation. Avoid the friction caused among staff when you intentionally or unintentionally show preference for one staff member over another.

 Confront an emerging conflict head-on.

Finally, if a conflict situation between you and a member of staff seems inevitable, tackle it immediately by discussing it with those involved. Never leave the scene, sulk, or withdraw support or cooperation when the going gets tough—such behaviour will not defuse the core issue. Ignoring conflict situations will only ensure greater problems later on.

Carl Rogers suggested that, to clear up misunderstanding promptly, each party should restate the other's position to the other's satisfaction, thereby forcing each to briefly adopt the other's frame of reference. The situation then becomes less emotional, with both parties doing more thinking and listening. The more rational people become, the greater the opportunity for conflict resolution.

? ask yourself

You *can* keep conflicts in your workplace to a minimum. But, for starters, to keep things running smoothly in your area, do you:

☐ Listen carefully to employees to prevent misunderstandings?

☐ Monitor employees' work to help you understand and coordinate their actions?

☐ Encourage employees to come to you when they can't solve problems with co-workers on their own?

☐ Clear the air with regular meetings that give employees a chance to discuss grievances?

☐ Provide a suggestion box, check it frequently, and personally reply to all signed suggestions?

☐ Offer as much information as possible about decisions (yours and management's) to minimise confusion and resentment?

☐ Use employee surveys to look for conflicts that haven't yet surfaced?

! viewpoint

"You never really understand a person until you consider things from his point of view."

– Harper Lee in *To Kill a Mockingbird*

437

How to deal with complaints

The way in which managers deal with complaints or grievances
can make the difference between satisfied, cooperative
complainants and those who become constant sources
of irritation and trouble. Your response to complaints must
demonstrate two things—your interest and willingness to get
involved, and your commitment to a fair deal for everyone. Here
are some basic principles that will leave complainants feeling
positive about how you've handled their concerns…

1 Show your concern and remain calm.

Complaints are important to the
aggrieved, so give them a chance to let
off steam and to express their feelings.
If they have a problem, you might
have one, too. It's OK for them to be
upset, but you need to remain calm, in
control, tactful, and ready to respond.

2 Be objective.

Your job is not to judge—the issue
is not really about who is right.
The complainant is simply seeking
satisfaction. You must make it clear
that you are interested in the problem
and are concerned with fair treatment.
Often the opportunity to complain is
just as important to some people as
any resolution of the issue.

3 Be prepared to listen.

Every story has at least two sides, and
you are about to hear one of them.
Listen to, and empathise with, the
complainant. This not only shows

respect, but might also enable you to
find out what the real problem is—
including any hidden agenda—and the
depth of feeling associated with the
complaint. Your considered response
will demonstrate that you have
taken the matter seriously. If you are
particularly busy at the time, make an
appointment to meet within a day or
two. Never allow people to gain an
impression that you're not interested.

4 Assemble the facts.

Although you will want to avoid
any escalation of the perceived
problem, you should resist making
a decision until you've probed for
the facts. Complainants may attempt
to minimise their part in a problem
by selectively omitting certain
details, so search beneath the surface
to understand what is involved
without trying to manoeuvre them
into admitting the complaint is
unfounded. Finally, state your
interpretation of the key issues and
allow the complainant to clarify
where necessary. Effective handling

of the complaint at this early stage could avoid complications later.

Direct the complainant to the right person.

Sometimes the best help you can give complainants is to put them in touch with the person who can help to solve their problem. You should make the necessary arrangements for discussions to take place.

Use creative techniques.

Complaining is a form of attention-seeking. By understanding the complainant's motivation, you will be able to adopt an appropriate strategy. For example:

- *Passivity*. Respond when you're ready; just sit; let the complainant exhaust the verbal tirade to the point of repetition before responding.

- *Positive reframing*. Change negatives to positives. Whatever someone complains about, counter with a good point. You might get the complainant to stop and think, even back off.

- *Monkey manoeuvring*. Avoid taking care of other people's monkeys by asking them, 'What are *you* going to do about it?' or 'Do *you* have a workable solution?'

Adopt and follow a grievance procedure.

If you have ISO 9000 certification, you will have in place documented procedures and accompanying work instructions for reporting and handling 'non-conformances', including complaints. If not, develop procedures for handling complaints and educate employees and

customers about those procedures. Though not every complaint will require strict adherence to formal, documented procedures, you can't afford to ignore a grievance or complaint.

Address the complaint; advise of the decision.

It's safe to assume that anyone coming to you with a complaint or grievance would like a direct answer. Either give it in clear, definite, understandable terms, or guarantee a response by a certain time. If further time is required to investigate, unanticipated delays should be communicated to the complainant. Once you've made your decision, tell the person yourself. Any misunderstanding can be clarified at this point. Though complainants may not always agree with your decisions, they should understand that their complaints were given very serious consideration.

And don't forget...

Other important points worth remembering include:

- Avoid 'off-the-cuff' remarks.
- Practise patience.
- Concede any point that you can.
- Admit any errors.
- Never laugh off a complaint.
- Help people to voice their complaint.
- If you're at fault, admit it, apologise, take steps to ensure it won't recur, and move on.
- Alert your superiors if you feel the grievance could escalate.
- Review your procedure to see if you could have handled the process better.

! **viewpoint**

"After listening to his gripe, I don't tell the employee with the complaint what I'm going to do – I ask him what he wants me to do for him. I've had men look at me in astonishment and say, 'Mr Feldman, I honestly don't know. I hadn't thought about that. I just wanted someone to listen to my side of the story for a change. You've done that for me, so that's enough. I'm satisfied.'

Sometimes they will tell me what they expect me to do. Ninety-five times out of a hundred, I find they ask for much less than I'd have offered them. Then, when I give them more, they're really impressed with my generosity.

Either way, when they leave, they're fully satisfied. You see, in both cases, they supplied themselves with their own answers, so they're bound to be completely happy with the end result."

– Roy Feldman, American Motors

How to handle an angry person

When an angry employee or customer bursts into your office, rarely do you have time to prepare yourself. Often, you are not the target of that anger; but you must be able to bear the brunt of the emotional onslaught. How do you normally respond? Do you become confused? Defensive? Disoriented? Are you always tempted to return anger with more anger? What is needed is self-control, calmness, a touch of assertiveness, and (most importantly) a sincere desire to solve whatever problem has caused the outburst...

Acknowledge the person's anger up front.

Nothing adds more fuel to the fire of anger than to have it brushed aside, ignored, or challenged. Anger is a symptom of a greater problem so make it clear immediately that you realise the person is upset: 'I can see that this is important to you—so it's important to me too. Let's go and have a talk about it.'

The message you thus send is twofold: first, it says that you're interested in helping with the problem; and, second, it makes clear that you're not going to combat rage with rage. Your supportive comments don't condone anger, but drive home the need to redirect these emotions constructively.

Be calm and confident.

It is essential when confronted by an angry person to remain calm, dignified, express confidence in your face and body language, and speak in a steady voice that says you are concerned but not intimidated.

It's vital not to respond aggressively to another's anger. If faced with shouting and profanity, draw a line: 'I have no intention of raising my voice during our discussion, and I ask that you extend the same courtesy to me'. No-one can win with an angry exchange of words.

Provide a non-threatening environment.

Your aim is not to shut them up or outshout them, but to devise a solution for their problem. The search for a solution can only begin in a non-threatening environment, so move any confrontation to a private setting such as your office. Get the person seated (it's harder to continue an outburst from a sitting position) and at ease.

Come out from behind the barrier created by your desk. Try a less formal setting such as adjacent, on one side of a table.

Listen to what the person has to say.

If the other party is still fuming,

let them get it all out before you start responding. If you maintain eye contact and listen actively without saying anything, the angry person will run out of steam much sooner—it's not easy to keep yelling at someone who doesn't respond. By letting the person get it off the chest, you are going a long way towards defusing a volatile situation.

Ask questions.

As anger subsides, to get at the seat of the fire you'll need to smoke out the real problem, which the person may not readily be honest about. You may need to ask plenty of questions— you're now moving the discussion more clearly into the objective, rather than the subjective, phase.

Focus on facts. People often get more and more angry because they're confused as well as disappointed. The more you and your angry client or staff member focus on cold, hard facts, the less you'll get caught up in red-hot emotions. You'll get less stressed and you'll have a happier client sooner.

Summarise the situation as you see it.

Without being aggressive or defensive, work through the facts as you now understand them, being as objective as possible. The other party can confirm, correct or add to your understanding of the issue.

Work towards a solution.

By now you will know whether you are dealing with a reasonable person. If you've listened calmly, asked questions in a courteous and concerned manner, and are now about to explore solutions, then the other person's anger should have cooled so that you can talk rationally about the problem. However, if the person is still too angry to consider solutions, it may be best to postpone the discussion, allowing time to reflect and regain composure.

But if discussion is now possible, explore with the other party the various options for a fair and equitable solution. Finally, agree on the solution that meets your mutual needs as fully as possible within the bounds of any existing constraints.

Act on the solution.

If the organisation or you are to blame, admit it. Apologise and assure the person that it will not happen again. If the other party is in the wrong, be firm in stating this without overreacting. If another person is involved, state your intention to gather further information before deciding on any action. Indicate that you will advise later of your decision. Above all, demonstrate fairness and an interest in the person and the problem.

Express appreciation.

Thank the other party for sharing the problem with you and guarantee your continuing interest, concern, and intention to use the opinions of customers and staff in serving their best interests as well as the interests of the organisation.

441

How to use anger constructively

Anger is a destructive human emotion. Rarely do we profit in any way from a spontaneous outburst of temper. It accomplishes nothing, regardless of whether it is aimed at others, inanimate objects, or ourselves. But at times, provided it is well timed and used to create energy rather than drain it, anger can be a powerful management tool. Here are some useful considerations to help you use anger constructively...

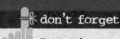

don't forget

Four rules to defuse anger...

The best way to manage a potential conflict situation between you and a colleague is to anticipate it and defuse it. These four rules always help...

- *Do something about whatever you're angry about – or forget it.* Never hold a grudge.

- *Write down your anger.* This lets you organise your thoughts and react constructively, rather than passing on your anger to someone else.

- Use *'I' statements, not 'you' statements.* Talk about how *you* feel and how *you* see things, not about the other person in the conflict.

- *Remember the future.* Before sounding off now, think about the effect this might have on future working relationships.

1 Realise you get angry; no one forces you to.

Each of us has our very own emotional buttons that just wait to be pushed; they reach out like antennae and actively pick up trouble. It's these buttons that hurt us. It's not what someone says or does that hurts—it's our *own* buttons that do it. The incident simply pushes our provocative, sensitive button and— clunk!

Anger is one such button. You're the only person who can be in control of your anger button, so don't relinquish that control to others by getting angered in situations of *their* making where *you'll* be sorry afterwards.

2 Put the lid on spontaneous anger.

It's been said that getting angry can be like leaping into a wonderfully responsive sports car, gunning the motor, taking off at high speed—and then discovering the brakes are out of order. Which is why you should always try to keep your immediate anger in check by considering those time-honoured coping devices—count to ten, bite your tongue, walk away.

The best coping strategy is to give your anger a raincheck. Provide yourself with a cooling off period. If someone upsets you, tell yourself, 'I'll get mad about this tomorrow'. Postponing anger is the best way to minimise its damage. If you spontaneously unload this potentially destructive emotion onto an employee or colleague, then minor mishaps can escalate into major catastrophes. Postponing an angry outburst can reduce the odds of that happening. Speak when you're angry and you may make the best speech you will ever regret.

Postponement also helps in that you can take a minute or two to remind yourself of the offender's good points and value to your organisation—which in turn may also prevent you from jumping in boots and all.

By postponing anger, you take the first vital step to using anger constructively.

Identify the cause and arrange a meeting.

Never resort to venting your anger on another person in public. To get the best results, tell the person concerned that a serious discussion is coming up. You might say, 'We have a problem and I'm going to talk to you about it later. When can we get together where we won't be interrupted for a while?' The news is unlikely to come as a shock to the other person, but your announcement will create a little healthy anxiety.

 Talk problems, not personalities.

People can normally justify behaving as they do; so try to understand why they behaved in the manner that resulted in your anger and this will help your discussions considerably. Separating the personality from the problem can be a challenge. But this can, and must, be done if you are to get people to help you rather than want to get even with you.

 Be precise.

When people earn your rejection, tell them. Let them know that you are angry, what precisely is making you feel that way, and exactly what has to be done to eliminate your anger. Express this in plain language, choosing words that will get the point across. Your choice of words must not only provide relief to your own frustrations but must also influence the other person to change. Remember: getting angry at this point is unlikely to get you anything else.

 Seek immediate feedback.

Don't forget: *you* don't own the problem (the cause of your anger) so leave the monkey where it belongs— with its rightful owner. Find out what actions the other person is going to take to remove the monkey and agree on a timetable for those actions. Any decisions made must be owned by the other person or your efforts will go unrewarded.

 Quit when you're in front.

You've relayed your concerns, communicated your feelings and hopes, and the other person has got the message. Quit. If you ramble on after you've covered the matter, the other person will decide that you're simply unloading your own problems rather than sincerely trying to achieve anything positive. Thank the person for contributing to a solution; offer help with any follow-up actions; and end the meeting. Make a note (mental or written) to touch base informally with the person over the next forty-eight hours. During that get-together you may decide to express your appreciation of their contributions.

 Review your performance.

Evaluate the way you handled the situation. Did your postponed display of anger achieve its desired outcome? Would you use a similar approach again in a similar situation? Hopefully, you will conclude that responding through anger to people, rather than reacting angrily to them, is the preferred alternative.

---

here's an idea

Whenever the famous inventor Thomas Edison was angry, he sat down and wrote a scathing letter – to himself. He left it on his desk for a day or two, and then he tore it up.

There is a message here for all of us: do not write anything, certainly not an email, memo or letter to anyone (other than to yourself) while you are angry. An emotional upset impairs rational thinking. Wait until you simmer down. What you write in fury you will almost certainly regret in composure.

 viewpoint

"When you are in the right, you can afford to keep your temper. When you are in the wrong, you cannot afford to lose it."

– Mohandas Gandhi

 don't forget

What anger really is

Anger is just one letter short of Danger.

Anger is never without a reason, but seldom with a good one.

Anger is a stone cast into a wasps' nest.

Anger is the wind that blows out the lamp of reason.

Anger improves nothing except the arch in a cat's back.

443

How to take the heat out of a confrontation

Confrontations are unpleasant but inevitable. What is important is that they can provide valuable opportunities to identify and deal with problems that otherwise might have simmered undetected. But there is a technique to handle them constructively. When you find yourself in face-to-face confrontations, here is what you can do to defuse, resolve, and profit from that potentially explosive situation…

quotable quote

By bringing conflicts out into the open and overcoming them, we develop honest, forthright, and loving relationships with ourselves and others. We turn heat into light.[6]

here's an idea

During a confrontation, if you reach an impasse, consider calling in a third party, depending on the seriousness of the conflict:

■ Experts are neutral third parties. Their responsibility is simple: to provide data, facts, and information that may help the involved parties improve their understanding of the objective issues in a dispute.

■ Mediation is a process in which a third person helps the parties in conflict to collaborate. Mediators do this by listening, asking questions, and creating a supportive and constructive environment.

■ Arbitration rulings may be binding or voluntary. You get an answer but since the involved parties don't participate in the solution, they may be less committed to implementing it.

■ Litigation is the process of going to court to get a ruling on an issue. The main benefit is that the solution is binding. Litigation, however, is a final solution, and it's costly, time consuming, and creates a very competitive situation.

1 Make confrontation constructive.

For a confrontation to become a beneficial episode, it should provide the following outcomes:

• The other person's behaviour changes in the manner desired.

• The self-esteem of the other person is preserved.

• Your relationship with the other person remains intact.

These outcomes can be realised if you remain objective about the other person's undesirable behaviour, listen to the other person's response, identify the effects, describe future expectations, and commit or agree to future behaviour.

2 Choose the time and place.

Don't fuel the fire by initiating any conflict in public. Also avoid confronting people after a hard day, before an event at which they have to be at their best, when they are dealing with a mistake or loss, or when they're working under the cloud of

an imminent deadline. Choose time and place carefully. Sensitivity to the other person's circumstances is always important, but in a conflict it is critical.

3 Keep your cool and listen.

Listen to everything the other party is saying and not just for what you want to hear. Don't let the other person's tactics unsettle you. Remember the adage: Never answer an angry word with an angry word. It's the second one that turns anger into confrontation.

Give yourself time. Keep calm and tell your adversary that you would rather discuss the observable facts and not personal opinions. You'll find that your actions will enable a focus on solutions rather than an attribution of blame.

4 Develop strategies to cope with confrontation.

Learn to accept conflict as inevitable and develop tactics to handle it

444

when it occurs. Coping mechanisms include:

Count to ten. Deep breathing helps to lower your emotional temperature, and can even cool the other person's anger.

Take 5. If you're not getting anywhere, postpone the encounter.

Set a time. Regroup, get your house in order, and resume.

Go for a walk. It is often easier to talk about difficult issues during a long walk. It also solves the problem of what to do with your hands and any difficulty you have with eye-to-eye contact.

Use 'I-language'. State your case in terms of your own feelings.

Agree. Where appropriate, agreement defuses most confrontations.

Side-step. Maintain strong and confident eye contact for a second or so—then move on.

Rehearse your responses. Thinking afterwards, 'I wish I would have said that', indicates you weren't prepared.

Control voice tone, tempo, volume, and nonverbals. It's not what you say, but how you say it.

Switch from content to process.

You *talk* about 'content'; how you *deal* with content is 'process'. When no progress is being made with content, it is often because the process is not working. So, try to negotiate a better way of dealing with the process. You might say, 'John, I'm getting a bit frustrated because I'm not getting anywhere. You don't wait for me to finish what I'm saying, and I don't

believe I'm conveying what I want to say to you. I can't operate that way. Can we work out a different way of doing it?'

Settle it now or postpone it.

If you can resolve the issue without attempting to allocate any blame, do so. But, if necessary, don't be reluctant to call a halt to things and set a time and date for resumption. Your actions will show that you're taking the problem seriously and want to resolve it in the fairest way possible.

Consider involving a third party.

A 'win-lose' outcome is really 'no-win' because it usually means that people are locked into their set positions, any goodwill is gone, and the goal is to win only. You need to break out of that mind-set by considering other options—like using a third party. Often the dynamics of a situation will change in the presence of a third person. If there is someone who is trusted and respected by both you and your adversary, enlist that person's help to see the problem through to a successful conclusion.

Arrange a follow-up.

Just as it is helpful to keep your conflict focused on the specifics of the problem, it pays to keep the solution focused on the specific *action* that will be taken. Set a follow-up date to meet again to discuss progress—and to strengthen any shaky bridges.

445

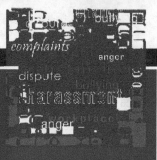
How to mediate a staff dispute

In a dispute between staff members, attitudes tend to polarise; perspectives usually get set in concrete; the middle ground is ignored; and a feeling of 'win-lose' predominates. To prevent this conflict from reaching such an impasse, you may find it necessary to intervene as a third-party mediator (as opposed to an arbitrator who makes the final decision after both sides have presented their cases). Your aim as a mediator would be to defuse the emotions of the combatants and to catalyse their own efforts to reach a mutually acceptable resolution...

1 Intervene before it's too late.

You need a reason to get involved in a staff dispute. Clearly, if you allow the conflict to get out of hand, it will disrupt the workplace and impact eventually on total staff harmony and effectiveness. So, state your concerns to both parties, either separately or together, and indicate that you wish to meet with both to establish, at least, a better working relationship.

2 Prepare both parties for the mediation process.

Explain the process to both staff members and inform them how the session will be conducted. Emphasise your role: you are not there to judge who is right or wrong; you will not be telling them how they will resolve their differences; you will not be taking sides. Your role is as a catalyst, to help the parties generate for themselves a solution with which they both are comfortable and to which they can commit themselves.

3 Get the issues out into the open.

'Getting it off the chest' is a very important part of the process. There are various approaches that might be considered. For example:

(a) Have each person explain the dispute from his or her perspective—without interruption. Encourage open and honest expression. After each has concluded, you then summarise the facts (not the emotions) of what you have heard from both parties. Confirm with them the accuracy of your summaries.

(b) Alternatively, have both parties complete two lists responding to, firstly, 'What I like about your behaviour and want you to continue', and, secondly, 'What I don't like about your behaviour and want you to change'. This information is then exchanged one item at a time so that each person understands the other's perspective. You dictate when each party responds, using this process:

• Sue takes one item from one of her

lists and outlines it as clearly as she can and, if possible, without blame, criticism, or demand.

- Ken then seeks clarification, if necessary, before responding to Sue's statement.
- When this sequence is complete, Ken then presents one item from his lists and the above procedure is repeated in reverse with Sue responding.
- Continue this process through the lists.

Continue this approach until all relevant information has been exchanged and understood. Even if the conflict remains unresolved, a better understanding of the problems by both parties will have resulted.

 Identify the issues.

Because you are not directly involved, you are in a good position to help both individuals see the conflict as a difference of issues rather than personalities. Separate the people from the problem. Only when the issues have been isolated will both parties see the conflict as a shared problem that will require the cooperation of both to resolve.

 Generate solutions.

Having pinpointed the real issues fuelling the dispute, encourage both parties to identify possible solutions to the conflict. Resist the temptation to put forward your own solutions or to evaluate their suggestions. Challenge both to consider what they want to see occur in the future rather than

allow them to dwell on the past. If the process is in danger of bogging down, lead with 'Let me offer a suggestion...' or 'Why not consider trying...?' Continually express your pleasure at any shift towards resolution of the dispute.

 Reach an agreement.

Write down solutions or areas of agreement as they are mutually accepted. Ensure that this record of agreement is clear and concise, and that both parties have a mutual understanding of what each is promising to do to resolve the conflict. Congratulate both individuals for their ability to resolve the dispute cooperatively and productively.

7 **Follow-up the agreement.**

While agreement is a major achievement, implementation is the key to success or failure. Discuss how the situation might be reviewed over an agreed period.

8 **Remember also...**

- Try to build the discussions around questions rather than demands or recriminations.
- When language gets strong, ask people to repeat the statement. The tone is usually less strident second time round.
- Don't speak on behalf of one to the other.
- Sometimes the process of mediation can take considerable time.
- Avoid 'I win-You lose' endings at all costs.

 don't forget

Advice for mediators:

- Stress the goals that are common to both sides. Build upon common goals and keep reviewing areas of agreement.
- Be a good listener. Take notes and show concern.
- Avoid working with groups that are too large. Triads do not work well, neither do groups in excess of seven or eight members.
- Emotions may be unavoidable, but do not allow decisions to be made while emotions are high.
- Continually express confidence in the group's ability to reach a fair solution.
- When the conflict is resolved, ask participants to state their perception of the solution and what will be accomplished by it.

How to handle harassment in the workplace

Legislation today requires companies to create a working environment free from harassment; they must have procedures for dealing with any reported incidents of harassment. You should have mechanisms for preventing workplace behaviour that attacks—verbally, physically, or psychologically—an employee's sex, colour, age, religious beliefs, disability, or race. These suggestions may help…

Acknowledge the possibility…

Cynthia Berryman-Fink cautions managers everywhere:

'One outdated approach to sexual harassment is that harassment does not occur in "our" company and that women who accuse men of sexual harassment are overreacting to or misinterpreting certain types of behaviour. That view trivialises the subject, maintaining that allegations of sexual harassment stem from romances that have gone sour, from women taking offense at well-intentioned compliments, or from overly sensitive women employees who are not tough enough to handle a normal work environment.

Managers who hold this view will dismiss reports of sexual harassment by indicating that boys will be boys, that the accuser must have behaved provocatively, that women have no sense of humour, and that no harm was intended. In short, sexual harassment is regarded as nonexistent, as an overreaction, or as a misunderstanding between two people. By perceiving harassment as an interpersonal rather than an organisational matter, managers who adhere to this school of thought either refrain from getting involved or try to protect the accused party.

Although some organisations seem to operate smoothly with this perspective, there is no way to determine the costs of absenteeism, medical benefits claims, turnover, or decreased morale or productivity resulting from unresolved incidents of sexual harassment. Such organisations and their managers clearly expose themselves to financially disastrous lawsuits, in light of contemporary EEO guidelines.'[8]

Establish and publish a policy.

Familiarise yourself with your organisation's policy on harassment. If no policy exists, campaign for one. It should define harassment, provide clear examples of harassment, and explain the organisational procedure for reporting and dealing with complaints. Provide copies of your policy to all employees.

Educate your employees.

A policy alone may not be sufficient.

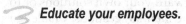

Provide training to clarify the issue, to show management support in preventing harassment, to encourage staff to discuss the matter, and to teach employees how to deal with offensive behaviour in the workplace. Managers themselves also need to know how to detect signs of harassment, how to intervene, and how to process complaints received.

 Establish investigative procedures.

Knowing how to conduct a fair investigation can ensure you take action appropriate to the offence. Consider these guidelines:

- *Interview the complainant.* Determine what happened, when, who else might be aware of the incident, the background, and attitudes towards the accused.

- *Interview the accused.* Have a third person present and allow the accused to choose that person. Tell the accused what the accusation has been and make sure the nature of the claim is understood. Again, identify the facts of the incident.

- *Interview all key witnesses.* Discretion is insufficient reason not to interview someone. Be aware that third parties often tend to take sides, so isolate and document facts rather than opinions.

- *Mediate a meeting between the complainant and the accused* if such a meeting would not be too traumatic or sensitive. This can clarify perceptions, reveal management's concern, and often resolve the incident.

- *Make an objective decision.* The final decision must be based on facts, not personal attitudes or relationships. Weigh up the evidence. Objectivity is essential.

 Consider the range of disciplinary measures available.

Once a complaint has been judged to be accurate, disciplinary action is required. Decide on whether the action was one of deliberate, recurrent harassment or a one-off act of thoughtless behaviour. Depending on the nature of the incident, disciplinary action might include a warning, apology, close supervision, reprimand, transfer, suspension, or termination. Some organisations also act against employees who knowingly file false allegations or against managers who do not follow established procedures in handling reports of harassment. Note also: if you unfairly dismiss someone accused of harassment, the courts may be forced to send them straight back to the workplace.

 Remember...

☐ You must act immediately when any harassment issue is brought to your attention.

☐ When collecting the facts, do so assertively and confine your investigation only to those involved and to witnesses.

☐ For minor offences, warn the offender promptly in writing.

☐ Seek legal advice if serious disciplinary action such as termination is warranted or if an employee threatens legal action.

☐ Legislation usually demands that you must ensure harassment does not take place. An employer cannot claim ignorance. You are, by law, responsible for providing a harassment-free work environment.

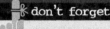 **here's an idea**

Make it easy for complainants to bring matters to the attention of management. Use staff newsletters and post notices throughout your workplace detailing to whom and how employees should bring their complaints.

don't forget

Watch for the warning signs

- A noticeable change in an employee's behaviour – tardiness, absenteeism, mood swings, for example.
- An employee avoiding another, or shrinking from another's physical proximity.
- Openly sexual behaviour between employees, even if it seems welcome.
- Frequent after-work partying or drinking.
- Unprofessional behaviour during business trips or conferences.

If you observe such behaviour, don't assume there is a sexual harassment problem – but it is a possibility.

 quotable quote

Sexual harassment is usually *not* about sex; it is about power. Harassment reflects a misguided sense of superiority.[10]

How to prevent violence in the workplace

In the United States alone, over one million employees annually are victims of violent crime while at work. Murder is now the second leading cause of occupational deaths in that country. Elsewhere, workplace violence is also increasing: domestic violence spills over on to the work site, disturbed employees commit violent acts. Sometimes the location of the workplace leaves it open to violent incidents such as robbery. What can managers do to prevent workplace violence? Begin by considering the following advice...

1 Be aware: you can be legally liable.

Society expects organisations to provide safe working environments —and that includes safety from violent acts. Whatever the origins, violent episodes have the potential to result in legal action against your organisation, or individual employees or management. However, if it is apparent that you have installed early, appropriate preventative measures or actions aimed at defusing lethal situations, then the likelihood of liability diminishes.

2 Devise strategies for minimising staff violence.

To minimise the possibility of workplace violence resulting from staff attacks on co-workers—whether they be threats, harassment, assaults or more serious acts—develop a set of procedures aimed at defusing the potential for such incidents. Consider the following actions:

- *Screen all job applicants.* Should you risk employing someone with a record of domestic violence, erratic behaviour, harassment, aggression, or an obsession with weapons?

- *Compile a written policy.* This should indicate clearly that threats, menacing behaviour, and actual violence will not be tolerated; incorporate processes for consistent and thorough investigation and handling of such incidents; and state the consequences of policy violations by staff.

- *Circulate the policy.* Ensure this policy is communicated to and understood by all employees.

- *Implement procedures for raising concerns.* Develop a process that enables staff to alert management to aggressive behaviour by co-workers. Be on the lookout for potentially violent employees—those exhibiting a recent decline in work performance or unusual behavioural changes; those with work stress, in conflict situations with co-workers, with domestic, financial, or medical problems, with short tempers and personality disorders; and those with prior records of threatening behaviour, violence, or substance abuse.

- *Create procedures for handling such*

> ❝ **quotable quote**
>
> Key research findings demonstrate a strong relationship between job stress and workplace harassment and violence. Substance abuse, layoffs, societal issues, and financial insecurity all contribute to the problem. Violence prevention programs and crisis response planning help reduce not only the possibility of workplace violence, but also reduce employee anxiety and improve productivity.[11]

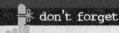 **don't forget**

Why violence occurs

Very few people engage in violence for the sake of violence. In most cases, aggression and abuse in the workplace result from escalating frustration over a short time span. There are many instances where staff and customers can start to get angry, frustrated, even violent:

- Being kept waiting
- Unhelpful staff attitudes
- Mindless bureaucracy and red tape
- Invasion of privacy
- Feeling aggrieved (bypassed for promotion, treated unfairly, in receipt of shoddy product or service, etc)
- Alcohol.[12]

problem staff members. The key here is to establish a means which allows disgruntled employees to have their complaints and grievances addressed openly and promptly.

3 Devise strategies for improving security.

There is clear evidence of increasing violence in those work locations, particularly retail establishments, which involve the exchange of money, routine contact with the public, staff working early or late hours, solitary work assignments, or businesses in high crime locations. For example, the Australian Institute of Criminology reported that in 2008 there were nearly 6000 incidents of armed robbery recorded in Australia: 40% occurring in a retail setting, with 67% between 6 p.m. and 6 a.m. (see www. aic.gov.au for further details).

Attend to the safety of your staff and customers by considering the installation of lights and mirrors, personal and silent alarm systems, drop safes, bulletproof enclosures, 'limited cash on hand' signs, and by increasing the number of staff during high risk time slots. Provide professional training for staff on how to react to violent situations such as robbery—basically, stay calm and controlled, act on the offender's instructions, remember details for later, and don't disturb the evidence.

4 Install a formal program to defuse violence.

US workplace violence prevention consultants Davis & Associates recommend that organisations adopt a formal approach to ensure the safety of staff and customers and to reduce potential litigation. They claim that focusing a formal program on four component areas will considerably lessen the chance of violent incidents:

Violence Prevention Program. This delineates the organisation's systems and procedures to ensure staff and customer safety—security systems, dysfunctional behaviour identification, conflict resolution, mediation programs, pre-employment screening, supervisory training, discipline procedures…

Personal Safety Program. This provides staff with skills to perform their jobs effectively and free from hostility—including interpersonal communication skills, personal safety training, and conflict management skills…

Crisis Response Planning. This provides a plan for staff to recognise, evaluate, and intervene before workplace violence occurs; and includes pre-planned responses and the organisation's responsibilities to deal with any incidents—notification and evacuation plans, crime scene response plans, media relations, press release plans, post-event debriefings, counselling services…

Crisis Survival Plan. This provides staff with specific action to take if violence erupts in the workplace—threat recognition, emergency notifications, personal protection, 'fight or flight' actions…

Davis & Associates believe that 'only through dynamic leadership, effective communication, planning, and training can organisations create employee awareness, reduce anxiety, and implement action plans to improve productivity, effectiveness, and safety'.

don't forget

Employers may be liable

According to the Australian Institute of Criminology, bosses should formally record all cases of workplace abuse, threats and bullying, and conduct regular staff surveys to identify potential security risks. The Institute says that violence should be taken as seriously as any other occupational health and safety issue.

It warns employers could be legally liable for acts of bullying, abuse and violence committed by one employee towards another if they did not move to assess the risk of workplace violence, and prevent it.

it's a fact

The initial 'trigger' to an act of workplace violence may be a single event such as a lay-off, disciplinary charge, or a series of minor incidents. The perpetrators are often loners who lack the necessary support system to cope with such events. They feel they have no control over their problems and survival becomes the goal because they perceive the world is closing in. There is 'no way out', and they can find no reasonable alternatives or solutions to the predicament. They embrace a violent act. In seeking to gain control of the situation, they see violence as a way of achieving this control.

How to respond if you are bullied in the workplace

Bullying is the deliberate, hurtful, and repeated mistreatment of one person by another. The perpetrator's desire to control the other person sometimes causes bullying, which not only undermines organisational peformance but can also destroy employees. In recent times, workplace legislation and media disclosure have revealed bullying as a significant issue in many organisations. If you have personally been the victim of bullying in your workplace, the following advice will prove helpful...

1 Be sure you are being bullied.

Do not confuse bullying with the stresses and pressures of normal worklife. We must meet deadlines, do more than resources sometimes allow, deal with difficult colleagues, perform under adverse circumstances. From time to time, we all experience conflict, differences of opinion, perfectionist bosses, personal rejection, criticism, and personality clashes. Bullying goes *beyond* the strains of daily worklife.

2 Do nothing. Ignore the bullying.

In career terms, weigh up your options and circumstances: It may be in your best interests careerwise to ignore the aggressor. The bullying could stop if the bully feels no progress is being made with you—although, on the other hand, the bullying could worsen.

3 Confront the bully assertively yourself.

If used early, this can be an effective strategy, especially if the 'bullying' was unintended behaviour. Meet with the bully in private, detail the behaviour and its effect on you, and ask that the behaviour you find unacceptable cease. Or, ask a third party, such as a senior colleague or mutual acquaintance, to raise your concerns informally with the aggressor.

4 Seek support.

Whether you decide to ignore the bullying or to take further action, you may wish to explore various sources for support and advice. For example, bullying affects mind and body: your doctor can help—and medical records could be important later. Your trade union or professional association can provide legal advice, and family, friends, and close colleagues can give valuable moral support. Relevant government agencies can also provide appropriate advice. And check out www.bullybusters.org as well.

5 Gather evidence.

If you are convinced that you are a victim of bullying behaviour, and

😊 smile & ponder

'OK. That's it, Fred! It's time to have a little chat.'

your informal requests have not resolved the problem, you will need to consider taking more formal action. To do this, you will need documented data to support your case:

- Familiarise yourself with a copy of your organisation's policy on bullying or harassment.
- Log every incident of bullying—the action, time, date, and witness.
- File any relevant documentation such as memos or emails.
- Explore the possibility of gaining the support of witnesses.

Armed with such information, you are better placed to consider adopting one of the following options…

Make an informal complaint.

Approach your supervisor and discuss your concerns. (If the bully is your supervisor, you'll need to talk to the supervisor's supervisor.) The supervisor should 'have a word' with the bully to help resolve the issue without having to take formal action.

Consider making a formal complaint.

If your informal approach proves fruitless, there may be a reason for this:

- the organisation has no anti-bullying policy, and no response is an attempt to deny the issue
- the bully has denied any guilt
- the identified behaviour may be acceptable in the organisation
- the supervisor may not believe your accusations
- the organisation may be unwilling to deal with the bully, because of his or her standing, even though the actions are provable.

In making a formal complaint through the appropriate internal channels, be aware that you should:

- be absolutely sure of your facts before making any accusations
- have a documented record of events from the time your problem began, including times, places, witnesses
- be familiar with procedures as detailed in the organisation's anti-bullying or harassment policy
- put your complaint in writing, and request that its receipt be acknowledged in writing.

Make an external complaint.

For organisational inaction, or bullying charges of a serious nature, you can turn to relevant outside agencies. Criminal action can be taken for such serious offences as threats of or actual physical assault, damage to property, and stalking. Complaints can also be made directly to relevant government agencies in those cases where employees have been treated or dismissed unfairly, harshly, and unjustly or for invalid or unlawful reasons in relation to, for example, sex, racial, political or disability discrimination, and in human rights, workplace health and safety, and industrial relations matters.

Look for another job.

When all else fails, or you do not want to challenge the workplace culture, or you find your situation intolerable, resign. Remember, however, that you may receive no reference, you may not find equal work, and you may have to explain your resignation to a potential employer. But this may be the only realistic option for some.

quotable quote

As soon as you think you may be a victim of bully tactics, seek help. Acting promptly can help to circumvent more serious situations such as a disciplinary or incompetence claim made against you. The longer you leave it to act, the harder the situation will be to resolve. There is a wealth of support for victims of bullying – you don't have to suffer alone.[13]

viewpoint

"Stop being a victim. You're in charge of your own attitude. *You* decide to be a winner or a loser. Choose winning. Remember, bullies pick their victims. If you stop acting like a victim, the bully will have to go elsewhere for satisfaction of his or her superiority needs."

– Patricia King
US management consultant

quotable quote

Most workplace bullies get away with such conduct due to the victims or other staff being unwilling to come forward and make a complaint to management. Victims inevitably suffer from low self-esteem and start to believe that their behaviour has caused the bullying.[14]

NOTE: You can adapt the anti-bullying guidelines on pages 452-463 to deal with other forms of workplace harassment.

How to uncover bullying in your workplace

There is no place for bullying in your workplace—and you can be legally liable if it occurs. To prevent bullying from taking subtle or overt forms, you need to consider whether it exists and to assess the risks of its occurring. Then you can adopt appropriate policies to deal with it. So the following advice is provided…

1 Know what workplace bullying entails.

Bullying has been defined as:

> Persistent, offensive, abusive, intimidating, malicious or insulting behaviour, abuse of power or unfair penal sanctions which make the recipient feel upset, threatened, humiliated, or vulnerable, which undermines their self-confidence and which may cause them to suffer stress.[15]

Or as:

> Aggressive behaviour arising from the deliberate intent to cause physical or psychological distress to others.[16]

2 Be aware of the implications of bullying in your organisation.

It is possible that an employee could be subject to bullying without others being aware of the problem. Because an employee tolerates this type of behaviour does not mean that it is acceptable, that it is not workplace bullying, or that the employer is not vicariously liable. Its presence can undermine workplace performance, crush the employee victim—and could lead to costly legal implications if not dealt with by the organisation.

To prevent bullying from happening, it is first useful to know whether it already exists in your workplace and to determine if your workplace is one that actually fosters it.

3 Determine if bullying behaviours exist in your workplace.

Using surveys, brainstorming, focus groups, check lists, and discussions, consult with key workplace groups to identify evidence of risk behaviours present in your organisation:

Physical: pushing, shoving, assaults, threats, offensive gestures, pinching, patting, touching, damaging or tampering with another's property or equipment…

Verbal: insults and name-calling, swearing, shouting, slandering, rumour-mongering, ridiculing, non-ending criticism and trivial fault-finding, ridiculing in front of others, constant put-downs, offensive jokes, wolf whistling, public reprimands, cutting comments about lifestyles or appearance…

Nonverbal: singling out for no reason, suggestive looks or jeers, meaningless tasks, tasks beyond one's skills, overwork, unnecessary pressure, offensive material in workplace, impossible deadlines, denial of reasonable requests, mimicking, constant overrulings, unwelcome practical jokes…

4 Identify any negative human resource management trends.

Through consultation again, explore the following signals that may indicate a workplace environment ripe for bullying behaviour:

Personal disability: withdrawal, depression, loss of self-confidence and self-esteem, high stress, panic attacks, aggressiveness, increased absenteeism and sick leave, irritability, tiredness, migraines, suicide…

Workplace indicators: increase in such areas as absenteeism and sick leave requests, staff turnover, accidents and first-aid treatments, recruitment costs, informal complaints, industrial disputes, workers compensation stress claims, counselling demands, mediation, and actions in relation to discrimination and harassment; reduced efficiency, productivity and profitability; poor morale, and erosion of staff commitment and loyalty…

Cultural indicators: an authoritarian management style, negative culture with little employee support, no clear codes of conduct, little staff participation or consultation, lack of training, no respect for others or their views, excessive demands on staff and workloads, no grievance procedures in place, difficult or aggressive clients, a very competitive commercial environment, the continual threat of organisational change…

5 Consider your findings.

Having gathered this wealth of data, you are now better placed to assess the likelihood of bullying occurring in your workplace, how well your organisation can handle incidents of bullying, even the costs incurred if bullying is not addressed. In this regard, consider:

- What is the probability of bullying occurring in your workplace?
- What are the organisational factors that might give rise to bullying?
- What financial and legal costs could result from bullying in your organisation—in terms of lost working time through illness and absence, staff turnover, reduced efficiency and productivity, high recruitment and retraining costs, potential legal costs and penalties?
- Just how effective are your current procedures to prevent and to address complaints relating to workplace bullying?
- How aware is management that a lack of effective policies and procedures could be seen as negligent in court?
- Do your current control measures such as a code of conduct, anti-bullying policy, and complaints procedures need to be modified? Do new controls need to be devised and implemented?

6 Document your assessment, decisions, and reasons.

If you have taken all reasonable measures through consultation to identify inappropriate behaviour and related risks, you will have taken the first step in eliminating the legal, moral, and financial consequences of bullying in your workplace. Record the results of this process for follow-up action and possible legal protection.

7 Derive and implement strategies for dealing with the issue.

You are now better placed to understand the problem of bullying in your workplace. The next step will be to develop an anti-bullying policy and effective control measures…

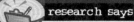 research says

In 1999, the Australian Institute of Management calculated that, for a fictitious company of 100 employees, the cost of workplace bullying, which is not managed, could be in excess of $A600,000. The costs related to such issues as sick leave, absenteeism, turnover, compensation, loss of productivity and organisational property costs, surveys, training, coaching, and recruitment.[17]

research says

An ACTU 2012 submission into workplace bullying in Australia found that:

- Associated stress claims have risen from 4440 in 1997-8 to 7850 in 2003-4.
- 53% of respondents reported an unhappy, oppressive workplace featuring intimidatory behaviour.
- 40% of workers were afraid to speak out.
- 70% claimed the manager or supervisor carried out the bullying.
- 18% said something was done to stop the bullying behaviour.
  - www.actu.org.au

NOTE: You can adapt the anti-bullying guidelines on pages 452-463 to deal with other forms of workplace harassment.

How to develop an anti-bullying policy for your workplace

Most organisations consider policies and procedures to deal with bullying behaviour in the workplace only *after* the damage has been done. Appropriate organisational policies should obviate complaints of bullying. To be effective, such policies should already have been adopted. Potential bullying should never reach crisis point: prevention is always better than cure. Are your staff members clear about your anti-bullying attitude? To develop an effective policy for your workplace, consider the following advice...

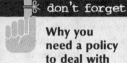

don't forget

Why you need a policy to deal with workplace bullying

1. There could be serious psychiatric or medical outcomes for victims.
2. There are legal and legislative issues involved.
3. There are extremely high economic costs.

here's an idea

The words 'bullying' and 'bully' can be highly emotive and you may choose to avoid their use in policies aimed at eliminating such behaviour. Your specific policy may instead refer to 'personal harassment' or 'physical and emotional harassment', or a broader policy may become your 'Dignity at Work Policy'.

quotable quote

Ambiguity is a big problem for an individual or an organisation. It is sometimes hard to agree on what constitutes bullying and, except in the most obvious or clearly witnessed cases, it can be hard to establish the truth about what has happened.[19]

1 Follow the guidelines suggested in Topic 554.

Revisit Topic 554 outlining the procedures for developing policy through the use of collaborative and consultative processes. Refresh your understanding of these basic guidelines before commencing work on an anti-bullying policy for your workplace.

2 Choose between a stand-alone and an incorporated policy.

Depending on your circumstances, an anti-bullying policy can be developed as a stand-alone document or incorporated into an existing policy relating to equity, harrassment, or workplace health and safety. If bullying is a problem, however, a specific policy should be adopted to highlight the issue. If written into a broader policy, it is important to ensure bullying does not become lost among the other issues.

3 Develop an anti-bullying policy for your workplace.

In preparing an effective anti-bullying

policy[18], you should :

1. **Open with a statement of intent.** This statement should clearly reveal your organisation's commitment to promoting trust, respect, and courtesy and to providing a workplace free from bullying. Affirm that your organisation finds bullying unacceptable and that it will not be tolerated.

2. **Define workplace bullying.** Provide a succinct definition and make it clear that bullying can occur at all levels—between senior managers and supervisors, between supervisors and employees, between employees, and between staff and clients. List examples of the types of actions which typify bullying behaviour—yelling, threats, belittling, public reprimands, ostracising, excessive supervision, offensive jokes, maliciousness, unwanted physical contact or assault, trivial fault-finding, and so on.

3. **Outline the impact of bullying on the organisation.** Make it clear, through examples, how destructive workplace bullying can be

to the organisation—through reduced productivity and morale, absenteeism, loss of trained and talented staff, unsafe working environment, loss of profits, and costly legal implications —and to individuals who become stressed, depressed, ill, withdrawn, aggressive, even suicidal, and so on.

4. *List your strategies for eliminating bullying.*

These could include developing a code of conduct to be signed by all staff, general training of all staff aimed at the elimination of bullying, the availability of complaints mechanisms, ongoing review of the issue, and so on.

5. *Make clear the role of management.*

Clarify the difference between management practice and bullying. Make it clear that critical comment relating to performance deficiencies, and constructive feedback or counselling on work performance is appropriate and reasonable, and does not constitute bullying behaviour. (The line between the legitimate use of authority and the beginnings of bullying behaviour is sometimes grey, particularly for a supervisor with a strong management style exercised in a pressured environment.)

Affirm that managers and supervisors must ensure that employees are not bullied, and that they themselves must demonstrate appropriate behaviour, promote the anti-bullying policy, treat complaints seriously and confidentially, and ensure that targetted employees and their witnesses are not victimised.

6. *Confirm procedures for making complaints of bullying.*

List the avenues by which a victim can obtain help or make a complaint relating to workplace bullying—for example, through a nominated contact officer, a supervisor, the human resource manager, the occupational health and safety officer, the union delegate, and so on.

The policy should also summarise the various options available to an employee victim in dealing with a workplace bully (see page 452).

7. *Record your organisation's commitment to prompt investigation of a complaint.*

Convey an assurance that any employee complaint relating to workplace bullying will be treated seriously and investigated promptly, confidentially, impartially, and that the victim and any witnesses will be protected from victimisation.

8. *Outline the consequences for those who breach the policy.*

Disclose clearly that disciplinary action will be taken against those who bully fellow employees or who victimise the person who has made or is a witness to a complaint. List the types of disciplinary actions which may be enforced; for example, depending on the circumstances, an apology to the victim, an undertaking that the behaviour will cease, a warning, training, counselling, suspension, demotion, or dismissal. Dismissal might occur after three warnings concerning the same breach of policy.

---

don't forget

In the public service, there are established policies and grievance procedures which must be followed in making and investigating workplace bullying complaints.

Smaller organisations could consider adopting or adapting anti-bullying policies and procedures developed by their relevant industry group.

---

here's an idea

If your organisation employs significant numbers of ethnic staff, you may need to prepare and provide anti-bullying material in languages other than English.

---

viewpoint

"The popular view of bullies as socially inept oafs who bully out of inadequacy has been proven wrong. They are more likely to be highly skilled people capable of sophisticated manipulation. And like other toxic types in the workplace, they are not always easy to recognise."

– Helen McGrath, Consulting psychologist, Deakin University

NOTE: You can adapt the anti-bullying guidelines on pages 452-463 to deal with other forms of workplace harassment.

How to implement your anti-bullying policy in the workplace

If you are establishing a workplace culture in which bullying is proactively discouraged, you will need a written policy that includes strategies for dealing with the problem. As well, a series of implementation measures will be necessary if you are to promote the policy and gain the support and confidence of management and staff. So, to 'sell' your policy enterprise-wide, you should consider the following advice…

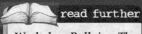
1 Develop an anti-bullying policy.

The foundation of any anti-bullying strategy is an anti-bullying policy. This should include a statement of management commitment, a code of conduct, complaints procedures, and disciplinary measures. Do you have such a policy in place? See page 456.

2 Obtain management commitment and publicise this.

Release a statement from the employer or management to clearly demonstrate commitment to a bully-free workplace, announcing the policy and a starting date. This would entail a commitment to prompt and proper investigations into complaints, a firm undertaking to deal with breaches of the policy, an ongoing review of the process, and the provision of adequate resourcing for implementing the anti-bullying strategies which follow.

3 Seek employee commitment to the policy.

The use of a collaborative and consultative approach to the development of your anti-bullying policy (see page 554) would facilitate employee acceptance of the document. The greater the level of consultation, the greater the level of commitment.

4 Adopt an enterprise-wide approach.

Explore the possibility of integrating your anti-bullying strategies into other organisational vehicles, such as your strategic plan, performance planning and review, business plan, risk management plan, workplace health and safety agreement, EEO and harassment policies, employee assistance programs, and industrial agreements.

5 Disseminate the policy.

The effectiveness of your dissemination strategy will ultimately determine the effectiveness of your policy. If your staff members are unaware of the policy, do not understand it, or do not adhere to it, then it is ineffectual and exposes your organisation to greater vicarious liability.

In communicating your policy to staff, you might consider using strategies that could include :

- Distribute copies of the policy to all employees, e.g. with pay slips.
- Include details of the policy and the complaints procedures in the staff newsletter.
- Develop posters, brochures, and leaflets. Display where appropriate.
- Ensure the policy is included in any organisational personnel manuals or computer network databases.
- Include discussion of the policy in staff induction and training programs.
- Request supervisors to discuss anti-bullying policy and complaints procedures at staff meetings and team briefings.
- Ensure new appointees receive the policy and agree to the policy as part of their employment contract.

6 Undertake training programs.

Training is a key to reinforcing the tenet that bullying has no place in your organisation. An understanding of the policy, legislative requirements, and management and staff responsibilities and accountabilities, is necessary. As well, focus on the development of those skills that are able to raise awareness, develop coping skills, and reduce bullying behaviours (including conflict resolution, interpersonal skills, assertiveness, negotiation, leadership, communication, team building, stress management). In particular, emphasise the development of people's 'softer', interactive skills. As Ruth Wheatley advises: 'We all need

to learn:

- to be aware of our own behaviour, particularly when under stress or going through organisational changes
- to assist others in coping with change or high pressure at work
- to deal with our own emotions and be aware of the feelings of others.'

She continues: 'Training in these skills will have the added advantage of developing an individual's self-esteem, confidence, and assertiveness. This will help him or her to become less likely to accept or attract bullying behaviour, as well as less likely to inflict it on others.' [20]

7 Establish a system of contact officers.

A team of trained contact officers should be established and available in larger organisations to provide confidential and unbiased advice and information to employees on how to submit complaints relating to workplace bullying, or on other available options. Contact officers, preferably volunteers, should demonstrate appropriate behaviours; but they would not provide advocacy or counselling services to colleagues.

8 Monitor and review the process.

Monitoring and regular reviews are vital to ensure the ongoing success of your anti-bullying strategies, and identification of potential problems. Keep a check on such indicators as turnover, absenteeism, complaints, and contact officer records; conduct general attitude surveys occasionally; and probe for bullying feedback at exit interviews.

 quotable quote

The level of bullying in the workplace is difficult to gauge. If the 'horror stories' that surface at any mention of this subject are an indication of how widespread this problem is, then there is an urgent need to address this issue, by documenting incidents, finding the source of the abuse and what and who perpetrates it, and developing a procedure to eliminate the bullying behaviour. [22]

 don't forget

An absence of complaints does not necessarily mean an absence of workplace bullying. It could mean that…

- there is *no* bullying – although it's best to have a policy in place, because you'll have procedures ready when there is.
- there *is* bullying, – but your staff do not know how to raise the issue.
- there *is* bullying – but your strategies are not working. For example, your staff may fear reprisals for making a complaint.

NOTE: You can adapt the anti-bullying guidelines on pages 452-463 to deal with other forms of workplace harassment.

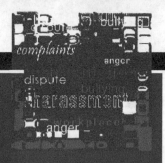

How to investigate a complaint of workplace bullying

Every formal complaint of workplace bullying must be taken seriously and investigated thoroughly. An investigation not only reveals the source of a particular interpersonal conflict: it also affirms to other employees that the organisation has a set of core behavioural standards in which there is no place for bullying. For any formal investigative process, the following procedures are recommended... [23]

1 Appoint an investigator.

The investigator of a formal complaint into bullying should be equal in status to, or more senior than, the accused employee. As part of a transparent process, an external investigator might be appointed if the organisation is small, or if internal staff lack appropriate skills, or bias is a concern. The investigator should meet with management to be briefed on the purpose of the investigation.

2 Ensure the investigation is just and ethical.

The underlying principles of procedural fairness must be known and followed by all involved in the investigation. These would embrace:

• *The principle of natural justice for the accused.* Here the accused is informed in writing of the complaint and by whom; will be allowed to respond by way of explanation; is assured that the investigator is without bias; has access to union representation or other support; and can be confident that procedural fairness is a paramount consideration.

• *Complainant support.* The complainant and witnesses must be assured that they will not be victimised before, during, or after the investigation.

• *A guarantee of confidentiality.* The complainant, the accused, witnesses, and senior management must agree that they will engage in no external debate or gossip relating to the issue.

• *Standard of proof.* Here the contested facts must be proved on 'the balance of probabilities' (rather than, for example in a criminal case, where they must be proved 'beyond all reasonable doubt').

The investigator may also require all parties to sign an interview protocol which affirms statements relating to natural justice, representation, co-operation and true and accurate disclosure, professional conduct, notetaking and signing-off of any written record as true and accurate, and confidentiality demands.

3 Conduct the investigation.

The investigator could consider adopting the following process:

• *Do your homework.* Become familiar with the background to the issue: Does this incident relate to overt or covert bullying? What is the relationship between the complainant and the accused? Was this a repeated behaviour? Was the matter addressed at the time? Were there witnesses?

Review any background documentation to determine if the alleged behaviour violates any Anti-Discrimination, Industrial Relations, or Workplace Health and Safety legislation, or any organisational codes of conduct or policies. Check files for any previous warnings issued to the accused.

• *Inform all parties about the process*. Advise all parties in relation to duration, procedures, natural justice, the need for confidentiality, representation, the accused's entitlement to documentation relating to the case, that all parties must be treated with respect, and that victimisation will not be tolerated.

• *Interview the complainant.* Compile a summary of the complaint and evidence which results from such questions as:

Who was involved? What was specifically done or said? Time, place and witnesses? Previous incidents, if any? How did the incident arise? Contributing factors? Nature of injuries? Was the accused told to stop? What outcome is the complainant hoping for?

The complainant should sign this summary as a true and accurate record.

• *Interview the accused.* Ensure the accused is provided with a summary of the complaint and has time to consider it. Conduct the interview, recording the accused's responses on each of the evidentiary points. The accused must also sign the summary as accurate.

• *Interview any witnesses*. Inform both the complainant and the accused of those to be interviewed. Seek direct observations of what each witness saw or heard. Do not seek opinions,

interpretations or impressions.

• *Weigh up the evidence.* Having considered the background to the case, and the statements of the complainant, the accused and the witnesses, recommendations can be compiled. Where there is disagreement over what occurred, or there are no witnesses and no way of verifying the information offered, substantiating the complaint is often difficult. Not substantiating a complaint does not mean that no recommendations can be made relating to the need for a reconsideration of existing workplace anti-bullying policies and strategies.

 Prepare and submit a report.

The investigator, having prepared a report, submits it to the person responsible for implementing the recommendations. It would include:

- A list of claims and, based on the evidence and statements, whether the claims were substantiated or not.
- Recommendations and reasons for any proposed disciplinary actions.
- Recommendations and reasons for changes to policies, procedures or control measures.
- An estimate of costs incurred as a result of the affair and investigation.

Once acted upon, the report itself should be kept securely, but not in the accused's personnel files.

Anticipate the outcomes.

Letters outlining the findings of the investigation, the action taken, and the reasons for the decisions made must be forwarded to the complainant and the accused prior to any follow-up actions being implemented…

NOTE: You can adapt the anti-bullying guidelines on pages 452-463 to deal with other forms of workplace harassment.

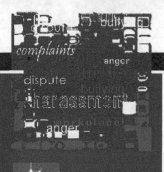

How to respond to the findings of an investigation into workplace bullying

After investigating an employee's formal complaint of workplace bullying, a written report is usually submitted to the manager responsible for implementing its recommendations. The report will reveal whether the complaint was justified or not. Sometimes the report will suggest how to tighten the policies and procedures intended to minimise the incidence of bullying within the organisation. In responding to such a report, you may consider using the following strategies...[23]

Reflect upon the findings of the report into the incident.

The investigator's report into a formal complaint of bullying will disclose whether the claims were proven and the justification for this decision. It may also provide a list of recommendations relating to possible disciplinary action and suggested changes to current policies and procedures as they relate to workplace bullying. Be familiar with these findings and prepare your responses before reporting back to the complainant and the accused.

Consider if any disciplinary action is warranted.

If the complaint was substantiated, you will need to decide upon the form of disciplinary action to be taken. Its severity will depend on the nature of the bullying, the intent of the perpetrator, his or her prior history of bullying, the need to set an example to others, the extent to which anti-bullying policies have previously been made clear to staff, and the degree to which your organisation has tolerated such behaviour in the past.

Bearing such factors in mind, the disciplinary action could include one or more of the following: an apology, a commitment to cease such offensive behaviour, a formal warning, training, counselling, transfer, withholding a pay increment, demotion, suspension with or without pay, or termination.

If the investigation found the complaint to be vexatious, the complainant may be subject to disciplinary action. Remember, however, that because a complaint was not substantiated does not mean that it was necessarily mischievous, frivolous, dishonest or malicious.

Advise the complainant of the investigation's outcome.

If the complaint has been substantiated, advise the complainant, indicate what actions will be taken in relation to the bully, possible changes to organisational procedures, and the availability of support for the complainant, if required. Clarify the policy as it relates to possible future victimisation if this should occur.

---

here's an idea

All documentation relating to an investigation into workplace bullying, including the final report, should be kept in a secure place. Such material is required if disciplinary action is involved, or if further breaches occur, or if legal or statutory action results.

here's an idea

If bullying is proven, a complainant should not have to work with the bully again.

here's an idea

No proven bully should gain from the experience. If your chosen option is to transfer or shift the bully to another job, s/he should not be moved to a *better* job. What kind of demotivating message would that send to other employees?

here's an idea

A proven bully should only be promoted when sufficient time has elapsed – say, two years – after demonstrating that s/he has succeeded in eliminating bullying behaviour.

If the complaint has not been substantiated, advise the reasons for this and indicate that no further action will be taken with respect to this particular episode. Reiterate any general preventative measures currently in place or planned.

 Advise the accused of the investigation's outcome.

If the complaint has been substantiated, advise the bully of this, and indicate what disciplinary actions are available to management. A consideration of any mitigating circumstances might be warranted. But for gross misconduct, or repeated breaches, instant dismissal is a likelihood. For an employee receiving an initial warning, this should be in written form, signed, and placed on his or her personnel file, with a copy given to the employee. The document should briefly summarise the results of the investigation, listing all substantiated complaints, and state that such behaviour clearly contravenes the organisation's policy on bullying and must stop. It should also include the consequences of further breaches, details of any monitoring provisions, and agreement that the employee will abide by the required code of conduct.

If the complaint has not been substantiated, advise the employee of this. If the incident and investigation has become common knowledge in the workplace, discuss with the employee the appropriateness or otherwise of acknowledging publicly that the complaint was not substantiated.

It may also be appropriate to indicate any intended changes to organisational procedures which have been consequential upon this episode, and to clarify again the policy relating to victimisation of the complainant if you suspect this is warranted.

5 Deal appropriately with the bully.

If retention and rehabilitation is an option, the organisation might, in addition to any disciplinary action, take responsibility for offering support to the bully. This might take the form of training in appropriate areas, such as interpersonal skills and conflict resolution, or counselling, group therapy, or psychotherapy. Close monitoring of future behaviour could also be a requirement.

 Deal appropriately with the complainant.

Some bullied complainants can become very demoralised and might require professional counselling or psychotherapy. Confidence and morale can be rebuilt if necessary by involving the bullied staff member in a small peer support group, in the context of facilitated, confidential supportive workgroup meetings, allowing all members to come to terms with their own role, and encouraging them to act differently if the same circumstances were repeated.

7 Implement any recommended organisational changes.

Attend to any report recommendations which proposed the introduction or modification of preventative strategies, or monitoring measures.

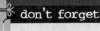
don't forget

The legislative implications of workplace bullying

Legislation can outlaw bullying or can provide redress for both the bully or the bullied…

Health and safety legislation. Employers may be held vicariously liable for the actions of their staff, or failure to take appropriate action to resolve risk issues relating to illness or injury in the workplace.

Anti-discrimination legislation. Employers can be held vicariously liable if they fail to act when workplace bullying involves acts of discrimination or harassment relating to race, disability, religion, sex, and human rights.

Industrial relations legislation. Employees forced to resign because of bullying can lodge unfair dismissal claims under most industrial awards and some workplace enterprise agreements.

Workers compensation legislation. Workers can claim compensation if bullying contributes significantly to a workplace injury.

NOTE: You can adapt the anti-bullying guidelines on pages 452-463 to deal with other forms of workplace harassment.

How to prepare for emergencies

Fire, bomb scare, wall collapse, chemical spill—we all hope emergencies will not occur, but a sad fact of life is that they do. So we need to adopt procedures for use in emergencies well before they happen if we are to minimise their traumatic effects...

1 Install smoke alarms and fire extinguishers.

Some of the most common emergencies are fire-related. You can be prepared by taking some simple precautions.

Contact your local fire service and ask them to visit your premises and provide advice on the strategic placement of fire extinguishers, smoke alarms, and other necessary precautions. Several smoke alarms and fire extinguishers will be required on most sites. The key is to install and maintain. Prepare a schedule that ensures you test your equipment on a regular basis. Clean the equipment annually and have regular alerts to check the efficiency of equipment and procedures.

2 Introduce procedures for bomb threats.

The bombing of businesses and public places has increased in recent years and can no longer be seen as an occurrence common only to politically sensitive areas of the world. Take bomb threats seriously and ensure your team is trained in the correct procedures. Specialists in this field can help you with your training, but general guidelines would include:

- Train the team in procedures for tracing telephone calls.
- Ensure your team knows how to attract the attention of another team member without tipping off a telephone caller.
- Record the time and date of threatening phone calls.
- When a caller phones, try and obtain information on where the bomb is, what it looks like, when it is set to explode, what will detonate it, why it was set, and who the bomber is.
- Ensure people do not use radios, walkie-talkies, or cellular phones in the area of the bomb.
- Contact the police immediately.

3 Know what to do after a break-in.

Professional thieves may break into your premises after you have closed for the day. If you arrive next morning and discover a break-in, take the following steps:

- Do not enter the premises.
- Use the nearest telephone to call the police.
- If you do go into the workplace, do not touch anything.
- Wait for the arrival of the police before cleaning up or allowing access to customers and staff.

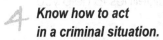 **Know how to act in a criminal situation.**

Make sure your staff know how to act and respond in the case of criminal intrusion during work hours—such as an armed hold-up or hostage situation. Refer to page 474.

 Compile a crisis phone directory.

It's the directory you'll never want to use, but it is an essential list that should be located near designated phone points. It should contain the phone numbers of:

- local police station
- fire station
- ambulance services
- Poison Control Centre (if relevant)
- water, gas and electricity utility services
- your closest doctor.

 Train your team in emergency phone use.

In Australia the emergency phone line is 000, in the United Kingdom 999, and in the United States it's 911. Such lines should only be used in an emergency. It is important that the caller stays calm, states the problem accurately, gives the location of the

emergency, and answers all questions asked by the tele-communicator. Let the emergency operator guide the conversation and do not hang up until help has been organised.

 Keep an emergency first-aid kit ready.

Every business should have a well-stocked first-aid kit available to staff. It is important that a list of essential supplies is also with the kit; or supplies will be used and may not be replaced. A basic kit should include: towels and wash cloths, cold packs, assorted bandages, adhesive tape, antiseptic, sterile gauze pads, allergy kit, and disposable rubber gloves.

 Know how to deal with the media in a crisis.

Emergencies are 'news' and it will not be long before the media arrive. You need to deal with the media in a professional manner that will not damage consumer confidence in your business. Check the following tips:

- Your goal is to inform the public with accurate information.
- Only talk to the press when it is appropriate to do so.
- Be patient with the press and avoid using 'no comment' answers.
- Minimise media distraction.
- Do not embellish your answers.
- Never lie to the media.
- Tell the bad news and get it over with.
- Do not assume anything is 'off the record'.
- Decide who in your organization should talk to the media.

Suspected bomb on the premises?

Except in an emergency presenting immediate danger to life, inexperienced personnel should never handle or attempt to dispose of any suspected bomb or explosive material found on your premises.

Take the following steps:

- Clear the area of all personnel, evacuate the premises, and establish a guard around the danger zone.
- Anything that might be connected with the bomb or that might act as a trigger mechanism must not be touched by anyone other than an expert.
- Send for the experts – notify any security services, police, and fire department.
- Shut off power, gas and fuel lines leading into the danger area.
- Wait at a safe distance for qualified explosive disposal personnel to give the all clear.

The terrorist attacks of September 11 (2001) reminded employers of the importance of being prepared for workplace emergencies. Companies need to update their crisis and evacuation plans and establish ways to provide employees with food and shelter for up to 72 hours in the event of a disaster that prevents them from leaving the premises.[1]

How to manage an emergency

An earthquake, a plant explosion, a shooting, a poisonous gas leak, a terrorist attack, a security alert of any kind—are you ready to handle a major crisis in your organization? Do you have a disaster plan? Those first few moments are going to be crucial in controlling events. Good crisis managers are decisive; they have recourse to procedures that will protect employees and customers, and minimise disruption to the organization's operations. Here are some guidelines to help you prepare for the unexpected...

1 Prepare for an emergency—now.

Now is the time to think about the unthinkable. It will pay off when you least expect it. Among the items you should consider immediately are:

- Have a crisis response team in place. Allocate specific responsibilities to team members (and their back-ups) and work together to outline each person's role.
- Imagine what crises your organization might experience within and external to it. With the crisis team, develop a plan for responding to those events. The plan should include specific timelines, contingency plans to deal with extra-ordinary developments or emergencies, and longer-term solutions to be adopted and implemented at the right time.
- Ensure your records are always up to date—next-of-kin and contact names and telephone numbers for emergency services and helping agencies.
- Know where to access any information you will need in a hurry.
- Assemble the crisis response team periodically to review the overall plan and provide necessary training—handling phone calls, dealing with the media, alerting customers and staff.
- Be clear on how traumatic support services and care-givers will be used during and after the event.

- Check that your crisis plan is kept up to date with industry guidelines.

2 Analyse the situation.

When a emergency occurs, assess it as coolly as you can and consider:

- Is it really a crisis?
- What is its probable impact?
- How much time do we have?
- Who else is involved and who is likely to be involved?
- What resources do we have in place and what will we need?

3 Stay calm.

There are three essentials for remaining cool in a crisis:

- *It's OK to be nervous.* Sports psychologists and athletes have exposed the myth that, if you get nervous, you'll perform poorly.
- *Try to relax.* This is a time when your mind and body need to be in sync. Breathe deeply; talk yourself through the situation; and repeat positive affirmations.
- *Remain calm.* Nervousness is OK; panic is not. Work through a process methodically, confronting problems rather than avoiding them.

Call your crisis team into action.

Earlier preparation will pay off when assembling your crisis management team. Members know their roles, they are familiar with procedures in the crisis plan, and the crisis management centre is quickly established.

At the time of the crisis, of course, nothing else matters except people's safety and the safety of their families:

- Make sure the injured are cared for.
- Implement your plan to take care of the personal needs of employees.
- Encourage staff to take time off to check on families and to tend to home concerns.
- Check for damage to the building and, where possible, arrange repairs. Some staff will want to return to normalcy as soon as possible to work in an environment where they feel safe and protected.

 Remember: post-trauma communication is vital.

A quality communication strategy will allow you to weather the trauma with humanity, integrity and credibility. Consider the following:

- All communication should emanate from one spokesperson.
- Communicate openly with employees. After making sure any injured workers are treated, let other staff know what has happened by holding a thorough briefing, or sending out a mass email or voicemail, or issuing an internal press release containing a straightforward statement about the incident. Employees don't want rumours, they want to know the facts. It is important to talk to the staff, acknowledge that the company had experienced some pain, but is working hard to return to normalcy.
- Outline the coping mechanisms which the company is adopting.
- Liaise with the media (see page 468).
- Inform customers and clients as soon as possible to combat gossip and allay fears.
- Keep your bosses informed.

 Provide counselling and follow-up support.

Depending on the nature of the crisis, staff can experience wide-ranging, distressing, and emotional reactions. Counsellors and other professionals should be made available. For staff, a critical incident debriefing will help stabilise the workplace after the emergency, hasten the return to work, lower the long-term incidence of generalised anxiety, and reduce the likelihood of litigation.

 Be a personal support for your staff.

This will be a time when it is even more important than usual to set an example for your workers and to provide support and comfort. Continue to provide clear, up-to-date details, in face-to-face situations if you can – the context will give you the warmth, the tone, the body language. Management by walking around and asking 'Is your family safe?' or 'What can we do for you?' is essential. Avoid spending too much time talking about the actual crisis and help people to focus on what they have—their health, their future, and their purpose.

 Evaluate actions and reactions.

Monitor progress continuously so that you can modify your disaster plan and take corrective or pre-emptive steps. When the crisis has passed, assemble your crisis response team for a thorough debriefing; and evaluate the appropriateness of existing procedures.

 research says

According to the Institute of Management in the United Kingdom, the top five 'disasters' that managers perceive as threats to business are: [3]

Loss of IT capacity	82%
Fire	62%
Loss of skills	59%
Loss of site	55%
Damage to corporate image or reputation	50%

here's an idea

Management experts are now saying that pessimists make great managers. Why? Because they're always thinking of what could go wrong, and are therefore coming up with solutions to problems – just in case the worst happens. The message for you then is this: If you're an optimist, force yourself to write down anything that could go wrong with new projects, initiatives, employees, and so on. If you do this, you'll have a head start if disaster strikes.

 don't forget

You need insurance

Insurance is designed to help you survive unexpected hazards:

fire and other perils, loss of income, burglary, theft, goods in transit, public, professional and product liability, workers' compensation, motor vehicle...

Seek professional advice.

467

How to handle the media during a crisis

Your organization may look to you for strength and continuity during a crisis, when you certainly cannot 'play it by ear' with the media. A traumatic incident is news; the media will be quickly on the scene. Any lack of preparation on your part could result in erroneous information, distortion of facts, and publicly embarrassing gaffes. If disaster strikes at your organization tomorrow, will you be ready to handle frenzied media? Here are some guidelines to prepare you for such a situation…

quotable quote

Whenever a major crisis strikes, you can be sure that representatives from the media will be some of the first to arrive on the scene. It's their job to report details of the incident as quickly as possible and the pressure is on to be first to report the story. Under such circumstances the correct handling of the media is essential.[4]

here's an idea

Recognise that there is a difference between an incident and a crisis. Management overreaction may indicate to staff and media alike that a situation is more severe than it really is and can cause undue alarm. That can do as much or more damage than the problem itself. Remember: Not every problem that has received media attention ranks as a crisis that requires top management attention and an all-out 'war room' approach. Deal with incidents for what they are, react accordingly, and use appropriate measures.

don't forget

Handling a crisis is a process, not an event.

1 Avoid being uncooperative.

Invariably in a company crisis a manager will be under immediate pressure from the media to make a practical response, so you'll need to weigh up the implications if you adopt a stance of being 'unavailable' or 'reluctant' to comment.

Silence breeds suspicion. If you are not prepared to give an interview, or you respond with 'no comment', then you must show that the company is not being deliberately obstructive or 'hiding' something. Offer good reasons for your silence. These might legitimately include insufficient information; legal proceedings, or the potential for such; a head office statement is pending; or a police inquiry is underway.

Remember also that the media have the ability to get the information they need—with or without you. So, as Diane Thomas says in *Crisis Communication*, 'almost without exception, your organization will be more favorably presented *with* your input'.

2 Advise relevant parties first.

Make no comments to the press until relevant authorities, company executives, legal representatives, and next-of-kin affected by the incident have been notified.

3 Appoint a spokesperson.

You or a senior company executive usually assumes responsibility as sole spokesperson, immediately available to reporters who arrive on the scene or who telephone. This ensures consistency of comment throughout the crisis.

The spokesperson should take time to reflect on the facts of the incident and have them clear before interview. Two sets of information will need to be gathered: the actual information about what happened, how, when, where, to whom, why and the consequences; and collateral information that puts the incident into perspective—for example, if a worker dies in a chemical spill, details such as the company's emergency action plan, safety record, staff competency and training, and investigation procedures should be outlined.

 Be judicious in your comments.

A tragic event is usually followed by a company, departmental, police, or coronial inquiry. Media comments on public record may have a bearing on future proceedings, so any comments should be made judiciously and, if possible, free of emotional reactions.

Consider these points:

- Some companies require that head office approval be sought before granting media interviews. If necessary, make such contact promptly to avoid delaying your media response.

- Restrict answers to those facts you know clearly to be true. Do not allow the media to elicit details of which you are unsure.

- To keep reporters (and their editors) from dicing an interview into digestible morsels, list the points for them by saying, 'I would like to make three points.' Expand on each point as necessary. Numbering the points makes it harder for the reporter to interject. And editors can't leave point number two, cut number one and three, and expect a seamless presentation.

- A momentary lapse in concentration could give the media the opportunity to question in the area of negligence or blame. Avoid commenting in this area at all times, as there could be significant legal implications.

- When a matter is under police investigation, do not respond to any questions that fall rightly within the police department's purview. Discuss such parameters with police beforehand.

- Record the details of interviews as soon as they have been completed for possible future reference.

 Protect employees against media intrusion.

Under stressful situations associated with a traumatic incident, it is appropriate for a manager to protect staff members from unwarranted intrusive interviews by the media. At times this can be difficult. Be aware of these two points:

- Even if the media are denied access to staff on company premises, contact can still be made as they are entering or leaving the workplace.

- It is wise, therefore, to counsel staff on their rights and responsibilities. They have the right to speak to the media if they so wish, but they have a responsibility to speak truthfully and not spread rumours or speculate about matters where they may not know the facts.

 Promote post-event services available.

As counselling staff could be needed to reduce stress after traumatic events, there is a need to promote these services to staff and community. It is highly likely that the community will be interested in knowing about the support available to your employees and their families. Consider involving a spokesperson for such services in any media interview.

Foster cordial relations with the media.

Cooperation from your organization evokes a similar response from the media—so cultivate cordial relations with the media in good times to help ensure fair, balanced treatment in times of crisis.

---

here's an idea

Oil giant Chevron takes great pride in the fact that its managers are well equipped to deal with business crises. One technique managers are taught is the 'bridging method' for dealing with reporters. It entails answering a volatile question (e.g., "What caused the explosion?"), followed by a 'bridge' phrase (e.g., 'in the meantime') to give additional information that puts the company in a favorable light (e.g., 'In the meantime, our emergency response crew is working around the clock…'). Here are other crisis dos and don'ts Chevron managers are taught:

Crisis management don'ts:

- Don't speculate about cause, consequences, or liability.
- Don't talk 'off the record'. Assume that anything you say will be reported on.
- Don't try to be funny. Such attempts can easily embarrass you and the company.
- Don't estimate the cost of the damage, clean-up, or containment.
- Don't assign blame to any employee, equipment, or contractor.

Crisis management dos:

- Do be as accessible as you can be.
- Do be prepared with the most current information available; provide a written fact sheet if possible.
- Do try to anticipate questions.
- Do rehearse what you will say – but rehearse quickly.

How to crime-proof your workplace

Offices, shops, and factories everywhere are becoming increasingly vulnerable to an expanding variety of non-violent and violent crimes—pilfering, shoplifting, vandalism, burglary, embezzlement, insurance fraud, arson, assaa, even murder… Just how far a security-conscious organization can go without upsetting employees or losing customers is the question facing most companies today. Is it time for you to become more security conscious?

Develop and distribute a security policy.

What type of environment fosters productivity for employees, openness for customers, and protection of the business from fraud, theft, and harm? This should be the basis of joint management-employee discussions in the process of preparing a security statement for your organization. Having developed a statement, hold employee meetings to discuss reasons for the policy and ask for possible improvements or changes. Disseminate the final document.

Train your employees to be security-conscious.

Contrary to popular belief, your staff will not inherently know what they should do and how they should act to protect your business assets. You need to create performance standards to define the parameters of their jobs, inculcate honest work habits, and educate them in the basics of security relating to your organization, e.g.

• the swift and certain consequences for dishonest employees.

• how to recognise and report all suspicious behaviour.
• awareness of personal security—such as after-hours safety and valuables.
• an anonymous in-house system for reporting possible crimes.
• the economics of crime and how it can affect pay-packets.
• the purpose of working in pairs in certain sensitive work areas.
• what to do if a break-in is discovered.
• what to observe when a crime takes place…

Protect your premises.

Whatever assets a business possesses, someone can always be tempted to steal them. To thwart overt and covert criminal theft or damage, you'll need to protect your premises. Consider the following precautions for starters:

• Keep all supplies areas locked.
• Use deadlocks throughout.
• Improve external lighting.
• Install movement sensor alarms.
• Install closed-circuit TV cameras in hard-to-see areas.
• Keep curtains closed.

- Re-key locks frequently.
- Reduce excess inventory.
- Limit the number of entrances and exits.
- Post signs outlining security and prosecution policies.
- Provide patrols in vulnerable areas.
- Seek neighbours' help in security awareness.

 Review your procedures.

Slack operating procedures can make you vulnerable in terms of pilfering, theft, embezzlement, and the like. Think about how you can tighten up procedures. To begin with:

- Don't keep excess cash on hand. Adopt a 'no cash after hours' policy.
- Hold employees liable for money under their control.
- Mark equipment and merchandise with owner-identification information.
- Stagger work shifts to reduce the amount of unsupervised time.
- Monitor computer programs used by employees.
- Don't leave valuable material or tools in view of external windows or doors.
- Engage a reputable auditing firm to conduct regular audits.
- Consider potential problems with briefcases, purses, shopping bags…

 Be cautious about whom you hire.

Many employee security violations can be averted through proper hiring procedures. For sensitive positions, screen potential employees carefully and make clear at this time the severe penalties for dishonest dealings.

 Review employee tasks periodically.

Keep this often-quoted advice in mind. 'The weakest link in your business is your most trusted employee, because that person is in a position to inflict the greatest damage.' An employee who tends to blend into the background can be in a good position to defraud the company. So, by regularly conducting task reviews, you can keep your staff in check.

 Use covert investigating techniques.

Most employees and customers are honest—which is why any suspicion of wrong doing must be backed up with irrefutable evidence. This should be obtained covertly. An overt get-tough approach will not only send a perpetrator to ground; it will upset loyal, honest employees and customers if they feel they are also under suspicion.

 Get assistance if necessary.

Remember, apathy is the friend of crime. So be vigilant, and seek help if necessary. Consider hiring a professional firm to conduct an audit of your internal and external security and your administrative procedures. At the very least, consult a reputable publication such as *Crimeproofing Your Business: 301 low-cost, no-cost ways to protect your office, store or business* by Russell Bintliff (McGraw-Hill, New York, 1994, 372pp.). Don't ever think: 'It can't happen to me!'

 it's a fact

Computer technology has revolutionised the way businesses work, but there are those employees who insist on demonstrating that their brain is still smarter than the microchip, and their bosses'…

- An employee at a New York stockbroking firm programmed the computer to siphon off funds from a company account into his own account. In eight years he stole nearly $500,000. His employer found him out – and then together they milked funds from a rival company's computer, forcing that company into bankruptcy!

- When accused of transferring stocks to his own possession, using a bedside telephone and teleprinter to talk to the computer, one Manfred Stein told the computer to erase all traces of the transactions – but the message was intercepted by a telephone maintenance man who by chance was making a routine check of his phone line.

- A German corporation paid $400,000 in 1973 to retrieve 22 reels of customer records and marketing data, stolen by one of its computer operators.

- A ransom of over $1 million was paid for software snatched in Japan, and several ransoms have been paid in similar cases in the United States.

We are told that only one in 100 computer crimes is ever detected, much less successfully prosecuted – which is one reason why managers must pay particular attention to crime-proofing their organization.

471

How to secure your business against theft and robbery

Businesses large and small can be targets for criminals. The wise manager anticipates, recognises, and appraises the risk of crime in the workplace and takes action to reduce or remove it. At all times, personal safety is paramount. Although prevention of crime should be the key issue, no security plan is universally applicable. But there are some basic strategies to minimise risk and deter the criminals. Among them are the following...

Take steps to secure your premises.

The opportunity for crime can be considerably reduced by attending to the physical environment of your workplace in a number of ways.

Externally:
- trim trees and shrubs to minimise hiding places and to ensure the view of your premises is not obscured.
- install exterior lighting to act as a deterrent, and to allow the public, security services, and police to clearly observe any unusual activity.
- fit solid wooden or metal doors, preferably with double cylinder deadlocks.
- ensure solid door and window frames are not subjected to shrinkage.
- protect exposed hinges to prevent hinge-pin removal.

Internally:
- keep the premises well lit.
- install on all windows key-operated locks, keyed alike, with ready access to the key in case of emergency.
- consider film protection or use of alternative material when replacing glass panels.
- install security grills on all accessible windows, but have some hinged in case of fire.
- fix mesh grills on skylights.
- where appropriate, consider separate doors for entry and exit, controlled with one-way turnstiles.
- place height markers on doors and adopt suspect description forms to assist police identify offenders.
- consider the use of intruder alarms, cameras, or monitored closed-circuit television.

Implement secure cash-handling procedures.

If your business handles cash, particularly if you employ a lone attendant at night, ensure you:
- count and transfer cash behind closed doors and away from public view.
- minimise the cash held on the

472

premises and advertise this fact.

- locate cash registers away from doors and separated from the public.
- establish clear cash register procedures, e.g. open cash drawer only while being used; close drawer before packaging merchandise; warn cashiers to avoid distractions; lock drawer and remove key when not in use.
- have only one entrance, clearly visible to the attendant.
- resist the temptation to place posters and other promotional material on windows, which perhaps obscures an attendant's vision from inside or outside.
- isolate the attendant with a high counter, say 120 cm high.
- implement a system whereby a nominated amount of cash is regularly removed to a secure area, perhaps a safe with a 'posting slot'.
- place emergency numbers where an attendant can easily see them.
- leave tills open and empty when unattended overnight to avoid possible damage by intruders.

Be careful moving cash.

Money on the move is vulnerable, so reduce the opportunity for crime when transporting cash. Ensure you:

- assign more than one person to the journey.
- send well-trained, able-bodied staff.
- avoid using public transport.
- keep to busy streets if walking.
- keep the doors locked if using a private car; vary the routine; and avoid quiet streets.

- never advertise the fact you're carrying money, e.g. by using a marked bank bag.
- keep cash movements private.
- ensure a time of return is known so an alarm can be raised if necessary.
- if using a night safe, never expose cash until the safe is open.
- be aware of vehicles or people behaving suspiciously.
- consider using a cash transit company, particularly for large sums.
- investigate banding together with other businesses in your area to hire cash transit companies for regular use.

Check your safe.

Safes are designed to keep your money secure—but be aware of the following safeguards:

- Buy only a quality safe.
- Make sure you select the type that best suits your purposes.
- Consider purchasing a model with a lockable 'post-feed' device.
- Understand the advantages of having a torch and drill resistant (TDR) model.
- Limit the number and control of keys and/or combinations.
- Anchor your safe to the floor.

Know what to do during and after a crime situation.

Make sure your staff know how to handle a potential offender and, if an offence occurs, what steps must then be taken to assist the police to apprehend the criminal.

here's an idea

Preventing pilferage

While most employees are honest and disapprove of theft, pilferage of materials and resources is an ever present concern in many organizations. Strategies for prevention of pilferage within your company could include:

- Install adequate inventory and control measures to account for all material, supplies and equipment. Poor accountability, if its existence is commonly known, is one of the greatest temptations to the casual pilferer. One control method is the requirement for signing for all tools and equipment to be used by individuals.

- Identify all tools and equipment by some mark or code.

- Conduct an aggressive security education program to convince employees that they have much more to lose than gain by stealing. It is important for all employees to realise that pilferage is morally wrong no matter how insignificant the value of the item taken.

- Demand that supervisory personnel set a proper example and maintain a desirable mans, propose spot searches of employees and vehicles leaving the installation at unannounced times and places. Publicise widely.

- Impress upon all employees that they have a responsibility to report any loss to proper authorities.[8]

How to handle a crime situation

We live in an increasingly violent society; many businesses are becoming more and more vulnerable to criminals. Not so long ago, most businesses believed that robbery, for example, was something that happened to others, never to them. But times have changed, and it is best to be prepared for the day when your business also falls victim to an armed hold-up, an assault, or some other crime…

1 *Make safety your first priority.*

Armed robbery is on the increase and your safety, and that of your staff and customers, must be your prime consideration. Your responsibility is, first and foremost, to protect people's lives in a situation where the armed assailant is usually nervous and unpredictable. Take CARE…

C alm and controlled
A ct on instructions
R emember details
E vidence.

2 *Remain calm and controlled.*

It's not easy to remain calm in these circumstances, but if you can take deep breaths, insist that you keep control of yourself, and stay calm, you'll be better able to cope.

3 *Do what the offender tells you to do.*

The first few seconds of the encounter is when the offender is most emotional and most likely to be violent. It is imperative that at this time you do what the offender tells you to do. Keep quiet and speak only when spoken to. Do nothing to aggravate the situation. Don't try to be a hero. There's a difference between bravery and bravado. The latter can be life-threatening.

If possible, ensure there's a physical barrier between you and the offenders. Raise your hands, the sign of submission. If the offenders can see your hands they will, most likely, be less nervous. Stand side-on to the offender if you can; this reduces your profile and is less threatening to the intruder. Advise the offender of any movements you may have to make, which could appear sudden or unexpected. Activate an alarm, or call for help, only if it is safe to do so.

4 *Keep your wits after the encounter.*

After the offender has fled, check to ensure that nobody has been injured; if they have, administer first-aid. Activate the alarm if you have not already done so. Contact police and cordon off the area of the crime. Take names, addresses, and phone numbers of witnesses and ask them to stay until police have arrived.

Remember details for later.

The accompanying bandit description form is designed to assist police in the apprehension of the offender. Have your staff complete the form immediately and independently after the encounter. Talk to no one until you have completed the form because you do not want other people's perspectives coloring yours.

Protect the evidence.

Close the premises to the public and do not disturb the crime scene until police arrive. They will want to know what the offenders said, what they touched, where they walked, their escape route, and how they got away. Refrain from making statements to the media before talking to the police; or discussing with anyone the amount of money or goods stolen. Finally, your adrenalin will be exceptionally high at this point. Rest up.

BANDIT DESCRIPTION FORM

Separate form required for each person. To be compiled immediately after incident by each staff member, customer(s) or other witnesses. If answer is unknown, write U/K against heading. Do not consult others during compilation. Senior staff members to collect forms and hand to police.

Name/Nickname used: ....

Gender: ☐ Male ☐ Female

Age approx.: ....

Complexion:
☐ Fair ☐ Dark ☐ Pale ☐ Fresh
☐ Pimply ☐ Ruddy ☐ Suntanned

Accent: ....

Stature: ☐ Erect ☐ Stooped ☐ Slouchy

Walk: ☐ Quick ☐ Limp ☐ Slow
☐ Springy ☐ Pigeon-toed

Hair: Color: ....
☐ Wavy ☐ Long ☐ Thick ☐ Straight
☐ Crewcut ☐ Curly ☐ Bald

Eyes: Color:......... Size:...........................
☐ Squint ☐ Starey

Ears: Size: ....
Shape: ....

Nose: Size: ....
Shape: ....

Mouth: Size: ....
Shape: ....

Teeth: ☐ Good ☐ Bad ☐ Protruding
☐ Uneven ☐ Spaced ☐ Missing

Height: ....

Nationality: ....

Build: ☐ Thin ☐ Stout ☐ Medium ☐ Nuggety

Voice: ☐ Clear ☐ Loud ☐ Thick ☐ Slangy

Eyeglasses: ☐ Color ☐ Tinted ☐ Thick
Shape:...

Disguise: Beard– ColorType.............................
Moustache—Color/Type ....

Hands: Size: ....
☐ Soft ☐ Hairy ☐ Calloused
Missing/deformed fingers:......................

Nails: ....

Gloves: Color/Type ....

Jewellery (describe): ....

Scars/Marks: (describe) Tattoos, scars, location, discolorations ....

Weapon: Type ....
In which hand: ....

Clothing (describe): hat, tie, coat, trousers, dress, skirt, jeans, sweater etc. ....
....

Method and Direction of Escape: ....
Registration No. ....
Color of car: ....
Make: ....

Method of operation: What did bandit do, say, touch?...
....
....
....
....

How to protect your organization against fraud

A recent survey found that more than half the world's largest companies were victims of fraud during the previous fiscal year, 25 per cent of them losing millions of dollars each during the previous five years. Online fraud has exacerbated the problem. Many organizations are too embarrassed to admit publicly that their employees have stolen from them. They fire the employees—but fail to fix the underlying problems. In some places, trivial fraud and pilfering are accepted as normal practice. Fraud, to any degree, should not be tolerated. Before it's too late, it may be wise to implement fraud protection measures...

1 Be aware: your staff are usually the villains.

Regretfully, your own employees pose the greatest threat when it comes to fraud—some are highly motivated to get rich quickly; they usually know what controls are in place; and they often have the ability to circumvent those controls and exploit company weaknesses.

Remember, the core element in all fraud is people; so effective human resource management in all forms is vital.

2 Check the references of potential employees.

Although previous employers are often reluctant to provide anything but confirmation of employment dates and positions held, as a rule they also do not want any other organization burned by an unscrupulous worker. So, check all references—not just the last job held. As well, verify education qualifications and certifications—'She *claimed* she was a CPA!' comes too late when the damage is already done.

3 Document and enforce policies and procedures.

Ensure that all internal control policies and procedures are well documented, communicated, and enforced. Your policies should address such issues as: Can staff accept gifts? When do perks and hospitality become corruption? When does pilfering become fraud? How can suspicions of fraud be raised? Who is responsible for dealing with it, and how? If necessary, put in place an audit committee with a policy-development, monitoring, and investigative role. Written guidelines are needed so employees can differentiate between accepted custom and what is not acceptable. These guidelines need to take into account whether or not employees have online access.

4 Install safeguards to limit computer misuse.

Our dependence on computer technology has meant that almost all major fraud committed today involves the misuse of computers by staff who:

- establish phony accounts
- drain legitimate accounts
- purchase assets for private use
- change ownership of assets or ship assets to false addresses
- create phantom sales transactions
- give individuals rewards they have not earned.

The key to preventing this is to restrict access to sensitive transactions to those with a legitimate need and to monitor employee activities to ensure that misdeeds are detected and addressed. Consider the use of:

- *passwords* which authenticate those seeking access to the network. To limit misuse of passwords, you may need to change them frequently, depending on the sensitivity of the material.
- *firewalls* which are programs that sit between your network and the Internet or other networks designed to reduce unauthorised access.
- *encryption* which prevents data intercepted by a criminal from being read, by encoding it with a special key known only to legitimate users.
- *audit software* which detects and responds immediately to suspicious or threatening computer transactions.

Databases integrated across departments also allow organizations to cross-reference information, and thus provide security checks against fraudulent behaviour.

 Review your vendor lists periodically.

A common fraud technique is to establish a fictitious vendor account. When authorising a payment (electronically or otherwise), would you know the difference between, say, IBM itself and a phony IBM? And importantly, how would you know if the products were authorised or the services performed? Regularly print out and review your vendor master list to check that each vendor is authorised to supply goods and services, and compare this list with all payments made. Any discrepancy could be a cause for concern.

6 Regularly review bank statements.

Spotting fraud is like spotting pornography: 'I can't define it, but I know it when I see it'. Regularly review bank statements to keep you 'up-to-speed' with all payment issues.

7 Consider taking out insurance against fraud.

Insurance protecting employers against fraud is relatively inexpensive and worthwhile for all employees with finance-related responsibilities.

8 Take a stand against fraud.

The message about fraud and corruption must come loud and clear from the top and be reinforced with action. Be adamant that you treat the problem seriously. Define it clearly. Call it fraud if you find it. Use newsletters, seminars and other communication techniques to explain your commitment to tackling it. Open up channels that allow staff identifying fraud to communicate their suspicions—around line managers if necessary. Never brush fraud under the carpet or be easy on it. Be seen to act when you uncover it. Remember, everyone in your organization has a role in the process of spotting and preventing fraud.

 don't forget

Stop fraud before it starts

The US Association of Certified Fraud Examiners suggests…

- Set an example. Employees tend to emulate the behaviour of honest and ethical employers.
- Implement a written code of ethics that states what you expect from employees.
- Prescreen job applicants. Screen references and perform background checks.
- Don't have one person keep the books and write cheques. Separate those duties.
- Know your suppliers. If an employee shows favoritism for one supplier, ask why.
- Ensure bank statements are delivered unopened to a high-level executive, who has no links to bank reconciliations, to detect any cash skimming and false disbursements. Look for inconsistencies and names you don't know.
- Create a positive workplace so that staff don't have any motivation for revenge.
- Ensure your computer system is set up so that only those needing access to various areas have it.
- Hire the right people, treat them well, and don't subject them to temptation.
- Don't think that because you pay someone a good salary, s/he won't steal from you.
- Be sure your employees know whom to contact if they uncover a problem or suspect a fellow employee of fraud.

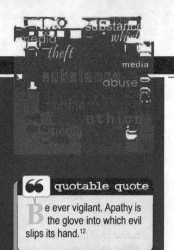

How to avoid being caught in a scam

From large corporations to small stores, businesses are increasingly becoming the targets for a range of schemers and scam merchants. Such tricksters rely on your being too busy to give a second thought to giving them the information they ask for, purchasing a bogus service or product, or paying an unjustified invoice. Whether the con-artist uses the telephone, the mail, or the Internet, your best defence against scams is to be vigilant and to follow these rules…

viewpoint

"You may also be surprised to find out that most con artists are never put out of business. Because of the time and resources required to bring a criminal case against a con artist, very few are prosecuted for criminal offences. The ones who are prosecuted are those who have stolen millions and millions of dollars or have blazed a new path in the area of fraud by doing something outrageous and bringing a great deal of attention to themselves."

– Marsha Bertrand in *Fraud: How to protect yourself from schemes, scams and swindles*

don't forget

The golden rule for avoiding investment scams is as sound today as it ever was: 'If a deal appears to be too good to be true, it probably is'.

1 Be aware of how you can get scammed.

There are many ways clever con-artists try to catch you out, but the two most common are:

Passing off: They try to mislead you into thinking they are someone or something they are not—often called 'passing off'. Here they may try to pass off that they are from a registered charity or a government agency.

Fake billing: They try to convince you to pay for something you have not asked for. Fake billing often involves offering advertising, usually in bogus magazines or directories, or trying to get you to pay for something never ordered or delivered.

2 Ensure you have enough information to decide.

Understand any offer being made, particularly if you are not dealing with a known company. It pays to get all the details and promises in writing, especially if the offer is being made over the telephone. And, prior

to making any decision, consider the following:

Who are they?
- Whom do they represent?
- Why have they contacted you?
- What service do they provide?

Find the organization's telephone number in the white pages directory and make contact. Verify that they are who they say they are.

Do you really need their service?
- What do you get for your money?
- Why is their offer better than others?
- Have you seen or checked their previous work or references?

How much will it cost?
- If it's free, is there *any* way this service will cost you money later? Will you automatically be charged for anything in the future?
- If it's not free, what will all the costs amount to? When will you have to pay? Is there a money-back guarantee? Get it all in writing.

Only when you have enough information to feel confident about the service and the provider should you make the decision to proceed.

3 When in doubt, check the contract.

If you suspect deception, and the con-artist tells you that they already have a contract with you, you should:

- Ask them to show you evidence of the contract.
- Check any evidence to see if it shows what you received, how much it costs, and that you did indeed accept those conditions.

If it seems that you have entered into such a contract, and you think you have been conned, seek legal advice.

4 Remember these essential rules...

- Do business with companies you know and trust. If you don't know them, check them out.
- Be clear on what is being offered. Seek details and get it in writing.
- Ask for the name of the person you are speaking to and whom they represent.
- Take notes of conversations including date, time, names, and important points.
- Read any written documents carefully. Seek the professional help of a solicitor or accountant if significant money, time, or responsibilities are involved.
- Never be pressured into making an immediate decision. Reputable companies will be happy to answer all your questions and to give you time to decide.
- Shop around locally to compare services and prices.

- Ask for references and contact them to check out the quality of services performed or products provided.
- Be suspicious of incredibly cheap prices. Unrealistic prices can be the warning bell of a scam. Don't forget: you get what you pay for.
- Don't pay the full amount upfront. Pay the balance only when satisfied.
- Check all bills and invoices carefully. It's hard to get your money back once you've paid a con-artist.
- Have a number of people authorised to make online payments and issue cheques. Keep the number to a minimum and keep a tight control on them.
- Guard your financial and other account information. Never give out or clarify any sensitive information about your business unless you know what it is being legitimately used for.
- Never agree to anything on the telephone. Ask for the offer in writing.
- Educate your employees about the hazards of scams. Ensure they understand their roles and responsibilities.
- If you are approached by somebody with what you think might be a scam, contact the appropriate State consumer affairs and fair trading agencies. Discuss any suspicions, seek clarification, or report any instance where you have fallen victim.

don't forget

How to check out a scam

Regardless of the type of scam that may be perpetrated against you, you can help to protect yourself and your organization if you do the following:

- Check out the person, the company, the investment, or the offer through the state attorney-general's office, or other appropriate agency in your state.
- Ask for and read written information that explains the offer or investment.
- Get the opinion of a trusted advisor, friend, or colleague.
- Verify the claims the person makes.
- Don't do business with strangers over the phone.
- Be very wary about the type of personal or financial details about yourself or your organization you give out over the phone.
- Never allow yourself to be rushed into making a decision.

Knowing how to recognise a con artist and a fraudulent offer and taking the time to check them out will help to keep you fraud free. Knowledge is power, and power is what you need to keep the con artists at bay.[13]

How to deal with substance abuse in the workplace

When dealing with drug and alcohol abuse in the workplace, managers are today expected to take increasing responsibility in an area for which they have little or no formal training. The problem is exacerbated further because drug dependency does not discriminate: anyone can be an addict, from your CEO to your back-room employee. Here are some practical ideas that will help...

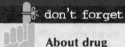
1 Adopt and circulate a substance abuse policy.

By having a policy, employees know what is acceptable behaviour, the consequences of abusing drugs and alcohol at work, and the level of support provided by the employer in the event of a problem. The policy should contain information about where employees need to go voluntarily for help and advice on drugs and alcohol abuse, time off for treatment and counselling, whether drug and alcohol abuse is a disciplinary matter and at what level that issue will be addressed, and the employees' rights under the disciplinary procedure.

2 Be aware of tell-tale symptoms.

Drug or alcohol impairment is more than an isolated incident. Indicators usually include performance problems, physical appearance, lack of coordination, mood swings, excessive tiredness, and thought disturbance. These are usually 'flagged' by:

- excessive absenteeism, particularly on Mondays
- regular tardiness
- diminishing performance and declining productivity
- increased injuries and accidents
- personal problems—legal, financial, or family
- constant and/or suspicious phone calls
- physical deterioration, dilated pupils, slurred speech, runny nose, scratching, and dry skin
- changes in interactions with others
- increased isolation from or conflict with peers
- rebellious behaviour towards authority
- erratic behaviour, moodiness, disorientation
- increased visits to the washroom or toilet.

3 Record observations.

If you suspect impairment, you must act on it and document signs and obvious patterns. If the person is performing a dangerous task, they must be removed from that task. Engage them in conversation to assess for slurred speech or disturbance in thought. Involve others if possible to verify your observations. Be careful not to make accusations until you've collected the facts, particularly if the employee tries to deny that there is a problem. Ultimately, you may be left with no other option than to tell the offending employee that disciplinary proceedings will be instigated unless their performance improves.

4 Act in the best interests of all persons.

Chemical abuse affects more than the one person. As the manager responsible, it would be wrong for you to:

- ignore or excuse unacceptable behaviour
- take on the person's responsibilities
- make excuses to others, cover up the problem, pick up the slack, or fill in for them
- feel responsible
- enable the person to get away with poor job performance.

5 Confront the person with your evidence.

This should be done privately and in a supportive manner. Be firm but positive, have your facts on hand, don't label, and give the employee a reasonable amount of time to address the problem, insisting that help

be sought if necessary. Additional guidelines are:

- Avoid blaming, using guilt tactics, or getting sidetracked with the person's personal problems. Stick to work issues.
- Clarify goals and standards set in your policy document. The person should refocus on what is expected of him or her.
- Let the person know the consequences of poor performance. If the employee has been involved in drug offences outside of work, it is likely that you will be able to act only if you can show that the employee's actions have damaged the organization in some way.
- Refer the employee to a professional to deal with personal problems. Programs exist to deal with these issues.
- Don't counsel on your own.

If performance does not improve, follow disciplinary steps according to company policy; this may involve a union representative.

6 Provide internal and external counselling.

Use the resources available to offer help—sooner is better than later. One of the conditions of your disciplinary actions may be that the person attends counselling sessions conducted by a qualified professional. An in-house substance-abuse prevention program could be considered for the entire staff.

👊 don't forget

If you're discussing an alcohol problem

■ Don't apologise for raising the matter. Make it clear that job performance is the focus.

■ Encourage the staff member to explain why behaviour or performance has deteriorated. The issue of substance abuse may be raised.

■ Don't discuss the person's right to drink or make a moral issue of it.

■ Don't you counsel that the person change or moderate drinking habits. Alcoholics Anonymous claims that alcoholics usually need professional help.

■ Don't be distracted by excuses. Your focus is the drinking itself, and how it affects the work scene.

■ Stress that the primary concern is the employee's work performance. Advise that if behaviour does not improve, disciplinary action will result.

■ Indicate that the decision to seek help is ultimately the staff member's responsibility.

💡 here's an idea

If you have to send an employee home under the influence of a drug or alcohol, don't let them drive – you or your company may be liable if the employee has an accident. Don't ask another staff member to do the driving either – call a taxi.

481

How to deal with dishonest staff

Once upon a time, if an employee was caught stealing in the workplace, instant dismissal would follow. Staff members caught red handed were found to have breached their duty of good faith to the employer; termination of service was an expected outcome. But these days, industrial legislation can protect even dishonest employees. Employers must, therefore, tread carefully when dealing with such staff members…

1 Stay alert.

Staff dishonesty is difficult to eliminate from the workplace; it is certainly difficult to detect. The natural loyalty of employers towards their staff often permits such crimes to go undetected. In most cases this loyalty is justified; however, when it is not, the resulting loss can be high for the simple reason that employees have easy access to cash, goods, or valuables. Stay alert.

2 Be scrupulously fair in any investigation.

Even if you believe that theft can be proven beyond doubt, a court could find the dismissal to be harsh, unreasonable, or unjust unless you have treated the employee with 'procedural fairness'. To ignore this just process could mean that you may have to suffer dearly in terms of time, aggravation, back pay, damages and compensation, even continued employment, if the terminated staff member seeks court judgement on unfair dismissal.

3 Gather clear evidence of any dishonest behaviour.

Remember that, for dismissal, you will need to show:

- that the theft was so serious that the employee should be no longer bound by the contract of employment
- that the employee's behaviour was not subject to any mitigating circumstances or alternative explanations.

4 Be aware of any mitigating circumstances.

Consider any underlying causes for an employee's dishonest actions. Were there any personal problems? Or major concerns with family? Or stress factors which may have affected the staff member's conduct?

Courts have even favored employees who actually showed no sense of guilt—who 'didn't realise that I wasn't supposed to take the item from the site'. So check out any underlying causes for the dishonest behaviour.

5 Put your allegations to the employee clearly.

State in clear terms your findings to the employee; provide the staff member with an opportunity to respond to your statement and to explain his or her own side of the story. It is important that you encourage the employee to respond and for you to listen sympathetically to that explanation. If the employee admits to a serious offence and shows little remorse, there may well be a case for dismissal on the grounds of seriousness and a breach of duty of good faith to the employer. Remember, 'procedural fairness' is an essential consideration in this process.

6 Provide the contrite employee with a second chance.

On the other hand, if the employee admits to an indiscretion, expresses genuine remorse, and can provide a sincere explanation for the dishonesty, then this should be noted and the employee given a second chance. Courts have been very sympathetic to employees who express genuine contrition and legal actions have gone against employers who have ignored such pleas.

7 Ensure the employee receives a written warning.

A written warning that an instance of employee dishonesty has been identified and that the employee's future behaviour will be carefully monitored should be provided to the employee. This will ensure that a further breach will make the employer's case for dismissal so much stronger.

8 Become familiar with legislatory provisions.

Forewarned is forearmed. Industrial relations legislation is ever-changing. It is important for employers to become familiar with the latest laws and requirements on dismissal. By knowing your local provisions, you will be prepared to act promptly and legally in cases of employee dishonesty.

9 Eliminate the opportunity; eliminate the crime.

If you want to reduce the discomfort of having to deal with dishonest staff members, then take steps to eliminate, or at least reduce, theft by employees. Consider this advice:

- Acknowledge the problem. Dishonest staff could be costing you money. US government studies show that employee theft from manufacturing plants alone amounts to $8 million a day nationwide!
- Conduct regular pilferage vulnerability assessments in your business operations.
- Recognise the many techniques dishonest employees use to pilfer your assets; devise effective counter measures.
- Create an effective inventory system that will alert you to a potential problem.
- Include your employees in the inventory control program—participation increases awareness and responsibility.

quotable quote

Employee pilferage causes more businesses to close or go into bankruptcy than any other crime. Studies by the US government and by a variety of business organizations indicate that employee pilferage accounts for 38-75 per cent of business losses. I need to add that business owners and management often resist the idea that employees steal from them. Others know or suspect it but ignore the problem, believing it's only a temporary situation.[15]

ask yourself

■ Do you have provable evidence, or mere suspicion?

■ Have you meticulously recorded your evidence?

■ Will you deal with the dishonesty in-house, or will you involve police?

■ In an in-house inquiry, did you scrupulously apply the principles of natural justice?

■ Will you require restitution or compens-ation? Will you need to instigate court action?

■ If dismissal is warranted, are you following the legal requirements?

■ If the case is proven or admitted, and if you are giving the person a second chance, did you make the necessary notation on the employee's staff file?

483

How to handle threatening phone calls

Whenever an employee answers a telephone, an unexpected threat can be an unwanted, distressing, even frightening experience. Unfortunately, such calls are increasing. In earlier times many were hoaxes by schoolboys and other pranksters. Now, increasingly, they are not. For this reason, your staff should be prepared for the unexpected. The following advice is provided to help you to prepare them...

Ignore mischievous callers.

The appropriate way to handle anonymous telephone calls (or letters) that peddle mischievous gossip is to ignore them. The letters should be thrown in the waste basket and the calls forgotten. This applies to the majority of anonymous communications, complaints or mischievous comment about the personal lives of staff members. Don't tell the employee that an anonymous call or letter has been received. It tends to give some kind of official sanction to the call.

Consider the following response if an anonymous phone call comes through to you as manager: 'My name is Sue Shaw. I'm the manager. Unfortunately, unless you give me your name, I'll have to hang up the phone. However, if at any time in the future you want to call and identify yourself, I'll be pleased to discuss with you any matter involving our organisation.' Then, if the caller doesn't identify himself or herself, hang up.

This advice, of course, is not totally binding. The exceptions are the threatening letters or calls; managers must have a separate set of procedures to handle those.

Treat threatening callers seriously.

If your organization receives a bomb threat by telephone, or a call which threatens the physical safety of a staff member, it is important to record as much information as possible to help police with their inquiries, or for you to take other appropriate action immediately. For this reason, it is wise to compile a Threatening Phone Call Check list which should be kept handy to each telephone on your premises. The check list should comprise six components:

- The wording of the threat
- Questions to ask the caller
- Caller's voice characteristics
- Background noises
- The language of the threat
- Staff response policy.

Staff taking any threatening phone calls should complete the check list during and immediately after the menacing call is taken.

Record the wording of the threat.

Try to record, or record later, the exact words of the threat. It is important to keep the caller talking so that, for accuracy purposes and for police follow-up action, you can obtain as much information as possible.

Ask appropriate questions.

In the case of a bomb threat, for example, keep the caller talking by trying to obtain answers to such questions as:

- When is the bomb going to explode?
- Where is it right now?
- What kind of bomb is it?
- What does it look like?
- What will cause it to explode?
- Who put the bomb there?
- When was it put there?
- Why?
- Where are you?
- What is your name?

Be aware, of course, that the caller may be reluctant to disclose such information.

Make a judgement about the caller.

After the caller has hung up, you should attempt to describe the characteristics of the caller's voice—angry, calm, excited, slow, rapid, soft, loud, laughing, crying, normal, distinct, slurred, nasal, stuttering,

lisping, raspy, deep, ragged, clearing throat, deep breathing, crackling voice, disguised, accented, familiar… elaborate where possible.

Record also the sex of the caller and the caller's estimated age.

Note any background noises.

Be aware of any background noises which might help to locate or identify the caller—street noises, voices, music, house noises, crockery, phone booth, children, local call, mobile phone, STD call, factory machinery, animal noises, clear, static, motor, PA system… elaborate where possible.

Describe the language of the threat.

Was the caller well-spoken, educated, foul-mouthed, irrational, incoherent, intoxicated? Did the caller read the message? Was it a recorded message?

Record the final details.

Make sure you record the number at which the call was received, the time of day and date, and the name and position of the person who took the call.

Report the call immediately.

Don't hang up the telephone, even though the caller may have done so. It may be possible for the call to be traced—which is why another line should be used to call the police. Take any other immediate action, e.g. notifying the CEO, or the fire warden.

485

How to break bad news

The need for managers to break bad news can occur without warning (a family crisis, for example). But bad news can be associated with everyday work life (such as redundancy, failure to gain a promotion, or refusal of a major project proposal). Whatever the situation may be, breaking bad news can be difficult—even distressing. Although no one likes delivering bad news, the process can be handled effectively and empathetically, leaving the recipient appreciating your help and communicating to others your managerial ability…

1   *Prepare yourself.*

Delivering bad news is a difficult, often unpleasant task; but it is one of your responsibilities as manager. Preparation is vital and an important part of that preparation is that your ego be removed from the process. The issue should not be what the person will think of you or how you feel about delivering the news. Your focus must be on conveying the message accurately, taking into account the recipient's feelings.

2   *Select an appropriate medium.*

Although extremely personal situations—redundancy, firing, family crisis—require face-to-face communication, some bad news may best be delivered by other means, such as letter or email. Cheryl Maday[18] claims that people are more effective at conveying bad news via computer than on the phone or in person. In face-to-face situations, she says, people have a tendency 'to tune out the worst and sugarcoat bad news, (while) email facilitates

straight talk because senders don't see the discomfort of their recipients'. And people react less defensively to computer messages, she concludes.

3   *Avoid delays.*

Although the grapevine and rumour mill will often foreshadow some areas of bad news—retrenchment, for example—you should break such news to those concerned as soon as you have assembled all the necessary information. If the news concerns an event external to the workplace, ensure that your facts are accurate before going public with the information.

4   *Plan the meeting.*

If you've decided on a face-to-face meeting, focus first on location, timing, and support. If the location is to be your office or an interview room, ensure a non-threatening layout. Ideally, there should be no physical barriers—table, desk, workbench—between you and the recipient. Chairs should be of the same height.

Notepaper, pen, water, even tissues should be available. Timing, too, is an important consideration. If the bad news concerns the person's redundancy, Friday afternoon would not be a good time because of the lack of professional support over the weekend, leaving the person to brood about the situation. Early in the day might be a good time because it allows the recipient time to think over the situation and access available support. In addition to counselling and outplacement support (if the issue is redundancy), provide all relevant paperwork including lists of networks, entitlements, and references.

Consider involving one other.

Depending on the nature of the bad news, consider inviting a third person to sit in on the meeting. In the case of breaking the news of a person's redundancy, for example, the presence of another person could be a demonstration of the immediacy of the support being provided. A third person also acts as a witness should any litigation result. Breaking some bad news can cause demonstration of emotions. A third person can provide valuable support should this occur.

Check for understanding.

After delivering the news clearly and in a straightforward and unambiguous manner, invite the recipient to ask any questions and generally confirm that the message is being understood. Avoid information overload. Listen, empathise, provide all necessary support. The recipient must be the focus of the discussion.

Accompany the person.

If the bad news concerns an event external to the organization, offer the person access to the telephone. You might arrange a taxi and accompany the person to the cab and deliver the appropriate instructions. Perhaps ask a trusted colleague to accompany the person to his or her destination, and to report to you after returning to the workplace. If the bad news concerns a termination, accompany the person to his or her workstation or office. You, or your nominee, can then follow established procedures to ensure that issues of security and physical and intellectual property are taken care of.

Communicate outcomes.

Keep other employees informed about the news and the outcomes. You may decide to issue a memo, send an email, or assemble the group for a brief announcement. The way you handle this situation will help to build others' confidence in you and defuse a potentially harmful staff grapevine.

Stay in touch.

Demonstrate genuine concern for the recipient's well-being by remaining in contact, a task made easier if the person remains in the organization. In the case of a redundancy, your enquiries about the person's well-being are likely to be appreciated.

How to be a whistleblower— the right way

People who consider going public with serious allegations of organizational wrongdoing or malpractice should be aware of the potentially serious consequences of their actions. Normally, having identified an area of major concern to the organization or community, the troubled employee should bring the matter to the attention of a higher level executive within the organization. Only when the organization fails or refuses to investigate the complaint should the employee feel compelled to go public with the allegations—and thereby become a whistleblower…

Know what whistleblowing entails.

Whistleblowers are watchdogs in organizations who bark loudly and publicly if they perceive that a company policy, practice, or product is unethical, dangerous, immoral, or illegal. Normally, and wisely, they will only alert the media or regulatory body if they believe the organization has refused to take their complaint or concern seriously. Heroes to some, troublemakers to others, whistleblowers should exercise this right with caution, because the consequences of their actions can have very serious implications for the organization and for themselves.

Be aware of the hazards of whistleblowing.

If whistleblowing can save lives or taxpayers' dollars, or protect the environment, then a whistleblower can become an organizational or community hero. There is also great satisfaction in knowing that one has served an important role as a responsible and concerned watchdog.

There is a downside, however. By going public and making allegations of organizational wrongdoing, a whistleblower can suffer considerable professional and personal pain. For example:

- Whistleblowing can be an extremely stressful exercise.
- Those colleagues who may have encouraged you, indeed voiced their undying support of your actions, often back down when your claims are made public.
- Others in the workplace may resent your actions and despise you— whether you are right or wrong with your accusations.
- You may ruin your chances of promotion within the organization. Indeed, you may be dismissed, only able to gain reinstatement after a costly and stressful legal process.
- Even if you are not fired, then ostracism within the organization may be so great that you have no option other than to resign anyway.
- You may be branded a

troublemaker within your industry or profession, a label which may hinder your future prospects for promotion or employment.

Clearly, whistleblowing is a course of action not to be taken lightly.

 Get your facts straight.

If you are making formal accusations internally or in public, it is imperative that you have solid evidence of wrongdoing or malpractice. Keep accurate records and obtain relevant documentary proof to verify your claims before approaching a superior or the media with your claim. Be warned, however, that some of your genuine concern could be faulty or misconceived because you may never have all the relevant facts in your possession.

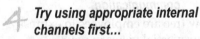 **Try using appropriate internal channels first...**

It is inadvisable to blow the whistle on your organization without having first exhausted all available avenues within your organization for rectifying the concern. Follow established complaint or grievance procedures where they exist. Be persistent in voicing your concern to supervisors and executives. Consider blowing the whistle in public only when the organization refuses to listen.

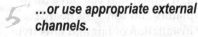 **...or use appropriate external channels.**

Consider using other safe channels if you do not have the confidence to

raise your concerns internally. Some organizations actually nominate well respected, impartial individuals or agencies outside the normal chain of command to address such matters. Explore these alternative avenues before exposing your organization publicly through the media.

 Seek the support of others.

Whistleblowing can be a lonely job. If you have a strong case, try to get other highly principled and troubled colleagues to join you. In this way, your case will be strengthened and much of the inevitable stress can be shared. It also helps to determine if any legislation, regulations, and court decisions support your stance.

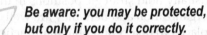 **Be aware: you may be protected, but only if you do it correctly.**

Legislation is increasingly being introduced to protect the authentic whistleblower. No matter how principled or confident you are, it is important to check current state and federal leglislation, together with recent court decisions, before committing yourself to exposing your organization's wrongdoing in the public arena. Normally, a whistleblower will have the court's protection if:

- the motive is not personal vengeance
- all internal avenues of complaint have been explored fully
- the whistleblower did not harm the organization in a reckless manner.

 it's a fact

Whistleblowers can save society considerable heartache. Consider these cases:

- Engineers on the Challenger space shuttle who tried to point out problems on the vehicle that eventually caused it to explode.
- Citizens who expose the immense damage caused by illegal waste dumping.
- Public servants who expose fraud in government costing billions of dollars.
- Accountants who expose business fraud involving large sums of money.
- Others who reveal practices resulting in the deaths of consumers.

research says

Queensland research has revealed that whistleblowers have suffered reprisals for their disclosures as follows:[21]

Official. Experienced by 71% of respondents: deliberate, punitive responses veiled behind policy and procedure to avoid charges of illegality – including selective redundancy, poor performance reviews, formal reprimands, punitive transfers, compulsory referrals to psychiatrists, demotion, suspension, dismissal.

Unofficial. Experienced by 94% of respondents: offensive but subtle, ambiguous or deniable workplace interactions – ostracism, spreading of rumours, close scrutiny of work, questioned motives and personal attack, abuse by colleagues, physical isolation, overwork, underwork.

489

How to minimise whistleblowing in your organization

Around the world, whistleblowing activity is increasing. In any but the most scrupulous of organizations, wrongdoing will occur to some extent; and well-intentioned and highly-principled employees or ex-employees will be motivated enough to stop it. In the right workplace environment, any improper practice can be addressed internally, quickly, and safely before an employee is tempted to blow the whistle in public, to the detriment of the organization. So consider the following advice...

1 Be aware of who your potential whistleblowers might be.

Whistleblowers can be either disgruntled troublemakers or highly-principled, dedicated, competent, and committed employees. They usually hold strategic positions in the organization and here they are well placed to detect potential malpractice and wrongdoing. Their well-intentioned public dissent is often the result of a lack of response within the organization to their voiced concerns. The larger and more bureaucratic the organization, the less likely these concerns will be heard or dealt with— and the more fertile the ground for whistleblowing.

2 Appreciate the value of dissent in your organization.

Differences of opinion and rational debate should be encouraged in any healthy organization. It is in such environments that illegal, unethical or dangerous practices are less likely to develop because staff are free to question and express dissension or concern over policies and procedures

in the workplace. So, take the raison d'être out of whistleblowing: encourage your employees to raise issues when concerned about any potentially damaging practice within the organization.

3 Nip whistleblowing in the bud: open the paths of communication.

How free are employees to express controversial views in your organization? Do you regularly provide through formal meetings and informal conversation the opportunity for staff to exchange diverse views relating to practices in your workplace? Ensure safe routes of communication are in place for your staff to discuss irregularities or other concerns.

4 Put formal grievance procedures in place.

Do you have formal mechanisms through which staff can have their complaints and concerns heard? The installation of fair and effective procedures for addressing staff discontent is a first step to eliminating public whistleblowing. Consider using such mechanisms as an organizational ombudsman, or a review board consisting of a cross-section of staff, or an impartial and trusted outside consultant. Ensure that your employees are aware of the processes and that they feel at ease raising an issue without fear of reprisal.

Minimise reprisals against dissentients.

If senior managers and other employees react over-defensively or aggressively against a dissentient, then your organizational culture is not open; staff with legitimate concerns will not be prepared to voice their concerns internally; and the potential for public whistleblowing will escalate. Take a firm stand against retaliation and harassment. Remember, the public and the law are increasingly taking the side of legitimate whistleblowers.

Conduct periodic audits of areas of concern.

If yours is a responsible and progressive organization, you should adopt a proactive stance in conscientiously reviewing your approach to such issues as health, safety, the environment, and employment. Are you fully aware of and do you comply with the relevant regulations in such areas? Do you regularly review and revise your practices and policies in these areas to ensure that no questionable activity

occurs? There is no reason for anyone to blow the whistle on an organization which operates responsibly, ethically, fairly, safely, and legally, and is constantly aware of its obligations to staff and community.

Insist on an ethical and open culture.

Senior management should ensure staff understand that malpractice, unethical behaviour, and fraud will not be tolerated; and that a company policy of fostering open and safe communication channels is intended to help staff freely disclose and discuss any concerns relating to a breach of ethical conduct.

Develop a policy to minimise whistleblowing.

The larger the organization, the more difficult it is to ensure a culture of openness and transparency. With journalists ever alert to a good story, a prime target for them today is the whistleblower, a principled or disgruntled employee or former employee, who is prepared to reveal instances of fraud, mismanagement, breaches of health and safety laws, malpractice, or any other illegal or unethical activity by management or employees.

For many organizations, whistleblowing has become a policy issue—and perhaps it is time for your organization to develop and implement a policy that sets guidelines for minimising and handling whistleblowing situations…

viewpoint

"To know what is right and not to do it is the worst cowardice."
– Confucius

it's a fact

Whistleblowing refers to the employee who publicly discloses unlawful, improper, or wasteful activity that is occurring within the workplace. The term has its origins from the practice of the British Bobby who, upon discovering a crime being committed, blows a whistle to attract the attention of fellow police officers.

research says

Methods used by organizations to suppress critics include:

- blocking of appointment
- blocking of promotion
- forced job transfer
- reprimand
- legal action
- ostracism, harassment
- blacklisting
- spreading of rumours
- censorship of writing
- denial of research opportunities
- dismissal.

In almost every case, those who take such action against dissidents say that the reason is poor performance by the dissident or something else that is the *dissident*'s fault.

491

How to implement a whistleblowing policy

The last thing an organization needs is for an employee or ex-employee to disclose unexpectedly in the public arena details of malpractice, unethical behaviour, or dishonest activity within the company. Such a crisis can be avoided by developing and implementing an effective whistleblowing policy, aimed at helping employees to disclose their concerns internally, freely and without fear. They will not then feel the need to blow the whistle to the media. Here's how you might tackle such a policy...

1 Understand the benefits of a whistleblowing policy.

Any progressive organization that takes the decision to develop and implement a whistleblowing policy is aware that the policy is capable of:

- exposing wrongdoing and malpractice early, providing the opportunity to eliminate the contaminating impact of improper activity on the company and its reputation
- detailing the internal avenues for potential whistleblowers to express their concerns—without having to do so in the public arena
- preempting any resulting bad publicity and the associated costs of the public disclosure and any possible legal action that might follow
- promoting internal accountability
- demonstrating that the company is committed to being honest, fair and ethical in all its activities.

2 Understand the problems arising from such policy.

Be aware of the problem areas associated with the introduction of a whistleblowing policy. For example, the policy can actually encourage troublemakers to increasingly blow the whistle on petty issues. There is the danger too that staff might see the policy as one of encouraging employees to spy on each other. And, by raising the issue of retaliation, whistleblowers may in fact now fear reprisals, despite policy to the contrary. As well, such a policy will be hollow if the organization does not have in place a code of conduct that defines the company's honest and ethical workplace standards.

3 Create a policy through staff involvement.

The evidence indicates that successful implementation of any policy depends on the extent to which employees are involved in its development. Appoint a project manager and select a team which is representative of all sectors of the organization to assist in the development of the whistleblowing policy. To expedite the process, raise the issues, explain the reasons, deal with concerns, and circulate drafts for comment by staff. During the writing phase, focus on such issues as these:

Commitment to an ethical culture.
Without a code of conduct and ethics, you will have no yardstick against which to measure proper and improper behaviour in your organization. The code must make management's view clear: the organization will tolerate no fraud, corruption, malpractice, or related unethical behaviour. Incorporate this code into the whistleblowing policy.

Commitment to an open culture.
Indicate that all employee concerns will be taken seriously and that dissentients will be protected. Reveal how the organization will support an open and communicative culture where staff are free to speak up.

Company-employee confidentiality.
Acknowledge that employees by law are prohibited from disclosing in the public arena any of their employer's confidential data, unless in the public interest.

Open channels for staff to communicate concerns safely.
How will the hierarchy accommodate staff members with concerns to raise? With whom can employees speak in confidence? What role might well respected outsiders or agencies play in providing a safe alternative listening channel for concerned employees?

Fair and impartial investigative procedures.
Remember: don't shoot the messenger; focus on the problem! Ensure the dissentient is listened to, indicate how the matter will be addressed, and advise promptly or regularly of what action has been taken (or not taken) and why.

Measures to guard against abuse of the policy.
The policy should indicate that the raising of petty, unfounded, or malicious allegations will be viewed as a disciplinary offence.

Protection for whistleblowers.
The policy should make it clear that harassment of genuine dissentients by management or other staff will not be tolerated. Anonymity may be granted where appropriate—although openness is usually advised since others will often know the instigator of any internal inquiry.

4 Publicise and promote the policy.

A final document, filed away and neither communicated nor acted upon, condemns any policy. So, circulate and discuss the policy at appropriate forums and reinforce its value through relevant and regular publicity.

5 Review the policy periodically.

Over time, keep the policy under review—for example, the project manager should discuss with any dissentient employees their experience with the process and the policy, and if they were harassed in any way. Conduct staff surveys to determine if staff are comfortable with procedures and the organizational support in place to make easier the airing of their concerns.

✔ it's a fact

■ A Tasmanian government veterinarian spoke out about the risks in dismantling animal health surveillance in Australia. He was dismissed from his position and, after more than four years of struggle, finally received a public apology from the government.

■ An auditor in a large NSW government utility discovered evidence of safety problems, fraud, and sexual and racial harassment. In response to her allegations, management did nothing except try to silence her, and eventually dismissed her. Her allegations were given to the Independent Commission Against Corruption – which referred them back to the employer.

■ A Sydney engineer expressed concern about the discharge of sewage and industrial waste into the ocean. Many engineers on the relevant Board were extremely hostile to anyone who questioned its policies. In the end, a code of ethics was invoked by the engineer's professional institute to silence the dissident.[20]

66 quotable quote

When employees in government or industry are inhibited from speaking out through fear for their jobs, society suffers. Powerful organizations that claim to serve the public interest should be able to tolerate critics. Indeed, they need criticism to make them more effective.[20]

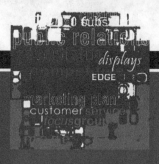

How to get the public image you want for your organisation

Sensible organisations are careful to develop and sustain a good public image. They strive to become good neighbours, showing concern for the affairs of the community in which they operate. And if they don't live up to community expectations, they will rightly be subjected to community criticism. Public support is therefore of the utmost importance. But many managers expect this support without taking positive steps to win it. Here are some principles essential for gaining a good public image...

1 Plan your program.

Planning is essential. In devising ways to win community support for your organisation, you must take into account information that the public has, wants, and needs about your organisation. Consider also such basic factors as your audience, program timing, techniques you will use, and potential media coverage.

2 Become a good neighbour.

Do your activities upset the local community in which you operate? If so, do something immediately about noise, fumes, smells, waste disposal, parking, visual pollution—things that can create antagonism locally. Or do your activities receive warm local acknowledgement—because you support local development, contibute to local community associations, donate to charities, support schools, sponsor student awards, offer assistance with local sport, art and youth activities? Think about the many ways in which you can keep your local community on side by becoming a good neighbour.

3 Know your community.

No effective program can be planned without a knowledge of the local community. What problems are of concern locally—lack of recreation facilities, youth unemployment, historic sites, pollution? What are your community's main interests—sport, culture, gardens? Who are the political leaders? Who are the opinion leaders? What is the current economic situation (the spending power of a prosperous mining town would be greater than that of a declining pastoral town)? Are there any special emotional issues—resulting from a racial, religious, or industrial past? And so on. Only with such background information can your image-building efforts be directed into the correct channels.

4 Identify and assess all available avenues.

If you now know what it takes

don't forget

Building a good reputation

1. There is no quick and easy way to have a good reputation.
2. A good reputation is everyone's job, not just management's.
3. You cannot have a good external reputa-tion unless you have a good internal reputa-tion.
4. Important decisions by stakeholders are based invariably on trust.
5. It may take years to build a reputation but only a moment to destroy one.[2]

to be a good neighbour, and you know your community, then your organisation can now explore ways of demonstrating good citizenship and of developing the image of a good neighbour. List all possible options from which a balanced selection of program strategies can be made, for example:

- *media relations:* keeping journalists aware of company projects which impact favourably on the local community
- *participation* in community activities
- *newsletters:* for distribution to staff, clients, opinion leaders, libraries, local businesses
- *speechmaking:* addressing schools, clubs, and civic groups on activities of your organisation
- *sponsorships:* from financing the local pet show to purchasing a new bus for the local retirement village
- *product donations:* donating products or services as prizes in local raffles, at school fetes or for other community fundraising events
- *open days:* inviting the community to view your facilities, and featuring demonstrations, tours, exhibits.

Select your strategies in terms of the nature of your message and business, coverage required, cost, time, and your particular situation.

5 Foster two-way communication.

Image building goes beyond advertising and is built on planned, systematic two-way communication. The greater the two-way flow of information, the easier it is to find out how effectively your message is getting across to the community.

Encourage and welcome expressions of opinion—good or bad; such views should be seen as opportunities for dialogue which can promote improved understanding and, possibly, even stronger local support for your organisation.

6 Remember the fundamentals.

The nature, content, and presentation of your message will vary with circumstances but there are basic principles which must be adhered to:

- *Be honest.* By all means accentuate the positive; but propaganda, dishonesty, and exaggeration are rarely forgiven.
- *Be continuous.* By repeating your message in a variety of ways, you will produce a stronger community response.
- *Be comprehensive.* All the important aspects of your organisation's activity should be considered in planning an image-building program. No activity should be singled out for undue emphasis; nor should others be ignored or minimised.
- *Keep it simple.* Language, content and presentation of information should be adjusted to the intellectual and interest levels of your particular community audience. Beware of mumbo-jumbo and jargon. Make things clear and interesting.
- *Present information rationally.* Your information should be presented objectively, constructively, unemotionally, and without sensationalism. Such an approach is more likely to convince intelligent and reasonable people.
- *Timing is important.* Schedule your campaign for the greatest effect.

✔ it's a fact

One day while on his way back to the office from an important lunch in the best restaurant in town, Ray Kroc, owner of the McDonald's chain in the United States, asked his driver to pass through a few McDonald's car parks. In one he spotted papers caught up in shrubs along the outer fence.

He immediately called his office to get the name of the manager, then called the manager to offer to help him pick up the offending rubbish.

Both the owner of the McDonald's chain in his expensive business suit and the young manager met in the car park and got down on their hands and knees to pick up the paper.

■ As managers we are frequently more interested in the activity inside our business premises than in the building's outside appearance. The appearance of your building and its surrounds is at the front line of your organisation's public image – as Ray Kroc was well aware.

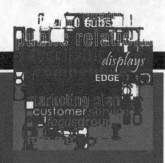

How to ensure your organisation makes a good first impression

Sometimes the most basic things can determine an organisation's public image. For the visitor, first impressions are very important. A pleasant, welcoming environment will put even the most apprehensive visitor at ease. But, regrettably, we often unknowingly place interpersonal and physical barriers in the way of clients, customers, and other visitors. The result? Outsiders leave with a less-than-favourable impression. If you want your organisation to create a good initial response in your visitor, note these points…

1 Remember: first impressions count.

Regularly put yourself in the shoes of your customers, clients, or visitors. What you may routinely notice every day may not at first seem important in your eyes because it's so familiar to you—but it can present an entirely different image to a client. When it comes to first impressions, three vital points must be noted:

- A visitor's first impression is gained in only ten seconds. The visitor may be charitable, and give you a second chance. You will rarely get a third chance to get it right!

- The impressions we gain from the world around us are based on our five senses. Research tells us that first impressions are gained through sight (83%), hearing (11%), smell (3.5%), touch (1.5%) and taste (1%).

- Visitors always remember vividly the worst impression, not the best impression. Your challenge is to know what it is that must be improved on.

The key is to always see and think like your visitors.

2 Locate on-site signage strategically.

Make sure that your premises are well signposted so that visitors can readily find their way from the street entrances or the carpark. Well-placed, friendly signs should also direct people to the reception area, the manager's office, drop-off points for deliveries, and to parking. Consider multi-lingual signs where appropriate. Pay special attention to the main display board fronting the street: company name and logo prominently displayed, address, phone numbers, friendly welcome…

3 Check the premises' physical appearance.

The appearance of your premises, both outside and inside, has a continuing and cumulative effect on public attitudes. Litter, peeling paint, unrepaired damage, graffiti, noise, dripping taps, broken furniture, that flickering fluorescent tube, unkempt gardens, cobwebs, cracked footpaths —all convey a powerful message that conflicts with a caring and well-run organisation. An attractive site, even if the buildings are old, is generally regarded as an expression of achievement. Have someone check with you the impression your business gives from the street. And what impression do you get as you walk from the carpark, through the front door, to reception, past the offices or workplace, or in the rest-rooms? Compile a list of concerns.

4 Pay attention to the reception area.

The reception area is often the visitors' first contact with your organisation—and often the only part of your enterprise they see—and the experience can have a lasting impact. Establish procedures to welcome them warmly and attend to their needs. Don't leave visitors waiting too long; the offer of tea or coffee creates a good impression. The reception area can be your showcase for the outsider, so be imaginative with decor and setting. This may be an ideal location for details of staff awards and accomplishments; visual explanations of processes; displays of product; company posters; historical items; copies of company brochures, newsletters, or annual reports for visitors to browse. Install pot plants and appropriate furniture.

5 Test your organisation's telephone technique.

The telephone is often the initial contact a customer or client has with your organisation. Check out your company's telephone technique—Is the phone answered promptly and pleasantly? Is the organisation identified? Does the person answering the phone always convey a willingness to help the caller? Is the caller kept too long on hold? Is the caller frustrated if required to press buttons and listen to music? Is the caller made to feel important and welcome? Do you have an effective message distribution procedure? Are calls returned promptly?

6 Check that your premises give off good vibrations.

Does your organisation 'feel' like a vibrant, successful enterprise to the visitor? Is it a friendly hive of activity? Is there evidence of staff, attired appropriately, enjoying their work in bright, co-operative surroundings? Visitors have an uncanny knack of picking up such vibrations.

7 And, finally...

- Encourage staff members to say hello to visitors when they pass to emphasise the organisation's friendly atmosphere.
- Always strive for quality first impressions. Lead by example. Others will follow.
- Remember, you and your team will often be judged outside work as well as during trading hours.
- At least once a year, have one or two trusted colleagues run the gauntlet of your premises as a visitor or phone caller, and have them report to you on the kind of impression your organisation generates.

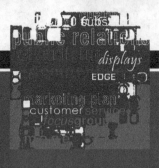

How to improve your organisation's visual image

Your company's visual image is often the first impression you give your customer or client; it should therefore be a good one. Your logo, product brochures, signs, letterheads, business cards, leaflets, newsletters, newspaper advertisements—all should have impact and increase sales. But, to be effective, such visual images must be eye-catching and professional; and the best way to achieve this result is to engage a graphic designer. The following suggestions will assist you to make the right decision…

1 Resist the temptation to do it yourself.

Graphic design is a professional activity and it cannot be done on the cheap. Despite the inroads of desktop technology, while many people in your organisation may be able to work a computer, few have the necessary design skills. Nor do local printers; while they employ in-house designers, their work is often dull and unexceptional. Remember, your visual image is something you will have to live with for many years.

2 Appreciate the value of a professional designer.

The use of a good designer is a long-term investment, and may be the best advertising investment you make. An experienced designer will bring both a lack of preconceptions and an entirely new perspective to the way you see your organisation. Indeed, a good one may force you to look at your business in a different way, encouraging you to clarify and strengthen previously unspoken attitudes, dreams, and directions.

Designers risk their reputation every time your logo, advertisement, or brochure appears in public. They have as much to lose, if their work is not first-class, as you do. But they do a better job than you; so let them do it.

3 Know how to select a good designer.

There are the large advertising agencies who normally cater for large businesses; and there are hundreds of freelance designers and graphic artists in the suburbs who keep small businesses in business. Having checked the Yellow Pages or your professional contacts, you can set about selecting a designer best suited to your company. In making your choice, consider this advice:

- *Find one you can work with.* You're entering a partnership: if the designer is not helping you make a profit, you will soon be a reluctant client. So it's important for both of you to be on the same wavelength.
- *Ask for testimonials* and the endorsements of the designer's

---

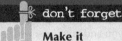

Make it simple

Any trademark, logo or symbol that requires more than a few seconds of thought to get its message across is not doing what it is supposed to do – and that is to communicate the nature of the bearer's business or synthesise how it perceives or positions itself in the marketplace.

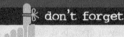

Hallmarks of a successful symbol

Your corporate symbol must meet most or all the criteria governing good visual communication – which include:

- clear, not confusing; original, not imitative; functional, not frivolous; distinctive, not forgettable.
- meaningful, instantly conveying the purpose and personality of the corporation.
- easy to recognise, pleasing to the eye; has no unfavorable visual connotation in countries of registration.
- adaptable to advertising in all media and capable of serving as the unifier of a total identity program.[6]

other customers. Discuss the designer's successes, creativity, and solutions.

- *Have a good look at examples of the designer's work.* You can also judge a lot by visiting the designer's office.

- *Ensure the designer is committed to meeting deadlines.* Check this out with other customers or by commissioning a small project to begin with.

- *Consider cost last of all* because if the other points don't make the grade, price will not come into it. Don't forget, you are buying creativity, individual talent, artistic flair, advertising skills, and these don't always come cheap. Discuss the designer's approach to budget, cost estimates, and total project charges. Some charge by the hour, some by the project, and some according to your set budget. If you're clear about the designer's policy on fees up-front, you'll avoid hassles later.

Always prepare a design brief.

Designers work from 'design briefs'. Your designer may want to know what you make or do, your business identity, long term plans, market strategy, your customers, your budget, and the way your mind works. The designer will need your ideas as a foundation to develop graphic concepts, an image, that will reflect your company's values and style. Many designers provide a creative brief form; if not, prepare a written statement of your own—the more detail, the better for all involved.

Be consistent with your visual imagery.

Consistency is important when it comes to visual imagery, which is one reason why you should try to use the same designer for all your work. A corporate identity is not developed from a rag-bag of diverse ideas and styles, the result of using a variety of designers for different items. If you remodel your company logo several times in a decade, change your letterhead design every two years, and dazzle your customers with ten different type styles in your latest product leaflet, how can you retain client confidence? Make the changes, make them well—and stick with them.

Remember also...

- Consider launching your company's new visual identity with a splash.

- Implement visual imagery changes quickly and thoroughly. When Coca-Cola released a new logo several years ago, every old Coke logo around the world was replaced *overnight!*

- Know where your old visual imagery will need to be replaced: stationery, signage, livery, publications, memorabilia, vehicles…

- While a letterhead or business cards may be your only project in the short-term, think long-term. Every visual item must eventually reflect your company's image—a professional image. People like to deal with businesses that look familiar and professional.

499

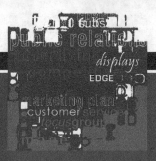

How to position yourself in the marketplace

The purpose of business is to get and keep customers—something that's difficult to do without a marketing plan. Such a document provides you with direction. It tells you how to develop products or services that will satisfy customer demands, communicate the benefits of your products and services to customers, and guarantee satisfaction. In essence, it is a plan that enables you to encourage people to do business with *your* organisation. Here are some important aspects to consider…

1 Remember: marketing is everybody's job.

Everyone in your organisation is involved in marketing your company's products or services. They may not actually work in the marketing department, or be directly responsible for finding customers, but they will all in some way be in a position to contribute to the organisation's success in gaining and retaining customers. For this reason, you, and your key employees, should have some understanding of what the process of marketing involves as it applies to your organisation…

2 Generate marketable products or services.

Do you have products, ideas, concepts, or services that you have screened and tested to ensure they will satisfy customer need and that are potentially profitable? Have you analysed your product's life cycle in order to predict its sales pattern over a period of time? Do you continue the search for new products and services? If you don't have a durable,

marketable product, you won't build up and hold a customer base.

3 Profile your competition.

How well do you know those organisations that compete for your customers? Who exactly are your competitors? What are their strong and weak points? Gather as much information as you can on their marketing and communication strategies, types of advertising, their product, price and markets, and how they take advantage of changes in the industry. Identify any areas in the market that are not filled by your competitors' products or services, and that could be exploited by yours. Remember, your competitors will probably be watching you also.

4 Analyse market opportunities.

Market research is essential. Assemble information about your organisation's current and potential markets, about the users of your products or services, and about

---

those areas where your company has the competitive advantage when it comes to introducing new products, improving current products, or entering new market territories.

This market profile should include your current and future markets' size, growth potential, barriers, key players and the existence of particular niches. If yours is a small to medium business enterprise, remember that research tells us that 75 per cent of your customers come from within a five kilometre radius of your business. In Australia, print and electronic rssources are available providing demographic information to assist you build a viable customer base.

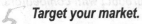

Target your market.

Based on the information you have gathered, and on the skills and resources of your organisation, you should now be able to select specific target markets. If you are not in the mass marketing business, i.e. you don't offer your product or service to all-comers, then are you in a position to pinpoint those segments of the market at which your specific products should be targeted?

Develop an appropriate marketing mix.

Your preliminary research will now enable you to consider the 4Ps of marketing. This is the set of controllable variables that all companies attempt to blend into the right combination to achieve the dominant position in the marketplace.

The four key factors are: Product, Price, Place, and Promotion. In the long run, the success you have in addressing these four components will determine your success in the marketplace.

Forecast sales potential.

You will need to produce a detailed outline of your sales targets, a plan for achieving those goals, and costs to be incurred in attracting customers.

Develop a strategy for publicising your product.

If you have the products or services people want, and are prepared to pay for, then your next step is to bring these to people's attention. You will need to develop a strategy to address advertising and promotion of the product, new product launches, sales campaigns, and distribution policies. How can you get value for your advertising dollar? Are there more cost-effective ways to promote your product? Should you be using more than one method? Do you need to promote your product all year?

Review your performance regularly.

Unless you monitor the progress of your marketing plan, you will run the risk of not finding out until too late that the plan is not working. Check sales results constantly to ensure targets are being achieved within expenditure budgets. Amend your plan as required in the light of your findings.

 don't forget

Remember the fast route to failure...

■ *Pushing a poor product.* Marketing won't make a poor product or service good.

■ *A short-term focus.* Don't get bogged down on a lone brochure. Think in years, not months. Work from a long-term strategic marketing plan.

■ *Decisions based on hunches.* Only objective research will give realistic feedback on customer needs and values.

■ *Communication overload.* Don't cram all your messages into one communication channel. Avoid customer confusion. Aim at one message per hit, and deliver it clearly and succinctly.

■ *Staff sabotaging your image.* Negative vibes from unhappy staff travel like electricity on a wire to your customers and clients.

■ *Lack of integration.* Marketing is a team effort. All employees have a role to play.

■ *Budget blow-out.* Don't blow all your marketing budget in one big show. Maintain a year-long presence.

■ *A focus on tools, not relationships.* People matter most. Focus on relationship training.

■ *Slow response to the future.* Have you embraced the burgeoning world of electronic communication?

■ *Forgetting the feedback.* How do you measure your success – and follow it through?[10]

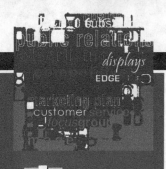

How to find out what your competitors are doing

To some it's 'corporate snooping', to others it's simply research; but 'competitive intelligence' (CI) means finding out as much as possible about your competitors—what products they are developing, what the strategic thrusts of their businesses are for the next few years, how they are faring, and their levels of profitability. If you want a more accurate picture of how your competitors are shaping up, here are a few tactical suggestions…

it's a fact

A US software company received more ideas than their R&D people had come up with in years by simply spending $5000. The small ad simply said: 'We'll pay $5000 for the most unusual and beneficial use of our product…'

The ideas flowed in, many from employees of rival companies…and they were all free to be used in future project development.

And the winner? An employee of a company competitor, which clearly was not exploiting the talents of its own staff.

it's a fact

J.P.Morgan, Rothschild, Rockefeller, Gates – they all used 'competitive intelligence' or 'analysed information'; they just never gave it that name. By actively seeking intelligence and learning how to use it, you too can turn information into a powerful weapon that will give you a competitive advantage.

Attend trade shows and conferences.

Trade shows are excellent places to check out competitors' products and services. These exhibitions are more than just booths and displays. Most expositions also offer seminars, product demonstrations, and other special events that can be good sources of competitive information. If you play your cards right, you can even gain access to a competitor's senior management, often by simply chatting with the salesperson who works the booth. By networking in the right circles at conferences you will learn lots of useful competitor information.

Become a shareholder—of your competitor.

There are a number of perfectly legal and ethical ways to get information on your competitors. If your competitor is a publicly listed company, for example, you can purchase a limited number of their stock making you a recognised shareholder. You'll be

amazed how much financial and strategic information that this tactic will deliver to your door on a regular basis.

Trade product with competitors.

Competitors may not let you inside their plants, but there are other ways to analyse their operation—as long as you don't mind reciprocating. You can start things rolling by offering to provide samples of your products in return for your competitors' samples.

Conduct a company search.

For a small fee, you can initiate a search of your competitors to see how they are travelling. The practice is legal and quite ethical. After all, it is possible that some of your smart competitors have already conducted a search to ascertain *your* position to help with *their* business planning.

Examine legal records.

Every time your competition applies

for a patent or becomes involved in a lawsuit, a public record is created. These sources can tell you much about the health of their businesses. Your legal adviser will direct you to the best places to find this valuable information.

Subscribe to investment research.

The Internet is a valuable resource. A search for 'investment research', for example, identifies many sites (such as Nelson's *Corporate Research E-Letter*) providing details about public companies in the United States. In Australia, the Australian Stock Exchange (ASX) and individual brokers also provide company review information. If your competitor is not a public company or a major firm, however, you will need to resort to other tactics—like requesting direct from the company copies of its Annual Reports.

Subscribe to a clipping service.

For a fee, clipping services will scan newspapers, trade journals, and consumer magazines for articles in areas that you identify, including your field of business or your competitors. In this way you can keep up to date with reported competitor activities. And don't forget to check out the Internet too: your competitor may have an interesting home page.

Talk to former employees.

If a competitor has a high employee

turnover or is laying off employees, and you can make contact with them, you can learn a lot. Keep in mind they may have an axe to grind and will be only too willing to provide information that will benefit you.

Scan the employment advertisements.

Keep a check on the display and employment ads in your local and national newspapers. Jobs on offer and their descriptions are often good indicators of changes in your competitors' strategies or organisational structures, whether they're hiring, how fast they're growing, whether they have a high staff turnover. At the very least, such advertisements can help to confirm or dispel marketplace rumours.

Don't rest on your laurels.

In the minds of many managers, the goal is to get the business up and running smoothly so that it will then 'run itself'. But such a model is defective, because it assumes that it is possible to establish a pattern or system that can meet both present and future challenges. If this was ever possible in the past, it isn't today.

Most successful organisations already have the capability of accessing most of the information required to stay competitive. But CI provides competitive advantage only when it's acted upon. So be prepared to take appropriate action to put your accumulated information to work for you.

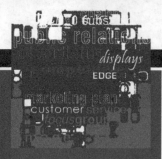

How to use focus groups to gain a competitive edge

Successful managers are always looking for ways of gaining and maintaining a competitive advantage over their rivals. One of the best sources of information about those advantages are your customers or clients—existing, potential, or lost—and those of your competitors. If you want to discover the views of customers so that you can transform those views into a winning edge for your organisation, you should consider using focus groups...

1 Decide on the focus for the group.

They're called 'focus groups' because they allow you to assemble a select group of people to investigate a specific issue—and there are many issues to consider: customer service, product reliability, responsiveness, company image, communication, promotion, and so on.

2 Target a specific group.

Focus groups can be conducted successfully for all categories of clients or customers. Different customer groups can provide different information for you to transform later into specific actions. So consider inviting your participants according to your focus: for example, potential clients might be invited to participate in a group assembled to discuss ways that the organisation can attract new clients; or former customers could be invited to contribute so that ways the organisation can retain its customers can be identified; or current clients can identify ways to improve services.

3 Plan to maximise the group's effectiveness.

Your planning should consider:

- Who should be invited? That often depends on the focus.
- How many should be invited? The ideal individual group size is considered to be 7 to 9 members.
- When is the best time for the meeting? Its duration? After work, for no longer than forty-five minutes, can be a good time.
- Personal invitations. First contact should be by telephone, followed up with a letter or email confirming the meeting.
- Should employees be invited? If so, which ones? This is your choice, but the guests must outnumber staff.
- Networking. Allow time to welcome guests and make sure they get to know one another.
- Who will act as facilitator?
- Seating arrangements. A round table configuration is best.
- Refreshments. Certainly.
- Record keeping. Arrange to have a scribe who does not participate in discussions.
- Follow-up. Contact every participant personally to express your appreciation and to provide a brief outline of the results of the meeting.

Start the meeting on time.

Get the meeting started on time with a welcome and a brief description of the purpose of the meeting. Give an undertaking to conclude at a particular time. Explain how the meeting will proceed. If another person is acting as facilitator, introduce that person followed by an invitation to proceed.

 Get people talking.

Slowly does it… you want contributions from every participant, not just the more vocal ones. A useful approach is to start with the broad picture and gradually focus on the issues of most concern to you. When you ask specific questions, try preceding those with 'softeners' like, 'I'm hoping you can tell me. . .' or 'I'm wondering if you know. . .'. Softeners not only encourage open questioning but also discourage the use of 'why'.

 Don't become defensive.

You have invited guests to participate in an event that should improve your organisation, so you could well be receiving some bad news with the good. Disclosure of your company's faults is valuable information, and you should not get defensive about such bad news. Indeed, you need to adopt an encouraging style by using prompters like, 'Would you be able to expand on that?' and 'Tell me what you mean by that' and 'Are you saying that…?'. Responses that surprise you, even upset you, could represent valuable information.

 Summarise often.

Clarify comments by offering regular summaries. This approach keeps the meeting on track, ensures the group is proceeding in the desired direction, and helps your scribe keep up with the action. If individual participants disagree with your summary, seek their help in getting it right.

 Wrap-up, on time.

Participants are donating their time, so fulfil your part of the arrangement by ending on time. Summarise outcomes, thank participants, and make a commitment to provide a written summary within a set time, say fourteen days. Personally thank each participant as they leave, then get with your participating staff for their general comments and a consider-ation of the lessons to be learnt by the organisation from the activity.

 Remember the qualities required...

The best focus group facilitator has

unobtrusive chameleon-like qualities; gently draws consumers into the process; deftly encourages them to interact with one another for optimum synergy; lets the intercourse flow naturally with a minimum of intervention; listens openly and deeply; uses silence well; plays back consumer statements in a distilling way which brings out more refined thoughts or explanations; and remains completely nonauthoritarian and nonjudgemental. Yet the facilitator will subtly guide the proceedings when necessary and intervene to cope with various kinds of troublesome participants who may impair the productive group process.[12]

 don't forget

Why focus groups are often preferred

■ Focus groups provide data from a group of people much more quickly and at less cost than if each individual were interviewed separately.

■ Focus groups allow you to interact directly with respondents, providing clarification and probing if necessary, and allowing you to observe nonverbal reactions such as smiles, frowns, gestures and the like.

■ The open response format provides the opportunity to obtain large and rich amounts of data in the respondents' own words, and you can seek deeper levels of meaning if required.

■ Focus groups allow respondents to react to and build upon the responses of other group members, resulting in the production of data and ideas that might not have been uncovered in individual interviews.

■ Focus groups are very flexible. You can explore a wide range of topics with a variety of individuals in a variety of settings.

■ The focus group is one of the few tools available for obtaining data from children and those who are not particularly literate.

■ The results are easy to understand, and this is not always the case with more sophisticated survey research that employs complex statistical analysis.[14]

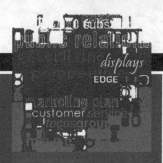

How to compile a questionnaire

Questionnaires are used for a variety of reasons—to gather information, to survey opinions or attitudes, to measure customer satisfaction, or to drive market research. But although sophisticated questionnaires usually require professional expertise to compile, administer, analyse, and interpret, you can construct simple instruments for surveys, interviews, and focus groups by following these guidelines…

1 Be clear about what you're looking for.

Before you begin designing any questions, articulate clearly what need or problem you want to address using the information you intend to gather from the survey. Why are you doing the evaluation? What do you hope to accomplish? For example, questionnaires can measure attitudes, market trends, consumption patterns, beliefs or expectations about your services or products, the effect of competition, media, etc. Having a clear focus will help you frame your questions.

2 Select the appropriate method.

How will you administer your questionnaire – by post, telephone, fax, personal interview, online, email? Each method has disadvantages and advantages relating to issues such as speed, cost, ability to reach a scattered sample, response rate, and interviewer bias. A combination of methods may be considered, such as using the post to elicit basic data, and following up with phone interviews to explore some issues in greater depth.

3 Select and define your sample.

To whom will the questionnaire be administered? Whose views are you seeking? Consider clients, customers and non-customers, age, sex, socio-economic groupings, and the sources of names, addresses and telephone numbers. Will you be sampling randomly or targeting a specific group or strata?

4 Know how you will handle the results.

Questionnaires can generate a great deal of paper and even more data. Determine in advance who will do the work, how the information will be sorted, how it will be analysed, how the responses will be used. By rightly focusing on these issues up-front, you will be forced to put more thought into the construction of the instrument.

5 Construct your questions carefully.

Consider the variety of ways

questions can be posed—closed questions where respondents simply 'tick a box' or 'circle a number'; open-ended questions where respondents are asked to write the answer in their own words; attitude questions where respondents are asked to mark their response on a 5-point Likert-type scale (ranging from 'strongly agree' to 'strongly disagreee').

Consider the following advice:

- Begin with a couple of fact-based questions (e.g. demographic data), followed by general, easy questions to get the ball rolling. Move from the general to the specific.
- Sensitive questions should be asked towards the end of the questionnaire.
- Follow a logical sequence to avoid confusing the respondents.
- Limit the number of questions or the respondents may be put off answering.
- Attempt to get also the respondents' comments or perspectives to supplement their ticked-box answers.
- Make sure you don't put ideas in early questions which may influence respondents' answers later.
- Consider concluding with a question which seeks the respondent's view of the questionnaire itself and any suggestions for improvement.
- If using multiple-choice questions, make sure the choices are mutually exclusive and embrace the total range of answers. Ensure that respondents won't have a clearly preferred answer that is not among your alternatives.
- As a general rule, keep it short, to the point, and easy to complete.

Questions to avoid are those that:

- are too difficult to answer
- assume the respondents have certain information—but they don't
- do not provide enough information for the respondents to answer intelligently
- point respondents to the answer desired by the researcher

- require the respondents to put more effort into answering than they are willing to give
- are too confusing to answer, e.g. use of the word 'not' can cause confusion when a yes or no response is wanted.
- are emotion-laden, e.g. use of the phrase 'our prompt, reliable service'
- use slang, cultural-specific, or technical words
- are, in reality, two different questions in one.

 Pay attention to the questionnaire's design.

An attractive layout for a printed questionnaire can have a major influence on the response rate. Focus on legibility of the typeface used, its size, generous use of white space, and, importantly, allow sufficient room for recording responses.

Give clear directions.

Include a brief explanation of the purpose of the questionnaire, how to complete the questionnaire, how to return the survey forms, and any details relating to confidentiality of the information or the respondent. And don't say it will take 5 minutes when it will take 15. Finally, remember to thank the respondents for their time and assistance.

 Conduct a pilot.

Test your draft questionnaire on a small group of staff or clients, to check on the clarity of the questions, their sequencing, the layout, the time taken to respond, and whether you get the type of data you really were seeking. Use this information to develop the final version of your questionnaire.

 it's a fact

Measurement, by using a questionnaire or any other tool, by itself changes nothing. If it did, there'd be very few overweight people. Measurement is a forerunner to action, so appropriately administered consequences are the only thing that will change behaviour for the better. Any performance can be measured, but the trick is how to apply those measurements. As well, if measurements are to be used to punish, people will try to avoid punishment by falsifying data.

 don't forget

Pros and cons

Although questionnaires have obvious limitations, many of these can be minimised by carefully thinking ahead and pilot testing. Good questionnaires do not just happen: they involve careful thinking, numerous drafts, thorough evaluation, and intensive testing. Despite shortcomings, questionnaires have the great advantage of generating a systematic variable by case matrix, of enabling coverage of a large representative sample, and of being relatively efficient. They are, however, only one method of collecting data and one unsuitable for many research problems and situations.

507

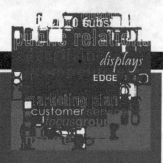

How to prepare a marketing plan

If you don't believe in your product or service, or if you aren't being consistent and regular in the way you promote it, you could be in trouble: you probably don't have a marketing plan for your business. Like your business plan, a marketing plan is a key ingredient in business success. Its primary aim is to ensure that you have the vision, the resources and the wherewithal to do what it takes to make your product or service work. If you don't want to plod along in uncertainty, you'll need a marketing plan. Here are the basics to get you started…

1 Think strategically.

Assuming your product or service is one that people want and are prepared to pay for, your strategic actions should include clarifying (for yourself and others) what business you are in, deciding on a mission, identifying areas of competitive advantage, considering value-adding possibilities leading to developing a value proposition. Conducting an internal and external audit, or SWOT analysis, will allow you to consider such key issues as the business environment in which you operate, perceived potential demand for your product or service, competitors, trends, operational issues, service provision, skills and competencies of employees, and available resources.

Armed with such data, you will be in a position to draft your marketing plan, a process which would have you address the following actions…

2 Prepare an introductory statement.

In compiling the scene-setting introduction to your plan, respond to the following issues:

- A brief statement about your company and what you provide
- Why you are writing this plan and the period it will be in use
- Specific objectives of the plan—so you can measure them on the way
- A vision statement for staff and customers.

3 Know your product and its benefits to the consumer.

The only products or services that succeed are those that offer benefits that make users' lives better. Don't confuse features with benefits. Marketing guru Jay Levinson clarifies:

> Think about the last time you went to buy a car. You probably thought about what you wanted: safety for the family, low operating costs, lots of room for the kids, etc. It's not too hard to translate these benefits into features: airbags, good gas mileage, an extra-large trunk, etc. But it's the benefits, not the features, that sell the car.[15]

Being able to list and communicate the benefits of your product or service is a vital step in creating a successful plan.

Know your target market.

Having established the benefits of your product, you have largely identified your target market. For example, a hunting gun with a foolproof safety device is probably not intended for infants, vegetarians, or animal rights advocates—it's for hunters. Next, segment your target group further to arrive at a list of those who need your product. Here, consider age, income, magazines they read, TV shows they watch, and so on. Assemble a focus group of likely consumers: what do they currently use? what do they think of the benefits of your product? how much would they pay for it? what do they read? You'll need your findings to locate a marketing niche and to generate marketing slogans, your target media, and advertisements.

 Know your position in the marketplace.

Who are your competitors and how well do they perform? How well does this competition serve the market? How will your competition react to your plans when implemented?

List the features of your product or service that are different from or better than your competitors'. Now list the benefits of using your product. They will need to be better than your competitors'—if not, what will compel consumers to switch to you and become loyal customers?

 Compile an advertising strategy.

Having a clear understanding of your product or service, the target market, the competition, the product's benefits, and how your product can be differentiated from the competitions', you can now devise an advertising or promotional campaign. Use an agency if necessary. Remember the essential requirement of an ad: if the reader is to get one idea out of the ad, what should it be, and what precisely do you want the reader to do as a consequence? Will your ad have this clear message?

 Develop a budget.

A good rule of thumb is to set aside ten per cent of sales to your marketing budget—leaders in the field often spend more. You could be in trouble if you spend a lesser percentage of sales on marketing than your competition.

 List the techniques and tools you'll be using.

How will you communicate with your customers and others? Explore the possibilities—publicity, focused advertising, direct mailouts, personal selling, telemarketing, special events, television, radio, posters, catalogues, inserts, newsletters, business cards, billboards, yellow pages, newspapers and magazines, gift certificates, frequent flyer programs, contests... Establish a framework and a schedule.

Devise a month-by-month schedule.

Having selected and ranked the tools that appeal to you, compile and implement a month-by-month marketing grid showing tool, budget, timing and evaluative strategy.

 don't forget

Seek value for money

Marketing initiatives must return at least 100 per cent of the money outlaid on the promotion.

 here's an idea

Keep your marketing plan private. If a potential financier requires a copy, ensure that you mark it 'Private and Confidential'. The only people who should be privy to the contents of your plan are those who have a genuine stake in its success.

 don't forget

In all your marketing...

- Never spend a dollar without having a marketing plan.
- Never run a major ad campaign without testing it first.
- Never pull an ad campaign while it is still producing.
- Never focus only on the mass media.

And always make sure your marketing plan meets your tactical and strategic goals. If not, revise it!

How to make your business grow

Managing a business is like being a top-flight athlete—always looking for ways to become better and better. The consensus among respected writers in the field of business growth is that there are three main ways for a business to grow successfully: get more customers; sell existing customers more products or services; and increase back-end sales. Here's an extension of those ideas. . .

ask yourself

Why should your customers do business with you? What makes you unique? What is your Unique Selling Point (USP) – that advantageaomething that the customer can't get anywhere else. It should be the flag under which you advance your sales and marketing efforts. Consider...

- Your USP may be that you maintain a 24-hour, 7-day week service.
- It may be that you provide more practical information and advice that anyone else.
- It may be that you have everything in stock at all times– no waiting or back-ordering necessary.
- It may be that you sell your products at the lowest mark-up in the industry.
- It may be that you guarantee same-day service.

What is your USP?

Attract more customers.

Your customers are those people who buy from you at least once. So one way to extend your business is to get more and more people to buy from you or use your services—at least once. Although there are many different approaches to attracting more customers, the one thing those approaches have in common is that they must either satisfy an existing demand for what you have to offer or create a new one. Supply and demand are key considerations when it comes to attracting more customers.

Develop a marketing plan.

Creating or satisfying a demand involves more than a trial-and-error approach. Given the product or services you have to offer, you need to plan *how* to create a demand and *how* to satisfy it. A simple, straight-forward marketing plan can achieve that. The plan needs to be specific enough to provide the necessary focus and be flexible enough to adapt to

changing circumstances. Remember, no one person can hope to know your product or service better than you do. By all means consult with outside marketing gurus if your strength is not in this area.

Sell customers more products or services.

It is considered to be five times easier, and much less expensive, to sell to existing customers than to find new ones. So it's a sound strategy to focus your energies and other resources on selling additional products to existing customers. Accountants, for example, often provide information technology services, management consulting, and financial planning services in addition to their normal range of services. Successful organisations are finding that existing customers respond positively when asked for additional business or referrals to new customers.

Focus on adding value.

Adding value occurs when the service

provider suggests additional products or services that dovetail with the selections already made. For example, a laundromat might include phone and fax facilities, exercise machines, movie hire, dry cleaning, and confectionery as add-ons to the basic laundry services provided. Wal-Mart adds value to the shopping experience with people-greeters at the door and distinctively friendly salespeople. In value-adding, the 'whole' is seen as being worth more than the sum of the parts.

 ### Train, train, train.

Staff training is important if value-adding opportunities are going to be recognised and exploited. Selling customers additional products or services is going to require staff who can bring those products and services to the customers' attention. Recent research indicates that it is six times more expensive *not* to train than to train. If you're into the right training program, additional sales made by well-trained staff will exceed associated training costs.

 ### Increase back-end sales.

As your customer base increases and your relationship with those customers improves, you will get to know other services, not directly associated with your business, that customers would value and be prepared to pay for through you. Your main task may only require that you advertise the service or product and then act as the go-between, linking

customer demand and the supplier. Video stores, for example, could offer a VCR maintenance, repair, and hire service. That service, though provided by another party, would benefit the customers, and you, through increased customer loyalty and commissions paid to you by the third-party service provider. Back-end sales should be considered as a profitable growth feature by all organisations with a well-developed customer data base. And, of course, the approach fits in well with the whole idea of value-adding.

 ### And finally...

The following advice from David Bangs Jr, US expert in small business management, is worth remembering:

- Put your customers first and the profits will follow.
- Give your markets reasons to buy your product.
- Look at what you sell through the eyes of your customers and prospects.
- Business is too competitive to allow your attention to lapse.
- 98% of small business failures stem from managerial weakness.
- Businesses stand or fall on the strength of their personnel.
- The importance of establishing a market niche cannot be overstated.
- Increased sales do not necessarily mean increased profits.
- Keeping control of operating expenses is immensely important and easily overlooked, perhaps because so much emphasis is placed on generating sales.

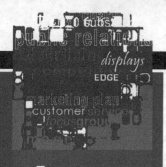

How to provide responsive customer service

Without customers, you don't have a business. So your employees must provide the best possible customer service. You can't afford not to if profit is your goal. Here are some more ideas for you and your employees to develop to provide high-quality customer service and a sustainable competitive advantage...

1 Ensure your team is honest and open.

The foundation of strong customer relationships is trust. Truthfulness and integrity are essential qualities for exceptional customer service, because when you hide the truth, invariably the customer will find out (or at least suspect it). Nor should there be any variations of the truth—white lies, half-truths, distortions, or excuses. In customer service, it's surprising what heights you will attain by simply being on the level.

2 Provide customer-service training for your staff.

In the long run, it is more expensive *not* to train than to train employees. You can't afford not to provide essential training that will lead to a more responsive organisation in terms of customer service. Identify those factors that affect customer service in your organisation and focus on improving those. Dealing with difficult customers, effective listening, problem-solving, courtesy, and using the telephone, are just some examples of the training required by all staff—even backroom employees. If your training is not making your organisation more responsive, don't scrap the training, change the program.

3 Remember the key word—RESPONSIVENESS.

Whatever your business, responsiveness is the umbrella covering all organisational activities. Responsiveness is giving customers what they want, courteously, when they want it, at a price that matches their expectations. Customers are prepared to pay more for a product or service delivered when *they* want it—not when it suits you. Responsiveness is an individual as well as a group quality.

4 Empower employees.

You must give employees the decision-making powers that will allow them to always act in the customers' best interests and help them to solve their problems.

Empowering employees does not mean that you are abrogating responsibilities, but making sure that customers receive a response in the minimum amount of time. Research tells us that most complaining customers will buy from you again if their problem is resolved on the spot.

Set the example.

Employees will not treat their customers any better than they themselves are treated. So make sure that you look after your employees. In addition, the way employees hear you talking about customers and the way they see you interacting with them will go a long way to determining the service culture at your workplace. In many ways, you and your actions set the standard for employees to aim for.

Establish benchmarks.

Emulating, even exceeding, leaders in the field of customer service is an established method of improving customer service. You will find that some of the approaches used by your competitors can be applied to your operations. Wal-Mart staff, for example, adhere to this principle: 'Every time a customer comes within ten feet of me I will smile, look them in the eye, and greet them, so help me Sam.'

Be accessible.

You need to remain informed about all aspects of the relationship between your organisation and its customers. Let employees and customers know that you value their feedback and encourage them to make regular contact with you. And when a customer takes you up on your offer and makes a complaint to you, don't go on the defence; accept the information as a way to further improve your service.

Add value, add profits.

A customer service focus will be one important way that you and your organisation can add value to the way you do things. Adding value goes beyond customer satisfaction to customer confidence. It will also improve the profitability and prosperity of your organisation.

Hold regular meetings on customer service.

Schedule regular discussions with your staff on service issues. Make 'The customer' an agenda item at all your staff and management meetings. Become aware of anti-customer policies and practices, and act to eliminate such things. Speak regularly about the importance of exceptional service. Create a company award which recognises excellent examples of customer service. Check that all in-house talk shows respect for the customer—ban those negative stories, customer nicknames, and amusing but damaging jokes which are capable of eroding a positive customer culture. Your aim must be to have every employee live the service commitment culture.

viewpoint

"Customers perceive service in their own unique, idiosyncratic, emotional, irrational, end-of-the-day, and totally human terms. Perception is all there is."
– Tom Peters and N. Austin in *A Passion for Excellence*

quotable quote

In this business environment, *satisfy the customer* is a sacred cow. Even most car dealers are doing that. Sales managers and store managers everywhere are imploring their people to put the customer first. But they're all playing catch-up. In the new world of commerce, *satisfying* is only the beginning... So don't satisfy customers; everyone does that. *Surprise* them. Give them something they don't expect.[19]

don't forget

Customer clues

- Don't use names in your customer database solely for invoicing.
- Don't use form letters and voice mail to respond to customer complaints.
- Acknowledge customer compliments.
- Spend money showing your customers that you appreciate their business.
- Make it easy for customers to get in touch with your company.

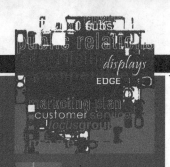

How to keep contact with hard-won customers

If every sale you made had to be to a new customer or client, you'd soon buckle under the pressure. Whether you're offering a service or selling a product, repeat business is the best business: it allows you to build on contacts already made. The really productive and satisfying relationships, in business as in life, are those that last. Usually a little work is needed to retain them. Here are some of the ways you can build long-lasting client relationships…

Make a contact soon after the initial sale.

The key to holding customers is to give superior customer service. Remember when you bought a washing machine and the salesperson said to you that this is the cycle, this is the switch, and this does something, and this does something else? When you got the machine home, chances are you probably forgot just about everything that was said. But imagine how appreciative you would have felt if the salesperson had phoned to ask how the machine was going and to refresh your memory with user instructions.

The message is clear. A day or two after you make a sale, make a brief phone call to your customer to check that everything is in order. If there's a problem, do something about it immediately.

Make a second contact two weeks after the sale.

A fortnight later, make another telephone call. This is not a courtesy call. Its purpose is to check once more on the customer to ensure that there are no problems with the product or service. Attend to any concerns immediately.

Stay in regular contact.

During the year, give customers a call for no reason other than to touch base with them. This is an important part of relationship building, indicating to customers that you value them as individuals. If you feel apprehensive about giving them a call, it could be an indicator that the relationship needs working on. Find out what they like and don't like—an initial discussion of their individual interests is a useful entrée to discussing other issues.

Take an interest in family successes.

Your customer's favourite topic is likely to be his or her family and the achievements of its members. Get to know family members' interests or their expertise and find opportunities to acknowledge their achievements.

Monday's papers usually record results of weekend activities that may have involved family members. Your recognition of those achievements will enhance your relationship with the customer.

Encourage customers to contact you.

Show you care by giving your home and mobile numbers to customers. Let them know that you don't consider it an imposition if they call you outside of business hours. Research indicates that your chances of successful sales are increased fourfold when the customer calls you.

Drop in if you're in the area.

Help customers to see that you have an ongoing interest in them and their businesses. Rather than plan the minimum number of times you must make face-to-face contact with customers, exploit every opportunity to increase your contact.

Keep them informed.

Write to inform your client about any new product or service, or just send a brochure with your business card attached. Often bulletins and other readings that come across your desk are likely to have applications for some individual customers. Mail or fax them copies, attaching a personal note. It's often those little things that will make the biggest difference.

Play Santa Claus.

Every now and then send the client a small inexpensive gift with a personal note or labelled with your business inscription—key ring, coaster, calendar, diary, year planner. Occasionally you'll receive referrals from such items. Establish a mailing list for Christmas cards or birthday greetings.

Provide networking opportunities.

Many business people are too busy to devote time to getting with other business people with similar interests. You can help by providing those opportunities—boardroom lunches, seats at the football, etc. Customers will look to you to provide networking opportunities—and remember you for it.

Develop your own after-sales strategy.

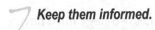

Using some of the above ideas, establish a follow-up action plan of your own. Keep an after-sales diary. As soon as you make a sale, record when you intend to contact your new client and what type of contact you intend it to be. Make subsequent entries to dovetail into your follow-up strategy. Selling never finishes with the sale!

As Napoleon Hill once counselled:

Render more and better service than you are paid for, and sooner or later you will receive compound interest from your investment. It is inevitable that every seed of useful service you sow will sprout and reward you with an abundant harvest.[20]

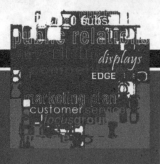

How to maximise the benefits from customer relationship management

If you think customer relationship management is what you have been doing long before you heard about the acronym 'CRM', you're probably right. CRM is a new name for the ways in which businesses interact with their customers. CRM's focus is the customer, aligning business processes with strategies to build loyalties and increase profits from existing relationships. Here's how to get the most from CRM...

research says

A recent survey by Exchange Application concluded: 'Companies who have the most success in implementing customer relationship management solutions always involve the CEO.'[24]

research says

Research tells us two things about customer migration, reinforcing the need for your company to consider using CRM:

- a typical business loses half of its customers in less than 5 years
- it is seven to ten times more expensive to gain a new customer than to retain an existing one.

read further

The CRM Pocketbook by D. Alexander & C. Turner, Management Pocketbooks, Alresford, Hants, 2001.

Be clear about CRM.

CRM can be difficult, expensive, and complex. It is a software-supportable philosophy that involves:

- identifying customers
- differentiating them in terms of both their needs and value to your company
- interacting with them in ways that improve cost efficiency and the effectiveness of your interaction
- customising some aspect of the products or services you offer that customer.

A successful CRM strategy relies on three critical components—a CRM vision, a strategy to tailor its operations to suit its customers, and the technology to support that strategy.

Get key people involved in the vision.

Consider the introduction of CRM as you would any top-down, change-management project, including the demonstrated support of key people, and the development of a skilled and motivated workforce that:

- is aware of changing customer needs
- understands the need to retain existing customers and acquire new ones

- develops attractive and appropriate value propositions
- follows best practices in all of their dealings with customers.

Demonstrated leadership support will include a preparedness to work with CRM support teams, show them how to achieve their goals by applying new processes, organise and support training, and reaffirm the importance of staying in contact with customers.

Initiate a clear strategy.

CRM's business strategy must have a clear customer orientation to create competitive advantage and superior performance. The strategy will help to align business processes before implementing any technology. Customers must experience the benefits of any renewed or extended focus on service provision and employees must understand clearly the focus on customers. Five main questions will help to define any strategy:

- How can we (our organisation) earn greater customer loyalty?
- What changes will be required to the

ways that we do things?
- How much customisation can we provide, profitably?
- What is the potential value we can expect from increasing customer loyalty?
- How much time and money can we afford to allocate to CRM right now?

4 Select appropriate technology.

The best way to optimise customer transactions, and become truly customer-centred, is through the knowledge and insight provided by appropriate, analytical software—here Siebel, PeopleSoft, Oracle and Microsoft are key players. Analytical CRM involves using data to understand customers even better, measure and monitor key customer metrics, and aligning the organisation around building customer value. The analysis identifies patterns and trends allowing you to predict variations so that you can respond or act before it's too late. Armed with the right information, you can initiate actions to increase customer loyalty and the total revenue from each customer, and increase intangible benefits such as the number of referrals that the customer sends to the company.

Outsourcing is an option.

5 Keep it simple.

A common cause of failure of CRM initiatives is that organisations attempt to build systems that are just too complex. The 'C' in CRM can often be forgotten. Studies show that investing in CRM technology without a customer-oriented cultural mindset, driven or promoted by the CEO, can be like throwing money in

a black hole. The principal focus must be employees' increased sensitivity to customers' needs—not in the use of new, state-of-the-art software. GE Capital's successful implementation of CRM provides a useful example: adopt customer-centric philosophies, change structures and processes, and alter corporate cultures accordingly.

6 Train your people.

Don't brush over the people side of CRM—training, education, communication. Training needs to focus on:
- developing an appropriate, 'can-do' attitude
- building and enhancing relationships with customers—including exploiting the particular technology, solution selling, and building customer loyalty
- effective selling skills—sales training should be provided to everyone involved in the CRM process.

7 Exploit benefits.

CRM provides two value-adds:
- It provides the potential to predict customers' behaviours
- It provides the ability to monitor competitors' behaviour and the effects of that behaviour on customers.

CRM can, therefore, be expanded to include marketing goals, with information generated affecting the products and services being offered to customers. Data provided on customers' buying patterns, and how they use and perceive products, can help to tailor services and incentives that can inevitably lead to increased sales. CRM provides a win-win situation for the customer and the organisation.

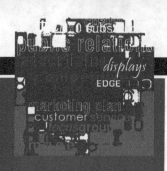
How to pitch your services to a new client

If your business is to achieve its potential in a competitive marketplace, you must first find possible clients or customers and then pitch your services to the most likely prospects. Your success in doing so will depend on how well you can identify prospective clients and how well you can present your services to them. To expand your client base, consider the following advice...

Build up a prospect file.

Compiling a prime prospect file is an essential task for any organisation intending to sell products or services. Such a list can be generated as follows:

Canvass the possibilities. Research and creativity are the keys to locating potential customers and clients. Through a variety of sources—such as directories, Yellow Pages, trade associations, publications, end-user lists, chambers of commerce, seminars and conferences, networking— identify the names of prospects, their location, size, and type of business.

Select the prime prospects. From this list isolate those with the best potential by applying such criteria as:

- being able to afford and pay for your product or services
- being sure that your contact person has the authority to buy or make the appropriate decisions
- being convinced that the prospect has need of your product or services.

Target the hot prospects. These are the ones who have a need to buy—now. Arrange a meeting with these people immediately to pitch your services...

2 Thank the prospect for meeting with you.

Thank your prospect for providing you with an opportunity to present your company's credentials. For people in business, time is valuable, so make sure they know you appreciate them giving you some of theirs.

3 Outline the agenda for the presentation.

Most people feel comfortable and safe when they know what to expect and, by providing your prospect with an outline of your intentions in the form of an agenda, you will put them at ease for what is to follow.

4 Outline what they can expect from the proposal.

Disclose briefly to your prospect what you believe they will get out of your presentation. Your statement should reflect something along the following lines: 'By the time I conclude this presentation, you will have a clear picture of why our organisation's services provide a perfect match to your needs.' In this way, you will have indicated to your prospect how you would be wanting them to respond, that is—yes, I see the match and agree that we could do business with you.

 Confirm you are still on target.

At this point, check to see that you are on target in terms of addressing your potential client's needs. Clarify if necessary. If your focus is astray, the presentation could be a waste of everyone's time. If all is in order, this might now be a good time to introduce the strengths of any of your team who may be present, emphasising their experience and talents without appearing boastful.

 Discuss the results that can be expected.

Outline your vision of anticipated results. Explain how long work on any project for this organisation may take and what the outcome will be on completion.

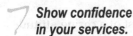 **Show confidence in your services.**

Present a confident front without being outlandishly so. Tell your prospective client you're going to be effective, but more importantly

show them exactly how you plan going about it. Checklists, graphs, plans, products, testimonials—all will help in making your prospect feel confident about your organisation.

 Discuss the deal.

Take your prospect through any written agreement which may be necessary. Don't be reluctant to discuss money, because being able to focus on sensitive issues confidently will reflect well on your experience in dealing with and serving clients.

 Build in follow-up action.

Your presentation may well be only your first step in ultimately closing a deal. Keep the process moving by suggesting a next step, such as having the client visit your premises. Be proactive in marking out the next step and a timeline, anything that will bring you closer to capturing a new client.

 Never give up.

If you are unsuccessful with your initial pitch, don't give up. When a prospect says 'no', they probably mean 'not now'. The needs of business today are ever-changing. 'No' today might be 'yes' tomorrow. For this reason, continue to make contact with the prospect through mailings, phone calls, invitations, and so on.

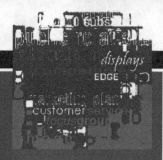

How to provide exceptional customer service

It has been said that service management is a total organisational approach that makes quality of service, as perceived by customers, the main driving force of any business. But often managers pay only lip-service to customer service—they're hampered by the day-to-day concerns of production, union negotiations, meetings, paperwork, budgets, and personnel matters. What can you do to improve your organisation's service? Start with these basic ideas…

1 Let no customer wait more than three minutes.

Time is money—for the customer too. If you work at minimising customer waiting time to no more than three minutes, you'll gain more customers than you'll lose.

2 Do a little extra each time.

Always try to exceed customer expectations by providing an unsolicited little extra—it's called value-adding. When your car is serviced—and the dealer cleans the windscreen and blackens your tyres at no charge, and leaves a chocolate bar on the driver's seat—chances are you'll return.

3 Redress a customer concern immediately.

There are no 'little' problems when it comes to customer service. You must take action, without hesitation, to redress any shortfall in service or any product defect. Any delay in meeting a dissatisfied customer's

needs could result in alienation and loss of business. On the other hand, prompt action can create a perception of a higher standard of company performance than if the problem had not occurred in the first place!

4 Take five seconds to answer the phone.

The telephone is often the first—and often the final—point of contact for some customers. Get that phone answered before its fourth ring. Any undue delay, any unanswered call, any engaged signal—and your company's goodwill could suffer, to say nothing of additional business.

5 Attend to detail.

The ultimate test of a caring attitude towards the customer is your attention to detail. It's been calculated that 80 per cent of customer alienation comes from getting 20 per cent of the detail wrong. While customers don't expect perfection, they do expect you to respond quickly and sympathetically.

Seek staff ideas on how to improve service.

Many of the best ideas for improving customer service come from those who deal with your customers—your staff. Implement their ideas whenever possible and provide encouraging feedback on suggestions that can't be used.

Monitor those things you often don't notice.

How do your face-to-face people (your officers of first impression) present themselves dress-wise and in terms of attitude? Do your people smile and say thank you? How's your receptionist's telephone answering technique? What about the appearance of that ageing sign, tired company logo, or old-fashioned letterhead? Have you checked lately? Such basic outward signs are vital in securing a customer's confidence that the service you provide is reliable, courteous, and of high quality.

Keep those promises.

Companies win customers by making promises about service—and retain customers by keeping those promises. The more promises you, your company or your staff make about quality, responsiveness, reliability etc, the more they must be kept. So, if a staff member promises to 'get back to' a customer today, they'd better do it—even if there's nothing to report.

Make sure your staff are 'in the know'.

Your company can only be judged as the best provider if your staff are 'in the know'. Are your employees familiar with the product? Do they know what service is really about? Do they know the company? How to get things done? How to solve problems? Do they know regular customers by name?

Be confident that everything works.

A failure in the system is simply a breakdown in management. If you are guaranteeing a service, make sure the system works—the television set in the hotel room, the lift to your office, the car park barrier, the pay phone in the foyer, the photocopier, the escalator in the department store, the broken chair in reception, the cold drink dispenser…

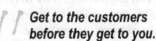
Get to the customers before they get to you.

Things inevitably go wrong. Often it's not your fault—perhaps your service person gets held up in traffic. Sometimes it is your fault—perhaps you underestimated the spare parts required. Whatever the reason, if you've made a promise to customers that cannot be kept, it's essential that you inform them before they inform you. Chances are then that they'll be sympathetic rather than angry, and they might even thank you for keeping them advised.

> ## quotable quote

Customer expectations for all organisations are now coming through loud and clear:

- Be efficient in giving me what I want.
- Be courteous and treat me with respect.
- Be responsive – react quickly when I need you.
- Use empathy – understand my needs and anticipate them.
- Treat me as an individual –my needs are very special.
- And above all, be reliable.[29]

don't forget

Frank's advice

Frank Pacetta has been the top Xerox sales person in the United States. He offers this customer service advice:

■ Never say 'No' to a customer... everything is negotiable.

■ Make customers feel good about YOU – not just your product – by sending thank you notes, cards for birthdays and promotions, taking them to lunch, football, and so on.

■ Meet customers' requests, even if it means fighting your bureaucracy.

■ Solve customers' problems.

■ Know your competitors' products better than your competitors do.

■ Be early for all meetings.

■ Dress and groom yourself sharply so YOU look like a superior product.

521

How to be the rainmaker in your organisation

Rainmakers in organisations have a special role: to help the business grow and prosper by attracting and introducing new business through personal contacts, professional networks, and personal reputation, and by adding value for existing clients. They're supersalespersons and project initiators. But rainmakers can never succeed in isolation—they need to be team players, confident that the new business generated will be supported by everyone involved. Successful rainmaking requires specific actions such as these...

here's an idea

The key to being an effective rainmaker is to communicate confidence and consistency. Successful rainmakers always have their client's confidence.

here's an idea

One simple strategy to remain in touch with your prospects or clients is to become familiar with their interests and concerns and, every so often, forward to them a photocopied article on that topic with a Post-it stuck to it. Handwritten on the Post-it is your brief note... 'Stuart, I thought this might interest you. Regards, Ron T.'

here's an idea

Ensure that your business cards, letterhead, website, and any other material are coordinated and communicate a clear message of quality and service. The help of an image and design consultant can be a valuable investment for rainmakers.

1 Work where rainmakers are appreciated.

Accept that some companies will never be able to make the best use of a rainmaker. Although they may appreciate the added business a rainmaker can encourage, they may not be able to appreciate the energy and expense required to produce that outcome. As a result, you will be spending an inordinate amount of your time dealing with in-house issues instead of focusing your attention on rainmaking activities. Successful rainmaking, for example, requires a budget sufficient to target the people you (and the company) want to attract. You can't 'make rain' for free.

2 Sell your services in-house.

Work colleagues need to know what you actually do, including the sorts of services you provide. In fact, the majority of client-contacts and referrals are likely to come from—or at least emanate from—within the organisation. This will mean that you will need to spend plenty of one-on-one time with people helping them to identify possible referrals. Discuss also how, and to whom, your services will be billed. Remember, it is considerably easier to sell to existing clients than to find new ones. Ensure also that your plans and activities dovetail with those of your marketing group.

3 Identify what you have for offer.

Continuing success for a rainmaker demands that the company being promoted has products or services that customers will want, and be prepared to pay for. A rainmaker without credibility and saleable products or services soon experiences drought conditions. Offerings should also include value-adds to make products or services even more attractive. Your one-on-one meetings with key people within your company will have helped to identify possible value-adds.

4 Establish ground rules with your own people.

Even when people within an organisation acknowledge the

importance and role of a rainmaker, the rainmaker's contributions can often be undervalued as part of the entire, completed project. A rainmaker's contribution to a complete project can be as high as forty-five per cent—without a rainmaker's involvement, there may never have been a project in the first place. Issues that need to be resolved from the outset include

- a role description
- the nature of the rainmaker's involvement in the entire project
- the way that billings will occur, including the rainmaker's contribution to the project
- responsibilities for debt collecting
- the level and form of recognition and reward
- the support required in-house
- the training required for those supporters.

 Build networks.

Establishing and maintaining networks is hard work, and there's a financial cost to many of the activities. As well as the seemingly endless lists of breakfasts, lunches, and dinners, there are the other need-to-be-seen-at events from ballet to football. Any spare time in between is spent on the telephone staying in touch. Active membership of professional and business associations is important. Don't neglect media exposure—a regular column in the local daily is worth considering. Ensure also that you get maximum exposure from involvement in project-related activities.

 Work on your communication skills.

Your oral, written, and nonverbal skills all need continuing

development. Given that most meaning will be communicated non-verbally, make sure that you pay attention to image, appearance, and the quality of those with whom you associate. Successful rainmakers can be expected to have their own dress consultant who advises them on all aspects of wardrobe. Oral communication can be improved by private tuition and involvement in groups such as Toastmasters International and others established specifically for the purpose of individual improvement. The Dale Carnegie program 'How to win friends and influence people', continues to cater for this need. Written communication, too, is a skill that can be developed with professional assistance. Remember the saying that 'all good writers need an editor'. Professional editors will help you to say what you want to say more clearly and precisely while retaining the individuality of your written communication style.

 Ensure back up.

You must be able to confidently guarantee deliverables. So you will need to ensure that those in-house who will take control of the project will deliver the client exactly what you have promised. It's your credibility that is on the line: the client will attribute to you the success or otherwise of the project. Ensure also that agreement exists regarding billings and debt collecting—the job is never complete until all of the bills have been paid.

 don't forget

The 90-day Rule…

As a rainmaker, it is essential that you stick to the 90-day rule.

You can be sure that if you haven't made contact with your client in 90 days, a competitor will have done so. Use whatever technology you choose to stay in touch with clients regularly. You might call to invite them to events; wish them a happy 'birthday', 'anniversary', or 'holiday'; seek feedback on a particular service provided; ask them for a referral; or call for no other reason than to say 'hello'.

The 90-day rule ensures that you will never become a stranger to them… and will continue to make rain for your company.

 quotable quote

Rainmakers can sometimes choke the life out of too few prospects. So, don't get caught up in pursuing twenty prospects when you can be gently nudging two hundred or more.

So don't let that sense of being held by the throat happen to your prospects. People don't mean 'no', they mean 'not now'. What is important is that you are still there when it is the right time for them to buy.[30]

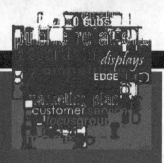

How to develop a successful website

If yours is a successful organisation, you will understand the importance of meeting customers' and clients' needs and wants—which is why you can spend millions of dollars designing memorable experiences for your consumers. You hire knowledgeable, helpful staff, provide expensive training programs, and build brightly-lit showrooms—all ultimately increasing market share. But are you prepared to expend the same energy in developing your online presence? Start by embracing several well-proven principles...

1 Understand your website users.

The problem with unsuccessful and unused websites is that they have been developed to disseminate what the organisation believes should be disseminated, rather than first finding out what the targeted user wants and needs. So, the first step must always be to ask: Who are our users? Are they novices or experts in computer use? Are they new or repeat users? Are they males or females? What information or services do they require? How do they prefer to access that information? Under what circumstances? What will they do with the information? And so on. Websites are for users.

2 Hire a specialist website designer.

If you want a site that brings real value to your users, you'll need to employ a professional website designer who has experience in coalescing your company's goals with user needs, who can cater for both proficient and novice web users, and for both browsing and directed users. There is no substitute for quality.

3 Know what you want to accomplish.

In developing your website, the designer will need to work with you to determine the purpose of the site. Your needs might include:

to establish a presence; to increase public awareness; to increase sales; to generate business leads; to offer customer support; to supplement existing advertising and promotional efforts; to generate requests for information; to build business or store traffic; to survey customers; to provide the latest information on products, services, events or sales; to post job opportunities; to build a database for mailings; to provide directions...

You will also need to detail for the designer the kind of information you want to get from the site, for example:

number of visitors; when they visited and for how long; their email and postal address; their phone and fax numbers; visitors' comments; which pages or products are most popular...

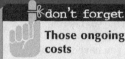

don't forget

Those ongoing costs

While businesses tend to focus on the start-up costs of e-commerce, a recent report by Ernst & Young found that the cost of maintenance can far outweigh the initial costs. For example, the highest cost for small investors can be the value of time spent responding to email correspondence generated by their website.

According to Kristian Page of Logic Commerce. Com, there are many unique costs associated with e-commerce that vendors might not take into account. It's vital, for example, that a website has a merchant facility from a bank that offers an e-commerce gateway. An organisation that handles secure transactions on your behalf will probably demand a start-up charge plus monthly fees, in addition to transaction fees. As well, a virtual shopping cart facility could cost between several hundred and several thousand dollars.

The bottom line? Be aware of the ongoing costs before committing your organisation to e-commerce.

Evaluate similar websites.

Get a head start when developing your site by noting the best features on your competitors' and other websites. See what they do (and do not do) well. Well-established, high-profile sites have usually invested considerably on usability features. Don't be constrained, however, by what others do if there's a better way to support your users' goals.

 Keep it simple.

You want visitors but, more importantly, you want regular visitors. This will to some extent depend on what your site provides. But it also relates to the simplicity factor, which acknowledges that people are busy and don't have the time to become familiar with the intricacies of every site they visit. So, remove every feature that is not absolutely necessary, even if it is graphically or functionally 'cool', for 'coolness' usually adds complexity (and cost). People will return to a simple, comfortable, functional site.

 Ensure your users are free from risk.

You should guarantee confidentiality and privacy if that's what users want. Most prefer to be anonymous, with research showing that users can be driven away from sites that demand personal information from them. For example, your site shouldn't entice users with the promise of

information—but only if they call or email to get it; nobody will relish the thought of being deluged with emails or promotional material after only one visit. Give users the right to dictate the degree of information they're willing to disclose. In some circumstances, registration is appropriate, including credit card details, but you'll lose potential clients if you require personal details without a legitimate reason. And you should never close the door to users who change their mind about a purchase or decision.

 Explore ways to humanise the technology.

Your website must be geared towards efficiency, but the challenge is to have it build relationships with users. It must be more than just a cold, heartless database. It should be somewhat like visiting a department store where a friendly sales assistant knows the customer's name, as well as likes and dislikes. If you intend to become a forward-thinking online organisation, you need to be continually on the lookout for ways to leverage the technology and to provide web users with a more emotional experience.

 Take the time to get it right.

If you don't get your website right and launch something unusable, you've achieved little. It takes time to develop a consumer-friendly site and the majority of organisations that take the time to do the job properly actually save time in the long run.

How to raise the profile of your business using the internet

Internet use has increased exponentially during recent decades. Creative businesses anticipated its growth and established an internet presence because they knew their clients expected them to do so. Today, avante-garde and establishment organisations alike recognise that an internet presence is essential for business success. If you want to raise the profile of your business, you should know how you can make the internet work for you. If you don't know, you can be sure your competitors

here's an idea

If you're thinking of getting your organisation into cyberspace, here's what it takes to be the best at e-commerce, says Eddie Lloyd of Internet-based Horizon Tours:

1. Put a lot of time into your website.
2. Be creative
3. Give people a reason to keep coming back, such as giveaways and free information.
4. Sell quality products.
5. Provide a way for people to give you feedback about what you're doing.

1 Use the internet to establish a presence.

No matter what your business is, you can't afford to ignore billions with access to the internet. To be part of that cyberspace community and to show that you are available to service their needs, you'll need to be on the internet. You can bet your competitors will be. Indeed, the internet will be the equivalent of today's business card in your organisation, a vital 21st Century networking tool.

2 Use the internet to keep people informed.

'This is what we do, here's how we can help you, and here's how you can contact us.' Whether you're a large corporation, a public service organisation, or a small business, you can tell this to potential and existing clients and customers, or the general public, anywhere in the world, simply, inexpensively, and 24 hours a day on the internet. The world can have immediate access to information about *your* business.

Use the internet imaginatively...

- to heighten public interest
- to publicly release time-sensitive material (e.g. press releases, prize winners, merger news, quarterly earnings statements) any time, at your discretion, without embargo
- to answer frequently asked questions about your organisation
- to make changes instantly and inexpensively to public company data, prices, information etc.
- to reach the media, the most wired profession today, with up-to-date information and images, quickly, cheaply and easily.

3 Use the internet to serve clients and customers.

Making business information available is an important component of customer service, but creative use of your website will also allow customers to, for example, complete forms to pre-qualify for a loan, track down that hard-to-locate jazz CD or book, inquire after the sizes and colours of coats available through your store, check on houses for sale in the northern suburbs, seek your latest DIY gardening hints, and so on.

By building an email response into your website, you can ask for instant client or customer feedback about your services or products, without the cost and lack of response often experienced through traditional business reply mail.

4. Use the internet to sell services or products.

As cyberspace becomes increasingly consumer-friendly, Internet shopping will be embraced as the norm. The introduction of universal codes of practice together with security and privacy safeguards and effective payment processing will pave the way for consumers to purchase everything from cars to home insurance without leaving home. You'll need to prepare yourself for the e-commerce boom if you are to compete.

5. Use the internet to expand your markets.

The internet enables you to reach your neighbourhood market and anywhere else in the country and overseas. As well, since there are nearly 200 million users out there, and even if you sell only nuts, fish tanks, or courses on basket-weaving, or you provide free or subscriber information or services to lawyers, astronomers, or caterers, the internet will allow even the most specialised groups to find you through available search engines.

The internet provides you with the opportunity to open up a dialogue with international markets as easily as with a company across the street.

6. Use the internet to stay open 24 hours a day.

The internet can serve your clients, customers and employees 24 hours a day, seven days a week—and with no unnecessary overtime. It can customise information to match needs and collect data to put you ahead of your competition, even before they get into the office next day.

7. Use the internet to stay in contact with your staff.

If you have employees on the road, they'll need up-to-date information to help them make the sale or pull together the deal. Keep them posted in complete privacy on the internet. A quick local phone call can keep your salespeople supplied with the most detailed information, without long distance phone bills or the need to inconvenience staff at central office.

8. Use the internet as a demo site.

You have developed a new product but people would really love it if they could see it in action. Or you know your new TV commercial is great but you want your boss interstate to hear and see it. In support of text information, the internet allows you to make pictures, sound, and film accessible to customers, clients and staff. No printed brochure or prospectus can do that.

---

viewpoint

"The Internet is the fastest growing alternative to customary distribution channels in all sectors of the market. Yet many managers are slow to come to terms with the new medium or have failed to assess its likely effect on the way organisations will engage in commerce in the future."

– Max Franchitto in *Management Today*

---

ask yourself

Are you ready? Your company's future is dependent on the decisions you make as to the relationships you want to develop with your customers. To assist in defining the Web challenge, you'll need to consider the following:

- What parts of your business could you conduct with customers over the Web?
- What is the cost of providing services to customers over the Web?
- What are the costs of not providing such services?
- How would your organisation use the information it collected?
- Would your organisation be significantly disadvantaged if your competitors were to find customers over the Web before you did? [32]

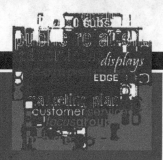

How to prepare your organisation for an online presence

The Internet is big. Millions upon millions of websites out there are competing for the attention and custom of hundreds of millions of users. If your organisation wants to establish an effective presence on the Internet and attract your share of the world-wide market, before developing your organisation's website, you need to consider, in the decision-making process, several important prerequisites...

it's a fact

Products best suited to e-commerce are:

- Those that do not have to be tried on or handled
- Those that are difficult to find in the customer's local area
- Those where the consumer requires information –banking, travel, books
- Those for which the sale can be very conveniently carried out online
- Those with a high value relative to their cost of delivery
- Those that can be down-loaded – information and software.

 Know why you need an online presence.

Your organisation can gain a more visible presence in the marketplace by using a website. It can:

- allow consumers to achieve their goals easily (e.g. in purchasing, or in obtaining sought-after information)
- increase customer retention
- invite repeat visits or purchases
- enhance brand loyalty
- increase organisational productivity
- decrease costs associated with supporting customers or with alternative forms of access such as mail, phone or fax.

In preparing for an online presence, keep those intentions to the fore.

 Be aware of the possibilities.

In their book *The Clickable Corporation*, Rosenoer, Armstrong and Gates recommend that businesses consider the following essentials prior to establishing an online presence. You'll be wanting a website that will:

- allow customers access to information that was previously inaccessible, difficult to find, or available only at great cost and trouble.
- provide customers with a range of products and services, and help those customers to make the best purchasing decisions
- offer customers as much convenience as possible
- offer customers products tailored to their specific needs and give them the personalised service they demand and deserve
- streamline your business processes and incorporate them into the online environment at a reduced cost and with an efficient supply chain that benefits everyone
- help build and maintain a sense of community or family online
- emphasise the security of your technology to ensure that information exchanged between you and your customer remains private.

 Get to know the Internet.

Know what you're getting into. Do plenty of exploring of the Web yourself, even if you end up outsourcing the development of your organisation's site. Check out and note the look and feel of effective sites around the world. Explore typical sites in your industry before focusing on your competitors' sites.

4 Define your business.

In the world of e-business, there are three main types of online companies —portals (entry points like Yahoo), e-commerce businesses (product or service sellers like Amazon), and those that combine the two (like Google). Each has a different focus, affecting their site designs and marketing strategies. Knowing what e-business you're in will allow you to be far more critical of the services on offer and of key site qualities such as visual appeal and ease of use.

5 Remain focused on your customer.

Think about the kind of online experience you would want if you were a customer of your business. Organise your site around your customers, not around your products or services. Streamline your business processes accordingly. Make it easy for people to do business with you. Remember, research tells us that e-business customers want predictable web experiences and a feeling of being in control of the process. You must give customers and clients reasons to keep coming back.

6 Aim to make your site a resource.

Web users normally seek information—so make sure your message is more than just hype. Whatever else your intention, add value by being an information provider as well. Give details and background on your industry, and advice on your specialities. Plan to draw customers to your site by turning it into an expert location.

7 Always conclude with a clear call to action.

What will you want the user to do after having considered your site presentation? Make a purchase? Join a mailing list? Request a price quotation? Ask for more information? Let users know what you want them to do and ask them to do it in clear terms. And make it easy for them to respond—a button to click, a form to complete, a direct email link.

8 Be prepared to keep changing your site.

To entice users back to your site, you'll need to keep it changing. Update your content. Take advantage of new technology as it appears. Add new features, new information, new products, new resources. Repeat visitors become clients or customers who will in turn recommend your site to others.

9 Understand that 'online' is only one part of your total thrust.

Your aim in online business should be to integrate it into your overall business strategy, where it supports and is supported by your offline marketing and service activities. Understand and explore this objective and you will make best use of the web's unique characteristics in attracting and retaining market share.

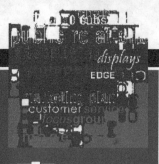

How to attract users to your website

viewpoint

"The 'If you build it, they will come' axiom no longer applies. Sites can invest thousands, even millions of dollars on website development. But without campaigns in place to effectively promote sites, even the most compelling commerce sites will have a hard time standing out in the clutter. As the number of websites continues to increase, the chances someone will randomly 'surf' onto your site dramatically declines. So does the chance they might be directed to you by a search engine. So publicising your presence on the Web is vital.
– Kate Maddox in *Web Commerce: Building a Digital Business.*

There's much more to establishing a successful business presence on the Web than simply designing attractive web pages, getting them into cyberspace, and then simply waiting for customers to call. Whether your organisation is looking for hits on the website or for actual online sales, your aim should be to attract as many users, potential clients, or customers as possible to your site. Just what can you do to generate traffic? The following suggestions provide a good starting point…

Name your website sensibly.

Pick a site address that is easy to remember, has some relevance to your line of business, is short, and is spelt exactly the way it sounds—a site name that readily sticks in a client's or customer's memory is ideal.

Make sure your staff know your website.

The people most familiar with your organisation—your staff—are the best marketers of your website. Be sure to familiarise them with its contents and purpose, and of any additions made from time to time.

Keep promoting your website offline.

Add your web address (URL) to every piece of communication that comes from your organisation, right up there with phone/fax/postal details—on business cards, brochures, letterhead, press releases, fax cover sheets, signs, newsletters, and catalogues. And don't neglect traditional media. In all your advertising in journals, television, radio, and newspapers, be sure to include your URL. Catch your readers' attention with the advertisement, and refer them to your website for additional details, even for placing orders.

Register with leading search engines.

It is essential to register your website with the major portals, search engines and directories—such as Yahoo!, Excite, AltaVista, WebCrawler, Google and Ask.com. As an example, go to www.yahoo.com.au, and work through the directory until you find the category that best suits your site. Complete the details as prompted, and your site will subsequently be reviewed for inclusion. It also pays to position your site to appear towards the top of search engine listings—all the more reason to seek advice on how to write page titles, keywords, and page descriptions.

Publish online.

People will keep coming back to your site if you have something fresh to offer them each time.

Provide freebies. It can be expensive in energy and time, but if your site gains a reputation, for example, for offering free advice in your area of expertise, or providing tips on how to get best use of your products (with a subtle crossover to the sales area of your site), then they will come.

Write online articles. People go to their computers to learn something. Use what you know about your business to become an online expert. Submit articles to some of the thousands of relevant online publications now on the Web—with a link to your own site.

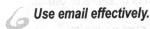 Use email effectively.

Sign all emails. Remember to include, as a fixture at the end of your email messages, a 'signature' that includes your organisation's URL and a one-line description of your business focus.

Publish email newsletters. Publish a regular newsletter for members, clients or customers to keep in touch, generate trust, develop awareness, and build business. Distribute it via email or install it on your website.

Capture visitor email addresses. Ask visitors if they would like to receive your newsletter. Unsolicited emails, or spamming, could do you more harm than good.

Try contests. Announce via email that something can be won by visiting your site, and the traffic will increase.

 Seek online links.

Try reciprocal links. Make an effort to have other quality sites include links to your site on a reciprocal and complimentary basis. Be careful, however, with the links you provide on your site—don't make it too easy for your visitors to leave. They might not come back.

Investigate links to related industry sites. Various trade associations, for example, will be prepared to feature member sites. Even if a fee is required, the link may bring you the targeted traffic you desire.

Encourage bookmarking. Make sure you ask visitors to bookmark your site.

Buy banner ads. Another way to encourage traffic is to buy banner advertisements that lead to your site. These can be expensive but, if strategically located, can increase visits—although not all visitors turn out to be buyers. Banner exchange schemes are an inexpensive option.

Seek expert advice.

If your organisation is serious about making an impact online, there are a plethora of expert companies available today to assist—website developers, search engine optimisation specialists, and online merchants who will help you find the right package for your particular business and who will provide facilities to accept online card payments for you.

Finally, for valuable information and articles on matters of website promotion, marketing and e-commerce related issues, sites such as www.practicalecommerce.com are well worth a visit.

> ## viewpoint
>
> "If you're not willing to pay for people's attention, get out of the business. But the trick to staying in e-business is to keep the cost of bringing people to your site below the value you can extract from those users. Some organisations lose heaps because it cost them too much to set up and too much to get clicks. And they had no feedback loop to get callers to come back. Getting attention will cost you money."
>
> – Seth Godin
> President, Yoyodyne

> ## here's an idea
>
> Nothing turns people off more quickly than a website with stale information. If you don't hook them the first time they visit, it's unlikely that they will ever return.

> ## here's an idea
>
> One of the best ways to improve your website marketing is to analyse the existing traffic to your website. Until you understand who is coming and why, it'll be difficult to improve. There are four ways to analyse site traffic:
>
> - Install a counter on your web page
> - Use your ISP's statistical package
> - Purchase web traffic analysis software
> - Employ an outside firm to audit your web traffic.[34]

531

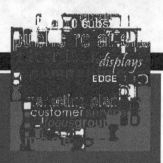

How to sell online

In the days before the Internet, if you wanted to sell direct to customers, you needed to build a shop or establish a mail-order business using catalogues. Doing so would require the outlay of many thousands, if not millions, of dollars. With the arrival of the Web, you now have an inexpensive sales channel that gives access to millions of consumers worldwide. The Web provides an exciting commercial opportunity—provided you adhere to several important rules…

Be sure online selling is for you.

As a general rule, whatever can be sold in a print catalogue can also be sold on a website. But if a customer has to see, hold, or try something before buying, neither avenues are appropriate. Remember, when it comes to selling online, it's not where you are, but what you're selling and how attractively you present the offer that count. The key is to select a niche small enough for you to dominate. For example, you may be hard-pressed to compete with Amazon.com in selling books; you may succeed, however, by specialising in books on folk poetry. One obvious way to dominate the market is to be the manufacturer. That way, you cut out all the middlemen who eat into your profits.

Ensure your site looks inviting.

Your website needs to inspire visitors with confidence. Consumers are reluctant to buy from an amateurish site; if your organisation cannot put up a good website, then potential customers will assume, rightly or wrongly, that you cannot deliver good products or services either.

Make sure your site is easy to use.

Internet users can be spooked very easily; potential customers or clients will leave at the slightest obstacle, e.g. having to register, or confusion over navigation, or an inability to find the product they seek on the site.

Check that your site looks credible.

Your website visitors need to be reassured that yours is a real and viable company. Convince them— include your name, a toll-free contact number, a street address, a brief company history, and customer testimonials. Ensure you display a healthy range of products or services. The larger the inventory, the more seriously your organisation is taken (e.g. Amazon or CDNOW). And if your ordering facility is shaky or questionable—are you really serious about wanting their business?

Make service your primary aim.

There are ways an online business can gain a reputation for quality service:

- Reassure reluctant customers. Outline how you will be providing top quality service, and guarantee they will be satisfied—or their money will be cheerfully refunded.

- To set a good impression and establish reliability, respond quickly to customer email messages and inquiries. Check your emails several times daily.

- If a visitor asks for additional details about your business, a product, or service, have a brochure prepared so that you can email back immediately.

- Offer a variety of credit card payment options. Some people prefer to pay by cheque. Make this possible. Include a privacy or confidentiality statement.

- For those customers nervous about sending their credit card details into cyberspace, have options available for them.

- Prepare a standard order-confirmation notice which advises the order number, shipping date, and estimated time of delivery. Email this back to customers after receiving their order.

- Email new customers a few days after delivering their order to thank them for their business and to seek feedback about your product and service.

- Explore ways to keep in contact with hard-won customers and clients. Send monthly or quarterly email bulletins about new products, current specials, ideas for getting the most out of your product, and ideas for maintaining it.

 Promote your site.

Success will depend on attracting people to your website. Explore the possibilities: promote the site on all your printed matter, tell the media, build email lists, get on search engines, write articles, buy banner ads, cross-link with other sites, publish email newsletters, have visitors bookmark your site, run contests, and so on.

 Keep your site fresh.

Your site will evolve over time. Constantly seek ways to improve your site; it will never be perfect. As well, a site that has not changed for months is boring. It looks abandoned. Why should a customer return to it? Explore ways to change your site regularly—monthly, weekly, even daily—by rotating featured items on the front page, by including some news, or by upgrading its appearance.

 Remember: it's hard work!

The good news about selling online is that it should be a lot cheaper, and you can reach a very large and scattered clientele. The bad news is that, just like any other successful business, it requires hard work. You don't simply build an online site that looks after itself. You must work hard to build a site that people will want to buy from, to attract visitors, to give good service, and to make sure your customers return, and bring their friends with them.

 Be patient.

For most online sites or stores, growth in customer numbers is slow at first. Don't be discouraged. Work hard, promote your site, provide value adds, and your customer base will increase.

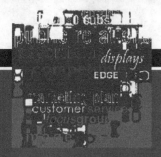

How to get the most out of your advertising dollar

Increased sales depend on a unified, coherent, and consistent marketing program; and advertising is one of marketing's major activities. The success of many businesses depends on effective advertising, which these days can be quite expensive. The following guidelines will help you to maximise your advertising dollar...

Be aware that advertising can work.

'I don't believe in advertising. We ran an ad three years ago and didn't get one call!' Plenty of businesses say this each time the idea of advertising is raised—but they never get around to evaluating where the ad was placed, what it said, its size, its audience and particularly why they thought a one-shot ad would produce results. If only they had considered the following advice...

Select the appropriate media.

The key to successful advertising is to use the right medium to reach the right people—national, state, and local newspapers and magazines, radio, television, letterbox flyers, posters, Internet, direct mailings, sandwich boards, etc. Different media can reach different audiences, so again you'll need to do your homework to achieve the best result. Avoid basing your buying decision solely on the price of the advertisement. In fact, for best results, it might be best to advertise through several media outlets at the same time.

Get inside the customer's head.

In planning your advertisement or campaign, always start with the customer or prospect. You may need to seek the assistance of research to answer such questions as: What problem can we solve for the customer? What does the customer want? What do we have on offer that other organisations do not? Do we have a solution for the customer—or just a product?

Use a quality advertisement.

It will cost you more money to produce a quality advertisement but, if results are what you are looking for, investing in quality is well worth the cost. Remember, you'll be competing with other businesses for the attention of the reader, listener, or viewer. The longer you can hold your potential customers' attention, the better your chances of convincing them that they want what you are offering—and you'll have more chance of doing that with quality advertisements. You may well require the services of an advertising agency to generate a quality ad.

5 Make it easy for the prospect to respond.

Whatever and however you're advertising, it's essential that you make it a simple process for an interested customer to seek further information or to make a purchase. Display a toll-free number prominently, or provide a credit card facility, or offer a pre-paid postcard or envelope for the reply.

6 Attract prospects with irresistible benefits.

The aim of your advertising should be to convince customers that they will derive immense benefit from what you are offering. In addition to old-fashioned 'reliability', 'dependability', and 'after sales service', we now see attractive discounts, free steak knives, two-for-the-price-of-one and buy-one-get-one-free offers, delayed payments, free gifts, and a range of other eye-catching sweeteners. What can your business offer prospective customers or clients in terms of traditional values and sweeteners?

7 Plan and follow an advertising schedule.

If you run your advertisement once, it is highly unlikely that a majority of people will even see or hear it—let alone respond to it. And just because it appears, does not mean that

everyone is even ready to respond. The aim of advertising is to be out there just when someone needs you, your product, or your service. Little wonder that research tells us, to be effective, an advertisement must run three to seven times.

8 Get value for your money.

Stretch your advertising dollar by making each advertisement work and work and work. For example, be sure to reprint your advertisements and mail them, together with a personal note, to existing customers and prospects. Tell them where the advertisement appears and why. You'll be getting double value for your outlay as well as ensuring that those who missed it haven't after all.

9 Remember: advertising is only part of your total marketing program.

Check out the opportunities to produce and distribute additional promotional materials to support your advertising. Some years ago, for example, one major petrol company's 'put a tiger in your tank' advertisements followed up with such gimmicks as tiger tail petrol tank caps, and another company's 'reliable, cheerful, trustworthy Stanley' in the advertisements was then transported around the country for guest appearances. Combine your advertising with press releases and media stories about your company and its services and products.

Finally, remember that when business is good, it pays to advertise; when business is bad, you've got to.

✔ it's a fact

In 1977, an enterprising New York bookstore mounted a novel promotion to sell a new book. It placed a large ad in the *New York Times*, which asked 'Have you ever been kissed in a bookstore before?' The ad went on to guarantee that anyone who bought a new paperback called *The Art of Kissing* would be rewarded with a kiss by an expert.

A stand was set up in the shop, and a man and a woman stood ready to deliver. Customers who bought the book were presented with a paper token and, armed with it, went to the male or female attendant (presumably according to gender).

On the day, the shop was crammed with voyeurs, photographers, and others were standing three deep on the footpath outside, peering through the window.

What happened, of course, was that more people came to *watch* than to take part in the kissing promotion or to buy the book – a point picked up by one advertising guru, who wrote after the event:

'Most advertising doesn't actually sell a product or service (unless an order form is included), and it's not meant to do so. Advertising is intended to persuade, to convince, and to bring the buyer to the point of sale...the sale has still to be made.'

It's a point worth remembering if you have a product or service to advertise. And, at the end of the day, that's why there were still many unsold copies of *The Art of Kissing* on the shelves of that New York bookstore.

535

How to select the right media for advertising

When business is good, it pays to advertise; when business is bad, you've got to advertise. Advertising is the mouthpiece of business. It is essential. Retailers are offered a multitude of avenues to promote their products; the greatest challenge is deciding where to invest your advertising dollar to get the maximum return. Advertising your business, services, and products does not have to be haphazard. You can plan, measure and monitor your advertising activities...[36]

1 Consider your audience.

If you do not know your target audience, and you blanket advertise, you will be wasting your advertising budget. Everyone's target market will be different, which is why you need to consider, firstly, such general variables as:

- the geographic location of your business and your audience—passers-by, workers, or residents
- the age group you wish to attract
- the gender you are targeting
- the primary socio-economic group you are hoping to draw upon
- the occupations of your audience.

2 Target your specific audience.

Having reflected upon your general advertising framework, you should become more focused on the individual customer. Marketers often use the term SPADE to focus retailers on their real target audience:

Starter	The person who initiates the enquiry
Purchaser	The person who pays for the goods
Adviser	The person who influences the decision
Decider	The real authority on what to buy
End user	The consumer of the product.

This may be one person or five different people. At each stage they are looking for different benefits. Your final advertising thrust should reflect this customer analysis by promoting to the selected target audience the benefits of your product.

3 Select the appropriate advertising media.

Once you have decided on your target audiences, you can then decide on the appropriate advertising media you should use to get their attention. Among the media available to you are:

National newspapers—Expensive, but ideal for nationwide retail chains.

Regional newspapers—Have immediate impact but remember, yesterday's newspaper is old news.

Local newspapers—Have excellent

household penetration and can be very cost effective.

Trade magazines—Well read and very targeted.

Local directories—Very effective, but you must plan well in advance.

Radio—Local radio and community radio are becoming more and more popular. This is a useful medium to consider.

Posters—Often linked to major advertising campaigns.

Street benches—Useful in high traffic areas. The message should be rotated every few months.

Public transport advertising—Moving messages on buses, trains and taxis must be simple, bold and short. Get them right and they work.

Television—Regional television is very cost effective. Only large retailers can afford metropolitan television. Ask your local television station; their advice is valuable.

Sponsorship—Always sponsor local events attended by your target audience. It gives credibility to you as a neighbourhood retailer and one of the 'local good guys'.

Parking meters—These work in the United Kingdom: over 35,000 meters are used by 5.5 million motorists a week.

Point of sale display—Remember, internal advertising is always more cost effective than external advertising. You know you will hit your target.

Letterbox-flyers, direct mailings, the Internet, sandwich boards... and the list goes on.

Do your homework before deciding.

Before deciding on which medium best suits your business, do your research. Contact as many advertising outlets as possible that suit your target audience. Ask for details on costs and evidence of how effective they are at reaching your target. Always keep notes of discussions so you can refer to them at a later date.

Keep to the advertising standards.

Most countries have advertising standards and an authority that monitors such standards. Regulations on advertising vary from country to country, but the following guidelines should always be adhered to:

- Advertisements should be legal, inoffensive, and truthful.

- Advertisements should be prepared with a sense of responsibility to the consumer and society.

- Advertisements should conform to the principles of fair competition.

Monitor the penetration cost of advertising.

It's important to look beyond the cost of the advertisement. Look at its penetration rate. This is not an easy assignment but—how many of your target audience did it reach? Begin with your team. Advise them of what advertisements you have taken out and have them monitor the number of new customers who come in as a result of your advertising campaign. In this way, you can determine how much it costs to get a new customer. In many cases, a new customer or client has to return to your premises three times before you make a profit from them. Your staff need to know this and commit themselves to your advertising initiative.

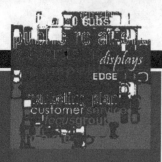

How to stage successful exhibits and displays

People usually show a great deal of interest in visual presentations. Many organisations have discovered that a well-planned exhibition or display can be a valuable vehicle for presenting information about themselves. Importantly, because they require a minimum of effort on the part of viewers, they allow key messages to be communicated quickly and conveniently. But no matter what kind of exhibit is staged, or what the particular message may be, the results are always better after careful planning. Here, then, are some useful suggestions to help you get the most out of your next exhibit…

1 Plan for your exhibit well in advance.

There is no point in staging an exhibit or display unless you have a clear purpose, an enthusiastic co-ordinating group, and a well thought-out strategy and schedule. Basic questions for the planners must be why, who, what, where, when, how and at what cost?

2 Focus on a key message.

It can be difficult to try to tell everything about your organisation in one display. Focus on one theme. What do you want people who view the exhibit to go away thinking? Communicating one idea forcefully is much easier and can be much more effective than confusing viewers with a series of scattered and disjointed messages.

3 Determine the nature of the event.

Displays can be static (featuring projects, products, services, the workforce, environmental issues, the company's community involvement etc.) or active (staff performances, demonstrations, parades etc.), or a combination of both.

To choose the content for the exhibit you should consider such questions as: Does the item fit the focus of the key message? How well will the item be received by the audience? Is it simple and concrete enough to be understood? Does it lend itself well to the exhibit's form of communication? Will the ideas, concepts, and facts capture attention and leave a vivid impression? What message-sending vehicles will be used—bulletin boards, posters, display panels and cases, tables, pedestals, videos, transparencies, photographs, performances, computer interactivity, products? Will printed handouts be available to reinforce your message? Any other give-aways?

4 Gear your message to the viewer.

Know your audiences and focus your display on their specific interests. Here you should consider such things as the level of language, the complexity of the message, the ease of viewing, and the time available to the viewer.

5 Consider the full range of possible locations.

Exhibits must be planned for specific locations to reach specific audiences. For instance, to reach your staff or visitors to your site, exhibits can be placed in foyers and corridors, in display cases, and in waiting rooms.

To reach the wider community, the best locations could include shopping centres, libraries, banks, service clubs, civic centres, shop windows, malls, local shows, trade exhibitions, and special civic occasions—depending on the theme and purpose.

6 Determine the best date for the display.

Why are you staging your display at a certain time? Trade exhibitions and conventions are usually well planned at a time to attract large numbers. If you're planning a public display of your own at another time, will it clash with another crowd-drawing event? Will people be available to staff your display on the day? At what time of week or year will the crowds be largest? Timing is an important consideration.

7 Use the experts where appropriate.

Exhibits developed inhouse have their place but, for public displays, a high-quality product should be your aim. By all means involve your staff, but there are times when professionals

should be hired to ensure the greatest impact. Consider the specialised skills required to plan, design, construct and assemble your exhibit: writing, window dressing, cabinet making, furnishing, promoting, photography, publicising, signwriting, announcing,…

8 Have competent people staff your display.

For public displays, roster people with the ability to meet-and-greet others and answer questions about the exhibit's focus. Static displays serve their purpose, but visitors generally have questions and you will always have additional messages to convey about your organisation. That's why the people factor is so important.

9 And don't forget...

A few important points to note:

- Don't take things for granted at the exhibit site: check power points, ceiling height, access, lighting etc.
- Publicise your event widely.
- Exhibit personnel should dress appropriately.
- If you want a photographic record, take it early when everything looks the best.
- Does the display have a visual centre of attention? Is its message clear?
- Consider souvenir give-aways (balloons, stickers), prizes and competitions.
- Accuracy is absolutely essential! Check the spelling and grammar.

Finally, peruse the latest in the how-to literature by consulting www.redcliffe.co.uk/resources/planning_for_exhibitions.htm.

How to become a sponsor

Sponsorship is an ideal avenue for you to display the name of your business in front of potential and existing customers. Choose events where those attending share the values and interests of your company. Increasingly, consumers want to purchase products from suppliers who share their values. By being associated with (or sponsoring) an appropriate event, you can get closer to your targeted customers, and, in doing so, affirm that you care about them and their lifestyles… [40]

1 Understand the meaning of sponsorship.

Sponsorship is not a donation from your organisation to those seeking sponsorship. It is an act which rewards both sponsor and sponsored. The UK Association of Business Sponsorship makes this key point:

> The common interest between sponsor and sponsored demands that their relationship be based on mutual respect, candour and understanding, with each investing the necessary time and attention to define clearly the aims of sponsorship, the expectations of the deal, and the provisions for evaluating and publicising projects. They must also try to understand each other's motivation.

As a sponsor, you will want to know how your money will be spent by the sponsored group and how you will benefit from the relationship through either more sales, greater exposure, or both. Remember, the aim of sponsorship is to put both sides in a win-win situation.

2 Ask the appropriate questions.

Before accepting a role as sponsor, consider the advantages to you:

- What does the sponsored group want from your sponsorship?
- Do your values match those of the sponsored group and the event?
- How will the sponsorship affect you?
- How can you maximise your exposure?
- Will the sponsored have the people and resources to maximise your involvement and the return to your business?
- Is there evidence that they have done their homework on your business and personalised their invitation?

3 Be aware of the types of sponsorship.

Whether you envisage a 'one off' event or a long term relationship, give consideration to the type of involvement, which might include…

Sole sponsorship. The sponsor wants the event to be named after their product or name, e.g. The Whitbread Cup, The Coca Cola Challenge, Optus Oval.

Graded Sponsorship. A number of sponsors are involved, their return based on the degree of sponsorship.

Special Event Sponsorship. A single event in the program is sponsored by an individual company.

Underwriting Sponsorship. Here the sponsor will fund any losses the event makes.

Endorsement Sponsor. To give the event credibility, the sponsor lends its name, but no money.

Sponsorship comes in many forms. You may be asked for financial support, the provision of goods or a site, or to fund a coffee break at a conference, and so on.

Target the market.

An event will have a highly defined market. For example, a flower show will be aimed at keen gardeners and flower arrangers; a trade show on hardware will attract handymen. Such events provide a great opportunity for those retailers to promote their business to a specific market and ensure they get maximum benefit from their financial involvement.

Ideally you should aim at heavy users of your product, develop a strong association with the event, and get your name upfront—The *Coca Cola* Olympics, The *Greengrowth* Flower Show, The *Product X* Home of the Year.

Consider your products and sales.

Apart from linking your name and products to an event, you can also use this as an opportunity to launch a new product or revitalise your products and services. But you will need to check beforehand whether this is purely sponsorship, or if you will be able to promote and sell products at the same time. A camera retailer, for example, might sponsor a tea break at a conference on the clear understanding that it would have a sales booth in the conference hall on the day of the sponsorship.

People are more inclined to buy at this moment than after the event when the euphoria has declined.

Ensure you embrace the target market's lifestyle.

Selling product is not the aim of sponsorship. Building loyalty is. For this reason, ensure that your potential customers at the event relate to you in their lifestyle. For instance, if you sell chemicals you would not sponsor a back-to-nature event, but a sporting goods retailer would find this an ideal opportunity for involvement.

Make sponsorship work for you.

How will your sponsoring of an event affect your company's stature?

- If it is an environmental, charity or educational occasion, it is an ideal public relations exercise.
- Sponsoring an event will involve you with customers in a non-sales relationship. It allows you to spend quality time with them, the result of which should mean future sales contacts.
- Sponsoring the right event will win you new friends *and* build employee relations. The New Zealand Post Office, for example, found sponsoring the New Zealand Olympic team was a major boost in building employee morale.
- Oddly, only 10 per cent of companies forge a marketing campaign around their sponsorship, unlike Coca Cola, Nike, Reebok, and Telecom who built excellent marketing campaigns around their Olympic involvement. Link your sponsorship to marketing.
- Forty per cent of sponsors do not even advertise their involvement with an event. If you are going to spend on sponsorship, budget an equal amount on advertising and promotion linked to the event.

How to get the most out of the press

Just doing a good job isn't enough any more. We are in a competitive environment these days; and the local newspaper is an important channel for communicating good news about your organisation. As a manager, you must know how to work effectively with representatives of the print media to build support for your organisation. Reporters appreciate cooperative, accurate, and available sources for their stories; so here are some useful tips for getting the best deal from your local journalists...

1 Know your local newspaper contacts.

Is your organisation one that might be able to use the print media more effectively than others? If so, you'll need to get to know your local newspaper reporters as soon as possible. Meet with them personally over coffee or lunch, and ask how you can meet their informational needs. Act on the practical advice they give you.

2 Develop procedures for generating good news stories.

Set up an internal reporting system through which your staff can funnel news and feature story ideas to one person who has the responsibility for working with the newspaper. A good backlog of story possibilities may be just what the reporter needs on a slow news day. Develop attractive news release formats for future use, and facts sheets and background materials for distribution to the press on a range of company themes and issues.

Become familiar with the skilful art of writing a news release.

3 Respond promptly to all inquiries from the press.

If a reporter calls and you are busy, make sure you get back to the caller as soon as possible or you may miss the paper's deadline.

Always be aware of deadlines. Both weekly and daily newspapers have to work to fixed deadlines. Remember, old news is no news—so work to those deadlines.

4 Be professional in your dealings with the newspaper.

Be professional in all your business with the media. For example:

- Show no favouritism. Don't give one reporter a scoop and withhold details from others or you'll end up losing the trust of all of them.
- Be open and honest. Always tell the truth or you'll live to regret it. Your credibility will be destroyed as soon as a reporter finds out you haven't been honest.
- If you don't have the answer, don't try to make something up. If you can't answer specific questions, say

so—and promise to get back to the reporter with the answers before the deadline.

- Never ask a reporter to show you a story before it is published.

Because you are open and honest, things might not always go the way you'd like them to. But your candour puts your relationship on a firm footing and this can be a bonus in a time of crisis or when you request a favour.

5 Go out of your way to help reporters.

Newspapers usually respond positively to organisations which put themselves out to make the reporter's task easier. So:

- If the reporter can't make it to cover a story, offer to deliver some information to the newspaper.
- Keep reporters informed of upcoming events, projects or products suitable as stories or photographic features.
- A package of background material for reporters about your organisation, the project or the event will always help them present your story fairly and accurately.
- Remember to alert reporters when you have to cancel an event. Time is money in the news-gathering business.

6 Never try to be too smart with the reporter.

If you expect the media to provide a balanced, fair, accurate, and interesting coverage of your organisation, make sure that you are always balanced, fair, accurate, and interesting in your dealings with them.

Therefore, particularly in a time of crisis, be aware of the following:

- Never say 'no comment'. This tells the reporter that you're probably trying to hide something. The result could be 'bad press'. Say rather: 'I'm sorry, I can't answer that. The matter's under investigation and if I were to answer, I'd jeopardise my position.'
- Silence is never golden. Being unavailable for comment doesn't help much either. If a reporter is on to a story about one of your directors or an incident at the factory, your silence will only breed suspicion.
- Use 'off-the-record' statements judiciously—if at all. Certainly you should never go off-the-record if you do not know the reporter well. Remember also that if the reporter gets the same information on-the-record from another source and uses it, then your agreement has not been violated. And jumping erratically on- and off-the-record causes absolute confusion.

7 Tell reporters when they've done a good job.

A telephone call or a brief note of thanks is appropriate when a reporter has done a good job for your organisation. Occasionally, let the reporter's boss know it as well.

543

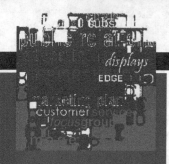

How to plan for a major public relations initiative

If you want to increase public awareness either of your organisation and its program or services, or of your company's attitude to a vital community issue, you have to plan the publicity: it won't just happen. Planning such a special initiative or campaign is really nothing more than preparing a blueprint of what is to be done and how and when each task will be accomplished. Start with a simple PR project, using this approach...

Appreciate the value of a planned PR approach.

A planned approach can help your organisation in a number of ways. In addition to providing clear direction for a special public relations thrust, it can also, for example:

- inform the community and customers about your organisation's overall programs and activities.
- build confidence in what your organisation and its staff are doing for the community.
- provide staff members with a common purpose which in turn will clarify their own concepts of the organisation's worth.
- raise awareness of common issues.
- rally support for the organisation's program.
- improve the relationship between your organisation and community.

Establish a task force.

Large organisations often employ specialised public relations staff; others outsource this responsibility. If your company is not in a position to use such services, however, a self-help approach could be considered. In this instance, responsibility for developing and implementing a plan is best vested in a small task force or committee comprising capable staff, community representatives, and even customers.

Define the challenge and identify the objectives.

A one-off public relations initiative is usually designed to correct a negative situation for the organisation, to achieve a well-defined once-only objective, or to maintain or improve an existing positive situation. Whatever your motivation, your first step is to define the message you wish to give the community. In 30 words or less, be able to answer the question: 'What precisely do we wish to accomplish?' A vague goal such as 'To get publicity for our company's environmental program' is relatively meaningless. This aim might be better stated as: 'To make clients, customers, and community aware of our company's concern for the environment and to induce community participation in our efforts to be concerned about our local environment.' Next, break this over-arching aim down into two sets of specific objectives—informational and motivational. Try to make them realistic, achievable and, hopefully, measurable.

4 Identify the target audiences and catalysts.

Specify as precisely as possible the groups of people who comprise the primary audiences for your message —clients, customers, local residents, other businesses and industries, local government agencies, community organisations, non-English speaking groups. Should a variation of your message be aimed at different groups? List also any community catalysts, such as schools, the local newspaper and radio, trade outlets, civic associations, or service organisations, who can help carry your message to the target audiences.

5 Develop a strategy and specify your tactics.

Compile a list of the ways you can use catalysts to carry your message to your audience. Remember, to convey your message, it isn't always necessary to initiate grandiose new events. Rather, it might be possible to focus on existing activities presented in novel ways. Take each idea in turn and subject it to long hard critical review. Is it feasible? Have you the time, skills, finance? If not, where can help be found? A wide array of

avenues is available—newsletters, displays, newspaper columns, videos, awards, ceremonies, community projects, public debates, news releases, stunts, T-shirts, speaking engagements… Target your strategies to specific audiences.

6 Draw up a calendar of events and activities.

Conceptualise your ideas and events into a schedule of activity to form a consistent flow of stories or events over a period of, say, six months or a year. This timetable, usually in chart form, should show starting and completion dates for each component event in the overall initiative and will provide an essential check list of progress.

7 Determine a budget.

Consider the financial aspects by outlining in sequence the costs of all activities. Balance aspirations and financial reality to arrive at a final list of usable proposals.

8 Specify evaluation procedures.

To provide essential feedback for the planning of future projects, determine in advance what criteria will be used to evaluate the success of each activity in your overall initiative. Short questionnaires, discussion, and simple response slips might suffice. The effectiveness of the total initiative can be assessed by comparing the overall community response with your original objectives.

 it's a fact

Campaigns need a cause. In the aftermath of the September 11 terrorist attacks on New York and Washington, for example, the US National Restaurant Association launched its *Cornerstone Initiative Public Relations Campaign* to encourage fearful Americans to support the nation's 858,000 restaurants during this most challenging period. The multifaceted and successful campaign included advertising in publications well-read by opinion and government leaders, and aggressive and creative public relations initiatives nationwide.

 quotable quote

Early steps in any public relations campaign are to identify the 'public' to whom the message is directed and to devise a strategy to ensure the credibility of the message. The strategy should also establish objectives relative to the various publics and define means to reach these groups.[46]

smile & ponder

The greatest public relations campaign can't turn a flawed product into a great one. As Yogi Berra once said about a slumping baseball club playing to empty seats, 'If the fans just don't want to come to the stadium, there's no way you can stop them.'

545

How to enhance your organisation's culture

Culture comprises tangible, intangible, and symbolic elements in organisational life—those customs, stories, practices, assumptions, values, symbols, ceremonies, and traditions that are shared by all members of an organisation. The culture indicates how employees should dress, think, work, behave, communicate, and make decisions in the workplace. Culture can be a most powerful influence; and leaders must work at enhancing their organisation's culture through maintenance, sustenance, or change...

1 Do not underestimate the role of culture.

The culture of your organisation is the set of beliefs that are shared, often subconsciously, by people in your organisation. It is a powerful influence that shapes behaviour, influences morale, and creates your organisation's identity. For example:

- It determines how individuals act and what they should value. Do men wear ties? Do superiors get called by their first names? Are meetings formal affairs? Staff who fail to come to grips with your organisation's culture will have trouble fitting in.

- It helps you understand employee motivation, performance standards, and actions. So, your company rewards individual effort—and yet you still wonder why some people have trouble working in a team?

- It can explain the presence of intergroup conflict. Do you ever wonder why your slow, analytical, patient, deliberate R&D people have trouble working with your action-oriented, flamboyant marketing group?

- It explains why change is so difficult to bring about. The targets of change are invariably those deeply imbedded cultural values, habits, behaviours, and images.

2 Appreciate that culture is not easy to change.

Organisational culture is usually so deeply rooted and pervasive that it is very difficult to change. However, because of a perceived need for more effective management approaches, a major restructuring, or changing market conditions, a decision to consciously reshape the corporate culture may be warranted. But remember, change could take years to achieve, be expensive, and create disruption for management and employees alike.

3 Begin with a vision.

The successful creation of a new organisational culture goes hand in hand with strong and respected leadership. Such leaders always have a vision of the type of company they want to develop and devise workable strategies to actively reshape the culture of the organisation.

4 Be patient in bringing about cultural change.

What steps might an effective leader take to bring about a change in the organisation's culture? Consider:

- *Intervention strategies*—such as team building, organisational development, or training.

- *Role modelling*—through your own behaviour, reveal the values and practices you want others to adopt.

- *Deliberate action*—such as participative decision-making, greater delegation of responsibility, or management-by-walking-around.

- *Recruitment*—hire and promote those people with the sought-after values and beliefs.

- *External consultants*—these are often needed to help your organisation cope in periods of confusion, upheaval, and anxiety.

- *Visible support*—particularly from top management, committed to change and clearly prepared to assist staff through a difficult period.

- *Resourcing*—equip the organisation with skills and materials to cope with change.

5 Focus on the elements of organisational culture.

If managers are seriously concerned with excellence and quality, then they cannot avoid becoming involved in maintaining or reshaping the elements and outward symbols that express what their organisation stands for. So, if you intend to examine, retain, change, or nourish your organisation's culture, the following aspects should be your focus:

- ☐ **Values**. Values are guidelines for behaviour. When operationalised, they permeate and shape the company. Strong leaders know what values they consider to be important —creativity, teamwork, persistence, accuracy, quality, etc.—and over time these become embedded in the organisation's culture. In turn, they are reflected in outward manifestations—customer creeds, slogans, mission statements, policy documents, logos, ceremonies, even architecture.

- ☐ **Tradition**. An organisation's culture is an accumulation of the influence of its major leaders and landmark events of the past, apocryphal stories, hero figures and colourful characters; and how these personify the values that the organisation wishes to sustain. The past invites emulation and helps to maintain group entity. The key is to capitalise on a rich history if it's there.

- ☐ **Procedures**. Decision-making processes, communication patterns, power-authority relationships, reward systems—every new and existing procedure should be consistent with the organisation's values.

- ☐ **Symbols**. Organisations have emblems, symbols, signs and slogans to represent what they stand for. Furniture, buildings, uniforms, logos, company literature, letterheads— they all contribute to organisational identity and should be a source of pride and loyalty.

- ☐ **Rituals and ceremonies**. What image do these public displays of culture portray and what values do they embody?

547

How to create a workplace where employees want to be

A workplace where employees want to be will be far more productive than one where they literally force themselves to come to work. Happiness is one of the most powerful and fundamental of the elements necessary to attract and keep the right people. Employees who are happy in their jobs will work hard and well—and will be reluctant to leave. Here's how you can create a happy and encouraging workplace...

viewpoint

"In order that people may be happy in their work, these three things are needed: They must be fit for it, they must not do too much of it, and they must have a sense of success in it."

– John Ruskin

it's a fact

CEO Herb Kelleher helped to make Southwest Airlines a place where employees want to be. Indeed, the airline is voted consistently one of America's most successful. Workers recently collected about $80,000 for a full-page newspaper ad thanking Kelleher 'for being a friend, not just a boss'. Imagine it.

don't forget

Do your share

- Be friendly and helpful to all staff.
- Greet your staff each morning; say goodbye on the way out.
- Share information and ideas with staff.
- Explore shared interests – holidays, hobbies, sport...
- Make compliments.
- Attend social events.

Create the right environment.

Given the cost of hiring new employees, and the destabilising effect of a high turnover of staff, you can't afford not to make your organisation a happy place to be. You need to look critically at the physical, social, and achievement environments to ensure that the mix of those three promotes a place where employees want to be. Ask staff periodically what they need to improve their person comforts and productivity and, where possible, undertake to have those needs met.

Know what makes people happy—and unhappy.

Research tells us that, if we were asked to remember the last time we felt unhappy, we would probably be thinking about what we don't have. As a manager, therefore, your task must be to affirm the positive, reinforce individuals' and groups' accomplishments, and share their successes. Keep employees focused on achievements and discourage dwelling on what could have been or what they don't have. Napoleon's description of leaders as 'dealers in hope' seems appropriate.

Develop a pleasant management style.

Managers who enjoy their work will do their job in more positive and constructive ways than manaaeir jobs. You and your attitude help set the tone. Employees are happier in a workplace run by managers who enjoy themselves, their work, and their employees. (The opposite also applies.) So target these things:

- *Manage your thoughts.* Think positively, choose to think the thoughts and stories about your work that you enjoy thinking about—and avoid thinking about the rest.

- *Enjoy your work.* The most important thing for you and for all those around you is that you like what you're doing. If you're not enjoying work, do something about it.

- *Act spontaneously.* Share those qualities that make you special.

4 Promote openness and trust.

An open, trusting environment provides a platform for growth; so authentic behaviours must be encouraged—even if you don't agree with that particular behaviour. There will always be plenty of opportunities for you to discuss the appropriateness of particular behaviours on a one-to-one basis. You must be able to rely on your employees at all times.

5 Recognise contributions.

One of the most common reasons for employees leaving an organisation is that they did not receive adequate recognition for their work. Employees' expect recognition and won't be happy until their expectations are satisfied. Your recognition will get the best results when it is of a type that is valued by the employee. Remembering an employee's birthday, for example, may be valued more by that person than a pay rise.

6 Involve families.

Families help to provide balance in people's lives. When things are going well at home, people are usually much happier and more productive at work. So you should take every opportunity to involve employees' families in the organisation's incentive bonuses scheme, in out-of-hours conferences and training sessions, and in social get-togethers. Keeping life partners happy is a productive investment. They, too, become committed to seeing the organisation succeed.

7 Encourage team identity.

The adage, 'a champion team beats a team of champions', proves itself in organisational life as well as in sporting life. You can promote the team identity by referring to your staff as a 'team', using 'we' instead of 'I' when talking about things to be done and, wherever possible, encouraging decision making by those likely to be most affected by the decisions.

8 Fight boredom in the workplace.

Any job can become boring and some jobs *are* boring. To combat boredom, continually re-examine all routine work, explore ways to alleviate the tedium, encourage suggestions, cross-train staff to do a variety of tasks, and vary procedures. Few employees look forward to turning up each morning to a boring job.

9 Empower your employees.

Make empowerment more than just a management 'buzzword'. Give people the authority and associated responsibilities to make decisions considered to be in the organisation's best interests. But remember that empowerment does not mean that you, as manager, can abrogate responsibility.

quotable quote

If you show people you don't care, they'll return the favour. Show them you care about them, and they'll reciprocate.[2]

How to turn your organisation into an empowered workplace

More frequently now, managers have to empower the workforce to reach new levels of performance. This means participative work practices and delegation of appropriate authority and responsibility. Empowerment, however, can't simply be conferred. It has to grow. To create it, conditions must be nurtured. Here's how you can foster conditions that will lead to empowerment in your organisation…

1 Tackle the barriers to empowerment.

One of the first steps in empowering staff is to deal with blockages to the empowering process and to overcome them. Examples of such barriers could include:

- Doubt that the system is sincerely committed to empowerment.
- Suspicion that 'empowerment' is simply another fad or buzzword. A feeling that 'what we do won't make any difference anyway'.
- Unhappiness with new roles that may be required. Reluctance to accept added responsibility without additional pay.
- Dislike of frequent meetings.
- Lack of time to take on the extra load.
- Unwillingness to give up authority and a preference for the comfort of routine.
- Concern that others may not carry their weight or share the increased workload.
- Fear of failure or, for some, success.

Many of these fears can be overcome if you strive to cultivate conditions that foster a climate of empowerment. But remember, as Ken Blanchard says: empowerment is not something you do to people, but *with* people.

2 Develop a culture and climate of trust.

Trust is the mortar for the bricks of empowerment. You can't have empowerment without trust at every level of your organisation. Trust breeds a climate of mutual respect that is conducive to open, frank discussions. Set the example: build trust by keeping your word and discussing your concerns openly.

3 Open up the channels of communication.

Communication is the key to empowerment. As an empowering leader you not only need to communicate well yourself, but you also need to facilitate communication among all staff. You must foster not only the movement of ideas and information to and from yourself, but also to, from, and between every other unit within the organisation. And by sharing feelings, goals, and information you ultimately build a sense of community within your group. So, practise empowering communication:

- Share your knowledge and skills.
- Offer and welcome constructive criticism or suggestions.
- Work with others in planning projects and initiatives.
- Respect the views of others by listening attentively.
- Form a network with others to hear and offer new ideas and information.
- Keep everyone in touch with news, ideas, suggestions, and information.
- Reduce the isolation of individuals and groups, a factor which can inhibit trust and empowerment.

 Foster creativity and risk-taking.

Empowered people are willing to take personal and professional risks. By so doing, they gain new insights about themselves, meet challenges, stretch their limits, solve problems, and test their mettle. They grow in self-assurance and, in turn, are better able to empower others.

Listen to and support new ideas in your organisation. Creativity and innovation are likely to flourish when people feel they can experiment, receive encouragement, and be defended (not penalised) for making honest mistakes.

 Be aware of your changed role.

In sharing power, you may feel you are giving up long-held authority. But you are, in fact, increasing your power because power shared is power multiplied. In an empowered organisation, instead of 'controlling subordinates for the good of the organisation', you now embrace a consultative and consensus-building role. Individuals and teams within the organisation coordinate with and support each other, while you facilitate the process and intervene only when problems occur.

 Be supportive.

Show ongoing support for your staff:

- Focus on results and acknowledge personal improvement.
- Foster a climate in which people enjoy what they do and are recognised for their contributions to the organisation.
- Help staff succeed. Be tolerant, sympathetic, and encouraging.
- Ensure resources are readily available.
- Promote understanding and support of staff efforts by focusing public attention, through media, newsletters and ceremonies, on outstanding work.

 Encourage personal and professional development.

Knowledge and skills are power—so personal and professional development is important for empowerment. Consider such strategies as these:

- Consult with staff about the types of professional development and training they need and provide it, along with the necessary time.
- Give staff time to think, plan, share, and learn from each other.
- Involve staff in discussions about budgets, staffing, resourcing, and so on.
- Encourage them to share with others what they have learned from training courses and reading.
- Provide technology together with adequate training and technical support.

don't forget

Empowerment means sharing

Empowerment doesn't mean giving up the power invested in your position – it means *sharing* it. Here's how:

- Delegate responsibility to the lowest level that can handle the task.
- Assist others in uncovering new opportunities for them to reveal their abilities.
- Encourage others to initiate projects or tasks that they think are important.
- Act as 'coach' as opposed to a 'player' when working with your staff members.
- Create a sense of ownership in those who do the work.
- Encourage your staff to take responsibility even when it has not been clearly assigned.
- Involve your people in the planning stages of all areas of activity within your organisation.
- Share your power in the interest of the overall organisational goal.
- Reward your staff for being innovative and for taking calculated risks.

Remember, however, that true empowerment always goes beyond 'participative management'. Your staff not only participate in decision making, but are also authorised to make decisions on their own without seeking approval from a higher level.

How to manage a learning organisation

A concept that continues to attract the management experts and practitioners is 'the learning organisation'. Such an organisation encourages everyone who works in it, or who has contact with it, to learn. It focuses on the 'learning habit': so that any activities undertaken for reasons of production, marketing, problem-solving, or customer service, for example, will also yield a harvest of learnings, reflections, insights, and new ideas for action. To turn your company into a learning organisation, take account of the following points…

1 Learn to learn—or you won't survive.

Mike Marquart writes that our large dinosaur organisations with pea-sized brains that flourished in the past cannot breathe and survive in today's new atmosphere of rapid change and intense competition. The survival of the fittest is quickly becoming the survival of the fittest-to-learn, he says. The advocates of learning organisations warn that traditional models won't cope in today's rapidly changing and increasingly technological society. The real issue today is one of knowledge management.

2 Focus on your people.

A learning organisation is achieved only if its people are eager to learn new ways of thinking. Peter Senge's message in *The Fifth Discipline* is simple—the learning organisation values and believes that competitive advantage derives from continued learning, both inductive and collaborative. He believes that people should be encouraged to put aside their old 'mental models', learn to be open with others, understand how their organisation really works, agree on a shared vision, and work together as a team to achieve a common purpose. In Senge's own words, a learning organisation is

> 'a group of people who are continually enhancing their capability to create their future… by changing individuals so that they produce results they care about and accomplish things that are important to them'.

From hiring the right people to creating an environment in which people are free to fail, your influence as manager will be vital in this regard.

3 Reflect on your new leadership role.

Senge sees the manager of a learning organisation as an ideal—the 'servant leader'—appealing to deeply held beliefs in the dignity and self-worth of people and the democratic principle that a leader's powers are given from those led. Together, manager and staff must develop towards a shared vision based on mutual trust and risk-taking.

Identify the knowledge you want to cultivate.

Three main types of knowledge will be present in your organisation—public knowledge (what everyone knows), industry-specific (what most people associated with your industry know), and firm-specific (what your people know about their own workplace). You need to define 'knowledge' for your organisation and consider how it can be converted into products and true competitive advantage. Intelligence, like any other asset, needs to be cultivated through action.

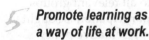
Promote learning as a way of life at work.

Work and learning should not be seen as separate forums. For example, it is your task to ensure that you transform into your organisation's 'way of life' such values as 'people are valuable resources', 'people must be nurtured and developed', 'people are partners in our enterprise', 'people need to be empowered', and 'structures that manipulate and control people are demeaning and outdated'. Unless such values are lived and modelled daily, they remain platitudes and a growing source of cynicism.

Encourage growth of 'human capital'.

Knowledge can grow in two ways: unleash the human capital already in existence, and channel talents to where they are needed and are most productive. The first can be achieved by using more of what people know and minimising mindless tasks, meaningless paperwork, and other unproductive activities. The second implies applying knowledge. Using interdisciplinary teams, for example, is one way of capturing, formalising, and capitalising on individual talents that might otherwise be lost to the organisation.

Promote a passion for experiment and risk.

Encourage learning through a work culture in which experimentation is valued and mistakes are accepted and promoted as learning experiences. Reward risk-taking. Though it may be difficult at times, in the interests of learning and progress, you need to be prepared to take a back seat.

Make a note...

Be familiar with and work towards the development of the attributes of a learning organisation. You should:

- have everyone reflect on practice
- consciously evaluate and live the company's goals, norms, and values
- have everyone experiment and question, searching for new strategies for innovation and action
- use teamwork and group approaches
- focus on self-esteem, self-discovery, and self-directedness
- value the whole person, including feelings and emotions, in learning
- motivate through empowerment
- foster continuous, informal, on-the-job learning
- focus on service and contribution to the whole
- take charge by giving control
- encourage people to act as if the business is their business
- recognise that the manager is the leading learner.

quotable quote

The phrase 'learning organisation' has become a handy label to talk about almost any company. The fact is, we don't know a lot about organisational learning. Sure, we know how to improve the learning of an individual or small team, but we don't know how to systematically intervene in the culture to create transformational learning across the organisation. For instance, we've discovered that a lot of individuals learning the same does not automatically mean that the organisation as a whole is learning.[4]

don't forget

There are prerequisites

The basic assumptions about learning which must be in place before you can create a learning organisation are:

- Learning is 'a good thing'.
- The quantity and quality of learning can be greatly enhanced if it is done deliberately and consciously, rather than left to chance.
- Learning is an ongoing, continuous process with no beginning and no end.
- Learning which is shared with others is much easier to sustain than solo learning.

The key to becoming a learning organisation is to begin with the right attitude.

553

How to develop policy using collaborative and consultative processes

Many companies have written policy statements on certain aspects of organisational life. Often, those policies outline consistent and coherent behaviour for staff and management. Policies can deal with a range of issues—leave, training, discipline, incentive schemes, recruitment, and so on. But they can become dated and decrepit. You can turn your policies into fresh and workable statements by actively involving your staff in creating and revising them—and gain commitment at the same time...

don't forget

Remember these rules...

To successfully facilitate a collaborative meeting...

- Treat everyone as a colleague.
- Speak with good intent.
- Ask questions from genuine curiosity, not from cynicism.
- Openly disagree with anyone in the group.
- Avoid attributions about other motives, thinking, etc.
- Invent new options that break log-jams.
- Retract proposals until agreement is reached.
- Embrace breakdowns as part of reaching breakthroughs.
- Respect confidentiality.[5]

viewpoint

"Collaboration involves:
- different views and perspectives
- shared goals
- building new shared understandings
- creation of new values.
It can be used to reach goals, solve problems, create policy, or resolve conflicts."

– Robert Hargrove in *Mastering the Art of Creative Collaboration*

1 Determine a need for the new policy.

The most effective policy stems from a grassroots need for it. For example, concern among staff that on-site training is inadequate and neglected, creates a feeling that 'We need to do something about this'. It is often difficult to create commitment to a training policy when it is management that senses the need, and then compiles and imposes a written policy statement. When presented with it, employees are likely to become defensive and resistant to the new policy's implementation. In short, there must be a clear articulation of need, preferably from the staff members themselves, if a policy is to have both credibility and direction.

2 Establish a representative policy committee.

As well, the more a policy statement is seen as the outcome of representative review and drafting, the more likely it will be approved and accepted by the employees. The process of formulating a specific policy should be outlined to all relevant groups before their participation is sought on a small representative policy committee. Ensure that the members of this committee possess skills in information-gathering, managing an extensive consultative process, writing policy statements, and communicating with the organisation. The committee is responsible for carrying the development of the relevant policy to completion using collaborative and consultative processes.

3 Gather data through wide involvement.

The policy committee can create opportunities for expansive discussion of the topic being reviewed. Strategies for staff involvement can include meetings, workshops, discussion sheets, morning teas, and other formal and informal consultation. Group discussions should be held at times convenient for all participants and include relevant special interest groups.

In a discussion of a possible change to the company uniform policy, for example, a local uniform manufacturer could be represented. First gain agreement on a clear 3-5 line rationale to underlie the final policy; then raise all relevant issues—in discussions relating to uniforms, for example, consider such aspects as the existing dress code, the case for and against uniforms, availability, equity issues, relevant legislation, design, cost, and so on. Outline the decision-making process to be adopted.

 Draft the policy statement.

Having obtained data and views from organisation-wide consultation, the policy committee should now produce a draft policy statement. Key points to consider would include:
- Ensure the statement is concise, unambiguous, readily linked to identifiable practice.
- Limit the document to 2-3 A4 pages.
- Group the details logically and as numbered cumulative points.
- Make sure each point can be adequately addressed by this question: 'How can we put this into practice?'
- Consider drafting a couple of alternative policies to stimulate discussion and ensure that the final adopted policy will indeed result from active consultation.

 Gain support for the policy.

A consensus policy statement should be arrived at only after reasonable consultation and debate. Publicise and promote the document through presentations at staff meetings, leaflets, or items in the company newsletter.

These are the important questions to address when considering the appropriateness of the policy statement:
- Does the policy statement convince me that the topic needed to be addressed?
- Does the statement give me a clear message? If so, what is it?
- Is the statement easy to follow? Do I clearly understand the language used?
- Is there enough information in the statement to guide me in implementing this policy? If not, what is missing?
- Does the statement cover all important issues? What other issues should have been treated?
- Are there any other documents or resources needed to help me understand the policy more fully or to implement it effectively?
- How will the policy benefit me? How can I use it?

Support for the drafted document can be obtained through resolutions passed at meetings or forums, or through negotiation, surveys, ballots, or petitions. Circulate the refined policy statement.

 Convert the policy into practice.

An accepted policy must be linked to short-, medium-, and long-term implementation plans. These should outline roles and responsibilities of those involved, timelines for the introduction of the various components, and procedures for periodic review and evaluation.

smile & ponder

A centipede consulted an owl about the pain it felt in its legs.

Said the owl, 'You have far too many legs! If you became a mouse you would have only four legs – and one-twenty-fourth the amount of pain.'

'That's a very good idea,' said the centipede. 'So show me how to become a mouse.'

'Oh, it's no good asking me about details of implementation,' said the owl. 'I only make the policy in this place.'[6]

quotable quote

Good policy identifies and articulates the values and the basic principles to be applied to specific needs in an organisation... Effective policy sets direction, but it does not give directions. Staff and administrators are left to apply the policy with discretion required by circumstances and their own professional judgement. Professionalism is given guidance. If effective consultation has occurred, that guidance will be welcome and professionally enhancing.[7]

 it's a fact

It is a proven fact that a flock of birds flying together in a V-formation has the lifting power to carry twice the distance of a single bird flying alone.

How to safeguard your intellectual property

Intellectual property (IP) has become one of today's most important business issues. People work hard to nurture their businesses and establish their names or reputations—but fail to protect (through patents, trademarks, copyright and other devices) the ideas, inventions, processes, and logos they create. The result is that such valuable assets can fall into the hands of rivals, and the creators can lose their competitive advantages. It is essential, therefore, that businesses identify their intellectual property, protect it, and develop initiatives to manage it. Consider these preliminary steps in that process...

1 Be clear about the concept.

In Australia, the federal agency administering intellectual property is *IP Australia*, which defines intellectual property as 'the property of your mind or intellect', and embraces proprietary knowledge. Securing legal protection today is absolutely essential. If you don't protect it, you could lose it.

2 Keep your smart idea confidential – until it's protected.

Be tight-lipped about your new ideas and do everything to ensure others don't take and use your intellectual property. If talking to others about your new idea or invention, use a confidentiality agreement, prepared preferably by your legal advisor. Once signed by the other party, the agreement prevents them from disclosing to others, or using, your ideas without your permission.

3 Check that your idea is unique by conducting your own research.

To obtain patent protection, any idea must be both novel and inventive. So, early in the process, you need to ascertain if your idea or invention is new or if it has already been claimed by others. A keyword search online might determine if someone else has already published, manufactured, or patented your idea. If, for example, you believe you have a new handgrip for a golf club, a search using key words like 'golf', 'golf clubs', 'grips', 'handgrip', 'sporting equipment', etc., could provide initial answers. If the idea still appears novel, you can try an Internet patent search using similar key words and visiting such sites as www.uspto.gov or www.ibm.com/ibm/licensing.

4 Determine what kind of IP protection you may need.

IP protection takes various forms...
- *patents* protect new or improved products or processes, business methods
- *trademarks* protect words, symbols, pictures, sounds, scent, or combinations, to distinguish the goods and services of one trader from those of another
- *design registration* protects the shape or appearance of manufactured goods

---

it's a fact

In 1972, Kambrook developed the electrical power board. It became an immediate success, creating massive company growth. Kambrook, however, neglected to patent the idea and lost millions of dollars to competitors who were free to copy the product. Don't fall into a similar trap.

viewpoint

"If the Internet economy has taught us anything, it's that the physical world determines less and less of what we value....The stuff between workers' ears has become treasure to today's managers. The challenge now for managers is how to capture, harness, develop, and protect that knowledge."
– *Fortune*, 22 November 1999

ask yourself

Do we own the IP we're using? Can we prove it?
☐ What are the processes or knowledge critical to our business success? If unique to our business, how are we keeping them confidential?
☐ Did an external agency write and/or design our software, or marketing material and leaflets? Did the contract specify who owned the IP?
☐ What strategies do we have to monitor our IP?

- *copyright* protects original material in literacy, artistic, dramatic or musical works, films, broadcasts, multimedia and computer programs
- *circuit layout rights* protect three-dimensional configurations of electronic circuits in integrated circuit products or layout designs
- *plant breeder's rights* protect new plant varieties
- *trade secrets* protect know-how and other confidential or proprietary information.

5 Take steps to formally register your IP.

Having identified your IP type, you can then register that protection formally. In Australia, check out www.ipaustralia.gov.au. You may, for example, take out a patent, register its design, and develop a branding strategy based on a registered trademark, including both colour and shape. Registration can be undertaken by an individual or, for stronger protection, by a patent attorney.

6 Lodge a provisional patent.

If you believe your idea is patentable then, before its public release, lodge a provisional patent—in Australia, with IP Australia. The do-it-yourself cost to record your legal ownership of the idea will be minimal. This provides twelve months' protection while you ascertain whether there is any interest in your idea and whether you can licence it, sell it, or raise capital to progress the idea. Following this twelve-month period, you can then lodge a full patent specification for a standard or an innovation patent. A patent attorney can assist in suggesting the best option for you.

7 Keep an eye out for infringers.

Use the vast resources of IP Australia's trade marks and patent registers, the internet, industry publications, and libraries to keep abreast of technological developments and to monitor your competitors. IP rights give you a legal basis to protect your ideas from unauthorised use. If you find that your rights are infringed, you can seek legal action and even compensation through the courts against the offender. Remain alert for copycats and rivals who infringe. Seek legal advice to ensure prompt action.

8 Access expert advice.

Smart innovators obtain the advice of IP professionals sooner rather than later. To assess what coverage your business may need, check with a patent attorney, IP consultant, or local inventors' association for advice to help you understand the method and costs of protecting, commercialising, and managing your intellectual property. And don't forget, with new ideas or inventions, keep track of all your development costs to help you and your lawyer place a value on your IP.

9 Monitor staff confidentiality.

A few vital points on matters of staff…
- Trust only those you absolutely must with any information or trade secrets integral and vital to your business.
- Rather than lose staff and possible trade secrets, do all you can via rewards and incentives to keep good people.
- Ask those with any knowledge of trade secrets to sign confidentiality agreements before departing your organisation.

don't forget

Advice from IP Australia…

- Identify all IP linked to your business.
- Check that you own all IP used in your business or that you have the right to use it.
- List registered IP and unregistered IP; place a dollar value on each.
- List other valuable assets such as clients' lists and corporate knowledge.
- Identify key staff involved in developing, maintaining, and protecting your IP and get them to sign confidentiality agreements.
- Educate staff on the nature of IP and how to protect it.
- Consider ways you can use the IP system in your overall business strategy.
- Develop an infringement strategy such as insuring your IP against infringement of someone else's IP.
- Search the patent, trademark, and design databases, as well as other literature and the Internet to ensure that your ideas are new and to avoid infringing the rights of others.
- Maintain secrecy and be first to market.
- Make effective trademarks the core of your brand and image building strategy. [8]

557

How to manage your organisation's intellectual capital

An organisation's most valuable resource is its knowledge—an aspect of its intellectual capital. Knowledge can be tacit (embedded in the minds of employees and, therefore, difficult to manage) or explicit (expressed in some record from which it can be retrieved). Knowledge is a vital corporate resource, on which an organisation thrives and survives. Like any other resource, however, it needs to be managed and successful organisations have developed ways of doing so. We can learn from their experience…

viewpoint

"Knowledge Management is the process through which organisations generate value from their intellectual and knowledge-based assets.'

– Santosus & Surmacz
in *The ABC of Knowledge Management*, 2001

ask yourself

The events of September 11 (2001) demonstrated the vital part that knowledge plays in everyday organisational life.

World Trade Centre tenants lost many of their employees. Some lost all. The accumulated knowledge and know-how – skills, general knowledge, contacts, experience, ways of doing business, networks of communication, institutional memory, organisational culture –all were lost forever. Some organisations were unable to overcome that loss.

It's almost impossible to place a value on an organisation's knowledge and intellectual capital.

Have you reflected lately upon the importance to your organisation of its workers' knowledge and intellectual capital?

1 Understand what is meant by intellectual capital.

Intellectual capital (IC) is often confused with intellectual property (IP), but is a much broader concept. IC consists of all the intangible assets of your organisation—skills, general knowledge, technological leadership, and learning ability. Most IP relates to tangible assets—databases, for example—and intangibles such as trademarks, patents, and copyright.

You have two forms of intellectual capital: human and structural. Human capital is your employees; structural capital is what remains behind when all your employees go home— manuals, training materials, etc.

Knowledge is developed and transmitted by two different networks of people who interact:[9] *communities of practice* (individuals and groups within your organisation that emerge around a discipline or problem) and *networks of practice* (peers from other companies, groups, and associations outside your organisation). The challenge is to develop, manage, and protect that knowledge by bringing people together across different structures, functions, and hierarchies.

2 Recognise knowledge as the basis of competitive advantage.

Properly managed, knowledge can provide a competitive advantage that might be expressed in doing things faster, cheaper, and better than your competitors. As CEO of General Electric, Jack Welch claimed that 'releasing the ideas of our people is what we've got to do if we're going to win.' To understand the influence your organisation's storehouse of knowledge has on your bottom line, you will need to:

- identify and evaluate the role of knowledge in the business you are in
- match the revenues with the knowledge assets that produce them
- develop a strategy for investing in and exploiting your intellectual assets.[10]

3 Create the right environment where people want to be.

As part of your strategy you will need to build a corporate environment—a knowledge culture that fosters a desire for knowledge among your people, rewards their efforts and achievements, and ensures its continued creation, dissemination, and application. An appreciation of how communities of practice generate, refine, and disseminate ideas will help you to build a place where people want (choose) to be. Your efforts will be rewarded as you retain key people and attract others who want to be part of your team, and tap into your organisation's intellectual resource and knowledge-creating capabilities.

To cultivate this situation, you will need to embrace a wide variety of activities such as cultivating creativity, fostering innovation, encouraging personal networks, providing mentoring, supporting appropriate training by experts in particular fields, overseeing the development of an infrastructure providing data networks and access to resources, participating in product development teams, and using job rotation and other strategies to provide opportunities for people to share data and work in close proximity to others engaged in similar endeavours.

Demonstrate flexibility.

Management expert, Peter Drucker, believes that every organisation's success depends on the performance of its knowledge workforce, thereby placing increased demands on those managing this vital resource.[11] Knowledge workers can be genuine wealth-creators, but most of them require a more flexible style of management than a traditional top-down approach. In fact, any

attempts to manage knowledge workers top-down is likely to result in an exodus of talent. Remember, in a traditional workforce, the worker serves the system; in a knowledge workforce, the system must serve the worker. In a knowledge workforce, the workers are not labour; they are capital that requires investing in. You need to identify ways to increase the productivity of knowledge workers.

Invest in your best.

If you fear that some employees will leave your organisation with valuable know-how, the property of the organisation, you will succeed only in stifling creativity. A far better use of your energy would be to invest in those with a desire and capacity to absorb and use knowledge and who are prepared and willing to transfer that knowledge to other parts of your organisation so that everyone benefits. Drucker advises leaders in knowledge-based businesses to spend more time with promising professionals: get to know them, mentor them, challenge them, and encourage them.[11]

Forget looking for shortcuts.

If you believe people are your greatest asset, knowledge management must touch almost every aspect of organisational life. There is no one way, and certainly no quick way, of building a knowledge organisation. An ongoing and comprehensive review of values, goals, policies, and measurement will be essential; and new programs and initiatives are likely to be required.

 quotable quote

Knowledge is as fundamental and versatile as electricity. It can do almost anything. You must first ask what the business needs, then ask how knowledge management can help.[12]

 it's a fact

According to the US Association of Executive Search Consultants, 2001-02, the number of Chief Knowledge Officers (CKOs) and Chief Information Officers (CIOs) is rising 21 per cent per year.

 viewpoint

"The power of intellectual capital is the ability to breed ideas that ignite value."

– Annual Report 2000, J.P. Morgan Chase

quotable quote

Knowledge management has become one of the more trendy topics in management circles.[13]

 viewpoint

"Ideas are capital. The rest is just money."

– Deutsche Bank advertisement, *Wall Street Journal* April, 2001

How to cater for diversity in the workplace

Embracing equal employment opportunities (EEO) and affirmative action has delivered far-reaching benefits to organisations and to the main groups (women and ethnic minorities) immediately affected. Although often linked to EEO legislation, age, religion, sexual orientation, and disabilities are also being widely recognised. Effectively managed diversity can become a competitive advantage for organisations prepared to seize the opportunities it presents. Here are some key considerations…

viewpoint

"Diversity is our reality. We need to make it our strength." [14]

– Roosevelt Thomas

research says

US Research by the Hudson Institute and Workforce 2000, in conjunction with the US Department of Labor, found that:

- The net growth in the US labour force will come predominantly from immigrants and women, with women accounting for more than 47 per cent of the total workforce. Sixty-one per cent of all women in the United States will be participating in the workforce.
- African-Americans will comprise up to 12 per cent of the labour force, Hispanics 10 per cent, and Asians 4 per cent.
- The US workforce will continue to mature, with people aged between 35 and 54 representing 51 per cent of the workforce.

Diversity is a workplace reality in the United States.

1 Take note of the numbers.

According to the Department of Immigration and Multicultural Affairs, Australia is the most ethnically diverse country in the world, with people from more than 130 language backgrounds and 220 nationalities. Some 23 per cent of the population was born overseas; a further 27 per cent has at least one overseas-born parent. Diversity is here to stay and it's set to increase even further. Organisations must embrace diversity. Any perceptions of discrimination will inevitably take a heavy toll on job performance. You simply can't afford not to cater for, and promote, diversity.

2 Realise the benefits.

A diverse workforce can provide a wide variety of benefits. People from a variety of backgrounds bring their own unique and special experiences and know-how that facilitate the way things happen and the way problems are solved. They can contribute to competitive advantage in an increasingly global marketplace. In addition, a better understanding of cultural idiosyncrasies can contribute to and attract a much broader range of customers. Anecdotal evidence suggests that many customers feel more relaxed about dealing with a more heterogeneous organisation that demonstrates an awareness of cultural differences.

Diversity has competitive implications, too—especially for smaller organisations. These have an even better chance of establishing a truly diverse culture and managing it successfully. Smaller organisations are typically not burdened by a large, entrenched bureaucracy, and it is easier for them to make changes while the business owner maintains greater control over the process. Customers expect small businesses to be more mindful of differences and to better serve their needs.

3 Ensure a committed leadership.

Changing hiring policies will not, of itself, ensure success. A strong commitment from the organisation's key people is also critical. When he was executive director of the American Institute for Managing Diversity in Atlanta, Roosevelt Thomas recommended that the question leaders needed to ask was: 'Given the diverse workforce I've got, am I getting the productivity, does it work as smoothly, and is morale as high, as if every person in the company was the same sex, race, and nationality?' A leadership role, according to Dr Thomas, is to '…create an environment where no one is advantaged or disadvantaged, an environment where "we" is everyone and in which people feel their contributions are valued'. He urged that everyone, from the boss down, must demonstrate sensitivity to cultural differences.[14]

Demonstrate open communication.

A key step in the effective management of a diverse workplace does not involve any financial outlay and usually warrants few dramatic changes to the way you operate. It simply requires that you create a climate in which people feel free to raise issues without fear or reprisal. To achieve this, you need to:

- make sure you make every attempt to really hear what your people are saying
- get to know and understand individuals' needs
- ensure that two-way dialogue is taking place
- act immediately on any negative issues that come to your attention
- empower people to be part of solutions.

Open dialogue and open minds are the essentials.

Build personal relationships.

In *In Search of Excellence*, Tom Peters defined business as 'a series of relationships between people'. The need to build relationships in diverse workplaces is even stronger as these relationships are a key communication medium. This relationship-building can include mentoring and coaching programs. Familiarise yourself also of the types and nature of external support that is available—often free of charge— for initiatives to build workplace relationships across diverse groups.

Invest in training.

Diversity provides additional opportunities for everyone in the organisation. People usually jump at an opportunity to demonstrate their skills with colleagues, so training needs can often be satisfied by using the in-house resources. And training can become an effective team-building opportunity. Successful diversity training needs

- to be developed through a partnership of internal employees
- to involve a senior-level advocate or champion
- to be based on sound research
- to occur in a supportive corporate culture
- to be skills-based
- to focus on improving observed behaviour in the workplace
- to be supported by other initiatives and activities
- to be thoroughly planned, implemented, and measured for its impact on the organisation.[15]

don't forget

A matter of size

In smaller organisations, people are often less threatened by diversity. They develop trust more quickly and are more open, and there tends to be a greater level of confidentiality. Smaller organisations develop approaches that use the most-qualified people available, regardless of their backgrounds.

Conversely, diversity can be a more complex issue for management to address in larger organisations.

don't forget

Be prepared to learn

When dealing with racial differences in the workplace:

- get over the fear of making mistakes
- be prepared to learn about your own cultural biases
- understand the importance of relationships, especially in Asian and Islamic cultures
- encourage dissent in people from more communitarian cultures.

561

How to manage diverse ethnic groups

An increasing number of employees come from different countries, cultures, and social backgrounds. The more managers learn about, understand, and become sensitive to those differences, the greater their influence over discriminatory and politically incorrect practices. Here are some important guidelines for dealing with diverse cultures...

it's a fact

Diversity: A variety of conditions and activities that create an environment where people can achieve their fullest potential – regardless of the many ways they may differ from each other.

quotable quote

All people hold cultural beliefs – norms, rules and values, which have developed through their experiences at home, in school and in the wider community. Most people also, perhaps unconsciously, believe that their own particular set of values is the 'right' set – the idea of 'how things have always been'. The resultant actions or non-actions from this prejudice affect relationships with those who hold different values. An awareness of one's own conditioning and sense of values is required if one is to grasp the significance of and understand the values held by others. An awareness of the effect of cultural conditioning on behaviour will increase sensitivity to both clients and colleagues whose behaviour and values are different.[16]

1 Be aware of the issue.

If your staff comprises men and women who come from different cultures or hold differing beliefs, it can sometimes lead to misunderstandings and conflicts. As a manager, you must not ignore this situation, since it is your responsibility to develop a smooth-running and collaborative workplace. But it isn't always easy to change deeply ingrained perceptions held by newcomers and by English-speaking nationals. Newcomers must embrace our ways and we must also learn to understand their attitudes and customs.

2 Find out about ethno-cultural backgrounds.

No one can be expected to know everything about every cultural group, but there is no excuse for not doing your homework about your own employees' cultural backgrounds. You should know about their preferred ways of greeting, sense of humour, emotions, perceptions of time and punctuality, particular gestures, attitude towards authority and the opposite sex, and status symbols. Good bookshops carry a wide selection of information to help you improve your knowledge of different cultures. Government agencies can also assist.

3 Adopt politically correct behaviour.

By being aware of cultural traits and idiosyncrasies you will become an even more effective communicator—and your flexibility will be acknowledged and admired by others. Set an example. Demonstrate your commitment to equal employment opportunity by always employing and promoting the best person for the job. Use terminology that is not offensive when referring to race, beliefs, or cultural background. Never let racial, religious, or homophobic slurs in the workplace go unchecked. Language can be potentially a powerful vehicle of discrimination; through language we can, intentionally or unintentionally, describe people in derogatory, hurtful, condescending, or alienating ways.

4 *Understand the idiosyncrasies of communication.*

'Communication' means different things to different people; and its interpretation differs across cultures. In Australia, for example, criticising the Prime Minister (the person elected to that position) seems acceptable. In some countries, however, this would be seen as a criticism of the position and, therefore, would be totally unacceptable—and punishable.

 5 *Encourage social events.*

Every opportunity should be taken to encourage employees to get to know one another through formal or informal social activities. When new employees join your organisation you may use a 'buddy system' or mentors as part of the induction process. Later you may celebrate their various national days—even include information about cultural groups in your organisation as part of your staff training. Much more will be achieved from building on individual differences than ignoring them.

 6 *Recruit, promote and train.*

Your organisation can only improve by virtue of the high calibre of your people. Employees representing a variety of cultural and belief groups can add a new dimension to your organisation—if you take the time to identify and use their particular skills. Don't pay 'lip service' to equal employment opportunity; let your actions do the talking.

 7 *Be aware of your nonverbal signals.*

Experts tell us that our body language communicates more than half the meaning when we communicate face-to-face. So we need not only to be aware of our body language but also to use it to ensure we communicate appropriate messages. Use all of your skills to eliminate any chance of mistaken perceptions of prejudice.

 8 *If in doubt—don't.*

If you're unsure how something will be interpreted—don't do it. It is far better to err on the side of conservatism than to create an embarrassment. Take humour, for example. What may be seen as fun in one culture may be taken as a personal affront in another. Similarly, an assertive stance may be interpreted differently in different cultures. Consideration of an individual's cultural sensitivities will always remain a key management quality.

 9 *Recognise and deal with problems immediately.*

Inevitably, problems among minority groups will occur. Denying prejudice if it exists in order to avoid problems is unrealistic, stressful, and could be, in terms of anti-discrimination legislation, disastrous. Never try to handle such problems by ignoring them or believing that they will just go away. Let employees see that you are committed to dealing with problems as they occur. You will gain the respect of all people for your actions.

 quotable quote

Diversity is a concept that recognises that many kinds of people are in today's workforce. It is often misused to suggest only race or race and gender. In reality, there are many other kinds of diversity. They include age, religion, varying abilities and disabilities, sexual orientation, education and so on. Diversity generally refers to employees already in place.

Some people speak of *managing diversity*, a phrase that experts generally discourage because it suggests that diversity is a problem that somehow must be contained. A better phrase is *valuing diversity*, which describes the process of recognising and appreciating differences, and using those differences for the benefit of the whole organisation.

It sees diversity as an opportunity, not a problem.[17]

mini seminar

To discriminate against the physically challenged is now illegal. But because accommodations must sometimes be made to assist this group, other workers can become resentful. This is a typical challenge for the manager in a diverse workforce. Integrating women into positions traditionally held by men (or vice versa) is another such challenge of diversity.

How might your organisation cope with such possible resentment?

How to ensure a healthy and safe workplace

Today, managers have legal and moral responsibilities to attend to their employees' health and safety at work. Managers must introduce and apply safeguards and procedures guaranteeing the physical security and welfare of employees; and if an accident occurs, managers must be able to do whatever is appropriate. The following strategies might be considered...

1 Make workplace health and safely a priority.

Consult the Workplace Health and Safety legislation governing your area. Advise your employees of these requirements, provide the necessary training, and demonstrate clearly your commitment to a healthy and safe work environment.

2 Make use of any available advisory services.

Most government agencies are only too willing to advise you on the legislatory requirements and will usually accept an invitation to review your procedures and help you develop workable policies.

3 Appoint a workplace health and safety officer.

Find an employee willing to assume the role of a health and safety officer—some legislation actually demands that. Relevant training programs are usually available through tertiary training institutions. The trained employee will play an invaluable role in implementing the health and safety program for your organisation. A safety committee may provide a support option.

4 Involve employees.

A healthy and safe workplace is the responsibility of everyone in the organisation; so provide opportunities for employees to be involved in a consideration of this initiative. Employees must know that management is committed to occupational health and safety, and that all staff are empowered to act in the organisation's best interests.

5 Keep records.

Your safety record is one measure that others will use to judge your organisation. Many potential employees are reluctant to join an organisation that is not serious about the safety of its employees. Reviewing statistics is one way of making sure that health and safety issues have been dealt with satisfactorily.

Prevent problems before they happen.

Document your procedures and train employees to follow them. Start with your staff induction program. An Australian study, reported by the Australian Institute of Management, claimed that it is six times more expensive not to train than to train—findings which would be conservative when the costs resulting from accidents are calculated.

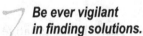

Be ever vigilant in finding solutions.

Be wary of quick-fix solutions. If employees are required to engage in excessive overtime, this could be indicative of inadequate staffing levels or ineffective procedures. Remember that productivity levels not only decline when employees are required to work long hours but workers are also adversely affected on the following day. Procedures also need to be in place to ensure that areas of non-conformance are identified, addressed, and monitored through a management review process.

If an accident occurs, take immediate action.

Make sure that documented procedures are carried out during any accident. Your first concern must be the health and safety of staff and any customers. Review the procedures after the accident and make any changes that will improve accident prevention and that will deal with any accidents should they occur. Keep a detailed record of the incident for possible workers compensation claims, litigation, or future corrective action. Provide any rehabilitation necessary, and recognise any significant staff achievements in coping with the incident.

Conduct regular checks.

Work closely with your Workplace Health and Safety Officer and insist on regular audits and reports. One of the added benefits of management-by-walking-around is that you keep your own close check on health and safety issues in your organisation. Adopt the Western Australian government's approach to health and safety program: *Thinksafe SAM* reminds us to:

Spot the hazard.
Assess the risk.
Make the changes.

Focus on continuous improvement.

When (or if) problems occur, initiate corrective actions that will ensure there is no recurrence of that problem. The importance of documented procedures cannot be overemphasised.

---

research says

Research by the World Health Organisation has revealed that workers who are desk-bound for long periods are at a greater risk of developing cancer. WHO stated that workplace inactivity, already linked to heart disease and diabetes, also increased risk of diseases such as colon and breast cancers, and possibly endometrial cancer and prostate cancer.

---

viewpoint

"Employers must understand, if only for productivity and morale reasons, that workers who are stuck at desks and computer terminals need breaks. Prompts, reminders and enforcements about ergonomic guidelines for spending time at a computer terminal should be put in place, because many people won't take a break unless the employer demands that of them."

– Professor Neville Owen
University of Wollongong

---

 quotable quote

Companies that turn their attention to health and safety at the workplace, have found rewards surpassing their expectations. Gains include enhanced productivity, improved industrial relations, cost effectiveness, a more skilled workforce, efficient communities, greater flexibility, and better informed decision making.[18]

How to run a better office

Managing a modern office can be demanding. It requires some sensible and well-considered strategies to deal with people, resources, time, and paper. Depending on the size of your organisation and your administrative style, your office and its adjuncts can act as Mission Control, or the Fortress of Solitude, or something in between. Over time, it will become what you make it. Meanwhile, here are some suggestions to start you thinking about running a better office...

Consider the premises.

It may not be possible to improve your existing office arrangement, but it's amazing how often people are prepared to accept an unsatisfactory layout just because they're used to it. Life is already filled with an ample supply of distractions and discomforts—so why make life in your office more difficult than it needs to be?

Take a look at your office. The office area should be efficient, neat, attractively arranged, and business-like. The work environment should be well-lit, equipped with appropriate furniture, and easily accessible in terms of visitors and work flow. Are phones, equipment, files and materials conveniently placed? Do you have adequate privacy? Has all unwanted furniture or dated equipment been removed? Have you added some greenery and art?

And pay special attention to the reception area: it must be welcoming, comfortable and informative; after all, it is the first port of call for customers, clients, and suppliers. Be imaginative with decor and setting.

Provide the appropriate equipment.

Research has shown that communication consumes over 70 per cent of a manager's time—phone calls, visitors, conferences, correspondence, writing, meetings, in- and out-trays, and so on.

For starters, then, investigate the communicative tasks that you and your office staff are required to handle; determine if you have the appropriate tools to carry out these functions efficiently. Focus for example on technology—phones (multi-feature units, conference, smartphones), answering machines, computers, ancillary equipment, appropriate software, photocopiers, facsimile machines, modems, intercoms, email, pagers, security systems. And check out also the many valuable and often inexpensive administrative aids now available—multi-purpose diaries, visual wall planners, modern filing, software

it's a fact

Apparently, having an office which looks like a bomb hit it isn't such a bad thing, particularly in the case of the American writer who recently won a $20,000 office refit for having 'the most disorganised office in America'.

Wendy Badman's office, full with paper, keepsakes and dead potted plants, was judged to be the country's most abominable and worthy of the award.

For her part, Ms Badman said her office is 'creatively cluttered' rather than disorganised – which, after all, is what messy people always say.

viewpoint

"Nothing is really lost. It's just where it doesn't belong."
– Suzanne Mueller

quotable quote

If your surroundings are depressing, your work may suffer. So brighten up whatever you can to create a pleasant and comfortable working environment...

Paper processing, perhaps more than any other office function, depends on a responsive physical environment: easy access to files and equipment.[19]

programs, pocket and digital diaries, to-do lists, and so on.

Is your office equipment ready to carry you well into the twenty-first century, or are you more appropriately equipped for the 1980s?

 ### Focus on your office staff.

If you're lucky enough to have a personal assistant and other support staff, ensure that each has helped compile a clear list of responsibilities relating to mail, telephone, paperwork, appointments, visitors, filing, office organisation, human relations, typing, accounting, confidentiality, and so on. How can you help your assistant make better use of time—by providing training? by improving conditions? by altering work schedules? How can your assistant become even more effective?

Remember too that, for many people, their first impression of your organisation is the one formed when first greeted by office staff. When did you last discuss with your office personnel the importance of this up-front role—their appearance, and their manner and attitude in responding to public, customers, clients, and suppliers.

 ### Establish workable procedures.

When did you last analyse the way things are done in the office? Many 'procedures' aren't—they're just habits. What *are* your current procedures? How is mail, for example, best opened, screened, and distributed? What procedure do you

have for weeding out irrelevant files and records? Do you create work with endless forms? Have you recently checked telephone etiquette? Or reception area courtesies? Take a look at each office task and ask:

- Is it really needed? If not, stop doing it.
- Is it being done at the right time?
- Is the right person doing it?
- Can the process be simplified without losing effectiveness?
- Can the process be computerised?

How effective are your office procedures for tackling the paper war? Does your office staff try to adhere to such basic rules of office management as:

- Never handle a piece of paper twice.
- Never leave the office until your desk is clean.
- Don't write it; phone it.
- Never stack paper.
- Work from a to-do list. And so on.

 ### Check the access to your office.

Do staff have ready access to you? Do you have an open door policy, or do you require appointments to be made? Just how accessible are you? With all the demands placed on a manager's time today, this can become a crucial factor in your relationships with employees.

 ### Remember: the final image is important.

Courtesy, respect, availability, accessibility, appearance, efficiency— all are vital elements for you to consider in fostering for your office a positive image within the organisation.

 ### it's a fact

Don't become obsessed about how neat and orderly your desk is – or how neat your employees' work areas are. People work effectively in different ways: some need to be neat, others don't. Sloppy people are certainly capable of churning out the work.

Witness this passage describing someone's office:

'Picture to yourself the darkest, most disorderly place imaginable… blotches of moisture covered the ceiling; an oldish grand piano, on which the dust disputed the place with various pieces of engraved and manuscript music; under the piano… an unemptied chamber pot; beside it a small walnut table accustomed to the frequent overturning of the secretary placed on it; a quantity of pens encrusted with ink, compared with which the proverbial tavern pens would shine; then more music. The chairs, mostly cane-seated, were covered with plates bearing the remains of last night's supper, and with wearing apparel, etc.'

That's how one visitor described Ludwig von Beethoven's 'office'.

Whether we possess the talent of a Beethoven or not, few of us would be excused by those around us for working in such an environ-ment today. Which is why effective office management is an essential consideration for the modern manager.

How to set up a filing system that works

The amount of material copied and stored—both physically and electronically—has increased as a result of the information explosion. Whatever means you use to file your information, an effective system allows ready access to stored material. If your filing system works for you, it satisfies the most important criterion of effectiveness. Whether you're setting out to develop a new filing system or reviewing your existing one, these are some of the essential points to note...

Decide what to file.

The number and types of files you need will depend on the kind of job you do, and the amount of information you need ready access to. As a general rule, the main types of material that need filing include:

- copies of incoming and outgoing correspondence
- papers, documents, and records
- reference or research materials
- warranties and instruction booklets
- memos, announcements, and notices of upcoming meetings or events.

Analyse what information you need to file to access later.

 ### Keep it or flick it.

Develop a system that helps you decide whether or not to file an item. You'll need to screen documents ruthlessly—remembering that Stanford University research found we never look a second time at 87 percent of the documents we file. One strategy to help you decide whether to hoard or bin/delete incoming documents involves asking yourself:

- Will it help me make a decision? (If no, dump it.)
- Is saving it worth the cost and hassle of storing it? (If no, dump it.)
- If I need this information, could I obtain it from someone else? (If yes, dump it.)
- Have I used this information in the past? (If no, dump it.)
- Am I likely to use this type of information in the future? (If no, dump it.)
- Is an electronic or paper copy readily available? (If yes, dump it.)[20]

 ### Separate 'active' from 'inactive'.

Accessibility, speed, and efficiency are essential when it comes to retrieving information. Designating files as 'active' and 'inactive' is one way of facilitating this process. Active files are day-to-day or priority documents that you'll need ready access to; inactive ones will be any remaining categories. For your active files, plan a system of topic categorisation, and know who will have ready access to these files, and a way in which active material can be rendered inactive. Inactive files can be filed and their status reviewed annually. You're now ready to begin implementing your filing system, purchasing necessary supplies, etc. Physical and electronic systems are commercially available. Remember to retain any planning notes, just in case.

 Select an organising strategy to follow.

Having identified your active files, use a basic organising theme for sorting and labelling, such as:

- Chronological—current to previous is suggested.
- Numerical—items listed or displayed in a master file are given a number.
- Alphabetical—last name followed by first name or, for topics or titles, file by the first letter of the first key word.
- According to subject or topic category.
- According to immediacy or importance of the response required.
- By colour (if you're using a physical file)—a master file identifying what each colour signifies.

 Learn from the experience of others.

Don't try to reinvent the wheel when it comes to filing strategies. Explore the valuable lessons others have learnt before you—such as…

- Check out systems used by other organisations in your business or industry. Modify to suit your needs.
- Label files clearly for easy and quick retrieval. Efficiency expert David Allen claims that printed labels, as opposed to written labels, upgrades the usability of a system considerably.
- Date every document you keep.
- Get into the habit of placing a 'dump date' in the top right-hand corner of a filed document—that is, the date after which it can be safely thrown out.
- Use a simple cross-referencing system to

avoid having to make duplicate copies.

- For a large system you may need to compile a contents list or index.
- Be disciplined. Every time you create a new document, date it, and place it in the correct file straight away.
- Always keep handy a stack of filing materials (folders, hanging files, tabs, labels). Prevent paper build-up. Create a new file when you need it.
- Make effective use of subcategories (subfiles), whether paper-based or electronic.
- Budget time for file management.
- Keep your file drawers less than full. If they are full, you'll resist trying to file anything.
- Purge your files periodically. Discard any you clearly will not need. Separate any inactive files from the active files.
- If your files are electronic, take the time to set up meaningful folders and subcategories. Make sure electronic file and directory names are long enough to show specifically the contents of the file. File in specific folders with a facility to back-up. Label folders clearly for easy retrieval. Regularly delete unwanted data. Archive what you want to keep.
- If you use paper and electronic systems in parallel, make sure they mirror each other in their terminology.

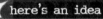 **Focus on thinner files.**

If your filing system is going to continue to support you, it needs to be kept in check. So you need to be prepared for regular filing purges, where you focus on discarding multiple copies and outdated information. If the task is a major one, you should involve others who access the files. This may mean selecting a time free from interruptions. The important first step in having thinner files is to have a system.

ask yourself

Consider your current filing system and ask yourself three questions:

- In a month, a year, or ten years, will I be able to quickly find a particular document or file again?
- Can I easily explain to someone else where a particular file is located?
- If I am not there, could others locate that file for themselves?

If your answer is 'yes', you are probably using an effective system.

here's an idea

Coloured hanging files can be very effective. For example, if one drawer in your filing cabinet contains only files of accounts that have been paid and they're all blue folders, and all the debit accounts are in red folders in another place, the likelihood that someone will accidentally file a debit account in a paid account is reduced. By grouping related files in the same place, you use less space and minimise error.

viewpoint

"A well maintained file system will enable you to find what you need quickly and efficiently, thereby contributing to your goal of creative time management."
– G. Yager in *Creative Time Management for the New Millennium*

569

How to manage ethics in the workplace

The effective management of ethics is sound business practice. Employees' morale is raised; bottom-line performance is improved; your corporate image is enhanced; and customers choose to form business relationships with companies that adhere to high standards of ethical conduct. One of your key management tasks is to persuade employees to accept your organisation's ethical values. Here are some points to consider…

1 Understand the benefits of ethical conduct.

All key parties benefit from ethical conduct within the organisation. **Employees** who have confidence in their management contribute to their organisation's prosperity. Conversely, in an unethical climate, employee productivity declines, creativity is channelled into seeking ways to profit personally from the business, loyalty diminishes, and absenteeism and staff turnover increase.

Customers prefer to be associated with and remain loyal to companies that adhere to codes of ethical behaviour.

Shareholders derive up to fifteen times greater return from companies with a dedicated commitment to ethical conduct. US research in the 1990s identified companies across industry sectors that had outperformed their peers. The one common quality among those companies was a demonstrated commitment to their stated values.

2 Focus on ethical conduct.

When referring to codes of behaviour, the term 'ethical conduct' is more comprehensive and more meaningful than 'ethics'. The best ethical values and intentions are relatively meaningless unless they generate fair, just, and observable behaviours in the workplace. Ethical conduct focuses on demonstrated behaviour—doing, not just saying.

3 Develop a code of ethical conduct.

The best way to handle ethical dilemmas is to avoid their occurrence in the first place. The process involved in developing a code of ethical conduct helps to sensitise employees to ethical considerations and minimises the likelihood that unethical behaviour will occur. A process is outlined in *How to develop a code of ethical conduct* on page 572.

4 Promote process.

When it comes to managing ethics and, in particular, developing a code of ethical conduct, the journey is just as important as the destination. Codes, policies, procedures, and budgets are important. So, too, is the process of reflection and dialogue that produces those deliverables. Where possible use group decision making to actively involve participation in, and ownership of, the final outcome.

Link ethics to other management practices.

The development of a code of ethical conduct should not occur in isolation. The creation of a values statement, for example, should occur as part of a strategic planning process. A link to ethical conduct fits ideally with this process. Similarly, any discussion about personnel policies could also reflect ethical values as they apply to the organisation's culture.

Demonstrate ethical practices.

The best way for you and your organisation to gain a reputation for operating ethically is to demonstrate that behaviour—the most important way to *remain* ethical is to *be* ethical. And the best advertisement your ethics management program can have is everyone's commitment to it. Be prepared for an increase in the number of ethical issues to be dealt with. As staff become increasingly aware of the importance of ethics management, it is to be expected that more issues will be identified. As Helen Vines says: 'The most damaging thing is for management to come out with a code of ethics, or a value statement, and model a *different* type of behaviour.'[22]

Allocate roles and responsibilities.

The approach will vary according to the organisation, but an appropriate

structure could include the following:

■ An ethics management committee, representing the entire organisation, with responsibilities to include implementing and administering an ethics management program. The creation and monitoring of a code of ethical conduct would be part of that overall program.

■ An ethics officer who ideally should be a senior executive but not from HR or the Legal Department. He or she must be trained in matters of ethics in the workplace and have ultimate responsibility for managing the program.

■ Demonstrated involvement and support of top management. Staff and Board must see that senior management takes ethical conduct seriously.

Identify and model industry benchmarks.

An increasing number of companies strive to match practices with espoused values. *The Soul of a Business* (Bantam, 1993), for example, is an account of the way in which ethical considerations guided the day-to-day operations of the American company, Tom's of Maine. One of the company's stated values was its commitment to the health of the environment. The company, therefore, used glass containers instead of plastic, even though plastic was cheaper to purchase, label, and ship. Tom's of Maine was also committed to supporting its regional economy. Only when it couldn't purchase a resource in its local area would Tom's go farther afield. This demonstrated commitment to espoused values contributed to the company's growth and profitability and inspired others to follow its lead.

! viewpoint

"What makes an ethical executive tick? Nobody knows for sure, but the consulting firm London House thinks they may be happier, less tense, and more responsible than people who are more willing to tolerate unethical behaviour....

The most striking finding: The more emotionally healthy the executives, as measured on a battery of tests, the more likely they were to score high on the ethics test. High-ethics executives were also less likely to feel hostility, anxiety, and fear."

– *The Wall Street Journal*

66 quotable quote

We cannot quit our job over every ethical dilemma, but if we continually ignore our sense of values, who do we become?[24]

How to develop a code of ethical conduct

Codes of ethics have long been associated with professional bodies and groups. In fact, members of those associations must abide by their codes of ethics. More recently, business organisations have become aware that they need their own codes of ethical conduct. So you may have to develop your own code, providing an ideal opportunity to tailor one that fits the specific needs of your organisation and its people. Here are some important steps to follow…

1 Get started on your code of ethical conduct.

Following recent global corporate events and scandals, we have become increasingly aware of the need for ethical business conduct. The print and electronic media continue to reveal examples of unethical conduct by global and emerging corporate organisations, as well as smaller local businesses. The need for higher ethical standards in business is obvious.

2 Conduct initial research.

As a first step, check for two important ingredients:

- Investigate any current legislative requirements guiding ethical conduct in your field, and be prepared to take immediate action if any anomalies are uncovered.
- Check the top-five traits or values espoused by your own professional association. Those, for example, could be 'honesty', 'integrity', 'objectivity', 'confidentiality', and 'accuracy'. Aligned with those values should be desirable behaviours.

3 Secure commitment.

Staff need to see that management is serious about ethical conduct and not just protecting itself and its interests. The type of consultative process will depend on the size of your organisation, but key staff discussions will focus on values. Don't assume that people share common values; identifying those beliefs can't be rushed. Provide opportunities for people to discuss in practical terms how a code of ethical conduct will fit into, and enhance, their day-to-day operations.

4 Focus on your organisation.

Try this three-step approach:

- Identify and collect descriptions of major issues in your workplace.
- Select those issues considered to be ethical in nature—dishonesty, discrimination, unfairness, etc.
- Identify behaviours needed to eliminate the causes of those issues and which values would generate your preferred behaviours. To minimise dishonesty, for example, you might promote the value 'respecting the property of others.'

Consider a social audit.

A social audit involves asking employees, customers, suppliers, and other stakeholders whether they believe the organisation meets its stated aims on key issues such as customer service, honesty, integrity, etc. The audit could be conducted as a survey or involve focus groups. Ideally, the skills of an independent expert would be used with a brief to provide a snapshot of the organisation's performance and areas for possible improvement. This information will assist your next step.

 Assemble high-priority ethical values.

From your various forms of data collection, compile a top-ten list of ethical values. Your list will probably resemble existing values lists, such as the Josephson Institute of Ethics' 'Pillars of Character' (see panel, *left*).

 Compose and circulate a draft code.

Having arrived at your top-ten ethical values, align key behaviours with each of them. In addition to your top-ten, you could document requirements in relation to, for example, dress codes, substance abuse, promptness, adhering to instructions from superiors, conflict of interest, reliability, confidentiality, acceptance of gifts from stakeholders, use of the organisation's property for personal purposes, reporting illegal or questionable activity. It is likely that this list will result from your consultative process. Your completed draft will probably include:

1. an introduction
2. a clear definition of mission, objectives, and values
3. guidance on dealings with colleagues, shareholders, stakeholders, suppliers, and the community
4. clear expectations of acceptable conduct
5. operating principles and realistic examples
6. a formal mechanism for resolving issues.

Invite feedback from as many people in the organisation as possible.

 Adopt the final code.

Provide everyone in the organisation with a copy of the code, and include it in induction programs, staff training, and performance appraisals.

 Institute a procedure for dealing with issues.

Appoint an internal ethics management committee, which will, among other things, elect an ethics officer who is ideally a member of executive (international company Raytheon has a Director of Ethics Compliance). Additional training for this person is desirable, on ways to deal with issues that may arise and how to mediate in grievances raised by employees. If anonymity needs to be protected, you may decide to use the services of an ethics counsellor.

 Review biannually.

To review ethical issues too frequently will risk alienating staff. Indeed, the review process must be quick, to the point, involve representatives of all areas of the organisation, and acknowledge examples of outstanding ethical conduct.

How to promote a code of ethical conduct

If ever you needed convincing of the importance of a code of ethical conduct, the events surrounding the collapses of several global and national organisations in 2001 and 2002 should have done so. Enron was America's seventh-largest company at the time, and HIH was one of Australia's largest insurance companies. Their failures helped to focus attention on the need for ethical conduct by everyone in an organisation. This renewed emphasis means that you need to be prepared to respond to questions from your employees and stakeholders. Here's some information to help in your preparation…

1 Define 'ethics' clearly.

Ethics in the workplace is values management (there are those, of course, who believe that values can't be managed), achieved when desired values are prioritised; appropriate workplace behaviours are aligned with those values. Business ethics defines responsibilities in relation to business dealings and social issues. A code of ethical conduct, a more appropriate term than 'ethics', helps to ensure that, when people are struggling in times of crisis and confusion, they are not tempted to divert from a strong moral code.

2 Know what 'ethics' is not.

Detractors will be quick to point out that what people say and what they do can differ quite significantly. And their comments are justified. The Chairman of the Board and Chief Executive of US energy giant Enron, for example, continued to espouse the virtues of ethical conduct while cashing in more than $US1 billion in

stock before its crash. These responses to frequently-made comments will help your cause:

■ 'Ethics is a just another fad.'
There is nothing faddish about ethical conduct. Business ethics is a management discipline linked to practical applications.

■ 'Business ethics is a new form of policing.'
Business ethics has been around for thousands of years, but since the 1960s has received more attention at the corporate level.

■ 'A code of ethics will end up as another door stop or dust collector.'
A code of ethical conduct is an organic instrument affected by organisational and social change.

■ 'A code of ethics is management's way of separating the goodies from the baddies.'
Ethical conduct in the workplace requires all staff to work together to help each other remain ethical and to work through ethical dilemmas.

■ 'Ethics in the workplace is an attempt by lawyers to generate more fees out of business.'

A code of ethical conduct can be developed independent of legal help. Intervention is required when unethical behaviour is detected.

■ 'Ethics is a social responsibility not a business one.'
Ethical behaviour rarely changes with context. A person who behaves unethically in one situation is likely to repeat that behaviour in other situations.

 Promote the benefits.

It is likely that you will need to promote the importance of ethical conduct in your workplace. In doing so, you can support your case by considering such benefits as:

- *Attention to ethical behaviour in the workplace is a sound business practice.* Recent events have made people even more aware of the importance of ethical conduct by everyone in the organisation. Staff also expect that a code of ethical conduct will impinge upon policies for workplace health and safety, equal employment opportunities, and sexual harassment.
- A *code of ethical conduct helps to promote high morale.* It provides clear directions about what is acceptable and unacceptable. People respond positively when they know where they stand on issues that affect them.
- *A code of ethical conduct promotes teamwork.* When people are pulling in the one direction on issues of mutual ethical concensus, teamwork is enhanced.
- *A code of ethical conduct helps people to grow and find meaning in their*

work. Staff act with confidence when they know what behaviours will be supported. They know also that they can have input to ongoing changes to the document.
- *A code of ethical conduct can prevent potential problems before they occur.* The process followed when developing a code of ethical conduct should consider scenarios that can lead to uncovering potential problems.
- *Ethical behaviour is linked to all aspects of an organisation's day-to-day operations.* Whether it's quality improvement, strategic planning, or collating and using information collected by the balanced scorecard or six sigma, a code of ethical conduct encourages people to be more sensitive to their own and others' behaviours.
- *Ethical behaviour promotes a strong public image.* Customers choose to do business with organisations that adhere to advertised codes of ethical conduct.
- *Ethical conduct has a major effect on an organisation's culture.* People experience at first hand how their values and actions contribute to their organisation's culture.

 Live it!

No-one will believe the message if they don't believe the messenger. The boss's behaviour sets the example or standard for others to follow. Employees have every right to expect that management will undertake their tasks responsibly and ethically. As Benjamin Franklin said, 'A good example is the best sermon.'

---

viewpoint

"The reputation of a thousand years may be determined by the conduct of one hour."

– Japanese proverb

smile & ponder

Kenneth Lay, the disgraced chief executive of US energy giant Enron, at a Centre for Business Ethics Conference, three years earlier in 1999, said:

'It's no accident that we put strength of character first. Like any successful company, we must have directors who start with what is right, who do not have hidden agendas, and who strive to make judgements about what is best for the company, and not what is best for themselves or some other constituency.'[26]

'Some people are like dirty clothes. They only come clean in hot water.'[27]

quotable quote

An ethical organisation is one that strives to live its values and to make these clear to all who have a relationship with it. It is perhaps not a perfect company but simply one that is still learning and growing, always keen to improve its performance.[28]

How to manage an ethical crisis

Most people experience pressures to achieve goals; and different people respond differently. Some may even resort to unethical conduct that, over time, is likely to affect both the individual and the organisation adversely. As a result, you may have an ethical crisis to deal with. Because in most organisations the approach to ethics is usually crisis-driven, it is appropriate to be prepared for such an event. Here are some important considerations...

Adhere to established management practices.

To put a positive spin on a negative situation, an ethical crisis within your organisation provides a great opportunity to demonstrate your managerial capabilities. Ensure that you:

- *Act immediately.* Management is all about action and implementation—getting things done. Although staff under pressure may not fully understand the implications of inappropriate and hasty actions, inaction on your part can never be excused in relation to behaviour that breaches the organisation's code of ethical conduct.
- *Provide support.* You need to be sensitive to individuals' needs, and to shape, direct, and focus them for the benefit of the group as a whole.
- *Show leadership.* Your exemplary behaviour will demonstrate that to be ethical is to focus on the cultural goals of the corporation as well as the business goals.

Keep the crisis in context.

Ethical dilemmas are an ongoing struggle for organisations everywhere. First, in any crisis, ensure that the event constitutes a genuine ethical crisis. A perceived crisis could involve resolving a conflict, clarifying ambiguities, dealing with stress, or managing problems associated with ongoing change. Genuine ethical crises are most often associated with far more stressful ethical predicaments—too-good-to-be-missed opportunities, superordinate goals, and other adrenaline-raising activities—or ambiguous situations such as indiscriminate use of sick leave or disregard by management for workplace safety. Dealing with the ethical dilemmas stemming from these situations is the real challenge.

Adopt a mechanism for dealing with crises.

Establish a group within the organisation with responsibility for dealing with ethical crises. This ethics committee, representing all groups within the organisation, is a much better alternative than having one person try to deal with such dilemmas.

The committee structure would also allow staff to raise concerns without fear of recrimination.

Construct an accurate picture.

An ethics committee first needs to establish the facts that lead to a clear understanding of the situation. Some of the questions to be considered at this stage would include:

- Do we have a problem—a genuine crisis?
- What is the problem?
- What are the known facts?
- What has caused this situation to arise?
- Who are the stakeholders involved?
- What options are available to us in dealing with the problem?

Adopt an organisational perspective.

Identify which of the organisation's ethical principles or codes of ethical conduct have been breached. The ability to take this action illustrates the importance of ensuring that the organisation's code of ethical conduct is a practical document. Having made clear the organisation's position, the committee needs to ask the following questions:

- Is additional information required before a decision can be made about the particular behaviour?
- What would happen if we did nothing?
- Are there loyalties that may be threatened?
- Are there other people who need to be involved in making a decision to act?

Deliberate prior to making any decision.

Decisions on ethical issues should not be made as knee-jerk reactions. You may, for example, consider applying a worst-case scenario as a tool to help the committee choose between competing options. The committee might ask whether a report of the crisis would be likely to be reported on the front page of your major daily newspaper. If so, what would the public response be? What actions, therefore, should apply? When the issue of broader community concern has been addressed, consider these questions:

- Should the problem be discussed with the affected parties before a decision is made?
- How sensitively should the situation be handled to prevent or minimise harm to stakeholders while at the same time upholding the organisation's values and arriving at a workable and acceptable situation?
- Is the committee confident that the position adopted will be valid over a long period?
- How can we ensure that such a situation will not arise again?

Implement a plan of action.

When the decision has been made, the committee should compile, implement, and monitor an action plan including details of how to inform all those who need to know the outcome of the investigation. That list could include the boss, the board, some or all employees, affected families, and the broader community.

How to safeguard people's privacy

The exponential growth of the Internet and electronic facilities has heightened concerns about people's privacy. Some governments have tried to address the problem by introducing new privacy laws. Australian legislation in 2001, for example, required most businesses to rethink how they collect and use information about clients and customers. Even if you're not affected by formal legislation at this stage, it is in your own interests (and those of others) to review the way information is collected and used in your organisation…

1 Review how you collect and use data in your business.

Most difficulties associated with the expected use of personal information can be overcome by obtaining individuals' consents when any information is collected. The main privacy concern for most people is whether and how their information is being accessed by organisations other than the one undertaking the collection. Be open about planned usage. If, for example, information being collected will be used by a contractor to whom a particular project has been outsourced, individuals should be informed of your plans as they affect the information provider. Individuals have every right to know who has access to their personal information.

2 Create a privacy policy for your organisation.

Policies are useful management tools. A privacy policy encourages you to outline in detail the ways in which individuals' privacy is protected in the day-to-day activities of your organisation. A privacy policy helps prepare you to be able to respond to requests from individuals to inform them what sort of information about them you hold, for what purposes, and how you use and disclose that information. In Australia, the National Privacy Principles (NPPs), under the *Commonwealth Privacy Act*, stipulate a need for organisations to be able to provide a privacy policy on request.

3 Appoint a privacy officer in your organisation.

An increasing number of issues will continue to be associated with individuals' rights to privacy and the ways in which information is collected and used. It makes good sense, therefore, to appoint a person whose responsibilities will include issues of privacy. This person's role will deal with key issues such as use and disclosure of information, data quality, data security, individuals' access to and correction of personal information, maintaining individuals' anonymity, and ensuring individuals'

mini seminar

You pick up your son's wallet that he inadvertently left behind the last time he visited. A licence to own and use a firearm falls out. What do you do? Do you ignore it? Do you ask him about it? Parents on a regular basis face dilemmas like this one.

Managers, too, face issues of personal privacy. What are some of the lessons learnt by parents that could help managers with their responsibilities relating to employees' privacy?

read further

In Australia, the Federal Privacy Commissioner has produced information sheets and guidelines to assist businesses to comply with legislative requirements. Consult: www.privacy.gov.au

consents have been obtained for collecting any information considered to be 'sensitive'.

4 Check your marketing and IT initiatives.

Many of the issues of privacy—data security, for example—are linked to marketing and IT. Your privacy policy will need to set out the requirements of both areas to comply with any legislation or organisational demands. Your marketing and IT personnel should be made aware of individuals' rights to access any information held about them. If the size and scope of your marketing and IT activities are large, a formal audit may be appropriate. This could require new or upgraded software, particularly in the interests of data security.

5 Collect only the information you need.

If you don't need particular information, don't collect it. Recent concern for individual privacy should result in more succinct requests for information that make it clear to the provider the need, or your intention, for the information collected. Take, for example, your company's website. Many websites collect needless information. In many instances, it is only after the information is collected that decisions are made about what to do with the information. Websites should be under continuing review, not only for updating content and visual appeal but also regarding the type and quality of information being collected. Data quality—its accuracy and completeness—must receive the continuing attention it deserves.

6 Analyse critically others' requests for information.

You, too, will be the recipient of requests to provide information— telesales, mail lists, etc. When in doubt, check any current legislation regarding the manner in which information is being collected. The collector must be prepared to respond to your request to inform them what sort of information it holds, for what purposes, and how it collects, holds, uses, and discloses that information. The collector's response will help you to refine further your organisation's collection procedures. Do not underestimate the public relations impact of perceived non-compliance. Research continues to show the importance of ethical behaviour in building customers' confidence in dealing with an organisation.

7 Make secure any information you collect.

Data security can involve misuse, loss, or unauthorised access. Employees who don't need access to personal information—about colleagues or customers—must be prevented from accessing databases containing that information. 'Need-to-know' information is different from 'nice-to-know'. Institute internal security measures to eliminate the possibility of open access. Again, while legislation is likely to address this issue, it is a further example of sound management practice establishing the boundaries of acceptance. Similarly, unauthorised external access must be denied.

don't forget

Privacy standards

Make it a practice to treat all personal information as if it were subjected to legislative enforcement. Use the following list, adapted from the former Australian law firm Deacons Lawyers, as your core standards for the collection, use, and disclosure of personal data contained in the National Privacy Principles (NPPs) under the Commonwealth *Privacy Act*:

- Ensure that the collection of personal information is fair, lawful and not intrusive.
- Disclose how information will be used and invite individuals' access to it.
- Maintain data that is up to date, accurate, complete.
- Guarantee that information is safe from misuse, loss, or unauthorised access.
- Be open with people about any information concerning them that is collected, held, used, or disclosed.
- Provide individuals with access to their personal information and be prepared to make any corrections on request.
- Provide anonymity whenever it is lawful and practical to do so.
- Keep the flow of data strictly controlled.
- Take extra precautions when dealing with sensitive information.

How to embrace the concept of equal employment opportunity

As well as creating conditions in which all workers have an equal chance of employment and promotion, Equal Employment Opportunity (EEO) is a legal requirement of most governments. In Australia, for example, the process of introducing EEO is linked to the *Affirmative Action (EEO for Women) Act 1986.* The *Equal Opportunity in Public Employment* (EOPE) legislation specifies the steps required to develop an EEO management plan. Those steps provide useful assistance in developing a plan for most organisations…

1 Adopt and circulate an EEO policy statement.

Inform your employees that your organisation has adopted or reaffirmed a policy commitment to EEO, thereby ensuring that staff will not be disadvantaged in any way on gender, religious, or racial grounds when it comes to employment within your company. Your immediate target groups covered by the policy would be: Aboriginal and Torres Strait Islander people, women, those with disabilities, and those from non-English speaking backgrounds. Senior management endorsement is vital.

2 Appoint an EEO officer for your organisation.

Appoint a person or persons to be responsible for ensuring compliance with any EEO legislation. EEO officers must have sufficient authority and resources to enable them to carry out that role effectively. Given the importance of assuring equal employment opportunity, it is likely that your chief executive officer will feel obliged to assume overall responsibility. Group ownership of the plan, however, will be achieved by involving all those affected.

3 Consult with those whose support is required.

Unions and employees are likely to be the two affected groups. A consultative committee comprising representatives of staff and unions should be considered. Additional consultation with employees can occur through meetings and surveys. Target relevant group networks—for example, indigenous people, single parents and the disabled. Use newsletters to get your message across; and establish a help desk for quick response to individuals' queries. Consultation is invariably a time-consuming, but essential, activity.

4 Construct an employment profile.

To manage something effectively you must understand it, and a statistical picture will help that process. In fact, comprehensive statistical data will prove to be one of the essential

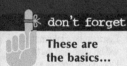

ingredients in evaluating the effectiveness of an EEO plan. Most organisations will not have all that information immediately available, but the picture will become clearer over time through surveys and using other information already in existence.

Review existing policies.

Make sure that existing personnel policies and practices do not contribute to any systemic discrimination. Check the policies of other companies. If you identify areas of incongruence, make the necessary amendments and include those as part of your overall EEO management plan.

Set objectives and make forward estimates.

Having now gathered all relevant information, you can now formalise your EEO plan or policy statement. In this regard, focus on:

- job descriptions
- selection and recruitment practices
- staff qualifications and training needs
- targets for under-represented groups
- timeframes for achieving these
- assignment of responsibilities
- flexible working arrangements
- grievance procedures
- appropriate schemes for parental leave, child care, flexible hours…

State the plan's objectives clearly to give the plan focus and structure. The corporate and strategic goals of the organisation should be taken into account; close consultation with senior management is essential. A clear, concise, usable plan is what's required

if you are to give direction to your company in terms of EEO policy.

Prepare your plan.

A typical EEO plan might comprise the following elements:

- an executive statement outlining organisational support for the plan
- an overview of the plan, its scope and its content
- a clear statement of objectives
- a timeframe for the achievement of those objectives
- a statement of how the policy will be implemented and monitored.

Communicate, monitor, and evaluate the program.

Disseminate the policy to applicants, new staff, and current employees. Review the operation of the plan annually to monitor and evaluate its progress and to set the objectives and forward estimates for the next year. Its progress can be measured against the stated objectives and forward estimates. If your organisation fails to meet its goals, then a satisfactory explanation should be sought and relevant corrective actions should follow. Training will be a feature of this action.

Use your plan to promote your organisation.

Your organisation's commitment to equal employment opportunity can be a useful tool in attracting the right people to your organisation. The plan will help to further differentiate your organisation from others, so advertise your commitment to EEO whenever the opportunity arises.

smile & ponder

The sign in the window of the local business read…

HELP WANTED.
Must be able to type, must be good with a computer, and must be bilingual. We are an Equal Opportunity Employer. Apply within.

A dog trotted up to the window, saw the sign and entered. He looked at the receptionist, wagged his tail, walked over to the sign, and whined.

Getting the idea, the receptionist led the dog into the manager's office. Inside, the dog jumped up on the chair and stared at the stunned manager, who began: "You realise I can't hire you. The sign says you have to be able to type."

The dog jumped down, went to the typewriter and proceeded to type out a perfect letter. He took out the page and trotted over to the manager, gave it to him, then jumped back into the chair.

The manager was stunned, but then told the dog, "Look, I'm sorry but the sign says you have to be computer-literate."

The dog jumped down again and went to the computer where it proceeded to whiz flawlessly around MS Word.

The manager, amazed, responded: "I realise that you are a very intelligent dog and have some interesting abilities, but I can't give you the job."

The dog jumped down and pointed to that part of the sign that said 'We are an Equal Opportunity Employer'.

The manager said, "Ah, yes, but the sign also says that you have to be bilingual!"

The dog looked at the manager and said, "Meow".

How to make the right decision on outsourcing

The drive to concentrate on core business activities and to increase value for shareholders has encouraged many organisations to examine opportunities for outsourcing. But any decision to outsource should never be a simple, quick-fix to hive off what management considers non-core activities. Outsourcing decisions are complex business initiatives, requiring considerable investigation. Here are some essential precursors to a final decision…

Be aware: outsourcing isn't always the answer.

The motto of 'core in, and non-core out' is a gross oversimplification of the outsourcing process—even if 'core' and 'non-core' could be clearly distinguished. For example, take IT, an activity frequently identified as 'non-core'. One study involving organisations outsourcing more than 80 per cent of their IT operations found high levels of dissatisfaction with the results achieved. Another study found that one-third of 116 large organisations outsourcing IT in the US and the UK experienced dramatic cost blow-outs, disputes, high levels of failure, and loss of control. So, rather than try to distinguish 'core' from 'non-core', try discriminating between 'effectiveness' and 'risk'.

Weigh up first your case for outsourcing.

First, discriminate between effectiveness and risk.

Use a simple four-squared matrix to decide whether to outsource an activity. On the one side are the risks associated with outsourcing the activity, e.g. costs or loss of know-how, and, on the other side, the *effectiveness* of the activity when performed in-house rather than outside:

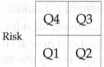

Effectiveness

If effectiveness is low and the associated risks are low (Quadrant 1), the logical action could be to outsource the activity.

If effectiveness is high and the associated risks are low (Q2), it would be logical to keep that activity in-house (assuming that the company can maintain that level of effectiveness in the future).

If the effectiveness is high and the associated risks are high (Q3), the activity would be better controlled in-house.

A problem arises when effectiveness is low and risks are high (Q4). The challenge for management is to redesign the task so that either it becomes more effective or the risks become lower. Only after the job has been moved out of this quadrant should outsourcing be considered.

Second, assess the pros and cons.
Some of the most common reasons

given for outsourcing are these:

- Cost efficiency
- Inability to develop in-house competencies quickly enough
- The need for a quicker response
- Small production runs too costly
- More effective and profitable asset management
- Economies of scale—providers can usually handle sudden hikes in demand
- Emergence of efficient supply market—transport, for example
- Improved operating performance
- Reduces overhead costs
- Some training and other employee-development activities become the provider's responsibility.

Some of the most common reasons for not outsourcing include these:

- Loss of know-how—outsourcing companies later become competitors
- Managing outsourcing too expensive or too difficult
- Cultural dissonance between the organisations involved.

Having weighed the advantages and drawbacks of outsourcing a task, you will be in a better position to make a confident decision.

 Refocus your attention on specific activities.

Evaluating an outsourcing alternative can often improve the activity under review. An activity not considered central by top management might not have received much attention and therefore might have been allowed to become inefficient. Renewed attention to the activity, brought on by looking at possible outsourcing options, can cause the activity to be revisited. That attention may be all that's required to increase the in-house effectiveness of the activity—and to suppress thoughts of outsourcing.

Keep people informed.

Keeping employees informed about outsourcing considerations prevents misinformation and unsubstantiated rumours from causing unnecessary anxiety about job security. Provide relevant employees with updates about the project plan, costs and performance analyses, proposal outlines, short-listed candidates, the nature and content of any agreements being negotiated, and any contract that allows the transition to begin.

 Make the decision to outsource and invite tenders.

Having made a decision to outsource, send an outline specification (services, activities, targets...), and a request for expressions of interest and supporting information, to reputable agencies in the particular field. Forward a detailed tender document to the most promising respondents. Evaluate the final tenders submitted, knowing that you seek not only a qualified and efficient agency, but also one that embraces your organisation's values and management style. Make your selection, and prepare and sign a contract, incorporating a trial period to allow for any necessary adjustments to the formal agreement.

 Consider developing a strategic partnership.

With your strategic goals in mind, outsourcing can provide an ideal opportunity to develop a strategic partnership with the selected provider. Viewed in this way, many of the key considerations in choosing the provider take on a different perspective.

How to hire a consultant

The decision to hire an outside expert to help your organisation in a specific area is always important. Although good outside consultants can provide you with invaluable service, the most difficult task is selecting the right person for the job. There are consultants—and there are consultants; and they can also be expensive. So, in choosing one, always remember the well-proven caveat 'Let the buyer beware!' As well, the following advice will prove helpful...

don't forget

What consultants will bring...

Knowledge. They specialise in an identified area of business, e.g. total quality management, marketing, or strategic planning, and may also practise in specific industries such as food processing, engineering, textiles or advertising.

Experience. Most have had experience as managers and this, with their consulting experience, makes them valuable as advisors.

Objectivity. They can bring to a business an objectivity which it may not be able to achieve with internal personnel.

– Institute of Management Consultants

don't forget

You'll need a contract

According to the Institute of Management Consultants, a contract should include:

Terms of reference; fees and payment arrangements; timeline for completion; milestone dates; circumstances for terminating or amending contract; copyright, i.e. ownership of contract material, including intellectual property; use of your resources; confidentiality aspects; professional liability.

Know exactly why you are using a consultant.

External consultants are brought in for a variety of reasons—to solve problems, give advice, perform specialised services, inject expertise currently lacking in the organisation, bring about change, and so on. Presumably no one in your organisation possesses the required knowledge or expertise and, for that reason, you are prepared to pay for this short term service. Consultants are usually able to see the wood through the trees; are usually seen by employees as being more credible and impartial; and their recommendations are often more readily accepted by the rank and file. But remember this key point: the consultant's job is to provide you with the best advice to enable *you* to make the final decision.

Identify your needs and what you want from the consultant.

To consider using a consultant, you must first take the time to determine the following:
- Why are we using a consultant?

Identify a problem or a need. Remember that it is important to define your problem in enough detail to target the kind of consultant you'll be requiring. And be warned: in the process of defining, you can also fall into the common trap of dictating, or partially stating, a solution to the consultant. Never use consultants to substantiate pre-conceived points of view, practices, or ideas. Simply determine the problem you want solved and set about hiring an expert to find the best solution.

- What are the specific areas of the project or effort the consultant will work on?
- What are your expectations of the consultant?
- How will the consultant's performance be evaluated?
- Who will be working with the consultant?
- What are the roles of those working with the consultant? What is the role of the consultant?
- What is the approximate budget we can allocate to the project?
- What is the timetable for the project?
- Will there be any flexibility for changing direction midstream?

584

Shop around.

Finding the right consultant means playing detective: some are self-employed, some are associated with large consulting firms, others are affiliated with universities. Don't accept just any consultant who comes along. Be wary of those offering standard or prepared packages which might not be able to meet your specific needs. Check out the Yellow Pages, your network of colleagues, directories of consultants in libraries or on the internet, professional or technical associations, and universities. In Australia, you can get lists of consultants from the Institute of Management Consultants, email: imc@imc.org.au.

 Screen potential consultants.

Matching the right consultant with the task at hand is the key to success. If necessary, call tenders from two or three firms and ask for details about:

- technical competence and training
- ability to carry out the task
- back-up available
- recent experience on similar tasks
- availability
- testimonials
- compatibility with your staff
- their understanding of your problem
- fees.

In most circumstances you should call for proposals from a small number of selected consultants. When all tenders have been received, applicants should be interviewed. This is helpful because:

- Written proposals do not always give an accurate picture of the tenderer's suitability.
- Consultants often indicate the type of methodologies they would use if granted the tender. This is a valuable source of ideas for you, and at this stage no charge has been made.

Finally, don't be misled by a smooth-talking principal who may be the firm's salesperson or rainmaker. You want doers, not sellers; so check out specifically the particular consultant to be assigned to your project. Perhaps hire the consultant to complete a small trial project first.

 Be clear on fees.

Don't be shy when talking about money. Understand precisely how the fees are to be charged—by the hour, on a predetermined scale, flat fee, or contingency basis, etc. Ask what preliminary work can be done by your staff to reduce costs. Never make a decision on the basis of cost alone: often the lowest bid simply provides a shoddy quick-fix. Good solutions often take time—and cost money.

 Pay particular attention to the contract.

Make sure the contract covers the nature of the project, who will perform the actual work, deadlines, number and type of interim reports, when, where, and how the final report will be made, and the total cost of the project. Don't assume related services or 'expenses' are included. Be thorough before commissioning the project: ensure all your specific requirements are part of the written agreement.

 don't forget

Why consultancies sometimes fail

Know upfront why the relationship between client and consultant might not work:

- Client fails to properly screen a prospective consultant.
- Client does not seek clarification of how the consultant will operate.
- Client fails to seek clarification of what his money will buy.
- Client fails to accurately identify the problem.
- Client fails to explain his resource limitations.
- Client fails to adequately inform his organisation of the consultant's role and goals.
- Client fails to adequately try to solve his own problems.[35]

How to work with a consultant

A cynic has described consultants as 'those people who borrow your watch to tell you what time it is and then walk off with it'. Perhaps that used to be true. Provided that you have wisely selected a consultant to start with and that you abide by certain rules during the consultancy period, the highly specialised services of an outside adviser may well prove to be one of the best decisions you have ever made...

 ### Make sure both parties understand the brief.

Having hired your consultant, you should have in place a written contract that specifies the expectations of both parties—who will do what, by when, how, and for how much. Written contracts vary in detail but, initially, the early interactions between you and your consultant should be characterised by explicit written statements. Over time, as trust develops, the relationship may continue to thrive on oral agreements. Either way, it is essential that both parties are clear on the details of such items as the objectives, resources, deadlines, costs, and so on.

Develop a sound working relationship.

You and your consultant are a team working together to solve a problem. Both parties should appreciate the collaborative nature of the relationship, being willing to exchange opinions and information freely and to make mutual decisions on the way. You have to be open and honest with each other.

A typical client-consultant relationship might build on the following steps:

- Agree on what aspects are to be investigated.
- Decide on what investigative methods will be used—study of reports and files, interviews, surveys, observation, research, measurement of deficits...
- Select those to be involved in the project to assist the consultant.
- Advise staff of consultant involvement to allay fears of probing activities.
- Analyse the data. Work with the consultant in this analysis to see first hand what's happening and to learn the skills of data analysis.
- Have the consultant present results and make recommendations.
- Decide on what actions should be taken in response to the recommendations proposed.

Do not expect miracles from your consultant.

Consultants are employed to *help* solve an organisation's problems.

They rarely *solve* the problem. They have no magic wand. Change in organisations comes slowly and will depend not only on the quality of your consultant's advice, but also on your ability to implement the advice.

Beth Fowler comments further:

> Consultants are not miracle workers. Consultants summoned to fix emergencies are at a disadvantage. Pro-active clients call consultants when opportunities for improvement exist—*not* when the patient is dying. Consultants' fees are better spent on preventative measures rather than damage control.[36]

4 Try not to become too reliant on your consultant.

A consultancy is a short-term, temporary relationship so you should remember that your aim is to work towards the successful completion of the project and then put an end to the relationship. Resist the temptation to cling too long to your expert adviser. Be aware also that some consultants create circumstances or systems to foster this dependency.

5 Insist on regular meetings.

Keep in touch with your consultant. Consultants shouldn't be left to their own devices for too long. Regular reporting to clear roadblocks and to discuss progress and direction is vital to the success of the project.

6 Be careful not to hamstring your consultant.

You will cripple your consultant's effectiveness if you place too many restraints in your adviser's path. The consultant will need to access freely all people, records, and information in your organisation. On the other hand:

- Do not allow the consultant to change the agreed program without consultation.
- Insist on making the decisions yourself when it comes to spending money.
- Ensure that the final outcome takes the form of a practical proposal which you can implement yourself or with the minimum of help.

7 Get the most for your money.

Capitalise on the outside adviser's expertise, knowledge, and skills. Don't waste your consultant's time, and your money, on those components of the project that your staff can do in-house. Appoint a member of staff to chase up basic information, to liaise or even work full-time with the consultant.

8 Remember: the final decision is yours.

In the end, the consultant will provide advice and recommendations that might challenge many cherished notions. It is your responsibility to act on those suggestions that are workable—and to reject those that you consider to be, after objective evaluation, unrealistic or contrary to your organisation's best interests.

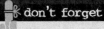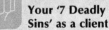

don't forget

Your '7 Deadly Sins' as a client

1. Failure to define your requirements clearly to yourself and effectively asking the consultant to find the problem as well as the solution.

2. Changing your mind and altering your decisions on the basis of casual and ill-informed criticism from colleagues or friends.

3. Reacting to criticism from superiors by putting all the blame on the consultant, even though you have approved what the consultant is doing.

4. Not bringing worries and criticisms out into the open and confronting the consultant with them: terminating the consultant's services without warning, or not having the courage to terminate when you should.

5. Interfering and second-guessing on matters that lie within the consultant's expertise and are outside your own.

6. Blurring responsibility for the consultant's work, so that all those involved try to arrange it so that they take the credit if it succeeds and avoid the blame if it fails.

7. Freeloading, that is, employing a consultant on a small, well-defined project and then trying to milk him/her 'informally' for free advice over a wide range of other, unrelated problems.[37]

How to assess the potential of letting staff work from home

For various reasons, employees increasingly want to work from home—to telecommute or telework. Telecommuting is becoming a preferred option for many employees. Indeed, in the United States more than one in ten white-collar workers now work from home for at least part of their time. So when you're approached by a worker keen to telework from home, it's important that you have all the information that will allow you to act in the best interests of the organisation and the individual. Here are some important pointers...

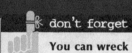

it's a fact

During the 1996 Olympics held in Atlanta, BellSouth – the Atlanta-based Company –encouraged its employees to work at home to help reduce downtown traffic jams. About 2,500 of them have barely set foot in the office since.[38]

don't forget

You can wreck the process

If you want to ensure failure of a teleworking scheme in your company, here's what you can do:

• Ring your teleworker four times a day to check on progress.
• Ignore your teleworker.
• Demand status reports constantly.
• Expect unrealistic deadlines for projects.
• Assume that everyone can be a successful teleworker.
• Ignore any problems that you may find or your teleworker may raise.
• Set unachievable goals.
• Expect perfection in the teleworker and the process.
• Agree that one unsuccessful attempt is enough to doom the process completely.

1 Determine if the job lends itself to telework.

Telecommuting is not for everyone, and certainly not for staff who are either not meeting expectations in the office or simply looking for an alternative to child-care. As a general rule, those who are effective in their office jobs will be just as effective if they work from home—provided they want that arrangement and it fits within their employment contract.

A bigger issue for you will be deciding which jobs qualify for teleworking. Salespeople and consultants, for example, have been operating successfully from their home offices long before the term 'telecommuting' was invented. Staff in management positions, however, and those whose duties require face-to-face contact with customers, are unlikely to be able to telework on a regular basis.

Sound out other companies with programs already established. You'll find that their insights, experiences, and policies are likely to prove invaluable.

2 Weigh up the pros and cons.

A study by the Society for Human Resource Management found that a person who worked from home for just two days a week in 1998 saved the employer between $US6,000 and $US12,000 a year in office space requirements, equipment costs, turnover, and increased productivity. Telecommuting, as a cost-effective work option, has other benefits:

• a significant boost in productivity
• elimination of travel time
• a reduction in direct supervision time
• time saved in readying oneself to go to work
• working in an environment free from day-to-day crises and office politics
• having performance judged on the work and results produced.

On the other hand, potential downsides could include:

• non work-related interruptions
• inadequate self-discipline
• removal from the organisation's culture
• an increased possibility of 'moonlighting' (doing work for other companies).

Collect your facts.

Try telecommuting yourself for a brief period as part of your information-gathering process. Not only will this experience help you to understand some of the real benefits but it will also develop an appreciation of equipment needs and the need for a written schedule detailing how to get the best value for time spent. Your experiences could result in a trial or pilot by others for an agreed period.

 Focus on communicating.

To maintain contact between the office and home, immediate access through Internet, email, and other forms of technology will be essential. Deciding who meets the costs of providing, maintaining, and upgrading these technologies can be negotiated. To help break down any feeling of isolation teleworkers may have, hold regular team meetings, both face-to-face and online, as part of the communication process. A daily email newsletter will keep teleworkers and co-workers in touch and up-to-date.

 Establish performance goals.

Telecommuters expect that their performance will be measured against results; so, in your management role, you will need to establish goals, monitor progress, provide feedback, and do all the other tasks associated with effective management. By involving the people concerned in the goal-setting process, the criteria established will receive the necessary

commitment. The bottom line is that performance appraisal will continue to focus on results, and your handling of performance-related issues will be similar to the way you have always handled them.

 Appoint mentors and coaches.

Mentors and coaches provide valuable support for teleworkers. A mentor will act as a trusted adviser, challenger, encourager, counsellor, and guide, and be able to support telecommuters develop new, more efficient ways to get their jobs done. A coach acts as problem-solver, skill-developer, and one who helps individuals achieve their full potential. Mentors and coaches will be ideally placed to suggest training and who will provide it. As well, by allocating mentors and coaches to all telecommuting staff, you are ensuring that the training needs of individual telecommuters do not go undetected.

 Stay in touch, but...

Maintaining regular contact with teleworkers is just as important as it is with on-site employees, and your telecommuting policy is likely to deal with this issue. But this contact should be restricted to office hours. Any visits to a telecommuter's home should be well planned and occur with at least three people present. Remember, too, that telecommuters have their own private lives and that must be respected. Unless it's an emergency, wait until the next workday to make contact.

 research says

A 2001 report by the Australian Bureau of Statistics revealed that, of 8.5 million Australian workers:

- nearly 1 million were classified as persons employed at home
- 49% were female
- 76% were aged 35 and over
- 38% were self-employed
- For males employed at home the most common occupation groups were managers and administrators (35%) and professionals (28%), while females were most likely to be employed at home as professionals (23%), advanced clerical and service workers (21%) or intermediate clerical, sales and service workers (19%)
- 51% had worked in that job at home for 5 years or more
- 64% used information technology in that job at home.

 don't forget

Wise words

- Teleworking is not suitable for every job or every employee.
- Let the employee withdraw from the program – or terminate it yourself – if it is clearly not working out.
- Distribute work so that in-office personnel and teleworkers are treated equally.
- Teleworking won't always be smooth sailing.
- Trust is vital to an effective teleworking program.

How to help women rejoin the workforce

Women take time out from paid employment for a variety of reasons —to start a family, to take care of relatives, to up-skill, to have a break from work. But these reasons are usually only temporary; women soon find themselves preparing to return to the work force. Although the responsibility rests initially with the individual (see 'How to ready yourself for re-entry to the work force' on page 100), a caring organisation has an important role to play in preparing for, and facilitating, the process. Here's how you can help in the transition…

Be prepared.

Being prepared for re-entry involves two things—understanding the advantages and disadvantages of re-entry, and having a clear policy to deal with this important and increasing phenomenon.

The majority of women re-entering the workforce are highly motivated, mature, experienced, talented, relatively settled and stable, and committed, and they possess practical organisation and time management skills. The downside could be that they demand more flexible working arrangements and display an initial lack of confidence, particularly if they have been absent for an extended period. Your policy and procedures should address this area of equal employment opportunity. Other organisations' policies in this area will be a valuable source of information.

Promote the 'right' culture.

Any feelings of apprehension about re-entering the workforce can dissipate if the environment is supportive and employees make the newcomers feel welcome. You are ideally situated to judge whether the prevailing attitude within the organisation is supportive of a smooth transition. If it isn't, training or some other form of educational intervention may be necessary.

Your aim should be to take whatever action is necessary to help the new or returning staff member become, in the shortest possible time, a fully functioning member of the organisation.

Review current work practices.

To maximise the benefits of women rejoining the workforce, more flexible working hours and work practices may be required, and this could be good news for everyone in the organisation. The need to review some practices can lead to an overall review of work practices, resulting in increased efficiencies. More flexible operating procedures can benefit employees and customers.

Put yourself in their shoes.

Understandably, the person rejoining the workforce may have competing priorities—child-care, home support, etc. Your response to those priorities could not only make life a lot easier for the employee but also build the employees' commitment to the organisation. All that may be needed is that you put the new employee in contact with others in the organisation who have faced, or are facing, a similar challenge. By seeing things from her perspective, you should be able to respond in a way that promotes a win-win situation.

 Provide appropriate training opportunities.

Women returning to work have special anxieties, says The British Industrial Society: 'One of these may manifest itself as lack of confidence— feeling that they will not be able to cope because of the changes in working practices and technology. An effective induction program should recognise this and place a particular emphasis on skills training. This will build confidence and enable the returning employee to feel that they can make a worthwhile contribution to the organisation.'

So, although your induction program will take care of the need-to-know information, it is likely that additional training will be required in areas such as specific skill building, confidence training,

assertive communication, and so on. Again, the timing for those sessions will need to take into account family responsibilities and other demands that might limit breakfast and evening training sessions.

 Gain recognition for your achievements.

Other organisations, too, are devoting their attention to helping women rejoin the workforce. By applying your energies to make this transition as smooth and as successful as possible for the person involved, you will gain an enviable reputation among peers. And when you have achieved this recognition, others will model their practices on yours. Your commitment to re-entry and any initiatives you take will, therefore, be mutually beneficial.

Stay in touch.

Women may take leave from, and rejoin, the workforce several times in their working lives. It is in the interests of both the individual concerned and the organisation to maintain contact during periods of leave. Appoint someone in the organisation to provide regular mailouts of in-house newsletters, magazines, and other communications. Although on leave, people could be invited to attend training sessions, social functions, and other regular events occurring in the organisation.

> **quotable quote**
>
> When women return to the workforce, it is essential that there is enough flexibility and consideration at the beginning of the job or training or educational course to allow for any settling-in periods due to changes in domestic circumstances.
>
> For example, we should be sure that women returners are aware of any provisions for staff welfare that could assist them in times of difficulty. More than this, those organisations that in the future make provision for child care, after-school care, or nurseries will be in a better position to attract and retain a wider choice of candidate offered by the inclusion of women returners.
>
> In order to attract women returners, some companies have decided to gear their production to the availability of female employees, by adopting flexible working rather than ask employees to fit into rigid shift patterns. Such flexible working includes: flexible working round school hours, term-time working only, teleworking, home working, and job sharing.[39]

> **research says**
>
> The survey of 350 professional women found that 60% of working mothers returned to the workforce before their baby's first birthday; 16.4% returned when the babies were less than four months' old and 11.2% returned when the baby was aged between four and six months.[40]

591

How to decide whether a strategic alliance is right for your organisation

When Jack Welch was CEO of General Electric, he observed that 'If you think you can go it alone in today's global economy, you are highly mistaken'. Clearly, Welch supported the practice of pursuing appropriate strategic alliances. But it does not necessarily follow that alliances fit every situation. Like others before you who have considered strategic alliances, you too may need answers to questions that will make your decision easier. Here are answers to some of those frequently asked questions...

What is 'a strategic alliance'?

The term 'alliance' generally describes a broad range of relationships that can include business-to-business collaborations or business networks. Alliances usually fall between the extremes of conventional outsourcing/service arrangements and mergers and acquisitions. Strategic alliances are typically alliances of equals, linking the core capabilities of each partner to increase value to the customer. The alliance becomes a partnership between two or more strong companies that have something to exchange. They are often global; involve a broad range of products or services; and allow one or both of the partners to achieve things that they simply couldn't manage on their own, or that could be done more effectively in partnership than by acting alone. The more familiar alliances are generally characterised by:

- a commitment to at least ten years
- a linkage based on equity or on shared capabilities
- a reciprocal relationship with a shared strategy in common

- an increase in the companies' value and competitiveness in the marketplace.

Are there different forms of alliances?

There is a variety of forms of strategic alliance. Five of these include:

- alliances between non-competing companies in different but related industries
- alliances between companies in the same industry that do not compete in the same markets
- alliances between direct competitors
- alliances between firms from unrelated industries
- alliances between entrepreneurs pursuing common goals.

What are the main benefits of alliances?

Effective alliances can provide access to global markets without the capital-intensive risks associated with mergers and acquisitions. Other benefits include:

- developing new products and services to reach new markets
- creating additional values and sharing in the rewards
- producing a consistently high return on investment (about 20 per cent among

it's a fact

Companies form strategic alliances for a wide variety of reasons which may change as the relationship develops. In the United States, Powersoft entered into an alliance with Lotus to share manufacturing space and soon discovered that sharing Lotus's new packing technology was even more valuable.

Sometimes, particularly in Asia, partners are selected more for their potential to open future doors than for immediate benefits. Lippo Group tapped a network of Japanese, European, and US partners to expand from its Indonesian home base to Hong Kong and China.[42]

it's a fact

The number of alliances among US companies has continued to grow at 25% over the past decade.[43]

viewpoint

"To decide whether an alliance is worth making or keeping, it is necessary to undertake a review which will measure each alliance against the company's overall strategic direction."[44]

– John Meacock, Head of Mergers and Acquisitions, PricewaterhouseCoopers

the top 2,000 companies in the world for nearly 10 years)
- achieving advantages of scale, scope, and speed
- increasing market penetration
- enhancing competitiveness in domestic and international markets
- increasing diversity
- reducing costs
- expanding market development
- creating new businesses.

4 Is there increasing interest in pursuing strategic alliances?

In the 1980s, when competition was simpler and companies did not need to excel in all capabilities to compete effectively, alliances were few and were generally limited in scope. If a company lacked a capability, it either took the time to develop it or bought it through acquisition.

Since 1987, in the United States alone, the number of strategic alliances has grown 25%. Since 1995, according to McKinsey & Company, the number of traditional alliances has grown at a compound annual growth rate of 14.8% while e-alliances grew at 103.5%. Between 1996 and 1998, more than 20,000 alliances were formed worldwide. The OECD (1998) claimed that 'strategic alliances are now considered one of the most powerful mechanisms for combining competition and cooperation and for industrial restructuring on a global basis'. During a similar period, research by Booz Allen indicated that companies using alliances as a major strategy achieved an average ROI of 18% compared with an average of 12% for those that did not.

Alliances clearly can pay off for participants.

5 What sort of a track record do strategic alliances have?

A 1998 US study identified that the three major forces motivating the formation of alliances were
- globalisation of markets
- the search for additional capabilities as technology tended to blur industry boundaries
- scarce resources and intensifying competition for associated markets.

Despite the support for alliance forming, more than 70% of strategic alliances fail. Two of the main reasons identified for these failures were inadequate planning (when deciding whether an alliance was worth making or keeping) and poor management (getting people from different groups to work together productively).

6 Are there any key messages for newcomers?

According to Michael Yoshino and Srinivasa Rangan[41], there are three important lessons.
1. All partners must remain independent firms but with different goals. A merger that creates a new company out of two formerly independent ones is not an alliance.
2. No partner in a strategic alliance can be dominant. If one partner has strategic control over the alliance, the partnership is not serving the strategic goals of the other firm.
3. Both partners must make equal and continuing contributions of technology or products to the alliance.

? ask yourself

Is an alliance your best strategy? If you rate your company highly on these issues, then perhaps you should give some thought to forming a strategic alliance…

☐ Your industry is experiencing a rapidly escalating technology base.

☐ You are frustrated with the difficulty of penetrating a foreign market where the opportunity is attractive.

☐ You are dissatisfied with leveraging your strength with a new growth opportunity.

☐ Your company is not adopting new productivity methods as quickly as you would like.

☐ An increasing research-and-development burden is being felt by your company and your industry.

☐ Your edge in core competencies is under pressure from capable competitors.

☐ You are faced with increasingly heavy investment burdens, and you want to leverage scarce resources.

☐ Destabilising conditions are forcing a new look at delivery and distribution alternatives in your markets.

☐ You want to strengthen value-added skills and raise the level of competitive intensity within your industry.

☐ Opportunities are limited because of size and geography.[45]

593

How to form an effective strategic alliance

You've done your homework about alliance-forming—explored the benefits, identified best practices, and gained the support of top people in the organisations involved. And you have decided that a strategic alliance will provide the appropriate opportunities and competitive advantages. Here, then, are the steps you need to consider...

1 *Sketch a business plan.*

Once you have made a decision to form an alliance, you need to establish what you are looking for from that alliance. A business plan of what you want to achieve will assist that process.

2 *Define strategy and objectives.*

Clearly defined business objectives are vital if you are to forge a successful alliance. Your objectives must be concise, straightforward, quantifiable, and easy to communicate. Personal factors may be more intangible and difficult to measure but can be what really makes or breaks an alliance.

3 *Screen potential partners.*

Research the experience of the many organisations which have formed successful alliances. Use this data to be proactive in screening potential partners—their strengths and weaknesses and the options that different partner choices can offer. Analyse this information to narrow the field to those providing the best possible fit. Consider prospective partners' alliance histories. By openly taking each partner's needs into account, you'll build trust to ensure sound relationship-building.

4 *Assess deliverables and leverage opportunities.*

Determine what you have to offer and what you stand to gain. You should:
- assess which of your capabilities have the potential to make a difference in the alliance
- define potential partners' deliverables
- explore the potential advantage of the alliance products over existing products
- be aware of the customer perspective
- qualify value creation and its source
- acknowledge whatever disadvantage might accrue under the alliance.

5 *Define opportunities.*

Quantify the size of the opportunities to assist in negotiations and subsequent implementation of an alliance. Such opportunities can act as the 'sizzle' to keep alliances on course and progressing when rough spots inevitably occur.

Consider the effect on stakeholders.

Thoroughly assess the concerns of all stakeholders—investors, workers, suppliers, customers, unions, and regulatory officials. What might be done to alleviate any identified concerns? For example, what might you do to counter a perceived impact of an alliance on jobs or share price?

 Assess bargaining power.

As in any negotiating situation, you'll need to assess your own bargaining position. This might include:

• defining the contributions required of all partners to make an alliance succeed
• knowing why the other company is at the table
• making it clear to a prospective partner what your core competencies are and why are you protecting them
• analysing other alliances that the prospective partner has entered into
• assessing the type and depth of resources and commitment that the prospective partner will bring to the alliance.

Once general agreement has been established, the alliance partners should prepare a memorandum of understanding to provide a framework for more detailed discussions. Future meetings should cover the alliance structure, financial requirements, partner resource contribution levels, and technology inputs.

 Be patient: it takes time.

Strategic alliances take time to develop and maintain. A potential partner who seems reluctant may be besieged with other invitations—an indicator to you that you need to rework your case, to help you stand out from the crowd. As well, make sure the potential alliance partner can see what's really in it for them.

 Integrate companies to an alliance.

Get the alliance off to a good start by planning the integration of partners into the alliance. You can do this by:

• structuring the alliance to meet the needs of the alliance rather than those of the partners
• assigning high-calibre managers to the alliance in which compensation is tailored to the alliance objectives
• coupling performance and pay as an incentive
• linking strategic objectives to budget and resources
• adopting a periodic review process
• defining divorce procedures, penalties, and exit obligations.

 Base the implementation process on the experience of other successful alliances.

Build your implementation process on the lessons of successful alliances by:

• creating a flexible and lean organisational structure
• basing the structure and process on alliance strategy and requirements rather than partners' demands
• tracking the competitors' reactions to the alliance along with the progress of the alliance itself
• preparing timetables and measurement tools, along with periodic reviews
• relying on open communication to provide flexibility in resolving issues, rather than turning only to the original alliance agreement for guidance
• defining management's roles early, empowering managers to accomplish goals, and communicating lessons learned to alliance partners.

 don't forget

Here's where agreement will be needed

An agreement negotiated among alliance partners should include the following:

• Clear objectives and defined levels of commitment.
• An organisational structure that fits the alliance strategy.
• Rewards that reflect the risks that alliance employees assume.
• Investment and compensation rewards tied to clear performance measures.
• Clearly defined benchmarks that the alliance will be measured against.
• Finance, tax, and legal considerations.
• Detailed penalty, arbitration, and divorce clauses.
• Specification of level and degree of support necessary should the alliance dissolve.
• Provisions to renew the commitment to the alliance.
• Formulas for transfer of pricing, earnings, and equity clearly defined and linked to resource and capability contribution.
• An alliance board of directors reflecting the resource contribution of each partner.
• A formula for tallying asset and capabilities contributions.
• The ability to accommodate changes.[45]

How to avoid the headaches often associated with strategic alliances

In recent years, forming alliances—even among competitors—has become a preferred strategy for many organisations. In 2002, more than 35 per cent of participating companies' revenue came from those alliances. One of the benefits of alliances is that, by studying the experience of others, we can better understand how to avoid many of the pitfalls associated with alliance-building. In fact, best practices in alliance-building have resulted from our growing knowledge and accumulated experience. Here's a list of such practices...

Learn from the experience of others.

Forming strategic alliances is not new so the experiences of those companies who have gone before have alerted us to some of the pitfalls...

- avoid thinking too small—be prepared to give something substantial to get something substantial
- take the time to make sure that you have found the right partner(s)
- make sure that the alliance attracts the best people
- agree explicitly on goals and objectives
- build and continue to develop trust
- focus on making a bigger pie rather than getting a bigger slice of the existing one
- maintain open and consistent communications
- value the independence of alliance members.

Be realistic about possibilities.

As one would expect, direction-setting in an alliance is considerably more complicated than in an individual company. A suggested starting point is to develop an analytically sound alliance plan that has the support of key people from all the organisations involved. This would consider variables such as competing cultures, harmonious communications, available and dedicated resources, and strategies pursued. The point of any strategic alliance should be to make an impact, and you can't do that without the active engagement of the top people involved—yours included.

Prepare a risk management plan.

Many companies new to alliance-building pay much more attention to opportunity than to potential problems. Alliance building can involve risks, and it is important that your preplanning considers responses to these. An effective risk-management plan should consider some of the most common stumbling blocks...

- the long-term competitiveness of the parent companies
- trade-offs that might be necessary in order to remain competitive
- interchange of proprietary information
- appropriateness of any new structure
- employees' resistance to changes

• communication problems between or among companies involved.

 Consider the costs.

Trying to build an alliance on the cheap will cost you dearly in the long term. So, too, will failing to establish priorities and developing resources, including personnel. Ensuring an adequate budget, considering priorities, and allocating resources will play important roles in attracting and keeping the best people.

 Select partners carefully.

Do your homework on potential partners. Alliances, as distinct from acquisitions or mergers, will require less of a focus on price and legal steps and more on the 'softer' issues like management culture, previous alliance experience, strategic objectives, and other perceived strengths and weaknesses. This is also a good time to consider divorce procedures, penalties for poor performance, and arbitration procedures.

 Adopt effective planning techniques.

For any alliance to deliver its desired potential, appropriate resources are essential. Each alliance partner needs to indicate up-front the level of resources that it will allocate. Discussing the resources and each partner's contribution helps to build relationships and, therefore, adds strength to the alliance. You might consider developing a timetable of when and how certain resources will be made available, secured, transferred, and delivered. You might even consider employing a facilitator for this planning process.

 Reward performance.

Making alliances work usually involves some risks, and the people involved need to be given both a sense of security and a level of motivation. Appropriate incentives, therefore, are an effective and necessary form of motivation; these will probably be different in an alliance than for the individual partner companies. Performance measures need to be linked to pay. Any incentive scheme needs to be straightforward, easy to understand, and sufficiently flexible to be adapted to achieve the outcomes desired.

 Define managers' roles clearly.

Key people in the alliance process must be aware of their roles, responsibilities, and authorities as they relate to the alliance rather than the original partner companies. Frontline managers in particular need to work towards building strong working relationships, sound reporting processes, and a demonstrated loyalty to the alliance.

 Listen.

Listen to your potential partners. What they tell you will not only give you the clues to their needs but may influence your thinking in ways you've never imagined.

quotable quote

When it comes to strategic alliances, the most common conflicts occur over money: capital infusions, transfer pricing, licencing fees, compensation levels, and management fees.[42]

viewpoint

"The 'three secrets of alliances' are:
1. There are no alliances between equals.
2. Your allies have hidden expectations.
3. All alliances are temporary."

– Ian Demack in
The Modern Machiavelli.
Power and Influence at Work

viewpoint

'Great deals are usually wrought at great risks.'
– Herodotus

read further

Building, Leading and Managing Strategic Alliances: How to work effectively and profitably with partner companies by Fred Kuglin & Jeff Hook, AMACOM, NY, 2002.

Trusted Partners: How to build mutual trust and win together by Jordan Lewis, Free Press, 2000.

597

How to develop an employment contract

An employment contract is a written, individual employment agreement setting out the wages, conditions, and working arrangements between an employer and an individual employee or group of employees over the age of eighteen. The signed agreement becomes legally binding when approved by the relevant legislative authority. If you adopt the suggestions made here, a workplace agreement can become a document for positive change and improved relationships within your organisation...

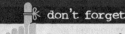

don't forget

Focus on work practices and arrangements

An employment contract could include the following examples of work practices and arrangements:

- flexibility in hours of work (e.g. starting/finishing times, varying meal breaks, 'banking' of time)
- flexibility in personal leave arrangements (e.g. sick leave, carer's leave, maternal leave)
- incentive programs (e.g. performance pay, bonus schemes, profit sharing)
- multi-hiring
- job sharing
- annualised salaries (e.g penalty rates and overtime)
- multi-skilling and job design
- establishment of a workplace consultative committee
- creation of performance indicators to measure productivity levels
- continuous improvement strategies
- training and development programs
- training and apprenticeship programs
- team-based work organisation
- flexibility in pay-period arrangements
- improved dispute-settlement procedures.[47]

1 Pursue mutually beneficial outcomes.

The focus of an employment agreement can go beyond wages and conditions if the preparation process encourages collective thinking about how the business could operate better. This requires consultation, negotiation, trust, cooperation, and agreement about what can be done to improve the performance of the business or industry and to create a work environment where everyone wants to be.

2 Focus on the benefits.

Both the employer and the employee should benefit from an employment agreement. The employer can reasonably expect:

- increased productivity, profits, and competitiveness
- better communication across all levels of the business
- less disruption and more harmony in the workplace
- more flexible and appropriate work arrangements
- lower staff turnover and reduced absenteeism

- improved skills; better work practices.

Employees can expect:

- a better working environment
- pay rises linked to productivity gains
- increased capacity to balance work, family, and lifestyle
- greater job security, job satisfaction, and career-path options.

3 Assemble relevant information.

Before commencing any consultation, conduct your own situational analysis of your organisation or business. A SWOT analysis is a good place to start and will help you to assemble an accurate picture of products and services, customers, competitors, human and physical resources, financial and budgetary requirements, and other marketing and operational issues. This process should enable you to develop a business plan including a list of actions to be taken in order to realise the goals outlined as part of those actions.

4 Decide on scope and content of the agreement.

Your preliminary research will help

you identify the issues you want to change or improve, and best served by an individual or collective agreement. The focus, therefore, becomes work arrangements that cater for the needs of the business, the employer, and the employee. The scope and possible content of the agreement should become clear. Do not, however, develop a draft agreement without involving employees in an initial consultation process.

Engage in consultation.

Successful negotiations should never start with the employer or employee presenting the other party with a draft agreement containing pre-determined wages and conditions. Effective employer-employee consultation and cooperation (never coercion) requires that you:

- canvass the desirability of an agreement
- discuss the content, terms, and conditions of the agreement
- consider how the agreement will affect wages, working conditions and productivity
- cater for special needs and circumstances—sex, age, ethnicity, literacy, and numeracy.

You might also discuss the possibility of employees appointing a bargaining agent to represent them in negotiating the agreement.

Structure the agreement.

Although your proposed agreement will be designed to meet the specific needs of employer, employees, and

the business, most agreements can be expected to contain:

- a nominal expiry date—say, three years
- dispute resolution procedures
- anti-discriminatory provisions
- approval for the employer or employee to disclose details of the agreement
- a no-disadvantage provision (see panel, *right*).

Model agreements, information booklets, check lists, details of procedures, and seminars are usually available through relevant state departments and employee and employer organisations.

Sign the agreement.

The agreement must be signed and dated by the employer and the employee and their signatures witnessed by a third party. (You will find that people will sign an 'agreement' but may baulk at signing a 'contract'.) Before the agreement is signed, give the employee a copy of the proposed agreement and a copy of any relevant legislation and supporting literature. Allow existing and new employees time to consider the agreement before signing, or not.

Submit for approval.

To be legally binding, the agreement must be approved by the relevant authority. So, complete the necessary application forms and supply all necessary information to accompany the proposed agreement. Ideally, the proposed agreement and completed application forms should be lodged with the relevant authority within 14 days of the agreement being signed.

it's a fact

One of the important principles in making agreements is that employees should suffer no disadvantage in their employment conditions as a result of the approval of the agreement – and this means definitively no reduction in employees' entitlements and protections. Legislative documentation points out that a workplace agreement which aims only to cut wages and working conditions will not be approved by the Commission.[47]

it's a fact

In Australia, if an employee's employment is terminated, any agreement involving the employee comes to an end. If, however, the ownership of the business changes, the new employer is bound by the existing agreement.[47]

don't forget

Why a contract?

A contract can:

- strengthen the link between pay rises and the achievement of improved work practices
- place prime responsibility for achieving results directly on employers and employees
- require employers and employees to abide by mutually agreed outcomes
- allow both parties to monitor the effectiveness of their agreement and plan changes if they are not working.[47]

How to prepare a budget

Thomas Paine, the great revolutionary writer, is supposed to have said 'People don't plan to fail, they fail to plan'. His words of wisdom can certainly be applied to budgeting. Planning (together with foresight) is acknowledged as the best way to avoid financial problems. A well-planned budget helps you to collect and use information about the day-to-day functions of your business and to spot problems before they derail your business plan. Here are the steps to follow in developing your next budget...

1 See budgeting as a vital management tool.

Your budget process consists of three main parts—forecasting revenue and expenditure, recording actual revenue and expenditure, and reporting and acting on variance between the two. Budgets usually evolve from business plans and, therefore, will change over time. Your first budget may be nothing more than a statement of targets. In subsequent years, with established benchmarks and an improving track record, you'll be able to make more accurate projections. Eventually, your budget will provide a detailed, accurate comparison of your actual and desired performance.

2 Consider revenue and expenses separately.

Avoid trying to balance your receipts to expenditure in the first instance. Revenue is a product of your business plan and will have a 'lag' component —a start-up period before the cash starts flowing, anything from a couple of months to a couple of years, depending on your business. Expenses are your costs of resources and they will probably dominate in the early days.

3 Identify and list expenses.

The first step in costing your resources is to identify what those line items might be. A useful definition of a line item is one to which a monthly dollar value is assigned, such as accommodation, staffing, advertising, electricity... Many of these items are fixed expenses and this makes the task relatively straightforward. Begin by selecting broad headings and list in detail the line items or resources associated with each. Under 'Administration', for example, you might include stationery and office rental. Under 'Utilities' may be listed electricity and telephone.

4 Forecast revenue.

Revenue is sales. So, using your business plan as a guide, make projections regarding the sales you hope to generate. Those projections will represent a target and should be broken down into monthly and weekly components—the smallest possible denominator, the better. Don't ignore historical data when setting those targets; and consider factors like the economy, inflation, whether your industry is growing, and any new technology that may improve productivity.

Prepare working papers.

Working papers are detailed calculations—cash-flow projections—that provide the monthly figures budgeted for each line item of revenue and expenditure. Produce separate working papers for each line item in the budget; this may be as simple as month-by-month predictions of revenue to be generated from one aspect of your business. Jottings may accompany individual papers as attachments. When a review of your budget is called for, your working papers will be a valuable source of information. For example, you may find that your revenue calculations were unreasonable and thus were contributing to a budget shortfall.

Check for variance.

Variance between your budget and your actuals must be identified and acted on regularly. Ensure that the person responsible for maintaining the financial records is provided with a clearly documented list of individual components designated as line items.

Using such information, this bookkeeper can logically record the actual transaction that can then

be compared with the budget. Any variance, positive or negative, between actual and budgeted, is highlighted in a budget action list for follow-up action.

Prepare a budget action list.

A budget action list is a result of the comparison (usually at month's end) of the actual versus the budget. Note any variance on the budget action list leading to a reassessment of the budget workings, to an amendment of the recording of actuals, or to action so as to address any variance.

Prepare a budget report.

A written budget report is a 'hands-on' summary, prepared on a monthly basis, setting out major variance between actual and budget items. The report should account for any variance and recommend relevant actions. The report is forwarded to the boss or nominee who will either confirm the actions recommended or suggest alternatives. 'What action is needed?', 'Who will take it?', 'When is it completed?' These are the outcomes of this reporting and review process.

Use your budget to help finance your business.

Potential investors or lenders will want to know how they are going to be repaid, and that's where your budget can help. Your budget gives you credibility, shows how your business is travelling, conveys the type of business needs you have to meet, and identifies the resources you must have to be competitive.

 quotable quote

Budgeting is a necessary activity and one that is required of most managers. Managers live and work in the future as well as the present. Planning is a major element of any management job and a budget is the numerical expression of the plans for the next year. Because it is specific and immediate, it is an important management tool.

From a positive point of view, the budget is the only instrument that can give reality to objectives, strategies, priorities and plans. Whatever you want to accomplish, it cannot be done unless resources have been provided for that accomplishment. Similarly, goals take on meaning when reflected in the budget and have no meaning when not so reflected.

From a negative point of view, the budget will be used to control managers' activities, and their performances will be measured against their budgets. Poor budgeting hurts credibility, an important asset for any manager. Anytime a manager gets approval to do anything, it is partly an expression of faith by higher management. An important element of that faith is the manager's track record – has he or she done what was promised in the past? Poor budgeting is a fast way to hurt your chances of getting your future favourite ideas approved.

The best weapons a manager can have for a new year are good plans and forecasts, with the approval of superiors who fully understand them – that is, good budgets.[50]

How to manage cash flow

Cash flow is the lifeblood of any business. So you must implement processes and procedures to ensure that you get paid on time, every time. Failure to adhere to these basic procedures will see your debtors' list grow, your cash flow dry up, and your business collapse. Effective management of cash-flow is essential. Here is what's required to keep the money flowing to you from your debtors...

1 Agree on a price before work commences.

Make sure from the start that the customer is told what the job will cost—and agrees to that cost—*before* any work commences. You have plenty of other more productive things to do with your time than to work for nothing. If you have presented a reasonable quotation but the potential customer is not prepared to accept it, then direct them politely to someone who may be prepared to work for a much lower rate. The practice of writing-off unpaid accounts becomes a thing of the past when both parties agree on an up-front price.

2 Build a sound personal relationship with customers.

Business is a series of relationships among people—the better the relationship, the more likely you are to win a customer's ongoing business. Your investment in getting to know more about individual customers will pay dividends when it comes to getting paid. Customers, too, who value the relationship, will feel an obligation to meet their commitments.

3 Adopt simple, straightforward procedures.

Customers and staff have to be educated to understand and follow a clear system of payment and collection. For example, when did you last consider your invoicing policy?

- Well-designed invoices rather than stuffy, standard computer stationery go a long way to boosting timely payments.
- Instead of the innocuous expression 'Amount due:.......' substitute the more powerful and action-oriented phrase 'Please pay:.......'.
- Make sure key information is highlighted by using different typefaces, underlinings, or bold text.
- Include only the payment address on the invoice.
- Incorporate a final date for making payments, e.g. 'Please ensure your payment reaches our office by...... in order to avoid our routine follow-up systems.'
- Print all legal matters, and terms

and conditions, of accounts on the back of the invoice.

- Send your invoice immediately upon delivery of the goods or completion of the service—the longer you delay in getting an invoice to the customer, the less urgency they will place on paying you.
- Set strict deadlines for payment of accounts—14 days from date of invoice has the best track record. Rarely allow more than 30 days.
- Use a no-fuss invoice and reply-paid envelope, phone, or online payment option—payment of your account must be as hassle-free as possible.

When you have your house in order, others will know it, and are likely to work with you to keep it that way.

4 Grab the attention of the debtor.

Lots of other creditors are competing for debtors' attention, so it is important that your package—envelope, invoice, and other information—gets the attention it deserves. Put yourself in your debtors' shoes and look critically at the material you send out. A simple initiative like offering incentives for prompt payment may be sufficient to distinguish your account from competing creditors'. No job is complete until you get paid, so make every effort to get your money where it belongs—in your bank.

5 Be persistent.

Once you have decided that a debt is worth pursuing—and not every one

will be—you must stick at the task like a blue heeler dog to a jogger's ankle. But remember Sun Tzu's (400 BC) advice: 'The purpose of war is victory, not persistence'. The focus of your persistence is results; so be flexible in adapting approaches to fit different situations. Making use of available technologies, phone, fax and email for example, can help you to be more flexible.

6 Deal only with the authorised bill-payer.

Heed the old saying, 'Don't waste time pow-wowing with the Indians when you know it is the Chief who makes all the decisions.' So, when it is time for you to follow up outstanding invoices, make certain that you talk to a person who can make a decision in your favour—the 'Chief'. Others can promise you everything, but they sometimes have no decision-making authority. So, if the Chief is not available when you call, find out the best time for your follow-up call.

7 Set an example.

Make sure you practise what you preach. You can't reasonably expect others to pay you when *you* make no attempt to pay your creditors. So play your part in keeping money on the move. Where possible, adopt a habit of paying a bill as soon as possible after receiving it. With the bill out of the way, you can then focus all your attention to the task at hand, and not waste time and energy carrying an overdue account with you.

How to collect outstanding debts

Every organisation seems to have errant debtors. And, although your formal management training might not have included debt recovery, you can be sure that others will look to you for guidance and assistance in collecting outstanding debts. By adapting the following simple suggestions to your own situation, you will largely satisfy those expectations...

smile & ponder

Maybe a letter is not always the best solution... The letter from Dorset & Chalmers Pty Ltd to Angus McCrae, 34 Bolstock St, Bentley 9012, read as follows:

Dear Mr McCrae
  Enclosed find our invoice for $106.95 for merchandise purchased in our Hepworth branch on 17 August 1999.
  Payment at this time would be appreciated.
  Yours
  S. Simpson
  Accounts
P.S. This invoice is now one year old!

The above letter was returned without a cheque – but under the postscript, in red, was scribbled:
Happy Birthday!!

Reject the myths of debt collecting.

Myths associated with debt collecting have plagued businesses for years. They're only myths. Reject them!

- *Bad debts are part of being in business. If you don't have them, you can't be doing too well.* The truth is: successful businesses ensure that their debtors' lists are minimal.

- *Pushing for payment of bad debts isn't good for business. Being too pushy will lose you a customer.* The truth is: do you need a customer who's costing you money?

- *Making people pay on time is difficult and expensive.* The truth is: it's possible to collect your money simply and inexpensively.

Decide if the debt is really worth pursuing.

Not all debts are worth chasing. Two variables to consider are the size of the debt in relation to your overall work in progress, and the time it will take to collect the debt. For example, a Fortune 500 company may be prepared to write off a $10,000 debt; a

small business could go to the wall if it ignored such an amount.

Be persistent.

Once you decide that a debt is worth pursuing, you must be prepared to persist, using a variety of techniques, until the money is recovered. Don't wait to see if something happens—make it happen!

Capture the debtor's attention.

If you want people to sit up and take notice, you must first attract their attention. So, when dealing with people who seem to have lost interest in paying-up, you must grab their attention, by fair means or foul, or your message will suffer a similar fate to previous reminders—collecting dust in their in-tray or filed in their wastepaper bin.

Be prepared to act decisively.

Never lose sight of the fact that it

is *your* money, so be prepared to take decisive action to get it where it belongs—in your bank account. For example, if your initial reminder is unsuccessful, telephone or visit the debtor. Both approaches can be combined successfully in the following way. Telephone the debtor and say, 'I will be in your area tomorrow and will call in to say 'hello'—and collect payment for my outstanding account.' Make sure you follow through the next day. Resist writing letters to debtors: the process is time-consuming, expensive, and rarely gets results for payment of long-overdue accounts.

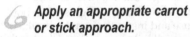

Apply an appropriate carrot or stick approach.

We usually use a 'carrot' or 'stick' approach when motivating or dealing with other people. While encouraging behaviours (the carrot approach) are often the most successful, you may, on occasions, have to resort to engaging a third party like a solicitor or collection agency (the stick approach). Choose the approach that will deliver the results you want, but knowing that to engage a third-party incurs an additional cost for you.

Think and act creatively.

If you send reminder after reminder, believing that these will eventually wear down an errant debtor, you may need to look for more creative ways of getting your message across, and collecting your money. Catch your debtor's attention—creatively…

Vary approaches according to the length of time the account is overdue:

☐ send your reminder invoice—but add a couple of zeros! Your debtor will be on the phone in a flash, so be ready.

☐ for a year-old debt, courier a small birthday cake, with candle, and reminder invoice attached

☐ courier an old broom, with a note attached about 'sweeping things under the carpet—including my invoice'

☐ send a faxed reminder marked boldly 'PRIVATE and CONFIDENTIAL'—so that *everyone* reads it.

Have your approach match your debtor's interests:

☐ to a manager, send a 'to-do' list with every item scratched off, except 'Payment of (your) invoice'

☐ to a cricket fan, send a note using cricket metaphors—being bowled out, stumped, or caught not paying your bill

☐ to a golfer, a golf ball and an appropriate reference to your invoice.

Remember: attract your debtors' attention, provide the information creatively (and with a touch of humour if that's your style), and make it easy for them to pay you (reply-paid envelope, credit card facility, payment by phone, online etc.).

Build up a resource bank.

Nothing succeeds like success and some approaches will be more successful than others. So keep a record of those approaches that deliver the desired results. For dozens of creative ideas, consult *Creative Debt Collecting* by Neil Flanagan, Plum Press, Brisbane.

How to save money by cutting costs

In tough economic times, it is vital for organisations to minimise running costs without jeopardising the welfare of employees or the productivity of the business. By examining some of the fundamental requirements of your organisation—such as telephones, photocopiers, lighting, office supplies, and outside services—you can make considerable savings. Over a year, these savings can markedly improve your financial bottom line...

here's an idea

Cut back even further on your office costs by considering the following:

- Keep office supplies in a controlled area.
- Order bigger paper clips. They might cost a little extra, but have far more application.
- Generic stationery brands can offer savings of 15 – 50% over name brands.
- Use lesser grades of paper for low priority documentation and correspondence.
- Use the correct size envelope to cut down on unnecessary postage costs.
- Always weigh up the speed option versus the cost factor. Often, you may pay extra for 'express' deliveries... only to have the documents sit on a desk across town or country for several days.
- Re-use product packing boxes as record storage boxes.
- Eliminate telephone lines or extensions that get little use.
- Double-check your stationery etc. orders on arrival. Never pay for what you don't get.

1 Recycle wherever possible.

By reusing material, you save money, reduce waste disposal costs, and help protect the planet. Consider:

- turning old file folders inside out and relabelling
- re-using letters or notes by answering them at the bottom or on the back
- stapling scrap paper together to make handy memo or phone message pads
- re-using large envelopes if they are still in good shape
- using the blank side of unneeded paper for future rough work or drafts
- taking an inventory of the forms or standard letters you use in your organisation and eliminating the unnecessary ones
- cutting back on memos to staff, and instead, posting memos on bulletin boards or circulating them
- having staff bring their own mugs instead of using Styrofoam cups
- preparing a sign for bulletin boards and waste bins: 'THINK BEFORE YOU TOSS'.

2 Reduce your interior lighting costs.

Get the most out of your lighting dollar by considering the following:

- Replace old lighting systems with high efficiency fluorescent lights. They use less energy and last twice as long.
- Train staff to turn off lights when not in use and institute procedures which ensure all lights are extinguished at the end of the day. Colour-code switches for lights and equipment which must remain on at night.
- If rebuilding or remodelling, consider the use of natural lighting, skydomes, skylights, glass bricks, light paint colours, and decorative mirrors.

3 Focus on the photocopier.

Photocopiers can be expensive technology in terms of purchase, rental, service charges, supplies, and time. Consider these points:

- New technology is designed to save you money in the long term. So make sure your staff know how to take advantage of all the special features on modern photocopiers. Two-sided copying saves paper; automatic feeding, collating, and stapling save time; reduction-enlargement options save time and money. Staff training sessions are often offered as part of the purchase deal—so use this service.
- Consider cooperative buying with

other businesses in your area for paper and supplies. Buying larger quantities almost always increases discounts.

- Place a tray beside the photocopier to collect bad copies; the other side can be put to a variety of uses.
- An alternative to photocopying could be to create digital files.
- Periodically, conduct an audit of photocopier use (or misuse)—you may be surprised at what you find.

Limit telephone usage.

Save on your phone bill by:

- letting your employees know you regularly review itemised accounts
- barring STD, ISD, and 0055 calls
- scheduling STD and ISD calls and faxes for off-peak times if possible
- charging clients for calls made on their behalf
- using an agenda for STD and ISD calls
- making greater use of Skype and VoIP
- addressing your staff's mobile bills, which are increasingly an issue to manage
- purchasing or leasing equipment outright—it's cheaper than renting
- checking phone bills for errors.

Minimise expensive professional fees.

When using outside consultants and professional advisers, know clearly what services you are 'buying'. To minimise expenses, remember to...

- be sure you really need this service
- shop around for the best deal
- consider using less expensive services for routine matters, e.g. use a debt collection agency instead of a solicitor
- talk about fees beforehand, and be clear on how fees will be charged—by the hour, flat fee, varying scale etc.
- consider 'group actions' to share costs with other organisations

- do whatever preliminary work is needed to reduce costs, and ensure the adviser has relevant files to eliminate the need for expensive searches later.

Seek the advice of your staff.

Try asking your key employees where costs can be reduced and you'll generate some productive discussion. Ask: If you had to reduce business expenses in your area by 10%, what would you cut? And where in other areas? Would any real value be lost? If we reduced just one expense each month by 5%, what savings would accumulate annually?

Check productivity.

Productivity leaks cost your business money. Consider the salary costs alone of starting meetings late, poor planning, duplication of effort, calling unnecessary meetings, non-essential overtime, socialising, and keeping unnecessary records. Focus too on pilfering, loss of supplies through faulty equipment, and loss through worker confusion or incompetence.

Introduce your cuts imaginatively.

When introducing an unpopular cost cutting policy, try to get the message across creatively and, if possible, with a little humour—as did Nippon Steel several years ago:

To reduce the excessive monthly phone bill, we tried a poster campaign to limit long-distance calls to three minutes. This failed. So a list of culprits was drawn up and each was presented with a gift-wrapped three-minute egg timer and call-monitor chart. Within a month, the plant's phone bill dropped 52%.

How to avoid bankruptcy

Bankruptcies continue to soar, particularly in small businesses. Indeed, analyses of why businesses go to the wall have found that up to 90 per cent of organisations that end in financial ruin made the same mistakes. The message is that, if your business repeats these mistakes, you too will walk the same path to financial ruin. So, before it's too late, consider the following sound advice…

1 Know why businesses fail.

Many businesses fail within five years of setting up. Early indicators on the road to bankruptcy would include…

Low profits. Likely causes are poor sales performance, wrong pricing strategies, poor purchasing, inability to control expenses, and poor decision making.

Falling sales. Likely causes are old product, poor marketing strategies, targeting the wrong clients, new competition, and poor staff performance.

Low productivity. Likely causes are low staff motivation, high absenteeism, old equipment, wastage, lack of staff training, and lack of operating systems.

Cash flow problems. Causes may be poor pricing policy, falling sales, high expenses, undercapitalisation, excess stock, debtors slow to pay, poor use of financial records.

Lack of customers. Likely causes are inappropriate marketing strategies, new competition, wrong location, poor signage, and poor visibility.

Overdraft at maximum. Causes could be poor financial control and record keeping, poor credit control, low productivity, poor choice of finance, poor stock control, and undercapitalisation.[55]

By addressing such symptoms early and taking control of business, the chances of avoiding bankruptcy are improved.

2 Develop and follow a business plan.

Successful businesses invariably have a business plan in place. For larger enterprises, such plans are vital. On the other hand, smaller businesses, too easily caught up in the excitement and minutae of the daily grind, tend to be easily distracted from the larger picture, are readily diverted from an essential strategic course—and falsely believe a business plan is unnecessary. Without one, however, they have no yardstick by which to measure their performance. Financial ruin can so easily sneak up on them.

3 Ensure you have sufficient capital.

Smaller businesses traditionally begin under-capitalised—which often means that they have no financial buffer for quieter times or for that unexpected expense. The problem compounds when they have no arrangements in place with their banks to bail them out of trouble in the tough times. It's vital to know how much capital your business will need at all times.

Manage your cash flow.

If you run out of cash, you're in trouble. Understand the cycles that occur in your business cash flow. To control your cash flow will demand strong discipline, an ability to differentiate between profits and cash flow, and control over stock and debtors.

Focus on running the business.

Never fall into the trap of believing that, because you're good at providing services, or you offer outstanding products, or negotiate great deals, you will also be good at running your business. If you focus only on what you're doing, leaving little time to manage your business properly, you'll find your business running down. Stay in control of your business; don't let your business run you.

Keep your records up to date.

In the flurry of daily business, it is often the paper work that is left to last or forgotten. Good quality records are essential—for your dealings with the tax office and other government agencies, as well as for keeping tabs on how well your business is running.

Install appropriate systems.

Too many small businesses are run out of their owner's head. They fail to put adequate operating systems

in place and, being dependent on the owner, they gain insufficient leverage. A lack of systems can cause standards to vary and an inability to provide consistency within the business.

Plan for taxation.

Bottom lines in the black are fine, but a failure to set aside funds for tax obligations has sent many business to the wall. Your business has to plan for, manage, and fund a wide range of tax responsibilities.

Focus on profit, not survival.

If you focus simply on survival, you'll be left with little in your financial reserves or to fund growth. Plan for profits. Know how much profit you'll need to make to allow your business to develop, and then organise your business around this target.

Know your break-even point.

Businesses often get into trouble because they trade below their break-even point. It is only when you know this critical piece of business information that you can make effective costing and pricing decisions.

Manage your resources wisely.

All businesses have a range of resources to manage—people, plant, equipment, time, cash, raw materials, and so on. To be successful, a business must manage its resources well for, in the long run, profit flows from good resource management.

---

research says

Why businesses went bankrupt…

27% – Lack of business ability, acumen, training or experience, resulting in such matters as under-quoting, mistakes in estimating, lack of super-vision and failure to assess the potential of business or to detect misrepresentations

24% – Lack of sufficient initial working capital

23% – Economic conditions affecting industry including competition and price cutting, credit restrictions, fall in prices, increases in charges and other overhead expenses, high cost of repairs and maintenance of equipment, and changes in the character of a business location (by-pass roads)

6% – Excessive drawings including failure to provide for taxation, either personal or wage tax deductions

5% – Personal reasons including ill health of self or dependents, domestic discord and other personal factors

4% – Excessive interest payments on hire purchase and loan moneys, capital losses on repossessions

3% – Inability to collect debts due to disputes, faulty work or bad debts

1% – Seasonal conditions, e.g. floods and droughts

1% – Failure to keep proper books of account and costing records

1% – Gambling or speculation

5% – Other business reasons or reason unknown.[58]

References

The quotations, quips, and ideas presented in this book were accumulated from a variety of sources over a number of years. Although every attempt has been made here to attribute fully the origin of each of these items, the authors have been unable to list some sources in the detail they would have preferred.

In response to... p. xiv

1. Daniel Goleman, author of *Emotional Intelligence* (1997) and *Primal Leadership* (2002). Quoted from 'Business Intelligence', *Business*, Bloomsbury, London, 2002, p. xxxi.
2. Jack Welch, former chairman and CEO of General Electric.
3. Helen Keller (1880-1968), blind and deaf from age two, rose above her disabilities to write eight books which were translated into more than 50 languages.
4. Aristotle (384–322 BC), the philosopher who mastered every field of learning known to the ancient Greeks, and whose books included *Politics, Ethics, Physics, Organon, Poetics,* and *Rhetoric.*
5. Stephen Covey, author of *The 7 Habits of Highly Effective People* (1989) and *First Things First* (1996).
6. John Adair, author of *The Skills of Leadership (1984)*, *The Action-Centred Leader* (1988) and *Great Leaders* (1989).
7. Michael Hammer, co-author of *Reengineering the Corporation.* Quoted from 'Viewpoint', *Business*, Blooms-bury, London, 2002, p. 250.
8. Daniel Tobin, author of *All Learning is Self-Directed* (2000). Quoted from 'Business Intelligence', *Business*, Bloomsbury, London, 2002, p. 336.
9. Edward de Bono, author of *Lateral Thinking* (1990) and *Parallel Thinking* (1995). Quoted from *Simplicity*, Viking, London, 1998.
10. Peter Drucker, US management guru and author of *The Effective Executive* (1967), *Management: Tasks, Responsibilities, Practices* (1973), *The Frontiers of Management* (1986) and *Managing in a Time of Great Change* (1995).
11. Albert Einstein, one of greatest scientists of all time, whose complex theory of relativity, encapsulated in the simple equation $E=mc^2$, became a foundation stone in the development of atomic energy.
12. Peter Senge, author of *The Fifth Discipline: The Art and Practice of the Learning Organisation* (1990) and *The Fifth Discipline Fieldbook* (1994).
13. Ken Blanchard, author of *The One Minute Manager* (1983), *Leadership and the One Minute Manager* (1986), and *The One Minute Manager Meets the Monkey* (1990).
14. Bill Newman, author of *The Power of a Successful Life* (1992) and *The Ten Laws of Leadership* (1994).
15. Alvin Toffler, author of *Future Shock* (1970), *The Third Wave* (1980) and *Powershift* (1990).
16. Warren Buffett, noted US investor par excellence.
17. Peter Block, author of *The Empowered Manager* (1991), *Stewardship* (1996) and *The Answer to How is Yes* (2001).
18. Rosabeth Moss Kanter, author of *The Change Masters* (1983) and *The Challenge of Organisational Change* (1992) Quoted from *Mastering Change* (1995).

Managing Yourself

1. Jeffrey Davidson, *Blow Your Own Horn*, AMACOM, NY, 1987, p. 29.
2. Denis Waitley, *The Psychology of Winning*, Brolga, Ringwood, Victoria, 1979, p. 41.
3. Denis Waitley, p. 101.
4. Toshihiko Maruta, *Mayo Clinic Proceedings*, August 14, 2002.
5. M. Brown, 'Survival of the fittest', *Management Today*, July 1996, p. 77.
6. Denis Waitley, *The Psychology of Winning*, Brolga, Ringwood, 1994, p. 62.
7. Jimmy Calano & Jeff Salzman, *CareerTracking*, Gower, Aldershot, 1988, p. 21.
8. Elaina Zuker, *The Assertive Manager*, AMACOM, NY, 1983, p. 59.
9. Lisa Davis, *Shortcuts for Smart Managers*, AMACOM, NY, 1998, p. 210.
10. John Mulligan, *The Personal Management Handbook*, Sphere Books, London, 1988, p. 121.
11. Elaina Zuker, *The Assertive Manager*, p. 198.
12. Elaina Zuker, p. 13.
13. Brian Tracy, *Maximum Achievement*, Fireside, 1995.
14. Mary Spillane, *Presenting Yourself*, Piatkus, London, 1993, p. 10.
15. Cited in *The New Professional Image* by Susan Bixler, Adams Media, Holbrook, Mass., 1997, p. 16.
16. Peter Drucker, *Innovation and Entrepreneurship*, Heinemann, 1985, p. 23.
17. Geoffrey Meredith, Robert Nelson, and Philip Nech in *The Practice of Entrepreneurship.*
18. After John Burch in *Business Horizons.*
19. Peter Hanson, *Stress for Success*, Pan, London, 1989, p. 19.
20. Greg Vance, *The Australian Manager's Guide to Success*, Hale & Iremonger, Sydney, 1994, p. 125.
21. Adapted from Stephen Covey's *7 Habits of Highly Effective People*, Simon & Schuster, NY, 1989.
22. Hendrie Weisinger in *Emotional Intelligence at Work*, Jossey-Bass, San Francisco, 1998, p. 102.
23. Fred Orr, *How to Succeed at Work*, Unwin, Sydney, 1987, p. 30.
24. James Kouzes & Barry Posner, *The Leadership Challenge*, Jossey Bass, San Francisco, 1995.
25. Chin-Ningchu, President of Asian Marketing Consultants, in *Thick Face, Block Heart.*
26. Source unknown.
27. James Kouzes & Barry Posner, *The Leadership Challenge*, Jossey Bass, San Francisco, 1995.

Managing Your Career

1. W.N. Yoemans, *Seven Survival Skills for an Organised World*, Dutton Signet, 1996.

2. Burdette Bostwick, *Résumé Writing*, John Wiley, NY, 1990.
3. Cynthia Berryman-Fink, *The Manager's Desk Reference*, AMACOM, NY, 1989.
4. Beverly Davis & Genevieve Brown, 'Your Interview Image', *The Executive Educator*.
5. *Sydney Morning Herald*
6. Anthony Medley in *Sweaty Palms: The Neglected Art of Being Interviewed*.
7. Connie Glaser & Barbara Smalley in *More Power to You!*
8. Arthur Young (UK), *The Manager's Handbook*, Crown, NY, 1986.
9. G.Morgan & A.Banks, *Going Up: How to get, keep and advance your career*, Collins Australia, Melbourne, 1988, p. 182.
10. Cheryl Reimold, *Being a Boss*, Dell, NY, 1984, p. 120.
11. Tom Peters, to a Stanford University audience.
12. Peter Drucker in 'The Deadly Sins of Administration'.
13. Derek Rowntree, *The Manager's Book of Checklists*, Gower, Aldershot, 1989, p. 129.
14. Paul Stevens, *Career Management: Whose Responsibility?*
15. Coleman Brunton Poll, NZ, 2000.
16. Arthur Pell, *Managing People*, Alpha Books, New York, 1999, p. 120.
17. Norman Cahners in IBM's *Think* magazine.
18. Jimmy Calano & Jeff Salzman, *Career-Tracking*, Gower, Aldershot, 1988, p. 228.
19. Jeffrey Davidson, *Blow Your Own Horn*, AMACOM, NY, 1987, p. 150.
20. Thomas Quick, *The Manager's Motivation Desk Book*, John Wiley, NY, 1985, pp. 107-109.
21. Hester Cholmon-delay, *Judas*.
22. Bob Rosner, Allan Halcrow, Alan Levins, *The Boss's Survival Guide*, McGraw Hill, NY, 2001, p. 31.
23. Lisa Davis, *Shortcuts for Smart Managers*, AMACOM, NY, 1998, p. 133.
24. Michael Armstrong, *How to Be an Even Better Manager*, Kogan Page, London, 1988, p. 263.
25. Mitchell Posner, *Executive Essentials*, Avon Books, NY, 1987, p. 287.
26. Sandra Wishner, 'Power: Wield it well and watch it multiply', *The Executive Educator*.
27. Derek Rowntree in *How to Manage Your Boss*.
28. Mary and Eric Allison, *Managing Up, Managing Down*, Simon & Schuster, NY, 1984, p. 17.
29. Arthur Young, *The Manager's Handbook*, Crown, NY, 1986, p. 196.
30. Christie Kennard in *Managing Your Boss*.
31. John Harvey Jones in *All Together Now*.
32. Glenn Van Ekeren, *The Speaker's Sourcebook*, Prentice Hall, NJ, 1988, p. 356.
33. Robert Ramsey, *Supervision*, February 1999, p. 4.
34. Eleanor Baldwin in *300 New Ways to Get a Better Job*.
35. Mary Ann Allison & Eric Allison, *Managing Up, Managing Down*, Simon & Schuster, New York, 1984, p. 75.
36. Susan Bixler in *The New Professional Image*, Adams Media, Holbrook, Mass., 1997, p. 237.
37. James Gray Jr., *The Winning Image*, AMACOM, New York, 1993, p. 63.
38. Mitchell Posner, *Executive Essentials*, Avon, New York, 1987, p. 631.
39. Robert Heller and Tim Hindle, *Essential Manager's Manual*, Dorling Kindersley, London, 1998, p. 137.
40. Mark McCormack, *Success Secrets*, Guild Publishing, London, 1989, pp. 205-208.
41. Mary Spillane, *Presenting Yourself*, Piatkus, London, 1993, p. 161.
42. Marie Jansen, 'Seven gifts and silvery laughter: Humour in educational leadership', *The Practising Administrator*, No. 4, 1994.
43. Terry Bravermann in *Training and Development* magazine.
44. Richard Nelson Boles, *What Color is Your Parachute?* (Workbook), Ten Speed Press, Berkeley, Cal., 1998, p. 102.
45. Ted Pollock, *Managing Creatively: 1*, Cahners, Boston, 1971, p. 168.
46. After US organisational psychologist Dr Al Bernstein.
47. Roger Black, *Getting Things Done*, Michael Joseph, London, 1987, p. 25.
48. Eleanor Baldwin in *300 New Ways to Get a Better Job*.
49. John Schiller, 'Timetable to Redundancy', *The Practising Administrator*, Vol. 18, No. 2, p. 8.
50. Gail Ginder, 'Completing the package: Balancing work and family as you press ahead', *InfoWorld*, August 1999.
51. Richard Nelson Boles, *What Color is Your Parachute?* (Workbook), Ten Speed Press, Berkeley Cal., 1998, p. 160.
52. William Cohen, *How to Make It Big as a Consultant*, AMACOM, NY, 1985, p. 2.
53. Linda Vining, 'Becoming a Consultant', *The Practising Administrator*, No. 4, 1997.
54. Dan Sullivan, Closing Keynote Presentation, 1996 IAFP Success Forum.
55. Les Taylor in *Starting and Managing a Small Business*
56. Wal Reynolds, Warwick Savage & Alan Williams in *Your Own Business*.

Managing Relationships

1. Norman Vincent Peale, *The Power of Positive Thinking*, The World's Work, Kingswood, Surrey, 1953, p. 249.
2. Norman Vincent Peale, p. 263.
3. Tom Hopkins, *The Official Guide to Success*, Warner Books, NY, 1982, p. 17.
4. Glenn Van Ekeren, *The Speaker's Sourcebook*, Prentice Hall, NJ, 1988, p. 299.
5. J.Allan in 'The power of persuasion', *Management Accounting*, December 1996, p. 26.
6. Richard Storey, *The Influencing Pocketbook*, Management Pocketbooks, Alresford, Hants, 2001.
7. Philip Chard, 'Managing workplace conflict', *Human Resources*, May 1997.
8. William Parkhurst, *The Eloquent Executive*, Times Books, NY, 1988, p. 118.
9. Robyn Henderson in *Be Seen, Be Known, Move Ahead*.
10. Frank Sonnenberg in *Managing with a Conscience*.
11. Gordon Shea, 'Building Trust in the Workplace, *AMA Management Briefing*.
12. Denis Waitley, *The Psychology of Winning*, Brolga, Ringwood, Victoria, 1979, p. 231.
13. Mary and Eric Allison, *Managing Up, Managing Down*, Simon & Schuster, NY, 1984.
14. Patricia King, *Never Work for a Jerk!*, Dell, NY, 1987, pp. 19, 26.
15. After Arthur Young, *The Manager's Handbook*, Crown, NY, 1986, p. 197.
16. William and Kathleen Lundin in *When Smart People Work for Dumb Bosses*.
17. Patricia King, *Never Work for a Jerk!*, Dell, NY, 1987, p. 19.
18. V. Clayton Sherman, 'Eight steps to preventing problem employees', *Personnel*, May 1988, p. 48.
19. Jimmy Calano & Jeff Salzman, *Career-

611

Tracking, Gower, Aldershot, 1988, p. 244.

20. Jeffrey Mayer, *If You Haven't Got the Time to Do It Right, When Will You Have the Time to Do It Over*, Simon & Schuster, NY, 1990, p. 107.

21. William Parkhurst, *The Eloquent Executive*, Time Books, NY, 1988, p. 100.

22. Bob Rosner, Allan Halcrow & Alan Levins, *The Boss's Survival Guide*, McGraw Hill, NY, 2001, p. 357.

23. After Bob Rosner, Allan Halcrow & Alan Levins, p. 356.

24. *Quotable Quotes*, Reader's Digest, Westmount, Quebec, Canada, 1998, p. 131.

25. Lisa Davis, *Shortcuts for Smart Managers*, AMACOM, NY, 1998, p. 200.

26. *Ecclesiastes*

27. Derek Rowntree, *The Manager's Book of Checklists*, Gower, Aldershot, 1989, p. 116.

28. Arthur Pell, *The Complete Idiot's Guide to Managing People*, Alpha Books, NY, 1999, pp. 310-11.

29. Sally Johnston, 'Dealing with grieving employees', *Management Solutions*, July 1987, p. 26.

30. After Hendrie Weisinger, *Emotional Intelligence at Work*, Jossey-Bass, San Francisco, 1998.

31. Weisinger, p. 20.

32. Weisinger, p. 5.

33. Kravitz, S.M. and Schubert, S.D., *Emotional Intelligence Works*, Crisp, Menlo Park, California, 2000.

34. Weisinger, p. 9.

35. Multi-Health Systems, Toronto, www.mhs.com

36. Goleman, D., *Working with Emotional Intelligence*, Bloomsbury, London, 1998, p. 317.

37. John Mayer & Peter Salovey, 'What is Emotional Intelligence', in *Emotional Development and Emotional Intelligence*, P. Salovey & D. Sluyter (eds.), Basic Books, NY, 1997.

38. Weisinger, p. 181.

Communicating

1. Roger Ailes in *You are the Message*.

2. Andrew Szilagyi, *Management and Performance*, Goodyear, Santa Monica, California, 1981, p. 396.

3. Cheryl Reimold, *Being a Boss*, Dell, NY, 1984, p. 120.

4. Robyn Johnston in *Leading the Way*,

Mandy Tunica, ed., Macmillan, Melbourne, 1995, p. 147.

5. Bill Marriott in *The Spirit to Serve*.

6. *Bits & Pieces*

7. Anne Evans, *Managing People*, Australian Business Library, Melbourne, 1990, p. 67.

8. Joseph Straub, 'Good first impressions on the telephone: There's never a second chance', *Supervisory Management*, March 1991, p. 1.

9. Leil Lowndes in *How to Talk to Anyone*.

10. George Fuller in *Supervisor's Portable Answer Book*.

11. William Nothstini, *Influencing Others*, Crisp, California, 1989, p. 3.

12. Linda Swink, 'Friendly persuasion', *Toastmaster*, November 1988.

13. David Lewis in *The Secret Language*.

14. Kris Cole in *Crystal Clear Communication*.

15. Leil Lowndes in *How to Talk to Anyone*.

16. M.J.Woodruff in 'Why companies should say thanks', *Supervision*.

17. John Milne, *Management Minutes*, Vol. 4 No. 2, 1992.

18. Karen Leland and Keith Bailey in *Customer Service for Dummies*.

19. Robyn Henderson & Marg McAlister in *Be Seen Get Known Move Ahead*.

20. Anne Evans, *Managing People*, Australian Business Library, Melbourne, 1990, p. 118.

21. The US Bureau of Business Practice, *For the President's Eyes Only*.

22. Robyn Johnson in Mandy Tunica, ed., *Leading the Way*, Macmillan, Melbourne, 1995, p. 151.

23. Aubrey Daniels in *Bringing out the Best in People*.

24. Rebecca Turner, 'Feedforward', *Financial Review Boss*, 9 May 2002.

25. Martin Edelston, CEO, Boardroom Inc.

26. Theo Haimann & Ray Hilgert in *Supervision: Concepts and Practices of Management*.

27. J.T.Straub, 'Productive gripe sessions', *Getting Results for the Hands-on Manager*, Vol. 41 No. 96, p. 8.

28. *Person to Person Managing*.

29. Cynthia Berryman-Fink, *The Manager's Desk Reference*, AMACOM, NY, 1989, p. 112.

30. Bob Rosner et al, *The Boss's Survival Guide*, McGraw Hill, NY, 2001, p. 188.

31. G. Simons with A. Zuckerman, *Working Together: Succeeding in a Multicultural

Organization, Crisp Publishing, Menlo Park, 1994, p. 33.

32. Candy Tymson & Bill Sherman, *The Australian Public Relations Manual*, Millennium Books, Sydney, 1990, p. 121.

33. Marian Hudson in *Surviving a Media Interview*.

34. Jimmy Calano & Jeff Saltzman, *Career-Tracking*, Gower, Aldershot, 1988, p. 140.

35. Ted Pollock, *Managing Creatively: 1*, Cahners, Boston, 1971, p. 141.

36. Mark McCormack, *Success Secrets*, Guild Publishing, London, 1989, p. 179.

37. Leslie Kindred, *The School and Community Relations*, Prentice Hall, Englewood Cliffs NJ, 1976, p. 234.

38. The Institute of Management (UK) report, *Taking the Strain*.

39. *Business Week*

40. Australian Government, *Guidelines on Workplace E-mail, Web Browsing*.

41. Mark McCormack, *Success Secrets*, Guild Publishing, London, 1989, p. 106.

42. Jarvis Finger, 'The school's image on paper', *The Practising Administrator*, Vol. 9 No. 3 1987, p. 16.

43. After Jim Macnamara in *Public Relations Handbook*.

44. *Evening Standard*, 13 November 1996.

Building Essential Skills

1. Edwin Feldman, *How to Use Your Time and Get Things Done*, Frederick Fell, NY, 1968, p. 266.

2. Rodger Black, *Getting Things Done*, Michael Joseph, London, 1987, p. 10.

3. Neville Christie in *Management Review*.

4. Mitchell Posner, *Executive Essentials*, Avon Books, NY, 1987, p. 23.

5. Jeffrey Mayer in *Winning the Fight Between You and Your Desk*.

6. Stephanie Winston, *The Organized Executive*, Warner Books, NY, 1985, p. 36.

7. Jimmy Calano & Jeff Salzman, *Career-Tracking*, Gower, Aldershot, 1988, p. 44.

8. Helen Reynolds & Mary Tramel, *Executive Time Management*, Prentice Hall, NY, 1989, p. 107.

9. Mark McCormack, *The 110% Solution*, Chapmans, London, 1990, p. 35.

10. Madeline Bodin, 'Making the Most of Your Telephone', *Nation's Business*, April 1992, p. 62.

11. Jack Collis & Michael LeBoeuf, *Work Smarter Not Harder,* Goal Setting Seminars, Sydney, n.d., p. 139.
12. R. Kemp & M. Nathan in *Middle Management in Schools,* Blackwell Education, Oxford, 1989, p. 165.
13. Lisa Davis, *Shortcuts for Smart Managers,* AMACOM, NY, 1998, p. 105.
14. Mary & Eric Allison, *Managing Up, Managing Down,* Simon & Schuster, NY, 1984, p. 165.
15. Lisa Davis, *Shortcuts for Smart Managers,* AMACOM, NY, 1998, p. 114.
16. Harold Taylor, *The Administrator's Guide to Personal Productivity,* Princeton Junction, NJ, 1993.
17. Lynne Wenig, *The A to Z of Time Management,* Allen & Unwin, St Leonards NSW, 1993, p. 37.
18. Cheryl Reimold, *Being a Boss,* Dell, NY, 1984, p. 67.
19. Michael Armstrong, *How to be an Even Better Manager,* Kogan Page, London, 1988, p. 118.
20. Willard Parker et al, *Front-line Leadership,* McGraw Hill, NY, 1969, p. 240.
21. Ted Pollock, *Managing Creatively: 1,* Cahners, Boston, 1971, p. 38.
22. Jack Parker, *The Collier Quick and Easy Guide for Running a Meeting,* Collier Books, NY, 1963.
23. Milo Frank, *How to Run a Successful Meeting in Half the Time,* Simon & Schuster, NY, 1989, p. 34.
24. Clyde Burleson in *Effective Meetings: The Complete Guide,* John Wiley & Sons, NY, 1990.
25. After Lisa Davis, *Shortcuts for Smart Managers,* AMACOM, NY, 1998, p. 187.
26. Conor Hannaway & Gabriel Hunt, *The Management Skills Book,* Gower, Aldershot, 1992, p. 171.
27. Jack Gratus, *Give and Take,* BBC Books, London, 1990, p. 20.
28. Clyde Burleson, *Effective Meetings: The Complete Guide,* John Wiley & Sons, NY, 1990, pp. 95, 104.
29. Abridged from *Give and Take* by Jack Gratus, BBC Books, London, 1990, pp. 39-41.
30. Milo Frank, *How to Run a Successful Meeting in Half the Time,* Simon & Schuster, NY, 1989, p. 31.
31. Jack Gratus, *Give and Take,* BBC Books, London, 1990, p. 112.
32. B.Y. Auger in *How to Run Better Business Meetings.*
33. William Pfeiffer and John Jones, *The 1980 Annual Handbook for Group Facilitators,* University Associates Inc, San Diego, Cal., 1980.
34. Anthony Jay in *The Articulate Executive.*
35. Harold Koontz & Cyril O'Donnell in *Principles of Management.*
36. George Idiorne, *How Managers Make Things Happen,* Prentice-Hall, Englewood Cliffs NJ, 1987, p. 194.
37. Thomas Quick, *The Manager's Motivation Desk Book,* John Wiley, NY, 1985.
38. Bob Nelson in *The Power of One.*
39. Adapted from *The Complete Idiot's Guide to Managing People,* Dr Arthur R. Pell, Alpha Books, NY, 1999.
40. Robert Luke in 'Meaningful praise makes a difference', *Supervisory Management,* February 1991, p. 3.
41. Source unknown
42. Kenichi Ohmae, Head of McKinsey Tokyo
43. Greg Vance, *The Australian Manager's Guide to Success,* Hale & Iremonger, Sydney, 1994, p. 70.
44. Ted Pollock, *Managing Creatively: 2,* Cahners, Boston, 1971, p. 99.
45. Buck Rogers, *Getting the Best Out of Yourself & Others,* Harper and Row, NY, 1988.
46. R. Kemp & M. Nathan, *Middle Management in Schools,* Blackwell Education, Oxford, 1989, p. 138.
47. Quoted in *Why Teams Don't Work,* Harvey Robbins & Michael Finley, Petersons Books, 1995.
48. Deborah Harrington-Mackin, *The Team-Building Tool Kit,* AMACOM, NY.
49. Linda Moran et al, *Keeping Teams on Track,* Irwin, 1996.
50. W.H. Weiss, *Decision Making for First-Time Managers,* AMACOM, NY, 1985, p. 29.
51. Robert Fitzgibbons in *Making Educational Decisions.*
52. Quoted in James Van Fleet in *The 22 Biggest Mistakes Managers Make,* Parker, NY, 1982, p. 49.
53. Source unknown.
54. After Edward Russo and Paul Schoemaker in *Decision Traps.*
55. John Harvey-Jones in *All Together Now.*
56. Mitchell Posner, *Executive Essentials,* Avon Books, NY, 1987, p. 255.
57. Patricia Hansen in *Heart Songs.*
58. W.H. Weiss, *Decision Making for First-Time Managers,* AMACOM, NY, 1985.
59. Lou Hampton, quoted in Jeffrey Davidson, *Blow Your Own Horn,* AMACOM, NY, 1987, p. 156.
60. Jim Sellars, 'If your yarn elicits yawns…', *American School Board Journal,* April 1987, p. 40.
61. Quoted by Granville Toogood in *The Articulate Executive.*
62. Cynthia Berryman-Fink, *The Manager's Desk Reference,* AMACOM, NY, 1989, p. 242.
63. David Peoples, *Presentations Plus,* Wiley, NY, 1988, p. 147.
64. *American Speaker: Your Guide to Successful Speaking,* Georgetown Publishing House, Washington, p. Int/3.
65. *The Speaker's Sourcebook,* Zondervan, Grand Rapids, 1960, p. 229.
66. Dick Smithies in *How to Develop a Winning Way with Words.*
67. Edward De Roche in *The Complete Public Speaking Handbook for School Administrators.*
68. Lisa Davis, *Shortcuts for Smart Managers,* AMACOM, New York, 1998, p. 211.
69. John Winkler in *Bargaining for Results.*
70. Anne Evans, *Managing People,* Australian Business Library, Melbourne, 1990, p. 67.
71. William Morrison in *The Prenegotiation Planning Book.*
72. Robert Ramsey, 'New year resolutions for supervisors', *Supervision,* January 1996, p. 8.

Planning

1. Robert Heller & Tim Hindle, *Essential Manager's Manual,* Dorling Kindersley, London, 1998, p. 709.
2. Timothy Nolan et.at. in *Plan and Die!*
3. Alexander the Great instilled a focussed passion among his troops with a clear mission to 'Kill Darius', the leader of the Persian army.
4. Jeffrey Abrahams in *The Mission Statement Book.*
5. After Timothy Foster in *101 Great Mission Statements.*
6. William R. Osgood, quoted in *How does your company measure up?,* Myra Faye Turner, Black Enterprises, 2001, p. 52.
7. Gary Hamel in 'Strategy as revolution', *Harvard Business Review.*
8. Neville Smith in *Down-to-Earth Strategic Planning.*
9. Timothy Nolan et. al. in *Plan or Die!*

10. Michael Porter, 'What is strategy', *Harvard Business Review*, November-December 1996, p. 62.
11. Zig Ziglar in *Steps to the Top*.
12. Andrew Szilagyi, *Management and Performance*, Goodyear, Santa Monica, 1981, p. 132.
13. Kris Cole, *Make Time*, Prentice Hall, Sydney, 2001.
14. Jarvis Finger and Neil Flanagan, *The Manager's 100*, Plum Press, Toowong, 1998, No. 17.
15. Les Bell, *Managing Teams in Secondary Schools*, Routledge, London, 1992, p. 151.
16. W.H.Weis, *Decision making for First-Time Managers*, AMACOM, NY, 1985, p. 116.
17. Harold Kerzner, *Project Management*, 5th edn, Van Nostrand Reinhold, NY, 1995, p. 18.
18. After Edwin Bliss, *Getting Things Done*, Charles Scribner's Sons, NY, 1976, p. 3.
19. After Kris Cole, *Make Time*, Prentice Hall, Frenchs Forest NSW, 2001.
20. George Odiorne, *How Managers Make Things Happen*, Prentice Hall, Englewood Cliffs NJ, 1987, p. 134.
21. W. Sahlman in 'How to write a great business plan', *Harvard Business Review*, July-August 1997, p. 98-99.
22. 'What is Facility Management?', The Facility Management Association of Australia, 1997.
23. 'A Degree in Facility Management?', *Managing Office Technology*, Volume 43, 1998.
24. Kit Tuveson, 'Facility Management in the 21st Century', *Managing Office Technology*, May 1998.
25. R. Beckhard and R. Harris in *Organisational Transitions: Managing Complex Change*.
26. Derek Rowntree, *The Manager's Book of Checklists*, Gower, Aldershot, 1989, p. 217.
27. Tom Payne in *From the Inside Out: How to Create and Survive in a Culture of Change*.
28. After John P. Kotter, *Harvard Business Review*, 1995.
29. Mary & Eric Allison, *Managing Up, Managing Down*, Simon & Schuster, NY, 1984, p. 189.
30. Gordon Sullivan & Michael Harper in *Hope is Not a Method*.
31. Robert Kriegel & Louis Patler in *If It Ain't Broke... Break It!*

32. James Sydow & Clark Kirkpatrick in *The School Administrator*.
33. *American Speaker*.
34. *Harvard Business Review*, Nov-Dec 1999, pp. 155-156.
35. W.J. Rothwell, *Effective Succession Planning: Ensuring Leadership Continuity & Building Talent from Within*, AMACOM, NY, 2001, p. 6.
36. Quoted in Neil Chenoweth and Anne Hyland, 'How companies choose their CEOs... and why so many of them get it wrong', *The Australian Financial Review Weekend*, March 28-April 1, 2002.
37. W.J. Rothwell, *Effective Succession Planning: Ensuring Leadership Continuity & Building Talent from Within*, AMACOM, NY, 2001, pp. 9-21.
38. Willard Parker et al, *Front-line Leadership*, McGraw Hill, NY, 1969, p. 318.
39. James Van Fleet, *The 22 Biggest Mistakes Managers Make and How to Correct Them*, Parker, NY, 1982, pp. 214-6.
40. Cathie West, 'Helping your successor succeed', in *Principal* magazine.
41. *Money*, Vol. 29 No.13, December 2000, p. 160.
42. 'Hello, Boss', An interview with Jack Welch, CEO General Electric, *Money*, Vol. 30, March 2001.
43. Michael Porter, 'What is strategy?', *Harvard Business Review*, November-December 1996, p. 61.
44. *Soundview Executive Book Summaries*, Bristol, VT, USA.
45. Michael Porter, 'Big Ideas', *Fast Company*, 1998.
46. Aubrey Daniels in *Bringing Out the Best in People*.
47. Lucy Gaster, *Quality in Public Services: Managers' Choices*, Open University Press, Buckingham, 1995, p. 74.
48. W.H.Weiss, 'Benchmarking', *Supervision*, March 1996, p. 14.
49. Michael Hammer & James Champy, *Reengineering the Corporation*, Allen and Unwin, Sydney, 1983, p. 2.
50. *Business: The Ultimate Resource*, Bloomsbury, London, 2002, p. 507.
51. Tubemakers SPD, *Australian Best Practice Demonstration Program*, 1995, p. 11.
52. Extracted from *Fortune* magazine.
53. Robert Kaplan & David Norton, *The Balanced Scorecard: Translating Strategy into Action*, Harvard University Press, Boston, 1996.
54. After Kaplan & Norton.
55. Mikel Harry & Richard Schroeder, *Six Sigma*, Bantam Doubleday Dell, 1999, p. 14.
56. 'Telstra pins future on Six Sigma', *The Australian Financial Review*, 24 October 2001.

Staff-Related Issues

1. Arthur Pell, *The Complete Idiot's Guide to Managing People*, Alpha Books, NY, 1999, pp. 170-174.
2. J. Smith, *The Advertising Kit*, Lexington Books, 1994, p. 26.
3. Robert Redmond in *How to Recruit Good Managers*.
4. Stephen Covey, 'How to hire people', *Executive Excellence*, December 1996, p. 3.
5. David Ogilvy in *Ogilvy on Advertising*.
6. James Black in *How to Get Results from Interviewing*.
7. Michael Meighan in *How to Design and Deliver Induction Training Programs*.
8. G.F.O'Shea, 'Induction and orientation', *HR & Development Handbook*, W. Treacy, ed., AMACOM, NY, 1994, p. 986.
9. Bob Nelson and Peter Economy, in *Managing for Dummies*.
10. Thomas Quick, *The Manager's Motivation Desk Book*, John Wiley, NY, 1985, p. 310.
11. Arthur Deegan in *Coaching*.
12. Bob Rosner et al, *The Boss's Survival Guide*, McGraw-Hill, NY, 2001, p. 307.
13. Michael Armstrong, *How to be an Even Better Manager*, Kogan Page, London, 1988, p. 128.
14. Larry Davis & Earl McCallon in *Planning, Conducting and Evaluating Workshops*, Learning Concepts, Austin, Texas, 1974, p. 223.
15. Adapted from *How To Run Seminars & Workshops*, Robert L. Jolles, John Wiley & Sons, New York, 2001.
16. Candy Tymson & Bill Sherman, *The Australian Public Relations Manual*, Millennium, Sydney, 1990, p. 156.
17. Marc Robert, *School Morale: the Human Dimension*, Argus, Niles, Ill., 1976, p.88.
18. Marshall Loeb in 'Ten commandments for managing creative people', *Fortune*.
19. B. E. Holm, *How to Manage Your Information*, Reinhold, NY, 1968, p. 151.

20. Philip Harkins, *Workforce*, October 1998, p. 75.
21. Gifford Pinchot III, *Intrapreneuring*, Harper & Row, NY 1985, pp. 202-3.
22. Gifford Pinchot III, p. xiii.
23. Gifford Pinchot III, p. 42.
24. John Bartunek, 'What to do when your employees plateau', *Supervisory Management*, July 1984, p. 26.
25. Arthur Pell, *The Complete Idiot's Guide to Managing People*, Alpha Books, NY, 1999, p. 250.
26. Robyn Quinn, 'Our Very Own Mid-Life Crisis', *Metro*, June 1995.
27. Bob Rosner et al, *The Boss's Survival Guide*, McGraw-Hill, NY, 2001. p. 212.
28. Glenn Van Ekeren, *The Speaker's Sourcebook*, Prentice Hall, Englewood Cliffs NJ, 1988, p. 48.
29. *The Financial Review Boss*, August 2002.
30. Ron Zemke, Claire Raines, Bob Filipczak, *Generations At Work*, Performance Research Associates, 2001.
31. Mark McCormack. *Success Secrets*, Guild Publishing, London, 1989, p. 119.
32. 'Managing for Growth', *The Economist*, July, 1999.
33. R. Alex Mackenzie, *The Time Trap*, McGraw Hill, NY, 1972, p. 154.
34. *Executive Edge Newsletter.*
35. After Arthur Pell, *The Complete Idiot's Guide to Managing People*, Alpha Books, NY, 1999, p. 325.
36. Quoted in Volunteering Australia's *Implementation Guide for National Standards*, 2001.
37. Linda Vining, *Working with Volunteers in Schools*, Lencross Publications, Carlingord, 1998, p. 28.
38. After Tom Philp in *Appraising Performance for Results.*
39. After Mark Edwards and Ann Ewen in *360° Feedback*, AMACOM, NY.
40. Tornow, W. & London, M., *Maximizing the Value of 360-Degree Feedback*, San Francisco, Jossey-Bass, 1998.
41. Adapted from 'Using Your 360° Feedback' by Dr Lynn Summers.
42. Louise Phelan, *Management Today*, July 2000.
43. *Person to Person Managing.*
44. James Van Fleet, *The 22 Biggest Mistakes Managers Make and How to Correct Them*, Parker, NY, 1973, p. 55.
45. Andrew Szilagyi, *Management and Performance*, Goodyear, Santa Monica, 1981, p. 561.
46. Thomas Quick, *The Manager's Motivation Desk Book*, John Wiley & Sons, NY, 1985, p. 427.
47. Peter Hanson, *Stress for Success*, Pan, London, 1989, p. 89.
48. Louis Imundo, *The Effective Supervisor's Handbook*, AMACOM, NY, 1980, p. 148.
49. www.qld.gov.au / workandfamily
50. *Management Today*, September 2002.
51. George Idiorne, *How Managers Make Things Happen*, Prentice Hall, Englewood Cliffs, NJ, 1987, p. 279.
52. After Arthur Pell, *The Complete Idiot's Guide to Managing People*, Alpha Books, Simon & Schuster, NY, 1999, p. 334.
53. Reported in 'The Secret's Out', *Workforce*, July 1998, p.24.
54. Albert Bernstein & Sydney Rozen, *Dinosaur Brains*, John Wiley, New York, 1989, p. 58.
55. Albert Bernstein & Sydney Rozen, p. 230.
56. After Waldroop and Butler, *Harvard Business Review*, September-October 2000.
57. R.Doybe, 'The new bargaining order,' *The QANTAS Club*, December-January 1994-5, p. 17.
58. Ron Visconti and Richard Stiller in *Rightful Termination: Avoiding Litigation.*
59. Joe Catansariti & Mark Maragwanath, *The Workplace Relations Act: A User Friendly Guide*, Newsletter Information Services, Sydney, 1997, p. 71.
60. Paul Stevens, *Staff Problems Solved*, William Brooks, Sydney, 1984, p. 123.
61. After Jack Deal of Deal Consulting (US).

Managing Conflicts

1. Brian Caldwell & Jim Spinks, *The Self-Managing School*, Falmer, London, 1998, p. 185.
2. Peg Pickering, *How to Manage Conflict*, Career Press, Franklin Lakes NJ, 2000, p. 110-111.
3. James Van Fleet, *The 22 Biggest Mistakes Managers Make and How to Correct Them*, Parker, NY, 1973. p. 190.
4. Janet Carter, 'How to cope with angry employees or colleagues', *Supervisory Management.*
5. Jack Collis & Michael LeBoeuf, *Work Smarter Not Harder*, Goal Setting Seminars, Sydney, n.d., p. 107.
6. Robert Bramson, 'Blaming isn't changing', in Jimmy Calano & Jeff Salzman, *CareerTracking*, Gower, Aldershot, 1988.
7. Cynthia Berryman-Fink, *The Manager's Desk Reference*, AMACOM, NY, 1989, p. 48.
8. Cynthia Berryman-Fink, p. 286.
9. Arthur Pell, *The Complete Idiot's Guide to Managing People*, Alpha Books, NY, 1999, p. 150.
10. Bob Rosner et al, *The Boss's Survival Guide*, McGraw-Hill, NY, 2001, p. 371.
11. Joe Davis, *Supervision*, March 1998, p. 14.
12. Peter Reynolds in *Dealing with Crime and Aggression at Work.*
13. Elizabeth Holmes, *Handbook for Newly Qualified Teachers*, The Stationery Office, London, 1999, p. 104.
14. Judith Himstedt, 'Is this really an employer problem?' in *Workplace Bullying*, Workplace Consulting Queensland, Brisbane, 1999, p. 2.
15. US Manufacturing, Science and Finance Union, cited in *Workplace Bullying*, Workplace Consulting Queensland, Brisbane, 1999.
16. Peter Randall, cited in *Workplace Bullying*, Workplace Consulting Queensland, Brisbane, 1999.
17. Carolyn Barker, 'Economic impact of bullying in the workplace', in *Workplace Bullying*, Workplace Consulting Queensland, Brisbane, 1999.
18. Adapted from the model proposed by the Queensland Working Women's Service in *Risky Business*, QWWS, Brisbane, 2000, pp. 19-20.
19. Ruth Wheatley, *Dealing with Bullying at Work...in a Week*, Hodder & Stroughton, London, 1999, p. 26.
20. Ruth Wheatley, p. 85.
21. Ruth Wheatley, p. 94.
22. Robyn Mann in *Bullying: From Backyard to Boardroom*, Paul McCarthy et al (eds), Millennium Books, Alexandria NSW, 1996, p. 83.
23. Adapted from recommendations of the Queensland Working Women's Service in *Risky Business*, QWWS, Brisbane, 2000, pp. 31-43.
24. *Risky Business*, p. 45.

Managing Crises

1. 'Lessons from September 11', *Workforce*, Vol. 81, March 2002.
2. John Ramée, 'Managing in a crisis', *Management Solutions*, 1987, p. 25.
3. *Professional Manager*, March 2001.
4. Candy Tymson & Bill Sherman , *The Australian Public Relations Manual*, Millennium Books, Sydney, 1990, p. 218.
5. Robert Ramsey, '101 ways to crime-proof your workplace', *Supervision*, May 1996, p. 10.
6. Marsha Dean Wilson, American Society for Industrial Security. Quoted in '101 Ways To Crime-Proof Your Work-place', *Supervision*, Robert D. Ramsey, June 1996.
7. Jock Neill in *Modern Retail Risk Management*.
8. Donald Schultz in *Principles of Physical Security*.
9. 'Defeating the Bad Guys', *The Economist*, Vol. 349, 1998.
10. Leaflet: 'Small Business – A Secure and Safe Workplace', Queensland Police.
11. UK Audit Commission.
12. Bodie Thoene in *Quotable Quotes*, Reader's Digest, Montreal, 1998, p. 86.
13. Marsha Bertrand in *Fraud: How to protect yourself from schemes, scams and swindles*.
14. Judith Howlings, 'Sober solutions to help tackle substance abuse', *People Management*, 5 December 1996, pp. 43-44.
15. Russell Bintliff, *Crimeproofing Your Business*, McGraw-Hill, NY, 1994, p. 112.
16. Keith Tronc, *You, Your School and The Law*, Fernfawn, Brisbane, 1996, p. 99.
17. Mark Stuart Gill, 'The phone stalkers', *Ladies Home Journal*, September 1995.
18. Source unknown
19. Nick Perry, *Organization Studies*, Spring 1998.
20. Dissent Network Australia, www.uow. edu.au/arts/sts/bmartin/dissent/
21. The Queensland Whistleblower Study, Paul McCarthy et al, *Bullying: From backyard to boardroom*, Millennium Books, Alexandria NSW, 1996.

Marketing

1. Linda Vining, *School Image by Design*, Spirit of Adventure, Randwick, 1994,
p. 4.
2. Davis Young in *Building Your Company's Good Name*.
3. Bobbie Gee in *Winning the Image Game*.
4. John McGillicuddy, 'Making a Good First Impression', *Public Management*, January 1999.
5. Julie A. Lyden, 'Impression Management: Implementation For Selection', *Supervision*, October 1997.
6. Elinor & Joe Selame in *The Company Image*.
7. D. Lanyon, 'Draw in more sales with a designer', *Australian Small Business Review*, July 1990, p. 33.
8. Theodore Levitt, *The Marketing Imagination*, The Free Press, NY, 1983.
9. Raleigh Pinskey in *101 Ways to Promote Yourself*.
10. After Linda Vining, *Marketing Matters in Schools*, Centre for Marketing Schools, Carlingford NSW, 2000, p. 26-27.
11. Robert Ramsey in *Supervision* magazine.
12. Tom Karger in *Marketing News*.
13. Neal Chalofsky, 'External evaluation', *HR Management and Development Handbook*, W. Treacy (ed.), AMACOM, NY, 1994, p. 1341.
14. David Stewart and Prem Shamdasani in *Focus Groups: Theory and Practice*.
15. Jay Levinson & Seth Godin, *The Guerrilla Marketing Handbook*, Houghton Mifflin, Boston, 1994, p.7.
16. Malcolm McDonald, *Marketing plans: How to prepare them and how to use them*, 3rd edn, Oxford, Heinemann Professional, 1995.
17. A.S. Slywotsky, *Value Migration: How to Think Several Moves Ahead of the Competition*, Harvard Business School Press, Boston, 1996.
18. Robert Kahn in *Retailing Today*.
19. Robert Kriegel and David Brandt in *Sacred Cows Make the Best Burgers*, Fontana, Glasgow, 1985.
20. Napoleon Hill in Matthew Sartwell's *Napoleon Hill's Keys to Success*.
21. Source unknown.
22. Quoted in *The Customer Care Revolution* by Stephen Dando-Collins.
23. Finbarr O'Connor, 'First-Class Service', *Ford Talkback*, October 2001.
24. 'The Seven Deadly Sins of CRM Implementation', META Group, November 1998.
25. D.K. Rigby, F. Reichheld, & P. Schefter,
'Avoid the Four Perils of CRM', *Harvard Business Review*, February 2002, p. 102.
26. 'Increasing Customer Value: Harness the Power of Predictive CRM', Sue Phelan, *CRM Project*, Volume 2, June 2001.
27. Wendy Evans, *How to Get New Business in 90 Days and Keep It Forever*, Millennium Books, Sydney, 1997, pp. 84-88.
28. Karl Albrecht & Ron Zenke in *Service America*.
29. Greg Vance, *The Australian Manager's Guide to Success*, Hale & Iremonger, Sydney, 1994, p. 107.
30. Wendy Evans, *How to Get New Business in 90 Days and Keep It Forever*, Millennium Books, Sydney, 1997, p. 13. (passim)
31. Lisa Davis, *Shortcuts for Smart Managers*, AMACOM, New York, 1998, p. 142.
32. Max Franchitto in *Management Today*.
33. *HyperW@rs*, Bruce Judson, Harper Collins, London, 1999.
34. Ralph F. Wilson, *Web Marketing Today*, Issue 24, November 4, 1996.
35. Phil Terry, CEO Creative Good, interviewed on US National Public Radio's *All Things Considered*, December 1999.
36. Acknowledgements to John Stanley, *Just about Everything a Retail Manager Needs to Know*, Plum Press, Brisbane, 1999, pp. 60-61.
37. Roy Morgan research, cited in John Stanley, *Just about Everything a Retail Manager Needs to Know*, Plum Press, Brisbane, 1999, p. 61.
38. Scott Cutlip & Allen Center, *Effective Public Relations*, Prentice Hall, Englewood Cliffs NJ, 1971.
39. Steve Miller, *How to Get the Most Out of Trade Shows*, NTC Business Books, Lincolnwood, Illinois.
40. Acknowledgements to John Stanley, *Just about Everything a Retail Manager Needs to Know*, Plum Press, Brisbane, 1999, pp. 224-225.
41. *Marketing Magazine*, July, 1992.
42. Candy Tymson & Bill Sherman, *The Australian Public Relations Manual*, Millennium, Sydney, 1990, p. 194.
43. Jarvis Finger, *Managing Your School: 3*, Fernfawn, Brisbane, 1995, pp. 84-85.
44. Candy Tymson & Bill Sherman, *The Australian Public Relations Manual*, Millennium, Sydney, 1990, p. 210.
45. Meg Whittemore, 'PR On a Shoestring,' *Nation's Business*, 79 (1), 1991, p. 31.
46. David Norman, *Public Relations*, September 1997.

Organisation-Wide Issues

1. Hedley Beare, Brian Caldwell & Ross Millikan, *Creating an Excellent School*, Routledge, London, 1989, p. 174.
2. Lee Bolman & Terrance Deal in *Leading the Soul: An Uncommon Journey of Spirit*.
3. Peter Senge, *The Fifth Discipline: The Art and Practice of the Learning Organisation*, Random House, Sydney, 1990.
4. E.H. Schein, 'The Anxiety of Learning', *Harvard Business Review*, March 2002, p. 103.
5. Robert Hargrove in *Mastering the Art of Creative Collaboration*.
6. Anthony de Mello S.J. in *The Prayer of the Frog*.
7. Peter Ryan, 'Cleaning up a dirty word – Policy', *The Practising Administrator*, Vol. 16 No. 2 1994, p. 30.
8. www.ipaustralia.gov.au
9. Brown and Duguid, *The Social Life of Information*, HBR School Press, 2000.
10. Thomas Stewart in *The Wealth of Knowledge*.
11. Peter Drucker in *The Australian Financial Review Boss*, March 2000.
12. Thomas Stewart, 'Making Knowledge Management Work', *Barely Managing*, April 2002.
13. Brown and Duguid, *The Social Life of Information*, HBR School Press, 2000.
14. Roosevelt Thomas, 'Managing Diversity in the Workplace,' *Business Development Success Series*, Vol. 8, p. 2.
15. The Diversity Training Group (askus@ diversityDTG.com)
16. *Cross-Cultural Communication*, National Centre for Vocational Educational Research, AGPS, Canberra, 1992, p. xxxiv.
17. Bob Rosner et al, *The Boss's Survival Guide*, McGraw-Hill, NY, 2001, p. 242.
18. M. Burdue & A. McLean, 'Integrated management systems', *Management*, 1994, p. 17.
19. Stephanie Winston, *The Organised Executive*, Warner Books, NY, 1985, pp. 56,

20. Kris Cole, *Make Time*, Prentice Hall, Frenchs Forest, 2001.
21. After G. Yager in *Creative Time Management for the New Millennium*.
22. 'The Core of Good Business' *HR Monthly*, June 1999 , p. 17.
23. *Speaker's Library of Business Stories, Anecdotes, and Humor*, Joe Griffith, Prentice Hall, 1990.
24. Bowen McCoy in 'When Do We Take A Stand?', *Harvard Business Review*, May-June 1997, p. 60.
25. Attracta Lagan, *Drake Business Review*, July 2000, p. 25.
26. Quoted in *Management Today*, May 2002, p. 15.
27. J. W. Sullivan, quoted in *Speaker's Library of Business Stories, Anecdotes, and Humor*, Joe Griffith, Prentice Hall, 1990, p. 109.
28. Attracta Lagan, *Drake Business Review*, July 2000, p. 24.
29. Derek Rowntree, *The Manager's Book of Checklists*, Gower, Aldershot, 1989, p. 258.
30. After Laura Nash in *Good Intentions Aside*.
31. Bob Rosner, Allan Halcrow & Alan Levins, *The Boss's Survival Guide*, New York, McGraw-Hill, 2001, p. 383.
32. Employment Equity Branch, Public Sector Management Commission, Queensland, July 1991, p. 17.
33. Mary Lacity & Rudy Hirschheim in *Information Systems Outsourcing*.
34. Peter Thomas, 'Calling in the consultants', *Certified Accountant*, January 1993.
35. Charles Ford in Bell & Nadler's *The Client-Consultant Handbook*.
36. Beth Fowler, 'Working with consultants', *Supervision*, August 1996, p. 15.
37. Antony Jay, former chairman of Video Arts (UK).
38. Quoted in 'Ask Annie', *Fortune*, 9 November, 1998.
39. Michael Meighan in *How to Design and Deliver Induction Training Programmes*.
40. Goss Cosmetics survey, reported in

169.
Courier-Mail, Brisbane, 18 July 2002, p. 7.
41. Michael Yoshino and Srinivasa Rangan, *Strategic Alliances*, Harvard Business School Press, 1995.
42. Rosabeth Moss Kanter, 'Collaborative Advantage: The Art of Alliances', *Harvard Business Review*, July 1994, p. 96.
43. Roberta Maynard, 'Striking the Right Match', *Nation's Business*, Vol. 84, May 1996, p. 18.
44. Quoted in 'Alliances still great weapon for expansion,' Mark Lawson, *Australian Financial Review, Special Report*, 3 October 2001, p. 2.
45. John R. Harbison & Pekar, P., *Smart Alliances*, Booz- Allen & Hamilton Inc., 1998.
46. A.A. Grikscheit & M.G. Cag, 'Extracting Value from Solid Alliances', *Mergers and Acquisitions Journal*, June 2002.
47. *Awards & Agreements*, Department of Employment, Training and Industrial Relations, Queensland, 2002.
48. Glen Walker, *Positive School Management*, Educational Consulting and Financial Services, Maleny, 1993, p. 49.
49. Robert Finney in *Basics of Budgeting*.
50. American Management Association.
51. Neil Flanagan, *Creative Debt Collecting*, Plum Press, Brisbane, 1992, p. 8.
52. Lesley Sly, 'How Do I Get Paid?', *Dynamic Small Business*, Feb/Mar 1996, p. 23.
53. Anthony Cordato, *How to Collect Business Debts*, Australian Business Library, Melbourne, 1990.
54. Bess May, 'How to cut your company's costs', *Supervision*, October 1994, p. 14.
55. Queensland Department of Tourism, Small Business and Industry, 1998.
56. Shira Levine, 'Sink or Swim', *American Network*, June 2001, p. 49.
57. Stephen Barlas, 'Looking for Cover', *Entrepreneur Magazine*, Vol. 26, 1998, p. 16.
58. Les Taylor in *Starting and Managing a Small Business*.

Index

To be effective in your role as a senior manager, supervisor, first-time manager or frontline manager, you will need quick access to essential management know-how.

Australian Management Essentials is written for busy managers looking for immediate access to vital management information. This information is presented in a clear, step-by-step fashion, with cross-references to help you drill down as far as you choose.

All the information is presented free of any management mumbo jumbo and gobbledygook, therefore guaranteeing that it's easy to read and easy to understand.

With more than 300 topics delivering access to this essential management how-to, *Australian Management Essentials* will become your constant companion.

But be warned: Share the content with colleagues and workmates, but don't let the book out of your sight. (Chances are that the book won't be returned to you!)

This book is an Australian bestseller. It won't take you long to find out why.